The Hippodrome Theatre
First Fifty Years

by Richard Gartee

LAKE AND EMERALD PUBLICATIONS

ISBN: 978-1-7363957-3-8

Library of Congress Control Number: 2023900012

Lake and Emerald Publications, LLC
PO Box 358381
Gainesville, FL

Front cover by Michael Eaddy from a design suggested by Franziska Raeber.

Back cover (clockwise from top left): *The Land of Point*, photo by John Moran; *Equus*, photo by Gary Wolfson; *The Great American Trailer Park Musical*, photo by Michael Eaddy; *Million Dollar Quartet*, photo by Michael Eaddy; *Amadeus*, photo by John Moran; *The Elephant Man*, photo by Gary Wolfson.

Photographs that appeared in the *Gainesville Sun* or the *Independent Florida Alligator* have been reprinted with permission of the editors.

To the founders of the feast

Bruce Cornwell, Gregory von Hausch, Mary Hausch,
Kerry McKenney, Marilyn Wall, and Orin Wechsberg

and to Dick and Caren Gorenberg

Acknowledgements

This book has been an enormous undertaking and I offer my deepest thanks to the Hippodrome Theatre, especially stage manager Amber Wilkerson, who organized the fifty-year archive of news clippings, photos, and playbills; also artistic director Stephanie Lynge, production and building manager Bob Robins, education director Gabby Byam, and marketing manager Franziska Raeber.

I owe special thanks to photographers Bryan Grigsby, Gary Wolfson, John Moran, Randy Batista, Michael Eaddy, and Allison Durham for helping locate and repair many missing or damaged photos from the early years. Also, thanks to Doug Ray and the *Gainesville Sun* and Alan Haley and the *Independent Florida Alligator* for granting permission to reprint photos from their newspapers. Every effort has been made to credit the photographer, if known; apologies to anyone whose name is missing.

Research for this book included interviewing Hippodrome co-founders and dozens of actors, directors, and key players in the Hippodrome's success. Thank you for taking the time to share your memories with me: Carlos Asse, Kelly Atkins, Margaret Bachus, Mark Barrow, Gabby Byam, Lauren Warhol Caldwell, Mark Chambers, Bruce Cornwell, Malcolm Gets, Caren Gorenberg, Greg von Hausch, Jessica Hurov, Dan Jesse, Gregg Jones, Stephanie Lynge, Jon Mills, Sara Morsey, Dana Moser, Liz Nehls, Marshall New, Kerry Oliver-Smith, Nell Page, Jennifer Pritchett, Kevin Rainsberger, Chad Reed, Bob Robins, Steve Robitaille, Mark Sexton, Catherine Fries Vaughn, Marilyn Wall, and Betsy Whitaker. Thanks also to the Matheson History Museum and UF School of Theatre and Dance for supplying historical information and photos.

Fellow writers Susie Baxter, Ken Campbell, Pat Caren, Joan Carter, Allison Durham, Skipper Hammond, Deborah Holt, Ronnie Lovler, and Bonnie Ogle critiqued each chapter and offered advice as I wrote. Signe Jorgenson copyedited the finished text and Pat Caren proofread the typeset text. Thank you one and all.

In closing, let us give thanks to the Hippodrome for fifty years of great theatre.

Contents

The Hippodrome Theatre First Fifty Years

Mary Hausch, Orin Wechsberg, and Kerry McKenney performing *The Land of Point* in the Gainesville Mall on NW Thirteenth Street.

1973

The Beginning

The houselights go down as the stage lights come up. An actor, dressed in a leotard and tights, enters and says, "You won't hear me talk again after this, but I want to welcome you guys. You are our first audience." The show, a pantomime titled *Did You Hear Something?*, opened August 8, 1973, and ran for five days. It was the Hippodrome's first production held in the theatre's original location on Hawthorne Road in Gainesville, Florida. Gregory Hausch remembers, "There were nine of us in the cast and eight people in the audience. We outnumbered them."

Cast of *Did You Hear Something?* (l-r) Chuck Haddad, Marilyn Wall, Greg Hausch, Kurt Hausch, Kerry McKenney, Mary Hausch, and Orin Wechsberg (bottom).

The six Hippodrome co-founders, Gregory and Mary Hausch, Marilyn Wall, Orin Wechsberg, Bruce Cornwell, and Kerry McKenney, had planned and worked toward opening night for over a year. Five were recent graduates of the University of Florida (UF), although Bruce was working on his master's degree. Kerry was still an undergraduate.

After graduating from UF in 1972, Greg and Mary had taken jobs in Miami to raise money for a theatre. Marilyn had worked as an artist for the UF Dental School. Bruce and Orin had scoured the Gainesville area, searching for a suitable building. Most places were too expensive.

Hawthorne Road Theatre

Finally, they'd found a place they could afford on East Hawthorne Road. It resembled a convenience store because it had large plate glass windows across the front. Even today, people still refer to it as "the 7-Eleven." Actually, it was a former plumbing supply store. The location was off the beaten path and it'd be a challenge to get audiences out there, but it had a rare feature for a Florida building—a basement where they could build sets and store props.

First Hippodrome theatre, 3401 SE Hawthorne Road.

Marilyn Wall teaches a workshop on UF Plaza.

Leasing the property was their next challenge. In the early 1970s, Gainesville was hippie central, and the Hippodrome founders were no exception. The owner was a conservative "good ol' boy" who, Bruce Cornwell recalls, gave them an ultimatum. "'If you boys go and shave off your beards and cut your hair, I'll rent you this building. But otherwise, get out of here.' A few days later, we came back clean-shaven with our hair cut, and he was so shocked that he rented us the building on the spot."

According to its Tenth Anniversary booklet, the Hippodrome considers its official founding date to be April 18, 1973, but the building was nowhere near ready for audiences in April. Greg and Mary moved back from Miami and everyone began working toward their dream, sanding the floors, painting the interior. To generate income, Kerry, Mary, and Marilyn taught children's theatre workshops over the summer. To generate interest in the theatre, the newly founded troupe performed an adaptation of a work by Harry Nilsson, *The Land of Point,* at music festivals, area schools, and even the Gainesville Mall on NW Thirteenth Street.

Meanwhile, construction continued, supplemented by what Greg called "dumpster diving" to get materials they needed. When the (UF) Florida Players ended a play, they would strike the set. Greg said, "We would be outside Constans Theatre, just like raccoons at a dumpster, waiting for them to bring out wood and nails or bolts." That spring, UF produced a large musical for which they'd built big I beams for the stage, then threw them away after the show ended. "Really well-built, glued, bolted together," Greg remembers. "They were fourteen or sixteen feet long, and we cut them in half to fit in my van. We made our seats out of those. We went to carpet stores, got carpet scraps for the padding underneath." They covered the seats in Naugahyde and added backrests. But the backrests were mounted at ninety degrees, so when you attended a show, you pretty much sat at attention.

The basement served as a coed dressing room, but the actors had to climb a set of old wooden stairs to make their entrance onstage.

They had no money to buy stage lights, so they went door-to-door asking people for empty three-pound-size coffee cans. They cut an opening in the bottom of each can, attached a light socket inside, and screwed in a parabolic aluminized reflector lamp. The cans then attached to the rafters with homemade hangers. That allowed them to aim the lights. Greg made the light control board by mounting household dimmers in a cigar box. Large rubber bands stretched around the knobs allowed them to fade all the lights together.

In college, Greg had been president of the Florida Players and Marilyn was vice president. Many current and former theatre students were good friends of the co-founders, and once the theatre opened, these same thespians appeared in many Hippodrome plays. One was Chad Reed, who is credited with naming the theatre. "They had a meeting to decide a name for the theatre," Chad recalls. Years ago,

Gainesville used to be called Hog Town, and during the hippie era, the name took on a tongue-in-cheek revival. "So, they said, 'Let's call it the Hog Town Players,' and I said, 'If you want to make this a successful theatre and attract audiences that are going to support you, I wouldn't call it the Hog Town Theatre.' I start suggesting some names. 'Well, you can call it the Hog Town Hippodrome, but I still think—'"

"The hippodrome? What's the hippodrome?" one of them said.

"The hippodrome in ancient Rome was a large oblong race track where they would hold spectacles," Chad said. "In Victorian England, there was a famous theatre called Hippodrome where the big lavish musicals and spectacles were held. In New York, at the turn of the century, there was also a Hippodrome Theatre. So, knowing the history of it, why don't we call it the Hippodrome Theatre? It gives a little panache, a little class. And everybody agreed."

First Show

They had a name, but money was tight. They all worked without pay for the first several shows. According to Greg, they opened with *Did You Hear Something?* so that "we wouldn't have to have props or buy costumes. It was cute and people seemed to like it." Even so, according to Greg, "We knew that pantomime and workshops weren't what we wanted to do." Their next show needed to be a real play.

The co-founders agree that the early Hippodrome was very much a communal process. They held meetings to decide everything from the next play to whether they could afford a gallon of paint. For several seasons, each member read plays and proposed ones they'd like to direct. While this produced eclectic seasons, it introduced theatergoers to plays they'd never seen before.

Although it was committed to becoming an avant-garde theatre, the Hippodrome was starting up in a conservative city. Greg suggested they do Neil Simon's *The Odd Couple* for their next play: "Something safe that people know of, and they'll come out." To appease those in the group wanting to do absurdist or existential theatre, he said, "We'll do it an inventive way."

The Odd Couple

Orin Wechsberg was someone who desperately wanted the theatre to focus on the avant-garde. He was doing the set design for *The Odd Couple,* which Greg was directing. Bruce was busy finishing his thesis for a master's degree in theatre but stopped by during rehearsal. "I saw this black Visqueen [polyethylene plastic sheeting] hanging around. Orin wanted the set to be just black Visqueen, so that the whole thing took place in a black void."

Marilyn Wall and Kerry McKenney offer Kurt Orwick a kiss in *The Odd Couple*.

"Orin says it needs to be avant-garde," Greg told Bruce.

"We're doing *The Odd Couple*, for God's sakes!" Bruce said.

"Yeah," Greg said, "I'm not wild about the idea either."

"Come on. We need to do something about this," Bruce said. He and Greg tore all the black Visqueen off the ceiling and started making flats for a more realistic set. Not that the theatre ever wasted a thing. The Visqueen was saved, and Orin used it for the set of their next play, *Exit the King*, which he directed.

The Odd Couple, a comedy about two friends with opposite dispositions sharing an apartment, had been a Broadway hit five years earlier but had not yet played Gainesville. The production worked beautifully and garnered the Hippodrome instant praise and recognition. Arline Greer, theater critic for the *Gainesville Sun*, wrote, "There is cause for rejoicing among Gainesville theatergoers. A new company, which calls itself the Hippodrome Theatre, has opened its doors, and the word is hurry, do not walk, to the Hippodrome to see a highly skilled, irreverent bunch of zanies do their thing in Neil Simon's *The Odd Couple*, the season's opener."[1]

"She single-handedly put us on the map," Greg recalled. Tickets were $1.50. "We filled up, and we were ecstatic. We still didn't have any money, but we could pay the $300 we owed for rent."

Enter the Gorenbergs

Not only did *The Odd Couple* bring success, it also brought two audience members who, by all accounts, are most responsible for the Hippodrome's survival. Dick Gorenberg was a new physician and his wife, Caren, was his office manager. They'd moved to Gainesville from New York, where they had loved theatre and seen many plays.

As Greg tells it, "After the show, I would run outside and direct cars, because in our little parking lot there was this huge sinkhole. I mean, a hole that would take a whole car into it. It was raining the night that the Gorenbergs came. I didn't know who they were, but I said, 'Why don't you give me your keys and tell me where your car is and I'll go get it.'"

After Greg brought their car, he stood in the rain talking with them and learned that Dick Gorenberg was a doctor. The Gorenbergs asked Greg a lot of questions and said, "We really enjoyed it. We should get together. Maybe we can help you."

Greg remembers thinking, "Here's a rich doctor who wants to help us. Thank God. Maybe we can get a thousand dollars or something like that." But the Gorenbergs had something much bigger in mind.

Caren's version of the story goes like this: "We were from New York, and there wasn't much theatre in Gainesville. We saw in the paper that this new theatre was going to be producing *The Odd Couple*, so we drove out to that fabulous site on Hawthorne Road. I believe Greg was out in the street with a cigar box, taking money and telling people where to park. We went in. They had a few benches and a bunch of cushions on the floor." The theatre seated sixty-five to seventy people. "We were really struck. They were very good. They did a great *Odd Couple*."

A few days later, one of Dr. Gorenberg's patients mentioned seeing him and his wife at the theatre. "Yes," he said. "My wife and I really had a good time. They're new. They're really struggling to make a theatre."

The patient very innocently said, "Well, it would be a shame if something like that would fail for lack of financing."

A day or two later, the doctor received a phone call. "We're calling from the Hippodrome and would like to invite you and your wife to dinner."

He came home excited and said, "We loved the show and now they've reached out to us and would like us to come to dinner."

Caren said to her husband, "Yeah, you're a doctor. It's saying to them, 'Money! There's money here! Let's talk to these people.'" She thought she'd really burst his bubble. Anyway, they went to dinner.

The Hippodrome members were poor, really poor. They hadn't started paying themselves yet, and even though they qualified for food stamps, recipients had to pay the government a token fee for them. They couldn't even afford that. Still, they wanted to impress the Gorenbergs. Marilyn scratched together some kind of meal, and they borrowed a bottle of wine from a friend.

Over dinner with the co-founders, Caren let them know that she and Dick couldn't give them money. He'd just opened his medical practice, and they'd taken out a loan to do it. However, that didn't mean they couldn't help.

The Hippodrome founders, all creative artists, lacked business acumen. Caren remembers balancing the books for them. "They were a very egalitarian group. They had a checkbook and anybody could write a check on it because that's the only equitable way." She told them to "start keeping track of it, not so much for signing the checks—that's fine—but there has to be money in the bank. And when you write a check, you've got to write down how much it's for. I can still see Marilyn to this day: 'Caren, I know you told me. After I did, I wrote it down on my hand, but then I took a shower.'"

The Gorenbergs advised the co-founders to form a board of directors and incorporate as a nonprofit organization. "We can't afford a lawyer," Greg said. But the Gorenbergs had friends who could help. Attorney Judy Miller joined the board and helped file the incorporation paperwork in 1974. Besides Judy and the Gorenbergs, the initial board included Carole Johnson, whose husband, Ed, was the editor of the *Gainesville Sun*. Dr. Albert Wehlburg, from the UF Theatre Department, rounded out the board. Dick Gorenberg was named president.

Three One-acts

From October 11 to 13, the Hippodrome presented a collection of three one-act plays followed by an hour of live music featuring Bill Hutchinson, Ginnie McCulloch, and David Darlington.

(l-r) Janis Teitler, Jon Schwartz, Ken Peterson, Yvonne Dell, and Mary Hausch in *Exit the King*.

The first one-act was *Sing to Me Through Open Windows* by Arthur Kopit. Directed by Marilyn Wall, the story portrays an old magician yearning for earlier times of his life as a clown and as a boy.

The second and third one-acts were directed by Kerry McKenney. *Maid to Marry*, by Eugène Ionesco, is a brief, witty game between the audience and two characters—Lady (Barbara Sizemore) and Gentleman (Rusty Salling). At the end of the repartee with the audience, Lady and Gentleman's daughter prances onstage wearing a lovely tutu and sporting a hairy chest and full beard.

In *Rats* by Israel Horovitz, the final play of the night, Marilyn Wall and Jon Schwartz were cheese-nibbling, baby-biting rats scurrying around a metropolis.

Exit the King and Orin

Their next full-length play was *Exit the King*, an absurdist drama by Eugène Ionesco. It was directed by Orin Wechsberg. The set was built around a giant horn-shaped speaker that emitted electronic music composed by David Darlington and played on a Moog synthesizer. After the play closed, Orin decided to leave the Hippodrome, saying this wasn't the kind of theatre he wanted to do. Now there remained five co-directors.

The Caretaker

Kerry McKenney directed the final play of 1973, *The Caretaker* by Harold Pinter. The story is a psychological study of the confluence of power, allegiance, innocence, and corruption among two brothers and a tramp. Its cast included Ken Peterson and two of the co-founders' former classmates who were destined to become mainstays of the Hippodrome: Dan Jesse and Rusty Salling.

Ken Peterson and Dan Jesse in *The Caretaker*.

Photo: Gary Wolfson

The Caretaker was set in an old decaying mansion in rainy London. With zero budget for special effects, the Hippodrome crew had to create their own rain machine. They started by putting gravel and broken tiles in a container behind the set. Next, they poked pinholes in the bottoms of several one-gallon plastic milk jugs. They filled these with water, screwed on the caps, and suspended them on ropes behind the set window. When rain was called for, the caps were loosened, and the entering air allowed the water to drip out of the bottom, creating that London drizzle. They could adjust the rate of rainfall by how far they opened the caps.

Contentious Past

As undergraduates, the UF theatre students had been close-knit. Marilyn Wall and Mary Hausch shared a house just off Thirteenth Street, behind the Krispy Kreme. Rusty Salling used to come over daily, sit on their porch, and smoke cigarettes.

While they were still students, long before dreaming up the Hippodrome, their creative energy pushed beyond the boundaries of UF's theatre department. In addition to their work with the UF Florida Players, the students formed an ad hoc group called The Lunchbox Theater. They performed what Mary Hausch termed "guerrilla theatre," where actors would dash onstage at coffeehouses, concerts, or protests, do a short skit, and then exit. A photo of one of these impromptu performances at an anti-war rally protesting the Vietnam War made the front page of both the *Gainesville Sun* and The *Florida Alligator* newspapers.

"Lunchbox Theatre members . . . present some antiwar skits," read the caption in the May 5, 1972, *Florida Alligator*.

Photo: Tom Kennedy/*Florida Alligator*

L. L. Zimmerman, head of the theatre department, called Greg Hausch, then president of the Florida Players, into his office and pointed to the news photo. "Have you seen this?"

"Yeah, I did," Greg said.

"You can't use our name like that."

"We didn't," Greg said, drawing Zimmerman's attention to the caption. "It says 'The Lunchbox Theater.'"

It would take years for the theatre department to get over that incident and begin supporting its former students' fledgling theatre. Not so for the founders' student colleagues. Their friends' names filled the cast lists of dozens of early Hippodrome plays. Foremost among them was Rusty Salling, who, by all accounts, became one of Gainesville's favorite talents.

Rusty, Dan, and Bacchus

Rusty loved the Hippodrome, but he didn't have any money when it started. In a 1978 article in the *Gainesville Sun*, he told the reporter, "When my friends first decided to form the group, they knew they would be working for free. They had savings to live on, but I didn't. So I couldn't afford to help out."[2] Marilyn Wall recalls that after they got the building on Hawthorne Road, they let Rusty stay in a little trailer on the property. Except for a brief stint in New York, Rusty remained part of the Hippodrome until he took his final bow in 2016 following a year-long battle with cancer.

Likewise, Dan Jesse, Rusty's fellow cast member in *The Caretaker*, had been a UF theatre student and knew the Hippodrome founders. *The Caretaker* was his first play at the Hippodrome, but far from his last. Dan frequently appeared in memorable roles up through the 1980s and was on the theatre staff from 1977 to 1980.

Gainesville was bursting with creativity in the early 1970s. Shortly after the Hippodrome's founding, other students formed two more theatre companies, Bacchus Productions and Vest Pocket Players. Bacchus Productions was a touring company founded by Jon Schwartz with Dan Jesse, Rusty Salling, and Janice Sizemore. Bacchus's biggest success was *Waiting for Godot* by Samuel Beckett with Dan in the role of Vladimir, Rusty as Estragon, Janice Sizemore, as Pozzo, Jon Schwartz as Lucky, and Janis Teitler as The Boy. The play toured throughout the Southeast, garnering rave reviews. Orin Wechsberg, who had just left the Hippodrome, directed the play, but once the show was running, he moved to New York to attend film school. In 1988, his first film, *Starlight*, won Best Feature at the International Children's Film Festival and was later picked up by Disney. Orin passed away in 2019.

1 Arline Greer, review of *The Odd Couple*, by Neil Simon, directed by Greg Hausch, Hippodrome Theatre, Gainesville, FL, *Gainesville Sun*, September 12, 1973.
2 Rob Elliott, "Rusty Salling Missed His Chance, but He's Back," *Gainesville Sun*, April 1978.

1974

Whatchamacallit

Still in their first season, the Hippodrome started 1974 with a three-day multimedia musical that ran January 10–13. It had a lengthy title: *The Experimental, Do You Want to Play Along? Song of the Eternal Nameless Whatchamacallit.*

Musician Bill Hutchinson, who was in the show, recalls, "It was a creature of the era. I believe the technical theatre term is 'Hippie Dippie.' Beginning with Om sounds and bells, it unrolled into an advertisement for consciousness through songs and stories."

Steambath

In February, they opened *Steambath* by Bruce Jay Friedman, a trail-blazer in dark humor. The quirky play presents the afterlife as a steam bath where many recently deceased souls do not yet realize they are dead. Gregory Hausch played a Puerto Rican steam bath attendant who is actually God. The play featured a large cast, some of whom the playbill lists with whimsical names like Pussy Willows, Dee Licious, Banana Baker, Lolly Pops, and Alpha Centauri. Bruce Cornwell, who had just completed his master's thesis on dark comedy, said, "This was pretty dark, as comedies go." But it was a hit. The play ran through February 17, 1974.

Steambath cast. Seated (l-r): Sandy Scott, Tim Glavin, Eileen Freid, and Greg Hausch. Standing: Rod White, Charles Barnett, Danny Brawley, and Larry Jurist.

Arline Greer, theater critic for the *Gainesville Sun*, wrote: "The Hippodrome... with their usual flair for the ridiculous and a sense of the comic unequaled on Gainesville stages, have given us an evening that vibrates with laughter, and, every now and again, with the pathos that underlies honest humor. Bruce Cornwell, who directed *Steambath*, has a fine feeling for the absurd and leads us very gently by the hand into the Hippodrome's *Steambath*, where we emerge, if not with a good sweat, with a hearty laugh at the human condition."[1]

The Owl and the Pussycat

Greg and Mary Hausch co-directed *The Owl and the Pussycat*, a 1964 play written by Bill Manhoff, which had recently been turned into a hit film starring Barbra Streisand and George Segal. In the Hippodrome's production, their roles were filled by Gerry Munn as a pseudo-intellectual bookstore clerk and Doreen Etherington as a call girl. Backgrounds for the set were large cartoons, and stage-hands dressed as clowns changed the set pieces.

Again, Arline Greer lavished praise: "It may be that in the last six years of reviewing plays in Gainesville, I have laughed harder than I did at the Hippodrome's production of *The Owl and the Pussycat*, but, if I did, I can't remember. *The Owl and the Pussycat* is the funniest play I have ever seen in Gainesville, and I would advise

Doreen Etherington and Gerry Munn in *The Owl and the Pussycat*.

any of you who have not yet made the journey to the Hippodrome, to do so forth-with."[2]

Except for the two-character play *The Owl and the Pussycat*, the remaining plays in the 1973–1974 season featured large casts made possible because the actors were unpaid. In later seasons, when the Hippodrome began to pay actors, the amount was low. This remained true until the Hippodrome became a member of the Actors' Equity Association (the union representing actors and stage managers). The union is a stickler about people getting paid.

The Hippodrome was on a roll. With exception of *Exit the King,* every play had been well received by audiences and, for most shows, they had sold out the seven-ty-five-seat theatre. They'd proven wrong the dire predictions of naysayers in the UF theatre department, who had said Gainesville couldn't support another theatre. In just six months, the founders could finally pay themselves $25 a week—enough to enable them to get food stamps.

Marilyn's Madwoman

Next up was *The Madwoman of Chaillot* by Jean Giraudoux. Marilyn Wall direct-ed the twenty-nine-member cast. The story concerns an eccentric woman who lives in Paris and her struggles against straitlaced authority figures—a struggle the Hippodrome founders understood.

Greg Hausch loved it. "I think of all the shows that first year, that was the one that created our identity. This was just joyous. We had people dancing in the street in these light, flimsy, see-through fabrics—a lot of, just, color and joy and life. The minute people came over the hill on Hawthorne Road, they would see the light of the fairies and spirits dancing in the middle of Hawthorne Road and then in the woods across the street, and were like, 'What's going on?' It was magical."

The company performing a number in *The Madwoman of Chaillot.*

The Serpent

The last play of the 1973–1974 season was *The Serpent* by Jean-Claude van Itallie. The theatre was reconfigured, and the Naugahyde bench seats were replaced by platforms hanging from the ceiling and cushions on the floor, creating an arena that immersed the audience in the experience.

Kerry McKenney directed a cast of eighteen in an experimental workshop-style performance which, instead of relying on makeup and costumes, required the actors to express every possible emotion with precise contemporary-style dance movements. Kerry recalls taking the entire cast to the beach to watch the sunrise and then rehearsing on the sand.

Company of *The Serpent* in rehearsal. Note platforms constructed for audience seating.

The Serpent is not a play in any normal sense of the word. It begins with the assassination of John F. Kennedy and moves back in time to Adam and Eve, and Cain's murder of Abel. And yes, the actors were naked in the Garden of Eden.

Playwright Jean-Claude van Itallie came down to watch rehearsals and the show. Kerry was thrilled. She said, "It was really great because that was a big name for us at that time." He was the first "name" playwright to come to the Hippodrome, but not the last.

If Greg's assertion was correct that *The Madwoman of Chaillot* created the Hippodrome's identity, then *The Serpent* added another wrinkle. Although actors doffing their clothing had made its way onto Broadway, off-Broadway, and off-off-Broadway stages with plays like *Hair* and *Oh! Calcutta!*, it was new to Gainesville. *The Serpent* begot the Hippodrome's reputation for baring all.

For years, infrequent patrons and people who weren't even theatergoers held onto the impression that Hippodrome plays contained nudity. That wasn't always true. Over the next four decades, only one or two plays per season had a nude scene. They were never egregious or titillating, but the Hippodrome didn't shirk from nudity, either. If a script called for it, or it served an artistic purpose, the actors were willing.

(above) Founders turned their cars into roving ads.

They were a success! In the nine months between their opening production of *Do You Hear Something?* and the close of *The Serpent*, the fledgling troupe had put on eleven plays. But it hadn't been easy. The founders weren't just the actors and directors. They also had to be the theatre's stagehands, set builders, costumers, lighting technicians, janitors, ticket takers, and publicists, operating on less than a shoestring. To create public awareness, they each painted the Hippodrome name on their personal vehicles. Mary and Greg also attached a full-size sheet of plywood to the side of their van to advertise the current show.

Summer Break

When *The Serpent* closed on June 2, 1974, everyone needed a vacation. For the first and only time in Hippodrome history, they turned the summer production over to another troupe—their former classmates. Bacchus Productions covered the rent and staged *What the Butler Saw*, a farce by English playwright Joe Orton. Directed by Jon Schwartz, the play featured Rusty Salling, Dan Jesse, Janice Sizemore, Jan Ford, and Tim Glavin. It ran from June through July 1974.

(below) Greg Hausch dons a caterpillar suit and climbs a giant spider web for *Hope for the Flowers*.

Photo: Bryan Grigsby/*Gainesville Sun*

In August, the Hippodromers returned, ready to start a new season. To publicize their return, they donned costumes for a photo shoot in the countryside capturing their improvisational skills. The result was a full-page spread in the *Gainesville Sun*, which generated publicity for a three-day run in August of *Hope for the Flowers*, a fable about two caterpillars based on the allegorical novel by Trina Paulus.

Enter the Gorilla

The first mainstage production of the second season opened September 5, 1974. Marilyn Wall directed *The Secret Affairs of Mildred Wild*, a bizarre madcap comedy by Pulitzer Prize-winning author Paul Zindel. The title character is a contemporary housewife living above a candy store who escapes her dreary life by imagining herself as a 1930s movie star. When the outside world intrudes, Mildred meets each crisis with a hilarious fantasy scene drawn from old movies. Her life is further complicated by such unlikely visitors as a TV camera crew, a nun, and King Kong.

(l-r) Mary Hausch, Elizabeth Winter, Gerry Munn, Kerry McKenney, Kurt Orwick, and Dana Preisler in a number from *The Secret Affairs of Mildred Wild.*

King Kong? Marilyn needed a costume. "I heard there was some guy who worked in the art department at UF that had a gorilla suit and I called. It was Marshall New."

"I have always had a fetish for King Kong," Marshall New recalls. "My wife, Becky, and a friend got a fake gorilla head, and hands, and feet from Disney World. Then, they built the body, which I was more than capable of filling out. Marilyn said there was a moment in *The Secret Affairs of Mildred Wilde* where Mildred has a fantasy about being molested by King Kong. She asked if they could borrow my gorilla suit. I said, 'Only if I come with it.' And that was my introduction to theatre at the Hippodrome."

Marilyn agreed to Marshall's terms, and he replaced the actor she'd originally cast for the role. Bitten by the theatre bug, Marshall would, a year later, leave his position teaching art history at the University of Florida to become a full-time member of the Hippodrome.

Reviewers for both *New Look* magazine and the *Gainesville Sun* disparaged Paul Zindel's script but praised the Hippodrome's production. Drama critic Arline Greer wrote, "It is a real tribute to the Hippodrome crew that they are able to take a piece of commercial claptrap like this, and elevate it to a dubious status that lies somewhere between Neil Simon and Woody Allen. The evening is filled with laughter and good theater fun, despite the fact that the author offers nothing more than a skeleton for the Hippodrome to flesh out and give life. Marilyn Wall, who directed the play, once again shows an instinctive flair for oddball comedy. You may not think *The Secret Affairs of Mildred Wilde* the end-all, be-all of tragi-comedy, but I don't think you can help yourself in enjoying this Hippodrome production."[3]

Two One-acts

At the beginning of October, the Hippodrome staged a pair of absurdist one-act comedies, *Cop-Out* and *A Day for Surprises* by John Guare, at their Hawthorne Road theatre. The troupe had premiered the show in a special performance at the University of Florida Reitz Union Ballroom earlier that summer.

Photo: Bryan Grigsby/*Gainesville Sun*

Promotional photo for *Cop-Out* and *A Day for Surprises*. Front: Greg Hausch and Kerry McKenney. Back: Bruce Cornwell, Marilyn Wall, and Mary Hausch.

Cop-Out, directed by Mary Hausch, had a cast of three. Gregory Hausch played a cop who fantasizes himself as supersleuth Bret Arrow. The story bounces back and forth between the cop's humdrum real life and his dream sequences of espionage heroics. Marilyn Wall played a protest demonstrator who, in Bret's fantasies, becomes Gardenia Gertie, an unhinged flower vendor seeking Bret's help after her cat is slaughtered. Rounding out the three-person cast was Kerry McKenney as Larue, a mysterious foreign temptress whom Bret Arrow interrogates.

For the second play, *A Day for Surprises*, Kerry McKenney and Mary Hausch changed hats, with Kerry becoming the director and Mary the actor. The setting is the New York Public Library where two sexually repressed librarians, Miss Jepson (played by Mary Hausch) and Mr. Falazano (played by Bruce Cornwell), learn that an unseen character, Miss Pringle, has been eaten by one of the stone lions that stand in front of the library.

The White House Murder Case

After a three-day run of the one-act comedies, the cast and crew turned their attention to preparations for their next big show that fall, the Jules Feiffer comedy *The White House Murder Case*. Gregory Hausch directed the play, which was openly critical of US military and political shenanigans. Written during the Vietnam War, Feiffer foreshadowed Watergate by including a plot to cover up a bungled presidential order with deceit and trickery. Only a month before the Hippodrome production opened, the Watergate scandal had forced President Richard Nixon's resignation, making the play even more timely.

Greg conceived the set as a football field and covered the stage with green Astroturf, with taped-on yard lines. On one side of the stage, the president, his wife, and advisers fabricated multiple cover-ups. At the opposite end of the field, US soldiers fought a new jungle war in Brazil some years hence. Underscoring the football parallel, the sixteen characters included six cheerleaders, a drum major, a majorette, and a member of a marching band who came on during set changes.

Sun drama critic Arline Greer confessed to her readers, "Reviews of Hippodrome Theatre productions have begun to sound like stuck records, or, worse yet, rewrites of rewrites, but I must reiterate that the Hippodrome company has done it again. And for those of you who are not conversant with this column, what they have 'done again' is to bring off another theatre coup, an excruciatingly funny, ingeniously executed production of Jules Feiffer's play, *The White House Murder Case*."[4]

David Lane, Associate Professor of Education at the University of Florida, played a general who had been blinded, burned, and partially paralyzed by a nerve-gas attack the president was trying to cover up. For the role of blind General Pratt, David wore dark glasses and stumbled around the stage using a cane for support.

Actors claim it is tough to act opposite animals or children because they grab the audience's attention. That's nothing compared to a scene-stealing cockroach. One memorable night, General Pratt was delivering his report to the president about what happened in South America when a large palmetto bug crawled onto the carpet. As the bug slowly made its way toward David's end of the stage, the audience's eyes were riveted on it, ignoring the actors. When the bug got near them, David, who was supposed to be blind, continued delivering his lines as he casually smashed the tip of his cane directly on the bug. The audience went ballistic with laughter.

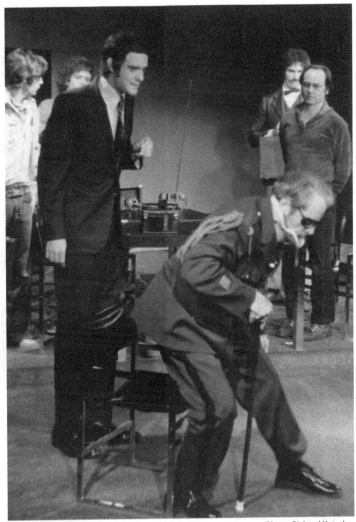

Photo: Richard Koterba

The White House Murder Case cast: (l-r) Rod White, Gerry Munn, Bruce Cornwell, Larry Winson, Grant Carrington, and David Lane with cane.

The White House Murder Case ran October 18–November 3, 1974, with only the onetime guest appearance by a palmetto bug.

Sade's Asylum

The Hippodrome exhibited an amazing ability to mount new productions in a short turnaround. Three weeks after their previous production closed, they opened *Marat/Sade*, which ran November 22–December 8, 1974. Bruce Cornwell directed the controversial play by Peter Weiss. It, too, had a large cast.

David Lane returned to the Hippodrome to play the lead, the Marquis de Sade. Kurt Orwick played Jean-Paul Marat. The role of the female lead, Charlotte Corday, went to Hippodrome newcomer Nell Page, who would go on to become an audience favorite and Hippodrome regular. Nell had a non-speaking bit part as a cheerleader in *The White House Murder Case*, but playing a main character was quite a leap forward.

Photo: Bryan Grigsby

(l-r) Kerry McKenney, Greg Hausch, David Lane, Nell Page, and (seated) Kurt Orwick in *Marat/Sade*.

The full title of the play, *The Persecution and Assassination of Jean-Paul Marat as Performed by the Inmates of the Asylum of Charenton Under the Direction of the Marquis de Sade,* tells us a lot. The story, set in 1808, after the French revolution, takes place in a lunatic sanatorium where the Marquis de Sade is an inmate. The hospital director allows de Sade to direct his fellow inmates in a play about Charlotte Corday's 1793 assassination of political theorist Jean-Paul Marat. This play-within-a-play takes up most of the show.

Sets for London and Broadway productions consisted of an enormous cage that covered the stage. In the much smaller Hippodrome venue, the bars of the cage came all the way to the edge of the seating, heightening the immersive experience for the audience. Pushing the effect, inmates in the Hippodrome production would reach through the bars and grab a patron's sweater or purse. Actors playing orderlies would then tussle with the inmate to get the item back and return it to its rightful owner.

Marat/Sade was a play with music, but not in the sense of traditional musicals of the day. The songs served not to further the plot or reveal a character's emotions, but rather to offer social or political commentary. For instance, one song celebrates the gaiety and excitement surrounding public executions, as a cart filled with shackled aristocrats headed for the guillotine. During the song, the cart driver flirts with newly arrived Charlotte Corday, trying to pick her up.

Charlotte's naiveté upon her arrival in Paris paralleled the wonder of young actor Nell Page on being cast in her first major Hippodrome role. Greg Hausch had seen her perform in a production at UF and encouraged her to audition for *Marat/Sade*. Nell didn't know what the play was. She recalls, "I rallied all my friends to go with me to audition. I was so scared." Her reaction when Bruce cast her as the female lead? "I remember calling my dad and crying on the phone."

"I guess I was able to channel this character in a way that was believable," Nell said. "After the opening night, Rusty and Dan came down to the greenroom to tell me what an excellent job I did. I had no idea the importance of their approval. At the time, I didn't know who they were, but that show pretty much put me in the loop—got me into the cast choices."

Again, the *Gainesville Sun* offered high praise: "They perform together as a company as beautifully as I have seen them. Each member of the collection of lunatics onstage is always in character. Each song is interpreted honestly, be it a rowdy rabble rouser or a ballad. Each dance is performed with precisely the correct feeling of madness for the moment. This is prime theatre by the Hippodrome... The cast of players is large for this production of *Marat/Sade*, and all play with some degree of brilliance. Of the many fine actors, I was most impressed by Rod White as Duperret, the raunchiest of lunatic noblemen, and Nell Page as a very lovely, quietly moving Charlotte Corday... Bruce Cornwell's direction is nothing short of brilliant, and the staging of *Marat/Sade* by Hippodrome regulars, Cornwell, Gregory Hausch, Mary Hausch, Jennifer Lane, Kerry McKenney, and Marilyn Wall is a work of art."[5]

The real-life Marquis de Sade actually was confined at Charenton, an institution for "socially impossible" people, until his death in 1814. His offense: sexual extravagances. While an inmate, he did numerous plays, which were often attended by upper-crust Parisians. However, the play's portrayal of de Sade's encounter with Jean-Paul Marat is fictional. The closest the two ever came was an address given by de Sade at Marat's funeral.

In retrospect, Gregory Hausch believes the fall 1974 plays further defined the breadth of the Hippodrome. He said, "We were really establishing our identity. Between *The White House Murder Case* and *Marat/Sade* and the lightness and fun of *The Secret Affairs of Mildred Wild*, that really showed kind of our personality."

1 Arline Greer, review of *Steambath*, by Bruce Jay Friedman, directed by Bruce Cornwell, Hippodrome Theatre, Gainesville, FL, *Gainesville Sun*, February 6, 1974.
2 Arline Greer, review of *The Owl and the Pussycat*, by Bill Manhoff, directed by Gregory Hausch and Mary Hausch, Hippodrome Theatre, Gainesville, FL, *Gainesville Sun*, March 13, 1974.
3 Arline Greer, review of *The Secret Affairs of Mildred Wilde*, by Paul Zindel, directed by Marilyn Wall, Hippodrome Theatre, Gainesville, FL, *Gainesville Sun*, September 12, 1974.
4 Arline Greer, review of *The White House Murder Case*, by Jules Feiffer, directed by Gregory Hausch, Hippodrome Theatre, Gainesville, FL, *Gainesville Sun*, October 23, 1974.
5 Arline Greer, review of *Marat/Sade*, by Peter Weiss, directed by Bruce Cornwell, Hippodrome Theatre, Gainesville, FL, *Gainesville Sun*, November 27, 1974.

1975

Absurd Zaniness

In a return to absurd zaniness, the Hippodrome opened 1975 with *The Red Eye of Love* by Arnold Weinstein, directed by Mary Hausch. The play depicts a bizarre yet familiar triangle involving Selma Chargesse (played by Christina Palacio), a girl who is forced to decide between moneyed butcher O. O. Martinas (Gregory Hausch) and poor but idealistic inventor Wilmer Flange (Gerry Munn). Greg, inspired by the film *The Godfather*, stuffed padding into his mouth and played Martinas a la Brando.

The set was cartoonish backdrops painted on muslin that could be rolled up and down like window shades. Taxicabs and other props were two-dimensional cutouts. The cast of fourteen threw everything they had into the show, including cartwheels and a girl riding a unicycle. A recurring piece of stage business was John Nichols as Bez, a baby wielding a large pink plastic hammer.

The Red Eye of Love Front row only: (l-r) Kerry McKenney, Greg Hausch, John Nichols, Gloria Johnson, Chuck Haddad, John Spangler, and Bruce Cornwell.

New Look magazine didn't care for the script, which the reviewer called "one of the most shallow pieces of the new 'artistic' literature in the world of theater," but admitted the Hippodrome people "cram it full of zany business and gimmicks... punctuated with some wonderful characterizations."[1] Not the least of which was Marilyn Wall's portrayal of a cleaning woman wearing large plastic beads as she mopped. Bruce Cornwell has compared Marilyn's ability to pull off roles like this to actress Lily Tomlin.

Papp

In February, Kerry McKenney directed *Papp* by Kenneth Cameron, starring Dan Jesse in the title role. The play was an absurdist religious satire. Papp's character was a thinly veiled substitute for the pope. Bruce Cornwell played Curio, Papp's Igor-like helper, whom Papp treated miserably. The set, designed by Marshall New, was the ruined shambles of Papp's private Vatican library. The script is essentially a satirical monologue filled with puns and blasphemy, such as the Papp's nightly conjugation with Marilyn Wall's character, Hoer of Babylond. Papp needs a successor. When Mak, a demolition expert played by John Spengler, arrives to blow the place up, Papp forestalls

Bruce Cornwell as Curio and Dan Jesse as Papp.

him with garbled versions of Bible stories. But Mak, who can read, starts correcting Papp, who cannot.

The *Gainesville Sun* called it "First rate satire."[2] Brian Jones's review in the *Independent Florida Alligator* said, "Within this simple framework pours forth the most fertile stream of twisted wordage heard around these parts in aeons. Puns, double meaning, and a thorough-going prevision of biblical parables combine to keep the dialogue dancing with bawdy surprises... fantastic acting by Dan Jesse, and a hilarious script to begin with, combine to keep the audience in smiles or better throughout the play."[3]

Macbeth

In April, the Hippodrome tackled Shakespeare with a Marilyn Wall-directed version of *Macbeth,* once again pairing friends Dan Jesse and Rusty Salling. Rusty played Macbeth, with Dan as Banquo, Macbeth's best friend. The role of Lady Macbeth went to Kerry McKenney after some contention with Mary Hausch, who also wanted the part.

Macbeth (Rusty Salling) surrounded by nine witches. Clockwise from Rusty: Laura Symons, Marilyn Hoey, Mary Hausch, Janis Falco, Celie Wolf, Christina Palacio, Chuck Haddad, Phyllis Hilenski, and Janice Sizemore.

Marilyn said she considered *Macbeth* her best work as a director, but her flamboyant nature didn't mind taking liberties with the Bard's work. The play traditionally begins with three witches foretelling Macbeth's fate. Marilyn had nine witches. She remembered that after rehearsing the first three acts, "the actors asked me about Act IV, and I said, 'Oh, let's just not do Act IV.'"

Macbeth also introduced the Hippodrome's best set designer and Marilyn's future husband, Carlos Asse. Cuban-born Carlos was a trained architect finishing a six-year program at the University of Florida. His schooling had been interrupted by a two-year stint in the army during the Vietnam War. "When I came back, I had my G.I. Bill and was not in such a hurry to graduate anymore," Carlos said. "So, I went to see a counselor at the theatre department, Michael Gillette.... I wanted to take some courses in scenic design."

Michael said, "Next semester, we only have a graduate program on this. It might prove a little bit too advanced for you, but you're welcome to audit."

Even though his classmates were graduate students, Carlos, trained in architecture, had no trouble building model sets and designing a show for the stage at the UF Constans Theatre. His work impressed the theatre students, one of whom was Kerry McKenney.

As director of *Macbeth*, Marilyn was looking for someone to help her with the set. Kerry suggested she call Carlos. He remembers, "They said they had big money to spend, they had, like, two hundred dollars." To which he said they could easily spend that much on costumes. But he took the job and designed a very stylized set, a perfect match to Marilyn's imaginative flair.

Chuck Haddad and Carlos Asse discuss construction of the *Macbeth* set.

It was relatively easy to rearrange the seating at the Hippodrome's Hawthorne Road location, so Carlos set the play in the round, with a revolving platform in the center. On the sides, four platforms had ramps that could slide out to meet the center revolve or be withdrawn to make the platforms stand-alone islands.

In the play, Macbeth takes the throne by murdering King Duncan. Shakespeare's script doesn't show the murder, but with Carlos's set design, Marilyn decided she would. She positioned two witches above Duncan's bed holding golden skins that dripped blood on him as Macbeth committed the act. The crew started rotating the stage, slowly at first, then faster and faster as Macbeth was killing Duncan. Carlos recalled, "Very gory, but very effective and very theatrical, the way it was done."

Dr. Sydney Homan, a recognized Shakespeare scholar and an associate professor in the UF English department, reviewed the play for the *Independent Florida Alligator*. "More than any other production I've seen since coming to Gainesville, this one raises the most exhilarating questions of the obligation of director to playwright and about the relation between Shakespeare's cosmic-reaching language and the present-tense physicality of the stage itself.

"Purists in the audience were doubtless shocked at the naked, writhing bodies, the overtones of the open theatre, the cuts in the text.... But what I saw here, and liked even more on reflection, was this, rather than striking a pose, a two-dimensional caricature to be rammed through successive scenes, Rusty Salling (Macbeth) and Kerry McKenney (Lady Macbeth) experimented with antithetical 'stages' of progression in the two characters.

"All the actors could take an object lesson from Daniel Jesse (Banquo) who knows how to fondle Shakespeare's marvelous language.... To be frank, you ought to beat down the doors to see it."[4]

"Carlos was a wonderful artist," Marilyn said. He stuck with the Hippodrome for the next forty-five years, eventually directing some of the plays. Future audiences marveled at Carlos's wonderfully detailed sets almost as much as the acting itself. But in the early years, he was forced to think frugally.

"The show was great," Greg Hausch said of *Macbeth*. He had the next show on the docket and said to Carlos, "I'm directing the next one, *Lysistrata*. We don't have any money. How can we make this set work for that?"

Aristophanes for the 1970s

Lysistrata, a classical Greek play by Aristophanes, was a sex romp, so Carlos covered the set with white muslin padding. Effective, yet economical. Marshall New, a skilled artist now on the Hippodrome staff, created huge drawings in the style of Aubrey Beardsley, who in 1896 illustrated the *Lysistrata* book. These were hung around the theatre and auctioned off when the play closed on June 1, 1975. Greg says the auction "made probably as much money as the show brought in."

The show was a huge hit, in part, Greg thinks, because of how much nudity it had. In the story, the women of Greece, aggravated that their men have spent the last twenty years going to war, decide to end it by withholding sex from every man in the land. Although originally performed in 411 BC, it is nonetheless a bawdy anti-war comedy. Aristophanes's message, "Make love, not war," was just right for the 1970s.

The play had scantily clad actors and duels with rubber dildos, but Greg needed someone to be fully nude for a particular scene. An amply endowed wife of one of the Hippodrome staff agreed to appear in the altogether, but only if she could wear a mask. At her day job, she taught kindergarten and was afraid her face would be recognized by someone from the school. Carlos made her a beautiful silver-looking mask that completely hid her face, and the show went on. Then, one night, her school administrators attended the show. Kerry McKenney graciously stepped in and took her part.

Clockwise from center: Bonnie Stauch, M. Catherine Piccalo, Debba Jean Rofheart, (back right) Gloria Johnson, and Deborah Kurman portray women who end war in Greece by withholding sex from every man in the land in *Lysistrata*.

The Hippodrome updated the text using modern vernacular, such as when Lysistrata's friend Cleo said, "What's up, Lys? Are you ever giving off bad vibes!" They also added music with a live band and song parodies with lyrics like, "You're doing fine, Lysistrata! Lysistrata, O.K." to the tune of the Rodgers and Hammerstein song "Oklahoma." Marshall New played the role of the commissioner, channeling a Rod Steiger-style Southern sheriff.

Although the reviewer for the *Gainesville Sun* thought there were too many four-letter words, she recommended readers see the Hippodrome production of *Lysistrata* and draw their own conclusions.

Marshall New, who went on to adapt and direct plays for the Hippodrome, found it freeing. He said, "Greg's adaptation of *Lysistrata* gave me permission to do whatever I wanted to do with the plays that I got to direct. It gave me a liberty, realizing that the directors and writers of the plays were not going to drop in on us like they do in New York."

Move to the Warehouse

After *Lysistrata* closed, it was time for the Hippodrome to find a larger home. The original space could only accommodate sixty-five to seventy-five people per show, depending on how the stage was configured. Their plays were a success, and they could easily sell more tickets if they had more seats. George Kirkpatrick, a local developer who would go on to become a state senator, was both a friend of Dick and Caren Gorenberg and a Hippodrome supporter. He had watched attendance grow until the place was filled wall to wall. One day he said, "I own this warehouse on North US 441. You guys should think about moving there." In those days, that was the outskirts of Gainesville, but so was their location on Hawthorne Road.

The warehouse had formerly been partitioned into individual bays that were rented separately, but now the entire space was available. Bruce Cornwell recalls that he and Orin Wechsberg had looked at it in the summer of 1973 when they were searching for a building to start the theatre. "But at that time," Bruce said, "the College of Dentistry had it, and all that was available was one of the little bays. It just didn't seem like it would work for our needs, so we decided to go with the store on Hawthorne Road."

By coincidence, Marilyn Wall had an office in the warehouse during her stint drawing illustrations for the UF College of Dentistry. The large steel building had eight enormous skylights made of translucent fiberglass that let in plenty of daylight. Good if you wanted a warehouse. Not so good if you were a theatre. But the 8,400 square feet of floor space would allow them to seat 280 to 375 people per show and still have room for an office, dressing rooms, and a prop/set shop.

Betsy Whitaker, founder of Trend Realty and the property's rental agent, recalls, "George [Kirkpatrick] reduced the usual rent, and I gave up my commission."

Even so, Greg recalls, "We were going to need like $1,500 a month. Mamma Mia! How were we going to swing that?" But somehow, they did.

Photo: Gary Wolfson/*Gainesville Sun*

The Hippodrome's second theatre, a warehouse on NW 53rd Avenue and US 441.

The Hippodrome didn't stage any shows that summer. Instead, everyone devoted their time to converting the warehouse into a theatre. First order of business, deal with the skylights. There were eight big ones over the main area that needed to be covered, and the Hippodromers got lucky.

The University of Florida was renovating its chemistry department building and throwing out all the chemical storage cabinets. "These had rows of drawers and were perfect for storage. We ended up using them in our scene shop to store tools. The tops were twelve feet long and thirty inches wide," Bruce said.

"They were made of oak, beautiful," Greg remembers. "We took all the drawer cabinets, and then we said, 'If you're throwing out these other countertops, we could use them.' The skylights would require two boards each. So, we took sixteen of those counters. They were heavy, in the vicinity of four hundred to five hundred pounds each. It took four people to carry one."

"Somehow we hoisted them up onto the roof and mounted them over the skylights," Bruce said. "A hurricane could go through and they weren't going anywhere. And they were perfect. They really blocked out all the light successfully, and at the same time, they also provided insulation."

Covering the skylights was only the first job. Kerry remembers, "We had to really work." That included constructing a whole new seating area. "Everybody was involved. I still have a scar from using the circular saw." They built multi-tier risers to hold seats that could be rearranged for different plays—a thrust stage for one play, in the round for the next. "At our original theatre, our equipment was very limited—like, the lights were coffee cans. Now we had this large space, we had to get serious, find some actual theatre lights. I don't know quite how we afforded that, but we did."

Greg credits Stuart Sachs, a UF engineering student, for designing their new lighting board. "It looked like a 1920s telephone operator switchboard with jacks to connect different lights to different dimmers. We also built our own grid to hang the lights."

Carlos Asse remembers the grid hung about seventeen feet above the floor and would sway. "We would use an extension ladder to hang lights. I remember one time, Bruce was standing on the ladder, and the grid moved enough that he went 'Oooo' and came down like Superman landing. He was okay but..."

"When we moved into the building out on 441," Bruce said, "we needed to let people know the new location. Marshall came up with this beautiful Art Deco design for a sign that we could put out by the road. Greg called around and found a company that would put telephone poles into the ground for us. We fabricated and assembled this Art Deco sign and then we rented one of those big cherry picker cranes to set the whole assembly up there. The sign was probably thirty to forty feet high and had space at the bottom for plastic letters like movie theaters use where we could change the name of what play was showing and the dates. It was wonderful."

Season Three

It took them all summer, but by September 1975, they were ready to open their first play in the new venue. They chose *Scuba Duba* by Bruce Jay Friedman, the author of *Steambath*, which had been a huge hit for them the previous year.

The plot concerned the misadventures of Harold Wonder (Kurt Orwick), a sweet but pathetically neurotic Jewish American vacationing with his wife (Mary Hausch) at a chateau in the South of France. Unfortunately, Mrs. Wonder starts having an affair with a Black scuba diver. While Harold tries to be non-racist and open-minded about the affair, he is kept busy by a steady stream of wacky visitors.

Nell Page played a sexy, bikini-clad American who is willing to comfort Harold. But what he wants and needs are his analyst, his mother, and his wife. A famous psychiatrist shows up with his crude girlfriend, Cheyenne, played hilariously by Marilyn Wall. In the Hippodrome production, Harold's mother was a wooden cutout that slid onstage whenever he called for advice. Harold's wife arrives with two Black men: Reddington, played by Dale McPherson, and Foxtrot, the hip, jive-talking scuba diver played to the hilt by Charles Washington. Other characters included a thief, a French policeman, an elderly landlady, and a loudmouthed ugly American.

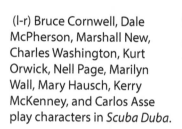
(l-r) Bruce Cornwell, Dale McPherson, Marshall New, Charles Washington, Kurt Orwick, Nell Page, Marilyn Wall, Mary Hausch, Kerry McKenney, and Carlos Asse play characters in *Scuba Duba*.

Greg Hausch directed the play, which was filled with racial slurs intended to be ironic and cause the audience to laugh at themselves. "I thought it was funny, and it was to audiences," he said, "but I guess it was a little too cutting-edge for the racial scene then. But it was definitely the biggest audiences we had had."

The new theatre had plenty of space for those large audiences, but no one had anticipated that inside the 8,400 square-foot metal building, Florida's typical tropical downpours would pound on the roof like a drum. A good, hard rainstorm would literally stop the performance. The audience couldn't hear and the actors couldn't shout loud enough to be heard. On those nights, there was no choice but to put the play on hold and wait until the rain let up.

One rain-related problem that the Hippodrome had to solve was the septic tank. The warehouse adjoined a wetland that would fill up after daylong rainstorms. This overwhelmed the building's septic system, which would cause the theatre's toilets to back up. When someone flushed and water flowed onto the stage, they knew it was time to fix the problem. On a dry day, the Hippodrome crew rented a tractor and mowed the swamp so the water wouldn't get trapped. Next, they rented an irrigation trencher and dug trenches out to the ditches that ran along US 441. That solved their stormwater problem, but it was something they had to do annually for the entire time they were in the warehouse.

Marshall Directs

The next show was two one-act plays staged October 22–26, 1975. Marshall New, having left his teaching position at UF, became a full-time member of the Hippodrome staff, although he still taught theatre part-time at Santa Fe Community College. He'd designed the set for *Papp*, done a lot of artwork for sets and posters, and had small acting roles in most of the productions following his role as Kong in *The Secret Affairs of Mildred Wild* the previous year. Now he wanted to try his hand at directing.

The two one-act plays were *Line* by Israel Horovitz and *Ravenswood* by Terrence McNally. Marshall had seen *Line* at a theatre in Atlanta and liked it. The play is an absurdist drama about five people waiting in line for an event. Each of the characters uses their wiles to be first in line, getting more and more vicious as the play progresses.

"I suggested they give it to me as a trial," Marshall said. They did. He cast Gregory Hausch, Brian Bradley, Marilyn Wall, Chuck Haddad, and Henry Fonte. "They were all pretty welcoming to me," Marshall recalled.

The second play of the night, *Ravenswood*, was directed by Marilyn Wall. Ravenswood is an expensive retreat for the unhappily married, where Dr. Pepper (Greg Hausch) dispenses his unorthodox marital theory of complete indulgence in bad habits such as smoking, drinking, and promiscuity. The cast of patients included Kerry McKenney, Mary Hausch, Marshall New, Gerry Munn, Chad Reed, Jerry Mason, and Tom Ambrosio.

Both plays were well received.

Photo: Gary Wolfson

Mary Hausch in *Ravenwood*.

A Midsummer Night's Dream

Next came their most ambitious production to date, William Shakespeare's *A Midsummer Night's Dream*. Bruce Cornwell and Kerry McKenney co-directed the cast of twenty, with several actors playing multiple roles. Among the cast was UF theatre student and Hippodrome newcomer Stephen Root. After performing in a few more Hippodrome productions and graduating from UF, Root went on to become a well-known film and television actor, nominated three times for a Screen Actors Guild Award and once for an Emmy.

Two supernaturals, Moth (Barbara Curtin) and Mustardseed (Becky McKee), feed grapes to Bottom (Marshall New) in *A Midsummer Night's Dream*.

In Marshall's opinion, "*A Midsummer Night's Dream* really redeemed us as far as the community was concerned." His words echoed *Gainesville Sun* critic Arline Greer's review: "This is one of the Hippodrome's outstanding endeavors in theatre, and it represents a return to the successful, innovative ideas it showed us when the company first set up shop two seasons ago."[5]

Kerry recalls that in the warehouse, they rearranged the seating and stage for almost every production. For *A Midsummer Night's Dream,* they suspended a platform from the ceiling to serve as the stage and set up audience seating in a horseshoe around it. A rope web over the audience members' heads became an extension of the stage. Actors swung on ropes out over the audience. The effect made the audience an implicit part of the play.

Shakespeare's story is quite complicated, with interwoven subplots concerning Athenian lovers, a group of players rehearsing a play, and a forest kingdom of fairies who manipulate the humans. Arline Greer said the Hippodrome's approach "fits the play and fits it most beautifully. It brings Shakespeare to life so successfully that a 10-year-old child could sit in the audience and rejoice in the intricacies of plot and counterplot."[6]

(below) William Hays conducts music he composed with Fernando Fonseca for the Hippodrome production of *A Midsummer Night's Dream.*

A Midsummer Night's Dream ran November 22–30, 1975, to sold-out crowds.

Shakespeare didn't write musicals, but the Hippodrome added original music to many of its early Shakespeare productions. William Hays composed and conducted a small chamber group for both *Macbeth* and *A Midsummer Night's Dream.* Multitalented Fernando Fonseca co-wrote the music for the latter, designed the crowns for Macbeth, and designed all the costumes for *A Midsummer Night's Dream.* Like Jon Schwartz, Dan Jesse, and Rusty Salling, Fernando Fonseca was an early member of Bacchus Productions (see 1974).

Free Money

The Hippodrome had received a small grant from the Florida Fine Arts Council and the National Endowment for the Arts (NEA) to produce *Macbeth.* It wasn't much—Greg thinks it was only a few hundred dollars—but it was important at the time for two reasons. First, any amount of money was a windfall to the struggling theatre. Second, they'd discovered a new source of funding. Up to that point, the theatre had survived on ticket sales (which never covered everything), selling ads in the playbills, and donations from a handful of generous locals. Grants were like receiving free money, and Bruce knew how to write grant proposals. Then, for their plays in the fall of 1975, the Hippodrome again received funding from the Florida Fine Arts Council and the NEA.

With a little encouragement from a staffer at the NEA, Greg and Kerry jumped on a plane to Washington, D.C. Greg remembers they'd been communicating by long-distance telephone because cell phones and email hadn't been invented yet, and only Fortune 500 companies had fax machines.

"Well, you sound like you got a really good thing there. You should talk to our director up here," the man told them.

"Okay, so we should come to Washington?" Greg asked. He and Kerry both remember the man saying, "Yes."

"So we told him when we were coming."

The troupe chose Kerry and Greg to represent them. They showed up at the NEA offices and said to the receptionist, "Hi, we're here to see Ray."

"He's not here. He called in sick today."

"What?" That was a problem. They didn't have a hotel room. They'd planned to meet and then to fly back that night. Greg said, "Oh, we have an appointment."

"What's your name?" the receptionist said. "Where are you from?"

"We're from Florida."

"That's odd." She called the director, Ruth Mayleas, on the intercom. "They're from Florida, and they have an appointment with Ray."

They didn't know Ruth Mayleas, except by her reputation as the Dragon Lady in charge of the NEA theatre grants program. Kerry and Greg could hear everything. "What! No, that's ridiculous. Send them home," Ruth said.

Greg leaned over the intercom. "Please, we had this appointment. Can we see Ms. Mayleas?"

"Let me go back and talk to her," the receptionist said, perhaps not wanting them to overhear any more of the conversation on the intercom.

Still, even from down the hall, Kerry and Greg could hear the exchange taking place in Ruth's office, and the woman was livid. Next thing they knew, Ruth stormed out of her office and lambasted them. "We would never in a million years tell a theatre company to come here to meet with us. If we want to talk to you, we would come to you."

Kerry and Greg were horrified. Looking back on the moment, they recall feeling crushed. They'd thought the meeting would be their big break.

Ruth continued lambasting them, asking rapid-fire questions, never letting them answer—or, if they did, telling them they were wrong. Finally, she started to ease. "Give me ten minutes," she said and strode back to her office.

A half hour passed. She called on the intercom. "Are they still here? Send them back."

They'd brought pictures and reviews, but she didn't want to see any of it. She just wanted to hear their story. So they started talking. Greg or Kerry would mention a play and say, "We did it very inventively."

"Oh, let me see that." Then she'd look at something they'd brought about the play. She continued looking through their stuff. Finally, she said, "Well, I don't know what I can do for you, but thank you for coming. I'm sorry I acted that way, but really..." Then she started scolding them again. At the end of the reprimand, she said, "Well, let me see what I can do."

While Kerry and Greg waited, she picked up the phone and called John Vos, the director of the New York State Council for the Arts and NEA on-site evaluator. "John, would you go down to Florida and see this company? They have a production of... what do you have coming up?"

"*Catch-22* will open in January," Greg said.

"Next month they're doing *Catch-22*," she said.

John told Ruth he'd put them on his schedule, and the following month, he came to see them in their tin warehouse.

1 K. Meyer, review of *The Red Eye of Love*, by Arnold Weinstein, directed by Mary Hausch, Hippodrome Theatre, Gainesville, FL, *New Look*, January 1975.
2 Arline Greer, review of *Papp*, by Kenneth Cameron, directed by Kerry McKenney, Hippodrome Theatre, Gainesville, FL, *Gainesville Sun*, March 5, 1975.
3 Brian Jones, review of *Papp*, by Kenneth Cameron, directed by Kerry McKenney, Hippodrome Theatre, Gainesville, FL, *Independent Florida Alligator*, March 6, 1975.
4 Sidney Homan, review of *Macbeth*, by William Shakespeare, directed by Marilyn Wall, Hippodrome Theatre, Gainesville, FL, *Independent Florida Alligator*, April 15, 1975.
5 Arline Greer, review of *A Midsummer Night's Dream*, by William Shakespeare, directed by Bruce Cornwell and Kerry McKenney, Hippodrome Theatre, Gainesville, FL, *Gainesville Sun*, November 27, 1975.
6 Ibid.

1976

Catch-22

1976 began with Mary Hausch directing *Catch-22*. The script was adapted by Joseph Heller from his novel of the same name. John Vos, the NEA evaluator, was impressed. His report gave the Hippodrome Theatre a glowing review, and because of that, the NEA awarded them $3,500 the following year.

Heller's adaptation reduced the novel's fifty characters to a more manageable thirty-nine. The roles were performed by fifteen actors, many playing multiple parts. Although set during World War II, the dark satire was actually aimed at subsequent wars and McCarthyism. The story centers around airman John Yossarian (played by Kevin McTigue). He is stationed at an airbase in the Mediterranean, flying sorties against German encampments in Italy.

Catch-22 actors (l-) Kenneth Bell, Kevin McTigue, Michael Quagliato, and Tom Ambrosio.

Photo: Bryan Grigsby

The play's title, which has become a common catch phrase, refers to a paradox from which contradictory rules prevent a solution. In Heller's story, an Army Air Corps rule says a man cannot fly if he is crazy; he only has to inform his superior that he is crazy. But if he asks not to fly, his concern for self-preservation shows he is rational and therefore not crazy, so he must fly. Although Yossarian is the oddball in the outfit, he turns out to be the only sane character in the story.

The *Gainesville Sun* called the production admirable and praised Mary Hausch for successfully juggling such a large cast which included Gregory Hausch, Marshall New, Michael Quagliato, David Lane, Chuck Haddad, Brian Bradley, Kerry McKenney, Gerry Munn, Tom Ambrosio, Antoinette Jourard, Kenneth Bell, and Cristina Palacio. The show ran January 30–February 8, 1976.

Three or Four One-acts

Henry Chalmers and Cory Munson in This Property is Condemned.

Twelve days after *Catch-22* closed, the Hippodrome had a show of three one-acts ready to go, which ran February 20–March 14, 1976. The plays were *This Property is Condemned* by Tennessee Williams, *Tango Palace* by Maria Irene Fornes, and *Aria Da Capo* by Edna St. Vincent Millay.

Although the plays were generally panned by *Gainesville Sun* critic Arline Greer, she praised the performance of fourteen-year-old Cory Munson as a waif in *This Property is Condemned*. Greer acknowledged that all three plays were flawlessly produced with acting of a "high order" but complained they were too abstract.

In the final five days of the run, the theatre troupe squeezed in another one-act play, Megan Terry's *Calm Down Mother*. This play, concerning female awareness and the rising identity of women, starred Mary Hausch, Kerry McKenney, and Nell Page. The play ran March 9–13, 1976.

Avant-garde *Frankenstein*

When the 1975–1976 season had been announced the previous summer, the three one-acts were scheduled to follow *Frankenstein*, but instead, the two productions swapped positions in the lineup after the season began. So, April 2–11, 1976, the Hippodrome performed a version of *Frankenstein* adapted from the Living Theatre and directed by Kerry McKenney.

Clockwise from upper right: Cathy Wolf, Mary Hausch, Marshall New, Bruce Cornwell, Helen Marietta, and Gregory Hausch in *Frankenstein*.

The Living Theatre was an avant-garde experimental theatre group founded by Judith Malina and Julian Beck in 1949 in New York City. By the late 1960s, they termed their work process collective creation—attempting to create the art in a true anarchist form. Kerry told reporter Jim Summers she considered them "the pioneers of experimental theatre."[1]

Although loosely based on the novel by Mary Shelley, the play was not the typical monster fare. The set was a two-story high structure of scaffolding divided into eight compartments on which the actors cavorted from level to level. The production depended less on dialogue than on the physicality of the actors' stylized movements. In the playbill, the actors' roles were not listed. In fact, most of the twelve cast members played four or five parts. "This production has no main characters," Kerry told the reporter. "The script was written so each character could be totally involved in the overall visual experience we are seeking."[2]

The Hippodrome was the first theatre in the country to produce an adaptation of the Living Theatre's version of *Frankenstein*. For the Hippodrome's production, Ron Sanzone composed an original score of synthesizer music to accompany the choreographed movements.

Hanging Chad

Apparently in the mood for monster tales, the Hippodrome followed *Frankenstein* with a production of Peter Barnes's *The Ruling Class,* directed by Marshall New. Although the title might lead one to expect a play somewhat akin to *Pride and Prejudice*, it is actually about Jack the Ripper, who in the play is the Fourteenth Earl of Gurney. The black comedy begins with the death of the Thirteenth Earl of Gurney, a wacko who gets off on asphyxiating himself by hanging and then calling his butler to save him. One night, the butler arrives too late and finds him dead. The Earl's nephew (played by Bruce Cornwell) then becomes the Fourteenth Earl and, secretly, Jack the Ripper. But during one performance, Chad Reed, the actor playing the Thirteenth Earl, nearly died for real.

Beneath his costume, Chad wore a special harness that held him from behind while he appeared to the audience to be hung by the neck. After standing on a stool delivering a soliloquy, Chad kicked out the stool, as scripted. But this time the body harness broke, and he was actually hanging by his neck. "I could see the people in the light booth as their mouths dropped open," Chad said. They knew what happened. "Someone came over, closed the curtain, got me down, and took me to the hospital." His friend and fellow actor Dana Preisler was in the audience. "I knew that something horrible had happened," Dana said. "Fortunately, he was tall so that he was on his tippy toes. Then, a little later, I feel something on my heel. He's underneath the bleachers passing me a note: 'I'm going to the hospital.'"

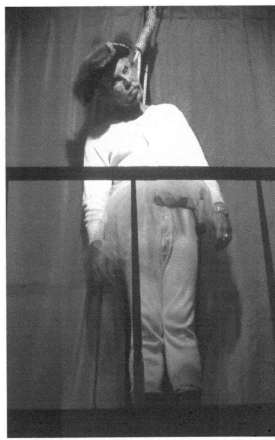

Photo: Gary Wolfson

Chad Reed as the Thirteenth Earl of Gurney in *The Ruling Class.*

The show went on without the audience ever knowing what had happened. Chad was all right. "I couldn't really sing after that," he said, "but it didn't matter. I was back in the play the next night with a very secure harness." The Hippodrome jokingly gave him an award for the best hanging that year.

Ralph Selfridge, playing Tucker, the butler, had his own mishap, albeit less life-threatening. The audience seats were set on risers, the highest of which was about six feet off the floor. When actors needed to make an entrance on the opposite side of the stage, they could go all the way around or scurry under the seating platforms between mazes of vertical supports and crossbeams. One night, Ralph was in the greenroom when he heard his cue to enter center stage carrying a large silver tray with teapot, cups, and tea. Already late, he dashed through the maze during the blackout, struck his head, and sent broken china and puddles of tea over the lobby floor.

The *Gainesville Sun* review praised the acting and called it "a hum-dinger of a funny, funny show."[3] *The Ruling Class* ran from April 30–May 9, 1976.

Meanwhile, the Hippodrome hired a business manager, John Wilson, a necessity for the growing theatre company whose founders readily admitted they weren't business minded.

Tom Jones

Less than three weeks after *The Ruling Class* closed, they were ready with *Tom Jones*, adapted from Henry Fielding's novel. The Hippodrome created its own adaptation, selecting the best elements from the stage play and film script. To this they added music, dance, singing, and a new character, the minstrel (Daryl Hunt) as narrator. Greg Hausch directed, setting it in the round with the audience on all sides, no backdrops, period costumes, and minimal props.

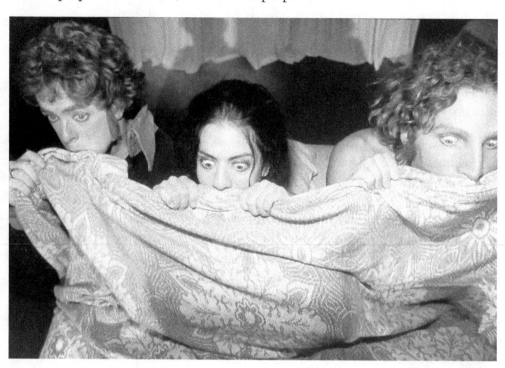

In *Tom Jones*, (l-r) Mr. Fitzpatrick (Kevin McTigue) catches Mrs. Waters (Mary Hausch) in bed with Tom Jones (Oren Leblang).

The show ran from May 28–June 6, 1976. Ads for the play declared it X-rated, which had the effect of packing the house. The *Gainesville Sun* drama critic called it "colorful, original, musical, risque, dramatically interesting, fast-moving, and true to the spirit of its origins." She went on, "*Tom Jones* is farce at its best tongue-in-cheek merriment that fairly makes your sides ache from laughing at the ingeniously convoluted shenanigans of the principal players."[4] Among the forty-member cast were Oren Leblang as Tom Jones and Hippodrome regulars Mary Hausch, Kerry McKenney, and Marshall New, all of whom the review praised effusively.

The Real Inspector Hound

In July, the theatre opened the Tom Stoppard play *The Real Inspector Hound*, directed by Mary Hausch. The show consisted of two simultaneous plays. One is the story of two theatre critics, played by Greg Hausch and Marshall New, watching a ludicrous murder mystery. Second is the play the critics were sent to review—a parody of an Agatha Christie-type whodunit, where a man has been murdered by his lover with an ax in the drawing room of an isolated country mansion. Mrs. Drudge, the help, played by Dana Preisler, cleans the room oblivious to the dead body. Later, the play restarts and the critics get trapped in it, mistaken for the characters in the play, while two of the original actors wind up in the critic's booth.

Sun drama critic Arline Greer wrote, "I have yet to see a nuttier, zanier, more kooky, downright mystifyingly hilarious satire in my entire life than this British comedy. That is not to say I understood one whit of it, nor that you will, necessarily... so I cannot make the unqualified assumption that you practically will fall on the floor from laughing as I did at *The Real Inspector Hound*. The likelihood of that happening, however, is good."[5]

The Real Inspector Hound ran July 16–31 and then was brought back September 16–18 for another three-day run.

Photo: Gary Wolfson/*Gainesville Sun*

Gerry Munn as *The Real Inspector Hound*.

NASA Calls

In 1976, the United States celebrated its bicentennial, and the Hippodrome was involved in several ways. First, officials from the City of Gainesville tapped Greg Hausch to emcee Independence Day events downtown, including dedication of the new community plaza next to the courthouse. The plaza (later named Bo Diddley Plaza) was built and funded mainly by volunteers because the city didn't have enough money. Since the Hippodrome was still in the warehouse out on US 441, being invited downtown probably felt like acceptance by the mainstream.

Then the NEA called, asking if the Hippodrome would be the official bicentennial players at Cape Kennedy. "NASA built a little theatre for us inside the Vehicle Assembly Building to seat about one hundred people," Greg Hausch said. "We performed a collection of thirty short cartoon-like sketches written by Jules Feiffer called *Feiffer's People*." Greg doesn't think the material would hold up today. "If you read them now, it's kind of like, *ouch*. But some were funny, and we made our characters funny. We were on their tour of the space center. They'd watch for a few minutes and move on. It was fine and lasted for the summer of '76."

Season Four

September 19–26, 1976, the *Gainesville Sun* hosted the eight-day Suntennial Festival to celebrate its one-hundredth birthday. The Hippodrome was selected to close the final four nights of the festival with a performance of its upcoming musical adaptation of William Shakespeare's *Two Gentlemen of Verona*, which was co-sponsored by the City of Gainesville. At the time, in addition to the stage that is presently in the plaza, there was also a water fountain in the grassy area where children played during the daytime festivities. In the evening, the Hippodrome staff laid boards

Performing *Two Gentlemen of Verona* at the downtown plaza. Note the stage is built over a water fountain that is no longer there.

Photo: Bryan Grigsby/*Gainesville Sun*

over the fountain, creating a makeshift second stage so some scenes of the play could be performed in the round.

During one of the festival's nightly performances, Greg Hausch, in the role of Valentine, was singing when a golden retriever ambled through the audience, walked onstage, and sat down in front of Greg. Quickly improvising, the actor kneeled, petted the dog, and sang the rest of the song to the dog. The audience loved it.

Producing *Two Gentlemen of Verona* challenged the Hippodrome's creativity. Shakespeare's play had been adapted into a rock musical that had won the 1971 Tony Awards for Best Musical and Best Book of a Musical. The Hippodrome secured performance rights and was well into rehearsal when the New York producers told them at the last minute, "We're not giving you the rights."

What a blow! Still, the New York producers didn't own Shakespeare's words, just the music and lyrics they'd added. So, the Hippodrome stripped out the songs and created their own. Bruce and Greg furiously wrote lyrics while Gainesville musicians Michael Gordon and Ray Van Shattenkirk composed the music over the next five days. The cast learned all the new songs, and the show went on.

The play is one of Shakespeare's early comedies, written when he was only about thirty years old. Lifelong friends Valentine (Gregory Hausch) and Proteus (Pete Colley) leave their rural hometown for life in the big city. There, Valentine meets and falls in love with Sylvia (Kerry McKenney), but her father, the Duke of Milan (Marshall New), has betrothed her to a wealthy undesirable, Thurio (Gerry Munn). Then, Proteus sets his sights on Sylvia, disregarding his friendship with Valentine as well as his sweetheart back home, Julia (Nell Page).

Complications arise. Valentine is banished from the duke's court. Julia disguises herself as a man to seek out Proteus, and Sylvia escapes from her betrothal to find Valentine. The duke comes to his senses and realizes Valentine should marry Sylvia the same day that Proteus weds Julia.

In addition to adding rock music, director Bruce Cornwell took other liberties with Shakespeare's script. "The play lent itself to this type of production because it's light material, geared primarily toward entertainment," Cornwell said. "We've taken some of the ideas Shakespeare created with words and recreated them onstage with actions."[6] Not above bending the Bard's plot, Cornwell added the twist that Julia's quest to find Proteus is because she is pregnant.

Kim Tuttle, co-founder and artistic director of Dance Alive National Ballet, provided the choreography. Nell Page, whose role as Julia required her to dance, recalls, "Kim Tuttle pulled me aside and said, 'Nell, I can't teach you to be a dancer, but I can teach you to dance. You just got to go with me on that.'"

Although the play was part of the *Gainesville Sun* festival, the newspaper's drama critic called it twaddle, but she did suggest that those who weren't picky would probably have a good laugh.

The play's premiere, scheduled for September 23, was postponed by a day when the *Sun* canceled the festival's Thursday night activities so as not to conflict with the presidential debate between Gerald Ford and Jimmy Carter. After performing three nights in the plaza, September 24, 25, and 26, the play moved to the Hippodrome Theatre on US 441 and continued its run through October 16, 1976.

Gainesville Gets Feiffer

While preparations were underway to open David Rabe's *In the Boom Boom Room* in November, the Hippodrome presented the aforementioned *Feiffer's People* to Gainesville audiences for a two-night run October 22–23.

Jules Feiffer's biting vignettes, which equally satirized virtually all aspects of American life, had not always gone over well with conservative tourists at the Kennedy Space Center performances. "Some of the people were offended by the contents. Anything alluding to sex was considered in bad taste," Greg Hausch said of the NASA audiences. "Mostly tourists in Bermuda shorts.... The people were so conservative that many left during a spoof on Ronald Reagan."

That wasn't the case in Gainesville, where the cast, made up entirely of Hippodrome artistic directors (Greg and Mary Hausch, Kerry McKenney, Marshall New, and Bruce Cornwell), brought the skits into the audience as a way of getting them involved. Gainesville audiences were far more receptive. This was possibly aided by free beer. That's right. Both nights, audiences were provided with unlimited free beer, making for a jolly crowd.

Photo: Bryan Grigsby

Marshall New and Mary Hausch in *Feiffer's People*.

In the Boom Boom Room

By mid-November, *In the Boom Boom Room* was ready with what was the Hippodrome's most elaborate set up to that point. The two-tier stage consisted of a fully realized bar and go-go nightclub with cages for dancers, as was typical of those clubs. On the upper level was the main character's apartment, including a bed, dining table, stove, refrigerator, and vanity. Experimenting with what director Marshall New called "environmental theatre," the first row of seats was replaced with round cocktail tables, and audience members seated there became patrons of the sleazy bar. Additional go-go dancers were stationed throughout the audience. To complete the immersive experience, audience members could purchase drinks from the Boom Boom Room bar during intermission.

(l-r) Kerry McKenney, Bruce Cornwell, and Brian Bradley in the apartment above the Boom Boom Room.

The play, billed as a tragicomedy, revolves around a young woman searching for her identity in the turbulent sixties. She dreams of becoming a successful dancer in New York but ends up working as a topless dancer at Big Tom's Boom Boom Room in Philadelphia. Working there, she is exploited, manipulated, and used by a bizarre pack of characters. Her lover is a hood. Her alcoholic father may have sexually abused her. Her mother wanted to abort her. The club's lesbian master of ceremonies wants to have sex with her. The homosexual man from the downstairs apartment wants her to pretend they are dating. The straight guy who wants to marry her promises he'll "make love to you so kindly, so gently, you'll hardly notice."[7]

Reviews in both the *Independent Florida Alligator* and the *Gainesville Sun* were critical of the script as lacking dramatic progression and the acting as too shrill. The two-and-a-half-hour play provided only a few scenes of comic relief. After the play, one theatergoer remarked, "That was a very heavy number!" The show ran November 12–28, 1976.

In terms of significant Hippodrome history, *In the Boom Boom Room* first introduced Gainesville audiences to actor Michael Doyle. A powerful, nuanced performer, Doyle, for whom the Hippodrome's current mainstage is named, was considered by his peers to be the company's most skilled actor. Until his untimely death at an early age, Michael's outstanding performances graced most of the Hippodrome's best-praised plays.

1 Jim Summers, "*Frankenstein* at Hippodrome Assaults Senses," *Gainesville Sun*, March 26, 1976.
2 Ibid.
3 Arline Greer, review of *The Ruling Class* by Peter Barnes, directed by Marshall New, Hippodrome Theatre, Gainesville, FL, *Gainesville Sun*, May 7, 1976.
4 Arline Greer, review of *Tom Jones* by Henry Fielding, directed by Greg Hausch, Hippodrome Theatre, Gainesville, FL, *Gainesville Sun*, June 2, 1976.
5 Arline Greer, review of *The Real Inspector Hound*, by Tom Stoppard, directed by Mary Hausch, Hippodrome Theatre, Gainesville, FL, *Gainesville Sun*, July 23, 1976.
6 John Snyder, "*Two Gentlemen of Verona*," *Gainesville Sun*, September 17, 1976.
7 David Rabe, *In the Boom Boom Room*, Concord Theatricals, New York, NY.

1977

An Odd Pair of One-acts

In January 1977, the Hippodrome returned to a favorite format of pairing two one-act plays. This time they chose David Mamet's *The Duck Variations* and *Rubbers* by Jonathan Reynolds. It was an odd pairing. *The Duck Variations* is a funny/sad gentle exploration of life by two elderly men sitting on a park bench watching ducks. *Rubbers*, on the other hand, is a satirical comedy with a cast of seventeen. *Rubbers* is based on something that actually happened in the New York State Legislature when the only female representative tried to pass a bill allowing prophylactics to be openly displayed in pharmacies. Kerry McKenney directed both plays, managing to preserve their opposite tones.

Photo: Gary Wolfson

The cast of *Rubbers* portray legislators opposed to letting pharmacies display condoms. Gale Nevill, David Lane, Chuck Haddad, Gregory Hausch, Jerry Mason, Gerry Munn, and Fran Watkins.

The pair of one-acts ran from January 21–February 6, 1977. *The Duck Variations* was performed again in March at the Florida State Museum for a convention of museum directors. In 1979, the Hippodrome received a grant to do a statewide tour of *The Duck Variations*.

Vanities

The most successful play of the 1976–1977 season was *Vanities* by Jack Heifner, which opened February 25. Directed by Gregory Hausch, the play follows three women, played by Mary Hausch, Nell Page, and Rena Carney, through three stages of their lives: as high school cheerleaders in the first act, later as college sorority sisters, and finally meeting again in a New York City apartment six years later. Rather than have intermission, the playbill advised, "There will be ten-minute transition periods between the acts in which you may mumble discretely and/or

Mary Hausch, Nell Page, and Rena Carney in *Vanities*.

perform anything you need to do."[1] During the transitions, the actors remained onstage, changing costumes and applying makeup to age themselves for the next act.

Gregory Hausch recalls that getting rights to the play was a coup for the Hippodrome. "We saw the production of *Vanities* at the Chelsea Theatre in New York, and we were just blown away by it." Playing one of the roles in the New York show was an unknown actress, Kathy Bates, who would go on to a long stage and screen career, winning Oscar, Emmy, Obie, Outer Critic's Circle, and Drama Desk awards.

"So after the show was over," Greg said, "we go backstage and talk to Kathy Bates and the director, Garland Wright. We tell them we've got this theatre and would really love to do *Vanities* there. And they gave it to us! We were the first theatre outside of New York City to do it."

Gainesville loved it, and *Sun* critic Arline Greer heaped on the praise. She wrote, "The acting by the three women cast is splendid, with Mary Hausch as Kathy, Nell Page as Mary, and Rena Carney as Joanne. Miss Carney is the acting find of the year, a joy to watch in all her innocent big-eyed pronouncements, her aspirations to the square, humble life, her literal interpretation of events around her. Nell Page is properly adept at developing the naughtiness of the young Mary into the degeneracy of the older Mary."[2] Greer said Mary Hausch had "some quiet, strong moments of revelation in the last act, when she recognizes the stupidity of the girls' high school and college years, when all they aspired to was leading cheers and being popular. *Vanities* is that rare species of play; a comedy that cuts through to the bone but leaves the body intact."[3]

One incident that occurred during the first act of *Vanities*, Nell Page will never forget. She said, "In the scene where we were cheerleaders in high school, we were chewing gum and sharing it. Well, Rena Carney loved potato chips and so she requested that there be chips, too, because she thought that would be a very teenage thing to do. So, she'd eaten a bunch of potato chips and chewed the gum, and then she passed this gob of gum to me. I thought, oh, here we go. You could hear the audience go, 'Ew!'"

Vanities ran through March 12. While they were striking the set, a director from the Sea Ranch Dinner Theatre in Lauderdale-by-the-Sea, Florida, approached Greg. He said, "Would you bring this down and open it up next week in Fort Lauderdale and run it for a month?" The Hippodrome said, "Yes." Rena Carney had another commitment, so Eileen Freid replaced her in the role of Joanne.

This was the first of several state tours the Hippodrome did. During the South Florida run, they garnered positive articles in the *Miami Herald* and the *Fort Lauderdale News,* the *Sandpiper,* and the *Sun Sentinel.* These and other touring plays gave the Gainesville theatre statewide recognition.

Butley

From April 8–23, 1977, the Hippodrome staged Simon Gray's dark comedy *Butley*, with Michael Doyle in his first leading role.

The play explores the complex relationships between Ben Butley (Michael Doyle), a brilliant, intellectual alcoholic university professor with unattainable literary standards, and the other characters in his life. Within a single day, he loses his wife plus his close friend, colleague, and possibly male lover, Joey (played by Bruce Cornwell).

Photo: Gary Wolfson

Butley hurls himself toward self-destruction, bullying students, friends, and colleagues (played by Mary Joye, Jenny Streiff, Dana Moser (formerly Dana Preisler), Marshall New, and Pete Colley). Bruce said of Butley, "In his personally charming way, he manages to alienate the people in his life who are closest to him."

The *Independent Florida Alligator* called the play "witty, vicious, clever and entertaining" and Michael Doyle's performance "an intense tour de force by one of Gainesville's greatest actors."[4]

Ben Butley (Michael Doyle) taunts Joey (Bruce Cornwell).

Sun critic Arline Greer wrote, "Kerry McKenney has directed *Butley* with complete understanding of its many levels of meaning. She moves the play tautly and subtly, creating one of the genuine theatre surprises of the season: a truly outstanding play."[5]

Carnal Knowledge

The following month, the *Gainesville Sun* equally praised Mary Hausch's direction of the Hippodrome's final play of the season, *Carnal Knowledge*. The Hippodrome had created its own adaptation of the controversial hit film written by Jules Feiffer.

The story revolves around two men, Jonathan (Jon Schwartz) and Sandy (Gregory Hausch), who search for identity through sexual exploits first in their college days and then, in the second act, during middle age. Sandy, the more naïve of the two, idolizes women while Jonathan, more interested in a woman's physical attributes, objectifies them. The play's five female characters each have their own flaws.

In act one, Sandy and Jonathan are college roommates looking to lose their virginity. Predictably, they fall for the same girl, Susan (Kerry McKenney), who ends up having sex with both men but marries Sandy. Jonathan, who measures perfection by a woman's bust size, takes up with voluptuous Bobbie (Margaret Bachus).

Twenty years later, in middle age, none of them are satisfied. Bobbie is depressed, and Jonathan finds her shallow. Sandy confides to him that perhaps sex is "just not meant to be enjoyable with the woman you love."[6] Sandy leaves Susan for eighteen-year-old Jennifer (Jackie Minari). After Jennifer leaves Sandy, he takes up with a

Jon Schwartz, Kerry McKenney, and Gregory Hausch in *Carnal Knowledge*.

Photo: Gary Wolfson

flower child (Lura Hartness). Jonathan hires a prostitute (Christina Palacio) to help him achieve sexual satisfaction.

Carnal Knowledge brought Margaret Bachus into the Hippodrome troupe of actors for her first role, but her part in the theatre's history became significant when she helped establish the Hippodrome's Theatre for Young Audiences.

Margaret recalled that her unique entry into the company began one night while attending a Hippodrome play earlier in the season. Just before the play was to start, Marshall New approached her and said, "We have something we'd like you to audition for at intermission, if you're interested."

She said, "Okay."

"But I have to tell you," Marshall said, "it has a bit of nudity."

Margaret's audition won her the role but, as the mother of three little children, she had stipulations regarding the nudity. "No photographs at all, and I will not do the scene in the nude until the final dress rehearsal."

The Hippodrome agreed to her terms and Margaret did *Carnal Knowledge,* playing the role for which movie star Ann-Margret had won a Golden Globe for Best Supporting Actress.

Season Five

Vanities, which was touring the state in the summer of 1977, returned to Gainesville July 1–16, 1977, for a short run while the next play, *Soap,* was in rehearsal.

Kerry McKenney, Larry Carle, and Darrell Hammond in *Soap*.

Photo: Gary Wolfson

Although audiences nowadays expect the Hippodrome to end its season with a summer play, 1977 was different. The first play of the 1977–1978 season, *Soap*, opened July 29, ran through August 13, and then resumed September 14–24.

A parody of television soap operas, *Soap*, written by Allan Albert, was directed by Marshall New, who also played a television show director onstage. In *Soap*, the actors play the cast and crew of *The Wanton Wind*, whose off-camera personalities closely parallel their TV characters.

In typical soap opera fashion, the plot thickens, and thickens, and thickens. The TV producers have brought *The Wanton Wind* to Gainesville in an attempt to get the show canceled. The Hippodrome stage is the television studio, and the audience is a Nielson rating family whose vote at the end of the play will determine the soap opera's fate, as well as the fate of one of the TV show characters.

The *Independent Florida Alligator* found the play to be generally successful and "on occasion side-splittingly funny," but qualified the review by adding, "However, listening to the seemingly never-ending verbal garbage of the characters is tedious."[7]

A New Level of Excellence

"Forget *Soap*," Greg Hausch said. "*Equus* was a hallmark production. Nothing we had done up to that time had come anywhere near that."

Gainesville audiences agreed. *Equus*, written by Peter Schaffer and directed by Bruce Cornwell, brought a new level of excellence to the Hippodrome and won the theatre statewide respect. The play opened September 30, 1977, and was held over repeatedly into November.

Photo: Gary Wolfson

Michael Doyle as psychiatrist Dr. Martin Dysart in *Equus*.

Set in a psychiatric hospital in Southern England, the play tells the story of psychiatrist Dr. Martin Dysart's attempts to treat Alan Strang, a seventeen-year-old boy with a pathological worship of horses. Dysart learns from Alan's parents that the boy grew up with conflicting views on religion. From the boy, the psychiatrist learns that his attraction to horses has morphed into a personal theology of a supreme godhead called Equus as a representative of God.

Dysart probes Alan's memory, revealing that he had become erotically fixated on a horse named Nugget that he secretly rode bareback while naked. When Jill, a young girl his age, attempts to seduce Alan in the stables, he hears the horses and cannot complete the act. After Jill leaves, he asks the god-like horses' forgiveness. Then, believing they have seen his very soul, he uses a steel spike to blind them.

The play includes overtones of Greek theatre, dramatizing the conflict between Apollonian and Dionysian values and using Greek human/animal imagery reminiscent of centaurs. The show had been a smash hit in London and later on Broadway. Leading actors of the day—Richard Burton, Leonard Nimoy, and Anthony Perkins—had played the difficult role of Dr. Dysart. Naturally, the Hippodrome wanted their best actor, Michael Doyle, for the part, but for some reason, he didn't think he could do it.

"So we bought him a ticket to see it in New York that summer," Marshall New said.

"We actually got seated on the stage and saw Anthony Perkins play the lead," Gregory Hausch recalls.

After the show, Mike Doyle told them, "I can do it."

The role of the boy, Alan Strang, went to Mark Sexton, marking his debut performance at the Hippodrome. Later, Mark would return to the Hippodrome to perform in over thirty plays and serve as its general manager for twenty years. But at the time, he was an undergraduate Fine Arts major at Florida State University (FSU).

Here's how Mark remembers it: "My first interaction with the Hippodrome folks was when they came up to Tallahassee to see a play called *In the Boom Boom Room* by David Rabe. They came backstage and said 'hi,' and then they left.

"Some time went by, then word got out that this interesting, avant-garde, fledgling theatre in Gainesville was doing *Equus*, and *Equus* was a really big deal at the time. It was getting a lot of buzz all around the world. It hadn't even been released to major cities yet, and the Hippodrome was doing it in Gainesville, Florida, of all places.

Mark Sexton as seventeen-year-old Alan Strang with the horses played by Kevin Cutts, Liddon Dell, Leigh Montanye, and Bryan Roy in *Equus*.

Photo: Gary Wolfson

"A friend of mine, a fellow actor at FSU, and I were familiar with the play. We decided to drive down to Gainesville and audition. We were both in a movement/ mime class at FSU, and we knew that there were elements of movement in the play, so we actually created this piece that we called 'The Boy and His Horse.' My friend was a big guy, so he was the horse and I, the boy. We did these scenes where I was grooming him because I knew that was one of the actions in the play. So we came down and read for some of the scenes in the play. The Hippodrome said, 'Thank you very much,' and we went back to Tallahassee. Then shortly thereafter, I got the call. I'm sorry to say my friend who played the horse didn't get called.

"It was kind of surreal. But one of the greatest things about doing it was getting to know Mike Doyle. Being onstage with him was a privilege, and a class in and of itself. Then, working with Bruce Cornwell as the director was just incredible. The play was very challenging, and my character in particular had some challenges that I had never experienced before onstage, and Bruce handled it with sensitivity."

Bruce Cornwell credits the wonderful collaboration. William Hays created the soundtrack. Choreographer Sandy Scott had the five actors who played horses visit stables to observe equine motion. Stuart Sacks devised a heavy revolving stage, while Marilyn Wall and Carlos Asse designed the horse heads. The heads appeared to be made of stainless steel or chrome, but that would have been far too heavy. Instead, they were made out of thin wooden dowels that were wetted and bent into shape and held their positions after they dried. The dowels were then wrapped in shiny silver tape that, under the theatre lights, made them look just like wire. The horses' hoofs were actual stainless steel platforms about six inches tall, culminating in a horseshoe.

The play had opened to rave reviews in London and New York. The Hippodrome's production received praise equal to that given in those larger cities. *Sun* critic Arline Greer effused, "Brilliantly acted, inventively staged, and directed with an uncommonly rare understanding of a complex, multi-faceted play, it offers theatergoers a once-in-a-decade opportunity to experience drama that is both intellectually provocative and emotionally moving."[8]

New Look magazine said, "*Equus*, one of the most awesome affairs ever undertaken by the Hippodrome, signals the opening of a new epoch for this community theatre."[9]

The rights had been expensive—a thousand dollars a week, the highest the Hippodrome had ever paid. But it had been worth it. Every show sold out. As a newbie, Mark Sexton recalls, "Having never done a show, I didn't know at first, I kept hearing, 'Wow! Another full house.' Then, 'Oh, we're extending the run. Oh, we're extending it, again.' Then, 'We're taking it on tour!'"

A professional theatre producer from the Tampa area was really excited about the production and approached the Hippodrome. He negotiated to take it on tour throughout the Southeast. Stuart Sacks and Carlos Asse worked up a plan for how to reconfigure the set so it could be taken on the road. Stuart accompanied Bruce and the company, rearranging the set to fit venues in Tampa, St. Petersburg, Miami, Orlando, Jacksonville, and other cities outside Florida, including 100 colleges and universities.

Mark took a semester off to tour. After he returned to college and graduated, he tried out in New York City, as many actors do. "The first audition I had in New York was to do *Equus* in New England," he said. "So, I rode that horse about as far as I could ride it."

The Gainesville production and tour were wildly successful. Even after the tour, *Equus* continued to earn the Hippodrome money as they rented the equine heads and hoofs to other theatre companies.

"Everything about the production was stellar," Nell Page said. "It was just the perfect storm."

Equus presented a level of professional theatre Gainesville audiences hadn't seen before. It set a new standard that the Hippodrome would be expected to meet on every play thereafter. "It raised our game," Marshall New said. "Make no mistake about it."

The Tempest

The Hippodrome immediately followed *Equus* with William Shakespeare's *The Tempest*. Director Greg Hausch and the Hippodrome crew threw all of their creative energies into a free-swinging version.

The story begins with a powerful storm that wrecks a ship on a remote island where Prospero, who is a sorcerer and former Duke of Milan, lives with his daughter Miranda and two servants, Caliban, a monster, and Ariel, an airy spirit. During the storm scene, actors and the ship below them roll and pitch onstage while another actor, sitting in the crow's nest of the ship's tall mast, tilts back and forth over the audience's heads.

The storm is no accident, but magic invoked by Prospero and created by Ariel. Among those shipwrecked are Antonio, the man who usurped Prospero's dukedom, and the men who helped him do it—the king of Naples, Alonso, and his trusted counselor, Gonzalo. Stranded with them are Alonso's brother, Sebastian, and son, Ferdinand.

Prospero separates the survivors into groups using magic. Then he finds Ferdinand, betroths Miranda to him, and instructs Ariel to bring some other spirits to celebrate the betrothal. Creating its own memorable bit of stage magic, the Hippodrome cast lithe young dancers as the spirits and had them hide in the space underneath the seats. At the appropriate time, a low bank of fog flooded the stage, and the spirits made their entrance from beneath the audience's feet.

Antonio, Sebastian, and Gonzalo plot to kill King Alonso and make Sebastian king. Caliban aligns himself with the king's jester and butler to attempt a coup against Prospero. In the end, Caliban and his cohorts are chased into the swamp. Prospero's title is restored. He forgives those who wronged him, and he sets Ariel free.

Caliban is symbolically a monstrous figure. Marshall New, who had made his Hippodrome debut dressed as a gorilla, decided to portray the character literally. He'd seen photos of an Edward Albee play in which a couple on the beach had a dialogue with two lizards. Marshall wondered if that costume was still available. "I wrote the company in New York and rented that costume personally," Marshall said. "I played him kind of as Peter Lorre." Caliban as a man-size lizard was a huge hit with audiences.

Reviewing the play for *New Look*, Richard Burkholder wrote, "To portray a cringing servant in lizard skin proved an inspired stoke; all New need do the night we attended was to step on stage and await applause."[10]

Chad Reed recalls, "Caliban, in that lizard costume, that's one of my favorite memories. Marshall never did anything halfway. He would throw his whole body into it."

Days before rehearsals were to begin, Greg had all the roles cast except for the most important one, Prospero. Dan Jesse recommended Greg audition Mike Beistle. "This guy can really do Shakespeare," Dan said. "You really got to see him."

"Okay, great," Greg said. "Then, I'm holding auditions in the warehouse and wondering, where is this guy Dan's talking about? He's out in the parking lot pacing. He was a chain smoker and nervous to

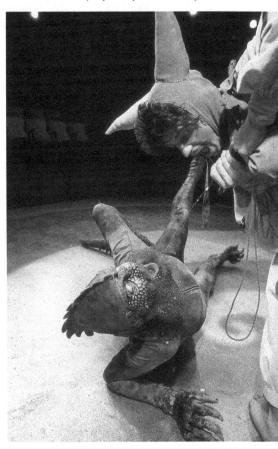

Wearing a lizard costume, Marshall New (as Caliban) receives a drink from a jester played by Pete Colley.

Photo: Gary Wolfson

audition with all these young people that didn't really have any resumes and were just starting out." Mike was considerably older than the others. He'd directed plays at the University of Florida and taught at Oak Hall, a local private school, where he'd been named Teacher of the Year. Eventually, Greg got Mike inside to audition and could tell he was going to be good. "But I had no idea," Greg said. "Oh, my God, he was just brilliant as Prospero."

Mike Beistle (center) making his Hippodrome debut as Prospero in *The Tempest*. Clockwise from lower left: Dan Jesse with back to camera, Craig Hartley, Leigh Montanye, Bruce Cornwell, and Rick Schneider. Sprites seated at Mike Beistle's feet: Susan Stewart, Ginger Pollini, Dawn Saurey, and Martha Williams at far right.

Photo: Gary Wolfson

Marshall added, "Thank God for Mike Beistle as he kept it together. You know Shakespeare's hard when you've got young people playing Shakespeare and having a hard time with his language." Marshall was referring to the fact that many of the supporting players were teenagers or younger, drawn from the Hippodrome's high school workshops and local ballet classes.

A late addition to the cast was Dan Jesse, who was doing a show in Miami when Greg went to see him. The actor that Greg cast as Gonzalo had dropped out. Greg told Dan, "I'd love to have you come up and do it." So Dan stepped into the role of Gonzalo. He and Mike Beistle were great friends and subsequently performed many comedies together at the Hippodrome that became the stuff of legends. After *The Tempest* closed, Dan was offered a full-time staff position at the Hippodrome, in which he remained for the next three years.

The Tempest opened November 11 and continued through December 11, 1977, after extending its run. Audiences loved it—the critics not so much, suggesting that the director had gone too far in pulling out all the stops. But, said Arline Greer, "I found Michael Beistle, as Prospero, to be the most successful in his ability to speak the Shakespearean tongue and act meaningfully. Bruce Cornwell makes a fine villain.... As always, New is able to transcend any difficulties, whether they be in production or play, and provide a character to savor."[11]

The Hippodrome didn't have a theatrical fog machine, so they concocted one of their own. They put 220-volt hot water heating elements in fifty-five-gallon drums and ran dryer hoses from the drum lids to beneath the seating platforms. Then drums were filled to two-thirds capacity with water and heated until the water was very hot. When it was time for fog, they'd drop dry ice into the water through a trapdoor in the lid and fog would then pour out of the hoses.

The fog it created looked great, but it was a wet fog that left a veneer of moisture on the stage so actors sometimes lost their footing.

Kerry McKenney, as Ariel, had her own adventures. The set had a steel wire strung from a platform above the top row of seats down to the back of the stage. There was a trapeze-like handlebar with which Ariel flew over the audience's heads into a scene. "When I was going to fly, people were supposed to be on the other side to catch me [backstage]," Kerry remembers. "They did okay in the beginning, and then they started getting a little loose, and then they just barely caught me."

Perhaps the wildest moment during the run of *The Tempest* was drug-related. Marshall New came offstage after a scene and a friend backstage gave him a quaalude, which was a strong prescription depressant popularly used recreationally in the 1970s.

"I went onstage and finished my last scene," Marshall said. "When I came off, my friend was still standing there. I said that I didn't feel anything."

"Have another one," his friend said. Marshall accepted.

"Onstage for the curtain call, I fell flat on my face. Everyone in the cast knew that I had taken something. Some of them grabbed me under the arms and picked me up. The audience screamed with laughter."

1 *Vanities* playbill, Hippodrome Theatre, Gainesville, FL, 1977.
2 Arline Greer, review of *Vanities*, by Jack Heifner, directed by Gregory Hausch, Hippodrome Theatre, Gainesville, FL, *Gainesville Sun*, March 3, 1977.
3 Ibid.
4 Mark Hoover, review of *Butley*, by Simon Greer, directed by Kerry McKenney, Hippodrome Theatre, Gainesville, FL, *Independent Florida Alligator*, April 11, 1977.
5 Arline Greer, review of *Butley*, by Simon Greer, directed by Kerry McKenney, Hippodrome Theatre, Gainesville, FL, *Gainesville Sun*, April 14, 1977.
6 *Carnal Knowledge*. by Jules Feiffer.
7 James Weinstock, review of *Soap*, by Allan Albert, directed by Marshall New, Hippodrome Theatre, Gainesville, FL, *Independent Florida Alligator*, August 8, 1977.
8 Arline Greer, review of *Equus*, by Peter Schaffer, directed by Bruce Cornwell, Hippodrome Theatre, Gainesville, FL, *Gainesville Sun*, October 7, 1977.
9 Richard Burkholder, "*Equus* the Hippodrome's Big Event," *New Look*, October 15, 1977.
10 Richard Burkholder, review of *The Tempest*, by William Shakespeare, directed by Gregory Hausch, Hippodrome Theatre, Gainesville, FL, *New Look*, December 1977.
11 Arline Greer, review of *The Tempest*, by William Shakespeare, directed by Gregory Hausch, Hippodrome Theatre, Gainesville, FL, *Gainesville Sun*, November 24, 1977.

1978

The Play That Didn't

The world premiere of a stage version of Vladimir Nabokov's novel *Lolita*, adapted by Marshall New, was set to follow *The Tempest*. One reason the Hippodrome got the rights to do plays before other theatres was that they had the chutzpah to ask the impossible, whether that was showing up in Kathy Bates's dressing room to ask director Garland Wright for *Vanities* or convincing the producers of *Equus* to let them have it. Such was the case with *Lolita*.

Marshall New thought the controversial book would make a good play and would enhance the Hippodrome's reputation for edgier material. So, he wrote Vladimir Nabokov that he'd like to adapt *Lolita* to the stage. Nabokov would receive 6 percent of ticket sales or $750, whichever was more. Nabokov wired back, "Sure, if you just send me your version of the script before you produce it." Marshall said he would.

The play was announced as part of the 1977–1978 season and tickets were sold. Marshall cast Bruce Cornwell as Humbert Humbert, Maggie Beistle as Charlotte Haze, Dan Jesse as the evil Quilty, and a handful of teenagers as Lolita's mates, but continued searching for just the right actress to play Lolita. After auditioning fifty girls, he settled on sixteen-year-old Maria Parkinson from Pennsylvania.

Photo: Gary Wolfson

Maria Parkinson was cast as Lolita, but the play was canceled.

Facing community criticism for not choosing a Gainesville actress, Marshall replied, "Our shows aren't training grounds for actors. We are trying to create the most effective interpretation of the material. So, if we have to go out of town to bring someone in because they would be more effective than what's available in town, we do it. This is our life. When we ask somebody to come in and join us for a show, they have to make an incredible time and energy commitment. The Hippodrome experience is incredibly intense, but what should art be if not everything you've got?"[1]

Maria began studying her role before Christmas—three weeks before coming to Gainesville to start rehearsals. Marshall told the *Independent Florida Alligator*, "Every night, when I see the script come to life and Maria Parkinson (Lolita) and Bruce Cornwell (Humbert Humbert) creating the roles and chewing them up, creating wonderful funny moments, I am just elated."[2]

In July 1977, Vladimir Nabokov died. Complying with the author's request, Marshall sent the final script to his widow, Véra Nabokova, before beginning rehearsals. According to the *Independent Florida Alligator*, Mrs. Nabokova gave Marshall and the Hippodrome approval for a limited fourteen-day run, with the caveat that he could not sell his script, extend the run, or take the play on tour. The Hippodrome publicized the play in local media, printed posters, and put them up.

Friday the thirteenth, five days before previews were to start, they received a letter from Mrs. Nabokova rescinding the non-contractual rights she had granted and suggesting there would be a lawsuit if they went ahead. Her son, Dmitri, was

WORLD PREMIERE!

LOLITA
VLADIMIR NABOKOV

JAN. 20 · FEB. 11
ADVANCE TICKETS AT REBEL DISCOUNT

HIPPODROME

Poster by Richard Ross

negotiating with a prominent Broadway producer who wanted Edward Albee to write the script. A sticking point for the deal was not having another adaptation around or a prior world premiere.

Without a legal leg to stand on, the Hippodrome shut down production. It was a disaster. The oft-impoverished theatre had already spent $5,000 on costumes and sets. Tickets were already sold. Lesson learned. The Hippodrome hired Jim and Debbie Peeples as business managers.

Steambath Revived

With only eight days to ready a substitute show, they opted to remount *Steambath* from their first season. It required a very simple set and inexpensive costumes. Originally staged before much smaller audiences in their Hawthorne Road theatre, it would be new to most of their current subscribers. Bruce Cornwell, who had helmed the 1974 version, directed the remount. Greg Hausch reprised his role as the steambath attendant (God). Current Hippodrome staff and UF students filled out the cast.

Dan Jesse, who switched almost overnight from his role in *Lolita* to that of Oldtimer in *Steambath*, said, "You know people were still hurting from the loss of *Lolita* because they really wanted that one so badly."

"We were just doing the best we could in the situation we were in," Marshall said. "After we lost our investment in Lolita, we went out to the junkyard and found a ton of white PVC piping. Greg, Bruce, and I looked at each other and said, 'Could this be a set?' We loaded the Hippodrome van until pipe was just pouring out of the back doors. At the theatre, we turned it into a giant mobile hanging over the stage. Our *Steambath* set, and it didn't cost us anything."

Working around the clock, they got the play open, although the first few nights included technical difficulties, missed musical cues, and rough choreography sequences. Marshall New remembers that "*Steambath* didn't have quite the charm or impact on audiences in the larger warehouse because it was so in-your-face in that smaller space, but it was still successful."

Photo: Gary Wolfson

Steam bath attendant (Greg Hausch) is God in *Steambath*.

Once *Steambath* closed, its director, Bruce Cornwell, got the *Equus* tour underway with most of the original cast. The only exceptions were that John Michael Fox took over the role of Dr. Dysart from Michael Doyle and Ron Culbreath replaced Larry Carle as Dalton.

Streamers

While *Equus* was on tour, the Hippodrome bounced back from *Lolita* with the very powerful David Rabe play *Streamers*, directed by Kerry McKenney. In the cast of eleven, audiences met for the first time two actors of future importance, Louis Tyrrell and Malcolm Meeks.

Louis would go on to stun audiences with his portrayal of the Elephant Man as well as help Margaret Bachus found the Hippodrome's Theatre for Young Audiences. Malcolm had previously broken racial barriers to become the first

Black UF basketball player. About *Streamers,* Malcolm said, "It's a well-written piece which relates to the struggle of Black people in this country." After his debut in *Streamers,* Malcolm starred in several more Hippodrome productions and co-found-ed Gainesville's Acrosstown Repertory Theatre.

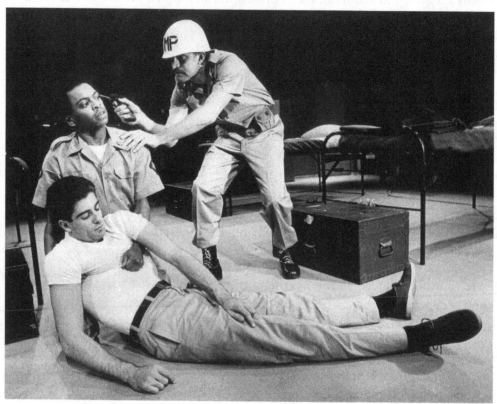

Drew Bongianni, Eddie Billups, and Gavin McConnell in a scene from *Streamers.*

Photo: Gary Wolfson

Streamers had won the 1976 New York Drama Critics' Circle Award for Best American Play, the Drama Desk Award for Outstanding Play, and had been nom-inated for the 1977 Tony Award for Best Play. That was a heady score for the Hippodrome—the first production of *Streamers* by an independent professional theatre in the Southeast. And the play was heavy stuff for Gainesville audiences. Set in an army training camp outside Washington, D.C. during the Vietnam War, the play climaxed with an all too realistic onstage murder.

Roger (Eddie Billups), a likeable, streetwise Black man, shares a room with Billy (Drew Bongianni), an educated all-American, and Richie (Louis Tyrrell), a self-in-dulgent homosexual. A second African American, Carlyle (Malcolm Meeks), frequently invades their room. Carlyle's demeanor is the opposite of Roger's. He is a militant bully, a bomb ready to go off. In charge of the barracks are gung ho Sargent Rooney (Larry Carle) and battle-weary alcoholic Sargent Cokes (Bert Taylor), who sing "Beautiful Streamers" (to the tune of Stephen Foster's "Beautiful Dreamer"), then explain to the men that streamers are paratroopers whose chutes fail to open. Conflicts over homosexuality and racial bitterness flare as the men of various backgrounds prepare to ship out to Vietnam.

"Their action and interaction in the course of the evening may not appear to be any more dramatic than a series of bull sessions," wrote *Sun* critic Arline Greer, "but, in actuality, they serve to build a finale in which violence is exposed in all its mind-numbing, inevitable horror.

"*Streamers* is a play that deals a blow to the gut at the same time it moves the soul to tears," Greer said. "That leaves us drained, limp, and filled with the pain and beauty of the evening, hardly able to move ourselves from the world of the stage in which we have been engrossed for two-and-one-half hours, back into our everyday worlds. Our thanks go to the Hippodrome for making it a part of our lives."[3]

The Fine Arts Council of Florida gave the Hippodrome a $500 grant to publicize *Streamers*, which ran February 24–March 18, 1978.

Doors Open

Since Greg and Kerry's first foray to the National Endowment for the Arts in December 1975, the theatre had been receiving regular funding from both the Fine Arts Council of Florida and the NEA. Equally important were the contacts they made. The fact that John Vos, NEA on-site evaluator and director of the New York State Council for the Arts, had been impressed with the Hippodrome's production of *Catch-22* also helped in other ways.

"Even today, if a company isn't from Chicago, New York, L.A., or London, there is a tendency to dismiss them," Greg Hausch said. "But John Vos didn't. He put us in touch with Bob Moss, who ran Playwrights Horizons, a respected off-Broadway theatre. Bob came down and then he introduced us to Eric Bentley, whom we got to come down when we did his play *Lord Alfred's Lover.*

"Doors started opening. A woman from the Chicago Theatre wrote a glorious review and sent down Arthur Ballet from the Guthrie Theater to see our production of *Otherwise Engaged*. Before we knew it, we were the second most NEA-funded theatre in the Southeast," Greg said. "Arthur Ballet loved the production and asked me to sit on the National Endowment for the Arts theatre panel reviewing theatres."

Otherwise Engaged

Perhaps the selection of *Otherwise Engaged* was inspired by the previous season's success of *Butley*, written by the same author, Simon Gray.

A bittersweet comedy, *Otherwise Engaged* has a plot similar to *Butley* in that it revolves around a witty intellectual whose world is falling apart. Director Mary Hausch cast Hippodrome regulars Gregory Hausch, Kerry McKenney, Rusty Salling, Lewis Moore, Jr., and Chad Reed, as well as Dan Jesse and Margaret Bachus, both of whom had recently been named Associate Directors of the company.

The play's title refers to the protagonist's answering machine message, which informs callers he is "otherwise engaged." A secondary meaning comes from the main character's emotionless detachment and refusal to become engaged in the human fray—for example, when his wife (Margaret Bachus) reveals she's been having an affair,

Photo: Gary Wolfson

(l-r) Gregory Hausch, Dan Jesse, and Kerry McKenney in *Otherwise Engaged*.

and again when a would-be author, played by Kerry McKenney, attempts to seduce him by walking around his apartment bare breasted.

The experienced cast did a wonderful job, and their performances received praise from the local press. *Otherwise Engaged* ran from March 31–April 22, 1978.

During the run of *Otherwise Engaged*, the Hippodrome participated in Celebration '78, a week-long festival of the arts at UF, presenting their 1977 hit *Vanities* on April 4, 1978. Rena Carney, who missed the state tour of *Vanities*, returned for the role of Joanne. The play was staged in the UF Reitz Union Ballroom.

Gemini a Déjà Vu

Although bursting with creative, innovative ideas, the Hippodrome's five artistic directors didn't always dot the i's and cross the t's with paperwork. Their next play, *Gemini,* a comedy by Albert Innaurato, was very nearly a déjà vu of the *Lolita* debacle.

It started simply enough. The Hippodrome artistic directors traveled to New York City in the summer to scout for new material. They'd seen *Gemini* at The Little Theatre, a smaller off-Broadway theatre. When they expressed interest in producing the play, the playwright's agent, Helen Merrill, referred them to Jerry Arrow, president of the Gemini Company at The Little Theatre. Marshall negotiated the rights and royalties. Having learned a lesson from the *Lolita* fiasco, he kept bugging the Gemini Company to send a written agreement.

With repeated assurances from the Gemini Company and a conversation with its treasurer that a license was forthcoming, *Gemini* opened at the Hippodrome May 5, 1978. The following Thursday, May 11, Helen Merrill telephoned the Hippodrome, extremely upset. She said they did not have a license to produce *Gemini* since they didn't obtain it from her and threatened to sue. Furthermore, she called the Theatre Communications Group, a national organization of theatres of which the Hippodrome was a member, and accused the Hippodrome of pirating Albert Innaurato's work.

Kerry McKenney responded to her in writing, detailing a full chronology of Marshall's negotiations with the Gemini Company, demonstrating that the Hippodrome had proceeded in good faith. The Hippodrome's position was strengthened by the fact that they had already sent royalty payments. Marshall New followed Kerry's letter with one to Jerry Arrow, asking him to clear up whatever misunderstanding existed between the Gemini Company and Helen Merrill. It must have worked, for the following week, they received a telegram from the New York producers giving them the go-ahead and a letter from Helen Merrill suggesting they let bygones be bygones.

Gemini takes place in a slum-like South Philadelphia neighborhood—replicated on a remarkable set of two-story brick apartment buildings. Francis Geminiani (Lewis Moore, Jr.) is home from Harvard when his girlfriend (Sharon Patrick) and her brother (Bill Abrams) make an unexpected visit. The first people the siblings meet are the Geminiani's neighbor, Bunny Weinberger (Maggie Beistle), and her mentally

(l-r) Marshall New, Maggie Beistle, Michael Beistle, Mary Hausch, Lewis Moore, Jr., Bill Abrams, and Sharon Patrick on a remarkable set of two-story brick apartment buildings created for *Gemini*.

Photo: Gary Wolfson

challenged son, Herschel, played to the hilt by Marshall New wearing a padded fat suit created by Marilyn Wall.

Francis's father (played by Mike Beistle) tries to hold on to his self-image as an "Italian Stallion" in the face of his son's wavering sexual identity and apparent attraction to his girlfriend's brother. Completing the Hippodrome cast was Mary Hausch as the father's widowed admirer, who is frequently offended by Bunny's crude language.

Director Bruce Cornwell kept the comedic pace of the outrageous characters frantic. From the moment 300-pound Hershel entered the stage riding a tricycle, the audience fell into knee-slapping laughter, which continued almost nonstop for the next ninety minutes. Reviewers for both the *Independent Florida Alligator* and the *Gainesville Sun* were especially delighted by the exchanges between Bunny and Hershel and called the actors' performances brilliant.

Marshall New recalls being surprised by the audience's reaction to a scene where Herschel runs onstage at the end of act two, says he ate his uncle's rat poison, and then collapses onstage. "I thought the audience would die laughing at that because when I saw the play in New York, I died laughing. When we did it at the Hippodrome, the audience gasped, like, 'Oh, my God, we lost Herschel.' I realized they saw the play totally different from the way I saw it."

Gainesville audiences weren't alone. Visiting representatives from the National Endowment for the Arts saw *Gemini* and told Marshall, "You guys produced a play full of humanity as opposed to being case studies of crazy people, which is what it felt like in New York."

Looking back years later, Marshall said, "That wasn't deliberate."

Summer Play

Gemini ran through June 3. Then, their summer play, *The Last Meeting of the Knights of the White Magnolia*, opened June 30 and ran through July 27. It was the first play of a trilogy written by Preston Jones, whom critics had compared to Tennessee Williams and Eugene O'Neill. Preston died the following year from a surgical complication, and the Hippodrome never got the rights to perform the other two plays in the trilogy.

The play is set in 1962 on the third floor of the Cattlemen's Hotel in a dead-end Texas town that the new highway has bypassed. It is a satire about a meeting of a Ku Klux Klan-like group, which Greg Hausch described as being closer to the *Hogan's Heroes* TV show.

The comedy, directed by Kerry McKenney, featured Malcolm Meeks in his second Hippodrome appearance playing a role exactly opposite his character in *Streamers*. David Lane, who played the blind general in *The White House Murder Case*, returned to play Colonel Kinkaid, a wheelchair-confined war veteran who is deaf, near-blind, and shell-shocked. The other members of the all-male cast were Hippodrome regulars at their funniest, of whom Arline Greer wrote:

"The parts are played so well and the situations are funny in the extreme. It will be difficult to forget such moments as the picky quarrels between horseshoe players, Gregory Hausch and Dan Jesse, as Rufe Phelps and Olin Potts... the wide-eyed enthusiasm of Lonny Roy McNeill, the new recruit to the 'White Magnolias,' played by Rick Lotzkar in a delectable southern 'shnook' fashion; the mama's-boy righteousness of Milo Crawford, as portrayed by Jerry Mason; the pompous bumbling of imperial wizard L. D. Alexander, performed with frantic compulsiveness by Bruce Cornwell; the booze-hungry bleatings of Skip Hampton, acted with redneck bravado by Gavin McConnell; and the half-cynical, half-accepting performance by Malcolm J. Meeks, as Ramsey-Eyes, the Black caretaker of the Magnolias' meeting place, who, ultimately, has the play's last laugh.

Photo: Gary Wolfson

The Last Meeting of the White Magnolia: (l-r) Dan Jesse, Marshall New, and Gregory Hausch.

"Marshall New plays Red Glover, a fat-bellied mean old southern boy, with a menacing humor that is so fine, so much in keeping with the role, that every eye in the house is riveted upon him whenever he opens his mouth or changes a facial expression.

"The high moment of the play is the initiation scene, when Lonny Roy is made a White Magnolia. This scene is so outrageously funny, so packed with idiotic, maniacal humor, that it should keep audiences laughing for weeks to come. It, plus the fine performances of so many talented actors, make this Hippodrome production a welcome summer attraction."[4]

At the end of July, the Hippodrome artistic directors traveled to Connecticut to attend the

O'Neill Center National Playwrights Conference and then on to New York City, scouting for plays to produce in Gainesville. Actor friends in New York let them sleep on their apartment floor to save money. Just before the trip, Hippodrome season subscriptions reached 2,000. This was a powerful negotiating tool that enabled them to guarantee sold-out shows to playwrights.

Season Six

Exactly which season *The Last Meeting of the Knights of the White Magnolia* belongs in remains unclear. The Hippodrome's June 1978 newsletter announced it as the first play of the 1978–1979 season. Then, after it closed, the September newsletter said *The Passion of Dracula* would start the new season.

They had seen *The Passion of Dracula* that summer at the Cherry Lane Theatre—the smallest off-Broadway stage. They loved the play, written by Bob Hall and David Richmond, and knew it would look even better in the Hippodrome's larger space. While in New York, they also secured rights for their second play of the new season, *Cabrona*.

Billed as a comedy thriller, *The Passion of Dracula* was a spoof of the Dracula legend, played as straight melodrama in an authentic-looking set created by Dennis Mauldin, Carlos Asse, and Stuart Sachs, supplemented with plentiful special effects and theatrical blood.

In this retelling of the Bram Stoker classic, Dr. Cedric Seward (John Harrison) presides over a mental hospital in the English countryside, where several village girls have died under suspicious circumstances. Into the good doctor's home enters the area's newest resident, Count Dracula, with an eye to make beautiful Wilhelmina Murray his bride. A trio of doctors, a young reporter, and an English lord battle the count to save the lovely heroine and dispatch Dracula in the traditional manner.

Directed by Mary Hausch, the play opened September 29, 1978, and ran, appropriately enough, through Halloween night. Special "family-friendly" matinees were added to the schedule "to provide an opportunity for children to enjoy the thrill of Dracula." Ads for the matinees stated, "Every adult must be accompanied by a child."

Photo: Gary Wolfson

Count Dracula (Ronald Gies) hovers behind Professor Van Helsing (Dan Jesse), Dr. Seward (John Harrison), and Dr. Helga Van Zandt (Margaret Bachus).

In a combination of community service and self-promotion, the Hippodrome gave a benefit performance for the Civitan Regional Blood Center, and the cast and crew were photographed donating blood while Dracula hovered.

Although the script didn't rise to the elevated expectations created by recent stunners like *Streamers* and *Gemini,* production values were high and delivered laughs and thrills to audiences. The *Sun* reviewer wrote, "The acting for *The Passion of Dracula* is on a high order, indeed. Three actors stand out for turning in exceptional jobs, with several others following closely behind them. Daniel Jesse, as Professor Abraham Van Helsing, a Freudian-style doctor who fights the infamous Dracula, gives one of his finest performances to date, which says a great deal, as all his Hippodrome performances have been first rate. Rusty Salling, as the very proper English Lord Godalming, is hilariously funny. His timing, facial expressions, speech, movement, all combine to epitomize a perfect caricature of the English gentleman. Bert Taylor as Jameson, the butler, gives us a classic interpretation of that much-represented species, inspiring laughter with his every phrase. Gregory Hausch, as Renfield, one of the sanatorium's loonies, is at the top of his form.... Kerry McKenney gives a beautifully restrained performance as Wilhelmina Murray, the reluctant bride of Dracula, so much so that you can almost believe her torment when the 'blood of Dracula courses through my veins.' Kevin Rainsberger, as the reporter, Jonathan Harker, makes a marvelously dashing, romantic, and amusing hero, whose efforts to save Wilhelmina enlist our undivided sympathy. Ronald Gies plays the role of Count Dracula in a soberly menacing style."[5]

The play was Kevin Rainsberger's debut at the Hippodrome, the first of many roles he would perform there. A recent graduate of UF, Kevin had been brought to the director's attention by Margaret Bachus, who had seen him act at UF. She also had a role in the play as one of the doctors.

One of Kevin's favorite theatre stories comes from that play: "At one point, Rusty Salling's character has been bitten by a vampire, so he knows he's going to turn into a vampire. Dr. Seward says, 'All right, we're going to have to take him out back and shoot him with a silver bullet.' That would put an end to him being a vampire. Rusty's character was all for it because he didn't want to turn into a vampire. So, they take Rusty offstage and you're supposed to hear the gunshot. Well, that particular night you hear click... click... click. Nothing happened. John Harrison—Dr. Seward—shouts, 'Use your knife.' Next, we hear Rusty going, ah... ah... ah. That was a good piece of ad-libbing."

Marshall New describes a special effect that intrigued many audiences. "We built a wireframe bat and painted it with luminescent paint. At one point, Dracula steps outside the mansion and starts flapping his cape. We set off this high-powered strobe light, followed by a poof of smoke. Then we turned on lights aimed at the audience, which temporarily blinded them. When the lights went out and their eyes adjusted to the dark, the luminescent bat was flying over them and the audience would scream.

"It was the cheapest theatrical trick in the book, one done for a long time. A guy dressed all in black had the bat on the end of a fishing pole and would fly it over all the audience. They had no idea how we did it. Many of them asked, 'Did you get an automated bat from Disney World?' Then one night, a man in a wheelchair was sitting in the handicap spot on the corner of the stage. When the guy with the fishing pole made his exit, he bumped into the wheelchair and knocked it over. The man fell out."

Marshall ran over and helped the man up. "Are you okay?"

"Yeah," the man said, "and I know how you did the bat."

"You sure do," Marshall said. "The bat ran over you."

World Premieres

The Hippodrome's successful foray to find new plays that summer had secured the rights to three world premieres. Cynthia Buchanan's play *Cabrona* would be the first. And the playwright was coming down! She had workshopped the play at the Arena Stage in Washington, D.C., with famous actors Ned Beatty and Lily Tomlin (for whom Cynthia wrote comedy material). Now, the Hippodrome would give the work its first professional production under the direction of Bruce Cornwell.

Photo: Gary Wolfson

Margaret Thomson as Verity Massey in *Cabrona*.

The tender comedy takes place just north of the Mexican border at Rancho Cabrona, with five characters whose emotional struggle for survival provides an unforgettable evening of theatrical fireworks.

The Passion of Dracula was still running when the *Cabrona* playwright arrived to begin work with Bruce. Naturally, she was invited to see the current show. On the night she attended, the theatre had added an extra performance with a special promotion: show up in costume and get in free.

"Not only did the University of Florida students show up in costume," Marshall New said, "but they showed up drunk. It was the most raucous audience ever. The seating platforms started rocking back and forth—a truly over-the-top evening. Not the evening to bring the playwright of a sensitive story about people in the Southwest and the delusions they lived under. I'm sure she thought, 'What the hell did I get into?' But we did her play, anyway."

Cabrona premiered November 10 and ran through December 9, but Cynthia Buchanan only saw the rehearsals. On opening night, she was in Spain due to a prior commitment. "I trust their instincts about it," she said.[6]

New Look magazine called *Cabrona* the Hippodrome's "most intelligent property since *Streamers*" and described Carlos Asse's set as "one of the most aesthetically satisfying we've ever seen."[7]

The First *Christmas Carol*

The Hippodrome was doing well and, as a gesture of goodwill, decided to give back to the community. Greg Hausch wrote an adaptation of Charles Dickens's novel *A Christmas Carol*, which the Hippodrome performed for free. Almost. Admission was two cans of food for the Salvation Army food drive or a toy to be distributed by Toys for Tots.

"It endeared us to so many people because of the way we did it," Greg said. "It was, in essence, a community production in every sense of the word. Boy Scouts packed the donated cans of food into boxes. The Brownies were the ushers. The Suzuki players and Gainesville Chorus serenaded arriving and departing audiences." Jaycees provided the Christmas tree. Cox Furniture underwrote the play and donated furniture for the set, and other merchants joined in as sponsors.

A Christmas Carol became a beloved annual tradition. Many who have seen it over the years automatically think of Rusty Salling as Ebenezer Scrooge, a role he refined to perfection. But during the first eleven years, Rusty wasn't Scrooge. He played Bob Cratchit, Scrooge's beleaguered clerk.

Dan Jesse was offered the part of Scrooge but turned it down. "This is your kind of role," they told him.

"Yeah, it's the kind of role I've done two or three times in this year already," Dan said. "I didn't want to get typecast as an old man. I was only thirty years old." Dan did join the cast, playing multiple characters, including the Ghost of Christmas Past.

Bruce Cornwell as Scrooge gets visited by three ghosts of Christmas played by Dan Jesse, Lewis Moore, Jr., and Jerry Mason.

Bruce Cornwell played Scrooge that first year. In subsequent seasons, Tom Nash, Kevin Rainsberger, and others took on the part while Rusty continued as Bob Cratchit until he decided to embody the legendary curmudgeon. Once he did, he remained in the role for twenty-five years, further perfecting it each time until illness forced him to step down in 2015.

A Christmas Carol had parts for many youngsters, including Shannon Wheeler and Margaret Bachus's son, Kyle. Justin Davis was that year's Tiny Tim. Also participating in that first production were two teenagers who would win leading roles in future plays, Malcolm Gets and Margie Llinas. Hippodrome regulars Kurt Orwick, Jerry Mason, and Lewis Moore, Jr., played multiple adult parts. Kathryn Nash played Mrs. Cratchit and Martha Williams was the daughter, Martha Cratchit.

The show, an overwhelming success, ran December 14–16 and 20–23. Wednesday, December 20, drew the biggest crowd the Hippodrome had ever had. "We had 410 people and had to turn away about 50 people," Greg Hausch told *Gainesville Sun* staff writer Dave Hunter.[8] So the Hippodrome added extra performances.

Malcolm Gets remembers, "It was such a success. We would do a show and Greg would say, 'Do another one at nine o'clock.'" Malcolm wasn't quite fourteen years old when he made his mainstage debut, playing dual roles of young Scrooge and Peter Cratchit. He said, "I had a line [as Peter] which was, 'Mother, our goose is cooked.' I was so young, I had no idea of the irony of the line, and the first performance it got a huge laugh. I thought I'd done something wrong."

"No," they told Malcolm. "It's good."

The community responded generously, donating enough toys for over two hundred families. They weren't skimpy with canned goods, either. Some gave whole canned hams and turkeys. They filled a truck plus a U-Haul trailer to take just a quarter of the donated food to the Salvation Army.

Each performance concluded with a Christmas carol sing-along with the cast, followed by free hot cider and Christmas cookies. "People came up after the show and said how they really got into the Christmas spirit for the first time this year," Greg said. Indeed, they did. People wrote letters of praise to the editor of the *Gainesville Sun*. Columnists Eloise Henderson and Margaret Shonbrun, neither of whom normally wrote about theatre, extolled the Hippodrome production in their columns. Furthermore, Shonbrun used the example of *A Christmas Carol* to make a case for giving the Hippodrome the old Post Office building—an idea that would eventually come to fruition.

A favorite memory of Dan Jesse's from that first year concerns the pudding. Those who have seen the play will recall the dinner scene. Mrs. Cratchit has put the traditional Christmas pudding on the windowsill to cool. While daughter Martha goes to fetch it, Mrs. Cratchit frets about whether it will turn out right. Then, when Martha returns with it, the family has a bit of dialogue raving about the wonderful pudding.

One performance, when the actress playing Martha went offstage to get the pudding, she found the prop table in complete disarray. Nothing is where it was supposed to be. Frantically, she searched everywhere for the prop pudding. The actors onstage, wondering what was taking Martha so long, were forced to ad-lib. Finally, unable to come up with the pudding, she went back onstage empty-handed and announced, "The dog ate it."

Without the pudding to admire, the rest of the dialogue made no sense, so the stage manager said, "Cut the lights." The bit about rejoicing over the plum pudding was lost, but the scene got a great laugh.

1 Marlena Reddy, "Can a 16–Year-Old Nymphet Make it for Marshall New?" *Independent Florida Alligator*, January 12, 1978.

2 Ibid.

3 Arline Greer, review of *Streamers*, by David Rabe, directed by Kerry McKenney, Hippodrome Theatre, Gainesville, FL, *Gainesville Sun*, March 2, 1978.

4 Arline Greer, review of *The Last Meeting of the Knights of the White Magnolia*, by Preston Jones, directed by Kerry McKenney, Hippodrome Theatre, Gainesville, FL *Gainesville Sun*, July 7, 1978.

5 Arline Greer, review of *The Passion of Dracula*, by Bob Hall and David Richmond, directed by Mary Hausch, Hippodrome Theatre, Gainesville, FL, *Gainesville Sun*, October 4, 1978.

6 John Snyder, "Cynthia Buchanan Wrote Cabrona, The Hippodrome Gives It Life," *Gainesville Sun*, November 10, 1978.

7 Richard Burkholder, review of *Cabrona*, by Cynthia Buchanan, directed by Bruce Cornwell, Hippodrome Theatre, Gainesville, FL, *New Look*, December 1, 1978.

8 Dave Hunter, "Bah Humbug?" *Gainesville Sun*, December 22, 1978.

1979

A Possible Dream

Since early in 1978, the Gainesville City Commission had been exploring the possible renovation/restoration of the old Post Office building into a theatre for the performing arts. The Hippodrome and the Gainesville Little Theater (now Gainesville Community Playhouse) were approached regarding occupancy of the building. The august historic structure that presently houses the theatre was at that time in possession of the Alachua County School District, whose board scheduled a February 1979 meeting to discuss its value. The Hippodromers were very excited by the prospect, but it would take the next two years to come about.

Anti-apartheid One-acts

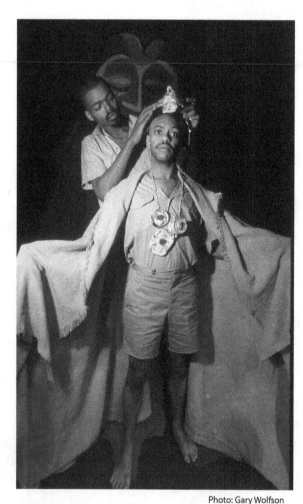

Photo: Gary Wolfson

Eddie Billups and Jonathan Peck in *The Island*.

The January 1979 show was a pair of one-act plays by Athol Fugard, *The Island* and *Statements Made After an Arrest Under the Immorality Act*. Both were directed by Margaret Bachus and sought to expose apartheid, the system of institutional racial segregation that existed in South Africa until the 1990s.

Eddie Billups and Malcolm Meeks each had the lead role in one of the two plays. They had previously appeared together in *Streamers*.

In *Islands,* two Black cellmates, imprisoned on an island, spend their days doing meaningless physical labor and their nights rehearsing the Greek play *Antigone* in their cells to perform for the other inmates. Both men have been incarcerated for violating apartheid laws. Eddie's character learns his sentence has been commuted and he will be released in three months. His cellmate Winston, played by Jonathan Peck, will not be. In the final ironic scene, Winston plays Antigone, who is sentenced to be walled up in a cave.

The second play, *Statements Made After an Arrest Under the Immorality Act,* is set in apartheid South Africa, where interracial relationships were a criminal offense. Two lovers—a Black man (Malcolm Meeks) and a white woman (Mary Hausch) meet secretly and make love. A neighbor reports them, and a policeman (Bert Taylor) secretly photographs and then arrests them for violating the Immorality Act.

Pairing the two plays did not work well. *Islands*, though a one-act, ran ninety minutes—about the same as a full-length play. By its end, audiences were emotionally exhausted. A fifteen-minute intermission wasn't enough to welcome another thirty-five minutes of drama after the intensity of the first play.

A Stage for New Plays

On the same day *Islands* and *Statements Made After an Arrest Under the Immorality Act* opened (Friday, January 12), the Hippodrome launched its newest venture, Second Stage. Offered on Friday and Saturday nights at 11:00 p.m. and Sundays at 7:30 p.m., it featured new plays "we've discovered, fallen in love with, can't live without, and yet can't fit into our main stage schedule," said the announcement in the playbill. Today, the Hippodrome uses its cinema when it needs a Second Stage, but while the theatre was in the warehouse, they just used the mainstage.

First up was *The Love Garden,* a short play by UF Professor of Humanities James Sunwall about the shift of power and possession between two men inspired by remote beauty. They paired it with David Mamet's one-act *Duck Variations,* which had been on the mainstage in 1977.

Lord Alfred's Lover

The next mainstage play was their second world premiere that season, *Lord Alfred's Lover* by noted theatre critic Eric Bentley. It, too, dealt with outdated immorality laws. This time, the setting was Victorian England, and the plot concerned the real-life trial and conviction of Oscar Wilde for his affair with Lord Alfred Douglas. Michael Doyle played Oscar Wilde, Mark Sexton played young Lord Alfred, and Rusty Salling portrayed Lord Alfred as an old man.

Eric Bentley was a big deal in the theatre world and it was a real feather in the Hippodrome cap to have him come for two weeks of rehearsals and the premiere. Kerry McKenney directed the play, which opened February 16, 1979, and ran through March 10.

Photo: Gary Wolfson

Playwright Eric Bentley autographing a poster for *Lord Alfred's Lover*.

The rest of the large cast was made up of Hippodrome regulars Dan Jesse, Kurt Orwick, Bruce Cornwell, Michael Beistle, Kevin Rainsberger, Margaret Bachus, Nell Page, Louis Tyrrell, Jerry Mason, Rick Lotzkar, and others. Making his second appearance was Malcolm Gets, who had just turned fourteen. Malcolm was, at the time, training with a renowned classical pianist from Julliard to become a concert pianist himself. Marshall New approached Malcolm's parents to ask if he could play piano in *Lord Alfred's Lover.* He told them Oscar Wilde was a homosexual and that Malcolm would be playing piano in a bordello scene. "My parents are British, so they were very cool and said 'sure,'" Malcolm recalls.

Because the original script was extremely long, Kerry made radical changes and cut out a lot. "She converted it into something really wonderful," was Marshall's opinion. The playwright didn't agree. When Eric Bentley arrived for rehearsals and saw what she'd done, he demanded she revert to the way he wrote it. She complied. Malcolm Gets remembers, "It was endless—like three-and-a-half-hours long." After opening night, Eric left town. The next week, they called the cast together and told them they were going to make major cuts in the show. "We were so happy," Malcolm said. "It was so much better and so much better for the audiences."

Photo: Gary Wolfson

Oscar Wilde charms Parisian youth in *Lord Alfred's Lover.* Clockwise from bottom: Malcolm Gets, Ralph F. Box III, Michael Massaro, Michael Doyle, and Lewis Moore, Jr.

The review by *Sun* critic Arline Greer gushed for four paragraphs about Michael Doyle's performance, calling him the consummate artist. She wrote, "To say his performance in *Lord Alfred's Lover* is a tour de force doesn't say it by half. There probably are no adequate words to describe the brilliance of his work. Quite simply, it must be seen."[1] She also praised the acting of the rest of the cast and called Kerry McKenney's work "the finest direction of her career."[2]

The Hippodrome played the abridged version for the rest of the run. Then they received a phone call. Eric was coming back for the final performance "to see how the play matured." Malcolm continues, "We had a show Saturday night of the edited version, then we stayed until midnight to rehearse the original version." The show closed the next day, with Eric in attendance for a performance of the full-length version.

After three weeks of playing the shorter version, something was bound to go wrong when the cuts were restored at the last minute. Kevin Rainsberger recalls, "After the blackout, Mark Sexton's character was supposed to be onstage with myself and Mike Doyle's character and Mark was nowhere to be found. So, Mike and I are kind of extemporizing."

"I was back in the green room listening," Mark Sexton explains. "The green room has speakers so you can hear what is going on. At one point I remember thinking, 'Wow, those guys are dying out there. They have forgotten their lines, and they are lost.' Finally, I hear, 'I'm sure he's going to be here any minute.' I realize I'm the one who had forgotten. When I walked onstage, the look in their eyes was this combination of wanting to strangle the life out of my body and yet grateful to see me."

Concurrent with *Lord Alfred's Lover*, the Hippodrome Second Stage presented on February 25 and March 4 Margaret Bachus's one-woman play about Emily Dickinson, *The Belle of Amherst.* Later, Margaret would tour the play in schools as part of the Hippodrome Theatre for Young Audiences, described in a later chapter.

The issue of turning the old Post Office into a performing arts center was still tied up in discussion between the city government and the school board. Not ones to sit idly by waiting for things to happen, The Hippodrome applied for grants from the National Endowment for the Arts to fund the purchase of the old building and the necessary renovations. It was an ambitious project that languished in a web of bureaucracy.

Making a Trilogy into One Play

Their next production, *The Norman Conquests* by Alan Ayckbourn, could have gotten the Hippodrome in a bit of trouble if anyone had known what director Greg Hausch had done. The source material was a trilogy of British farces that were first produced in London's West End and later on Broadway. Three plays were set on

Caught! *The Norman Conquests* cast: (clockwise from left) Rusty Salling and Katherine Hallowell; Kevin Rainsberger and Sandy McConnell; Nancy Seibert and Tom Nash.

Photo: Gary Wolfson

the same English estate, one in the garden, another in the kitchen, and the third in the living room. "I said this should be one play," Greg recalls. "I took the best out of each one of them and married it together so that we had one three-act play. I don't think it's ever been done that way." Undoubtedly it hadn't, because that sort of thing isn't allowed, but the Hippodrome was far enough from London and New York to get away with it.

Rusty Salling, recently promoted to Associate Director, played the title role, Norman. The *Independent Florida Alligator* said of his performance, "Salling somehow exudes charisma, seducing the audience—as well as the ladies of the play—with charm. As one of the characters put it, Salling looks alternately like a woolly sheep dog and an ever-so-innocent little boy."[3] Norman is neither. The plot concerns his seductive conquests of three women and the hilarious repercussions that follow.

Dashing, handsome actor Kevin Rainsberger wore padding to give his character a large belly. Kevin told a *Gainesville Sun* reporter, Beth Demauro, "I enjoy the fact that I'm out there making people laugh. I've really enjoyed the role I'm playing because it has given me the opportunity to blow myself up and be as bombastic as I want."[4]

A comedy of manners, the play relied on wit, facial expressions, and mannerisms. For instance, when Kevin's character asks his wife, played by Sandy McConnell, "What are we having for dinner?" She replies, "I'm making a salad."

"Great," he says. "All those lovely lettuces."

Making their Hippodrome debut were the actors playing Norman's other two conquests, Katherine Hallowell and Nancy Seibert. Joining the cast for his second mainstage appearance was Tom Nash, an old friend from Greg's UF days. Tom had given Greg his first big role in a play. Tom had previously acted at the Hippodrome in *Lord Alfred's Lover*, and in December 1979 would take on the part of Scrooge in the Hippodrome's second *A Christmas Carol*. There was also a cat who someone (probably Rusty) named Devil Kitty.

The Norman Conquests ran from March 30–April 21, 1979.

Great Depression Dance

Following *The Norman Conquests* was the Hippodrome's next world premiere, *They Shoot Horses, Don't They?* Marshall New secured the rights to create a stage adaptation of the screenplay written by James Poe and Robert E. Thompson for the 1969 film, which the screenwriters had based on a novel by Horace McCoy.

The play was set during the Great Depression, when couples entered brutal dance marathons during which they were required to keep moving until they could go no more, and many collapsed from exhaustion. The last still dancing would win prize money. The cast of thirty-two was the Hippodrome's largest so far. Twenty of them were UF theatre students in their first professional theatre roles. Margie Llinas, who had worked backstage on previous plays and served as Assistant Director of *A Christmas Carol*, finally made her mainstage debut as dance contestant Ruby Bates. Also making his first Hippodrome appearance as one of the contestants was a professional actor, Gregg Jones, who had just moved to Gainesville.

Scene from *They Shoot Horses, Don't They?* Referee Jerry Mason; dancing couples (l-r) Ken Martin and Margie Llinas, Kevin Rainsberger and Susan Elizabeth Mowrer, Kerry McKenney and Rob Ferguson, Marilyn Wall and Michael Stott.

Photo: Gary Wolfson

The play perfectly matched the Hippodrome's penchant for environmental theatre—making the audience part of the play. To that end, the entire warehouse theatre became a 1930s music hall and featured a live band. The audience became the dance marathon audience rooting for their favorite contestants. Margaret Bachus's sons, Kyle and Kurt, sold peanuts to the crowd. "What a mistake that was," Marshall said. "We had people cracking peanuts over some of the best lines."

In an inspired (or perhaps cruel) stroke of realism, director Marshall New made the actors continue to dance through the intermission, true to the nature of 1930s dance marathons. When the warehouse air conditioner stopped working, they threw open the warehouse's wide bay doors. Patrons, accustomed to the Hippodrome's environmental theatre approach, assumed it was a planned effect to invoke the hot, muggy experience of a Depression-era dance hall.

Perhaps Dan Jesse played Rocky Gravo too well. As the sleazy producer and emcee of the marathon, Rocky takes advantage of the poor dancers, treats them cruelly, and when a couple wins, cons them out of their winnings. Dan admits, "My character is a really evil person. He is horrible." But Dan's just an actor playing a character, right?

Someone who saw the play mistook art for real life. "One night I got this phone call," Dan remembers. "This guy on the other end of the line says, 'You really think you're something else, don't you, Rocky? I know who you are and the things you did to those people.'"

Dan thought it was one of his actor friends. "So, I'm laughing and joking, but as it's going on, my ear is tuned in because I know all the people that it could be. I'm saying, 'Oh, this is so-and-so.' He just keeps getting creepier and angrier throughout the call. I reach the point that I don't think this is one of my actor friends because by now they would be laughing with me. Finally, he just screamed, 'I'm going to kill you' and slammed down the phone."

They Shoot Horses, Don't They? Ran from May 3–June 2, 1979, without Dan being threatened again. *New Look* magazine praised Marshall New's masterful direction of the large cast, comparing it to the work of film director Robert Altman.

Photo: Gary Wolfson

Dan Jesse as Rocky Gravo in *They Shoot Horses, Don't They?* Clockwise from nurse played by Meredith Normington: Lawrence Seigel, Rick Lotzkar, Margie Llinas, and Dan Jesse.

The Duck Variations Tour

Before and after *They Shoot Horses, Don't They?*, Marshall New, along with Kurt Orwick and Bruce Cornwell, hit the road on two state tours of *The Duck Variations.* The Hippodrome had received a grant from the Florida Endowment for the Humanities to tour fifteen retirement communities with a somewhat unusual program. After brief opening remarks by a university humanities professor, Marshall and Kurt performed the short play about two elderly men sitting on a park bench, talking about the ducks in a lake. However, their characters were really talking about themselves, and since that is sometimes difficult, they "pretended" to talk about ducks. Once the play ended, the audience participated in a town hall-type meeting with the goal of learning "what Florida should do for its senior citizens."

Photo: Gary Wolfson

Kurt Orwick and Marshall New in *The Duck Variations.*

They presented the program in Miami, Tampa, St. Petersburg, Gainesville, Jacksonville, and smaller towns in between. The university humanists accompanying them on the tour were Dr. Sheldon Isenberg, Dr. Sidney Homan, and graduate student Steven Robitaille. Later, Robitaille produced a documentary about the program for broadcast on PBS.

Around the same time, things were beginning to move forward regarding the old Post Office building. Hippodrome subscribers, patrons, and fans directed their opinions toward elected officials, finally stirring them into action. A meeting with the Hippodrome's Board of Trustees followed resolutions passed in April by the Alachua County School Board and the Gainesville City Commission. All parties agreed to cooperate toward a plan of action. The legalities of property transfer took another year and required extensive negotiation. However, a new home for the Hippodrome was in sight.

Two Summer Plays and a Mime

During the summer of 1979, the Hippodrome produced two plays, *Same Time Next Year* from June 22–July 14 and *Sleuth* from July 27–August 18.

Hippodrome co-founder Marilyn Wall had recently taken a sabbatical to marry Carlos Asse and start a family, but she returned to act in *Cabrona* and *They Shoot Horses, Don't They?* And then direct *Same Time, Next Year*. Bernard Slade's two-character play starred Margaret Bachus and Nik Hagler.

The play had recently been turned into a film starring Alan Alda and Ellen Burstyn, and the Hippodrome got the rights to perform it shortly after it ended its Broadway run. The story is a bittersweet comedy about a couple's extramarital affair conducted one day each year for twenty-four years.

Doris (Margaret Bachus) and George (Nik Hagler) rendezvous annually in *Same Time Next Year*.

Photo: Gary Wolfson

Mary Hausch helmed the second summer offering, *Sleuth*, by Anthony Shaffer, a cloak-and-dagger tale of deceit. Carlos Asse, who had returned to the Hippodrome full-time, designed a magnificent set—an old English country home. Stars Michael Doyle and Bruce Cornwell traded snappy dialogue in a detective story heavy in gamesmanship with twists and turns aplenty.

Audiences were warned not to reveal any details about the plot to those who had yet to see the play. *Gainesville Sun* critic Arline Greer kept mum about the details but did say, "*Sleuth* contains some of the wittiest lines to be turned out by a British author; and a plot that, instead of thickening, runs like syrup through your hands. For mystery buffs and admirers of fine language and acting, *Sleuth* provides an evening of exciting theatre."[5]

It is worth mentioning the rest of the cast: a police constable, a detective sergeant, and an inspector, played by local luminaries Ed Johnson, publisher of the *Gainesville Sun*; Richard Gorenberg, MD, president of the Hippodrome Board of Directors; and Dr. Al Wehlburg of the UF Theatre Department.

Dr. Wehlburg's part in Hippodrome history had been significant since the beginning. Relations with the UF Theatre Department were rocky in the troupe's early years. Disgruntled over the co-founders' rebellious activities during their college years, department personnel were told not to have anything to do with them. Al, who taught technical directing at UF, ignored that dictum, offering advice or sending prize students undercover to assist them on sets. By the 1978–1979 season, the Hippodrome had become a recognized professional theatre, and UF became more supportive. But Al Wehlburg deserves considerable credit for supporting the Hippodrome from the start.

During the run of *Sleuth*, the Hippodrome Second Stage featured Jon Schwartz performing an evening of mime titled *You Show Me Yours and I'll Show You Mime*.

A deal to make the old Post Office into a performing arts center and new home for the Hippodrome was progressing, albeit at a much slower pace than the Hippodrome was accustomed to doing things. In July, the US Department of Interior listed the building on the National Register of Historic Places, ensuring its preservation. Then, in September, the National Endowment for the Arts awarded the Hippodrome $175,000 to aid in restoring the building even though they'd yet to iron out a lease.

Another announcement that stunned and excited the community was that the Hippodrome's next world premiere would be a play by America's greatest living playwright, Tennessee Williams, and he would be in residence for the rehearsals and opening.

Photo: Gary Wolfson

English mystery writer Andrew Wyke (Michael Doyle) catches houseguest Milo Tindle (Bruce Cornwell) stealing jewels in *Sleuth*.

Season Seven

The 1979–1980 season opened in September with *Sly Fox*, a play many think was one of the Hippodrome's funniest. The script by Larry Gelbart, head writer of the TV series *M*A*S*H*, was based on *Volpone* by seventeenth-century playwright Ben Johnson. Gelbart changed the setting from Renaissance Italy to nineteenth-century San Francisco and the play's tone from satire to farce.

Photo: Gary Wolfson/*Gainesville Sun*

The Judge in *Sly Fox*, played by Michael Beistle, confronts Abner Truckle (Rusty Salling) and his wife (played by Nancy Seibert). Cowering in the doorway are Miss Fancy (Shari Freels) and Simon Able (Gregory Hausch).

The plot revolves around witty, wealthy conman Foxwell J. Sly, who feigns impending death to dupe those around him of their fortunes as they vie for his inheritance. Jethro Crouch wills away his son's inheritance to Sly on the promise that Jethro will inherit Sly's money after Sly dies; Abner Truckle offers his wife to Sly under the impression that it will sway Sly to name him as his heir; Lawyer Craven defends Sly's dignity in court after Captain Crouch discovers Sly diddling Mrs. Truckle; Merrilee Fancy, the most popular harlot in the bay town, finds herself in the family way and hopes to marry Sly for his wealth. None of them realize they're being conned, and even Able, Sly's servant and closest confidant, is unable to outfox him.

It was the perfect vehicle for the Hippodrome's top comedic talents, whose individual performances had filled the theatre with laughter in many previous plays. Now together, trading witty lines and playing off each other, they brought audiences to tears of laughter.

Arline Greer raved, "It is a gem of a production, flawlessly produced, directed, and acted; filled with enough sly humor to keep audiences laughing even as they leave the theater, and then afterward; chuckling in memory at the wily inventiveness of the farce, the hilarious one-liners, and the impeccably comic characterizations of the actors.... There is probably no way to describe, adequately, the subtle, but robust, talents of Dan Jesse as Foxwell Sly; Gregory Hausch as Simon Able; Nino Barucci as Lawyer Craven; Louis Tyrrell as Jethro Crouch; Kevin Rainsberger as Captain Crouch, son of the old geezer Jethro Crouch; Rusty Salling as Abner Truckle; Nancy Seibert as Mrs. Truckle; Shari Freels as Miss Fancy; Rick Lotzkar as the lascivious chief of police; and Michael Beistle as the judge. Each characterization is a gem of acting expertise to be savored and remembered, all the more for the unity of style in which it's rendered. Even the 'bit parts' are meticulously handled by Jerry Mason, Sandy Scott, and John Bergh."[6]

Gregg Jones, listed in the playbill under the stage name Nino Barucci, played Lawyer Craven in his second appearance at the Hippodrome. Already a professional actor, Gregg had worked three years at the Living Stage Theatre Company in Washington, D.C., and a year and a half before that doing musical theatre in Atlanta, Georgia. Settling in Gainesville, he became a regular and continues to act in Hippodrome productions up through the present day. But his story from *Sly Fox* is legendary.

Gregg prefaces his tale with a caveat: "The rules about pyrotechnics and firearms onstage were much less stringent in 1979 than they are now." To make the play authentic to nineteenth-century San Francisco, the actors wore actual six-guns and fired blanks. They reloaded the blank cartridges themselves, using wax in place of the bullet. Wax wads aren't used nowadays in stage bullets.

Photo: Gary Wolfson

Michael Beistle wasn't this close to Gregg Jones when he accidentally shot him during a performance of *Sly Fox*.

In the courtroom scene, Michael Beistle's character, the judge, would enter and say, "All right, everybody sit down." Then he'd fire his gun in the air and the rest of the cast would sit down real fast because he's a mean judge.

Shortly after the judge's entrance, Lawyer Craven is supposed to approach the bench and say, "Your Honor, I have an objection!" The judge is supposed to stand up, wave his gun, and bellow, "I said, 'Sit down!'"

One night, Michael, standing about eight feet away from Gregg, waved his gun and delivered his line—"Sit down!"—when Bang! The gun accidentally went off.

"A wax bullet hit my forehead literally right between my eyes," Gregg recalls. "It started spurting blood immediately. My first thought was, 'I'm going to die onstage. This is going to be live death, but it'll be great for the audience because it'll look so real.'

"Then my next thought was, 'I'm going to be okay.' I reached into the breast pocket of my jacket and pulled out a handkerchief and dabbed my forehead. It soaked with blood and I was a little freaked out, but I looked at Michael, and he was looking at me in shock, like, 'Oh, my God, what have I done?'

"I came back with this improvised line just off the cuff, 'Well, your Honor, you don't have to be quite so rash about it. I'll sit back down.'

"I walked over and sat down at the defendant's table next to Greg Hausch. I turned to Greg and whispered, 'Does it look very bad?' He didn't say anything. He just looked at me with this look of horror on his face and turned away. So I stayed on and we finished the scene.

"I made my exit when I was supposed to and ran into the dressing room. My makeup kit had this wax compound called Plasto that's used under makeup to make warts and other features on your face. I stuffed the hole in my forehead with

Plasto and then took pancake makeup and covered it over. I went back onstage, thinking, *Man, I'm gonna be a real trooper and finish this play. The show must go on!*

"The way the play was staged, we were using the audience as the jury. I'm the lawyer doing my closing argument, so I walked right up to the audience and did my monologue. My lines were going fine, but I kept getting these strange, wincing looks. They're looking at me with looks of pain. I know I covered up my wound. What's the big deal?

"I finish, leave the stage, and come back for curtain call. After we came offstage, I looked in the mirror. The wound had continued to bleed, but the Plasto contained it in a bubble that grew larger and made this golf ball size bubble on my forehead. It looked like a third eyeball."

Arline Greer said she wished the Hippodrome's schedule permitted them to extend it for as long as there were theatergoers willing to buy tickets. Unfortunately, an extension wasn't feasible. *Sly Fox,* which opened September 14, had to end October 13, 1979. After all, Tennessee Williams was coming. The next year, however, the Florida Division of Cultural Affairs funded a state tour of *Sly Fox.*

Tennessee Williams

Tennessee Williams, considered America's greatest playwright, won the Pulitzer Prize twice, three New York Drama Critics Circle Awards, a Tony, and the Kennedy Center Honors. His plays are among the most acclaimed dramas ever performed on Broadway. The prolific author wrote thirty-nine full-length plays, a dozen of which were made into hit movies. He also wrote seventy one-act plays, two novels, twelve short story collections, two memoirs, three books of poetry, and an essay collection.

At age sixty-eight, he accepted a stint as playwright-in-residence at the Hippodrome to stage the world premiere of a new-ish play, *Tiger Tail.* The story is about a middle-aged husband with a child bride who refuses to consummate their marriage until she's of age. After the husband crosses a rival, the rival exacts his revenge by seducing her. Williams adapted it for the stage from his screenplay for the film *Baby Doll.* A prior trial run at the Alliance Theatre in Atlanta, Georgia, displeased him, so he rewrote the script and allowed the Hippodrome to premiere it twenty years before it premiered in New York.

It is customary in the theatre world for the premiering theatre to receive credit, and sure enough, the published work lists the entire Gainesville cast along with the following statement: "The text, which incorporates the author's final revisions, records the play as it was produced at the Hippodrome Theatre Workshop in Gainesville, Florida, in 1979."[7]

It won't be a surprise to learn that all of this was brought about by the play's enterprising director, Marshall New. Initially, the play had been scheduled to open on Broadway, and Marshall was in negotiations with the Broadway producers when the producers switched to a different Tennessee Williams play. Marshall then began negotiating directly with Williams and his agent, Mitch Douglas, and struck a deal.

Hippodrome co-founder Marilyn Wall said, "Marshall would just get on the phone and call anybody."

"I had always thought *Baby Doll* would make a great play," Marshall said. "The movie was based on two one-act plays that Tennessee had written in 1946, before he hit it big—*27 Wagons Full of Cotton* and *The Unsatisfactory Supper*. So, I wrote Tennessee a really long letter spelling out my ideas for producing it. He said that I had more ideas than the people in Atlanta did, and he sent me three versions of it.

"Well, the script they'd used in Atlanta and the other two attempts were just dreadful. I mean, all you needed to do was jam those two short one-act plays together. They were brilliant, perfect little gems. Adapting them didn't require a lot of work on my part. I just made a lot of little changes and wrote an extra scene or two to make things flow from one story to the next."

Marshall's proposed changes totaled sixteen. Tennessee told him, "Send them to me and I'll tell you yes or no, but more than likely, I'll say, 'Let's get together on them.'"

"He seems to be an easy man to work with," Marshall told the *Gainesville Sun*.[8]

Photo: Gary Wolfson/*Gainesville Sun*

Tennessee Williams (at top) with cast of *Tiger Tail*. Clockwise from playwright: Amar Long, Dana Moser, Jennifer Pritchett, Jon Schwartz, and Michael Doyle.

Meanwhile, negotiations with the City of Gainesville for the purchase or lease of the old Post Office building were moving ahead, but the Hippodrome had to raise funds to match the NEA grant. Tennessee Williams graciously agreed to help. He promised to attend a fundraising dinner at Gainesville's fanciest restaurant, the Sovereign, followed by the play's preview. The next night, he'd attend the opening and join the cast for a curtain call and an after-party with the audience, whose higher-priced ticket included a donation to the building fund.

Marilyn Wall recalled, "We built this beautiful set." The character Archie Lee was a down-at-the-heels owner of an antiquated cotton gin, and the set reflected that. "Jon Schwartz cut down a whole tree and dragged it into the theatre," Marilyn said.

Dan Jesse worked on the set, too. "The set had this old broken-down car out in the front yard. There was a junkyard very near the theatre, and I went over there and gathered up all the parts that I could find and put together this ridiculous-looking junk car."

Jennifer Pritchett, who played Baby Doll, recalled that to convey the characters as white trash, "Carlos Asse actually went to a dump and picked up garbage and trash and strewed it around the stage—around the perimeter of my [character's] house. It was so appropriate, authentic, and we had a real chicken." Yes, a chicken they named Rhonda, and Rusty Salling was the "chicken wrangler," watching over Rhonda when she was offstage. "He loved that chicken," Dan Jesse said.

Marshall also had to come up with a song. He said, "Tennessee had lyrics in the script, and I knew Malcolm Gets's musical talent was as great as his acting talent. I just handed it to him and said, 'Can you make this into a song?'"

Malcolm remembers it well. "It's sort of extraordinary, because I was fourteen, almost fifteen at the time. Marshall New came to me and said, 'We're doing this play by Tennessee Williams, and he is coming. Tennessee wrote some lyrics. Will you write the music?' He gave me a copy of the soundtrack of *In the Heat of the Night* and said, 'Write something like this.' Because the character was actually a prostitute, I wrote a blues song to it." Tennessee was very happy with the result and later autographed it for Malcolm. The song is titled "Ruby's Blues," and the published work reads, "Lyrics by Tennessee Williams, Music by Malcolm Gets." A heady credit for any performer's resume—let alone a fifteen-year-old's.

"I was so young," Malcolm said. "I didn't really know who he was. My mother had played Laura in *The Glass Menagerie* and she said, 'He's a very important man.'"

The Great Playwright Arrives . . . Almost

"Tennessee agreeing to come to Gainesville," Greg Hausch said, "is a really big deal, so Marshall and I go out to the Gainesville airport."

Back then, the tiny airport terminal was the size of a convenience store. Passengers dropped their luggage out on the curb. There weren't any concourses, Jetways, or airport security. The outdoor waiting area was a few park benches on the runway apron. When a plane landed, ground personnel pushed a mobile stairway over to the plane door.

"There was only one flight from Key West the whole day," Greg continued. "We waited and waited. Finally, a small plane lands. Everybody gets off. There's no Tennessee. So, we ask at the ticket counter."

"No, he's not on this flight," the woman at the counter said.

Crestfallen, they returned to the theatre and telephoned him.

Tennessee spoke with an accent much like his character Maggie from *Cat on a Hot Tin Roof*. "Ah was feeling poorly," Tennessee said. "Ah didn't feel like coming. I might be coming tomorrow."

"So, will you let us know?"

"I'll try."

"Let me know," Greg said.

"If I'm coming, you will know."

Greg doesn't remember Tennessee letting them know, but they still drove out to the airport the next day. "And sure enough, he was there," Greg said. "He gets off the plane with his bottle of wine, and we take him to the Hilton, which was the nicest place in Gainesville, and get him the presidential suite. We think it looks pretty fancy, but he didn't say anything. That was disappointing."

Tennessee took a nap and a swim at the Hilton, and then they took him to the university where he was going to read some of his poetry. Greg explains: "We got Student Government to help pay our expenses because we didn't have a sponsor. The hotel wasn't free, the airfare, and all that stuff. In exchange, we arranged with them for Tennessee to do a reading of his poetry at the University Auditorium, and then afterwards the faculty was going to throw him a party in a suite at the Reitz Union. So, we pick up Tennessee at the Hilton, and we don't get far before he says, 'Wait. I forgot my wine. I got to go back.' He never went anywhere without it. He walked around with a bottle of white wine all the time. Like people today walk around with water bottles."

They were already late, and everybody was waiting in the University Auditorium. "I'll pull over and get you one," Greg said.

"No, Greg, I need my wine. I have to have my wine."

"Can't I just go to a store?"

He agreed, and Greg pulled into a 7-Eleven, but Tennessee didn't like anything they sold. So, they returned to the hotel, got his wine, and finally got him into the auditorium. The audience was mainly bored freshmen and sophomores, no faculty, no upperclassmen.

Marshall New had told him in the car, while driving to the university, "You know, I think more people write poetry than read poetry."

"Do tell," he said.

Marshall also told him that he'd cut one scene from the script because it made act one a little tighter.

"Oh, really?" Tennessee said.

"That conversation would end up biting me in the ass," Marshall recalled. Anyway, Marshall was standing backstage with Tennessee while he was being introduced by someone from the English department. Kerry thinks it was Harry Crews, drunk and rambling off a list of all the things Tennessee had written.

Tennessee leaned over to Marshall and said, "You know, I think this introduction's gone on longer than my career."

"I think so, too," Marshall said.

Once the introduction finished and he got onstage, Tennessee said, "When I was driving here tonight, Marshall New told me he thinks more people write poetry than read it." The audience howled with laughter.

Marshall turned to Greg. "You, Kerry, and Bruce take care of Tennessee. Get him fed and bring him to the theatre. I'm going to go rehearse the show."

Remembering that night, Greg said, "His reading seems to go on forever. Finally, I go out onstage and say, 'Ladies and Gentlemen, Tennessee Williams!' And he looks at me mid-prose. I said, 'Don't forget the faculty reception.'" They left and went to the Reitz Union suite. "We open the door, and there's no faculty, not one. Outside there is a line of undergraduates as far as you can see holding copies of *Glass Menagerie* and *Streetcar Named Desire* for him to autograph. He signed a couple and then wanted to eat seafood, so we took him to a real cracker joint on Waldo Road where he had catfish and regaled us with stories."

After dinner, they drove him to their warehouse theatre where rehearsal had just ended. Tennessee said to Kerry, "Where the hell am I? I'm not only off-Broadway, I'm off-off-off-off-off-Broadway."

Photo: Gary Wolfson/*Gainesville Sun*

Michael Doyle as Archie Lee and Jennifer Pritchett as Baby Doll in *Tiger Tail*.

Marshall had cast Hippodrome veterans Michael Doyle as the husband Archie Lee, Jon Schwartz as his rival Silva Vacarro, and Dana Moser as Aunt Rose Comfort. UF alumni and Gainesville native Jennifer Pritchett, who'd had a small part in the Hippodrome's 1974 *Marat/Sade*, was by 1979 a professional actor based in New York City. Her mother telephoned Marshall and suggested Jennifer for the role of Baby Doll, Archie's child bride.

"Jennifer was perfect," Marshall said, "and Tennessee loved her."

Unfortunately, he didn't love Marshall's choice of Dana. Meeting her out of costume, he thought her too young and pretty to play the elderly Aunt Rose Comfort. With proper makeup and consummate acting skill, Dana performed the role wonderfully, but upon first meeting her, Tennessee considered Marshall's failure to cast the appropriate age as amateur theatre.

The Hippodrome was no longer working under the radar. To be considered a professional theatre by New York producers, agents, and actors, they had become an Equity theatre. Gregg Jones said he was the first Equity actor hired by the Hippodrome, but by this point, Michael Doyle and Jennifer Pritchett were also Equity members. Tennessee Williams, whose plays had been on Broadway for the past thirty years, didn't ask. He just expected they were all Equity actors.

The next morning, Marshall's conversation in the car the previous night came back to bite him. "I got a phone call from his agent saying, 'Tennessee wants to talk to you.'"

Tennessee was just boiling over with anger. He said, "I want that tampering you did with my play—that scene you cut—restored."

Marshall had cut the page before they'd even started rehearsal. The actors had never seen it. "But believe me, that day we rehearsed it," Marshall said. "I remember when it was performed that night. Jennifer looked up at where Tennessee and I were sitting together and gave a very quick little wicked smile like 'we did it.' Jennifer was spectacular as Baby Doll, and Tennessee loved her so much, he didn't feel like he was with amateurs. Oh, and he loved Dana. When he saw her as Aunt Rose Comfort, he looked at me and acknowledged the fact that she worked."

"I have a photograph somewhere," Dana said, "where I'm reaching out to shake his hand, and he was kind of drunk. When he reached out to shake hands, he fell down. I remember thinking to myself, 'There is the world's greatest playwright, dead at your feet.' Later, I read about an actress who said all her life she'd wanted to meet Tennessee Williams. I thought, 'Well, I did, but he almost died in the process.'"

Dana Moser shakes hands with Tennessee Williams on the set of *Tiger Tail* as Marshall New looks on. Moments later, Williams falls.

Photo: Gary Wolfson/*Gainesville Sun*

"Tennessee was very gracious," Dan Jesse said. But he was a handful for his hosts. A big fundraising dinner at the Sovereign preceded the preview performance. One hundred twenty-five season subscribers had paid extra to dine with the famous man. Marshall drove to the Hilton to pick up Tennessee and his agent for the dinner. "I couldn't find them," Marshall said. "I looked and looked and looked and finally found them in the Hilton restaurant." Tennessee was enjoying a shrimp cocktail.

"Tennessee," Marshall said, "I'm supposed to take you to dinner."

"Well, I've already ordered dinner from this charming young man here. Come here, sir." Tennessee motioned to a beautiful young student waiter whom he'd been flirting with. "I would never insult this young man by refusing his victuals."

"Well, he didn't cook it," Marshall said, "and you're expected at the Sovereign."

His agent pulled Marshall aside and said, "Tennessee is on the verge of leaving town. He was not happy with what he saw at your theatre."

"Well, let's hope he'll be happy tonight," Marshall said.

They arrived late. Everybody was sitting there drinking because no one wanted to start their salad until Tennessee got there. He came in and said his hellos. He wasn't keen on being there but signed a few autographs and said a few words. "He was actually quite shy," Dan Jesse said. "If you said things like 'I think you're our greatest playwright,' he would just go, 'Oh, pshaw.'"

The Sovereign restaurant was in downtown Gainesville, a block from the old Post Office. When they pointed out the beaux arts edifice the Hippodrome hoped to occupy, he said, "Y'all going from the warehouse to the courthouse." A different night, when the odor of hogs in the neighboring stockyard wafted over the theatre parking lot, he revised that line. "Ew-eee, y'all moving from the outhouse to the courthouse."

After dinner, everyone drove out to the theatre for the performance. The show was sold out. In addition to those who'd been at the restaurant, another 150 patrons had paid a premium to watch the show with the playwright.

"The good fortune was that everyone had gotten loaded," Marshall said, "so the audience was really receptive. They laughed at every last line in the play, and they just loved it. They loved Jennifer. They loved Mike Doyle. All the actors did a great job. Tennessee was very happy with it." Marshall drove them back to the Hilton after the show and had a drink with Tennessee's agent, Mitch Douglas, in the bar.

Mitch said, "You know, Tennessee really loved the show, and he's going home in the morning—"

"What!" Marshall said. They'd already sold out opening night with the playwright at elevated prices and had a major press conference scheduled the next day. Marshall called Greg. "What are we going to do? Tennessee says he's going to leave town tomorrow."

"I'll come down there," Greg said.

"Greg and I sat in the bar discussing what to do. Then, we realized that behind the bar was the young waiter that Tennessee had been flirting with when we came to pick him up to go to the Sovereign. So, we bought a bottle of wine and asked him to take it with two glasses to Tennessee's room, praying that would delay Tennessee's departure. No one knows for sure what happened, but all I know is, the next day, Tennessee was still there."

Missed Press Conference

Still in Gainesville, but not ready, as he was supposed to be, when Greg went to pick him up the next morning. "I'm at the door rapping and rapping," Greg said. "I go to the house phone and call him. Not a stir. I've got a press conference at the Hippodrome warehouse with reporters from all over the South. I keep pounding on the door."

Finally, "Hello?"

"Tennessee, it's Greg."

"I'm afraid I'm feeling poorly. I can't make it. Tell everybody I'll see you later."

"No, really. I've got press out there."

"I'll see you later, babe." Tennessee went back to bed.

"Holy crap!" Greg said. "This is the first time we had any real press from anywhere outside Gainesville. Here we had statewide coverage, even people from Atlanta." Greg doesn't call anyone at the theatre to warn them. "I just show up back at the Hippodrome, Tennessee-less. I walk onto the stage and there are thirty to forty reporters. I said, 'I am sorry to announce that Tennessee is not feeling well this morning, and he will not be attending.' Everybody ran into our office, fighting over the three telephones we had, then it went out over the wire service: 'Tennessee Williams on his deathbed in Gainesville, Florida.'"

That night, he was bright and shiny, ready to go to the theatre again. "It just was a wonderful evening of theatre," Marshall said. "He was very happy. When the curtain call happened, the cast got a standing ovation, of course. I nodded to Jennifer, and she ran up the aisle, grabbed Tennessee by the hand, and led him down to the stage to take a bow with the cast."

Photo: Gary Wolfson/*Gainesville Sun*

Jennifer Pritchett and Tennessee Williams at the *Tiger Tail* after-show party.

Jennifer, who has had a long, successful acting career, said, "That was probably the high point of my entire theatrical career—a bow with Tennessee to a standing ovation. I'm getting goosebumps even now re- membering it."

The next morning, newspapers statewide feature a large photo of him holding Jennifer in his arms at the after-show party with an article next to it: "Tennessee Williams suffers from nervous exhaustion."

Leaving the Hilton for the airport, an old lady recognized him. "Mr. Williams, I'm so glad to see you. I thought you were dead."

"Not yet," Tennessee replied, drolly. "Not yet."

Tiger Tail opened November 1. The night it closed, December 1, 1979, Tennessee received the Kennedy Center Honors.

Tennessee passed away in 1983.

Marshall New reflected, "He is the greatest American playwright, living or not liv- ing. We don't have another American playwright whose pieces will stand up against a few of his." Notable works such as *The Glass Menagerie*, *A Streetcar Named Desire*, *Cat on a Hot Tin Roof*, *The Night of the Iguana*, and *Sweet Bird of Youth* continue to be performed forty years after his death. A few years after *Tiger Tail* premiered at the Hippodrome, Marshall had the opportunity to direct it at the Tennessee Williams Theatre in Key West—with a different cast, of course. But Dan Jesse got to play Archie Lee in that production.

Christmas Carol, Again

The Hippodrome ended the year with *A Christmas Carol* for the second time, es- tablishing what was to become an annual tradition. Again, admission was two cans of food for the Salvation Army food drive or an unwrapped toy for Toys for Tots. Many of the adults in the previous year's cast returned, except for Bruce Cornwell, whose role as Ebenezer Scrooge was filled by Tom Nash. Of course, children in the cast changed from year to year as they outgrew younger parts.

Since its first year, *A Christmas Carol* has frequently served as an entry to acting for children of Hippodrome thespians. That year, Molly Beistle, daughter of Hippodrome favorites Mike and Maggie Beistle, made her debut.

The production, which ran from December 14–22, again warmed the hearts of Gainesville theatergoers who flocked to hear Tiny Tim cry out, "God bless us, every one!"

Photo: Bryan Grigsby/*Gainesville Sun*

Bob Cratchit (Rusty Salling) and Tiny Tim (Justin Davis) sit among a huge pile of canned goods collected for distribution by the Salvation Army at the previous production of *A Christmas Carol*.

1   Arline Greer, review of *Lord Alfred's Lover*, by Eric Bentley, directed by Kerry McKenney, Hippodrome Theatre, Gainesville, FL, *Gainesville Sun*, February 27, 1979.
2   Ibid.
3   Bob Cochran, review of *The Norman Conquests*, by Alan Ayckbourn, directed by Gregory Hausch, Hippodrome Theatre, Gainesville, FL, *Independent Florida Alligator*, April 13, 1979.
4   Beth Demauro, "People Can Find Themselves in GLT, Hipp Urban Comedies," *Gainesville Sun*, April 13, 1979.
5   Arline Greer, review of *Sleuth*, by Anthony Shaffer, directed by Mary Hausch, Hippodrome Theatre, Gainesville, FL, *Gainesville Sun*, August 3, 1979.
6   Arline Greer, review of *Sly Fox*, by Larry Gelbart, directed by Kerry McKenney, Hippodrome Theatre, Gainesville, FL, *Gainesville Sun*, September 27, 1979.
7   Tennesse Williams, *Baby Doll and Tiger Tail*, New Directions Publishing Corp., New York, NY.
8   "Tennessee Williams to Work With Hippodrome for *Tiger Tails*," *Gainesville Sun*, September 14, 1979.

1980

Next Stop, Greenwich Village

Whatever headaches Tennessee Williams had given the Hippodrome, his collaboration with them had vaulted their legitimacy in the theatre world. Bruce Cornwell approached screenwriter Paul Mazursky and asked for the rights to adapt the screenplay of his film *Next Stop, Greenwich Village* for the stage. Mazursky agreed, and the Hippodrome started 1980 with yet another world premiere.

Bruce wrote the adaptation himself and also directed it. He cast Michael Massaro in the lead as Larry, a nice Jewish boy who moves to Greenwich Village to be an actor, much to the chagrin of his mother, played by Maggie Beistle. Except for Sidney Bertisch, the piano player, and Kathryn Nash, who'd been Mrs. Cratchit in *A Christmas Carol*, and Derry Glenn, a professional actor from Atlanta, the rest of the seventeen-member cast were UF students. Several of them had played small roles in *They Shoot Horses, Don't They?*

(l-r) Derry Glenn, Kathryn Nash, Emily Kairalla, Michael Massaro, Graham Gilbert, and Maggie Beistle in *Next Stop, Greenwich Village*.

The story takes place in 1953, and the Hippodrome production was staged on a four-level set designed by Carlos Asse. Larry has left his overprotective, guilt-inducing mother for a chance at stardom. He ends up in Greenwich Village, hanging out with a bunch of eccentric characters while waiting for his big break, which finally comes. Arline Greer called the story trite but praised Bruce's adaptation and directing. The play ran from January 11–February 2.

Talley's Folly

Next up was *Talley's Folly*, a two-character romance by Lanford Wilson, directed by Marshall New. It was another coup for the Hippodrome. The play premiered on Broadway February 20, 1980, but opened in Gainesville five days earlier, on February 15. This wasn't the first time the play had been performed, though. It had played off-Broadway at the Circle Repertory for six weeks the previous May. But the Hippodrome had beaten Broadway to the punch (with the author's permission). Adding to the prestige, the play won the 1980 Pulitzer Prize for Drama.

Set at a boathouse on the Talley farm near Lebanon, Missouri, in 1944, the ninety-seven-minute play takes place in real time without scene changes or intermission. The story depicts a single night in the lives of two unlikely sweethearts, Matt Friedman and Sally Talley, played to perfection by Michael Doyle and Jennifer

Photo: Gary Wolfson

Jennifer Pritchett and Michael Doyle in *Talley's Folly*.

Pritchett. Having recently portrayed completely different character types in *Tiger Tail*, Greg Hausch said, "You wouldn't think of them as being a possible couple, but because they are both such fine actors, it worked."

Since the previous summer when Matt met Sally, a thirty-one-year-old spinster, his interest in her has never waned. He has written her a letter every day. Though Sally has given him no reply or encouragement, he arrives to ask her to marry him. Sally is in disbelief that Matt has shown up uninvited, even though he wrote her that he planned to come. His arrival creates a stir in Sally's conservative Protestant household, because not only is he Jewish, he's eleven years her senior.

Dick Gorenberg, president of the Hippodrome Board of Trustees, and his wife, Caren, saw the play at the Circle Repertory Theatre in New York and raved about it. However, soon after the Gorenbergs saw it, the *New York Times* named it one of the Ten Best Plays of 1979, putting it out of reach of regional theatres.

Explaining how the Hippodrome secured the rights to *Talley's Folly*, Marshall New said, "Basically, it boiled down to who we knew and our reputation out of town. Bridgett Aschenberg, Lanford Wilson's agent, met up with Tennessee Williams' agent. He was so happy with what we did with *Tiger Tail*, he put in a good word for us."

That got back to Lanford Wilson, who, upon meeting the Hippodrome artistic directors over lunch, decided to let them do the play. His agent sent Greg a contract, and Marshall got to work with only five weeks to go.

Creative geniuses? Definitely. But not so when it came to business matters. February 12, two days before the preview show, they got a telegram from Lanford's agent:

"Because of your failure to return counter-signed agreement for Talley's and non-payment of advance of one thousand dollars, we are putting you on notice that we will get a legal injunction against you and prevent you from opening."

Oh, no! But all's well that ends well. Greg rushed to the bank, got a cashier's check, took it to Western Union, and wired the agent the money. The show opened on time. Michael Doyle sent the New York cast, who hadn't opened yet, a mailgram that read, "Happy Valentine's Day, signed Jennifer Pritchett, Michael Doyle, and Marshall New." *Talley's Folly* continued at the Hippodrome through March 8.

Loose Ends

On March 21, the Hippodrome opened *Loose Ends*, marking its Southeastern premiere. The 1979 play by Michael Weller had just closed its Broadway run on January 27, 1980, and the Hippodrome was the first regional theatre to get it.

The bittersweet romance featured Kevin Rainsberger in his sixth Hippodrome appearance. He played Paul, a Peace Corps dropout. Paul's girlfriend and eventual wife, Susan, was played by Greta Lambert, a UF Theatre Department graduate student making her Hippodrome debut. The *Gainesville Sun* review called their performances "top drawer, exquisitely conceived and executed."[1]

The story spans the turbulent decade of 1970–1979, with each scene jumping to a new year and location. The audience is kept abreast of time's progression by the projection of the couple's slideshow on an overhead screen. Paul and Susan meet on a beach in Bali. Later, they live together in Boston, marry, separate briefly, then reconcile in a New York penthouse. She has become a successful photographer, he a successful film editor. Paul wants children and Susan does not. At her birthday celebration in New York, Paul bitterly denounces her for having had an abortion six months earlier without his knowledge or consent. They divorce. Not a happy play, but emotionally poignant.

Photo: Gary Wolfson

Kevin Rainsberger, Greta Lambert, and Marshall New in a scene from *Loose Ends*.

Kevin said, "The wonderful thing about acting is that you get to play all these characters, take on personas, and feel emotions that you would never necessarily feel in your lifetime. To me, that's the fun of performing; that's the greatest payoff that there is."

The cast, directed by Gregory Hausch, included Hippodrome regulars Mary Hausch, Marshall New, Dan Jesse, Rusty Salling, and four UF theatre students.

Candide

Loose Ends ran through April 12 and was followed less than two weeks later by *Candide*, which opened April 25, 1980. Kerry McKenney had written an adaptation of Voltaire's 1759 French satire and was also initially directing it. Voltaire had written the story largely to skewer the philosophy of German philosopher Gottfried Leibniz, a contemporary of Voltaire. Leibniz's philosophy of optimism—that everything would work out—seemed idiocy to Voltaire.

Candide is the illegitimate nephew of a baron. He is in love with the baron's daughter and the feeling is mutual. Naturally, the baron opposes their marriage. In both

Photo: John Moran/*Gainesville Sun*

(Back) Dan Jesse as Voltaire.
(Front) Greg Hausch as Candide
and Catherine Thompson as the
baron's daughter.

the novella and Kerry's adaptation, Candide's mentor, Professor Pangloss, represents Leibniz. Greg played Candide. Louis Tyrrell had the role of Pangloss, and Dan Jesse, as Voltaire, narrated.

The play was a lavish spectacle, an extravaganza with a beautiful set designed by Carlos Asse. Eighty-one characters were played by twelve actors performing quick costume changes. Rusty Salling and Gregg Jones each played a half dozen characters. Hippodrome regulars Rick Lotzkar and Jerry Mason, along with student actors Patti Avick, Beth Bigelow, Catherine Thomson, Molly Beistle, and Kyle Corley, filled out the rest of the cast. Marilyn Wall designed eighty-one innovative costumes to give each character a distinct look. Her costumes were described as "the stuff of which dreams are made."[2]

However, during rehearsals, Kerry had to leave for a bit. The Ford Foundation had given her and Marshall a grant to visit other theatre groups who had renovated historic buildings, as the Hippodrome was about to do with the old Post Office. With the impending acquisition bearing down like a juggernaut, they couldn't put the trip off. So, Kerry left Greg Hausch in charge of her play. When they returned, Kerry was unhappy, feeling Greg had turned her play into bawdy vaudeville-style slapstick. *Candide* closed May 31, 1980.

Summer Farce

The Hippodrome readied its summer production, *Bedroom Farce*, written by Alan Ayckbourn and directed by Greg Hausch. Unlike the gargantuan number of characters in *Candide*, *Bedroom Farce* required only four couples. Greg cast longtime Hippodrome regulars Marshall New, Dan Jesse, Kerry McKenney, Rusty Salling, Marilyn Wall, Nell Page, Yvonne Dell, and Bert Taylor.

Yvonne had acted in early Hippodrome plays *Exit the King* and *The Madwoman of Chaillot* when the theatre was on Hawthorne Road. More recently, she'd appeared in *Soap* and *Equus*. Bert Taylor, who'd been in *They Shoot Horses, Don't They?*, was perfect for British farce, being from England originally.

(l-r) Bert Taylor, Marilyn Wall,
and Yvonne Dell in *Bedroom
Farce*.

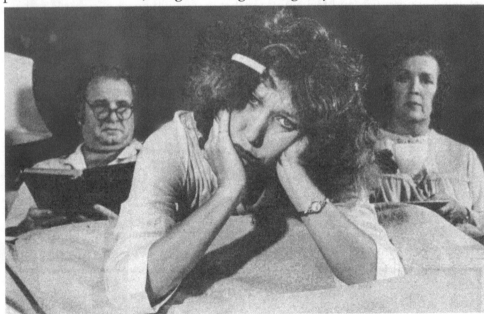

Photo: *Gainesville Sun*

The set was the bedrooms of three British couples, each lit in turn by stage lighting as the action switched rooms. The comedy comes from a melee of events among the four couples. The bedroom of the fourth couple, played by Rusty and Marilyn, is never shown. Nor does it need to be, because they chase each other through the other couples' bedrooms, drawing everyone else into their conflict. The characters jump into and out of each other's beds and argue about it. But for a play about four philandering couples, it was surprisingly tame. The *Florida Times-Union* said it was "funny without being too racy."[3]

Sun critic Arline Greer called it "farce at its best... audiences are reduced to helpless laughter of the belly-clutching variety."[4]

Bedroom Farce ran from June 20–July 19. During its run, two important announcements appeared in the local press.

First, on June 30, Richard Gorenberg, President of the Hippodrome Board of Trustees, signed on behalf of the theatre a twenty-year lease with the City of Gainesville for the old Post Office.

Second was that the Board had hired Daniel Schay, a Yale graduate with a degree in Theatre Management, to serve as the Hippodrome's Executive Director and Chief Administrator. Schay had worked at theatres in New Haven, Connecticut, and Pittsburgh, Pennsylvania, and was currently at Cincinnati Playhouse. He would start at the Hippodrome in August.

Season Eight

Although the deal for the old Post Office was signed, a lot of renovation needed to be done, and the first show wouldn't be staged there until January 1981. While planning and construction to convert the old building into a working theatre got underway, the Hippodrome kept producing plays at the warehouse. The new

(l-r) Kevin Rainsberger, Maggie Beistle, and Fred Thompson toast in *Deathtrap*.

Photo: Gary Wolfson

season kicked off September 19 with *Deathtrap* by Ira Levin, directed by Marshall New. This wasn't a world premiere, but it was the Southeastern premiere of the long-running Broadway hit. The cast featured a professional actor from New York, Fred Thompson, and Hippodrome veterans Kevin Rainsberger, Dan Jesse, and Maggie Beistle. Making her debut was Santa Fe Community College faculty member Ann Ritch. The set was designed by Carlos Asse.

The action takes place in the study of formerly successful mystery playwright Sidney Bruhl at his home in Westport, Connecticut. Sidney (Fred Thompson) has a serious case of writer's block. Then he receives a brilliant script penned by a former student, Clifford (Kevin Rainsberger). Sidney realizes the only thing standing in the way of another hit is this unknown playwright.

"Would you really kill someone to have another successful play?" asks Sidney's wife (Maggie Beistle).

"Don't be foolish, darling," he replies. "Of course, I would."

Billed as a comedy thriller, *Deathtrap* dazzled the audience with clever, often hilarious dialogue and a plot with more twists than Chubby Checker. After being initially led into fits of laughter by the witty repartee, the audience is shocked as one character after another dies. The playbill beseeched audiences not to spoil the surprises for others.

The *Gainesville Sun* called *Deathtrap* "a Delightful Thriller."[5] It ran through October 18, and two years later, the Hippodrome took it on tour.

Transplanted Shakespeare

Next was William Shakespeare's *As You Like It*. Director Bruce Cornwell transplanted the time and place from Renaissance France to early twentieth-century Italy, and Marilyn Wall costumed the actors like members of the Mafia. *Sun* critic Arline Greer wasn't pleased, calling the production "Flawed, But entertaining."[6] She asked, "Why is a theater company not satisfied with the challenge of rendering a faithful and beautiful enactment of the language of Shakespeare?"[7]

She wasn't wrong. The story probably worked better in the period Shakespeare set it, for the inciting incident is the heroine Rosalind's banishment from court by her uncle, a powerful duke who usurped his position from her father. Rosalind dresses as a man and escapes to the Forest of Arden with her cousin Celia, the duke's daughter. There, they meet a variety of memorable characters and fall in love after several identity mix-ups—a device Shakespeare loved to use.

Hippodrome veterans returned to play key parts. Rena Carney, Mark Sexton, Gregg Jones, Dan Jesse, Malcolm Gets, and Stephen Root stood out among the cast of fourteen. Atlanta actress Laura Copland played Rosalind and Stephen Root played the clown, Touchstone. Since his 1975 Hippodrome debut in *A Midsummer Night's Dream*, Stephen had graduated from UF and been touring the US and Canada with The National Shakespeare Company.

(l-r) Fritz Bronner, Jordan Lund, Malcolm Gets, Rena Carney, Stephen Root, and Dan Jesse in a scene from *As You Like It*.

Photo: Gary Wolfson

As You Like It contains some of Shakespeare's most famous soliloquies and lyrics for several songs. Malcolm Gets recalls, "Bruce Cornwell said, 'Will you write the music for these songs that Shakespeare wrote?' I played the part of the minstrel, Amiens. So, I wrote the music and Anna Freeman played the violin as I sang them." Anna played Audrey, a country wench. She would go on to become a founder of Gainesville's Acrosstown Repertory Theatre.

Dan Jesse played melancholy traveler and philosophical observer Jacques, who delivers some of Shakespeare's most memorable speeches, including the Seven Ages of Man: "All the world's a stage, and all the men and women merely players; they have their exits and their entrances, and one man in his time plays many parts, his acts being seven ages."[8]

Dan recalls how it was almost lost. "Malcolm wrote music to all the songs in the play—beautiful music. It was great, except he came back and said [to Bruce], 'I'm really sorry, but there's one song in here—I tried my best—but I cannot write any music for the Seven Ages of Man.'"

Bruce said, "Well, if you can't write music for it, I guess I'll just have to cut it."

"My jaw hit the floor," Dan said. "He's getting ready to cut the most famous speech in the play?" He told Bruce, "You can't take Seven Ages of Man out of this play. I'll tell you what. My character is a pensive kind of character. I'll just come out onstage right before the end of act one and just elocute the Seven Ages of Man."

"Well, okay, I guess that would work," Bruce said.

It worked for Arline Greer, who praised not only the soliloquy but Dan Jesse's entire performance: "Casting Daniel Jesse as Jacques is the play's redeeming grace, as he is one of the few actors who speaks Shakespeare's language with clarity and eloquence. It is to Jesse that the audience gives immediate, enthusiastic response when he renders that splendid speech."[9] She also commended Mark Sexton: "[Dan's] expertise is matched by that of Mark Sexton, who, in the role of Orlando, also shows his ability to render Shakespearean line and cadence with smooth flowing grace."[10]

As You Like It ran from October 31–November 29. During the same period, the Hippodrome took its 1979 hit, *Sly Fox,* on tour around Florida where it was well received. *The Tampa Tribune* said it was "possibly the funniest play you'll see in Tampa this year."[11]

Most of the actors from the 1979 production were in the tour version, except for Dan Jesse, who was playing Jacques in *As You Like It*. His role as Foxwell J. Sly was taken over by Michael Beistle. Gregg Jones switched roles to the Chief of Police, and his part as Lawyer Craven was filled by Michael Locklair. Jennie Stringfellow also replaced Shari Freels as Miss Fancy, and Barbara Kearns took over Nancy Seibert's role as Mrs. Truckle.

Third *Christmas Carol*

Kevin Rainsberger as Scrooge.

The tour returned to Gainesville for a two-week run December 2–13 while the rest of the company rehearsed *A Christmas Carol*, which played December 17–21. Again, admission was two cans of food for the Salvation Army food drive or a toy for Toys for Tots. Kevin Rainsberger became the third actor to play Scrooge at the Hippodrome.

1 Arline Greer, review of *Loose Ends*, by Michael Weller, directed by Gregory Hausch, Hippodrome Theatre, Gainesville, FL, *Gainesville Sun*, March 26, 1980.
2 Arline Greer, review of *Candide* by Kerry McKenny, directed by Kerry McKenny, Hippodrome Theatre, Gainesville, FL, *Gainesville Sun*, May 7, 1980.
3 Marjorie Anders, review of *Bedroom Farce*, by Alan Ayckbourn, directed by Gregory Hausch, Hippodrome Theatre, Gainesville, FL, *Florida Times-Union*, July 1, 1980.
4 Arline Greer, review of *Bedroom Farce*, by Alan Ayckbourn, directed by Gregory Hausch, Hippodrome Theatre, Gainesville, FL, *Gainesville Sun*, June 26, 1980.
5 Arline Greer, review of *Deathtrap*, by Ira Levin, directed by Marshall New, Hippodrome Theatre, Gainesville, FL, *Gainesville Sun*, September 24, 1980.
6 Arline Greer, review of *As You Like It*, by William Shakespeare, directed by Bruce Cornwell, Hippodrome Theatre, Gainesville, FL, *Gainesville Sun*, November 6, 1980.
7 Ibid.
8 William Shakespeare, *As You Like It*, Act 2, scene 7.
9 Arline Greer, review of *As You Like It*, by William Shakespeare, directed by Bruce Cornwell, Hippodrome Theatre, Gainesville, FL, *Gainesville Sun*, November 6, 1980.
10 Ibid.
11 Bruce Jones, review of *Sly Fox*, by Larry Gelbart, directed by Kerry McKenny, Tampa Theatre, Tampa, FL, *The Tampa Tribune*, November 15, 1980.

Old Building, New Theatre

Hear the name "Hippodrome" and people in Gainesville, Florida, who are even vaguely familiar with the community will instantly think of the magnificent beaux arts architecture of the historic building downtown on SE Second Place. Images of it appear everywhere, from the closing credits of the nightly news to brochures and billboards promoting the city. It truly serves as a symbol of Gainesville's vibrant local arts scene and lively downtown nightlife. But that wasn't always the case.

In the 1970s, Gainesville's downtown business district was a ghost town of empty stores. When the Gainesville Mall was built on NW Thirteenth Street, major department stores like JC Penney, Sears, and Silverman's abandoned their University Avenue locations. Their smaller neighbors went with them. At one point, the downtown area looked so unappealing that a civic group put Christmas decorations in the windows of a number of empty buildings to make the area seem less forlorn.

The Hippodrome's move from the warehouse on US 441 to its present location at 25 SE Second Place was key to revitalizing downtown Gainesville. But getting the building wasn't easy. It took two years, a lot of money, and the cooperation of local businesses and government entities.

Throughout efforts to save the old building and secure its use for the Hippodrome, newspapers and government entities alike referred to it as the old Post Office. It might more properly be called the old Federal Building, for it had housed not only the Post Office but also the Federal Court for the Northern District of Florida, the US Land Office, and the US District Attorney. Following completion of its construction in January 1911, it served as the Federal Building until 1964.

Image from an original blueprint for the front design signed by James Knox Taylor.

History of the Old Federal Building

On March 20, 1903, prominent Gainesville attorney B. F. Hampton and his partner J. M. Graham sold the land on which the building sits to the US government for one dollar. Hampton was instrumental in securing the University of Florida for Gainesville and is credited with persuading the federal government to build the handsome building the Hippodrome now calls home. His partner, Graham, was founder and president of the First National Bank of Gainesville.

The building was designed by federal architect Thomas Ryerson under the supervision of architect James Knox Taylor. Plans were finished and approved in November, 1908. Construction began May 1, 1909, with E. C.

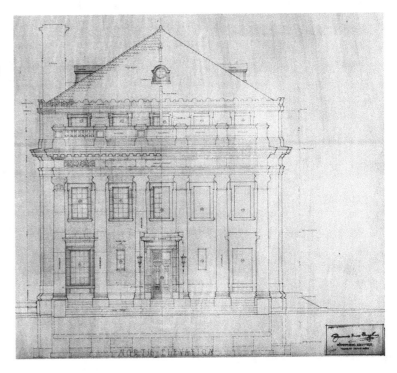

Two photos taken between 1910 and 1911 of building construction in progress. Column sections on ground await assembly. Orange blossom detail atop the six columns.

Carved limestone trims the columns, capitals, entablature, and balustrade beneath the clay tile roof.

Heald as Structural Engineer, J. E. Powell as Mechanical Engineer, and John Young as Construction Supervisor.[1]

The three-and-a-half-story building rests on a base of cut granite block at the first-floor level. At its core is a load-bearing riveted steel frame. Individual granite blocks provide bases for the building's most recognizable feature, six Corinthian limestone columns that support the pediment over the front facade. Carved limestone trim was used for the columns, capitals, entablature, and balustrade. The hipped roof is constructed of clay tile and is surrounded by ornate limestone scrollwork.

One needs only to stand some distance away and look up to see the semicircular copper-sheathed dormers with round windows that light the attic space. The building also has a basement that houses the mechanism for the electrically operated elevator and a furnace providing steam heat—both very advanced for 1911.

The original elevator, which goes between the first, second, and third floors, is the oldest elevator in Florida still in service. Sometime after the Hippodrome moved into the building, Marilyn Wall learned a hard lesson about safety in an old elevator. While carrying a bundle of costumes from her costume shop on the third floor down to the stage, she opened the elevator gate and, without looking, stepped inside. But the elevator was already on a lower floor, and she fell down the shaft, landing on the top of the elevator. To make matters worse, it happened on a weekend when no one was around to help her. She had to repeatedly jump to reach the edge of the opening she'd fallen through so she could pull herself out.

Gainesville Sun columnist Margaret Thomson Shonbrun wrote that in 1909, "The basement was excavated with shovels and the dirt moved by wheelbarrow.... that mountains of glistening white sand waited for construction workers on the lot, and... [her father] Hugh Thomson and other lively boys got into trouble for riding their bikes up and down those mountains.... that the columns were cast far away in sections and assembled on the site to be the glory and pride of growing Gainesville."[2]

Completed in March 1911 at a cost of $160,000, the building remains one of the finest examples of Palladium Classical Revival Architecture in Florida. Bronze entry doors, terrazzo floors, marble staircases, and richly plastered interiors were considered very elaborate for Gainesville in 1911 and still are today.

Interior Past and Present

The interior spaces might be best explained through orientation to their present application. The first floor held the Post Office. Postal customers entered through the oak double doors on the west side of the building, located between the present bar and cinema. The next time you're there, notice the columns are faced with marble on two sides and painted on the other two. Similarly, you will notice some of the floor is marble and the rest is not. These distinctions indicate the portion customers could see; the plainer area was where postal workers stood. While ordering a drink at the bar, look for the word "BULLETIN" etched into the marble above the bar menu. This is where the FBI used to post mug shots of their most wanted criminals.

The building entrance Hippodrome audiences use today wasn't for the Post Office. It was for the Federal Court and government offices. The white marble stairway on the first floor, opposite the elevator, led to the court, which took up the entire second floor. The judge's bench sat about where upstage center is currently located. Offices and chambers for two judges were located in the area that is the backstage today. In the rear corner was a private stairway for judges. It goes all the way down to the basement. Today, actors use it to come and go from the dressing room.

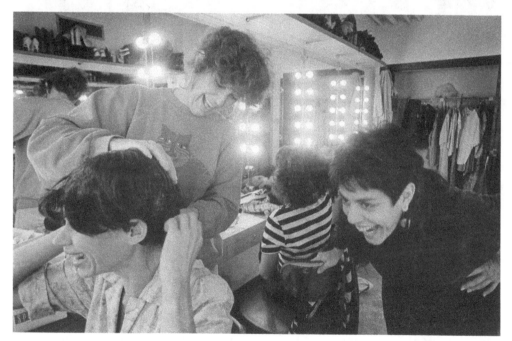

In the basement dressing room: (l-r) Nell Page, Marilyn Wall, and Mary Hausch. (Lauren Caldwell seated with back to camera.)

Photo: Randy Batista

The next time you attend a play, look to your right while standing in front of the ticket takers and you will see a set of red marble steps. These lead to the third floor, where the US Land Office, District Attorney's office, a jury room, witness waiting area, and additional government offices were located.

Visitors may not notice the cleverly disguised steel pillars that are the heart of the building's structural integrity. It was the first concrete-and-steel construction in the region. The pillars hold up the thick concrete slabs of the first and second floors, while the third floor is hung from steel beams above it. Even the attic roof is poured concrete—a very advanced technique for its time.

The pillars are evident in the basement, which is now used for opening night parties and special events. Today, the non-public areas of the basement house the utilities and elevator mechanicals, as well as actors' dressing rooms. On the first floor, directly above the dressing rooms, is the scene construction workshop. In 1911, that space was the mail sorting area, and the present dressing rooms were a holding area for prisoners awaiting court.

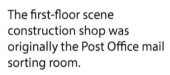

The first-floor scene construction shop was originally the Post Office mail sorting room.

Gainesville citizens were justifiably proud of the magnificent edifice when it was completed in 1911. A monumental portico with six limestone Corinthian columns dominates the front. The portico is richly detailed with carved limestone panels on the frieze and a decorated cornice that continues around the building's perimeter. The Hippodrome works hard to maintain the building and preserve the historical features of its beautiful exterior. But Gainesville's cultural icon was nearly lost to development.

Replaced

In 1963, a new Federal Building was built on SE First Avenue, and in 1964, the court, Post Office, and other federal offices moved there. The US Government listed the old building as surplus property and leased it to the Alachua County School Board for twenty years. The school board used it for office space and storage. Slightly over a decade later, the *Gainesville Sun*, then located behind the old building, was looking to expand. The idea of demolishing the old to make room for the new was floated. Nearby, the Duck Pond and Sweetwater areas were also targets for modernization. Citizens banded together to establish historic districts and protect certain houses and buildings by getting them placed on the US Department of Interior National Register of Historic Places. Two of those were the Thomas Center and the old Federal Building/Post Office. The latter was listed on July 10, 1979, forever eliminating the question of demolition and making it eligible for federal restoration grants.

Downtown Rejuvination

Back in 1974, downtown Gainesville was in sad shape. There were two restaurants, Phil-Nick's and the Primrose Inn. Both closed on weekdays after the only people downtown, attorneys and city workers, got out of work. The city tapped the UF College of Architecture to develop a comprehensive plan for downtown under the direction of Harry Merritt. One of their proposals was to convert the old Federal Building into a performing arts center.

On October 24, 1977, the City Commission received a detailed feasibility study from the College of Architecture: "Renovation and Uses of the Old Post Office." The report included a pictorial design for turning the building into a performing arts complex. Bruce Cornwell, Dr. A. F. C. Wehlburg of the UF Theatre Department, and a group of UF students developed a list of needs for creation of a 450-seat theatre. A few weeks later, the Hippodrome's artistic co-directors and Board of Trustees met with Merritt and concluded that undertaking the renovation was a possibility.

Complicated Negotiations

The city's original thoughts were that the Gainesville Little Theater (GLT) and the Hippodrome would share the space. Neither theatre group was crazy about that. Eventually, the GLT dropped out. In January 1978, the Hippodrome launched a letter-writing campaign through its subscribers to demonstrate public support for such a project to the City Commission. Over the next few months, Greg Hausch and Hippodrome Business Manager Jim Peeples traveled to Washington, D.C., three times to meet with US Senators Richard Stone and Lawton Chiles, US Representative Don Fuqua, several officers of the National Registry of Historic Buildings, and the National Endowment for the Arts (NEA).

Negotiations between the City Commission and the School Board (who held the property) were delayed while the School Board had the property value assessed. The board would also have to relocate fifty-three school district employees who worked in the building. It took until July 1979 for the deal to be settled. The US government transferred the title to the School Board on a quitclaim deed, and the City Commission approved $150,000 to purchase it from them. Still up in the air was the lease between the city and the Hippodrome.

In November 1979, the NEA awarded the Hippodrome a $175,000 Challenge Grant exclusively for renovating the building interior into a theatre. More money than they'd ever seen! But it came with strings attached. The Hippodrome had to match it four-to-one with money they raised themselves. One caveat, they had to raise the first $175,000 by July 1, 1980.

Success! Now Find the Money

Then in January, the City Commission unexpectedly approved the final version of the lease. Under the lease's terms, the Hippodrome would pay no rent for the first two years and then $675 monthly thereafter, subject to renegotiation every five years. Though the rent was only a token, the city was looking for the Hippodrome to reverse the decline of downtown. "I think the city will be well pleased with the effect we'll have on the downtown area," said Hippodrome chairman Richard Gorenberg.[3] They immediately hired Al Dompe as project architect.

Ribbon cutting: (l-r) US Representative Don Fuqua, Bruce Cornwell, Mayor Bill Howard, Director of Cultural Affairs Rebecca Kushner, and State Senator George Kirkpatrick.

On March 16, 1980, the Hippodrome kicked off its official fundraising drive with a ribbon-cutting ceremony on the steps of the old Post Office with Representative Don Fuqua, Director of Cultural Affairs Rebecca Kushner, Gainesville Mayor Bill Howard, and State Senator George Kirkpatrick. Once fundraising got underway, the Hippodrome tried everything: Wet Hippo Night at Wild Waters park, Skeeter's Biscuit Eating Contest, roller skating scavenger hunts, a Hippo Fun Run, a Hippo Sock Hop, concerts, raffles, contests, parties, car washes, and benefit performances. TV-20 also broadcast a Hippothon. But it wasn't enough.

Greg Hausch recalls, "We'd raise $350 at an event and then spend it all on our next event. We were getting nowhere. So we hosted a thing at the Hippodrome for the few corporate entities that we had. Dick Gorenberg gets up. We have these charts of what it's going to look like and he's talking and talking."

Their guests listened from church pews that made up most of the seating at the warehouse theatre. "Dick can be long-winded," Greg said, "So he's going on a little bit long."

Bob Hester, who was the president of First Federal of Mid-Florida, blurted from the audience, "I'll give you $50,000 if I don't have to sit on these pews again."

"Are you serious, Bob?"

"Yeah, I'm telling you right now. I'll give you fifty thousand dollars."

Greg calls that the turning point. "If it wasn't for Bob Hester, we would never have made it. We needed somebody to step up and say, 'I'm going to make a legitimate donation.' After he did that, then doctors, lawyers and law firms, hospitals, and everything started catching on."

The Hippodrome's first public event in the old Post Office, a fundraiser on May 31, put them over the first goal set by the NEA grant one month ahead of the deadline. On June 30, they signed the lease and started working on the building.

Trapdoor for the Shop

The old Post Office has several stairways, but each set of stairs makes at least three ninety-degree turns. Technical Director and scene designer Carlos Asse foresaw that carrying scenery, furniture props, and sheets of wood from the scene shop to the second-floor stage would be an ongoing problem. He beseeched his fellow Hippodromers to install a trapdoor and electric winch backstage, but they told him they couldn't spare the money.

Throughout July and August, 350 volunteers put in 15,000 hours of labor getting the third floor ready. One day, Carlos's team loaded a truck with sheets of plywood and drywall to be used for the administrative offices. He telephoned the co-directors at the old Post Office and said, "Hey guys, I'm going to need some help to carry all these sheets of dry-wall up to the third floor."

When he arrived, they all came down to lend a hand. After carrying a truckload of drywall and plywood up three flights of stairs, they were convinced. Al Dompe modified the plans to include a five-by-twelve-foot opening in the floor between the scene shop and the present-day backstage area, with a trapdoor. They installed an electric winch. "It is a very slow winch," Carlos said. "But you can bring up a lot. We welded two units large enough to hold sheets of plywood or whatever we need and lift them up to the stage."

Al Dompe on site during renovation.

Move in

On September 1, the Hippodrome moved its administrative offices to the new lo-cation, but the theatre portion wasn't even started, so fall productions continued to be staged at the warehouse. By September 15, contributions totaled $326,933 and M.M. Parrish Construction began converting the second floor into the mainstage theatre it is today.

Hippodrome artistic directors in front of their new theatre: (l-r) Bruce Cornwell, Kerry McKenney, Mary Hausch, Marshall New, and Gregory Hausch.

Photo: Gary Wolfson

The Hipp hoped to open their January play, *The Elephant Man*, in the new theatre. Carlos had the set designed but held off building it because it was uncertain if the second-floor construction would be finished in time. The stage downtown is smaller than what they had in the warehouse, so the size of the set would differ depending on which space they used. The directors and board kept delaying their decision. Finally, ten days before opening, they told him the play would open downtown.

Carlos's team built the set in pieces at the warehouse, trucked it downtown, and lifted it to the second floor through the new trapdoor. When they arrived, the seats were not in and the carpet wasn't laid, but he and his crew started erecting the set anyway.

Workers constructing the seating platforms.

With Herculean effort, the contractor finished, the lights were hung, and the show opened.

1 Hippodrome inauguration brochure, January 1981.
2 Margaret Thomson Shonbrun, "Old Post Office Is Too Fine a Building to Demolish," *Gainesville Sun*, December 28, 1978.
3 Maryfran Johnson, "Hippodrome Plans September Move," *Gainesville Sun*, January 24, 1980.

1981

The Elephant Man

The Hippodrome inaugurated its new home in the restored Federal Building on January 16, 1981, with a special gala performance of Bernard Pomerance's *The Elephant Man*, which ran through February 7. The emotionally charged drama had won the Tony Award, the New York Drama Critics Award, the Obie Award, the Drama Desk Award, and the Outer Critics Circle Award. It was currently in its second sold-out season on Broadway. In yet another coup, the Hippodrome had secured rights to its Southeastern premiere. Director Marshal New also received permission to alter the script and add an original score composed by David Smadbeck.

"I wanted the music to the scenes to emotionally describe locations, to create psychological states of mind, to introduce characters thematically," Marshal said. "David and I separately revisited the Broadway and touring productions. We then spent a gray Sunday in a Greenwich Village basement flat discussing ideas." David finished the score and recorded it at Gainesville's Mirror Image Recording Studio.[1]

Every night of its run, audiences, moved by the intense, touchingly truthful production, rewarded the players with round after round of applause. Reviews in the *Gainesville Sun*, *Ocala Star-Banner*, and *Florida Times-Union* were uniformly effusive in their praise. Hippodrome supporters, who had given generously to turn the old building into a wonderful theatre, watched in awe as the top-notch cast delivered a performance that rivaled Broadway for excellence.

British-born actor Bert Taylor, who played the dark-hearted freak show barker in *The Elephant Man*, had performed in London and New York in addition to touring America. Discussing the professionalism of the Hippodrome, he told *Ocala Star-Banner* reporter Alyse Lounsberry, "They're known better outside Florida than here. You can mention the Hippodrome in New York, and they know it instantly."[2]

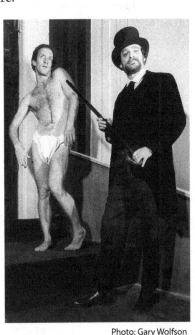

Louis Tyrrell and Dan Jesse in *The Elephant Man*.

The intriguing drama tells the real-life story of Joseph Carey Merrick (called John Merrick in the play), an unfortunate man in the nineteenth century who was grossly disfigured by a bone and skin disorder. For many years, he was exploited as a sideshow freak and called the Elephant Man. Then he was discovered by a London surgeon, Frederick Treves, who found a gentle, sensitive man beneath a hideous exterior. Treves took Merrick to the London hospital, Whitechapel, where Merrick lived from 1886 until his death in 1890. In order to get money for Merrick's care and for the hospital, Treves, played by Dan Jesse, publicized Merrick's condition. London society responded, making Merrick a cause célèbre visited by high society—bishops, dukes, princesses, and the famous actress Madge Kendal, who was played by Kerry McKenney.

The most powerful performance was that of Louis Tyrrell as John Merrick. Contorting his body and face, Louis managed to portray Merrick's monstrous deformity without makeup or prosthetics. His acting was brilliant.

Photo: Gary Wolfson

"The challenge of playing Merrick is trying to portray the contrast between Merrick's physical deformity and his high degree of sensitivity as a human being," Louis said. "Another interesting contrast is between Merrick and the very successful Dr. Treves. The doctor realizes many of his own values have come into question."[3]

"*The Elephant Man* is so successful because there is the same thing in Merrick that touches in each of us—his vulnerability," Louis added. "The vulnerability expressed in each of us that makes us respond, shiver, cry is what makes the story so good. I want to give a true portrayal of John Merrick and bring out the vulnerability in each member of the audience."[4]

Betrayal

The year was off to a great start. The Hippodrome scored a second Southeastern premiere, a new comedy/drama by Harold Pinter, *Betrayal*. They'd negotiated directly with Mr. Pinter's English agent and solicitor to obtain the production rights.

(l-r) Kevin Rainsberger, Nell Page, and Jimmy Richardson in *Betrayl*.

Photo: Gary Wolfson

The four-character play, directed by Kerry McKenney, featured Nell Page, James "Jimmy" Richardson, Kevin Rainsberger, and Jerry Mason. All four were polished professionals, but Jimmy Richardson was a Gainesville native who had become a Hollywood star. After earning his master's in drama from UF, Jimmy starred in Broadway and off-Broadway plays, then moved to Los Angeles. There he landed film roles in the Academy Award-winning *Coming Home* starring Jon Voight and Jane Fonda, *One on One* with Robby Benson, and eventually became the lead in his own television series, *Sierra*. Now he was doing a turn at the Hippodrome playing a man having an affair with his best friend's wife.

In an innovative twist, the playwright uses reverse chronology, so the play's first two scenes take place at the end of an extramarital affair, and the final scene of the play is set seven years earlier when the affair began. That wasn't the only juxtaposition. Although the scenes take place in London and Venice, Carlos Asse created a Japanese-inspired set with sliding shoji screens that Arline Greer called "exquisitely beautiful and effective."[5]

Of Kerry McKenney's direction, Greer said, "*Betrayal* is, perhaps, her finest Hippodrome effort. She moves her players like so many chess pieces on a board that is rigidly drawn, and from which she exacts precise moves and counter-moves."[6]

Greer's review called the acting first rate: "Nell Page, as the beautiful and paradoxical Emma, gives an inscrutable performance that is totally in keeping with the Pinter character. Kevin Rainsberger as Robert, her husband, brings a clenched-teeth kind of anger to his role, as well as an urbane, vindictive nastiness that scores a direct blow each time he appears. James G. Richardson as Jerry, Robert's best friend who dallies with Emma, is so totally likeable, it's hard to fault him as a guilty lech. He has the enthusiastic mannerisms of the boy next door combined with a doltish anxiety that is, somehow, winning. Jerry Mason, in a brief appearance as an Italian waiter, is very amusing."[7]

Betrayal ran from February 20 through March 14. It was Jimmy Richardson's only Hippodrome appearance. He died in a California skiing accident two years later.[8] His parents established a UF theatre scholarship in his memory. In the small world that is Gainesville theatre, Mark Sexton (who debuted with the Hippodrome when he played Alan Strang in *Equus*) won the Richardson scholarship when he enrolled in the UF Master of Fine Arts program.

Award-winning Choreopoem

Photo: Gary Wolfson

Cast of *For Colored Girls Who Have Considered Suicide / When the Rainbow Is Enuf*: (l-r) Carolyn Griffin, Margaret Carey, Janet Hayes, Lynn Pride, Brenadette Harper, and Phyllis Williams.

The Hippodrome followed *Betrayal* with *For Colored Girls Who Have Considered Suicide / When the Rainbow Is Enuf*. Billed as a twenty-part choreopoem, it combined highly theatrical stage movement and music with Ntozake Shange's bitter, funny, and powerful verse. Although it won the 1976 Obie Award (the off-Broadway equivalent of a Tony), it was not a typical play. It had no plot, and the playbill identified the characters only by the color of their dresses—Lady in Yellow, Lady in Blue, etc.

Director Mary Hausch cast six local Black actors/dancers: Margaret Carey, Brenadette Harper, Carolyn Griffin, Lynn Pride, Janet Hayes, and Phyllis Williams. LaVern Porter, founder and director of the LaVern Porter Dancers, choreographed the show.

Ntozake Shange was a Black feminist, novelist, poet, and playwright. Much of her work addressed race and Black power, but the experiences portrayed in the production weren't unique to Black women. Almost all the pieces dealt with women's feelings toward men and the way men treated them as sexual objects to be used, undervalued, and, ultimately, discarded.[9]

For Colored Girls Who Have Considered Suicide / When the Rainbow Is Enuf ran from March 27–April 18.

Space Pandas

Like a rising wave about to crest, a procession of praiseworthy productions had increased the number of season subscribers. The marvelous new facility pleased the public, who had given generously to make it possible. Then, in what many subscribers considered a misstep, the Hippodrome closed the season with *The Revenge of the Space Pandas or Binky Rudich and the Two-speed Clock*. The story is about a twelve-year-old boy named Binky, played by Steve Wedan, who travels through time and space with his friends Vivian (Mary Hausch) and Bob, a sheep (Marshall New). They find themselves trapped on the planet of the space pandas where the Supreme Ruler (Mike Beistle) wants to turn Bob into a wool sweater.

Audiences were not pleased. Some called it the worst play the Hippodrome had ever done. Marshall defended it, explaining, "Kids would come to see it and they would talk back to the actors onstage—especially Mike Beistle's character. The kids would yell, 'Watch out! Watch out!' That part was fun."

It surely would have been a hit in the Hippodrome's Theatre for Young Audiences program. David Mamet had written the play for children ages four to twelve. The problem was that they were playing it to grownups. Director Gregory Hausch adapted it into a musical with songs by Gainesville musician Ed Gwaltney, but at its heart, it was still a goofy children's play.

Photo: Gary Wolfson

Space Pandas Betty Breslin and Kyle Kulish surround Bob the Sheep, played by Marshall New.

Arline Greer said it recalled "a Younger Hippodrome."[10] Undoubtedly, she was referring to the troupe she used to call zanies and crazies, fresh out of college and just having fun. But the theatre and its audiences had matured. Productions like

Equus, Tiger Tail, The Elephant Man, and dozens more had raised expectations. And the Hippodrome no longer ran on a shoestring. It had become a big-budget operation, dependent upon generous donors to keep going. *Space Pandas* opened May 1 and closed May 30.

Elephant Man, Again

In a smart move, the Hippodrome remounted the highly successful *The Elephant Man* from June 9–20, with the same cast as the January production. Many patrons who had seen it then returned to see it again. In July, they sent *The Elephant Man* set, costumes, soundtrack, and lead, Louis Tyrrell, to the Caldwell Playhouse in Boca Raton, where it played through August 30. The Hippodrome received a small share of the proceeds.

Attentive readers of *The Elephant Man* playbill for the summer production might have noticed that Bruce Cornwell was no longer listed among the Hippodrome's artistic co-directors. If they did, no one commented on it. Bruce had moved to Milwaukee, having been awarded a fellowship called the National Fellow in Performing Arts Management and Artistic Direction. Bruce explained the terms of the grant: "They would pair you with a company that they felt was appropriate for whatever you wanted to focus on, where the growth was needed. So they sent me to Milwaukee Repertory Theater for a season. To relieve all parties of any pressure, the agreement was that the theatre that you were going to could not hire you and you agreed not to ask that they hire you." When his year was up, Bruce moved to the Circle Repertory in New York City, co-founded by Lanford Wilson, whose *Talley's Folly* the Hippodrome had previously staged. Thirty years later, Bruce would return to the Hippodrome to serve on the Board of Trustees.

A Sure Start for the Ninth Season

The Hippodrome was now down to four artistic directors: Greg, Mary, Kerry, and Marshall. Back in their first year, Greg Hausch had suggested a Neil Simon play for their season opener. The playwright's relatable comedies reliably drew audiences. It had worked for them in 1973, and it would again.

I Ought to Be in Pictures, Simon's newest play, had just opened on Broadway in April 1980, and the Hippodrome already had performance rights. A film version was being made, but that wouldn't be out until March 1982.

The Hippodrome's production ran from July 3–August 1, 1981. Audiences loved the three-character comedy, which also boosted subscribers, as the price of a ticket to the play could be applied toward the cost of a season subscription.

"There is much to laugh at in the course of this highly professional Hippodrome production," Arline Greer wrote, "not the least of which are three first rate performances by three first-rate actors. Margie Llinas, as Libby, the daughter in search of a father, is determined, awkward, cunning, and naïve by turns, and altogether pleasing. Linda Stephens, in the role of Steffy, the understanding mistress, gives a polished, likable performance that is engagingly real. As Herb, Michael Beistle, in his best Hippodrome role to date, makes a wonderful confused

Photo: Gary Wolfson

Michael Beistle and Margie
Llinas in *I Ought to Be in
Pictures*.

father of a nineteen-year-old, and creates a believable picture of a scruffy, untidy, rapidly aging writer, who is forced to come to terms with his life."[11]

Herb Tucker is a Hollywood screenwriter struggling with writer's block when his nineteen-year-old daughter, Libby, hitchhikes from Brooklyn, convinced her dad can use his Hollywood connections to help her break into the movie business. She barely remembers the father who abandoned his family sixteen years prior, and he knows nothing of parenting a teen. But over the course of the play, Libby forces Herb to accept the responsibilities of parenthood as well as deal with his on-again/off-again relationship with girlfriend Steffy.

Reviewer Jim Camp wrote, "It all comes together again—talent, direction and staging, transcending Broadway's proscenium to meld the players and the patrons in a camaraderie where emotions are shared rather than just observed."[12]

Many considered Margie Llinas's portrayal of Libby superior to the actress who had originated the role on Broadway. In fact, many felt the chemistry of the entire cast under Marshall New's direction turned out better than the chemistry in the film, which came out seven months later.

Margie, who had started at the Hippodrome while she was a senior at Buchholz High School, was by 1981 studying theatre and English at Wesleyan University in Connecticut. Marshall had previously directed Margie in *They Shoot Horses, Don't They?* and thought of her for the part of Libby as soon as he read the script. He said, "Margie is a very instinctive actress and has no problem with dialects (Libby has a Brooklyn accent)."[13]

Margie told the *Gainesville Sun* that Libby was her hardest acting role to date: "She (Libby) changes during the course of the play as she learns to let people love her, and she is tough. But Libby is also fun and outspoken."[14]

Morning's at Seven

Resident scenic designer Carlos Asse had a firm command of the Hippodrome's new stage space and designed Herb's dilapidated Hollywood bungalow for *I Ought to Be in Pictures*, followed by construction of two two-story 1930s-style houses for their next offering, *Morning's at Seven*. Carlos thought an old-fashioned swing would fit the period piece, but he couldn't hang anything heavy from the lighting grid because the auditorium ceiling to which it is fastened is covered with original decorative antique tiles.

While Carlos was designing the set for *Morning's at Seven*, M. M. Parrish workers were on site renovating the first floor into a lobby, gallery, bar, and Second Stage theatre. Carlos asked the contractor to take up the floorboards in two of the third-floor offices and drill holes to mount three-quarter-inch threaded steel rods that extended through the ceiling below. The building floors are extremely thick, so the rods had to be four feet long. After they were bolted in place, the office flooring was put back without a trace of what had been done. But below, on the mainstage, Carlos could fasten to the protruding rods anything his sets required. "We have hung many things up there," Carlos said, "but that swing was the first."

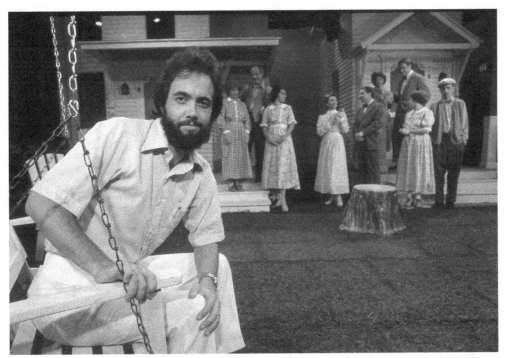

Photo: Gary Wolfson/*Gainesville Sun*

On swing, director of *Morning's at Seven* Kent Stephens; on the set behind him are cast members Roz Simmons, Richard Bowden, Laura Whyte, Sondra Barrett, Dan Jesse, Rena Carney, Marshall New, Theresa O'Shea, and Rusty Salling.

Morning's at Seven, a 1939 play by Paul Osborn, had recently been rediscovered and had won the 1980 Tony Award for Best Revival. In a break with the tradition of having Hippodrome artistic directors helm their plays, they brought down Atlanta theatre director Kent Stephens for the job. Kent and Hippodrome Executive Director Daniel Schay had been friends at Yale. The previous January, Kent had been sent by the NEA to report on the Hippodrome's production of *The Elephant Man*. He liked what he saw. Then his wife, Linda Stephens, was cast as Steffy, opposite Margie Llinas and Mike Beistle in *I Ought to Be in Pictures*.

Describing *Morning's at Seven*, Kent said, "It's like a Norman Rockwell fairy tale. America not as it was, but as we like to imagine it might have been."[15]

Set in 1928, in a small Midwestern town, the plot revolves around the families of four elderly sisters. Scenes take place in the adjacent backyards of Cora and Ida. Cora and her husband, Thor, share their home with unmarried sister Arry. Ida and husband Carl live next door with their son, Homer, who is in his forties and still single, having stretched out his engagement to fiancée Myrtle for seven or, some say, twelve years. Marshall New gave a brilliant performance as the reluctant bachelor who cannot bear to leave his mama to marry Myrtle (Rena Carney).

Visiting this mix of eccentrics is the eldest sister, Esther, whose husband David considers the family a bunch of morons. Dan Jesse's ability to deliver lines dripping in sarcasm was perfectly suited to the role of intellectual snob David. But Rusty Salling's subtle portrayal of husband Carl brought audiences to tears of laughter by simply leaning his forehead against the side of the house. "One thing about Rusty," Greg Hausch said, "is that he could take whatever you gave him, like the tiniest little part, and he would make a jewel out of it."

Equally skilled in the cast were professional actors brought in from other places: Richard Bowden from Knoxville, Tennessee; Roz Simmons from Miami; Theresa

O'Shea and Laura Whyte from Atlanta; and Sondra Barrett, who split time between New York, Los Angeles, and Miami.

Audiences laughed so hard their stomachs ached. *Sun* critic Arline Greer called it "a felicitous beginning to the fall theatre season."[16] The show ran from September 11–October 10, 1981.

Becoming a State Theatre

During the show's run, exciting things were happening. On September 18, the Hippodrome hosted the organizational meeting of the eleven-member Florida Professional Theatres Association, which the Hippodrome had been instrumental in founding. That same day, the Florida State Theatre Board voted unanimously to recommend to Secretary of State George Firestone that the Hippodrome become the third State Theatre. After his approval, and legislative action on the budget, the Hippodrome would receive 10 to 17.5 percent of its budget from the State of Florida. By the following spring, the Hippodrome was officially a State Theatre of Florida.

Pantomime

On October 1, the Hippodrome participated in UF's Celebration of Caribbean Culture by presenting two performances of *Pantomime*, a play by Nobel Prize winner Sir Derek Walcott.

Whose Life Is It Anyway?

Nurse Anderson (Maggie Klekas) administers oxygen to a patient (Rudolph Willrich) while Nurse Sadler (Darla Briganti) restrains Mrs. Boyle (Rena Carney) in *Whose Life Is It Anyway?*

Photo Gary Wolfson/*Gainesville Sun*

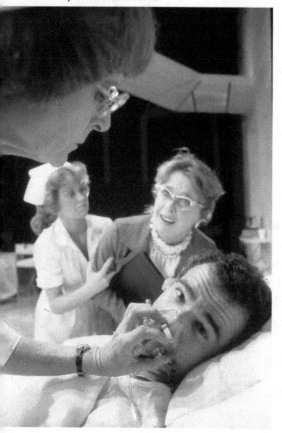

Next on the mainstage, Brian Clark's *Whose Life Is It Anyway?* opened under the direction of Gregory Hausch. Playing the lead was Rudolph Willrich, a New York actor recognizable to Gainesville soap opera fans for his recent six-month stint as a villain on *All My Children*. But from October 23–November 21, he played a courageous, wise-cracking quadriplegic confined to a hospital bed throughout the entire play. Staying in character, he remained in bed throughout intermission.

The main character, Ken Harrison, had been a sculptor and art teacher before his spinal cord was severed in an auto accident, paralyzing him from his neck down. He looks ahead into his future life and sees only an abyss of despair. The play's conflict arises over Harrison's right to die on his own terms and the medical professionals' desire and responsibility to keep him alive despite his wishes.

Such deep questions and the protagonist's dire situation could have made for a depressing night of theatre were it not for the extravagant and biting wit the playwright gave to the character. Instead, as Arline Greer noted in her review, "He is, perhaps, the best-ever lie-down comic to rat-a-tat-tat one-liners in a hospital room. There is very little of the sorry-for-myself attitude displayed in Harrison's exchanges with the hospital staff and with the legal experts who come to argue his case. Instead, he taunts them and himself with flashing witticisms, sparing no one in his desperate display of gags.... he does it with a slash to the funny bone that is true. The sheer virtuosity of the man's humor dazzles us so that we cannot help but be swayed to rooting for his success, an ironic success, in this case, as it represents death."[17]

As with the previous play, the cast was a blend of out-of-town actors and Hippodrome regulars. Rudolph Willrich, Maggie Klekas, Darla Briganti, Daniel Hagen, and Rennie Manning came to Gainesville for the first time. Richard Bowden had stayed on after his appearance in *Morning's at Seven*. Filling remaining roles were local actors Rusty Salling, Rena Carney, Yvonne Dell, Gregg Jones (using the name Barucci), Dan Leonard, Jordan Lund, and Maggie and Michael Beistle. In an interesting twist, the Beistles played the part of Dr. Barr on alternate nights.

Renewed Ties with UF

While the main character of *Whose Life Is It Anyway?* was giving the audience plenty to think about, another weighty issue was being dramatized on campus in the Florida Players' production of Jerome Lawrence and Robert E. Lee's drama *Inherit the Wind*, directed by David Shelton. The play is based on the famous 1925 Scopes Monkey Trial in which Clarence Darrow and William Jennings Bryan argued a case regarding a law against teaching the theory of evolution in Tennessee schools.

Inherit the Wind was staged at the UF Constans Theatre and billed as a coproduction between the UF Theatre Department and the Hippodrome. The Hippodrome's main involvement was to provide Equity actor Edward Stevlingson for the lead role of Henry Drummond. But, more importantly, it bridged the gulf that had once existed between UF and the Hippodrome. "The coproduction of *Inherit the Wind* is just one of many new ties between the University of Florida's theatre department and the Hippodrome this fall," said Department Chairman James Hooks.[18] "The two groups now offer a conservatory internship program, where theatre graduate students at UF can work in some aspect of theatre at the Hippodrome, and receive a stipend for their work. Undergraduate students in theatre will also have the opportunity to work as volunteers at the Hippodrome for class credit under an independent study program."[19] He added, "It gives our MFA students an opportunity to work at a professional level with a completely different organization than that of educational theatre. The Hippodrome has a well-deserved reputation as a progressive, young and aggressive professional theatre group."[20]

Photo courtesy of UF School of Theatre and Dance

Inherit the Wind coproduction with UF, staged at the Constans Theatre. (l-r) Edward Stevlingson, David Shelton, and James Hooks.

New *Christmas Carol* Set

In December, work on the first floor of the building continued. So did efforts to raise $70,000 to fulfill the next phase of the Challenge Grant requirement. But the Hippodrome pressed ahead, offering holiday cheer in the form of *A Christmas Carol.* "It generated a lot of goodwill that we did it for free," director Greg Hausch said. "All [the audience] had to bring was a toy or two canned goods."

Carlos Asse, now the Hippodrome Technical Director, designed a new set for *A Christmas Carol,* repurposing the windows he had used in the hospital set for *The Elephant Man* and the fireplace he had created for *Sleuth* in 1979. The windows remained in sets for *A Christmas Carol* for four decades.

Chad Reed as Scrooge visited by Michael Beistle as Marley.

1 *The Elephant Man* playbill, Hippodrome Theatre, Gainesville, FL, January, 1981.
2 Alyse Lounsberry, "Twice Bitten," *Ocala Star-Banner,* February 12, 1981.
3 Nancy Dahlberg, "Elephant Man Challenges Audience," *Artifacts,* Gainesville Department of Cultural Affairs and the Thomas Center Associates, January 1981.
4 Ibid.
5 Arline Greer, review of *Betrayal,* by Harold Pinter, directed by Kerry McKenney, Hippodrome Theatre, Gainesville, FL, *Gainesville Sun,* February 26, 1981.
6 Ibid.
7 Ibid.
8 "Gainesville Native Dies in Calif. Skiing Accident," The *Gainesville Sun,* February 25, 1983.
9 Arline Greer, review of *For Colored Girls who Have Considered Suicide / When the Rainbow is Enuf,* by Ntozake Shange, directed by Mary Hausch, Hippodrome Theatre, Gainesville, FL, *Gainesville Sun,* April 2, 1981.
10 Arline Greer, review of *The Revenge of the Space Pandas or Binky Rudich and the Two-speed Clock,* by David Mamet, directed by Gregory Hausch, Hippodrome Theatre, Gainesville, FL, *Gainesville Sun,* May 6, 1981.
11 Arline Greer, review of *I Ought to be in Pictures,* by Neil Simon, directed by Gregory Hausch, Hippodrome Theatre, Gainesville, FL, *Gainesville Sun,* July 12, 1981.
12 Jim Camp, review of *I Ought to be in Pictures,* by Neil Simon, directed by Gregory Hausch, Hippodrome Theatre, Gainesville, FL, *Hometown Shopper,* July 8, 1981.
13 Monica Moore, "Hippodrome Features Two Actresses Who Really 'Ought to Be in Pictures,'" *Gainesville Sun,* July 10, 1981.
14 Ibid.
15 Diane Chun, "Atlantan Stephens Joins Family to Direct Morning's At Seven," *Gainesville Sun,* September 18, 1981.
16 Arline Greer, review of *Morning's at Seven,* by Paul Osborn, directed by Kent Stephens, Hippodrome Theatre, Gainesville, FL, *Gainesville Sun,* September 18, 1981.
17 Arline Greer, review of *Whose Life Is It Anyway?,* by Brian Clark, directed by Gregory Hausch, Hippodrome Theatre, Gainesville, FL, *Gainesville Sun,* October, 1981.
18 Diane Chun, "Marriage of Talents Between Florida Players, Hippodrome to Produce Inherit the Wind," *Gainesville Sun,* August 21, 1981.
19 Ibid.
20 Ibid.

1982

Man Friday

From January 8–30, 1982, the Hippodrome presented the American premiere of Adrian Mitchell's *Man Friday*. Director Marshall New had scored again. "I saw *Man Friday* on a late show on TV, and I thought, this will make a great play. So, I wrote Adrian Mitchell in London and asked if it was available. He replied, 'Not only is it available, I wrote it as a play,' and he sent me a copy." Mitchell also flew to the States and became artist-in-residence for the rehearsals and opening.

Man Friday flips the story of Robinson Crusoe, telling it from the vantage point of the Black servant, Friday, and his tribe, letting the audience decide who is civilizing whom. Mitchell, an Oxford-educated author, playwright, poet, and journalist, originally wrote *Man Friday* as a one-hour teleplay for BBC television. Later, he adapted it into a one-act play that toured England before turning it into a film and novel.

Marshall thought the hour-long play was too short for the mainstage. To lengthen it, he had Eddie Gwaltney compose six songs for the show and asked LaVern Porter to choreograph dance sequences. LaVern had previously choreographed *For Colored Girls Who Have Considered Suicide / When the Rainbow Is Enuf,* and Eddie had written the music for *Revenge of the Space Pandas.*

"We added stuff that he [Mitchell] didn't find objectionable," Marshall said. "There was a dance sequence that he complained about, but he loved the cast."

"The tribe really works together marvelously," Mitchell said after seeing the dress rehearsal. He also loved Carlos Asse's set of sandy beach and palm trees. "Not many of those in England," he said with a laugh.[1]

Louis Tyrrell played Robinson Crusoe. Atlanta actor Jihad Babatunde played Friday. Completing the cast of five were Eddie Billups, who had debuted alongside Louis in *Streamers*, and Lynn Pride, who had been in *For Colored Girls*. New to the mainstage, but not to the theatre, was Lance Harmeling, a cast member of the Hippodrome's Theatre-In-Education Department plays.

Photo: Gary Wolfson

From bottom up: Louis Tyrrell (Robinson Crusoe), Eddie Billups (left), Lance Harmeling (right), Jihad Babatunde (Friday), and Lynn Pride in *Man Friday*.

After ninety minutes of Crusoe trying to "civilize" Friday into being his servant and Friday trying to educate the degenerate colonialist mentality out of white, Protestant, Puritan Crusoe, the audience votes on whether the lonely Crusoe can become a member of the tribe. "That was the whole point," Marshall said. "About how we treat each other and whether it makes us viable to be a member of the tribe or not."

On February 6, after *Man Friday* closed, the Hippodrome held a benefit to celebrate completion of the Federal Building restoration and the opening of the first-floor gallery and seventy-three-seat Cinema / Second Stage theatre. The evening included a champagne and dessert buffet, dancing to the music of the Phil Kay Trio, a chamber concert by the Kitts Family Players, and a retrospective look at the Hippodrome's seven-year history narrated by artistic co-directors Marshall New and Greg Hausch.

Since they would not always have enough plays for the Second Stage, they started the Hippodrome Cinema which showed its first film on January 21, 1982. Films ranged from 1930s classics like *Mata Hari* to recent movies that were no longer showing in mainstream theatres. In subsequent years, the Cinema offerings would expand to feature foreign and independent films. For a time, the Second Stage was also used for small concerts by local musicians.

Terra Nova

In March, the Hippodrome sailed from *Man Friday*'s tropical island moral comedy to bleak drama in Ted Tally's *Terra Nova*, the story of English explorer Robert Scott's doomed race to be first to reach the South Pole.

Photo: Gary Wolfson

(l-r): Edward Rudney as Amundsen, Terry Lumley as Kathleen Scott, and Ned Schmidtke as Captain Scott.

"*Terra Nova* is a drama of heroic proportions," wrote critic Arline Greer. "With a magnificent fusion of all the elements of theatre craft, director Kerry McKenney has achieved that stage rarity; a true rendering of the human heart, an honest, soul-searching enactment of words committed to paper by a gifted playwright. The feat is all the more remarkable as Ted Tally, the author of *Terra Nova*, has constructed a complex play which must be performed immaculately on several levels. Time sequences, past and present, flow into each other, overlapping in the minds of the protagonists. Dreams are superimposed on the time sequences. Characters step out of themselves as they address different stages of consciousness on the part of viewers. Flashbacks, dreams, the cold hard present, and visions of the future, all are fused into one remarkable whole that, performed with the clarity of this Hippodrome production, have a hypnotic quality."[2]

Perhaps too much so. The play was long. Even Greer acknowledged that. She wrote, "On the night I saw *Terra Nova*, the audience seemed quiet and almost deflated when the play ended. I could not tell if it was tired from sitting so long, or from the emotion it felt from the performance it had experienced. Its applause seemed respectful, rather than enthusiastic."[3] Director Kerry McKenney told Greer she was going to shorten the play for the remainder of the run, and she did. *Terra Nova* ran from February 12–March 7.

Funds and Management

In March, the Hippodrome toured their previously successful production of Ira Levin's *Deathtrap*. Greg Hausch took over for Marshall New as director for the tour. Richard Bowden replaced Fred Thompson as Sidney Bruhl, and Laura Whyte replaced Ann Rich in the role of the psychic. But the rest of the cast—Maggie Beistle, Kevin Rainsberger, and Dan Jesse—reprised their roles from the 1980 production.

They toured ten states, performing in thirty cities across the Southeast, and garnered winning reviews in each city, such as this one by Kathleen Hargreaves in the *Key West Citizen*: "It is a fine production, reminiscent of first-class theatre in major cultural centers across the country."[4]

The tour made money the Hippodrome desperately needed. Executive Director Dan Schay had left their employ during *Terra Nova*. Although he'd done important things for the Hippodrome, such as getting them into the League of Resident Theatres, which improved their position regarding Equity contracts, he hadn't done any fundraising.

"We could have spoken to him about that earlier," Marshall New said, "but we weren't very confrontational, and we didn't want to be involved in it after all we did to get the Post Office. We were burned out when it came to raising money for the Hippodrome—at least I was. But we had created this monster that had to be fed money for it to survive." Exactly what the other theatre groups he and Kerry had visited warned them about. "When you expand from one venue to the next big step up, you are going to have to turn your focus to fundraising on a continual basis," Marshall recalled.

"We were told what to expect," he added, "but we didn't believe it because we were so excited about getting into the Post Office." Even Tennessee Williams had warned them, calling their ambitions for the building an "edifice complex." He said, "You get too big and you can't sustain the magic that you had when you were poor and in a warehouse."

The Hippodrome issued a special plea to the community: "The building has been obtained and renovated, the artists recruited, potential long-term funding sources found—the future for the Hippodrome looks better than ever. But we have to get to that future. The next four months—February through May 1982—will be one of the most difficult periods financially in the theatre's history. Please, if you enjoy the theatre, if you agree that the Hippodrome is good for Gainesville, give now—and help assure the realization of that bright future."

While Greg toured, Mary got good at writing grant proposals, applying for every arts grant available. The Hippodrome's Education Department brought in money, too, winning grants for educational tours from organizations and school districts—entirely different funding sources from the arts grants that the Hippodrome was tapping. To fill the gap caused by Dan Schay's departure, Christina Tannen was named Interim Managing Director. Previously, she'd been managing the tours and assisting Dan Schay.

The Gin Game

Just twelve days after *Terra Nova* closed, the Hippodrome opened *The Gin Game* by D. L. Coburn. The two-character play had won the 1978 Pulitzer Prize for Drama. Set on the seldom-used sun porch of a rundown retirement home, the story evolves as an elderly man and woman play gin rummy. Neither seems to have any other friends, and while playing cards, they engage in lengthy conversations about their families and their lives in the outside world. Gradually, each conversation becomes a battle, much like the ongoing gin games, as each player tries to expose the other's weaknesses, to belittle the other's life, and to humiliate the other thoroughly.

Rather than put makeup on a couple of Hippodrome regulars to make them look old enough for the parts, director Mary Hausch hired two mature actors from New York who were nearer in age to the characters they were playing. Though not famous, each had decades of serious acting credits in stage, film, and television.

Photo: Gary Wolfson

George Hall and Marian Primont in *The Gin Game*.

The male lead, actor/director/dancer/singer George Hall, had made his Broadway debut in 1946. Later, he danced for Martha Graham and sang on the original cast albums of Rodgers and Hammerstein and Cole Porter musicals. His opponent in *The Gin Game*, Marian Primont, had worked in radio and television since the 1940s. She'd done plays on Broadway, founded her own theatre in Upstate New York, and taught dramatic arts at New York University.

About her own work, Marian said, "I think I experience more inner serenity when I'm building a character than I do at any other time."[5]

In her director's notes, Mary Hausch wrote, "The actors play fourteen hands of gin. These mechanics—plus the demands of lines, characterizations, and blocking—sometimes proved awesomely confusing. But the game of cards was worth mastering. It led me and my actors to Mr. Coburn's underlying game of life. The play is a challenging mixture of the bitter and the sweet. Every move of the cards led us from the funny, grumpy, idiosyncratic surface of these two social discards to revelations of malevolence and pain, and eventually, violence. It has been especially gratifying to work with George and Marian."[6]

The Gin Game ran from March 19–April 17, in addition to the special benefit performance on March 18 for the Interagency Council for the Elderly.

Summer Musical

After three heavy dramas in a row, audiences were ready for a little fun, and the Hippodrome brought them *The Robber Bridegroom*, a musical comedy based on a novella by Eudora Welty. Alfred Uhry wrote the script and lyrics and Robert Waldman, the music.

The action takes place in and around Rodney, Mississippi at the annual community hoedown. The story concerns Jamie Lockhart, a gentleman robber who steals for pleasure and takes love only when it is made sweeter by being forbidden. The object of his desire is Rosamund Musgrove, daughter of a wealthy plantation owner. Dual mistaken identities confound the couple but are resolved in the play's inevitable romantic conclusion.

(1- r): Rusty Salling, Lance Harmeling, Gregg Jones, Jennifer Pritchett, Marilyn Wall, Maria Mathe, and Ron Williams (as *The Robber Bridegroom*).

Photo: Gary Wolfson

Leads Ron Williams as robber Jamie Lockhart and Jennifer Pritchett as Rosamund were perfect. Both had previously starred in the show elsewhere. Ron had just performed the role in Texas, and Jennifer had done it three years earlier in Minneapolis. Equally requisite for a stage musical, both actors had excellent voices.

Reviewer Jim Camp said Ron was "All talent and several octaves wide.... The pretty Jennifer is Pritchett-perfect."[7] These sentiments were echoed by Arline Greer in her review: "Apart from the notable talent of Ron Williams as Jamie Lockhart, this production also offers audiences the opportunity to see and hear Jennifer Pritchett, a beautiful, accomplished actress, who, as the fetching and willing Rosamund, gives a performance that is tender, funny, enticing and altogether bewitching. She sings two ballads that, probably, are the best numbers in the score, with a sensibility that enhances their intrinsic value."[8]

Director Kerry McKenney cast current and past Hippodrome regulars in the remaining roles. Kurt Orwick, who had appeared in many plays during the Hippodrome's early years, returned to play Rosamund's father. Rena Carney played her stepmother. Rusty Salling played the innkeeper and Lance Harmeling a wagon chaser. Maria Mathe, who had debuted in *Revenge of the Space Pandas*, played Queenie Bodine. The most unusual role went to Gregg Jones as deceased criminal Big Harp, whose talking head sticks out of a trunk. Big Harp and Little Harp (Daniel Renz) sang a duet, "Two Heads Are Better than One."

Jamie Lockhart may have been the robber, but it was Greg Hausch who stole scene after scene as a gap-toothed simpleton named Goat. Marilyn Wall played Goat's sister and Dawn Bodnar, his mother. Recent UF grad Phoeff Sutton played a raven.

Eddie Gwaltney on guitar, Mike Peyton on banjo, and Bryan Sibley on fiddle performed live as The Lighter Knot Heads. The onstage trio, in costume, blended seamlessly into the hoedown theme. To add period authenticity, Kerry tapped David and Marietta Massey of the Cross Creek Cloggers to choreograph country dancing and teach the cast how to clog.

It was all good fun, and audiences enjoyed it so much the play had to be held over an extra week. But feminists objected to one aspect. Jamie may be a swashbuckler, but not a gentleman. He coldcocks his lovers, throws them across his shoulder, and carries them into the woods. Jennifer winks at the audience as she's being carried offstage to let them know she is in on it, too. She admits now that this element of the story would have to be changed for the play to be performed today.

The Robber Bridegroom, running from May 7–June 5, wrapped up the 1981–1982 season. Around this same time, Christina Tannen officially became Managing Director. "I can't tell you how thrilled I am to have this job," she told the *Gainesville Sun.* "To be in this town, working with this organization. There is so much excitement surrounding it."[9]

Florida Festival of New Plays

In July 1982, the Hippodrome put on the Florida Festival of New Plays, six plays selected from 400 submissions received in response to a call for new works the previous winter. Judging the contest were theatre critics from the *Atlanta Constitution* and *Miami Herald,* a UF professor of English, and the president of the State Theatre Board, who was also dean of the Florida State University (FSU) theatre department.

Photo: Gary Wolfson

Directors and actors of the Florida Festival of New Plays: (l-r) Mary Hausch, Marshall New, Bill Lewis, Iris Acker, Jeffrey King, Kerry McKenney, Theresa O'Shea, Mike Beistle, and Gregory Hausch.

Kerry McKenney told the *Gainesville Sun* the impetus behind the festival stemmed from a desire to work with original playwrights.[10] In Greg Hausch's recollection, it was more about trying to impress the theatre world beyond Gainesville. "The NEA was really into new works," he said, "and we were, too—to some degree. The NEA loved us, but we felt like our star was diminishing because we didn't do enough original things. So, we concocted this [festival] as a device to keep us in the conversation."

The *Gainesville Sun* sponsored it. In addition to the plays, the festival included musical performances, poetry readings, and an art exhibition in the Hippodrome Gallery. The newspaper gave the event a lot of coverage.

From July 2–July 25, the festival alternately presented the six winning plays, three plays on one night and the other three on the following night.

Night One:

- *Wild Rose Branches* by Phoeff Sutton. Directed by Kerry McKenney.
- *I Am Waiting* by Claudia Johnson. Directed by Mary Hausch.
- *The Boogey Man* by Edward Clinton. Directed by Marshall New.

Night Two:

- *Sanibel & Captiva* by Megan Terry. Directed by Michael Beistle.
- *The Showdown* by Shelley Fraser Mickle. Directed by Mary Hausch.
- *The Pie Rate's Off* by Jeffrey Smart. Directed by Phoeff Sutton.

What became of the playwrights? Phoeff Sutton, a UF Master of Fine Arts student who had the previous month played the raven in *Robber Bridegroom,* left Gainesville for Los Angeles, where he ended up writing most of the episodes of the hit television show *Cheers.* Claudia Johnson became a successful screenwriter, documentary filmmaker, and screenwriting instructor at FSU. Edward Clinton's *The Boogey Man* won first prize in the festival; at the time, he also wrote weekly scripts for the television soap opera *Another World.* He continued to write plays and became a fellow at the Eugene O'Neill Playwrights' Center. Megan Terry was already a well-established playwright before she adapted her *Sanibel & Captiva* radio play into a stage play for the festival. In a career that spanned 1955–1995, she penned thirty stage plays, three plays for television, and three for radio. Shelly Fraser Mickle became an award-winning author of more than a dozen fiction and nonfiction books. Jeffrey Smart graduated from UF, earned a Master of Fine Arts degree in playwriting from Indiana University Bloomington, and continued to write plays—mostly comedies and musicals.

Acting in three of the six plays, Iris Acker was new to the Hippodrome but not to theatre. She was undoubtedly the most experienced performer in the festival. She earned her actor's Equity card at age eleven and started dancing professionally with the June Taylor Dancers at age fifteen. By twenty-one, she was a Rockette at Radio City Music Hall. She was fifty-two when she appeared in the Florida Festival of New Plays, but in one play she played a sixty-five-year-old, in another, an eighty-five-year-old, and in the third, a woman near her own age.

Sun critic Arline Greer liked both nights of the festival. Of all six plays, she gave the most accolades to Edward Clinton's *The Boogey Man.* Her only complaint about any of the others was that the actors in *The Pie Rate's Off* rushed their lines, causing the audience to miss Jeffery Smart's marvelously funny dialogue.

Season Ten

In September, the Hippodrome took to the psychiatrist's couch with Christopher Durang's wickedly funny farce, *Beyond Therapy,* in its Southeastern premiere. The play poked fun at homosexuality and bisexuality and took gleeful whacks at psychotherapy with two analysts at least as certifiable as their clients.

Arline Greer praised Greg Hausch's lively direction and the job done by the cast: "Jeffrey King is first rate as Bruce, the uneasy bisexual. Kerry McKenney is funny as Prudence, the girl who can't quite believe what she sees and hears in Bruce's

Beyond Therapy cast: (l-r) Rusty Salling, Sandy Scott, Mary Hausch, Jeffrey King, Kerry McKenney, and Marshall New.

Photo: Gary Wolfson

company. Rusty Salling, who is able to express a whole range of feelings with a twitch of his lips, gives a gem of a performance as Bob, Bruce's lover. Marshall New makes a marvelously vain and pseudo-macho psychiatrist. And Mary Hausch is utterly hilarious as Charlotte, the nutty therapist, who tries word associations to remember names and objects."[11] Also in the cast was Sandy Scott, who had appeared in five previous Hippodrome productions dating back to 1974's *Steambath*.

Greer said she enjoyed the play. Not everyone did. Some thought the language too profane or objected to the subject matter. Three people walked out in the middle of the first act. Greer suggested the Hippodrome add a disclaimer: "For mature audiences only."[12]

Beyond Therapy ran from September 10–October 8, a week beyond the original closing date.

Cast of *The Dining Room*. Top row: Michael Beistle, Jeffrey King, Kevin Lauritsen. Bottom row: Sara Gotcher, Maggie Beistle, and Jennifer Pritchett.

The Dining Room

A. R. Gurney's *The Dining Room* was a comedy-drama that had been running off-Broadway for the previous year. As soon as it closed in New York, July 1982, the Hippodrome Theatre snapped up the rights for its Southeast premiere.

The play is set in the dining room of a typical well-to-do household, the place where the family assembled daily for breakfast and dinner and for all special occasions. The story is told through overlapping vignettes that chart the decline of upper middle class WASPs over an eighty-year time span. Six actors play fifty roles from little boys and giggling teenage girls to stern grandfathers and a senile grandmother, making constant character and costume switches as time periods overlap.

Arline Greer explained: "The action is non-stop, as one scene flows directly into another, often with a kind of discreet

Photo: Johnston Photography

overlapping of one on the other. A twosome, circa 1920, is seen having breakfast at the dining room table, while, simultaneously, another twosome, belonging to a time 20 years in the future, arrives to discuss remodeling the room. The play is designed in multiple layers that reveal life as it was at the turn of the century; as it evolved over the years; and as it is in the present. Its revelations are comical and sad, foolish and touching. It is a meticulously written play, and one that takes great skill to perform well."[13]

The Hippodrome production starred Jennifer Pritchett, Jeffrey King, Kevin Lauritsen, Sara Gotcher, and Maggie and Mike Beistle. Greer raved about Mike Beistle's performance but thought the rest of the cast needed more work. *Alligator* critic Danny Ball disliked the script, saying it had "little intrinsic worth."[14] Despite negative reviews, the play did well and was held over for an extra week, running from October 22–November 20.

Holiday Tradition

The year 1982 ended with what was now a firm tradition, *A Christmas Carol*. The Beistles made it a family affair as daughter Molly played Martha Cratchit. Maggie Beistle was Mrs. Cratchit, and Mike Beistle portrayed Marley's ghost. Rusty Salling was again Bob Cratchit, and Kevin Rainsberger returned to the role of Scrooge. The show ran from December 7–18.

Photo: Gary Wolfson

Bob Cratchit (Rusty Salling) gets scolded by Scrooge (Kevin Rainsberger) on a set designed by Carlos Asse that continued to be used for decades.

1 Jonathan Suskind, "Man Friday A Play—and a Playwright—with a Twist," *Florida Alligator*, January 8, 1982.
2 Arline Greer, review of *Terra Nova*, by Ted Tally, directed by Kerry McKenney, Hippodrome Theatre, Gainesville, FL, *Gainesville Sun*, February, 1982.
3 Ibid.
4 Kathleen J. Hargreaves, review of *Deathtrap*, by Ira Levin, directed by Gregory Hausch, Tennessee Williams Fine Arts Center, Key West, FL, *Key West Citizen*, March 18, 1982.
5 *The Gin Game* playbill, Hippodrome State Theatre, March 1982.
6 Ibid.
7 Jim Camp, review of *The Robber Bridegroom*, by Alfred Uhry, directed by Kerry McKenney, Hippodrome Theatre, Gainesville, FL, *Hometown Shopper*, May 26, 1982.
8 Arline Greer, review of *The Robber Bridegroom*, by Alfred Uhry, directed by Kerry McKenney, Hippodrome Theatre, Gainesville, FL, *Gainesville Sun*, May 14, 1982.
9 Joan Flocks, "Christine Tannen Knows Theater is Not All Entertainment," *Gainesville Sun*, July 2, 1982.
10 S.A. Carlton, "Hipp's Festival of New Plays is a Showcase of Talents," *Gainesville Sun*, July 2, 1982.
11 Arline Greer, review of *Beyond Therapy*, by Christopher Durang, directed by Gregory Hausch, Hippodrome Theatre, Gainesville, FL, *Gainesville Sun*, September 17, 1982.
12 Ibid.
13 Arline Greer, review of *The Dining Room*, by A. R. Gurney, directed by Kerry McKenney, Hippodrome Theatre, Gainesville, FL, *Gainesville Sun*, October 29, 1982.
14 Danny Ball, review of *The Dining Room*, by A. R. Gurney, directed by Kerry McKenney, Hippodrome Theatre, Gainesville, FL, *Independent Florida Alligator*, October 29, 1982

1983

Unlikeable Saint

In his negative review of *The Dining Room*, critic Danny Ball had wondered why the Hippodrome would seek to damage its reputation by producing it. And this was before anyone had yet seen their January 1983 production, *The Saint and the Football Players*, generally considered by audiences, other reviewers, and even the Hippodrome artistic directors as the worst play the Hippodrome has ever done. Interestingly, Ball liked it.

Not Kerry McKenney. "It was so..." she paused, searching for a suitable word, but couldn't find one. "This director, Lee Breuer, a famous guy in New York, came about once or twice and basically just left us hanging."

Marshall New said, "During the '82–'83 season, there was a lot of criticism about our choice of plays from people who had bought subscriptions. *The Saint and the Football Players* was their number one [complaint]." Marshall had the unhappy task of telling audiences before each show, "You will not see anything recognizable in the way of dramatic plot onstage." True. There were no characters for the audience to identify with and no real plot. A cast of sixteen actors dressed in football and referee uniforms danced around and simulated football plays in a slow-motion ballet to a score by minimalist composer Philip Glass.

Greg Hausch blames himself for bringing the fiasco to the Hippodrome. He was serving on the National Endowment for the Arts (NEA) theatre panel. "On the panel was David Mamet, Gordon Davidson, Lynne Meadow, Louise Valdez, Richard Foreman—all these big notables in avant-garde and regional theatre, and I was the only nobody," Greg said. Lee Breuer was also on the panel. "Everybody adored him nationally—people that never even heard of the Hippodrome, much less cared to hear about it. He was a big enchilada around the world."

Greg puts the choice of *The Saint and the Football Players* in the same vein as the Hippodrome's grasp for national recognition with the Festival of New Plays that opened the 1982–1983 season. "We thought it would be prestigious for us to have Lee Breuer. So, while I was up at the panel meeting, I said, 'Why don't you come in residence and do a play?'"

"Oh, that sounds good," Breuer said. "Can you pay me?"

They got an NEA grant to bring him in. Breuer had conceived, designed, and choreographed *The Saint and the Football Players* after a poem of the same name by Jack Thibeau. The poem was a series of Xerox images. Breuer brought down Steven Waryan to direct it and Michael Patten to assist. Both were members of Mabou Mines, Breuer's experimental theatre group in New York. They all stayed at Greg's house. "After I worked with him," Greg said, "I thought he was an emperor's-new-clothes type of thing. We all sat through this bullshit. I said, 'Just tell me where we're going. What are we trying to say?'"

With a strident tone, Breuer answered, "We're trying to say the commercialization of sports has invaded our society."

"Yeah, but how are we telling it to the people through what we are doing? How are we conveying that?" Greg asked.

"It's in there if you want it to be in there," Breuer snapped back.

"I'd really like that to be in there," Greg told him.

None of the Hippodrome cast had played much football—they'd been the kids in the drama club. To help them be more authentic, they brought in Steve Tannen. Steve was a Gator great, an all-American defensive back at UF who went to the NFL as a first-round draft pick. He'd played six years for the New York Jets. He was also the brother-in-law of Hippodrome Managing Director Christina Tannen.

Cast of *The Saint and the Football Players.*

Photo: Gary Wolfson

In addition to Steve, the team was made up of Hippodrome actors and UF theatre students: Ed Barriner, Randy Borden, Leroy Debose, Lance Harmeling, Gregory Hausch, Gregg Jones, Jeffrey King, Bill Messer, Sandy Scott, and Louis Tyrrell. The referees were all women: Mary Hausch, Kerry McKenney, Ginger Pollini, and Laura Pollini. Kurt Orwick was the announcer. Five televisions hanging over the stage played fictional commercials for Gainesville businesses featuring the "football players."

At halftime, Gregg Jones, who is really good at doing voices, imitates Howard Cosell in a halftime analysis of the game with Kurt Orwick as Frank Gifford. (Both Cosell and Gifford were popular sports commentators at the time.)

Gregg Jones remembers the play for a painful injury he received in practice. "Two days before the show opened, we went to a field at Kirby-Smith school for a scrimmage, just to get the real feel of hitting and playing in real time at real speed so that we could imitate slowing it down. I hadn't played football since the Boys Club when I was twelve. I got the ball, started running, got tackled, and I fell belly up on the ground. I got piled on by about five or six big guys and cracked three ribs. Opening night is the only time I've ever performed on any kind of drugs, but I was in excruciating pain. It's one thing to be in pain, but another to be in pain and have to move in slow motion."

The Saint and the Football Players ran from January 14–February 6 and definitely was not held over. In fact, they canceled the January 30 performance for the Super Bowl and then canceled another the following week. Greg Hausch wrote a tongue-in-cheek apology to subscribers in the playbill for their next play, *Key Exchange*: "Well, now that everyone has seen *The Saint and the Football Players*, and fathomed the meaning of life, we thought we'd bring you something completely different... and what better vehicle than a light, frothy comedy of love and bicycles to usher in the Spring season."[1]

Key Exchange

Gregg Jones, Jennifer Pritchett, and Kevin Rainsberger ride bikes on stage in *Key Exchange*.

Photo: Gary Wolfson

With warmth and humor, their next play, *Key Exchange* by Kevin Wade, looked at contemporary relationships among three young New Yorkers who zip around Central Park on bicycles. Audience favorite Jennifer Pritchett played Lisa, a liberated photographer whose sexual partner resists commitment. The most she can hope for is to get him to exchange apartment keys.

Paired with Jennifer were two Hippodrome veterans, Gregg Jones as reluctant boyfriend Phillip and Kevin Rainsberger as newlywed Michael. Between them, they'd previously appeared in twenty-seven Hippodrome productions, but never together in the same show. The three handsome actors rode ten-speed bicycles on the set, even making entrances and exits on bikes through the aisles by which the audience enters the theatre. Director Greg Hausch kept the pace moving. The script was funny in an unchallenging way. The modest comedy that let audiences forget *The Saint and the Football Players* ran from February 25–March 20.

Filmmaker Harkens

After *The Saint and the Football Players*, Kerry McKenney decided to leave. She applied for and was awarded a grant from the Theatre Communications Group to go to Spain and find a play to bring to the United States. But in March, her plans had to be put on hold when independent filmmaker Victor Nuñez came to recruit Hippodromers. He had cast Kerry, Marshall New, Bruce Cornwell, and Jennie Stringfellow in his 1979 adaptation of Marjorie Kinnan Rawlings's *Gal Young 'Un*. He'd been so impressed with Gainesville talent that he wanted to work with the Hippodrome again.

Victor Nuñez's new project was *A Flash of Green*, based on the novel by best-selling author John D. McDonald. Filming would start in the summer in South Florida, but preparation needed to start immediately. Kerry would act as assistant director, helping with casting and directing the secondary characters. Carlos Asse became art director, selecting locations and sets. Marilyn Wall did costumes and makeup. Dana Moser and Martha Williams joined the crew as assistants. Greg Hausch was the production manager. With so many key Hippodrome staff involved in the film, only Marshall New and Mary Hausch were left to direct the remaining plays for 1983. They took turns.

Photo: John Moran/*Gainesville Sun*

Filmmaker recruits Hippodromers to make *A Flash of Green* (l-r) Carlos Asse, Marilyn Wall, Victor Nuñez, Greg Hausch, Dana Moser, and Kerry McKenney.

Italian Comedy

Marshall New directed *We Won't Pay! We Won't Pay!*, an Italian comedy by Dario Fo that was first performed in Milan, Italy, then translated for the London stage, and then translated into a North American version by R.G. Davis. The Hippodrome production was the play's Southeastern premiere. It also marked the Hippodrome's tenth anniversary. A perfect choice to remind everyone that, since its earliest days, the Hippodrome had been able to make an audience double over in laughter.

Photo: Gary Wolfson

Cast of *We Won't Pay, We Won't Pay*: (l-r) Michael Beistle, Maggie Beistle, Jeffrey King, Margie Llinas, and Rusty Salling.

Although set in communist Italy of the late 1960s/early 1970s, the humor, plot, and action could easily have been an episode of *I Love Lucy*. At a protest demonstration against runaway inflation, a poor Italian housewife (Maggie Beistle) makes off with a load of groceries. For the rest of the play, she and her next-door neighbor (Margie Llinas) take extraordinary measures to hide the ill-gotten goods from their husbands, played by Mike Beistle and Jeffrey King. Hot on their trail is Rusty Salling, playing five roles: a police sergeant, a lieutenant in the Carabinieri, the Minister of Tourism, an undertaker, and even Mike Beistle's character's grandfather.

Running from one lunatic situation to the next, the women come up with an instant pregnancy and an impossible tale about a baby transplant. They also borrow a coffin to hide sugar. It was great fun and had audiences laughing nightly from April 8–May 1.

Ten-Year Celebration

By May 1983, the Hippodrome's annual budget had grown from the pitiful $15,000 in their first year to over a half-million. The need to raise money was constant. Their tenth anniversary seemed like a good opportunity for a big event.

UF Professor of Physics Rick Field is a genius who, with Nobel laureate Richard Feynman, co-developed the Field-Feynman algorithm for comparing the fragmentation of quarks. His sister, Sally, had achieved greatness, too. She'd won an Academy Award, an Emmy, and a couple of Golden Globes.

The Hippodrome contacted Rick and asked if his sister would help them do a fundraiser. She agreed. They quickly put together a Tenth Anniversary Celebration based around Hollywood star Sally Field.

The celebration began May 7, the day before Sally's arrival, with a nine-hour fundraising Dance-A-Thon where participants were sponsored for the length of time they kept dancing, à la *They Shoot Horses, Don't They?* The Dance-A-Thon was followed by a Gala Masquerade Ball with a live orchestra, a costume parade, a dance competition, and entertainment that lasted until 1:00 a.m.

Sunday was the star event. Gainesville Mayor Gary Junior proclaimed May 8 Sally Field Day and gave her a plaque. "She was great," Greg Hausch said. "We held a brunch with her at the theatre. She cut a PSA [public service announcement] for us out on the front steps. We did a cocktail party at Cox's Furniture (where Harry's Restaurant is today)." She sat in on rehearsals for their upcoming play, *Children of a Lesser God*, and was the star attraction at a benefit dinner. "We found out after Sally left that she was very ill at the time," Greg recalls. "She never let on or used it as an excuse. She showed up for everything. She was a real champ."

Sally Field (center) with Hippodromers (clockwise) Kerry McKenney, Christina Tannen, Gregory Hausch, Marshall New, and Mary Hausch.

Children of a Lesser God

Just as *We Won't Pay! We Won't Pay!* had reminded audiences that the Hippodrome was still hilariously entertaining, their next play, *Children of a Lesser God* by Mark Medoff, showed their dramatic chops.

The Tony Award-winning drama tells the story of a marriage between a young deaf woman who despises those who can hear and a well-meaning teacher who thinks he is doing her a favor by trying to force her to learn to speak.

Julianne Fjeld as Sarah and
David Fitzsimons as James in
Children of a Lesser God.

Consistent with the story, three of the six actors actually were deaf. Hearing-impaired cast member Mary Beth Barber told reporter Michael Farris, "Why not use the resources you have? If a hearing person were to really study, he could play a deaf person, but a deaf person could do it better."[2]

Arline Greer wrote, "The play is remarkable in that it is acted almost entirely in sign language. Sarah cannot speak. She signs rapidly and with great dexterity. James translates everything she signs and makes it seem as if a spoken dialogue is taking place. It is an extraordinary acting feat that is accomplished here by Julianne Fjeld as Sarah and David Fitzsimons as James. Both actors are so very fine that early into the first act, Sarah's (Julianne Fjeld's) signing actually becomes speech for us, speech with vivid imagery, speech with humor, emotion, and glowing intelligence.

"Fitzsimons' work is equally impressive in that he talks and signs, simultaneously, throughout the play. He plays two roles in that he is James, but he also is Sarah's voice. He must react to Sarah and tell us her reaction to him. His performance is altogether wonderful.

"Directed with meticulous care by Mary Hausch and acted by a gifted cast that does honor to a work of integrity and strength, it is a production of which all can be proud."[3]

Additional members of the cast included Michael Doyle, Rena Carney, Ellen Lau, and Mike Lamitola. The play ran from May 20–June 12.

A Flash of Green

As soon as *Children of a Lesser God* closed, Michael Doyle and Ellen Lau headed to Fort Myers with fellow Hippodromers Maggie Beistle, Gregg Jones, Margaret Bachus, Malcolm Gets, and Rusty Salling to start filming *A Flash of Green*. Other Gainesville actors included Nancy Griggs and Jennie Stringfellow. Already on site were the production staff: Greg Hausch, Marilyn Wall, Carlos Asse, Dana Moser, Martha Williams, and Kerry McKenney. The film's stars were established Hollywood actors Ed Harris, Blair Brown, and Richard Jordan. The shoot lasted nine weeks.

Marilyn Wall later worked with Victor Nuñez on three additional films, but for Dana Moser, one was enough. "I actually did not sleep from Tuesdays to Saturdays. I just kept taking cold showers," Dana said.

Photo: Gary Wolfson

Robert Alan Ferguson and Charles C. Welch in *Mass Appeal*.

Mass Appeal

Meanwhile, in Gainesville, Marshall New directed their summer offering, *Mass Appeal*, a two-character play by Bill C. Davis about an old priest and a young seminary student.

The old priest has become worldly and materialistic, bent on pleasing his affluent congregation rather than instructing them. He's been sent a young firebrand who scorns the old priest's reluctance to deal with social and moral issues and criticizes his need for popularity at the cost of integrity.

"The play itself is a charmer, a warm, witty, tender exposition of a friendship between vastly dissimilar men of the cloth," wrote Arline Greer. "More than that, it is an actor's dream. With a cast of just two, on stage non-stop, it offers those who perform in it the opportunity to create a tour de force... Charles C. Welch as Father Tim Farley, and Robert Alan Ferguson as seminarian Mark Dolson are more than equal to the task. Under Marshall New's direction, generous to every facet of the actors' development, as well as to the play's bittersweet nuances... *Mass Appeal* is a lovely play, done just right for a summer pick-me-up."[4]

While the name of the actor playing Father Farley might not have popped into a theatergoer's mind, audience members immediately recognized Charles Welch as the neighborly oldtimer on the Pepperidge Farm television commercials that were blanketing the airways that year. Marshall recalls, "He said [the money from] Pepperidge Farm allowed him to do [smaller] theatre all around the country. God knows we were paying Equity minimum."

Playing opposite Welch was Robert Alan Ferguson, a recent UF grad then living in New York City. During Robert's UF years, Marshall had previously directed him in *They Shoot Horses, Don't They?* "The chemistry between [Robert] and Mr. Pepperidge Farm was really great," Marshall said. *Mass Appeal* ran from July 8–31.

Season Eleven

The Hippodrome kicked off its eleventh season on September 9 with a contemporary musical, *I'm Getting My Act Together and Taking it on the Road* by Gretchen Cryer and Nancy Ford. It was directed by Mary Hausch with musical direction by Eddie Gwaltney.

In the story, the main character, Heather Jones, is a successful soap opera ingénue, who, at age thirty-nine, decides she should drop her current TV role for a career as a nightclub singer, against the advice of almost everyone, especially her agent, Joe, played by Dan Jesse. He urges her to stay with what's safe. Instead, she wants to reveal onstage what she feels as a liberated woman.

Lead actress Naima Eriksen found her character's life as a mature woman in an unliberated world not so unlike her own. After graduating from the UF Theatre Department in 1978, she'd moved to New York City where she was then playing a gossip reporter on the TV soap opera *All My Children* by day and trying to make it as a nightclub artist by night.

Hippodrome actors Sara Gotcher and Debbie Laumand portrayed Heather's backup singers, performing fourteen songs accompanied by the four-piece Liberated Man's Band. The musicians, James Wren, Lance Harmeling, Shishir Kurup, and Michael Derry, played onstage behind the singers.

"There are many truths spoken in this play," Arline Greer wrote in her review, "and it doesn't hurt a bit to hear them uttered with musical good humor.... The musical numbers are quite marvelous. They tell it like it is with a rueful smile, a bitter jest and, ultimately, a grand hoorah.... Naima Eriksen and Dan Jesse, as Heather and Joe, give performances that come from deep inside.... They perform brilliantly."[5]

The play was held over an extra week, closing on October 7.

On October 10, the Hippodrome announced a new Managing Director, Paul Bennett. He'd been managing the Actor's Workshop and Repertory Company in West Palm Beach when the Hippodrome's previous Managing Director, Christina Tannen, went on maternity leave. "Ms. Tannen will return to the Hippodrome as business manager sometime next year," he told the *Florida Times-Union*.[6]

Photo: Gary Wolfson

(l-r) Debbie Laumand, Sara Gotcher, and Naima Eriksen get their act together.

Amadeus Scores

Three weeks later, Marshall New directed Peter Shaffer's Tony Award-winning play *Amadeus* in its first Southeastern production. In Hippodrome history, it ranks alongside *Equus* and *The Elephant Man* as one of the theatre's most lauded productions. Not too surprising, since Schaffer also wrote *Equus*.

Amadeus is a fictional account of the lives of composers Wolfgang Amadeus Mozart and Antonio Salieri. When the play begins, Salieri is an old man, having long outlived his fame. He claims to have poisoned Mozart and tells the story as a flashback, starting when Mozart first comes to the court of the Emperor of Austria. Salieri adores Mozart's compositions and is thrilled at the chance to meet him. When he finally does, teenage Mozart is crawling around on his hands and knees, exchanging profanities with his future bride.

Salieri cannot reconcile Mozart's boorish behavior with the genius that God has inexplicably bestowed upon Mozart. Salieri renounces God and vows to do everything in his power to ruin Mozart. He pretends to be Mozart's ally to his face while doing his utmost to destroy his reputation and any success his compositions may have.

As befits the script, Marshall put together a powerhouse cast led by some of the Hippodrome's best. He knew Malcolm Gets would be a natural for Mozart. Before choosing a career in theatre, Malcolm had been studying for a career as a classical pianist under Bernice Maskin, who taught at Julliard and was on the faculty of the Manhattan School of Music.

Marshall went to see Malcolm and said, "There's this play called *Amadeus.*"

"I know," Malcolm said. "I've just seen the play on Broadway with my mother."

"We're going to do it," Marshall said. "I want you to play Mozart and I want you to do the music live. And Mike Doyle is going to play Salieri."

Malcolm recalled later, "It was one of the highlights of my life."

"I did a lot of research on Mozart," Marshall said, "and incorporated a lot of his music into the play that wasn't indicated in the script—because I had Malcolm."

Carlos Asse designed the set. He originally intended to place Mozart's pianoforte upstage. "Because I thought we would have to make a fake one and put a speaker in it."

The pianoforte was invented in the early 1700s as an improvement over the harpsichord. A woman who lived in the Duck Pond area of Gainesville had one—an heirloom her family had brought from England two hundred years before. She agreed to let the Hippodrome borrow it for the play.

"I couldn't believe it," Carlos said. It was in nearly perfect condition. "There was one key that was messed up and we had to fly in somebody from North Carolina who specialized in working on pieces like this and he fixed it. Since we had a real pianoforte, I turned it around so the audience could see the keys and see Malcolm play it."

"We start our rehearsals," Malcolm recalls. "I've got this [circa] eighteen-hundred pianoforte, but it was a tiny little instrument, and they were always saying to me, 'You have to quit playing so forcefully.' I wanted to make music with it, but it was

In a scene from *Amadeus,* Constanze (Debbie Laumand) speaks with Mozart (Malcolm Gets) while Salieri (Michael Doyle) and Baron Gottfried (Jeffrey King) observe.

Photo: John Moran

hard. I just kept thinking, 'If only Mozart lived to hear a modern piano, what else would he have written?'"

Marshall wanted to contrast the look of overfed dilettantes versus the wild and crazy kid. "So we padded Mike a little and had Salieri always eating sweets and puff bakery items."

Rusty Salling played the Emperor and Debbie Laumand played Mozart's bride. Also in the cast were Michael Beistle, Jim and Ann Wren, Michael Stevens, Jeffrey King, Michael Gioia, Elisabeth Speckman, Pauline Genduso, Eric Riley, Michael Fowler, and Shishir Kurup.

Sun critic Arline Greer described it as "a theater event of magnitude, a star in the crown of the Hippodrome."[7] The *Alligator* reviewer predicted it would "probably be the most talked about play of the Hippodrome's season."[8] *Sun* staff writer Laura Kelly called it "undeniably the richest and most powerfully executed play the theater has offered since *Equus*. For finesse, professionalism and an indelible theater experience, there are no parallels."[9] The play was so popular its run had to be extended twice, ending December 3. It probably could have run longer, but they had to ready the mainstage for the annual production of *A Christmas Carol*, which opened December 9 for fourteen shows.

Amadeus wasn't easy. Marshall New said, "It was a monster." Once the show closed, Marshall resigned from the Hippodrome and left for Key West to direct *Tiger Tail* at the newly christened Tennessee Williams Fine Arts Center. "This has nothing to do with being unhappy," Marshall told the *Gainesville Sun*. "It's just time to do new things."[10] After directing *Tiger Tail* in Key West, he moved to Los Angeles, where he wrote screenplays for a number of years.

Also gone was Kerry McKenney, who departed for Europe after *A Flash of Green* wrapped. Although her name continued to be listed in Hippodrome playbills as an artistic co-director, she wouldn't return until the end of 1984. For now, just Mary and Greg Hausch were left.

Equity Grinches

The Hippodrome's sixth annual charity production of *A Christmas Carol* almost didn't come off. First, the union ruled that no Equity members can participate in *A Christmas Carol* on an unsalaried basis, which meant most of the Hippodrome company who play the adult roles. Second, the theatre hadn't found any business sponsors to underwrite the production costs.

Fortunately, a week before it was scheduled to open, Barnett Bank and Shands Hospital stepped up. Greg Hausch directed the cast of 45, which included Hippodrome Equity actors. Greg didn't explain how. Admission was two cans of food or one new toy. Managing Director Paul Bennett announced that the performances resulted in donations of over 10,000 cans of food and 1,000 toys.

For the third year in a row, Forrest Harris and Rusty Salling reprise their 1981 roles as Tiny Tim and Bob Cratchit.

Photo: Gary Wolfson

1 *Key Exchange* playbill, Hippodrome State Theatre, Gainesville, FL.

2 Michael Farris, "Deaf Actors Sound Off in Play," *Independent Florida Alligator*, May 27, 1983.

3 Arline Greer, review of *Children of a Lesser God*, by Mark Medoff, directed by Mary Hausch, Hippodrome Theatre, Gainesville, FL, *Gainesville Sun*, May 27, 1983.

4 Arline Greer, review of *Mass Appeal*, by Bill C. Davis, directed by Marshall New, Hippodrome Theatre, Gainesville, FL, *Gainesville Sun*, July 15, 1983.

5 Arline Greer, review of *I'm Getting My Act Together and Taking it on the Road*, by Gretchen Cryer and Nancy Ford, directed by Mary Hausch, Hippodrome Theatre, Gainesville, FL, *Gainesville Sun*, September 16, 1983.

6 Ed McIntyre, "Hippodrome Opens with *Amadeus*," *Florida Times-Union*, October 28, 1983.

7 Arline Greer, review of *Amadeus*, by Peter Schaffer, directed by Marshall New, Hippodrome Theatre, Gainesville, FL, *Gainesville Sun*, November 4, 1983.

8 Danny Ball, review of *Amadeus*, by Peter Schaffer, directed by Marshall New, Hippodrome Theatre, Gainesville, FL, *Independent Florida Alligator*, November 4, 1983.

9 Laura Kelly, "*Amadeus* Is One of the Hippodrome's Finest," *Gainesville Sun*, November 25, 1983.

10 Dave Hunter, "Marshall New Resigns from Hippodrome," *Gainesville Sun*, December 9, 1983.

1979–1990 Workshops and Theatre for Youths

Since its inception, the Hippodrome has offered programs and workshops for school-age young people to train, inspire, and entertain future generations of actors and theatergoers. Before the Hippodrome ever had a building, Marilyn Wall and Mary Hausch were teaching children's workshops outside at UF's Plaza of the Americas, or wherever they could. Children's classes were their only source of revenue while they converted the building on Hawthorne Road into a theatre. Their first production, *The Land of Point* by Harry Nilsson, staged at the Gainesville Mall and elsewhere, appealed to children.

In subsequent years, the Hippodrome continued to offer theatre programs for youth. Workshops developed performance skills and interest in theatre among area children, many of whom were cast in annual productions of *A Christmas Carol*. Some, such as Malcolm Gets, went on to have lengthy acting careers. Others, like Margie Llinas, not only won mainstage roles but became part of the Hippodrome staff. But the Hippodrome Education Department really took off after Louis Tyrrell and Margaret Bachus joined it, and later, Kevin Rainsberger.

Louis Tyrrell and Margaret Bachus

Louis Tyrrell first learned of the Hippodrome while it was still on Hawthorne Road. Sarasota's Florida Studio Theatre, where he was working, borrowed the stage during a tour. By February 1978, when he was cast in *Streamers*, the Hippodrome had moved into the warehouse on US 441. Louis liked Gainesville. He said, "I've been abroad and I've seen and worked with different companies in this country, and all I can say is that it's been great working with the Hippodrome."[1]

Louis had been involved with theatre as a student at Antioch College in Ohio. He'd trained for two years at London's Guildhall School of Music and Drama and had studied mime in Paris for a year before starting with the Sarasota troupe. In January 1979, the Hippodrome hired him to be Educational Coordinator. Together, he and Margaret Bachus created the Theatre-In-Education program to take plays into schools.

Margaret had a late start as a thespian. "I always dreamed of working in theatre," she said, "but let it go and got a degree in elementary education. In my mid-thirties, I decided to go back to school and got accepted into the University of Florida Master of Fine Arts program." She was finishing her master's in 1977 when the Hippodrome cast her as Bobbie in *Carnal Knowledge*.

Louis Tyrrell and Margaret Bachus with the set of *Tree Tide*. At top is puppeteer Dan Leonard.

Photo courtesy of Margaret Bachus

By the time Louis joined the staff, Margaret was already a Hippodrome Associate Artistic Director and had premiered her one-woman tour de force *The Belle of Amherst* at the Reitz Union Ballroom. The play, written by William Luce and directed by Mario Hernandez, tells Emily Dickinson's story through her letters and poems.

The Hippodrome's Theatre-In-Education program toured *The Belle of Amherst* to high schools in thirteen surrounding counties at no charge. Adult audiences also got to see Margaret perform the play on the Hippodrome's Second Stage on February 25 and March 4, 1979. In April 1979, the Education Department announced an expanded slate of workshops with classes for all ages.

Waking Up and *Game Play*

Louis Tyrrell in *Waking Up*. In the back is David Smadbeck playing drums.

Louis, an accomplished mime, created his own one-man play, *Waking Up*, which used mime to portray the story of a boy awakening to the joys of his own life. It was accompanied by an original musical score that Louis's brother, David Smadbeck, performed live, playing dozens of percussion instruments from around the world. *Waking Up* was a hit at elementary schools.

For the Theatre-In-Education's next play, Louis and Margaret collaborated with Sarah Safford to write *Game Play*. The show combined Sarah's original songs with acrobatics, mime, dance, and drama in an exploration of values, competition, and cooperation. The story of a playground encounter between a boy and girl is an honest reflection of the feelings, concerns, and attitudes children express toward other children. As the two characters begin to interact on and around the playground, the familiar problems of communication among young people emerge.

The idea of bringing new works specifically created for young audiences into schools was a success. Each play was seen by over 15,000 students in Alachua County alone—even more when the programs toured the state. A 1987 tour brochure stated that since 1979, the Hippodrome's programs for children had played to over one million children. Study materials accompanied every production, along with workshops designed to integrate the theatrical experience into the academic curriculum.

Tree Tide

In 1980, the Education Department added *Tree Tide* to its repertoire, written by Margaret Bachus, Louis Tyrrell, and Dan Leonard, with original music by David Smadbeck. The play attempted to show elementary and middle-grade students how to cope with the changing environment as well as the physical and emotional changes they experience as they grow up. Margaret said, "The best time for children to see this play is the beginning of a new school year, as this time creates many changes in their lives."

The play drew from the Japanese Kabuki theatre. Its hub was an abstract tree made by Carlos Asse. The characters were three puppets, a kid, and an adult puppet master. "The kids got it," Margaret said. "It didn't matter that it was puppets. [To them] it was somebody climbing a tree, and that's what it's all about."

Profiles in History

In March 1980, Kevin Rainsberger became the third principal member of the Theatre-In-Education program. Margaret had directed his senior thesis at UF and got him his first part at the Hippodrome in *The Passion of Dracula*. With Kevin on board, Theatre-In-Education toured a new series for older students called Profiles in History. Kevin's one-man show *Clarence Darrow*, written by David Rintels, taught area high school students about the famous lawyer. Later, Kevin performed the play for the UF College of Law and for Ocala lawyers at the Golden Hills Theatre.

Photo: Gary Wolfson

Kevin Rainsberger as Clarence Darrow.

In addition to *Clarence Darrow*, the Profiles in History series included Margaret's *The Belle of Amherst* and a third play, *Ernie Pyle: Here is My War*, written and performed by Dan Leonard.

Sign Posts

For most of 1981, Louis was tied up performing *The Elephant Man*, so Margaret teamed with Rena Carney to write the next Theatre-In-Education play, *Sign Posts*. Its subject was communication between a deaf person and a hearing person working together in a sign shop. Initially, the parts were performed by Rena Carney and Margaret Bachus. Rena knew sign language, so she initially played the deaf person. But Rena wasn't deaf, and Margaret and Louis felt the part called for a deaf actor. They found one in New York, Lewis Merkin. He and Dan Leonard took over the roles for the tour. Bob McPeek collaborated with David Smadbeck on the music for it. About that time, Toni Gwaltney came on board to manage their tours.

Kevin Rainsberger and Jay Millman in *Sign Posts*.

Sign Posts was a great success. In 1984, they took it to a showcase in Detroit where schools buy plays. There, it received a standing ovation. People stood in line to book it for schools throughout the Eastern United States. They performed it at the Kennedy Center, and a Canadian company bought the rights to tour it in Canada and Australia.

With various co-authors, Margaret wrote thirteen plays for children. All featured music by David Smadbeck. Marilyn Wall did costumes for every show, and if it had puppets, she created them as well. Carlos Asse designed sets that could be packed for travel.

Original songs, combined with layered scripts, spoke to everyone. "My pieces could play just as well for adults as they could play for children," Margaret said. "I had to tour kindergarten through eighth grade. To me, moments in a play that speak to one child differently than another child are because of the levels of nuance in it."

The Theatre for Young Audiences also recorded a cast album of songs from their plays.

Ad for *Vaudeville Jazz*.

Vaudeville Jazz

In the summer of 1981, Margaret and Kevin Rainsberger co-wrote *Vaudeville Jazz* and started touring the show that fall. At a time when there wasn't much public awareness about Alzheimer's disease, Stephanie Tolan's book *Grandpa and Me* caught Margaret's attention and inspired her to write about the subject.

The play is set at a gazebo in the park where Lolly Pop and his granddaughter, Candy Cane, put on shows that remind him of his former days in vaudeville. Bill Rockwood played the grandfather. "Bill was just a sweetheart of a guy," Kevin recalled. Tina Smith played his granddaughter.

As the audience enters, Candy Cane confides to them that her grandpa is having some memory issues. Candy and Pop perform a series of routines, comic one-liners, songs, and a top-hat-and-cane dance number. During the last routine, Pop forgets what is happening and where he is. Still, the show ends on a positive note.

"We toured *Vaudeville Jazz* in schools several times," Margaret recalled. "Eventually, I wrote to the Florida Endowment for the Humanities for a grant. Then, we toured it to senior citizen centers throughout the state of Florida. It was an entirely different experience having seniors watch it as opposed to kids, but the show still worked."

Beneath the music and fun, Margaret's plays had depth and addressed real issues—like growing up, grandparents losing their memories, and the environment—in an entertaining way that never preached to the audience. "I'd seen so much children's theatre that I felt talked down to children," Margaret said, "and that's not what I wanted to create."

TYA touring company circa 1986. Standing: (l-r) Tom O'Neill, Michael Stevens, Steven Butler, Michelle Meade, and Elaine Coolidge. Kneeling: Brian Park and Michael McKay.

They toured schools throughout the state every spring and fall, rotating plays and writing new ones. Margaret said, "I wouldn't go back into a school with the same show until the kids who'd seen it before couldn't see it again." The plays toured for over a dozen years, albeit with different casts.

Most shows had only two or three cast members. "I couldn't afford more," Margaret said, "because we were under the Equity contract of the Hippodrome. Although there's a different scale for Theatre for Young Audiences—you don't pay the actors as much—but still, it's a lot of money."

The advantage for UF theatre students and recent graduates was that they could get their Equity card by performing with the Education Department. Equity membership is vital for an actor who dreams of working in New York or other major markets. Actors qualify for Equity by accruing fifty points—one for each week they work in theatre. However, an Equity theatre can help an actor skip all that and become an immediate member if it chooses. Such was the case for Malcolm Gets and Lance Harmeling, who got their Equity cards when Margaret and Kevin cast them in their 1982 fall play *Stages*.

Stages

In *Stages*, two stagehands, played by Malcolm and Lance, move from one stage of life to the next. The characters have been instructed to strike the set of a western musical that has just closed and reset the stage for a show in outer space, but they have forgotten the blueprints. As they solve their problem, they share their dreams and prepare to move to their own next stage of life with songs and humor.

"In this show," Malcolm Gets said later, "I learned that you have to be twice as honest and real in children's theatre or the kids will resent being played down to."[2] Margaret agreed. "Kids, particularly at the middle school level, are highly skeptical. They tend to pre-judge the play. But we try to show them 'truth,' and they respect it."[3]

From Inside a Swan's Egg

Meanwhile, Louis Tyrrell had found *From Inside a Swan's Egg*, a children's book about Hans Christian Andersen written by UF professor John Cech, which Cech wanted Margaret to adapt into a one-person play. Dennis Maldin from UF designed the set. Louis toured Alachua County schools with it in the spring of 1983 and then took it to South Florida under the auspices of his own company. About that time, the Hippodrome changed the Education Department's name from Theatre-In-Education to Theatre for Young Audiences (TYA) to sound less academic.

Portraits

That same spring, 1983, Kevin Rainsberger and Margaret Bachus wrote and toured *Portraits*. The plot concerned three people who received notification in the mail that they had won a trip around the world. To get their prize, they just had to meet at a photography studio and complete a challenge to make a series of portraits representing competition, kindness, and other concepts. "It was beautiful and simple," Margaret said. "Three strangers coming together, at first in competition, then they reconcile, and that's when they create their portrait of kindness." For the set, Carlos Asse designed large photo frames that appeared to be empty, then suddenly revealed a photograph as each task was accomplished. "We toured it quite a bit," Margaret recalled, "but every time the cast changed, we had to do a whole new set of photography to make it work."

Photo: Gary Wolfson

(l-r) Maura Hearden, Michael McLane, and Kevin Krop in *Portraits*.

The Water Log and The Energy Carnival

Besides providing the Hippodrome income from TYA tours, the Education Department also qualified them for grants and sponsorships from untapped sources beyond arts and humanities. For instance, actor Mike Doyle worked at Gainesville Regional Utilities (GRU). One day, he asked Kevin and Margaret, "If GRU commissioned a play on water awareness, could you write one?" That was the origin of *The Water Log*.

(l-r) Thomas Jarrett, Ann Hearden, and Mark Traxler in a scene from *The Water Log*.

In the story, two scientists and a water investigator conduct a laboratory experiment to duplicate water conditions of a test city and record the results in the water log. A panic button has been installed to keep experiments under control, but water conditions deteriorate rapidly, and the lab is nearly destroyed. Viewing the devastation, the three characters express a deepening understanding of the need to conserve and protect water resources. A pretty song closes the play with the message that it's too late to hit the panic button after the water is gone. For this play, Dan Leonard co-wrote the lyrics with Margaret. Joe Sinardi drew a coloring book and a comic book that were printed and distributed to kids at the performances. *The Water Log* premiered in 1984 and was a success.

The following year, GRU commissioned *The Energy Carnival*, a musical about energy conservation. Its cast of five—the largest of any TYA play—featured Malcolm Gets, Lance Harmeling, Debbie Laumand, Dan Sapecky, and Stephanie Smith.

(below) *The Energy Carnival* featured Lance Harmeling, Debbie Laumand, Daniel Sapecky, Malcolm Gets, and Stephanie Smith.

In the imaginative story, two energy auditors test three entertainment droids who are not operating at their designed efficiency. One robot is electrical, the second is chemically run, and the third is solar-powered. The auditors perform various tests on them. Conservation measures are applied and the robot team returns to its designed efficiency. Again, a comic book and coloring book accompanied this play.

Florida Power and other electric utilities underwrote a tour of *The Energy Carnival* throughout Florida, and eventually other states. In 1989, the South Florida Water Management District sponsored a 250-performance tour of *The Water Log*. The response was so positive that the district renewed their contract for another year.

Tours didn't always go smoothly. Once, during a tour of *The Energy Carnival*, someone stole all the costumes. No one could understand why. They called Marilyn, who remade all the costumes and shipped them overnight.

Captain Jim's Fire Safety Review

In Kevin and Margaret's next script, *Captain Jim's Fire Safety Review,* Jim is an old fireman who is retiring and has to pack up his office. But going through his collectibles, he winds up unpacking them instead. In the end, he finds a sign behind the door, "Captain Jim's Fire Safety Museum," and learns that the fire department has intended all along to turn his office into a museum. As with other plays, this one had songs and a small comic book-style pamphlet for the kids to take home.

Kevin Rainsberger in *Captain Jim's Fire Safety Review Revue.*

Margaret recalled how they found the props. At the time, Eastern Airlines supported the Hippodrome by donating tickets they could use for business travel. She and Kevin were working on the script for *Captain Jim's Fire Safety Review* when they learned that Rhode Island had a number of authentic old firehouses. So they flew there to research them.

"Our second day, we saw this big flea market on the side of the road, and a retired fireman was selling all this stuff," Margaret said. "We started telling him our story that we were working on. He said, 'Oh, you should see my collection.' He had a room filled with [firefighter] stuff, and we bought everything we could bring back on the plane."

The play began touring in 1986. Four years later, Margaret and Kevin decided to have a chili cook-off and invited Gainesville Fire Department personnel to enter the contest. After everyone ate, Kevin performed the show for them, and the firefighters were really touched.

(below) (l-r) Jimmy Jay, Melissa Weinstein, and Michael Johnson in *Just Florida.*

Just Florida

Their 1987 play, *Just Florida,* was a tribute to Florida through yesterday, today, and tomorrow. Two men deliver props on-stage, and the artist in charge has to have them assembled before the governor arrives. So she asks the deliverymen to help. After they stand up cutouts of a tree, an alligator, and a raccoon, one of the men, who is from the country, says, "Now, that's Florida," representing its past. The other man, from the city, sets up cutouts of a condo plus props representing Florida sports and says, "Now, that's Florida." Its present. Lastly, they set up the remaining pieces, cutouts of children, symbolizing the future of Florida. The play ends with a song about how children will be the ones to decide what Florida is going to become.

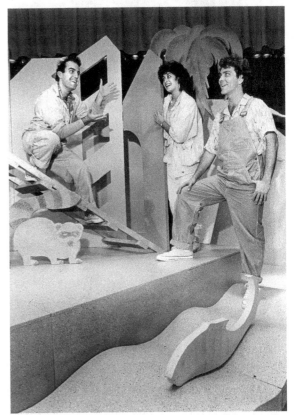

Photo: Gary Wolfson

Final Play

(l-r) Carroll Tolman, Jay Millman, and Madeline McGail in *Nickels, Dimes, & Dreams*.

The final play they wrote for the TYA series, *Nickels, Dimes, & Dreams*, premiered in April 1989. It tells the story of F. W. Woolworth, who started the first "five and dime" store. Margaret had asked Carlos to design a complicated set, but when it was finished, Margaret admitted, "It really was too much to tour with. It needed to be simplified, but we never had the chance to do that. We performed in the Alachua County schools, and it was the last one that I did [with Theatre for Young Audiences]."

In January 1990, the Hippodrome was in a financial crisis. To help the theatre raise funds, Margaret and Kevin wrote a musical fairytale with songs by Eddie Gwaltney. *The Wolf, Three Pigs, and Little Red Riding Hood* was staged in March 1990 at the University of Florida Auditorium.

By summer of 1990, management decided they could no longer afford the TYA tours. Since Margaret and Kevin owned the plays, the Hippodrome gave them the sets and costumes, and that year they became a separate entity, Creative Stages. They continued to tour their plays to schools for several more years. Meanwhile, the Hippodrome Education Department went in a different direction. More on that later.

For 52 hours straight, Kevin Rainsberger and Louis Tyrrell played racquetball against all challengers during a marathon fundraiser for TYA at Sports and Courts in Gainesville.

1 John Snyder, "Recruiting Billups and Tyrell for 'Streamers' Has Proven Successful for Everyone," *Gainesville Sun*, March 17, 1978.
2 Michael King, "UF Festival Features Two Plays for Young People," *Gainesville Sun*, December 3, 1982.
3 Hal Hubener, "To Live Is to Change," *Artifacts*, Gainesville Department of Cultural Affairs, October 1980.

1984

Italian Comedy

The Hippodrome kicked off 1984 with *The Servant of Two Masters*, a 1746 Italian comedy by Venetian playwright Carlo Goldoni. Director Gregory Hausch gave it an innovative opening. Drawing on the tradition of Italian commedia dell'arte, he had his costumed actors parade two blocks down SE First Street and enter through the Hippodrome's main entrance, passing among arriving theatergoers. Voices called out, "The commedia dell'arte players are coming! The players are arriving!" Once the audience members took their seats, the plot unfolded.

Beatrice (Peggy Rumble) has traveled to Venice disguised as her dead brother, who was betrothed to Clarice (Ann Wren). Beatrice's lover, Florindo (Kevin Rainsberger), has killed the brother so he and Beatrice can be together, but she has no dowry. She has disguised herself as her dead brother to collect the dowry he is due from Clarice's father. But since the brother's death, Clarice has become engaged to Silvio (Jeffrey King). Clarice's father (Michael Beistle) believes Beatrice to be her brother and tries to keep "him" from meeting Silvio.

Photo: Gary Wolfson

Ann Wren and Jeffrey King as Clarice and Silvio in *The Servant of Two Masters*.

Central to the story is Beatrice's always-hungry servant, Truffaldino (Sandy Scott). When the opportunity arises for him to be servant to a second master, Florindo, he takes the job to get extra dinners. In an outrageous scene, the starving Truffaldino, while desperately trying to satisfy his own hunger, must serve a banquet to entourages of both Beatrice and Florindo without either group becoming aware of the other.

Also in the Hippodrome cast were Rusty Salling, Betsy Speckman, Jerry Mason, Michael Alicia, Donald Holbrook, John Creveling, and Yvonne Weatherall. The show featured original music by Eddie Gwaltney and Bob McPeek, along with jugglers and clowns.

Arline Greer began her review with, "Silly season has arrived at the Hippodrome." She called its humor slapstick and compared it "with the antics of The Three Stooges." She liked Marilyn Wall's colorful costumes and praised each cast member by name. But the script, she said, "seemed too clumsy to carry the weight of its many trappings.... Some strong-armed pruning would help it considerably."[1]

The play ran from January 6–29.

Cloud of Ambiguities

Mary Hausch took the helm for their next production, Caryl Churchill's cross-dressing satire, *Cloud 9*. The play had won three Obies and two Drama Desk awards, and was, at the time, the longest-running comedy on or off Broadway.

The play is about the ambiguities of sexual and social mores and stereotypes. In two acts, it compares and contrasts our sexual development as a society. Act one shows sexual repression in 1880s Victorian colonial Africa. Act two portrays life in

Photo: Gary Wolfson

Cast of *Cloud 9*. Standing: (l-r) Gregory Hausch, Rusty Salling, Rena Carney, Jeffrey King. Seated: Maggie Beistle, Carol Ann Francis, and Malcolm Gets.

swinging 1980s London. Between the two acts, the characters' names stay the same and their situations are similar, but the actors switch roles and genders. For example, Malcolm Gets played Betty in act one and Gerry in act two. Rena Carney was Edward in the first act and Victoria in the second. Equally against type, Gregory Hausch, a white actor, played Joshua, a Black slave. In the second act, he was Cathy, a white woman. The rest of the cast included Rusty Salling (Clive/Edward), Maggie Beistle (Maud/Betty), and Jeffrey King (Harry/Martin). Carol Ann Francis played three roles, Ellen, Mrs. Saunders, and Lin.

The reviews were good. The reviewer from the *Independent Florida Alligator* called it "a crowd pleaser... one of the funniest, insightful, and most bewildering plays I have seen in some time."[2] Arline Greer wrote: "The production is first rate... an entertaining, if imperfect, theatre piece. It did not seem to me that either the action or language of *Cloud 9* was objectionable, given its context. This is not what I would call a gross play."[3] That last comment was aimed at theatergoers who took offense at the play's subjects of incest, homosexuality, adultery, bisexuality, and female self-pleasure. The Hippodrome responded by warning subscribers of explicit content and offered to exchange their tickets for a future play.

"It was very controversial," Malcolm Gets said. "I don't know if the audiences liked it. I loved it."

Nineteen-year-old Malcolm, wearing makeup and a floor-length frilly Victorian gown, made a beautiful young Betty. In act two, his Gerry is homosexual. Malcolm's father and mother attended opening night. "I knew it wasn't her cup of tea," he said. "I walked up to her after the show and said, 'Hi Mom, did you enjoy the show?' She said, 'You were so good in Amadeus.'"

Cloud 9 ran from February 17–March 11, after which South of Broadway theatre group rented the Hippodrome's *Cloud 9* set, props, and costumes to stage it at the University of Miami from April 11–May 5.

While *Cloud 9* was on the mainstage, the Hippodrome premiered Jamaican play-wright Trevor Rhone's comedy *Two Can Play* on February 20, 1984, on the Second Stage as part of UF's Latin American Studies Conference and Caribbean Festival, and Rhone attended. Later that same week, UF Theatre Department graduate students presented three one-act plays on the Second Stage.

Crimes of the Heart

Greg and Mary Hausch continued to alternate direct-ing duties for the rest of the year. Next, Greg direct-ed Beth Henley's Pulitzer Prize-winning drama *Crimes of the Heart*. In the story, three sisters, Meg, Babe, and Lenny, reunite at their granddaddy's old Mississippi home after Babe has shot her abusive husband. Past resentments bubble to the surface as the sisters deal with assorted relatives and past relationships. While coping with Babe's latest incident, each sister is forced to face the consequences of the "crimes of the heart" she has committed.

Photo: John Moran/*Gainesville Sun*

(l-r) Hope Jasper, Jennifer Pritchett, Kathy Tyrell, and Marilyn Wall in *Crimes of the Heart*.

Greg packed the cast with top-notch actors: Jennifer Pritchett, Malcolm Gets, Kathy Tyrell, Jeffrey King, Hope Jasper, and Marilyn Wall, whose performance Arline Greer called "entirely funny, providing the only caricature on stage that fulfills the author's inten-tion."[4]

Greer criticized the director's "rock-em-sock-em style."[5] She said, "Glib and fast-moving bordering on the overwrought, the play is delivered with a laugh a minute. This style lends itself well to lots of laughs, but what the author has given us in *Crimes of the Heart* is that genre known as bitter-sweet comedy, in which pa-thos underscores the humor of the situation. This Hippodrome production misses the human suffering that lies at the heart of its comedy."[6] Despite all that, Greer closed her review with this: "The audience laughed almost non-stop on opening night.... If anyone missed the pathos that should have been felt with the fun, it was not apparent. If it's laughter you're after, then *Crimes of the Heart* fills the bill."[7]

Crimes of the Heart opened March 23 and had its run extended an extra week, clos-ing on April 21. Less than two weeks later, on May 4, Mary Hausch had the next play running. Credit for the amazingly quick turnaround must also go to the set construction and technical crews who, with minimal time, struck the Mississippi set, replaced it with a California kitchen, and reset all the lighting in time for dress rehearsals.

True West

Sam Shepard's *True West* revolves around two brothers, Lee (Jeffrey King), a thief who has been living out on the desert because he can't make it in society, and Austin (Dan Leonard), a moderately successful screenwriter with a wife and kids. Austin is watching their mother's house while she is on vacation when Lee

Photo: Gary Wolfson

Jeffrey King and Dan Leonard in a scene from *True West*.

unexpectedly shows up. The rivalry between the brothers explodes. Also in the Hippodrome cast were Ellen Lau as their mom and Gregory Hausch as a stereotypical Hollywood movie producer.

In a case of life imitating art, an unkempt Jeffrey King was slouched on the stoop behind the Hippodrome wearing his thieving brother costume—a torn, stained T-shirt. "It was opening night, and I was scared," he recalled. "And then this cop pulls over and was going to run me off. I thought, 'If I can fool the cops, then I'll be okay.'"[8]

His performance was more than okay. Arline Greer wrote, "This Hippodrome production of *True West* is a corker, with some of the finest acting seen on stage all season. Jeffrey King, as the desert drifter, plays his role with sinister violence that demands tremendous physical strength. He is brutal, funny, wild, cunning, stupid and compelling."[9] The *Alligator* reviewer agreed: "King is a marvel. The part seems to have been written for him.... His is the performance of the year in Gainesville."[10]

True West ran through May 27 and was remounted in 1985 for a statewide tour.

Season Twelve

In recent decades, the Hippodrome's summer plays have ended each season. In the early years, however, they were considered the start of the next. So, *The Middle Ages* by A. R. Gurney began the twelfth season. It ran from July 6–29. A note in *The Middle Ages* playbill bragged that they'd reached a new milestone—5,000 subscribers.

(l-r) Consuelo Dodge, Kevin Rainsberger, Mariah Reed, and Michael Beistle in *The Middle Ages*.

The play's action spans three decades, from 1946 to 1976, taking place in the trophy room of a private men's club. The *Sun* review said, "The set, designed by Carlos Asse, is as fine a reproduction of this sort of room as you are likely to see. It is a warm, cozy place, all wood panels, plush furnishings, soft lights, a convenient balcony, and an appropriate array of trophies. *The Middle Ages* is romantic comedy at its most beguiling. Under Gregory Hausch's direction, it is funny, sweet, irreverent, quick-witted, and practically guaranteed to bring a glow to the heart of the steeliest curmudgeon.

"The acting in this Hippodrome production is first rate. Particularly fine is Kevin Rainsberger as the reprobate son, Barney. He does equally well as awkward adolescent, swinging porno king, and loving son grown to manhood. He gives a totally engaging performance. As Eleanor, the girl he loves, Mariah Reed is lovely, indeed. She, too, is able artfully to express the changes that occur in her character over a broad range of years."[11] The cast also included Michael Beistle and Consuelo Dodge.

Photo: Gary Wolfson

Autumn Romance

Greg directed the fall play, *Isn't It Romantic?* by Wendy Wasserstein. The lively comedy is about two women in their late twenties, best friends from college, navigating their post-college careers while struggling to escape from lingering parental domination. It is told in a fast-moving series of inventive scenes, alternately touching and hilarious, including parents dropping by unannounced with a Russian cab driver as a possible suitor.

Joining a cast of Hippodrome favorites—Ann Wren, Mariah Reed, Dan Jesse, and Mike and Maggie Beistle—were Lona Stein, developer of Santa Fe Community College's Children's Theatre program, and UF senior Michael Crider in his first Hippodrome show. Director Greg Hausch did a cameo as the cab driver. The play ran September 7–30 with great reviews.

Photo: Gary Wolfson

(l-r) Lona Stein, Mariah Reed, and Mike Beistle in a scene from *Isn't It Romantic?*

Block Party

October kicked off with Hippodrome Week, a publicity stunt advertised as "The Largest Outdoor Concert Ever Held." Beneath this headline, in fine print: "on SE 2nd Place." The Hippodrome never believed in doing things small. They erected a stage spanning the entire front of the Hippodrome, plus stage lights and a sound system. The city closed off the streets and a crowd of over 5,000 came to the festive block party/street dance, entertained by Gainesville's popular Rhythm & Blues Show Band and Revue. Rock legend Bo Diddley performed, and Gainesville City Commissioner Gary Gordon presented him with a proclamation declaring October 5 as Bo Diddley Day.

Gregory Hausch and Mariah Reed enacted the balcony scene from *Romeo and Juliet* with her sitting at the top of the three-story Hippodrome and Greg spouting Romeo's lines as he climbed the ladder of a fire truck provided by the Gainesville Fire Department.

At the block party, Gregory Hausch and Mariah Reed enacted the balcony scene from *Romeo and Juliet* with her sitting at the top of the three-story Hippodrome and Greg spouting Romeo's lines as he climbed the ladder of a fire truck provided by the Gainesville Fire Department.

The Dresser

From October 26–November 18, the Hippodrome presented *The Dresser*, a powerful tour de force starring Rusty Salling in the title role, playing opposite Michael Doyle—both actors at their best. Written by Ronald Harwood and directed by Mary Hausch, it is the story of the relationship between a great Shakespearean actor and his dresser—a combined nanny, prompter, ego-booster, and confidant—who has devoted his life to the actor.

Photo: Gary Wolfson

Rusty Salling and Michael Doyle in *The Dresser*.

"The great joy of *The Dresser* is the duet played between the two men, Sir and Norman," stated Arline Greer in her review.[12] She continued, "Greater joy still may be found in the rendering of these roles by Michael Doyle as Sir and Rusty Salling as Norman.

"Doyle can break your heart with the briefest of shudders, the smallest whimper. He fills the theatre with majesty as he raises himself from frightened, broken-down actor to the heights of a king. He is a totally commanding figure, his voice modulated for every nuance of the role he plays. It is a rare treat to watch him perform.

"Salling is no less accomplished as Norman, the prissy dresser, who so skillfully works the transformation of Sir. He moves on stage with supple assurance, tossing lines away with deceptive nonchalance. He is funny, sad, bristling with his own self-importance and, ultimately, undone by it."[13]

Also in the cast were Ruth Johns, Maggie Beistle, Missy Weinstein, Bert Taylor, Dan Jesse, Michael Crider, Kevin Rainsberger, Kevin Kolczynski, Joe Holden, and Gregory Hausch.

In the playbill, the Hippodrome announced the return of co-founder Kerry McKenney from her sabbatical abroad. Now home, she and her husband Tony (anthropologist Dr. Anthony Oliver-Smith) were busy creating the first English translation of a play by South America's leading novelist, Mario Vargas Llosa, for its premiere at the Hippodrome the following April.

A Christmas Carol

A Christmas Carol 1984 featured (l-r) Maggie Beistle (Mrs. Cratchit), Jamey Stern (Tiny Tim), Chad Reed (Scrooge), and Rusty Salling (Bob Cratchit).

The Hippodrome finished 1984 with its seventh annual production of *A Christmas Carol*, which ran December 9 to 16, again to benefit charity.

1 Arline Greer, review of *A Servant of Two Masters*, by Carlo Goldoni, directed by Gregory Hausch, Hippodrome Theatre, Gainesville, FL, *Gainesville Sun*, January 13, 1984.
2 Danny Ball, review of *Cloud 9*, by Caryl Churchill, directed by Mary Hausch, Hippodrome Theatre, Gainesville, FL, *Independent Florida Alligator*, February 24, 1984.
3 Arline Greer, review of *Cloud 9*, by Caryl Churchill, directed by Mary Hausch, Hippodrome Theatre, Gainesville, FL, *Gainesville Sun*, February 24, 1984.
4 Arline Greer, review of *Crimes of the Heart*, by Beth Henley, directed by Gregory Hausch, Hippodrome Theatre, Gainesville, FL, *Gainesville Sun*, March 30, 1984.
5 Ibid.
6 Ibid.
7 Ibid.
8 Laura Kelly, "Jeff King Had the Part Right, After a Run-in with the Law," *Gainesville Sun*, May 18, 1984.
9 Arline Greer, review of *True West*, by Sam Shepard, directed by Mary Hausch, Hippodrome Theatre, Gainesville, FL, *Gainesville Sun*, May 11, 1984.
10 Danny Ball, review of *True West*, by Sam Shepard, directed by Mary Hausch, Hippodrome Theatre, Gainesville, FL, *Independent Florida Alligator*, May 10, 1984.
11 Arline Greer, review of *The Middle Ages*, by A. R. Gurney, directed by Gregory Hausch, Hippodrome Theatre, Gainesville, FL, *Gainesville Sun*, July 13, 1984.
12 Arline Greer, review of *The Dresser*, by Ronald Harwood, directed by Mary Hausch, Hippodrome Theatre, Gainesville, FL, *Gainesville Sun*, November 2, 1984.
13 Ibid.

1985

Turning Over

Back in Gainesville, Kerry McKenney's first project was to direct the Hippodrome's January show, *Turning Over* by British playwright Brian Thompson. She had gone to Europe looking for a Spanish play to translate, but while working at the National Theatre in London she saw *Turning Over* and got the rights to stage it at the Hippodrome.

Photo: *Gainesville Sun*

Scene from *Turning Over*: (l-r) Debbie Laumand, Dan Jesse, Kevin Rainsberger, Jennifer Pritchett, and Lance Harmeling (on the floor).

On January 11, 1985, *Turning Over* made its American debut with a cast of Hippodrome favorites: Dan Jesse, Kevin Rainsberger, Lance Harmeling, Rusty Salling, Jennifer Pritchett, and Debbie Laumand. Pradeep Kumar, a newcomer, made his first stage appearance. His performance as an Indian tour guide won the praise of Arline Greer: "In mastering both the humorous and sorrowful elements of his role, Kumar is capable of making you want to cry, even as you laugh."[1]

The comedy is set in two locations: India, where a BBC crew is making a documentary, and in a London editing room where the film is being spliced together. Scenes alternate between the two sets, each one ending with a pointed one-liner. The play ran through February 3.

Money Problems

Twelve years into the Hippodrome's history, they were still having money problems. According to a Jacksonville reviewer, *Turning Over* only happened because the Board of Trustees had managed to raise $40,000.[2] Still, that wasn't enough to keep the theatre operating for the remainder of the season. On opening night, State Representative Jon Mills made a plea to the audience, who coughed up $4,121 and pledged another $2,000. A Hippodrome press release the following Tuesday reminded the community that the amount raised was only 6.3 percent of the $98,000 they needed.

To help raise money, the Hippodrome took a popular show from the previous summer, *True West*, on a state tour during January and February under Mary Hausch's direction. Jeffrey King and Greg Hausch reprised their roles, while Maggie Beistle and Michael Crider took over the parts previously played by Ellen Lau and Dan Leonard. The *Orlando Sentinel* called it "exhilarating" and raved about Jeffrey King's acting.[3]

The Comedy of Errors

While her fellow artistic directors were on the road, Kerry McKenney partnered with UF English Professor Sidney Homan, an internationally renowned Shakespearean scholar, to co-direct Shakespeare's *The Comedy of Errors*. With his help, could the Hippodrome produce something that would please purists? Dr. Homan hoped so, for in the audience on March 8 would be twenty Shakespearean scholars and critics who were in town to attend a national conference on Shakespeare at UF.

From *The Comedy of Errors*: (l-r) Michael Crider, Rick Lotzkar, Rusty Salling, Malcolm Gets, Lance Harmeling, Mariah Reed, Kevin Rainsberger, and Deborah Laumand.

Photo: Gary Wolfson

The Comedy of Errors is Shakespeare's earliest comedy, a farce of mistaken identities. A father, mother, and twin sons, all separated since the boys were children, fail to recognize each other when they meet years later in the Greek city of Ephesus. To add to the confusion, the servants of both sons are themselves twins separated at birth.

Rusty Salling and Malcolm Gets played the twin sons, Lance Harmeling and John Staniunas, their servants. Rusty's character is married, so, as is typical to farce, his wife (played by Deborah Laumand) mistakes the wrong twin for her husband. Mariah Reed, playing Deborah's sister, becomes the other twin's love interest. Jennifer Pritchett played their mother, who, after losing her family, had become an abbess. The twins' father (Mike Beistle) gives lofty speeches at the beginning and end of the play.

Mike had a reputation among the actors as a jokester. Jennifer recalls, "We're all out there at the end of the play, and Mike Beistle would improvise new Shakespearean language almost every night, just to make us crack up. We would have to listen to Mike's final speech, never knowing what it was going to be from night to night, and try to keep a straight face."

Instead of ancient Greece, the directors chose to set the play in a dreamy fantasy world in an unspecified time period for which Carlos Asse created a surrealistic set. Eddie Gwaltney composed a musical suite for the show, borrowing from Bach and swing music.

Marilyn Wall's creative talent was born to costume a play like this one. With an assist from skilled seamstress Leslie Klein, she went all out—blue velvet frock coat and Carnaby-style cap for Rusty and leather bomber jacket and leopard-pattern tights for Kevin Rainsberger. But Jennifer's costume for her grand appearance at the end of the play topped them all.

"There was never a better entrance than the one Marilyn created for me with that costume," Jennifer said. "I played Mother Superior [the abbess]. It had a tight bodice with this glittery red lace cross across my chest. The skirt was layers and layers of lace and tulle, black and red and netting. A black veil attached to my crown went to the ground, and when I made my entrance, the whole floor-length veil flew up and back. It was fabulous."

The show was a hit, running from February 22–March 17, after being extended an extra week. By the time it closed, the theatre's fundraising efforts had garnered $98,787. Even school children inspired by Theatre for Young Audiences shows helped. Students at Howard Bishop Middle School raised $200 for the Hippodrome by selling flowers donated by the Enchanted Florist, while fifth-grade students at St. Patrick's raised $50 with a bake sale. Efforts to raise another $55,000 continued with an all-day "Hippothon" telethon at the Oaks Mall, a Cabaret Night at the University Centre Hotel, and haircuts by local professionals on the Hippodrome steps with the proceeds going to the theatre.

(below) (l-r) Melanie Bridges, Michael Crider, Rusty Salling, Melissa Weinstein, John Staniunas, Gregg Jones, Mike Beistle, and Kevin Rainsberger in *Rhinoceros*.

Ionesco Visits

April brought playwright Eugène Ionesco, an important contributor to what is known as theatre of the absurd, to Gainesville to discuss his work and his latest play, *Parlons Français*, as part of the Florida Arts Celebration. One of the foremost figures in French avant-garde theatre, he stayed for the Hippodrome's opening of his 1959 play, *Rhinoceros*, directed by Mary Hausch. The Hippodrome had performed Ionesco's *Exit the King* during their very first year.

Photo: John Moran/*Gainesville Sun*

Rhinoceros is an absurdist comedy set in a provincial town mysteriously becoming inundated with charging rhinos. Soon, the rhinos' origins are understood. Residents are being transformed into the beasts one by one, lured by the strength and simplicity of the rhino. Ionesco said his inspiration for the play had been the delirium and mass hysteria associated with the Nazi movement of the 1930s and was mainly an attack on collective hysteria.

Reviewers for both the *Alligator* and *Gainesville Sun* thought that while the play was humorous, the script fell flat at the end. Both newspapers commended the fine cast, which included Rusty Salling, Kevin Rainsberger, Michael Beistle, Rena Carney, Gregg Jones, Mariah Reed, Michael Crider, Melanie Bridges, John Staniunas, and Missy Weinstein. The show ran from April 5–25.

Sweet Tango of Lies

Fifteen days later, director Kerry McKenney premiered *Sweet Tango of Lies*, which she and her husband Anthony Oliver-Smith had translated from Mario Vargas Llosa's 1983 drama, *Kathie y el Hipopótamo*. The project was the outcome of their year-long visit to Spain looking for a Spanish play to translate.

"I went to all the theatres [there] to see what they were up to," Kerry said, "and actually, they weren't very good. It was still Franco's influence, very conservative. But, in Spain at that time, they were doing great street theatre, spectacle kinds of work that were fantastic—just blew your mind. It was more like *Cirque du Soleil,* and the Hippodrome couldn't do that."

However, while living in Madrid, Kerry and Tony discovered a play called *Kathie y el Hipopótamo* by Mario Vargas Llosa, an internationally known Peruvian novelist and playwright who has won many writing awards, including the 2010 Nobel Prize for Literature. Almost simultaneously, they learned that the Ibero-American Institute in Madrid was hosting Vargas Llosa at an event there.

After learning what hotel Vargas Llosa was staying at, they left him a letter proposing to translate his play into English and produce it at the Hippodrome. He called them and set up a meeting, at which he agreed to let them do it. While working on the translation, they met together again in London, and once again in New York.

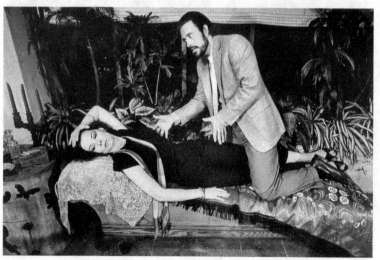

Suzanne Marlowe and Alex Pinkston in *Sweet Tango of Lies*.

Photo: Gary Wolfson

The title of Vargas Llosa's play translates as *Kathie and the Hippopotamus*. Kerry thought that sounded too much like a children's play and wanted to change it. Until the month before it opened, the Hippodrome advertised it as *Exotic Lovers and Other Beasts*, but Mario didn't like the title. They finally settled on *Sweet Tango of Lies*.

Sweet Tango of Lies is a fiction within a fiction. Wealthy, bored Kathie Kennety (played by Suzanne Marlowe) wants to turn her world adventures into a prurient romance novel by telling them to a ghostwriter (played by Alex Pinkston). The problem is, Kathie and Alex are both lying to each other. He is really a college professor who is henpecked by his wife, Ana (Jennifer Pritchett). And it turns out that Kathie's comical husband, Johnny (Kevin Rainsberger), is a mindless surfer, and her adventures are only fantasies.

Sweet Tango of Lies ran from May 10–June 2. Later in 1985, the performance of their translation won the Fringe Theatre Festival Award in Edinburgh, Scotland.

That concluded the twelfth season and ended Kerry's time as a co-artistic director with the Hippodrome. She resigned, enrolled in a doctorate program at UF, and raised a family. When the Harn Museum of Art opened in 1990, she took a position as curator of contemporary art. Her accomplishments there included starting the Harn's RISK Cinema program and two major grant awards from the Andy Warhol Foundation for exhibitions that ultimately travelled nationally. Kerry remained at the Harn until she retired.

Season Thirteen

The thirteenth season schedule and the playbill for *Sweet Tango of Lies* announced that *Pump Boys and Dinettes* would be the summer show, but the Hippodrome couldn't get the rights. Come July, *They're Playing Our Song* opened instead.

No one complained. *They're Playing Our Song* by Neil Simon, with music by Marvin Hamlisch and Carole Bayer Sager, was a rousing hit, and audiences had a good time. Neil Simon's script was filled with hilarious one-liners. Carole Bayer Sager's pop songs had won gold records, and Marvin Hamlisch's music had won multiple Academy Awards and a Tony. On top of that, Sager and Hamlisch were an actual couple on whom Simon loosely based his story of the on-again, off-again relationship between two talented, slightly neurotic, but basically romantic songwriters.

Back row, Voices of Vernon: Lance Harmeling, Bern Gautier, Andy Leech. Next to piano: Michael Crider (Vernon) and Debbie Laumand (Sonia). Front row, Voices of Sonia: Mariah Reed, Sharon Cline, and Ann Wren in *They're Playing Our Song.*

John Staniunas, who taught musical theatre at UF and had appeared in *Rhinoceros* earlier that year, directed and choreographed the show. Debbie Laumand and Michael Crider played the leads, Sonia and Vernon. Each of these characters has three alter egos, characters who contribute to the musical numbers and humor. Sharon Cline, Mariah Reed, and Ann Wren played Sonia's, and Bern Gautier, Lance Harmeling, and Andy Leech played Vernon's. All had excellent voices.

The reviewer for the *Independent Florida Alligator* said, "*They're Playing Our Song* fits the Hipp better than it did Broadway. Because the relationship between Laumand and Crider really clicks, this is a good play to get close to. It plays true up close, partly because John Staniunas, the director, has staged the play so cleverly. He's set it up for the smallest moments to succeed."[4]

They're Playing Our Song ran from July 12–August 11, being held over an extra week. Mary Hausch reported it was the

Photo: Gary Wolfson

Hippodrome's biggest moneymaking show up to that point, exceeding *Amadeus*, which held the previous record.

Ain't Misbehavin'

The Hippodrome kept the audience's feet tapping with its September production, *Ain't Misbehavin'*. A musical revue written by Richard Maltby, Jr., and Murray Horwitz, set in a 1927 Harlem jazz club, it featured the songs of Fats Waller. Fats (Thomas) Waller was an American jazz pianist in the stride piano style and a prolific songwriter. By age eighteen, he was a recording artist who had achieved critical and commercial success. Waller became one of the most popular performers of his time. *Ain't Misbehavin'* had won three Tony Awards in 1978, including Best Musical.

Gainesville wunderkind Malcolm Gets directed and choreographed the show—his first and only turn as director before he moved to New York and made his off-Broadway debut. He also played piano in the production's live onstage band, the Hot Chocolates, which included Michael Derr on drums, Bill Rode on trumpet, Roland Burns on saxophone, Christopher Dorsey on trombone, and Neil Jones on bass. Musical director Eddie Gwaltney kept the joint jumpin'.

The revue consisted of two dozen Fats Waller tunes performed by a cast of strong vocalists: Leah Bass, Elizabeth Graham, Mennie Nelson, Ron White, and James Randolph II. Leah had just spent two years on Broadway. Elizabeth had sung opera in the Tony Award-winning revival of *Porgy and Bess*. Mennie had just finished a national tour of *Ain't Misbehavin'*, and Ron had performed the musical in Maryland.

Cast of *Ain't Misbehavin'*: (l-r) Mennie Nelson, Leah Bass (atop piano), James Randolph II, Elizabeth Graham, Ron White (kneeling), and Malcolm Gets (playing piano).

Back in August, Malcolm hadn't been sure *Ain't Misbehavin'* would open. Actors Equity was on the verge of a strike against the League of Resident Theatres (LORT), of which the Hippodrome was a member. Since the entire cast consisted of Equity members, a strike would put them outside on a picket line instead of inside rehearsing. The union didn't have anything against the Hippodrome per se, but the Gainesville theatre operated under the LORT contract. A week before preview night, Equity and LORT reached an agreement, and the show opened on September 6. It was so popular that its run was extended through October 4.

Photo: John Moran/*Gainesville Sun*

A Fine Stoppard Play

For their next play, *The Real Thing*, by English playwright Tom Stoppard, Carlos Asse designed an ingenious revolving stage that allowed for multiple scene changes. Director Mary Hausch put together a fine cast with Mark Capri as Henry, married to Jennifer Pritchett's Charlotte, and Kate Alexander as Annie, married to Max, played by Rusty Salling. In the first act, the two couples engage in adulterous relationships, switch spouses, and part ways.

In act two, Henry has divorced Charlotte and married Annie, who is having an affair with a young actor (played by Andrew Watts). Then Annie takes up the cause of a young dissident (played by Michael Johnson). Henry's free-thinking seventeen-year-old daughter from his previous marriage (actress Caryn Rosenthal) declares that monogamy is a thing of the past.

Critic Arline Greer said, "The play is acted marvelously by a fine troupe," and she especially admired the script.[5] She wrote, "Stoppard uses all his gifts in a dazzling display of theatrical virtuosity in *The Real Thing*. It is perhaps his finest play, in that its dramatic construction mirrors its theme so faithfully, so honestly, that the theatergoer cannot help but admire the wholeness of the production."[6]

Kate Alexander and Mark Capri in *The Real Thing*.

The Real Thing had won the 1984 Tony Award for Best Play. The Hippodrome production ran from October 25–November 17.

Shortly after *The Real Thing* opened, Greg Hausch took *The Middle Ages* on tour with the original 1984 cast, except for Consuelo Dodge, who was replaced by Melanie Bridges.

A Christmas Carol

December 13–21, the Hippodrome presented its eighth annual charity production of *A Christmas Carol*. This time it was co-directed by Rena Carney and James Wren, and for the first time offered a performance accompanied by sign language for the hearing impaired. No doubt the idea was inspired by Rena's work on the TYA production *Sign Posts*. Another first, the Hippodrome offered advance tickets to *A Christmas Carol* and lines stretched around the block.

The Hippodrome estimated that during the eight years, their Christmas shows had collected more than 56,000 cans of food and well over 9,600 toys. The success of this annual event inspired theatres throughout the country to develop similar programs.

Line for tickets to *A Christmas Carol*.

1   Arline Greer, review of Turning Over, by Brian Thompson, directed by Kerry McKenney, Hippodrome Theatre, Gainesville, FL, Gainesville Sun, January 18, 1985.
2   Watch Hound, review of Turning Over, by Brian Thompson, directed by Kerry McKenney, Hippodrome Theatre, Gainesville, FL, Happenings, January 26, 1985.
3   Elizabeth Maupin, review of True West, by Sam Shepard, directed by Mary Hausch, Annie Russell Theatre, Rollins College, Winter Park, FL, Orlando Sentinel, February 5, 1985.
4   Timothy McShane, review of They're Playing Our Song, by Neil Simon, directed by John Staniunas, Hippodrome Theatre, Gainesville, FL, Independent Florida Alligator, July 18, 1985.
5   Arline Greer, review of The Real Thing, by Tom Stoppard, directed by Mary Hausch, Hippodrome Theatre, Gainesville, FL, Gainesville Sun, November 1, 1985.
6   Ibid.

1986

Season's Greetings

Although Christmas season was over in the real world, it continued on the Hippodrome stage with the January comedy *Season's Greetings* by Alan Ayckbourn. The play is a farce about several English couples celebrating Christmas under one roof. Besides being related by marriage, the other thing the couples have in common is that they're all involved in disastrous relationships.

Cast of *Season's Greetings*. Front (l-r): Cynthia Leigh Pierson, Dan Jesse, Mariah Reed, Daniel Sapecky, Rena Carney, and Kevin Rainsberger. Back: Marilyn Wall, Michael Beistle, and Rusty Salling.

Photo: John Moran

Arline Greer called it a winner and said, "The ensemble acting for the Hippodrome production of *Season's Greetings* is as fine as anything this company has produced. Every performance is a gem."[1]

She was referring to Michael Beistle, Rusty Salling, Dan Jesse, Kevin Rainsberger, Rena Carney, Mariah Reed, Cynthia Leigh Pierson, Daniel Sapecky—and Marilyn Wall as Rusty's character's boisterous, drunken wife.

Greer continued: "The play is expertly directed by Gregory Hausch, who sees to it that the constant interplay among various spouses, sisters, in-laws, and guests, moving here and there, with one scene falling into place directly as another has concluded, has a sustained flow. Here is the gift that makes for a satisfying farce, replete with improbable situations that take on a wild and wooly look, as they tumble along with comical frenzy."[2]

When it came to improbable situations, Rusty's character's bumbling puppet show of the *Three Little Pigs* had audiences hysterical with laughter at every performance from January 10–February 2.

Oh, Romeo

The opening of Shakespeare's *Romeo and Juliet* on February 21 missed Valentine's Day by a week, but the production was altogether romantic. Gregory Hausch co-directed it with Shakespearean scholar Sidney Homan, who had assisted Kerry McKenney with the previous year's well-received *Comedy of Errors*. The magical combination worked again, garnering accolades from every reviewer.

Praiseworthy performances by Mariah Reed as Juliet and Michael Stevens as Romeo were equaled by a strong supporting cast, including Michael Beistle, Rusty Salling, John Staniunas, Kurt Orwick, Kevin Rainsberger, Leticia Jaramillo, Charles Noel, Michele Grave, Mitchell Bronsen, and Robin Pennington.

The large-cast play created acting opportunities for UF theatre students Craig Foley, Mark Alan Harris, Michael Johnson, Galatea Ramphal, and Melanie Bridges, some of whom had already been in several Hippodrome plays. *Romeo and Juliet* also had parts for four middle school students: Heath Ward, Forrest Harris, Carly Asse, and Marisa Gwaltney. The show ran through March 16.

Last-minute Change

In keeping with the Shakespearean theme, the next play in the season's subscription package was supposed to be Tom Stoppard's *Rosencrantz and Guildenstern Are Dead*, which features two characters from *Hamlet*. However, the Hippodrome made a last-minute switch when seven years of perseverance paid off.

Since July 1978, they'd sought the rights to produce Howard Ashman and Alan Menken's off-Broadway hit musical *Little Shop of Horrors*, to no avail. Each year, they received the same reply: "Unable to grant your request at this time."

Then, the previous October, the Hippodrome had been suddenly informed that they would be the first state theatre in the US to receive production rights. Although the 1985–1986 season was underway, they jumped at the opportunity. "I was overwhelmed," said Mary Hausch, who directed it. "After eight years of rejection, the word 'approval' was like seeing your lottery number appear in the winner's column."

Little Shop of Horrors is the story of bizarre events that occur at a skid row flower shop. Seymour, a stock boy, has nurtured a strange and unusual plant and named it Audrey II after the ditzy blond shopgirl whom Seymour secretly adores. The odd plant brings unexpected fortune to the shop and wins Seymour Audrey's love. But it demands, in payment, a steadily growing diet of human blood.

A stage adaptation of Roger Corman's B horror movie, the play was a hilarious and madly entertaining comic feast that engulfed the audience in laughter. The script and lively songs parodied everything 1950s, from sentimental rock and roll songs to cheap horror films and Marilyn Monroe-type blondes.

Photo: John Moran

Rusty's character's bumbling puppet show of *The Three Little Pigs* had audiences hysterical with laughter at every performance.

Photo: John Moran

Michael Stevens as Romeo and Mariah Reed as Juliet.

Malcolm Gets as Seymour with Audrey II in *Little Shop of Horrors*.

Photo: Gary Wolfson

Mary persuaded Malcolm Gets to come back from New York to play Seymour. He had just completed his off-Broadway debut in *They're Playing Our Song*, where he'd worked with actress Debbie Birch, whom Mary had cast as Audrey in *Little Shop of Horrors*. Three New York City musical theatre veterans were cast as a 1950s girl pop group: Lynda Karen, Deborah Malone, and Leah Bass, who had been in the Hippodrome's *Ain't Misbehavin'*. Michael Scott, also from the New York stage, played a half dozen smaller roles. The head of the UF Theatre Department, Dr. David Shelton, made his first appearance on the Hippodrome stage as the owner of the flower shop.

Teaming up to animate the plant were Michael Crider, who, unseen, manipulated her limbs and mouth, and James Randolph II, who did the voice. "Feed me" was her frequent line. With each feeding, Audrey II grows until, by the play's end, she is very large with octopus-like limbs, a body resembling a fat toad, and the jaws of a shark. Carlos Asse not only designed the set but many different-sized versions of the carnivorous plant.

The *Alligator* reviewer called it "a pleasant and often amusing musical."[3] But the *Sun* critic wrote, "Three cheers and a big Bravo! Not only is it one of the funniest shows produced in the troupe's history, it is the best of its musicals, a whopping, wacky, wonderful hit that engages audiences from start to finish with outlandish antics.... as entertaining as anything you're likely to see anywhere."[4]

Little Shop of Horrors ran from April 4–27, ending each performance with an audience surprise as ninety-two vines with 688 leaves dropped onto them from the ceiling.

Lighter Side of Tennessee

David Shelton returned to the Hippodrome for their next play, *Period of Adjustment* by Tennessee Williams. Joining him in the cast were Kevin Rainsberger, Mariah Reed, Michael Crider, Ellen Lau, Kathy Tyrell, and Matthew Vought. Making their Hippodrome debuts were second grader Lashan Thompson and Bugsy Bordon, a large, shaggy dog with extensive acting experience at Busch Gardens.

Michael Crider, Mariah Reed, and Kevin Rainsberger in *Period of Adjustment*.

Period of Adjustment, one of Williams's less frequently performed works, is a gentle, lighthearted story. Following an unfortunate wedding night, a newlywed couple on their honeymoon visits the husband's Korean War buddy. There, they discover the buddy and his wife are having marital problems of their own. During a night of drinking, the couples individually confide their insecurities, problems, and plans. Both couples come to the realization that they have to reconcile their own relationships.

It has been said that Williams wrote this softer comedy in response to a criticism that his dark, brooding tragedies were always plunging into sewers. Arline Greer liked seeing another side of Tennessee Williams, but she complained that director

Photo: John Moran

Gregory Hausch had crammed three acts into two, causing the first act to be overly long and forcing the actors to rush.[5]

The play ran from May 23–June 15, ending the season.

TV Documentary

On June 28, 1986, *The Duck Variations*, which had previously been performed on the mainstage in 1977 and toured the state in 1979, was recorded before a live audience at WUFT, Gainesville's PBS station. This time, Michael Crider and David Shelton played the two elderly gentlemen. The performance was for a television documentary on aging produced by Steve Robitaille and Mary Anne Hilker. Mary Hausch directed the play, and Alan Saperstein directed the TV recording. The one-hour-long documentary, titled *Old Friends*, aired on public television the following spring (1987).

Fourteenth Season

For their summer musical, Gregory von Hausch (formerly Gregory Hausch) and Michael Beistle cooked up *'Cause Baby Look at You Now*, a jukebox of popular standards from the 1940s through the 1980s that included "Boogie Woogie Bugle Boy," "Rock Around the Clock," "I Want to Hold Your Hand," "Age of Aquarius," "I Am Woman," and more. Promoted as a Star-Spangled Musical Revue, it opened on July 4 and ran until the end of the month. Greg directed and Mike Beistle narrated. Belting out the tunes were three female singers: Kathy Tyrell, Debbie Laumand, Mariah von Hausch (formerly Mariah Reed), and three male singers: Malcolm Gets, Lance Harmeling, and James Randolph II.

Behind the cast, slides of events that occurred between 1946 and 1986 portrayed the changing times as Mike Beistle's tongue-in-cheek commentary provided a transition between songs. Arline Greer criticized the production, saying, "It lacks polish."[6] Greg defended it, saying it was "a work in progress."[7] Letters to the editor called Greer's review too harsh, and the letter writers said it had entertained and delighted them.

Cast of *'Cause Baby Look at You Now*. Back row (l-r): Debbie Laumand, Malcolm Gets, Michael Beistle. Front row: Lance Harmeling, Mariah von Hausch, Kathy Tyrell, and James Randolph II.

'Cause Baby Look at You Now closed on July 27, and five days later, the Hippodrome remounted their successful *Ain't Misbehavin'* for a three-week run from August 1–17. The show's previous director and choreographer, Malcolm Gets, took the helm again with only one cast change: Jacqueline Stroudemire replaced Elizabeth Graham. Greer loved it and recommended "seeing it again, and again."[8] Performances sold out even though it was not part of the season subscription package.

A Big Production

The Hippodrome could squeeze in an extra play that summer because their September production, *A Chorus Line*, was to be staged a few blocks away in the Florida Theatre. The former vaudeville theatre had changed with the times, becoming Gainesville's downtown movie theatre before succumbing to competition from multiplexes. In the 1970s, investors had resurrected it as a concert venue, the Great Southern Music Hall. The building was sold in the 1980s and opened again as the Florida Theatre just in time for the Hippodrome show.

The temporary switch to a larger space was a necessity for the show to succeed. Twenty-seven cast members and a nineteen-piece orchestra would never fit on the Hippodrome stage. Not to mention, their 276-seat theatre didn't hold enough people to recoup the cost of a production that large, but the 750-seat Florida Theatre did.

> **Book?**
>
> The text for musical plays is called the book instead of the script.

A Chorus Line was conceived by Michael Bennett, the book was by James Kirkwood and Nicholas Dante, with music by Marvin Hamlisch and lyrics by Edward Kleban. In 1986, it was the longest-running musical on Broadway and had won nine Tony Awards, the Pulitzer Prize for Drama, and the New York Drama Critics Award for Best Musical. It was a coup for the Hippodrome and their largest production ever. They pulled out all the stops, handing directing reins over to the chair of the UF Department of Theatre, Dr. Carole Brandt. For choreography, they tapped Judy Skinner, artistic director of Dance Alive National Ballet and the Gainesville Civic Ballet.

A Chorus Line cast:
Michael Alicia
Debbie Birch
Timothy Brantley
Jennifer Cook
David Earl
Jon-Michael Flate
Malcolm Gets
Tyrone Grant
M. Sayers Green
Kyle Ridraught
Mariah von Hausch
Jimmy Jay
Joanne Keith
Michael LaFleur
Debbie Laumand
Scott Leonard
Carol Liebman
Jenny Lynn Herwig
Keith Mottola
Andy Pratt
Becky Pusta
Laura Quinn
Jamie Robbins
Susu Sparkman
Charlotte Sternberg
Carole Stevens
Billy Vergara

Photo: Gary Wolfson

Full cast performing the finale of *A Chorus Line*.

Audiences and reviewers alike loved it. The show opened September 5, and the run had to be extended an extra week, closing on September 26. The *Alligator* praised the entire cast, "all of whom perform[ed] admirably in their extremely demanding roles."[9]

The *Sun* said, "With its altogether sophisticated and accomplished rendition of *A Chorus Line*, the Hippodrome has arrived at another milestone in its professional career.

"It is an exhausting show, an uplifting show, an exhibitionist show, and a show that is sheer razzle dazzle entertainment. Its finale alone is worth the price of admission, providing an almost indescribable feeling of elation, accompanied by an unaccountable lump in the throat. The actors... sing and dance their hearts out, and, in the process, they all but break ours."[10]

After finishing his role acting in and serving as musical director of *A Chorus Line*, Malcolm Gets led a Hippodrome state tour of *Ain't Misbehavin'* to fourteen Florida cities from October 17–November 22. Only he and James Randolph II remained from the original cast. New for the tour were Maleta Jefferson, Yvette Curtis, Gamalia Pharms, and Malcolm's old friend Lance Harmeling.

A Farce within a Farce

Meanwhile, the Hippodrome returned to their own stage for their next play, *Noises Off*, written by Michael Frayn and directed by Gregory von Hausch. The cast included Dana Moser, Kevin Rainsberger, Traber Burns, Rusty Salling, Michael Beistle, Mariah von Hausch, Caryn Rosenthal, Kate Alexander, and Tom Nash. Tom had been teaching theatre in Wisconsin and Idaho since his last appearance at the Hippodrome.

The play is a farce within a farce. The cast members play actors rehearsing the first act of a lamentable farce called *Nothing On*. Later, the set is turned around and the audience sees them perform it to an imaginary audience from a backstage point of view. When *Nothing On* is performed a third time, it is in shambles with its supposed cast missing cues, inventing dialogue, and stumbling and falling in and out of the set's seven doors.

For Kevin Rainsberger, it was a matter of sacrificing himself for his art. "In *Noises Off*, I had to fall down a flight of stairs. This was thirty days after I'd had back surgery. My doctor knew that I was going to do it. He said, 'You should be fine.' But Carlos was doing the finishing touches on the set until half an hour before our first audience. So, the first opportunity I had to fall down the stairs in rehearsal was a half hour before our first audience. I ended up going through the rails [on the side of the steps] a couple of times before I figured out exactly how to fall. But that wasn't until after the first weekend of shows."

Dana Moser shared her own mishap. In the inner play, *Nothing On*, her character is a maid who, in several instances, serves a platter of sardines. "For some scenes, the sardines were loose, other times they were in a gel, and sometimes they were glued onto the platter. Well, one night, I had the wrong sardines, and the gel got on the floor. I slipped and went up in the air, my feet went over my head, and I came down right on top of that mess. I lay there thinking I might have knocked myself out. I don't even know where I am. So, I get up and I start doing my lines, and in my head I'm going, 'No, no, no, these are the lines from act three.'"

In *Noises Off*, Kevin Rainsberger falls down the stairs and lands on his head—intentionally.

An audience member came up to Dana after the show and said, "Oh, I loved that bit when you went up in the air and came down."

"I'm glad you liked it," Dana said, "'cause that's the one and only time."

The play hit Arline Greer's funny bone: "Has anything funnier than *Noises Off* been produced in this town or anywhere else?" she asked her readers. "Not likely. To be sure, there was *Sly Fox*, a hilarious Hippodrome success of some years back; and, even farther back, the Hippodrome's production of the deliciously wicked *Tom Jones*, but *Noises Off* beats them both and any other farce that has been played before defenseless audiences, which can't help but wonder if a person's sides actually might split from too much laughing.

"Keeping the wild shenanigans of this farce within a farce on track with the split-second timing and demonic energy it demands is the task of director Gregory von Hausch, who is faultless in this extraordinary production. And speaking of the extraordinary, audiences watched gaga-eyed as Carlos Asse's set of a country living room was turned around completely for the play's second-act backstage scene and then reassembled for the play's third act."[11]

Dual Scrooges

Noises Off ran from October 17–November 9. When it closed, it was time to prepare for the Hippodrome's ninth annual production of *A Christmas Carol*. This time, Kevin Rainsberger took over the directing duties. That year Chad Reed and Mike Gioia both played Scrooge on alternate performance dates.

1 Arline Greer, review of *Season's Greetings*, by Alan Ayckbourn, directed by Gregory Hausch, Hippodrome Theatre, Gainesville, FL, *Gainesville Sun*, January 17, 1986.
2 Ibid.
3 Tom Yardley, review of *Little Shop of Horrors*, by Howard Ashman and Alan Menken, directed by Mary Hausch, Hippodrome Theatre, Gainesville, FL, *Independent Florida Alligator*, April 18, 1986.
4 Arline Greer, review of *Little Shop of Horrors*, by Howard Ashman and Alan Menken, directed by Mary Hausch, Hippodrome Theatre, Gainesville, FL, *Gainesville Sun*, April 11, 1986.
5 Arline Greer, review of *Period of Adjustment*, by Tennessee Williams, directed by Gregory Hausch, Hippodrome Theatre, Gainesville, FL, *Gainesville Sun*, May 30, 1986.
6 Arline Greer, review of *'Cause Baby Look at You Now*, by Gregory von Hausch and Michael Beistle, directed by Gregory von Hausch, Hippodrome Theatre, Gainesville, FL, *Gainesville Sun*, July 11, 1986.
7 Ibid.
8 Arline Greer, review of *Ain't Misbehavin'*, by Richard Maltby Jr. and Murray Horwitz, directed by Malcolm Gets, Hippodrome Theatre, Gainesville, FL, *Gainesville Sun*, August 8, 1986.
9 Michael Giltz, review of *A Chorus Line*, by James Kirkwood and Nicholas Dante, directed by Carole Brandt, Hippodrome Theatre, Gainesville, FL, *Independent Florida Alligator*, September 19, 1986.
10 Arline Greer, review of *A Chorus Line*, by James Kirkwood and Nicholas Dante, directed by Carole Brandt, Hippodrome Theatre, Gainesville, FL, *Gainesville Sun*, September 12, 1986.
11 Arline Greer, review of *Noises Off*, by Michael Frayne, directed by Gregory von Hausch, Hippodrome Theatre, Gainesville, FL, *Gainesville Sun*, October 24, 1986.

1987

Orphans

After three musicals and a farce, it was time for a drama. Mary Hausch directed *Orphans* by Lyle Kessler. *Orphans* has been described as a combination of theatre of the absurd, black comedy, and psychological melodrama. Grown orphan brothers Treat (Brian Cousins) and Phillip (T. Scott Cunningham) live in a dilapidated row house in Philadelphia. Treat, the brutal, violent older brother, provides for them by petty theft. Younger brother Phillip never leaves the house and spends his time lying in their dead mother's closet. One day, Treat kidnaps and ties up a Chicago mobster (Traber Burns) who, it turns out, is an orphan himself. He slips his bindings and turns the tables on the brothers. The ensuing power struggle, filled with profanity, violence, blood, and a killing, spans both acts. Ads for the show carried a warning: "Recommended for mature audiences."

The play won the 1985 Obie Award. The Hippodrome's production opened January 9 and ran through February 1, 1987. Reviewers for both the *Independent Florida Alligator* and the *Gainesville Sun* thought it was a tantalizing, emotional play and praised Mary Hausch for keeping the action moving.

Photo: Gary Wolfson

Brian Cousins as Treat in *Orphans*.

Cyrano

On February 13, the Hippodrome brought Edmond Rostand's classic *Cyrano De Bergerac* to the stage. Set in seventeenth-century France, the play is a romantic tale of love, poetry, and death centered around a flamboyant, swashbuckling hero with a big heart and nose to match. Cyrano, the man with the unfortunate proboscis, is hopelessly smitten with the beautiful and intellectual Roxanne. Although he is a remarkable duelist, a musical artist, and a gifted, joyful poet, self-doubt about his overly large nose makes him fear even an ugly woman would ever love him.

Roxanne's poetic soul is better suited to a man like Cyrano instead of the count she is being set up to marry. But just as Cyrano is about to reveal his feelings, Roxanne informs him she has fallen for a handsome new cadet, Christian. Lacking any gift with words, Christian convinces Cyrano to write letters to Roxanne, which Christian signs. With Cyrano's help, he wins the lady and they secretly marry. This angers the count, who sends the men into battle. While there, Christian persuades Cyrano to tell Roxanne the truth, but when Christian is killed, Cyrano decides it is better to preserve Roxanne's image of her husband's eloquence and say nothing. Fifteen years later, as Cyrano is dying, Roxanne finally sees the truth on her own.

Photo: Tim Jackson/*Gainesville Sun*

Beautiful Roxanne (Barbara Kearns) informs Cyrano (Rusty Salling) she has fallen for a handsome new cadet.

Rusty Salling starred as Cyrano, surrounded by a cast of twenty-two, including Michael Beistle, Dan Jesse, Kevin Rainsberger, Rena Carney, Gregg Jones, Jim Wren, and James Randolph II. A dozen UF theatre students played soldiers, thieves, pickpockets, bakers, nuns, and monks. Carlos Asse's sons played street urchins. Barbara Kearns came down from New York to play the beautiful Roxanne. Barbara had graduated from UF, had a role in the Hippodrome's *Sly Fox*, and then moved to television where she'd spent six months on the show *All My Children*.

Directed by Gregory von Hausch, *Cyrano De Bergerac* ran through March 8.

Brighton Beach Memoirs

The Hippodrome closed its fourteenth season with Neil Simon's humorous look at Jewish life in 1937 Brooklyn, *Brighton Beach Memoirs*.

Simon's memories of growing up during the Great Depression are told through the eyes of teenage Eugene, portrayed by Louis Martin. Eugene's two adolescent desires are to play for the New York Yankees and to eat an ice cream cone while seeing a naked woman. Older brother Stanley (Peter Bauer) provides Eugene with questionable advice. His mother, Kate (Mimi Carr), is an obsessive homemaker with the bawl of a staff sergeant. His father, played by Michael Beistle, had just gotten a foothold on prosperity when the Depression whittled it to bare survival. Other family members include Eugene's widowed Aunt Blanche (Linda Stephens) and her two daughters: restless older daughter Nora (Jennifer Grace) and coddled, sickly younger daughter Laurie (Cathy Chase).

The play was directed by UF Professor of Theatre Dr. David Shelton, whom Arline Greer said made "its different levels of action flow into each other with great beauty."[1] Her review closed with, "It will make you laugh and cry and, perhaps, recall the bittersweet time of your own youth. It's a hit and should please audiences for a long time."[2] She was right. The play, which opened on March 27, had to be held over an extra week, not closing until April 26.

Brighton Beach Memoirs was the first of Neil Simon's trilogy of plays about his life, told through his alter ego, Eugene. So what could be more perfect than to start the Hippodrome's fifteenth season with Simon's second autobiographical play?

Fifteenth Season

Moving forward in time to World War II, Eugene's story continues with Simon's *Biloxi Blues*. Eugene is sent to boot camp in Biloxi, Mississippi. At the camp, he experiences anti-Semitism, sees a friend persecuted for homosexuality, has his first encounter with a prostitute, deals with an authoritarian drill sergeant, and has problems making friends in what seems like a foreign territory. The play had won two Tony Awards.

The Hippodrome's oft-lauded set designer, Carlos Asse, directed the play in addition to designing one of his most creatively sophisticated sets yet. "*Biloxi Blues* was a show that went from place to place to place," Carlos said. Scenes take place on a train, inside and outside an army barracks, at a USO dance, and more. "I saw it in New York, and they had all these revolving scenes that would come in, and I said, 'Oh, my God, how am I going to do this?' But I thought the play was so good that we should do it."

His solution was to raise the stage by about a foot and cut grooves into the floor to act as tracks so large scenery could be slid onto and off the stage. One was the train. Another had the bunk beds in the barracks, and another the USO dance. "On the side, I had two sections that bolted together for the [prostitute's] bedroom and then it would reverse and become the [barracks] latrines where they were getting dressed for their outing."

Arline Greer's review praised Carlos's "handsome set" and said his directing "has given it a gentle, almost loving quality that mutes the choppiness of some of its scenes and colors them with a lingering backward look. *Biloxi Blues* is a funny play, filled with the kind of quick-witted one-liners we have come to expect from Neil Simon.... The audience laughed nonstop.... Score another hit for Neil Simon and the Hippodrome!"[3]

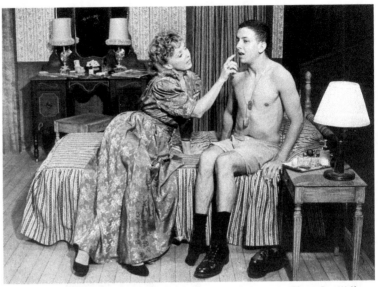

Photo: Gary Wolfson

Rena Carney plays the good-natured prostitute who helps Eugene (Scott Tiler) lose his virginity in *Biloxi Blues*.

Eugene was played by Scott Tiler, who had received critical acclaim for his role in the film *Once Upon a Time in America* and had just completed a film with Steven Spielberg before coming to the Hippodrome. Shawn Black, who played the homosexual soldier, was, like Tiler, a professional film and stage actor. Rena Carney played the good-natured prostitute who helps Eugene lose his virginity. The tough-talking Sargent was Kevin Rainsberger, who Greer said was "giving the best performance of the play and the performance of his career."[4]

The remaining cast members were UF theatre students or recent graduates: Joseph Cirnick, Stewart Clarke, Jon Beshara, Stephanie Disandis, and Jimmy Jay. Jimmy and Stephanie had previously toured with the Hippodrome's Theatre for Young Audiences.

Biloxi Blues was so popular it had to be held over twice, running June 26–August 2, 1987. Later that fall, its director, Carlos Asse, was awarded an Individual Artist Fellowship from the Florida Department of State. He used the money to research artistic and mechanical techniques for touring productions.

Aging Hippie Musical

When the Hippodrome chose *Hair: The American Tribal Love-Rock Musical* for its fall production, they expected it to be nostalgic fun, its controversy long past. Wrong.

Its story concerns a "tribe" of politically active long-haired hippies living a bohemian life in New York City while fighting against conscription into the Vietnam War and awaiting the dawn of the Age of Aquarius. Threaded through the plot are forty infectious songs, several of which became hit records and anthems of the hippie era.

Hair had premiered in 1967 at the New York Shakespeare Festival, then played off-Broadway for four months before moving to Broadway, where it ran for 1,750 performances. Brash and outrageous, it celebrated the generation gap, thumbing its nose at controversies of the day like free love, interracial relationships, religion, politics, and the length of men's hair.

Photo: Erik Lesser

Cast of *Hair* in a dance scene.

Truthfully, the twenty-year-old play *was* dated. Hypocrisies so evident in the sixties had disappeared. By 1987, no one cared if a man had long hair, free love was common, and the last US troops had left Vietnam a dozen years earlier. Director Jim Wren made no attempt to update the script. "To do so would be a sacrilege," explained Sidney Homan in the Hippodrome newsletter.[5]

During a joyous song near the end of the first act, the cast members tossed off their clothing. According to Mary Hausch, the nudity lasted about twenty seconds, but that was too long for a local Baptist church. The congregation made signs and protested on the sidewalk outside the Florida Theatre, where the show was being performed. The minister and others wrote letters to the newspaper, and the church took out an ad in the *Gainesville Sun,* calling the nudity in *Hair* pornography. Hippodrome staff and audience members responded with their own letters to the editor supporting the play. The two sides went back and forth, with some item about the show appearing in the paper every week of its run.

Dozens of Hippodrome shows over the previous fifteen years had contained far more nudity without a picketer in sight. So, why this play? One explanation might be that non-theatergoers who had never heard of *Streamers* or *Otherwise Engaged* had

heard of *Hair.* Equally likely, the play's overall "do what you feel" message offended them. A protester told a reporter the play "promotes the breakdown of morality" and reflects "an era which had no respect for authority."[6]

The protest marches on the sidewalks of Gainesville brought reminders of a bygone era. The cast reacted like flower children—handing the picketers flowers and offers of peace. The publicity didn't hurt. In fact, sales of season ticket subscriptions increased.

Protesters picketing *Hair.*

The cast consisted of eight principal characters played by Malcolm Gets, John-Michael Flate, Scott Isert, Lance Harmeling, Melissa Weinstein, Debbie Laumand, Arline Williams, and Ann Wren. They were joined onstage by fourteen actors identified in the playbill as "The Tribe" and a live band at the back of the stage. To accommodate the large cast and bigger audiences, the Hippodrome again rented the Florida Theatre.

James Rado and Gerome Ragni wrote *Hair*'s book and lyrics, with music by Galt McDermott. The Hippodrome production ran from August 28–September 20 and proved very popular at the box office. Besides local coverage, it received positive write-ups in Ocala and Jacksonville newspapers.

Although the Orlando reviewer thought it was dated, Arline Greer called it "that splendid, irreverent, energetic musical depicting the mood of the '60s, performed by a joyful cast.... It's a happy enthusiastic show, a visual and musical treat that makes you want to get up and dance right along with the performers."[7] At the finale of each performance, the cast invited the audience to do exactly that.

As Is

With infectious songs and antiestablishment rebellion, *Hair* brought up the social ills of its day. But by the 1980s, there was a tragic illness of a different magnitude that no one wanted to face—AIDS. In fact, until handsome movie star Rock Hudson revealed he was dying from the disease in 1985, most of the public had never heard of it. One segment of the population feeling its tragic impact was the theatre community. Playwright William M. Hoffman dramatized it with his award-winning play *As Is*.

HAIR CAST:
John-Michael Flate
Malcolm Gets
Lance Harmeling
Scott Isert
Debbie Laumand
Melissa Weinstein,
Arline Williams
Ann Wren.
THE TRIBE:
Irene Adjan
Michael Alicia
M. Clark Canine
Sharon Cline
Stephanie Disandis
Jennifer Grace
Elizabeth Homan
Joan Taylor Larrick
Andy Pratt
James Randolph II
Bruce Rise
Janet Read Rucker
Judith Walton
Reeves S. Watson

Photo: Stephen Morton/*Gainesville Sun*.

In a scene from *As Is*, Saul (Scott Winters) photographs Lily (Nell Page) while on the couch, Chet (Malcolm Gets) listens to Rich (Robert Browne).

The League of Resident Theatres, to which the Hippodrome belonged, encouraged each of its member theatres to host a benefit performance and donate the funds raised to a local organization involved in AIDS care. The Actors' Equity Association agreed to allow its members to waive their salaries for the benefit performance, and Samuel French, Inc., a publisher of plays, agreed to waive the royalty payment.

The Hippodrome production, running from October 30–November 22, was accompanied by an entire week of programs aimed at increasing understanding of the disease. These included an AIDS awareness forum, AIDS-related films in the cinema, and a sale of paintings by local artists in the Hippodrome Gallery to benefit the North Central Florida AIDS Network. Playwright William Hoffman joined director Mary Hausch, Sidney Homan, and county health officials for a panel discussion following a performance of *As Is*.

Mary said, "I've been wanting to do a public forum program for some time, and I thought that if we produced this play, we would want to use it to inform the public. AIDS is such a volatile issue, and Florida seems to be a hot spot." She added, "It's a particularly complex problem, because while it is an extremely emotional—sometimes hysterical—issue, it also brings up many, many ethical questions. We want to lend sanity and sensitivity to the issue, and to educate the public about the problem itself."[8] In line with that goal, teenagers in the Hippodrome's Gainesville Area Improvisational Teen Theatre held a special production aimed at their peers.

The play brings its message in the form of "a moving story about two gay men, and how they deal with AIDS separately and together.... [The story is] enriched by Mary Hausch's sharp and sensitive direction, and by outstanding performances from Robert Browne, as Rich, and Scott Winters, as Saul."[9] Arline Greer wrote, "Six other cast members appear in multiple roles. Most memorable is Kevin Rainsberger, as Rich's straight brother, who visits Rich in the hospital and awkwardly tries to approach him, revealing love mixed with embarrassment. Rena Carney is quite wonderful as the hospice worker, who serves as master of ceremonies. Rusty Salling and Reeves Watson play a couple of AIDS hot-line workers with unforgettable black humor. Nell Page Sexton, in the role of Lily, an actress and friend, is stunning to look at and brings her own stamp of drama to the stage whenever she appears. Malcolm Gets as the not-so-bright Chet, the new younger man in Rich's life, is just right."[10]

As Is wasn't the first time that Hippodrome had raised money for local causes. In addition to its annual *A Christmas Carol* production, the preview show of every play since 1978 has been a benefit performance. Recipients of the theatre's generosity have ranged from Civitan Blood Center to Kanapaha Botanical Gardens.

As Is was followed by *A Christmas Carol*, which ran December 4–18.

1 Arline Greer, review of *Brighton Beach Memoirs*, by Neil Simon, directed by David Shelton, Hippodrome Theatre, Gainesville, FL, *Gainesville Sun*, April 3, 1987.
2 Ibid.
3 Arline Greer, review of *Biloxi Blues*, by Neil Simon, directed by Carlos Asse, Hippodrome Theatre, Gainesville, FL, *Gainesville Sun*, July 3, 1987.
4 Ibid.
5 Sidney Homan, *Backstage*, The Hippodrome Theatre, Gainesville, FL, June-July 1987.
6 Carol Arnold, "Nudity in *Hair* Attracts Protesters," *Gainesville Sun*, September 17, 1987.
7 Arline Greer, review of *Hair: The American Tribal Love-Rock Musical*, by James Rado and Gerome Ragni, directed by Jim Wren, Hippodrome Theatre, Gainesville, FL, *Gainesville Sun*, September 4, 1987.
8 Benita Budd, "AIDS Awareness Forum," *Gainesville Sun*, October 28, 1987.
9 Arline Greer, review of *As Is*, by William M. Hoffman, directed by Mary Hausch, Hippodrome Theatre, Gainesville, FL, *Gainesville Sun*, November 3, 1987.
10 Ibid.

1988

Lighter Fare

Compared to the important but heavy message of *As Is*, Sandra Deer's *So Long on Lonely Street* was much lighter fare. In what was becoming a trend, the playwright came the week before the show opened to work with the theatre.

Billed as a comedy/drama, Deer's play fell somewhere in between, with genuinely moving moments interspersed with rowdy good humor. Its plot concerns a wealthy Southern family whose conflict over an inheritance uncovers skeletons in their family closet. Greer called the script "witty, compassionate and heartwarming... a beautifully crafted play, whose characters are unique individuals, transcending the stereotypes."[1]

Pivotal to the story are twins Raymond and Ruth, played by Kevin Rainsberger and Nell Page. He is a TV soap opera star and she a dark suicidal poet who has slept her way across Europe. For fifteen years, they have tried to deny incestuous feelings that become apparent to the audience the first time Raymond steps onstage and Ruth runs and leaps into his arms.

The family has gathered after the death of dear old Aunt Pearl, whose body lies in a coffin up stage. At issue is what will become of the ramshackle ancestral home and Pearl's elderly half sister, Annabel Lee, played by Lizan Mitchell. Lizan had originated the role in Atlanta. John Ammerman played King, the twins' cousin, and Mariah von Hausch played his pregnant wife. King wants to turn the place into a Christian Shopping Center. Annabel Lee wants to remain in the only home she's ever known. The lawyer, played by Rusty Salling, reads a will that leaves the decision up to the twins.

Cast of *So Long on Lonely Street*. Standing: Rusty Salling, Lizan Mitchell, John Ammerman, and Mariah von Hausch. Seated: Nell Page and Kevin Rainsberger.

Photo: Erik Lesser/*Gainesville Sun*.

Nell Page recalls how director Gregory von Hausch decided to stir things up. During a scene in the second act where sexual tension between the twins heightens, Nell's character drinks heavily. "Greg instructed the stage manager to pour out the juice and put wine in the bottle," Nell recalled. "My character [has to] drink like half a bottle. I was just trying to get through that scene." She expected it to be a onetime prank. "Then it would happen again. Every night he put real wine in."

"I don't think I ever knew that," Kevin said years later. He added, "*So Long on Lonely Street* was a great script. I mean, it is so well written. Here's a show about incest and by the end of the show, the audience wants this brother and sister to get together."

Greer praised all the actors' individual performances, but felt Kevin and Nell "[held] back, uncomfortable, perhaps, with spelling out their incestuous feelings."[2] Or maybe it was the wine.

The show ran January 15–February 7.

Political Satire

In March, Mary Hausch directed *Rum and Coke*, Keith Reddin's Obie Award-winning political satire, which takes a wry, poignant look at the optimism and patriotic naiveté that led the United States to stumble into the Bay of Pigs invasion. The play sensitively evokes the tragicomic excesses and the catastrophic outcome for the Cuban exiles, the involved Americans, and the governments they both served.

Except for UF grad student Carroll Tolman, the cast members were old Hippodrome favorites, including Michael Beistle, Dan Jesse, and Rusty Salling, who had not appeared onstage together since *Cyrano De Bergerac*. Gregory von Hausch

(l-r) Dan Jesse, Rusty Salling, Michael Beistle, and Mark Sexton play misguided CIA operatives in *Rum and Coke*.

Photo: Stephen Morton

played Richard Nixon and Gregg Jones was Fidel Castro. Kevin Rainsberger played multiple characters, among them a Cuban grandmother—a challenge to be sure because Kevin had a mustache. In another casting twist, Nell Page's real-life husband, Mark Sexton, played her little brother.

"Mark is a very physical actor," Nell said. "He didn't always separate himself from the character. There was a scene that he was supposed to shove me like a little brother would do, but he shoved me really hard. I'm thinking this character would not stand for that kind of shoving without shoving back. So, I shoved him back so hard that he fell to the ground and slid to the side of the stage." Later, the show's stage manager, Mike Johnson, told her he thought a domestic fight was about to break out. It wasn't. Nell explained, "The kind of thing that you have to do as an actor is to take these moments and make it believable."

Rusty Salling had to do exactly that in the same play. Mike Beistle was a great practical joker, and everyone knew it. Dan Jesse remembers a scene where Rusty's character has to pick up a box of Cuban cigars and pass them around to his fellow CIA agents. Dan said, "One night, Rusty goes over to pick up the box and he can't. Mike had glued it to the table. Of course, Rusty knows Mike did this. He tries to pull it up, then just grabs a fist full of cigars and hands them out to people, glaring at Mike all the time."

The headline for Arline Greer's review in the Gainesville Sun read, "*Rum and Coke* Often Walks Unsteady Line between Satire, Heavy-handed Moralizing." Her review said, "Many funny scenes... make audiences laugh for the better part of the evening. But when the crunch comes... the play goes flat. *Rum and Coke* is worth seeing for the performances of the Hippodrome's grand old cast. What *Rum and Coke* lacks as a well-constructed socio-comedy, it makes up for in enjoyable acting that provides a generally entertaining evening in the theater."[3]

Rum and Coke ran from March 4–27.

Pump Boys and Dinettes

The fifteenth season ended with the Broadway musical *Pump Boys and Dinettes*. But bringing it to Gainesville wasn't easy. It took the play's director Greg von Hausch three years of begging, pleading, and negotiating with the authors and producers.

When he'd first seen the title, he got the wrong idea. "I was in New York, walking through Times Square," he recalled. "To get to where you're going, you have to pass a lot of little porn theatres. They're all over the place. So I look up and see the marquee on the Princess Theatre, and it says *Pump Boys and Dinettes*. I thought, what a title! The pornography business has hit a new low!"[4]

Contrary to his first impression, there was nothing pornographic about the country-flavored musical set at a roadside diner across the highway from a full-service gas station. The cast of six featured Irene Adjan and Mariah von Hausch as sisters who own the diner, i.e., Dinettes. Guys who work at the station are the Pump Boys, played by Eddie Gwaltney, Matt Morrison, Randy Glass, and Clay Williams. They were also the onstage band.

Pump Boys and Dinettes
played by (l-r) Clay Williams,
Randy Glass, Irene Adjan,
Eddie Gwaltney, Mariah von
Hausch, and Matt Morrison.

Photo: Stephen Morton/*Gainesville Sun.*

Thin on plot and heavy on songs, the show is more a concert than a play. Spoken lines are mere links to the next song. "There's a lot less book to rely on, a lot less story," said actress Irene Adjan. "Usually a play is a lot more structured. This, a lot of it, evolved from our own imaginations."[5]

Pump Boy and guitarist Matt Morrison explained, "You're given the songs and the chords, and that's about it. A lot of the arrangements have been up to us." Matt, who had been in several other productions of *Pump Boys and Dinettes,* said, "The cast literally has to become a band, to think like a musical unit."[6]

That was the job of the musical director, Eddie Gwaltney, who ran the cast through weeks of intense vocal rehearsals. Eddie also played bass and piano onstage as one of the Pump Boys. This was Eddie's twenty-eighth production with the Hippodrome. His own band had performed everywhere from Birmingham to St. Augustine, but he had no aspirations to be an actor. When Greg first suggested Eddie should be in the play, Greg said, "How can you pass this one up? There's a character with no lines who is a bass player named Eddie!"[7]

Musical talent filled the entire cast. Clay, Matt, and Eddie each had country rock bands. Randy was a music major at UF who had played piano in the Hippodrome productions of *A Chorus Line* and *Hair.* Irene had also been in *Hair.* Mariah had been in Broadway and off-Broadway shows and had sung with a music group in New York City.

Given a script with a hazy set of instructions, Greg gladly added his own innovations. He brought the cast onstage ten minutes before curtain and had them mingle with the arriving audience. In character, with laid-on yokel accents, they told corny jokes and gossiped about the other characters, giving the play a homey touch.

The show, conceived and written by John Foley, Mark Hardwick, Debra Monk, Cass Morgan, John Schimmel, and Jim Wann, kept audiences' feet tapping. It opened on April 8 and didn't close until May 15, having been held over two additional weeks.

Resignations and a New CEO

During the run of *Pump Boys and Dinettes,* Hippodrome Board Chairman Charles Holden, Jr., announced that the theatre was advertising nationally for a new chief executive officer. "We want to have one person, instead of two or three people, reporting to the trustees," he told the *Gainesville Sun*.[8]

After the musical closed, Greg von Hausch resigned. "The theatre is going to be hiring a new chief executive officer soon," Greg said, "and I felt that the new person could be more effective and have more freedom if they didn't have to worry about someone second-guessing their actions."[9]

Founding board member Richard Gorenberg called Greg "the heart and soul of the Hippodrome."[10] He also said, "Any success the theatre has had over the last fifteen years has been tied to Greg's talents." Gorenberg also resigned at the same time. He said, "I just felt that when Greg left, I would leave, too. That way they can infuse new blood into the organization."[11]

Greg took a position as executive director for the Tampa Players for a year, then moved to Fort Lauderdale, where he founded an international film festival that continues to the present day. Of the original founders, Mary Hausch remained the sole artistic director, though co-founder Marilyn Wall continued as costume designer until illness forced her to retire in 2017.

Mid-August 1988, the Hippodrome announced they had found their CEO, C. David Black. His theatre credentials were impressive. He had begun his career with Joseph Papp's New York Shakespeare Festival, spending a decade as its general manager. Next, he had managed the Coconut Grove Playhouse, a state theatre like the Hippodrome, and served as the first president of the Florida Professional Theatres Association, which the Hippodrome had helped co-found.

Mary Hausch was optimistic. She said, "I've known David for about twelve years. He is tremendously capable and is a well-respected theatre manager. His having worked with Joseph Papp speaks for itself."[12] In September, Mary's title was changed to Producing Director.

Sixteenth Season

The new CEO announced that since they'd already set the sixteenth season, they would not make any changes to the lineup. Herb Gardner's Tony Award-winning comedy *I'm Not Rappaport*, directed by Mary Hausch, opened the season September 9 and ended up being held over through October 9.

Hippodrome veterans Mark Sexton, Nell Page, Gregg Jones, and Cynthia Leigh Pierson played smaller roles this time. The stars were sixty-year-old David Howard and forty-one-year-old William Hall, Jr., playing octogenarians Nat Moyer, a feisty Jew, and Midge Carter, a cantankerous African American. They spend their day sitting on a bench in New York's Central Park, sharing tall tales that Nat spins while dealing with the problems of aging.

When Midge accuses Nat of lying, Nat explains that he makes "alterations. Sometimes the truth doesn't fit. I let it out and take it in here and there."[13]

Nat (David Howard) and Midge (William Hall, Jr.) have words in *I'm Not Rappaport*.

Photo: Tim Davis/*Gainesville Sun*

The dialogue is funny yet moving and true, touching on society's treatment of the elderly. But it's not all talk. The eccentric old-timers take on a drug dealer, a mugger, and adult children who think they know what's best for their parents. High school students Gus Hughes and Henry Sommerville took turns playing the mugger. Both were veterans of the Hippodrome's teen workshops.

David Howard called it "a beautiful play. It deals with old age within a comical framework. It has warmth and humanity and is all the more beautiful to behold because of it." Asked what he wanted audiences to take from the play, David answered, "I want audiences to go home and think about these people."[14]

Asked the same question, William Hall said, "When the play is over, I'd like the audiences to go out to the box office and renew their subscriptions."[15]

Blue Plate Special

From November 4–27, the Hippodrome served up a delicious *Blue Plate Special* under the direction of James Wren, who had also directed *Hair*. Plot-wise, it resembled the Hipp's 1977 *Soap*, with the actors playing actors on a TV soap opera. But this one had country music composed by Harris Wheeler, with lyrics by Mary L. Fisher, and book by Tom Edwards.

Blue Plate Special originated in an Atlanta supper club, where it played for two years, then had a limited engagement in Manhattan before coming to the Hippodrome. As a soap, Jim Wren said he believed it could hold its own with the likes of actual TV soap operas *Dynasty* or *Search for Tomorrow*.[16]

It certainly had a mix of quirky characters with backstories as convoluted as any long-running soap. Della is a good-hearted, God-fearing cook at the diner where the TV show is set. Della was previously married to Preacher Larry, who died in a

Cast of *Blue Plate Special*: (l-r) Kevin Rainsberger as Ronnie Frank, Gregg Jones as Preacher Larry, Scott Isert as Ricky Jim, Rebecca Hoodwin as Della, Karen Hinton as daughter Ramona, and Jennifer Pritchett as Connie Sue.

Photo: Tim Davis/*Gainesville Sun*

helicopter crash but came back to life. Meanwhile, she'd married Ricky Jim. Her daughter, Ramona, is a rising country singer married to Ronnie Frank, who is determined to punish Ramona's son for murdering Preacher Larry. Toss into the mix Connie Sue Day, a former country music queen fresh out of jail and longing to resume her career.

Critic Arline Greer called the show fun and advised readers, "Just check your brain at the door and let the good times roll. *Blue Plate Special* has... a lively score that's mostly country rock with a little gospel thrown in for a hallelujah-clapping good time... and there isn't a clinker in the bunch. The cast for *Blue Plate Special* puts heart, soul and humor into every line and song. Each of them does first-rate work, singing; dancing; flashing 'who-me?' looks at each other and the audience; making the entire spoof as engaging as it can be."[17]

Marilyn Wall and Leslie Klein had fun with the show's costumes, dressing the country rock queens in flashy outfits with big wigs and ever-larger fake bosoms. "Marilyn really just made my character," Jennifer Pritchett recalled. "In the opening scene, I've just been released from prison. I've got on denim and look pretty drab. Then with each scene, I come out and I have bigger hair, bigger tits, and more glitter."

A New *Christmas Carol*

For its eleventh annual charity production of *A Christmas Carol*, the Hippodrome revamped the show into a musical with music by Jim Wren and lyrics by Carlos Asse, who also directed the show. "I think that the music not only adds to the festivity of the evening, but it really gives a different insight to the different ghosts and characters that have their songs," Jim said.[18]

Carlos promised theatergoers, "Scrooge sounds as grumpy as ever." Kevin Rainsberger, who played Scrooge that year, agreed. "You can be as nasty when you're singing as when you're speaking."[19]

The show ran December 9–18 and had a waitlist for tickets.

1 Arline Greer, review of *So Long on Lonely Street*, by Sandra Deer, directed by Gregory von Hausch, Hippodrome Theatre, Gainesville, FL, *Gainesville Sun*, January 19, 1988.
2 Ibid.
3 Arline Greer, review of *Rum and Coke*, by Keith Reddin, directed by Mary Hausch, Hippodrome Theatre, Gainesville, FL, *Gainesville Sun*, March 9, 1988.
4 "In the Margin," *Gainesville Sun*, May 3, 1988.
5 Bill DeYoung, "The Show Must Go On," *Gainesville Sun*, May 6, 1988.
6 Ibid.
7 *Pump Boys and Dinettes* playbill, Hippodrome Theatre, Gainesville, FL, April 8, 1988.
8 Dave Hunter, "Scene Around," *Gainesville Sun*, April 15, 1988.
9 Dave Hunter, "Hippodrome Founder Leaves Strong Legacy," *Gainesville Sun*, July 1, 1988.
10 Ibid.
11 Ibid.
12 Dave Hunter, "Hippodrome Names New Chief Officer," *Gainesville Sun*, August 17, 1988.
13 Arline Greer, review of *I'm Not Rappaport*, by Herb Gardner, directed by Mary Hausch, Hippodrome Theatre, Gainesville, FL, *Gainesville Sun*, September 16, 1988.
14 Arline Greer, "Nat and Midge Bring Their Act to the Hippodrome," *Gainesville Sun*, September 9, 1988.
15 Ibid.
16 Arline Greer, "Hippodrome Serves a Blue Plate Special," *Gainesville Sun*, November 4, 1988.
17 Arline Greer, review of *Blue Plate Special*, by Tom Edwards, directed by James Wren, Hippodrome Theatre, Gainesville, FL, *Gainesville Sun*, November 11, 1988.
18 Fataima Ahmad, "It's a 'Sing Along with Scrooge' at the Hippodrome," *Gainesville Sun*, December 9, 1988.
19 Ibid.

1989

Talk Radio

In January, Sidney Homan directed Eric Bogosian's *Talk Radio*, which had been nominated for the 1987 Pulitzer Prize. Kevin Rainsberger played Barry Champlain, a verbally abusive Cleveland-area shock jock, on the eve of his radio show's national syndication. Barry's producer, played by Mike Beistle, is afraid Barry will say something that will offend the sponsors. This, of course, makes Barry even more outrageous.

As Barry, Kevin was onstage during the entire show, usually alone, doing what Barry did best: insulting the pathetic souls who called in the middle of the night to sound off. The character says things like, "Everything's screwed up and you like it that way, don't you?" and "You're just a spoiled, spineless little baby," and "You're happiest when others are in pain! And that's where I come in, isn't it?"[1]

The thirty-five callers to his radio show are disembodied voices performed by actors in the theatre's sound/lighting booth. Nell Page was one of them. She said, "In those days, there were no stairs to the booth. So, you'd have to crawl up this ladder and kind of hunch down to get into the booth." And it was crowded. In addition to the techs running lights and sound were Nell's fellow cast members: Dan Jesse, Gregg Jones, and Lauren Caldwell, making her Hippodrome debut.

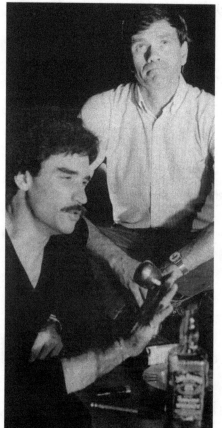

Kevin Rainsberger (left) rehearses a scene from *Talk Radio* with director Sidney Homan (right).

Photo: Spencer Weiner/*Gainesville Sun*.

Lauren remembers, "Those of us who played multiple characters were in the booth and actually talked on the telephone to him in real time. Lysol became very important. After you huddled down, phone in your ear, doing your bit, and then the next person comes up. The Lysol came out, the phones wiped off, so that they can slobber all over it, and so on."

The character of Barry was complex and the role challenging. Kevin and director Sidney Homan began meeting and talking about the character weeks ahead of rehearsal. Kevin recalls, "It was a tough play. There were a lot of big monologs and you had to be in the right frame of mind. Every night before the show, I would get into character by listening to heavy metal, and I don't really like heavy metal."

Most of the cast never appeared onstage until the curtain call. The exceptions were Rusty Salling, Amanda Fry, and John F. Lennon, a theatre student from Middle Tennessee State University. *Talk Radio* opened at the Hippodrome on January 13. As fate would have it, a film version of the play opened the same day. Sid Homan told the *Sun*, "*Talk Radio* is meant for the theatre. Anyone who sees the show and likes the movie better, I'll wash his car."[2] Sid didn't wind up washing any cars. The play ran through February 5.

Except for a bow at the end, Lauren Caldwell was heard but not seen in her first role at the Hippodrome. However, she would appear onstage later that month in the next Hippodrome production, *Absent Friends*. Thus began her thirty-year relationship with the Hippodrome, where she eventually became its sole Artistic Director and a key figure in the theatre's history.

Lauren already had a degree in theatre directing and design from Baylor University and was finishing her master's at UF. Her resume included several stints working for superstar Liza Minnelli. She admits that before she came to Gainesville, she'd never heard of the Hippodrome. At UF, she acted in a production of *The Dining Room* that Mary Hausch and Nell Page attended. She says, "Mary said something to Nell along the lines of, 'I want to know who *she* is.' I got a phone call to audition, and the rest is history."

Absent Friends

Director Mary Hausch cast Lauren Caldwell and UF directing instructor Sandra Langsner alongside Hippodrome stalwarts Kevin, Dan, Rusty, and Nell in *Absent Friends*, the fourth Alan Ayckbourn play the theatre had produced. The previous three were *The Norman Conquests*, *Bedroom Farce*, and *Season's Greetings*. In many ways, *Absent Friends* was similar—three couples, infidelity, fussy mannerisms, and bombastic pomposity.

Diana (Nell Page) is married to Paul (Dan Jesse), a blowhard womanizer who tyrannizes his wife. Small-time hustler John (Kevin Rainsberger) is married to vulgar, gum-chewing Evelyn (Sandra Langsner). Marge (Lauren Caldwell) is married to Gordon, who never actually appears in the play but telephones frequently. They have gathered to comfort their long-absent friend, Colin (Rusty Salling), who returns to the group after the drowning death of his fiancée.

(l-r) Dan Jesse, Sandra Langsner, Rusty Salling, Lauren Caldwell, Nell Page, and Kevin Rainsberger in *Absent Friends*.

Photo: Stephen Morton/*Gainesville Sun*

In her review, Arline Greer thought the characters unlikeable but praised the actors: "Nell Page... makes a wonderfully attractive and hysterical Diana.... Dan Jesse plays Paul the bounder, with just the right blend of bluster, alarm, and ennui. Lauren Caldwell makes a chatty, capable, fix-it-all Marge. As John... Kevin Rainsberger is immensely funny. Sandra Langsner plays Evelyn... with a marvelous understanding.... Rusty Salling has never been funnier."[3]

Carlos Asse's set of an elegant English home was so realistic and beautiful it was used in a fashion shoot for the Style section of the *Gainesville Sun*. The show ran from February 24–March 19.

Back to Brighton

In April, Carlos took the helm, directing *Broadway Bound*, the third and final installment of Neil Simon's autobiographical trilogy, following *Brighton Beach Memoirs* and *Biloxi Blues*, which Carlos had also directed. He said that *Broadway Bound* required the same set as he'd created for *Brighton Beach Memoirs*. That would save money. But he didn't know the Hippodrome had struck the *Brighton* set, so they had to rebuild it anyway.

Photo: Stephen Morton/*Gainesville Sun*

Peter Bauer as Eugene and Lauren Klein as Kate in *Broadway Bound*.

The story starts with Simon's alter ego Eugene, played this time by Pete Bauer, living back at his parents' home in Brighton Beach after serving in the army. He and brother Stanley (James Wren) are working to become radio show comedy writers. After they discover that their father (Frank Biancamano) has been cheating on their mother (Lauren Klein), their short, comic radio sketches begin to make fun of their own family. Their father hears the broadcasts, picks up on the similarities, and becomes outraged. Eventually, he moves out. Later, Eugene and Stanley get great offers and become successful, as did Neil Simon.

Frank Biancamano knew a thing or two about playing a father in a comedy, having performed the role of the father in the Broadway production of *Gemini* for two years.

Also in the cast were Herbert Rubens as the grandfather and Lynn Rudner Jamieson as Blanche, the brothers' matron aunt. Early Hippodromer Chad Reed did the voice of the radio play announcer.

Arline Greer's review was effusive: "Every once in a while, one of those moments comes along in theatre when everything works: play, production, direction, acting. It is then the theatre's legendary magic takes hold of an audience and lifts it right out of itself. Such a moment... is to be savored at the Hippodrome Theatre, where Neil Simon's *Broadway Bound* is on stage. A beautifully written play, directed with loving care for its human values by Carlos Asse."[4]

Broadway Bound opened April 14 and was held over two extra weeks, closing May 21, 1989.

Goodbye Mr. Black

During the run of *Broadway Bound*, C. David Black, the CEO the Board of Trustees had hired nine months earlier, left. Chairman of the Board Jim Fort said, "There is no search [for a replacement] going on. These are very competent people running the theatre now, so we don't really feel an urgent need to rush out and make a decision on anyone."[5]

A Walk in the Woods

Another change: the play scheduled to close the sixteenth season, *Laughing Wild*, was replaced with a two-character play, *A Walk in the Woods* by Lee Blessing. It was cheaper to produce, with just two actors and a simpler set. Hippodrome Director of Marketing Joe Buonfiglio put a positive spin on it: "The play just became available, so we grabbed it."[6]

Photo: Stephen Morton/*Gainesville Sun*.

A Walk in the Woods takes place during the arms race between the United States and Russia. Frank Biancamano (who played the father in *Broadway Bound*) was Andrey Botvinnik, the Russian negotiator, and Kevin Rainsberger played his American counterpart. The two men meet in the woods—away from the conference table—to find out what's really going on in each other's minds. Kevin remembers it as a "super-well-written show, but unfortunately it's a dated play now [that the Cold War is over]."

Kevin Rainsberger and Frank Biancamano in *A Walk in the Woods*.

The show, directed by Mary Hausch, ran from June 7–July 2. On June 22, in the true spirit of the play, sixteen Soviet citizens—part of the Sister City program—attended *A Walk in the Woods* and stayed after the performance to meet the people of Gainesville. Back in 1982, Gainesville had become the first US city to form a relationship with a Soviet city, Novorossiisk, USSR. The goal of the Sister City program, to promote ties between individual citizens rather than governments, perfectly matched the theme of the play.

Season Seventeen

Michael Crider as the wicked Valmont schemes with equally despicable Marquise de Merteuil (Nell Page) in *Les Liaisons Dangereuses*.

In September, Mary Hausch directed *Les Liaisons Dangereuses*, a Tony-nominated play by Christopher Hampton based on an eighteenth-century French novel by Pierre Choderlos de Laclos.

It is the story of two narcissistic aristocrats, Vicomte de Valmont and Marquise de Merteuil. The two are former lovers, now rivals, who use sex as a weapon of humiliation and degradation, all the while enjoying their cruel games and boasting about their talent for manipulation.

Valmont (Michael Crider) is determined to seduce the virtuous Madame de Tourvel (Leslie Witt). The equally despicable Merteuil (Nell Page) is determined to corrupt young Cécile (Sunday Theodore), whose mother (Lauren Caldwell) has brought her out of the convent to marry one of Merteuil's previous lovers, on whom Merteuil wants revenge. To get it, she wants Valmont to take Cécile's virginity.

Photo: Gary Wolfson

Their schemes and manipulations are documented in an exchange of letters. The rivalry ramps up to the point that Valmont is fatally wounded in a duel after making public Merteuil's letters, destroying her reputation.

Of the play, Arline Greer said, "It has the ability to take hold of viewers and, almost against their will, pull them into those decadent games, played by a decadent society."[7] She called Nell's acting "Brilliant... every inch the grand manipulator; cool, detached, the supreme lady, the supreme predator. She commands the stage with a cold fury that grabs an audience and twists it in her grip.... Michael Crider, who as Valmont, gives an incredible performance... Charming, insidious, beguiling, unyielding."[8]

Besides the actors previously mentioned, several smaller roles were played by Sandra Langsner, Rusty Salling, Michael Johnson, David Shatraw, and Jane Davis. *Les Liaisons Dangereuses* ran a full month, opening September 8 and closing October 8 after a week's extension.

The Boys Next Door

Next up was *The Boys Next Door,* Tom Griffin's play about four mentally challenged men living in a group home. Under Carlos Asse's direction, it did "what few, if any, dramas with a social message are capable of accomplishing. It mixes comedy and pathos in just the right balance to make audiences laugh and weep," wrote Arline Greer.[9]

The *Independent Florida Alligator* said Carlos "did a great job of both amusing the audience and heightening their awareness of these struggling survivors. The play effectively delivers sensitive material with comic relief, a delicate balancing act."[10]

Carlos also cast it well, populating his characters with skilled comedic talent. Rusty Salling played fussy, confused, paranoid Arnold. Michael Beistle as Norman, an overgrown child obsessed with doughnuts, was both loveable and hilarious. Michael Johnson played Barry, a schizophrenic who thinks he's a golf pro. Simplest of the four is Lucien (Larry Venson), whose mental acuity one character describes as "somewhere between a five-year-old and an oyster."[11] Kathy Tyrell played Norman's girlfriend, who is both physically and mentally challenged.

Caring for his charges at the group home is Jack, a social worker (played by Tom Nowicki) who finds his patience slowly running out. Playing three roles each were Dan Jesse and Martie McLean. Mitchell Carrey played Barry's father, who doesn't arrive until near the end of the play.

The Boys Next Door ran from October 27–November 19.

December 1989

From December 8–17 the Hippodrome continued its tradition of producing *A Christmas Carol* to support the Salvation Army and Toys for Tots.

On December 27, Mark Sexton, newly appointed Director of Development, announced that the scheduled play for January, *Burn This*, was being replaced by *The Mystery of Irma Vep*. "We had two pretty heavy plays in a row," Mark explained. "We'd been looking at this new play, and the rights came open. We thought it would make a nice change of pace."[12]

1 Eric Bogosian, *Talk Radio* (New York: Samuel French, 1988),

2 Arline Greer, "Speaking out on *Talk Radio*," *Gainesville Sun*, January 13, 1989.

3 Arline Greer, review of *Absent Friends*, *Gainesville Sun*, March 3, 1989.

4 Arline Greer, review of *Broadway Bound*, by Neil Simon, directed by Carlos Asse, Hippodrome Theatre, Gainesville, FL, *Gainesville Sun*, April 19, 1989.

5 Dave Hunter, "Hippodrome Won't Rush to Find a New Director," *Gainesville Sun*, May 12, 1989.

6 Ibid.

7 Arline Greer, review of *Les Liaisons Dangereuses*, by Christopher Hampton, directed by Mary Hausch, Hippodrome Theatre, Gainesville, FL, *Gainesville Sun*, September 15, 1989.

8 Ibid.

9 Arline Greer, review of *The Boys Next Door*, by Tom Griffin, directed by Carlos Asse, Hippodrome Theatre, Gainesville, FL, *Gainesville Sun*, November 1, 1989.

10 Susan Calvert and David Mann, review of *The Boys Next Door*, by Tom Griffin, directed by Carlos Asse, Hippodrome Theatre, Gainesville, FL, *Independent Florida Alligator*, November 9, 1989.

11 Ibid.

12 "New Hippodrome Play," *Gainesville Sun*, December 27, 1989.

1990

Vampire by Any Name

On January 12, 1990, the Hippodrome opened *The Mystery of Irma Vep* by Charles Ludlam following preview performances the preceding two nights. The play had been voted Best Play of the Year by *Time Magazine* and the *New York Times* and had won two Obie Awards. It was described as a psychosexual tour de force.

The play takes place in the 1890s in the library drawing room at an English estate and at various places in Egypt. Lord Edgar and Lady Enid find themselves taunted by Irma Vep, a jealous vampire, not to mention a werewolf with a wooden leg, a deceptive mummy of an Egyptian Goddess, and a mysterious intruder.

Photo: Spencer Weiner/*Gainesville Sun.*

Irma Vep (Kevin Rainsberger) frightens Lady Enid (Gregg Jones) in *The Mystery of Irma Vep.*

At the Hipp, two male actors performed quick changes to portray eight characters, male and female. Kevin Rainsberger played Egyptologist Lord Edgar; Lady Irma Vep, his deceased first wife; Jane, an outspoken maid; and a mysterious intruder. Gregg Jones played the new wife, Lady Enid; Nicodemus, the servant/werewolf; Egyptian guide Alcazar; and mummy goddess Pev Amri. The changes were indeed fast. Just seconds after Kevin exited dressed as the maid, he returned attired as a proper English gentleman, Lord Edgar. Gregg, as servant Nicodemus, limped offstage, dragging his wooden leg, and seconds later reappeared with blonde curls as Lady Enid. For nearly three hours, the two actors brilliantly moved in and out of their various characters with split-second timing. They didn't just switch costumes but also voices, demeanor, and personalities.

Gregg said, "I call it aerobic theatre because it was—literally. We got it down to five-second costume changes. Going from a cockney footman to Lady Edith, who talked way up here [in a high register]. Going back and forth, from this one to that one, over and over. Instantly changing the costumes and the wigs. We would just be cracking up backstage, having wig mishaps and all kinds of stuff. But that was a great, fun, fun play with Kevin Rainsberger."

Director Mary Hausch said, "*The Mystery of Irma Vep* combines all the elements of theatre that gave the early Hippodrome its reputation for wild, eccentric, visually stimulating and highly physical theatrical productions."[1]

Arline Greer called it "deftly crafted suspense comedy... as complex a pot-boiler as you're likely to encounter." She continued, "Ludlum's gift for dramatic invention is prodigious, equal to his gift for satire and for tossing out one-liners that are hilarious.... Pure talent on the part of Kevin Rainsberger and Gregory Jones makes for a tour de force quite unlike anything the Hippodrome has produced in its 17-years' history."[2]

The Mystery of Irma Vep ran at the Hippodrome through February 4 and then played another sold-out performance in Ocala at the end of the month.

Finacial Woes

The show may have done well, but the theatre was financially ill. Three days before *Irma Vep* opened, a newspaper headline read, "For Want of $100,000 Hippodrome May Close."[3] Hippodrome Board Chairman Jim Fort told the paper, "It's very serious... we're not crying wolf.... If we don't raise $35,000 in the next two weeks, the Hippodrome will basically be out of business. We will not be able to meet our payroll. We will not be able to meet our obligations."[4] Even if the theatre got the $35,000 in the short term, it needed $100,000 by June. A change in rules, preventing official state theatres from receiving certain additional state grants, had lost them $200,000. Their inability to broaden their base of subscribers and donors compounded their cash-flow problem Unlike comparable theatres in places like Louisville and Cincinnati, who received donations from major local employers like Humana and Proctor and Gamble, the Hippodrome's donors were small business-es—there were no major corporations locally.

The budget for that year was $775,000—cut from $1.1 million in an attempt to keep the theatre alive. Mainstage productions, cinema, and Theatre for Young Audience tours earned about half of that. Their place as a State Theatre brought in another $150,000. The rest had to come from donors to replace the lost grants.

Hours after the story appeared in the local newspaper, businesses who were members of the Downtown Owners and Tenants Association collectively pledged $14,000. Gainesville area radio stations banded together to air free public service announcements soliciting donations for the theatre and to advertise the January play. People responded, and the Hippodrome raised enough to hang on through its next production, *Romance / Romance*.

The Show Must Go On

Romance / Romance, a musical with book and lyrics by Barry Harman and music by Keith Herrmann, had won the New York Drama Desk Award for Best Musical two years prior. Carlos Asse designed a simple set and directed the cast of four: Steve Grojahn, Ellen Sachos, Wendy Woods, and J. Jonathan Austin. Judy Skinner, founder and director of Dance Alive, did the choreography.

The show was actually two musicals. Each of the actors played one character in the first act and a different character in the second. Act one, set in 1900s Vienna, was based on a short story by Arthur Schnitzler. A bored, attractive man of the world, tired of rich Viennese women, disguises himself as a poor artist. A rich woman, also bored, pretends to be a poor milliner searching for love. Inevitably, the two meet and fall in love with their false personas. The other two actors shadow their interactions with dance and song.

Act two takes place in the present day and is based on Jules Renard's play *Le Pain de Ménage.* Two couples, good friends, share a vacation beach house in the Hamptons and sing fourteen more songs. Arline Greer summed it up: "All together, *Romance/*

Romance is as refreshing as the summer breeze that blows through its second act and as charming as the operetta-like spoof in its first act."[5]

A unique fact about the play was that the Hippodrome staged it at UF's Constans Theatre. Judith Williams, newly arrived Chair of the UF Theatre Department, and Mary Hausch proposed swapping theatres. Judith was directing *Come Back to the Five and Dime, Jimmy Dean, Jimmy Dean*, a drama she thought would work better in the Hippodrome's more intimate setting. Likewise, the large dance numbers in *Romance / Romance* would benefit from a bigger space. In no time, the deal was in place.

Come Back to the Five and Dime, Jimmy Dean, Jimmy Dean was Lauren Caldwell's acting thesis for her master's degree. "I loved doing [the play] at the Hippodrome," Lauren recalled. "The smaller space really gave a sense of the tiny Texas diner where the play took place."

Romance/Romance opened at the Constans Theatre on February 16 and closed March 7, four days early to save money.

Desparate Measures

From the end of January through May, a weekly stream of letters to the editor appeared in the *Gainesville Sun* criticizing the Hippodrome's choice of plays and pointing out that theatergoers unhappy with plays would not make willing donors. Other writers responded in the Hippodrome's defense, touting its successes.

On February 28, a local businessman and Hippodrome board member was named Interim Managing Director. He resigned after one week. At issue was his proposal that the theatre cancel the season's remaining shows and regroup. The Board unanimously voted against it. Fellow board member Beverly Browning replaced him.

By March 2, the theatre had raised $43,000, but that was still a long way from $100,000. Cox Cable offered to broadcast a Hippothon, a twelve-hour live fundraiser similar to those frequently seen on PBS. They also held a subscription drive and staged a special family show at UF's auditorium, *The Wolf, Three Pigs, and Red Riding Hood*, a musical fairy tale written by Margaret Bachus and Kevin Rainsberger with music by Eddie Gwaltney.

Adding another blow to their budget woes, the Gainesville City Manager asked the City Commission to cut funding to "outside agencies" like food banks and cultural groups. The Hippodrome received $23,000 a year from the city. What would fill that hole? Mary Hausch pointed out, "The Hippodrome brings 500 visitors a night downtown from Thursdays through Saturdays, and 300 visitors a night on other days. Those visitors mean some $3 million annually to the city's economy, particularly Gainesville's struggling downtown area."[6]

The *Gainesville Sun* sponsored a Hippodrome Walk-A-Thon in which participants got people to pledge a certain amount for each mile the participant walked. It was held on Paynes Prairie. A free picnic lunch was provided and there were prizes for walkers who got the most pledges. Art auctions and other fundraising events continued throughout the spring.

A Road Paved with Turmoil

Hippodrome co-founder Kerry McKenney, who had left in 1985, returned to direct *The Road to Mecca* by South African playwright Athol Fugard. The play had won the 1988 New York Drama Critic's Circle Award for Best Foreign Play. It was also economical, with only a three-person cast.

Miss Helen, an eccentric widow living in a conservative South African village, has been working on an overgrown sculpture garden of concrete animal figures all pointing toward Mecca. Pastor Marius urges Helen to move into a home for the aged. However, Elsa, a schoolteacher played by Nell Page, travels from Cape Town to see Helen's art and encourages her to continue.

Photo: Jon Killen/*Gainesville Sun*

In *The Road to Mecca*, Pastor Marius (David Rogers) implores Miss Helen (Dana Moser) to move into a home for the aged.

The set is the interior of Helen's home, a temple of light; scenic designer Carlos Asse achieved this with ground glass, mirrors, and myriad candles. The audience never sees the sculpture garden, but Nell's character describes it so passionately, it is as if they have.

The script, addressing artistic freedom, human values, bigotry, love, friendship, and reasons for being, was excessively wordy. Too wordy for the New York actress originally cast as Helen. "She was completely miscast," Nell said. "She was not very good and was having a hard time learning her lines. Because she was an Equity actor, you can't just fire them. So Kerry announced during rehearsal that the next day this other actress and I were to be onstage in front of a panel to see how many lines we knew, and then they would decide our fate. I knew it was about her, but I was freaking out because I thought she probably knows as many lines as I do. So I got an intern and Kevin [Rainsberger] to help me run my lines. They ended up firing her a week before we opened."

Dana Moser, the original actress's last-minute replacement, said the fact that the other actress couldn't remember her lines "should've been a red warning to me. It was a three-person play and there were times when you had page after page after page of monologue. The reason I said I'd do it was the Hippodrome was in financial problems at that time. I thought, well, I can help them out this way."

Broadway playwright David Rogers had the role of Pastor Marius. "David was an author, a playwright," Dana said, "so I thought, 'He'll know his lines.'" He never did. "It was a terrifying experience."

Nell recalled that in David's opening scene, he was to toss a potato in the air, catch it, and say his first line. "Night after night, he would just throw that potato over and over, not saying anything. Dana and I would be dying." As a joke, she and Dana had T-shirts made that read "Better you than me."

The Road to Mecca ran from April 13–May 6. After it closed, Dana needed surgery for a condition caused by stress.

Daisy Saves the Day

Two out-of-town actors brought in for the final play of the season, Alfred Uhry's *Driving Miss Daisy*, were as professional as they come. Joining one of the Hippodrome's favorite actors, Rusty Salling, were Janis Benson and William Hall, Jr. Both had decades of theatre experience. Audiences saw stunning performances from everyone in the three-person cast, who not only knew their lines but expressed the nuance of every line with just the right feeling.

Janis Benson as Daisy and William Hall, Jr. as Hoke in *Driving Miss Daisy*.

The story revolves around the twenty-five-year relationship of Miss Daisy, a cantankerous elderly Southern widow, and Hoke, the Black chauffeur her son hired after she crashed her car.

William Hall, Jr., who had played the elderly Midge in the Hippodrome's production of *I'm Not Rappaport*, had just spent twenty months playing Hoke at Atlanta's Alliance Theatre.

Janis Benson (Daisy) had most recently acted at the Asolo State Theatre in Sarasota, but her long international theatrical career included performances in Nairobi, Rio de Janeiro, Stockholm, and Paris.

"A better production of *Driving Miss Daisy* than the one mounted at the Hippodrome is hard to imagine," wrote Arline Greer. "Those who have seen other editions of the Pulitzer Prize-winning play, or the Oscar-winning film, have a fresh treat in store for them in the Hippodrome's presentation.... *Driving Miss Daisy* makes us realize once more how good theater defines, illuminates, and enriches our lives."[7]

Driving Miss Daisy, directed by Mary Hausch, was a crowd-pleaser that had to be held over. It ran from June 8–July 8, and probably could have continued longer, except for some pesky fire safety rules.

Environmental and Fire Safety Upgrades

The 1911 building had to be closed while a contractor removed asbestos from its hot water pipes. Then, to bring it up to fire code safety requirements, a sprinkler system and outside fire escapes were added. Fortunately, the renovations and upgrades to the cash-strapped theatre were covered by a grant from the Historic Preservation Board. Still, being shuttered all of July and August meant the Hippodrome lost the revenue it would have earned from summer workshops, cinema, and an extended run of *Driving Miss Daisy*.

Education Department Cuts

During the closure, theatre management raised ticket prices, made staff changes, and enacted further financial cuts, eliminating all the children's programs except the Hippodrome Improvisational Teen Theatre (HITT). Lauren Caldwell became HITT's director. The successful touring program for young audiences, Creative Stages, was offloaded to Margaret Bachus and Kevin Rainsberger, who had written most of its plays.

Audiences were allowed back in September, even though construction wasn't totally completed.

Fear Thick as Quicksand

It is a rare and wretched experience when fear becomes so palpable one can actually feel it in the air. Yet that is exactly what happened to Gainesville in late August.

The Hippodrome was in rehearsals for *Steel Magnolias*, which was slated to reopen the theatre on September 3, when the news reported that two UF freshman coeds were found in their apartment on August 27, brutally slain and mutilated.

The next day, a third female victim was discovered. A day later, two more students were horribly murdered. Then the killings stopped, but the trauma caused by serial killer Danny Rolling shrouded the city in panic. Rumors flooded the streets like the aftermath of a hurricane, ramping up anxiety. Parents withdrew their daughters from college and took them home. Half the cast of *Steel Magnolias*, all out-of-town actresses, abruptly quit the show and left Gainesville.

For readers who don't know about Rolling, he was identified as the murderer and indicted a year later. The killings had stopped because he'd been arrested for robbing an Ocala supermarket and held in the Marion County jail since September 7, 1990. He was tried on five counts of murder, convicted, and executed four years later.

Women of Steel Open Season Eighteen

The female characters in Robert Harling's *Steel Magnolias* are strong, and so were the women of Gainesville's acting community. Down three actors, director Mary Hausch postponed the opening for a week and called actresses she knew had the professional-level experience the roles demanded. Jennifer Pritchett, then teaching drama at Santa Fe Community College, agreed to play the daughter, Shelby. UF theatre professors Judith Midyett and Melissa Hart signed on to play Ouiser and Clairee. Before coming to UF, Judith had acted in theatres across the US. Melissa, a Broadway actress, had once been nominated for a Tony Award.

Steel Magnolias is very much an ensemble piece—its characters are six Southern women of three generations. Mary's challenge was to meld her three replacements with the highly capable original cast members who'd stayed. They had to perform as women who'd known each other their whole lives. And they only had a week to do it.

Photo: Randy Batista

The women of *Steel Magnolias*: (l-r) Nell Page, Lauren Caldwell, Jennifer Pritchett, Judith Midyett, Melissa Hart, and Janis Benson.

The setting is Truvy's, a small-town beauty parlor where the women regularly gather to gossip and talk about their men. Lauren Caldwell played Truvy and Nell Page was her assistant, Annelle. The story spans three years, starting with the impending nuptials of Shelby (Jennifer Pritchett), then jumping forward in time to her decision to have a child. Her mother, played by Janis Benson, worries that Shelby's Type 1 diabetes makes pregnancy too risky. The town matriarchs, Ouiser and Clairee, frequently put in their two cents with biting one-liners. It's all great fun until Shelby's kidneys fail.

Mary Hausch said, "The play begins with six strong women, Steel Magnolias, talking about life and love. The play ends with a strong sense of community and the triumph of the human spirit. It is a high-spirited comedy that allows for hysterical laughter but also explores the other end of the spectrum."[8]

"This play... is about friendship," Jennifer Pritchett said, "the need to live life to the fullest; getting on with the business of living; and dealing with grief, is so timely for our community, considering all that's gone on. It allows people to laugh and cry, and cry again. In theatre, any time you can touch people, that's great."[9]

Janis Benson, one of the actresses who stayed, said she thought the Hippodrome's production would help to heal the community. She said, "*Steel Magnolias* can offer a catharsis to audiences."[10]

Nell and Jennifer both laugh about the night a patron in the front row knocked over a shelf that held shampoo, beauty parlor potions, and beverages. Diabetic Shelby's orange juice spilled all over the stage.

"I can just hear [Lauren] running across the stage," Nell said. "She was just in a panic."

Jennifer recalled, "Nell, without missing a beat, goes, 'Oh, Truvy, I'm so sorry.' She went behind the stage, somehow manifested a mop, and started cleaning up the orange juice as part of her character."

The use of humor and lighthearted conversations to cope with the seriousness of the underlying situations proved to be exactly what audiences needed to relieve the prevailing state of fear in Gainesville that September. Although the show opened a week late, September 11, its popularity caused it to be held over until October 7.

Don't Cry for *Evita*

After two blockbusters in a row and with their finances in the black, the Hippodrome was ready to try a bigger show. At the time, nothing was bigger than Tim Rice and Andrew Lloyd Webber's Tony Award-winning musical *Evita*. Director Carlos Asse called it "a powerful dramatic modern opera that will enchant, and at the same time move us."[11] The story follows Argentine political leader Eva Perón's early life, rise to power, charity work, and death.

Photo: Randy Batista

Entire cast in a scene from *Evita*.

To accommodate nineteen singing, dancing actors, the Hippodrome again chose to stage it at the larger Florida Theatre. The move also allowed Carlos to start rehearsals and sets while *Steel Magnolias* continued at the Hippodrome. Wendy Woods, who'd taught dance professionally since age fifteen, handled the choreography. Beth Nolan, Music Director for the theatre department at Santa Fe Community College, served as the play's musical director and conducted its orchestra.

Carlos filled the lead roles with experienced musical theatre talent. Chevy Anz, who played Eva, and Ricky Russell, as Che, had both performed those roles previously. In the role of Juan Perón was David Kelso. Kathy Tyrell played Perón's mistress. John D'Angese, a talented tenor, portrayed popular Argentine singer-songwriter Agustín Magaldi, who gave Eva her start. A chorus of ten adults and four children, symbolizing the people of Argentina, sang and danced in big production numbers.

The show opened on October 19. Arline Greer called it "a triumph... dazzling for both the eye and ear.... an exciting musical spectacle."[12] Even with the larger 750-seat Florida Theatre, *Evita* had to be held over until November 11.

Chevy Anz as Eva Perón in *Evita*.

Photo: Randy Batista

A Historic Role

A significant marker in the history of the Hippodrome's annual charity production of *A Christmas Carol* occurred in 1990. Rusty Salling, who had played Bob Cratchit for eleven years, decided to try his hand as Scrooge. He loved it, and audiences loved his portrayal of the crusty old miser. For the rest of his career, Rusty annually brought forth Scrooge, honing the character to perfection. Over the years, the Hippodrome changed versions of the script many times, but until 2015, Rusty's Scrooge was always at the center.

Tiny Tim (Kjell Ryerson) sits on the shoulder of Bob Cratchit (Michael McLane) with Rusty Salling in his first year playing Scrooge.

Photo: Stephen Morton/*Gainesville Sun*

1 *The Mystery of Irma Vep* playbill, Hippodrome Theatre, Gainesville, FL, January 12, 1990.
2 Arline Greer, review of *The Mystery of Irma Vep*, by Charles Ludlam, directed by Mary Hausch, Hippodrome Theatre, Gainesville, FL, *Gainesville Sun*, January 17, 1990.
3 Mitch Stacy, "For Want of $100,000 Hippodrome May Close," *Gainesville Sun*, January 9, 1990.
4 Ibid.
5 Arline Greer, review of *Romance/Romance*, by Barry Harman, directed by Carlos Asse, Hippodrome Theatre, Gainesville, FL, *Gainesville Sun*, February 21, 1990.
6 Cheryl Thompson, "Agencies Fear City's Ax on Funds," *Gainesville Sun*, March 30, 1990.
7 Arline Greer, review of *Driving Miss Daisy*, by Alfred Uhry, directed by Mary Hausch, Hippodrome Theatre, Gainesville, FL, *Gainesville Sun*, June 13, 1990.
8 *Steel Magnolias* playbill, Hippodrome Theatre, Gainesville, FL, September 11, 1990.
9 Arline Greer, "The Ladies at Truvy's Pull Together," *Gainesville Sun*, September 7, 1990.
10 Ibid.
11 *Evita* playbill, Hippodrome Theatre, Gainesville, FL, October 19, 1990.
12 Arline Greer, review of *Evita*, by Tim Rice, directed by Carlos Asse, Hippodrome Theatre, Gainesville, FL, *Gainesville Sun*, October 26, 1990.

1990–2022 Children's Workshops and HITT

Origin of HITT

The Hippodrome's 1990 cost-cutting measures, which resulted in splitting off the Creative Stages touring program as its own company, had left the Education Department without a director and eliminated Theatre for Young Audiences (TYA).

Mary Hausch then redefined the role of the Education Department and applied for a grant to reach at-risk youth. Back in 1985, she, Rena Carney, Marilyn Wall, and Denise Matthews had pioneered the Gainesville Area Improvisational Teen Theatre program. In 1990, they renamed it Hippodrome Improvisational Teen Theatre (HITT) and appointed Lauren Caldwell to run it. Besides HITT, the only remaining part of the original Education Department was the acting workshops. So, for the time being, Mary managed those.

In 1987, Mary Hausch, Marilyn Wall, and Rena Carney (not shown) received the Margaret Sanger award for developing the Hippodrome's GAITT program.

In the summer of 1990, HITT made a video about drugs and alcohol to be shown to teenagers at a runaway shelter, and they also performed at a camp in Ocala.

In 1991, Mary asked Lauren Caldwell to be head of the Education Department. Lauren agreed to the job, so long as she could also direct mainstage productions. During the summer of 1991, she and Marilyn Wall conducted two HITT programs at a halfway house for teenagers. The teens then presented what they had learned on the Hippodrome's Second Stage. That October, Lauren also got to direct *Accomplice*, her first play for mainstage Hippodrome audiences.

Teen Playwright Festival

With the theatre's finances improving, 1992 saw several innovations in the Education Department. While HITT programs continued, the Hippodrome also inaugurated its first-ever Teen Playwright Festival, a competition for teenagers nineteen or younger. The winning plays were produced on the Second Stage. Also, Lauren and Marilyn Wall started day camps for students to learn theatrical skills at the Hippodrome during summer break. Parents paid tuition, and the camps (which still continue as of 2023) earned money. In later years, additional camps were added for spring and winter breaks, and Nell Page took over from Mary Hausch as Workshop Director.

"We've done a lot of really wonderful work," Lauren said. "Our Education Department remained very full, not only with the touring programs but with the at-risk programs and all of those fabulous programs that were started by Mary writing a grant [application]."

Education Department Expands

Gabrielle Byam, who became Director of Education in 2013 and still holds the position as of 2023, first joined the Education Department when a friend of hers, who appeared in the 1992 mainstage production of *Nunsense*, suggested she would be a good fit. She started working part-time, but her HITT position soon became full-time alongside Marcia Brown, Sandra Dietel, and Bonnie Harrison. Bonnie joined the Hippodrome in June 1992 as an intern, but after her internship finished, she became Workshop Director in the fall of 1993, replacing Nell.

A revamped HITT took techniques from Augusto Boal's Theatre of the Oppressed into Loften High, Eastside High, and a charter school named Hogtown High. They'd ask students to describe a time when they felt oppressed, pressured to have sex, or use drugs. Then students acted out the scene, stopping at the point where trouble was about to happen and asking if anybody in the audience had an idea of how this character could make it come out differently. They used pretest and posttest surveys to measure attitude/behavior changes.

Participants in a HITT program.

Eventually, they added a whole new component to HITT—peer education. Research showed that students responded well to peers who were slightly older. "So, that became a kind of rehearsed improv," Gabrielle said. "We'd rehearse and rehearse their stories and when they were done, we'd take that into another school and have [them teach] younger students."

TYA Restarted

In the fall of 1993, the Hippodrome got a grant from Gainesville Regional Utilities (GRU) to write plays about recycling and tour them throughout Alachua County Schools. Lauren and David Boyce co-wrote *EcoHeroes*, the first of four they would produce for GRU, and started a new TYA program. But this iteration of TYA was different due to the cost-cutting measures in place. Lauren recalled, "The Hippodrome made the [new] TYA a non-Equity program. When [the former] TYA was an Equity program, UF theatre graduates were eager to work in those plays. Because you got your Equity card immediately, you were paid a good salary, and all the Equity rules had to be applied to you. [Once] it became a nonunion tour program, we began to hire acting interns to be in those shows."

By 1994, Lauren was regularly directing mainstage productions, so in September, Bonnie Harrison was made Assistant Director of Education and took over as Director of Education the following March. Bonnie remained in that position until 2003, when she became a teacher at Douglas Anderson School of the Arts in Jacksonville.

EcoHeros cast: (l-r) Jolynn Graham Keith, Richard Davis as Zelnar, and Jamie Stevens.

In 1995, at the National Service-Learning Conference in Philadelphia, First Lady Hillary Clinton presented HITT with the first-place award naming it the nation's best program of its kind. The program expanded into the Caribbean when Mary Hausch and Bonnie Harrison took HITT to Antigua in 1996. In subsequent years, HITT's outreach expanded to eight Caribbean nations.

From January through February 1996, the TYA program toured David Boyce's adaptation of *Alice in Wonderland* to schools in twelve Florida counties. The play had inaugurated the Hippodrome's mainstage Family Performance Series back in 1994. TYA also toured its second play about recycling, *4 Our Planet*, under a grant from GRU. In 1997, they toured *An Enchanted Land*, a one-woman show about Marjorie Kinnan Rawlings by Mary Hausch that starred Sara Morsey. In 1998, the City of Gainesville and the Department of Cultural Affairs funded two TYA shows. *To Be or Not To Be . . . that is two questions*, an original play by Lauren Caldwell based on *Hamlet*, and *The Canta Danca Dancer*, written by Ric Rose.

Cast of *To Be or Not To Be . . . That Is Two Questions.*

In 2000, TYA toured elementary schools with *Radio Active*, an original play by Lauren Caldwell about music. "In a lot of outlying schools, there are no programs for music and theatre," Marcia Brown told the *Gainesville Sun*. "There's been a great response to our program."[1] Actor Kim Kuykendall added, "When you put on a performance and see their little faces light up, you just can't beat that."[2]

Summer Spectaculars

Each year, the Education Department's Summer Spectacular camps culminated with the production of a show large enough for all the kids to participate in. In 1995, they did *The Sound of Music*. For 1996, it was *The Wizard of Oz*, then *Jungle Book* in 1997, which was reprised in 2007 and 2014. In 1998, they did *A Midsummer Night's Dream*, and in 1999 *The Chronicles of Narnia*. For 2000, the kids performed *Dreamcatcher*, and in 2001, *Charlie and the Chocolate Factory*.

After Bonnie Harrison's departure in 2003, the position of director remained vacant until March 2004, when Kelly Dugan became director. Sandra Dietel also left, and Jen Tyler joined education associates Marcia Brown and Gabrielle Byam.

In 2004, when Gabrielle Byam was director of the Summer Spectacular camp, she had so many children attending that she needed to stage three productions. Two casts performed *Tangled Tales*, an original play written by Marilyn Wall for the Family Performance Series back in 1995. One cast was directed by Samantha Sudduth and the other by Tharon Moore (both were interns). The third production that summer was a re-staging of David Mamet's *The Revenge of the Space Pandas or Binky Rudich and the Two-Speed Clock* directed by Gabrielle Byam. Regular subscribers in the 1980–81 season had not liked the play, but this time, performed by children for children, it worked.

In 2005, the kids performed an original script by Lauren Caldwell, *Red! Red! Red! What Does the Future Hold?*, plus two versions of *Peter Pan*. Other Summer Spectacular plays have included *The Hobbit* (2003 and 2013); *The Odyssey, 40 Thieves*, and *Snow Angel* (all three in 2007); *Holes* (2008); and *The Adventures of Babar* and *The Midwife's Apprentice* (both in 2009).

Kelly Dugan remained director until 2007. Kara Winslow joined the department as an associate that year, and Jasmin Robinson took over as Director of Education. In 2008, Jasmin handed the reins to Tiffany Dunn, who was followed in 2009 by Kimberley Alderson. Kara Winslow left the department to become the Hippodrome's Director of Development.

In 2010, Kim Berry became Director of Education and remained so until 2012. Katherine Delvaux was added as Education Outreach Coordinator in 2012, but after Kim Berry's departure, no replacement director was named. Marcia Brown and Gabrielle Byam continued their work as Theatre Educators and Prevention Specialists.

Julian Boal Workshop

Since HITT's techniques were based on Augusto Boal's Theatre of the Oppressed, they felt particularly fortunate to host his son, Julian Boal, to conduct a workshop and forum at the Hippodrome May 19–20, 2010. Gabrielle Byam had seen him teach when she attended a conference in Omaha. "He [Julian] is very passionate, and it transcends to the people at the workshop," Gabrielle said.[3] She contacted Julian through social media and invited him to Gainesville. He accepted.

Later that summer, the camp kids presented three plays: *The Pirates of Penzance, The Tempest*, and *Still Life with Iris*; in 2011, they presented *Jack and Jill and the Beanstalk, Little Women*, and *Gulliver's Travels*. For 2012, they did *Tom Sawyer, Alice in Wonderland*, and *Louder than Words*.

Out of Money

For many years, HITT brought the Hippodrome large amounts of grant money. Then, just prior to Mary Hausch's retirement from the Hippodrome in 2013, she told the Education Department that the grants were drying up and they'd have to shut down every Education Department program except the camps.

After Mary Hausch retired, the Board of Trustees hired Thomas Anderson to replace her as Producing Director. Once he wrapped his head around the state of the Hippodrome in 2013, he asked to speak with Gabrielle Byam. "Three hours later, I came out Director of Education," Gabrielle recalls. Today, she continues the theatre camps, including producing a Summer Spectacular on the mainstage at the culmination of each summer session. These have included *Fame* (2014), *James and the Giant Peach* (2015), *The Three Musketeers* and *Still Life with Iris* (both 2016), *A*

Wrinkle in Time (2017), *The Lion, The Witch, and the Wardrobe* (2018), and *The Wizard of Oz* in 2019.

Even when the COVID-19 quarantine shut the theatre building in 2020, the Summer Spectacular camp performed two plays at the Cade Museum, *Hush: An Interview with America* and *Harriet the Spy*. When the Hippodrome reopened in 2021, the Summer Spectacular camp did *Fantastic Mr. Fox*. In 2022, they presented *Anon(ymos)*, Naomi Iizuka's powerful retelling of Homer's *Odyssey*.

TYA co-founder Margaret Bachus once said, "When we produce theatre for children, we help define the taste of the theatre audiences of tomorrow."

As of 2023, the Hippodrome Education Department is alive and well.

1 Alexander Lim, "Hippodrome's *Radio Active* Teaches Music and Theater to Youth," *Gainesville Sun*, November 23, 2000.
2 Ibid.
3 Lauren Joos, "Renowned Director to Teach at Hippodrome this Week," *Gainesville Sun*, May 16, 2010.

1991

Good Play, Odd Title

Lee Blessing, who wrote *A Walk in the Woods*, which the Hippodrome had produced two years prior, also penned the troupe's January 1991 play. Its title, *Eleemosynary*, was a word so unfamiliar that newspaper articles included its phonetic pronunciation (el-i-mas-e-ner-ee). Dictionary definitions of the word include "charitable" and "dependent upon charity."

The three-character play examines the relationship struggles between three generations of women: a strong-willed, eccentric grandmother, Dorothea; her daughter, Artie, an intellectual biochemist who ran from her overpowering mother; and Artie's daughter, Echo, whom she left to be raised by Dorothea.

When Dorothea suffers a stroke, Echo is forced to reestablish contact with Artie through extended phone conversations, during which they skirt real issues. Despite many years of estrangement, Artie and Echo come to accept their mutual need and summon the courage to build a life together.

Janis Benson, in her third consecutive Hippodrome play, appeared as Dorothea. She said, "*Eleemosynary* is a play that touches all your emotions. It's funny, sad, and uplifting. It has a lot of tension, argument, and hurt in it, but the characters work through it all and finally come to understand each other."[1]

For Nell Page, who played Artie, *Eleemosynary* was her twenty-fourth Hippodrome show, but she said she broke down and wept the first time she read the ending. "Parents will feel this so keenly. To be accepted and loved by your child means everything,"[2] Nell said.

(l-r) Janis Benson, Candace Dian Leverett, and Nell Page in *Eleemosynary*.

The role of Echo was performed by Candace Dian Leverett, who was making her Hippodrome debut but had previously played Echo at the Asolo State Theatre. "She's a fighter," Candace said of her character. "She never gives up. Even though her mother's left her... she won't settle for abandonment. In the end, she prevails."[3] Working the title into the play, Candace's character says to her mother and grandmother, "We're all three of us, in our own way, eleemosynary—charitable."

In her review, Arline Greer wrote, "The Hippodrome production of this extraordinary play is every bit as good as the play itself. Mary Hausch has directed it with genuine sensitivity for the mood changes of its swing through time. And the three actresses are nothing short of brilliant."[4]

Eleemosynary ran from January 11–February 3, 1991.

Photo: Randy Batista

The Heidi Chronicles

On February 22, less than three weeks after closing the previous production, Mary Hausch brought to the stage Wendy Wasserstein's Pulitzer Prize-winning *The Heidi Chronicles*. The Hippodrome was one of only two Florida theatres granted the rights to produce it. "It's such an honor for us," Mary said.[5]

The play focuses primarily on the women's movement during two decades when the status of American women improved dramatically. Mixing humor and politics, Wasserstein covers consciousness-raising sessions, women's protests, the hippie era, the sexual revolution, and questions about relationships. A soundtrack of songs from each decade was used to indicate the progression of time.

Photo: Randy Batista

New York actress Deborah Anne Gay starred as Heidi, the heroine seeking self-determination as a woman. Kathy Tyrell played Heidi's childhood friend, Susan, who grows from hippie to TV mogul. Mark Sexton portrayed Heidi's sometimes lover, Scoop, and Robert Patrik Thompson was her gay friend. Rachel Tench, Michael McLane, Heather Hollingsworth, and Heather Storm played multiple characters who come in and out of Heidi's life.

(l-r) Deborah Anne Gay, Kathy Tyrell, Heather Storm, and Rachel Tench attend a demonstration in *The Heidi Chronicles*.

"Wasserstein's integration of politics and humor allows us to laugh at the intensity and confusion of this restless generation," Mary Hausch said. "But in the end we are very aware of the passion and conviction of the '70s and '80s and the social changes that they inspired."[6]

The Heidi Chronicles ran from February 22–March 17. Arline Greer said the play "lives up to its reputation for being absorbing theater."[7]

Blue Law Blues

In late March, the Alachua County Commission weighed a new law banning nudity from establishments that served alcohol in an attempt to get rid of Café Risqué, a club on Williston Road that featured nude dancers. Attorneys for the business kept pointing out that Hippodrome plays contained nude scenes, yet they were allowed to sell alcohol. It wasn't the kind of publicity the theatre wanted. After three weeks of debate, the commission passed the ordinance. The Café moved to Micanopy, and no one cut off the Hippodrome's liquor sales.

A Farce from Neil Simon

Carlos Asse, who had at this point directed three Neil Simon comedies at the Hippodrome, staged Simon's only farce, *Rumors*. Farces differ from Simon's usual character-driven comedies in that a farce typically includes sequences of preposterous situations presented at such a madcap pace that the audience is laughing too hard to question the absurdity. To pull this off, Carlos cast nine "marvelously gifted comic actors"[8] who played it to the hilt.

A scene from *Rumors*. Top: Dan Jesse. Middle: (l-r) Keith Cassidy, Rusty Salling, Michael McLane, Nell Page. Bottom: (l-r) Nancy Gray, Kathy Tyrell, and Rachel Tench.

Photo: Randy Batista

"The actors in this Hippodrome production are funny and know how to time a line," Arline Greer wrote.[9] "Funniest of the lot, almost unbearably so, is Dan Jesse, who plays Lenny. Kathy Tyrell, who plays Claire, Lenny's wife, is equally brilliant, tossing off bare-bone lines of undisguised disdain.... Rusty Salling makes a genuinely prissy Ernie, the psychiatrist. Rachel Tench, as Cookie, his wife... has many funny moments. Michael McLane plays a sheepish, not-so-bright, Glen, who aspires to being a senator. Nell Page Sexton manages to look stunning and comical as his suspicious wife. Keith Cassidy plays Ken, the hapless lawyer."[10] Ken's wife, Chris, was played by Nancy Gray. UF graduate student Adam Weiner played a policeman.

The play's setup is that Ken and Chris are hosting an elegant tenth-anniversary party for Charlie and Myra, who never actually appear in the play, but about whom all the guests exchange rumors. From the outset, the party does not go according to plan. All the kitchen staff are gone, Myra is missing, and Charlie has shot himself in the ear. While Chris is on the phone with the doctor, the other couples start arriving. Each couple is told a different version of what has occurred. The string of mishaps and misunderstandings that follows had the audience holding their bellies from laughter. The show opened April 12 and ran through May 12, being held over for an extra week. "We had a magic cast for that show," Dan Jesse remembers. "We had them rolling in the aisles."

Good Night, Sweet Prince

After Hamlet's death, his friend Horatio says, "Now cracks a noble heart! Good night, sweet Prince; and flights of angels sing thee to thy rest."[11]

The Hippodrome chose this Shakespeare quote for a memorial to actor Michael Doyle, who died from renal cancer on April 22, 1991. He was forty-six. Ten days earlier, in the *Rumors* playbill, Carlos Asse had dedicated the show to the man audiences and fellow thespians alike considered Gainesville's most talented actor. On the opening night of *Rumors*, the Hippodrome officially named the mainstage in his honor.

Arline Greer had once said of him, "There probably are no adequate words to describe the brilliance of his work."[12]

Looking back, Jennifer Pritchett said, "One of the best things about *Tiger Tail* was getting to play opposite Mike Doyle. He was so reliable and gave so much to work with. He was just a treat."

"Being onstage with him was a privilege, and a class in and of itself," said Mark Sexton, who had performed with Mike twice, in *Equus* and *Lord Alfred's Lover*.

The Season Must Go On

The evening of May 31, UF President John Lombardi and his wife Cathryn hosted a fundraising gala for the Hippodrome at the president's home. Melissa Hart sang for guests, followed by a fashion parade of costumes modeled by Hippodrome actors.

The next week, Jerry Sterner's *Other People's Money* opened, directed by Mary Hausch. It'd been named Best Off-Broadway Play two years earlier. The highly charged dark comedy concerns large conglomerates taking over small corporations. Mary said, it's "about money and how individuals are controlled by their desire and need for money."[13]

Mike Beistle played loud, crude, controlling, Larry "the Liquidator" Garfinkle, the force behind the conglomerate. Garfinkle's next target is a family-owned small-town company run by Andrew Jorgenson, who was played by New York actor Max Jacobs. Garfinkle's competition is Kate, played by Jennifer Pritchett. Kate wants money and power. She's a wheeler-dealer out to win in a man's world. And

Kate Sullivan (Jennifer Pritchett) confronts Larry "the Liquidator" (Mike Beistle) in a scene from *Other People's Money*.

the possibility of beating Garfinkel is irresistible to her. Rounding out the cast of five was Janis Benson as Kate's mother and Gregg Jones as the company president stuck in a no-win situation.

Jennifer described *Other People's Money* as "a very, very funny and very, very dark comedy which sorely tests ethical rights and wrongs in contemporary business practices."[14]

Arline Greer wrote, "Michael Beistle is giving the performance of his Hippodrome career. Jennifer Pritchett, as Kate, gives an equally dynamic performance. *Other People's Money* keeps audiences riveted to every word right up to the play's last lines."[15]

The show played June 7–30, 1991.

Summer Moments

Not since the end of their first season had the Hippodrome relinquished the main-stage to another company. But they made an exception for a good cause. Director, choreographer, and playwright Marion J. Caffey presented his musical *Moments in Time* to raise money for the Center for Excellence and to foster Black talent.

Although he was born in Texas, Marion grew up in Gainesville before making his way to Broadway. When the Hippodrome originally did *Ain't Misbehavin'*, he was in a Broadway show, but he'd sent other performers their way.

Marion described *Moments in Time* as a ninety-minute potpourri of theatre centered around vocalist Felicia Walton with guest artist Heath Ward, a full band, and three backup singers. The show featured songs from the 1920s to 1991 and ran from July 24–August 3.

The Nineteenth Season

After Greg von Hausch left, Mary had been the sole remaining Artistic Director, the theatre's Managing Director, and primary grant writer. Except for two shows, she or Carlos Asse had directed every play in the three years since Greg's departure. The previous June, she'd made Carlos Associate Artistic Director. In dividing up their directing duties, Carlos frequently chose Neil Simon comedies and musicals, and Mary the other plays. So, it was no surprise that September when Carlos directed Ken Ludwig's Tony Award-winning *Lend Me a Tenor*.

Set in 1934 Cleveland, Ohio, the manager of the Cleveland Grand Opera Company is anxiously awaiting the arrival of a world-famous Italian opera tenor. A sellout crowd will be on hand that night to see him perform. When the star and his jealous wife arrive, it is obvious he has overindulged. The manager's wimpy assistant is charged with keeping him sequestered until show time. Through a series of mishaps and misunderstandings, the famous tenor is believed dead. But the show must go on. So, the assistant manager is forced to get into costume and take the stage.

Although *Lend Me a Tenor* is a farce, closer in style to *Rumors* than a typical musical, at least some of the actors had to have voices good enough to be plausible

Photo: Randy Batista

(l-r) Adam Weiner, Sid Conrad, Jennifer Pritchett, Chevy Anz, Jennie Stringfellow, Kathy Tyrell, and Thomas Eldon in a scene from *Lend Me a Tenor*.

opera singers. And many of them did. "This play is so funny, you laugh and laugh," Carlos said, "and then you come to this point and think, 'Oh, my God! These people can sing too!'"[16] He'd cast Jennifer Pritchett, Kathy Tyrell, Chevy Anz, Grant Norman, Sid Conrad, Thomas Eldon, Adam Weiner, and Jennie Stringfellow. All of them also had impeccable comic timing.

Arline Greer called it a "Masterfully crafted farce.... With great energy and wicked humor, the cast of eight rides pell-mell on *Lend Me a Tenor*'s roller coaster. They play together as an ensemble should, each performer dovetailing his performance into the whole."[17]

The show was such a crowd-pleaser that it had to be held over an extra week. It played for a full month, from September 6–October 6, 1991.

Accomplice

Longtime Hippodrome Artistic Director Lauren Caldwell got her first shot at directing a Hippodrome play with Rupert Holmes's *Accomplice*. The comedy-mystery-thriller is in the vein of *Deathtrap*, which the Hippodrome had staged in 1980. As the plot unfolds, the audience tries to figure out who is doing what to whom and why.

The playbill listed four actors but didn't mention which characters each played. One reason it didn't was that the plot takes so many dizzying turns the actors had to play many roles. The other was a gimmick called for in the script in

Rusty Salling and Nell Page in *Accomplice*.

Photo: Randy Batista

which the audience was told an understudy was filling in for (fictional) New York actor Rex Stokman. The actual (unlisted) actor was Mark Sexton. Listed cast members were Heather Hollingsworth, who had appeared in *The Heidi Chronicles*, and Hippodrome veterans Nell Page and Rusty Salling.

Arline Greer called it a "dazzling puzzle" but thought the playwright overdid it with "complex, convoluted and crafty mechanical devices."[18] Even so, Greer complimented Lauren Caldwell, saying she "shows a flair for mystery dramas."[19] The show opened October 10 and ran through November 17.

A Christmas Carol

December 6–16, the Hippodrome presented its fourteenth production of *A Christmas Carol*, once more benefiting needy families through donations to the Salvation Army and Toys for Tots.

Full cast of *A Christmas Carol*, 1991.

Photo: Randy Batista

1 Arline Greer, "Stages of Development," *Gainesville Sun*, January 11, 1991.
2 Ibid.
3 Ibid.
4 Arline Greer, review of *Eleemosynary*, by Lee Blessing, directed by Mary Hausch, Hippodrome Theatre, Gainesville, FL, *Gainesville Sun*, January 18, 1991.
5 Arline Greer, "Four Plays Fill Weekend Theater Menu," *Gainesville Sun*, February 22, 1991.
6 *The Heidi Chronicles* playbill, the Hippodrome Theatre, Gainesville, FL, February 22, 1991.
7 Arline Greer, review of *The Heidi Chronicles*, by Wendy Wasserstein, directed by Mary Hausch, Hippodrome Theatre, Gainesville, FL, *Gainesville Sun*, March 1, 1991.
8 Arline Greer, review of *Rumors*, by Neil Simon, directed by Carlos Asse, Hippodrome Theatre, Gainesville, FL, *Gainesville Sun*, April 17, 1991.
9 Ibid.
10 Ibid.
11 William Shakespeare, *Hamlet*, Act V, scene 2.
12 Arline Greer, review of *Lord Alfred's Lover*, by Eric Bentley, directed by Kerry McKenney, Hippodrome Theatre, Gainesville, FL, *Gainesville Sun*, February 27, 1979.
13 Arline Greer, "Hipp Calls Greed into Question," *Gainesville Sun*, June 7, 1991.
14 Ibid.
15 Arline Greer, review of *Other People's Money*, by Jerry Sterner, directed by Mary Hausch, Hippodrome Theatre, Gainesville, FL, *Gainesville Sun*, June 14, 1991.
16 Arline Greer, "Laughter in the House," *Gainesville Sun*, September 6, 1991.
17 Ibid.
18 Arline Greer, review of *Accomplice*, by Rupert Holmes, directed by Lauren Caldwell, Hippodrome Theatre, Gainesville, FL, *Gainesville Sun*, October 30, 1991.
19 Ibid.

1992

Competition?

In January 1992, the University of Florida opened its brand-new Center for the Performing Arts facility (UFPA) with a touring production of *Cats*. In 2000, that facility was named for Curtis M. Phillips. From the time the UFPA construction was announced, there had been much concern behind the scenes at the Hippodrome that the competition would diminish their audiences. After all, Gainesville wasn't that large, and there were by that time five theatres producing stage plays: the Hippodrome, Constans Theatre, Gainesville Community Playhouse, Acrosstown Repertory, and Santa Fe Community College. In the end, UFPA rarely hosted more than one play a year, and those seldom stayed more than two nights. The real threat UFPA posed was competition for donor dollars.

Lettice and Lovage

For the January play, the Hippodrome had chosen *Lettice and Lovage* by Peter Shaffer. Shaffer had also penned *Equus* and *Amadeus*, two of the Hippodrome's biggest successes. Those were both dramas. *Lettice and Lovage* was a comedy. But it had enjoyed a long, successful run in England before landing on Broadway. So director Mary Hausch had high hopes that a Shaffer script would work box office magic again.

Central to the story is the battle between a passionate, inventive tour guide, Lettice, and Lotte, a strict, stick-to-the-facts administrator for the trust that operates tours of an old English mansion. Lotte fires Lettice upon learning that to spice up the place's boring history, Lettice has peppered her spiel with preposterously false anecdotes.

For the two leads, Mary cast Tony-nominated Melissa Hart as Lettice and another Broadway actress, Denise du Maurier, as Lotte. "When Melissa read for the role of Lettice," Mary said, "She just blew me away. The role is a marvelous vehicle for an actress who has her kind of fire and passion."[1]

"The role of Lotte is just as powerful," Mary added. "Lotte has to be strong. She has to be firm in her belief that the mediocre way is the only way to live. I saw Denise du Maurier do the role at the Caldwell Theatre in Boca Raton and was amazed at her strength. She has the disciplined, hard edge Lotte needs."[2]

Rusty Salling played a solicitor. Smaller roles went to Michael McLane and Marcia Brown. Seven UF students played visitors on the tours: Cindy Arnold, Brad Evans, Mathew Marko, Elise McKenna, Rigtje Passchier, Heather Storm, and Adam Weiner.

Tour guide Lettice (Melissa Hart) gets fired by Lotte (Denise du Maurier) in *Lettice and Lovage.*

Photo: Randy Batista

The show ran from January 10–February 2, 1992, and received a great review in the *Gainesville Sun*: "Two outstanding performances are to be seen by Melissa Hart, who plays Lettice, and Denise du Maurier, as Lotte.... and close behind them is one by Rusty Salling.... Salling's timing and delivery are so artfully accomplished, he's a treat to watch.... In fact, the entire physical production of *Lettice and Lovage* gives pleasure. It's no mere accomplishment, but a creation of extraordinary imagination."[3]

The Diplomat and the Spy

On February 21, David Henry Hwang's Tony Award-winning drama, *M. Butterfly*, made its Southeastern premiere on the Hippodrome stage. Arline Greer raved: "An extraordinarily beautiful production that encompasses the finest craftsmanship in set and costume design, musical arrangement, dance performance and ritual movement... does not disappoint. It is a glorious sensual feast."[4]

Director Mary Hausch said, "*M. Butterfly*, on every level, is the most challenging theatrical piece that the Hippodrome has staged to date. For the team of creative artists, it is the most difficult show to produce in two decades."[5]

Photo: Randy Batista

French diplomat Rene Gallimard (Sean Cullen) under the spell of Song Liling, played by Francis Jue, in *M. Butterfly*.

M. Butterfly was a ripped-from-the-headlines drama based on a recent (1991) espionage trial. A French diplomat had carried on a twenty-two-year affair with a Chinese Opera star. It created an international scandal. Not only was his lover a spy but, throughout their relationship, his loving "perfect woman" had also deceived him physically. Until the trial, the diplomat had never learned his lover's true gender. How could he have missed something so obvious? The facts of the play were essentially what newspapers had reported, except for changing the characters' names and creating some incidents. "Hwang takes this bizarre story and runs it up against the stereotypes of male and female relationships in Puccini's opera, *Madame Butterfly*," Greer wrote. "It is possible, and likely, that audiences will get caught up in the wonder of how the deception could take place.... The entire cast of *M. Butterfly* works as an ensemble to bring off a strong performance."[6]

Over half the cast had performed their parts in *M. Butterfly* at other theatres and in the national touring company. Among them were Sean Cullen, who played the diplomat Rene Gallimard, and Francis Jue, who played his lover, Song Liling. Also from the national tour were Erika Honda, Paul Keoni Chun, and Man Wong, who also served as the choreographer.

Gainesville actors included Nell Page as Gallimard's wife. Dan Jesse had dual roles, first as Gallimard's superior and later as the trial judge. Mark Sexton portrayed Gallimard's boyhood friend and then a character in the Puccini opera. UF grad student Rigtje Passchier played a woman with whom Gallimard had an extramarital affair.

Marilyn Wall and Leslie Klein designed forty-four costumes for the show, fourteen of which were for Francis Jue's character Song Liling. "When I first heard about doing *M. Butterfly*," Marilyn said. "I thought, 'We can't do that. Those kimonos cost $16,000 each in New York.'" She found material that cost $2 a yard. She and Leslie silk-screened, painted, and glued it into something Greer called "exquisitely beautiful."[7] But the highest compliment came from Francis Jue, who said, "The costumes here at the Hippodrome are better than any we had on Broadway."[8]

M. Butterfly played for over a month, closing March 29.

Gala at the Lombardis'

For the second year in a row, UF President John Lombardi and his wife Cathryn opened their home to host a fundraising gala for the Hippodrome. An expanded slate of entertainment featured performances by Melissa Hart, Michael McLane, Heather Hollingsworth, Richard Aycox, Shannon Parnell, and Jennifer Pritchett. Mark Sexton and Lauren Caldwell acted as masters of ceremonies. The party on March 28 celebrated the Hippodrome's upcoming twentieth anniversary.

Another gesture of cooperation between the university and the Hippodrome was the announcement that the university's new Center for the Performing Arts (UFPA) would be the location of the Hippodrome's next production, *West Side Story*. The show was advertised as "presented by The Hippodrome State Theatre in conjunction with The Center for the Performing Arts."

Broadway Classic

West Side Story is a Broadway classic with music by Leonard Bernstein, lyrics by Stephen Sondheim, and book by Arthur Laurents. Filled with memorable songs, its story reimagines the tragedy of *Romeo and Juliet* as a rivalry between two gangs of juvenile delinquents, the Jets and the Sharks. That the Sharks are Puerto Rican adds an element of racial tension.

Sharks and Jets look on as Maria weeps over Tony's body in the climax of *West Side Story*.

Photo: Randy Batista

West Side Story cast:

THE JETS
Riff... Michael B. Tapley
Tony... Chris Rempfer
Action... Charlie Marcus
A-Rab... John Kasak
Baby John... Rusty Mowery
Snowboy... John-Michael Lander
Big Deal... Darrell Scott Rushton
Gee-Tar... Kai Schmoll

THE JETS' GIRLS
Graziella... Laurie Sheppard
Velma... Joy Green
Minnie... Cindy Arnold
Clarice... Caylen Clark
Pauline... Lesley J. Tunstall
Anybodys... Trish Santini

THE SHARKS
Bernardo... Michael Martino
Maria... Andrea Burns
Anita... Justine DiCostanzo
Chino... Lou Lanza
Pepe... Bob Perry
Indio... Marion J. Caffey
Luis... Ric Rose
Juano... George Wainwright
Toro... Scott MacDonald

THE SHARKS' GIRLS
Rosalia... Jillian Johnson
Consuelo... Chrissi Guastella
Francisca... Susanna Velasquez
Teresita... Kathleen Thompson
Estella... Beth Chobaz
Margarita... Dawn Murray

THE ADULTS
Doc... John Henderson
Schrank... Gordon McConnell
Krupke... Jim Borda
Gladhand... Rusty Salling

Carlos Asse directed it with choreography by Jillian Johnson, who had worked on *West Side Story* before. He also found Mark Janas for musical director. Mark had served as Leonard Bernstein's assistant with the New York Philharmonic and the Boston Symphony orchestras, and he had also conducted for two national tours of *Les Miserables.*

"Presenting it at the Center for the Performing Arts, with its large proscenium stage and wonderful facilities, opened up a myriad of technical options to us," Carlos said. UFPA's 1,700 seats didn't hurt, either, because this was the largest and most expensive production the Hippodrome had ever undertaken. The show had thirty-three actors, a twenty-six-piece orchestra, ninety-three costumes, and sixteen scene changes.

"*West Side Story* is so much an ensemble show, it seems unfair to single out performances," Arline Greer wrote.[9] "Keeping that in mind and without meaning to take away anything from the impressive group performance, it should be acknowledged that Andrea Burns makes a lovely and believable Maria. She sings beautifully and with the innocence and passion her role demands. Chris Ramfer gives a sweet, guileless performance as Tony [Maria's star-crossed love].... In *West Side Story*, there are moments so heart-rending as to make audiences weep; others bring laughter. Through it all, the glorious sound of Leonard Bernstein's music soars with all its rich harmonies; and those beautiful young people dance their way through a story that's almost as old as time itself. *West Side Story* is a triumph for the Hippodrome."[10]

West Side Story is very much a dancer's piece, and two members of the dance chorus should be mentioned. UF Assistant Professor Ric Rose, who played Luis, had previously choreographed Hippodrome productions of *A Christmas Carol*, *Blue Plate Special*, and *The Boys Next Door*. The other is Marion J. Caffey, who, though already a Broadway dancer and choreographer, humbly took a dance role in the Sharks.

The show was a great success, playing from May 8–17.

Nunsense

The Hippodrome quickly followed *West Side Story* with another musical, *Nunsense*, written by Dan Goggin and directed by Lauren Caldwell. Jillian Johnson again handled the choreography. Kathy Tyrell was the musical director. The show was good-time nonsense, with five outrageous nuns singing thirty-one songs. The cast included three Broadway actresses, Catherine Fries as Sister Mary Leo, Elizabeth Harris as Sister Mary Amnesia, and Mary Jo Catlett as Mother Superior. Elizabeth Harris had already played Sister Mary Amnesia in three productions of *Nunsense* prior to the Hippodrome. But Mary Jo Catlett was the most famous, having made her Broadway debut in the original *Hello Dolly*, followed by *The Pajama Game* and many other shows. In films, she'd worked with big-name stars Burt Reynolds, Jon Voight, Ed Asner, and Mel Brooks. On TV, she starred in *Diff'rent Strokes* and appeared on dozens of other television programs, including *M*A*S*H*, *Kojak*, and *The Waltons*.

Rounding out the cast were two UF grads making their Hippodrome debuts: Gail Anderson as Sister Mary Hubert, Mistress of Novices, and Shannon Parnell as Sister Robert Anne.

The five nuns are the surviving members of a onetime missionary order, the Little Sisters of Hoboken. Mother Superior opens the show by greeting the audience and apologizing for their set constraints. All five nuns introduce themselves in the opening number, "Nunsense is Habit-Forming." The backstory is that their cook, Sister Julia, accidentally killed the other fifty-two convent residents with her tainted vichyssoise. Upon discovering the disaster, Mother Superior had a vision in which she was told to start a greeting card company to raise funds for the burials. The greeting cards were an enormous success and, thinking there was plenty of money, she spent it on the convent, leaving no money in the kitty to pay for the last four burials. With the deceased nuns on ice in the deep freeze, they decide to stage a variety show to raise the necessary amount.

Photo: Randy Batista

In *Nunsense*, Mary Jo Catlett as Mother Superior (center) is surrounded (clockwise) by the Little Sisters of Hoboken, played by Gail Anderson, Catherine Fries, Elizabeth Harris, and Shannon Parnell.

Providing the entertainment are Mother Superior, a former circus performer who cannot resist the spotlight; her competitive but dignified second-in-command, Sister Mary Hubert; Sister Robert Anne, a streetwise nun from Brooklyn; Sister Mary Leo, a novice who is determined to be the world's first ballerina nun; and wacky, childlike Sister Mary Amnesia, who lost her memory when a crucifix fell on her head.

Arline Greer wrote: "It's funny. Belly-laughing, thigh-slapping, giggle-goofy funny!... A happy good-natured show that doesn't seek to be profound."[11]

The show, which opened June 5 and was scheduled to close June 28, proved so popular it was held over until July 19.

Hooked on Broadway

The weekend after *Nunsense* closed, July 25 and 26, Marion J. Caffey returned to the Hippodrome mainstage with his one-man show *Hooked on Broadway*, in which he sang, danced, and tapped with the dexterity of legendary Gregory Hines, for whom he'd understudied and had an uncanny resemblance.

Photo: Randy Batista

Hippodrome co-founders Mary Hausch and Kerry McKenney smile as Cinema director Shirley Lasseter lights candles on the twentieth-anniversary cake.

Jennifer Pritchett and Sean Cullen in *Prelude to a Kiss*.

Photo: Randy Batista

Twentieth Season

The Hippodrome celebrated its twentieth anniversary with a gala party in the Sun Center on opening night of the new season's first show, *Prelude to a Kiss*. The party, hosted by the theatre's downtown neighbors, featured a live band and offered guests delicacies from five nearby restaurants. Guests were given an elaborately produced commemorative booklet recapping the Hippodrome's history.

Prelude to a Kiss

Mary Hausch directed *Prelude to a Kiss*, a comedy by Craig Lucas. It is a romantic fairytale with the message that true love endures for all time.

The leads were Jennifer Pritchett as about-to-be-wed Rita; Sean Cullen as her fiancé, Peter; and Max Jacobs as Julius, an old man who switches bodies with Rita. Sean had played the diplomat, Rene Gallimard, in *M. Butterfly* the previous March. Max Jacobs and Jennifer had acted together in *Other People's Money*.

In supporting roles, Rusty Salling and Cristine McMurdo-Wallis played Rita's parents. Thomas Eldon played Peter's friend. Pat Lennon was the wedding minister. Hippodrome interns Bonnie Harrison and Matthew Reed were Rita's aunt and uncle. UF theatre students Hanna Bondarewska, Kim Christopherson, Ana Cooper, Vinnie Jones, Thomas Mark Lowe, and Charles McWhorter filled out the ensemble.

In the story, Peter falls in love with lovely, quirky young Rita. On the day of their marriage, an uninvited old man at the wedding kisses the bride, and the two exchange souls. Rita, Peter's beloved, is now inside the body of the old man. The old man, in Rita's body, goes off to honeymoon with Peter.

For Jennifer, the challenge was to play a woman playing a man who's playing a woman. "I have to put myself in Max's shoes," she said. "I try body posture, standing like he does, or in the way men think a woman stands and walks."[12]

The *Gainesville Sun* didn't give it a great review, but a Jacksonville reviewer did. The show, held over an extra week, played for a full month, from September 4–October 4.

Fire Island Phobia

In the next play, Terrence McNally's *Lips Together, Teeth Apart*, two heterosexual couples gather for Independence Day weekend at a luxurious beach house on gay Fire Island. Sally, played by Susan Russell, has inherited the house from her brother, who died of AIDS. Her husband, Sam (Bill Ford Campbell), is homophobic, and the neighbors on all sides are gay men. Chloe (Rachel Tench) is a nonstop talker, and her husband, John (Thomas Eldon), is a snob. None of them will swim in the house's pool for fear of catching AIDS. Throughout the play, the characters skirt deeper issues with each other, revealing them only in monologs to the audience, which the other characters cannot hear.

For the second play in a row, the *Sun* critic failed to give a good review. She called the script wordy and didn't care for some of the acting, but heaped praise on the set by Carlos Asse. The script called for a pool deck behind a house on Fire Island with three sliding glass doors. Carlos managed to turn the small Hippodrome stage into exactly that, including a wood-shingled cottage with a deck and a swimming pool!

Photo: Randy Batista

Lips Together, Teeth Apart featured (l-r) Rachel Tench, Thomas Eldon, Bill Ford Campbell, and Susan Russell. The amazing set included an actual swimming pool.

Director Lauren Caldwell recalled, "It was one of the most complicated sets on that space that's ever been done. We had a pool company come in. [The pool] was wide as the downstage, was tiled, and had chlorine in it. Actors could stand in it."

The show ran from October 23–November 15.

Putting a Face on the Election

1992 was a presidential election year, and Bill Clinton and Al Gore were stumping in Gainesville. Marilyn Wall got a taste of the political spotlight when she was called to do the makeup for the candidates' appearance on ABC-TV's *Good Morning America*, which was broadcasting from Gainesville that day. Mary Hausch assisted her.

"It was a fascinating experience," Marilyn said, describing her meeting with Clinton and Gore in a carefully guarded reception room at the UF Reitz Union. "There were probably fifty Secret Service people around, just as you would imagine, with the little hearing aids, sunglasses, and dark suits. There were probably four hundred people buzzing around there on cellular phones or walkie-talkies. When Clinton and Gore came in, they were incredibly warm—so relaxed and energetic, as comfortable talking about jogging as they were about the state of the world. I told Senator Gore he didn't need any help with makeup because he was already gorgeous."

Rusty Salling as Scrooge is visited by the ghost of Jacob Marley, played by Jimmy Jay.

Fifteenth *Christmas Carol*

Photo: Randy Batista

In 1992, for the first time, the Hippodrome held a special preview performance of *A Christmas Carol* just for children who might otherwise not get a chance to attend. Children from Loften Center, Alachua County Halfway House, the Alachua County Substance Abuse Prevention Partnership, as well as foster children from Florida's Department of Health and Rehabilitative Services enjoyed a fun-filled theatrical experience.

1 Arline Greer, "Peter Shaffer's Comedy of Conflict," *Gainesville Sun*, January 10, 1992.
2 Ibid.
3 Arline Greer, review of *Lettice and Lovage*, by Peter Shaffer, directed by Mary Hausch, Hippodrome Theatre, Gainesville, FL, *Gainesville Sun*, January 17, 1992.
4 Arline Greer, review of *M. Butterfly*, by David Henry Hwang, directed by Mary Hausch, Hippodrome Theatre, Gainesville, FL, *Gainesville Sun*, February 28, 1992.
5 *M. Butterfly* playbill, Hippodrome State Theatre, Gainesville, FL, February 21, 1992.
6 Arline Greer, review of *M. Butterfly*, by David Henry Hwang, directed by Mary Hausch, Hippodrome Theatre, Gainesville, FL, *Gainesville Sun*, February 28, 1992.
7 Ibid.
8 Arline Greer, "The Hippodrome's Elusive Butterfly," *Gainesville Sun*, February 21, 1992.
9 Arline Greer, review of *West Side Story*, by Arthur Laurents, directed by Carlos Asse, Hippodrome Theatre, Gainesville, FL, *Gainesville Sun*, May 13, 1992.
10 Ibid.
11 Arline Greer, review of *Nunsense*, by Dan Goggin, directed by Lauren Caldwell, Hippodrome Theatre, Gainesville, FL, *Gainesville Sun*, June 10, 1992.
12 Arline Greer, "The Hippodrome's Leading Man," *Gainesville Sun*, September 4, 1992.

1993

Melba Moore

For their January play, *From the Mississippi Delta* by Dr. Endesha Ida Mae Holland, the Hippodrome brought in international superstar Melba Moore. She was undoubtedly the biggest star to play the Hippodrome. By 1993, she'd already triumphed in several Broadway productions and won a Tony Award. As an R&B and pop soloist, she'd recorded fourteen extremely successful albums and been twice nominated for a Grammy Award. Her singing performances included stage shows in Las Vegas, Atlantic City, and Paris; State dinners at the White House; and many television appearances.

Melba, in her first non-musical drama, shared the stage with actresses NeAnni Ife and Debra Walton. Both NeAnni and Debra were accomplished actresses that the playwright had seen together in a Dayton, Ohio production of *From the Mississippi Delta*. Dr. Holland was so impressed by their performances that she personally recommended them for the Hippodrome.

The trio plays a multitude of characters in hard-hitting, sometimes comical vignettes—often poetic, and at times hair-raising. The stories portray the experiences of Phelia, a young African American woman, and her midwife mother. They are largely autobiographical, drawing from the playwright's childhood, laced with bigotry, violence, and prostitution, and her struggle to rise and earn her PhD. The play had been nominated for the Pulitzer Prize.

Photo: Randy Batista

(l-r) Debra Walton, NeAnni Ife, and Melba Moore in *From the Mississippi Delta*.

Melba told the *Gainesville Sun* she had been touring the previous spring when she was introduced to Dr. Holland. "She wanted me in it, and did I mind working out of town? And of course, for me, that's a great plum because it's a lot better for me to get started, and working in a piece this challenging, out of town.... I don't feel it's out of my league, in that it's my life story as well. It's so much a part of our culture. There are so many things I was so familiar with, that I have a lot to bring to it."[1]

To direct the play, the Hippodrome hired Shirley Basfield Dunlap, a professor of theatre at Morgan State University in Baltimore, Maryland, who had directed four productions of *From the Mississippi Delta*.

The ensemble won over *Sun* theatre critic Arline Greer, who wrote, "Rare moments in the theater should be noticed and applauded long after they become part of memory. An evening of rare moments has come to the Hippodrome with Dr. Endesha Ida Mae Holland's play, *From the Mississippi Delta*."[2]

During its run, Melba Moore, a former educator herself, met with youths in the Hippodrome Improvisational Teen Theatre-At-Risk program. Director of Education Lauren Caldwell said, "This is a once-in-a-life chance for them to talk with someone who has been something of an idol to many of them. Getting to meet a celebrity like Melba Moore helps them to understand that the seemingly unattainable is attainable and provides them with a model that they can follow and from which they can learn."[3]

Melba's fellow actors also reached out. NeAnni and Debra traveled to a subsidized housing complex in Alachua to meet and talk with the women of the Nurturing Program Support Group. Following the visit, the women were given a chance to see the play.

The show ran from January 15–February 7.

Unscheduled Coups

In January, the Hippodrome announced changes to its 1992–1993 season schedule. The theatre had just received rights to two of the hottest plays in New York, *Dancing at Lughnasa*, which had just won the 1992 Tony Award for Best Play, and *Marvin's Room*, which had won the Drama Desk Award for Outstanding Play. Both plays made their Southeastern premieres at the Hippodrome.

Dick Kerekes, theatre reviewer for *First Coast Entertainer*, said, "Producing Director Mary Hausch should be given the key to the city for somehow managing to get the newest plays as soon as possible for the Hippodrome."[4]

The Lughnasa Festival

Throughout the whole of Ireland and in parts of Great Britain and France, a festival celebrating the beginning of harvest was held every year in early August. In Ireland, that festival was called Lughnasa. The festival varied from place to place and from generation to generation. But in all the records and recollections of the Lughnasa festivities in Ireland, dancing is the most prominent and persistent element.[5]

Carlos Asse directed playwright Brian Friel's *Dancing at Lughnasa*, the story of five unmarried sisters eking out their lives in a small Irish village in 1936, as narrated by their nephew, played by Michael Balin. Rena Carney, Joanna Olsen, Maggie Rasnick, Kathy Tyrell, and Patricia McLaughlin were the sisters. Their brother, a returning missionary with malaria, was played by Dan Jesse. Matthew Reed portrayed the youngest sister's ne'er-do-well suitor, Gerry.

Their sparse existence is interrupted by brief, colorful bursts of music from the radio, their only link to the romance and hope of the world at large. It is the time of the Festival of Lughnasa with its drunken revelry and dancing.

When the sisters finally dance to a wild pagan Irish tune, they embody the core of the human spirit that cannot be vanquished by time or loss, or even fully expressed in language. Ric Rose choreographed the dance sequences, which Arline Greer called "remarkable" and "luminescent."[6]

Photo: Randy Batista

(l-r) Rena Carney, Maggie Rasnick, Kathy Tyrell, and Patricia McLaughlin play sisters in *Dancing at Lughnasa*.

Dancing at Lughnasa opened February 26 and ran for nearly a month, closing March 21, 1993.

Twentieth Anniversary

Florida Governor Lawton Chiles proclaimed the week of April 16–23, 1993, as Hippodrome Theatre Week throughout the state of Florida. The Hippodrome marked its birthday with a cake-cutting ceremony on the front steps of the theatre at noon on Friday, April 16, followed by a special performance by the P. K. Yonge Blue Wave Marching Band. The *Gainesville Sun* featured a special section on the Hippodrome in its *Scene Magazine*.

Laughing at Death

The second big score that spring was Scott McPherson's *Marvin's Room*. It opened April 16, the first night of Hippodrome Theatre Week, and ran through May 9. Directed by Mary Hausch, *Marvin's Room* was a bittersweet play, yet also very funny, and had been compared to *Steel Magnolias* for its humor and poignancy.

Bessie (Nell Page) is a middle-aged spinster who takes care of her bedridden father and eccentric Aunt Ruth (Mary Jo Catlett). Ruth suffers from chronic backaches, relieved by an anesthesia device wired to her brain that also causes the garage door to open when it operates. When Dr. Wally (Rusty Salling) diagnoses Bessie with leukemia, her estranged sister, Lee (Lauren Caldwell), comes to visit and be tested as a possible bone marrow donor. The uncomfortable reunion between the sisters is aggravated by the behavior of Lee's two sons, Hank (Heath Ward) and Charlie (Dylan Thue-Jones). The two women eventually confront their shortcomings as sisters, reach out to each other, and arrive at an understanding about the importance of family. Also appearing were Maggie Rasnick as a stereotypical psychiatrist and Robert Patrik Thompson in two smaller roles.

(l-r) Dylan Thue-Jones, Nell Page, Heath Ward, Mary Jo Catlett, and Lauren Caldwell in a scene from *Marvin's Room*.

Photo: Randy Batista

Reviewers for both the *Gainesville Sun* and *First Coast Entertainer* praised the acting, especially that of TV and film star Mary Jo Catlett, who on her off days visited the Oaks Residential and Rehabilitation Center to meet the residents, sign autographs, and pose with them for pictures. "Mary Jo really brightened up the whole Center when she visited," said an aide working there. Mary Jo was also a champion supporter of the Retirement Home for Horses in Alachua and visited there several times.

Hippodrome cast of *Six Women with Brain Death or Expiring Minds Want to Know*: (l-r) Debra Walton, Kathy Tyrell, Geraldine O'Mahoney, Diane Bearden, Elizabeth Harris, and Sara-Page Hall.

Photo: Peter Thosteson

A Musical as Wacky as a Tabloid Story

Supermarket tabloids accost shoppers daily with screaming headlines and scandalous photographs. They wallpaper check-out lines and paint the world with the rancor of purple prose and yellow journalism. These papers provided the inspiration for the playwrights of the Hippodrome's next play.

While touring in a Stephen Sondheim production, six women grew bored and amused themselves by perusing supermarket tabloids. These women were Cheryl Benge, Christy Brand, Rosanna E. Coppedge, Valerie Fagan, Sandee Johnson, and Peggy Pharr Wilson. Collaborating with Ross Freese and Mark Houston, they wrote *Six Women with Brain Death or Expiring Minds Want to Know*, a hilarious musical spoof of *The National Enquirer*. Houston composed the music and lyrics.

Fourteen musical numbers portray ordinary women with ordinary problems, perturbed by the tabloids, fearful of high school reunions, nostalgic about Ken and Barbie, and fed up with soap operas. The women sing and speak truths about contemporary America as they see it. Song styles range from doo-wop to funk to opera. Ric Rose choreographed the show and A. Paul Johnson provided the musical direction.

"Nothing is sacred and everything is fair game for a joke," Arline Greer wrote. "Six actresses make the Hippodrome stage sizzle with energy, excitement, and ribald humor that has its own unique womanly—and decidedly non-feminist—charm. The actresses in *Six Women* work beautifully as an ensemble, and each has her moment to shine individually. Director Lauren Caldwell makes the musical bounce smartly from episode to episode."[7]

Six Women with Brain Death or Expiring Minds Want to Know opened June 11 and was scheduled to end on July 4, but it proved so popular its run was extended twice. "People who have already seen it are coming back again and bringing friends!" explained Lauren Caldwell. "One woman told me that she laughed so much that she hurt. She laughed until she cried and then couldn't see because her mascara was running into her eyes!" The show continued through July 18.

Twenty-First Season

The Hippodrome opened its twenty-first season on September 3 with *Breaking Legs*, a pasta-filled mobster comedy by Tom Dulack. The farce was a big hit off-Broadway and made its Southeastern premiere at the Hippodrome.

A cornball comedy filled with stereotypical characters, *Breaking Legs* takes place in an Italian restaurant owned by mobster Lou Graziano (Michael Beistle) and managed by his beautiful unmarried daughter, Angie, played by Patricia McLaughlin. The reviewer for *First Coast Entertainer* commented that the set looked so authentic he found himself wanting Italian food.

The action begins when Angie's former college professor, Terrence (Sean Cullen), arrives to ask for

Photo: Randy Batista

(l-r) Dan Jesse, Sean Cullen, David Preuss, Patricia McLaughlin, David Howard, and Michael Beistle in the dinner scene from *Breaking Legs*.

financial backing for a play he has written about a murder. Lou would like to get Angie married off, so he introduces Terrence to his mob connections, Tino (Dan Jesse) and a Mafia godfather played by David Howard. The idea of producing a play intrigues the mafiosi, and Angie takes a fancy to the playwright. But Terrence has second thoughts after Frankie Salvucci (David Preuss) is beaten for not repaying a loan. The show, directed by Carlos Asse, ran through September 26.

Ruthless to Win the Part

In October, Lauren Caldwell directed the musical *Ruthless!* The book and lyrics were written by Joel Paley and the music by Marvin Laird. Again, she tapped A. Paul Johnson for musical director, but this time Broadway choreographer Marion J. Caffey handled the choreography.

A savagely funny satire on the theatre world and stage mothers, *Ruthless!* had won the 1993 Drama Desk and Outer Critics Circle Awards for Best Off-Broadway Musical and was making its regional premiere at the Hippodrome.

Cast of *Ruthless!* Front (l-r): Kathy Tyrell, Abby Lindsay, Susan Russell, and Melissa Hart. Back: Elizabeth Harris and Diane Bearden.

Photo: Natalee Waters/*Gainesville Sun*

The story revolves around adorable, talented eight-year-old Tina (played by UF grad student Abby Lindsay) and her mother (Susan Russell). Much to her mother's chagrin, Tina's driving ambition in life is to be a star at any cost. She will do anything to get the leading role in her school play—including murder!

Tina is encouraged by hard-as-nails agent Sylvia St. Croix (Melissa Hart), who swoops into her life like a demonic fairy godmother. Another larger-than-life character caught up in the backbiting, backstabbing, glamorous, glorious world of theatre is Tina's grandmother, a sardonic theatre critic (Elizabeth Harris). Kathy Tyrell played dual roles, Tina's third-grade rival, Louise, and later, Eave, a wannabe Broadway star. Diane Bearden also had two parts, the girls' schoolteacher and, later, a journalist.

Ruthless! opened October 22 and enjoyed an extended run through November 21. Arline Greer gave it a rave review: "The Hippodrome's cast for *Ruthless!* has class, style, subtlety, brass and talent to spare.... Hart carries an intrinsically likable show to levels of brilliance.... Its laughter goes on all evening!"[8]

Christmas Loss and Gain

From December 10–19, the Hippodrome presented its annual benefit production of *A Christmas Carol*. This time it was co-directed by Pat Lennon and Michael McLane, who also played Bob Cratchit. Missing was the play's longtime director Carlos Asse who, after finishing *Ruthless!*, resigned to form his own architectural painting and fabrication company.

December also brought money worries. After a steep slump in state and federal funding, Mary Hausch said, "Without some public funding, there may not be a Hippodrome."[9] The theatre began an advertising campaign to win support for giving the theatre a cut of the "bed tax" paid by hotel and motel patrons. Monies from the tax contributed $200,000 to the Performing Arts Center. Linda McGurn of the Downtown Redevelopment Agency said, "The Hippodrome is in the same position as the Performing Arts Center in needing this extra support."[10]

At an Alachua County Commission meeting the following night, before an audience of two dozen theatre supporters, the commissioners voted unanimously to give the theatre $75,000. A jolly something for their stocking.

1 Bill DeYoung, "Straight Talk from Melba Moore," *Gainesville Sun*, January 15, 1993.
2 Arline Greer, review of *From the Mississippi Delta*, by Endesha Ida Mae Holland, directed by Shirley Basfield Dunlap, Hippodrome Theatre, Gainesville, FL, *Gainesville Sun*, January 22, 1993.
3 "Melba speaks for HITT-At-Risk program", *Ovation*, Hippodrome Theatre, February 1993.
4 Dick Kerekes, review of *From the Mississippi Delta*, by Endesha Ida Mae Holland, directed by Shirley Basfield Dunlap, Hippodrome Theatre, Gainesville, FL, *First Coast Entertainer*, January 23, 1993.
5 Máire MacNeill, *The Festival of Lughnasa: A Study of the Survival of the Celtic Festival of the Beginning of Harvest* (Dublin: Comhairle Bhealoideas Eireann and University College, 1982).
6 Arline Greer, review of *Dancing at Lughnasa*, by Brian Friel, directed by Carlos Asse, Hippodrome Theatre, Gainesville, FL, *Gainesville Sun*, March 5, 1993.
7 Arline Greer, review of *Six Women with Brain Death or Expiring Minds Want to Know*, by Cheryl Benge et al., directed by Lauren Caldwell, Hippodrome Theatre, Gainesville, FL, *Gainesville Sun*, June 16, 1993.
8 Arline Greer, review of *Ruthless!*, by Joel Paley, directed by Lauren Caldwell, Hippodrome Theatre, Gainesville, FL, *Gainesville Sun*, October 27, 1993.
9 Mark Hollis, "Hippodrome Hoping for Salvation from Taxpayers," *Gainesville Sun*, December 14, 1993.
10 Ibid.

1994

Melba Returns

In January 1994, Melba Moore returned to the Hippodrome to premiere *Songs My Mother Taught Me*, an original show she'd conceived and developed in collaboration with David Boyce, Lauren Caldwell, and Mary Hausch. For most of them, it was the first time they had worked on an original theatrical piece from beginning to end.

Co-creators of *Songs My Mother Taught Me*: (l-r) Lauren Caldwell, Melba Moore, Mary Hausch, and David Boyce.

The first step was to get material about Melba's life. Mary and Lauren flew to New York and, over several sessions, recorded hours of tapes of Melba recollecting influential people and events in her life. Upon their return, Hippodrome dramaturg David Boyce went through the hours of tapes, piecing together the most important people and events, and structured them into a workable script. After extended story conferences with Mary and Lauren, the script was revised. Melba discovered events and patterns in her life she had never noticed before. For example, that music had not been a part of her early childhood.

Mary and Lauren co-directed the show. To serve as musical director and Melba's accompanist, they brought composer, conductor, and arranger Donald Dumpson from Philadelphia.

The play had its world premiere on January 7, 1994. Arline Greer, who attended the opening, wrote, "Midway through the second act of Melba Moore's one-woman show, *Songs My Mother Taught Me*, an extraordinary reaction from the first-night Hippodrome audience brought the show to a halt. Moore was singing 'Stormy Weather' in her softly gently-rock-it-sock-it-and-float-it-highway-high style, when the crowd erupted. Applause mingled with loud cries of approval as, in a body, people leaped to their feet."[1]

Greer loved the songs and Melba's singing but didn't care much for the script's first act. She wrote, "The monologue with music, meant to be an autobiographical account of Moore's life, tends to be choppy and disjointed in its writing, particularly in the first act.... The facts of Moore's childhood are told willy-nilly. They have no cohesive flow."[2] But it got better.

"The second act of *Songs My Mother Taught Me* leaves behind the muddle of the singer's early life. It concentrates on her acting career in *Hair* and *Purlie* and tells of her misadventures with men. Here the writing is crisp, witty, fast-moving, wise. Moore's story knows where it's going. The songs come fast on the heels of pointed remarks and asides to the audience. By the time Moore concluded her last song, the audience was on its feet again," Greer said.[3]

The show ran through January 30, but before she left town, Melba met with young people in the HITT-At-Risk program as she had the previous year. She told them, "Whether you're rich or poor, there's gonna be some challenges in your life that are going to be heart-wrenching."[4] She had just revealed many of those challenges to audiences in *Songs My Mother Taught Me*.

A Stage Experiment

Frank Galati's adaptation of the Anne Tyler novel *Earthly Possessions* opened February 18, 1994. Originally scheduled for February 1993, it was bumped from that slot by *Dancing at Lughnasa*.

In the novel, the protagonist, Charlotte Emory, narrates her story in the first person. To keep his adaptation from becoming one long monologue, Frank Galati took the innovative approach of using two different actresses to portray different sides of the main character. Charlotte (played by Sara Morsey in her Hippodrome debut) is the principal narrator of a rambling story about a woman who wanted adventure in her life and got it. Her other half, Mrs. Emory (played by Nell Page) is a middle-aged woman who is taken hostage during a failed bank robbery attempt and swept away on a cross-country journey with a bandit (played by Patrick Lennon). Mrs. Emory had gone to the bank to make a withdrawal so she could leave her fuddy-duddy husband (Rusty Salling). Heading for the sunny South in a stolen car, the housewife and the incompetent thief learn strange and wonderful things about themselves and the other people in their lives.

Photo: Stephen Morton/*Gainesville Sun*

Foiled bank heist in *Earthly Possessions* featuring (l-r) David Preuss, Sara Morsey, Pat Lennon, and Nell Page.

Even with Sara and Nell portraying two aspects of Charlotte Emory, there was still a lot of exposition. Director Mary Hausch and Shirley Lasseter, head of the Hippodrome Cinema, came up with an ingenious solution. Shirley, who had an interest in filmmaking, made a movie that played behind the action during various scenes in the play. It was the first time the Hippodrome had ever tried such a gimmick.

Sara Morsey recalled, "The film played at the very beginning of the show. I would come out and stand in the middle of the stage talking to the audience, but everybody would be watching the film. This one night, I started talking and suddenly I see everyone is looking at me. That got my attention. Like, what am I naked? The light onstage was different when the film was playing, and it dawned on me that the film wasn't playing. They finally got it fixed, but anyway it was kind of a weird play."

Arline Greer praised "virtuoso performances by Nell Page Sexton and Sara Morsey."[5] But, she concluded, "That the sum of these admirable parts does not add up to total satisfaction is the fault of the vehicle itself. Some novels do not lend themselves to dramatization and, while Frank Galati has used clever theatrical devices to make Tyler's *Earthly Possessions* work on stage, it stubbornly resists moving from the printed page."[6]

The play ran through March 13. Also in the cast were Ellen Lau, Bonnie Harrison, Shannon Wright, Kathi Sanderlin, and David Preuss.

Although *Earthly Possessions* was Sara Morsey's debut in Gainesville, she was already an experienced professional, having acted in theatres from Chicago to Louisville to St. Petersburg. "I was living in Chicago at the time and what I wanted to do was work in a regional theatre and have an artistic home," Sara said. She found one at the Hippodrome. Over the next twenty-five seasons, she became the Hippodrome's Grand Dame, starring in many plays every year.

Equus Lost, *Yonkers* Gained

In the 1993–1994 season subscription package, a re-staging of *Equus* had been announced for April, and either *Lost in Yonkers* or *Oil City Symphony* for June. Instead, the Hippodrome skipped *Equus* and did the other two.

First up was *Lost in Yonkers,* a Pulitzer Prize and Tony Award-winning play by America's great comic playwright, Neil Simon. The Hippodrome had sold out the house with previous Simon plays, and *Lost in Yonkers* did as well. The show, which opened April 8, had to be held over an extra week, closing May 8, 1994. Reviews were effusive. *First Coast Entertainer* called it "the absolute must see play of the year."[7] The *Gainesville Sun* reviewer said, "The Hippodrome State Theatre has produced a play worthy of its talents. Brilliant acting, combined with a thorough understanding of Simon's marvelous blend of comedy and tragedy, make the Hipp's *Yonkers* come alive with characters who touch our hearts and minds."[8]

Set in 1942, the focus of the play is another battling odd couple—this time Grandma Kurnitz and her thirty-five-year-old daughter, Bella. As if Bella isn't enough for Grandma to manage, Grandma's broke son, Eddie, deposits his two young boys, Jay and Arty, in her care while he goes on an extended sales trip. Her other son, Louie, may have mob connections, and her other daughter, Gert, is a nervous type with a breathing problem.

Temporarily exiled in Yonkers, Jay and Arty must contend with tough, stern Grandma and the secret romance of their emotionally deficient, pathetically affectionate Bella. The boys' mission becomes how to raise money quickly so that they can move back with their father. Bella's mission is to find a way to tell the family that she wants to marry a movie theatre usher, while Louie's is simply to dodge some mob henchmen for the next couple of days.

Cast of *Lost in Yonkers*. Seated: (l-r) Richard Delia, Patricia Kennell-Carroll, Sara Morsey, and Elya Ottenberg as young Arty. Standing: Michael Balin, Rachel Tench, and Rusty Salling.

Photo: Peter Thosteson

Director Lauren Caldwell cast Patricia Kennell-Carroll as Grandma and Sara Morsey as the ditzy Bella. Rusty Salling was Eddie, Michael Balin played Louie, and Rachel Tench was Gert. About the youngest two actors, Arline Greer wrote: "Elya Ottenberg as young Arty has a face that speaks volumes.... he'll steal your heart. Richard Delia as Jay, the older brother, makes an ingenuous straight man for Arty, Bella, Louise and Eddie."[9]

Elya was a ninth grader at Eastside High School. Three years of the Hippodrome's summer camps had sparked his interest in theatre, and the previous December, he'd played a street urchin in *A Christmas Carol*. Bonnie Harrison, who directed the workshop programs, got him cast in an educational film about kidney transplants. None of that made him a shoo-in for Arty. Lauren Caldwell auditioned twenty kids before giving him the part. "Elya won the role through his talent, that's the bottom line," she said.[10]

Summer Musical

Starting with *Nunsense* two years earlier, the Hippodrome began closing its seasons with somewhat goofy musical comedies. Although they'd often presented musicals at other times, light summer fare seemed to draw people from outlying communities who weren't regular theatergoers. On June 3, they opened *Oil City Symphony*. It proved so popular that it had to be held over through July 3.

Cast of *Oil City Symphony*: (l-r) Mike Craver, Mary Ehlinger, Philip Cress, and Mary Murfitt.

Photo: Paul Perone

Now, there wasn't an actual symphony, or much of a plot, just a loose setup. Four geeky high school alumni musicians gather with their small-town neighbors at the Oil City school gym to honor their former music teacher with a recital. The gymnasium is decorated, as might be expected, with crepe paper streamers. The two males are wearing outdated tuxedos and the two women are in tacky formals that appear to be left over from a prom ages ago. Onto this is laid a charming mix of humor and eighteen songs—some original and some standards. Familiar tunes range from the "1812 Overture" to rock and roll "In-A-Gadda-Da-Vida," and even the "Hokey Pokey."

Silly? Certainly, but it had won both the Drama Desk and Outer Critics Circle awards for Best Off-Broadway Musical in 1988. The New York production had received good reviews from no less than the *New York Times*, *Time Magazine*, and the *New Yorker*. And half of the original cast and two of the co-authors were in the Hippodrome production, so it was a sure bet.

Mary Murfitt, who co-authored the play with Mike Craver, Mark Hardwick, and Debra Monk, directed the show at the Hippodrome as well as appearing in it. Co-author Mike Craver was also in the cast. With them were Mary Ehlinger and Philip Cress. Philip had performed the show with Mary Murfitt previously.

The talented quartet sang and played multiple instruments. Mike played synthesizer; Philip, piano and accordion; Mary Murfitt, violin, flute, and saxophone. Drummer Mary Ehlinger did a show-stopping solo. They also danced, and at one point got the audience doing the Hokey Pokey. Pushing the parody of small-town high to its limits, several old-fashioned metal folding chairs were brought onstage and audience members invited to sit in them so they'd have a better view. After the show, the cast served the audience cookies and punch in the Hippodrome lobby.

Local reviewers matched the praise of the New York critics, calling *Oil City Symphony* "a musical laugh-a-thon" that "elicited roll-in-the-aisles non-stop laughter."[11]

Not only was the show a success for the Hippodrome, but it came with its own director, cast, sets, costumes, and lighting plan.

Family Performance Series

The Hippodrome had made its reputation on bringing cutting-edge theatre to Gainesville. The language and/or themes were often inappropriate for children. To balance that, the Hipp inaugurated the Family Performance Series in 1994, which aimed to present a family-friendly mainstage play that both children and adults would enjoy. The first offering was an adaptation of Lewis Carroll's *Alice in Wonderland* written by Hippodrome play-wright-in-residence David Boyce and directed by Lauren Caldwell.

Alice was played by UF student and Hippodrome intern Kathi Sanderlin, who had made her Hippodrome debut in *Earthly Possessions* as Mindy, the bank robber's pregnant girlfriend. In the opening scene of *Alice in Wonderland*, where Alice falls down the rabbit hole, Kathi had to fall from a four-foot-high scaffold into the arms of a six-foot-five-inch cast member and was then passed around from person to person, simulating Alice's tumbling fall.[12]

Discussing the show's appeal, Kathi said, "There are moments that are in the head, intellectual, but they're very physical. The kids will get it on a physical level and laugh, and the parents will get it on an intellectual level and laugh."[13]

The White Rabbit was played by Jimmy Jay, who'd debuted at the Hippodrome in *Biloxi Blues*. He'd just returned to Gainesville after a four-year stint doing theatre and television in Los Angeles.

Photo: *Gainesville Sun*

Kathi Sanderlin as Alice surrounded by the cast of characters in *Alice in Wonderland*.

Brad Evans played multiple characters, among them the Cheshire Cat. Also performing multiple roles were Bonnie Harrison, Assistant Director of Education; Marcia Brown, who worked with the HITT program; and Jolynn Graham Keith, who had toured in the Education Department's play about recycling, *EcoHeroes*.

Alice in Wonderland ran from July 21–August 14. The following year, the Education Department toured it throughout Florida as part of state touring program.

Season Twenty-two

While *Alice in Wonderland* was still onstage, Brad Evans, Jimmy Jay, and Jolynn Graham Keith began rehearsing with Sara Morsey, Dan Jesse, and Patrick Lennon for the Hippodrome's season opener, *Beau Jest* by James Sherman.

Jolynn had the lead as Sarah Goldman, a nice Jewish girl with a big problem. Sarah's parents (Sara Morsey and Dan Jesse) think it's time for her to settle down with a nice Jewish boy. But her boyfriend, played by Brad Evans, is a WASP. To appease her parents, she invents a new boyfriend and hires an actor (Patrick Lennon) to play her imaginary beau. With a lot of luck and a little help from watching *Fiddler on the Roof*, he improvises his way through several family dinners and wins the approval of her parents. But things become complicated. He falls in love with Sarah and she with him, then her brother unravels her deception.

The *Beau Jest* dinner scene: (clockwise from left) Jimmy Jay, Dan Jesse, Jolynn Graham Keith, Patrick Lennon, and Sara Morsey.

The romantic comedy had been a big hit in Chicago and New York, but according to Arline Greer, playwright James Sherman held it back several years before he let it "be performed in cities lacking significant Jewish audiences. Why?"[14] Greer explained Sherman's rationale: "The *Beau Jest* humor is Jewish; its one-liners stem from the comedy of its Jewish dilemma; the language is sometimes Jewish. But Sherman need not have worried about his audience. The humor of the play's contrivances, combined with the universal themes of parents wanting what's best for their children and children wanting to please their parents are recognizable to anyone.... Director Lauren Caldwell has taken pains to make her characters identifiable to audiences of any religious persuasion."[15]

Beau Jest ran September 2–25, 1994.

Fall Musical

Following *Beau Jest*, the Hippodrome presented *The World Goes 'Round*. A musical revue conceived by Scott Ellis, Susan Stroman, and David Thompson, it strung together thirty numbers written by the team of John Kander (music) and Fred Ebb (lyrics). The two men were famous for Broadway mega-hits *Chicago*; *Cabaret*; *And All That Jazz*; *New York, New York*; and *Kiss of the Spider Woman*. The revue, featuring songs from those shows plus five others, had won the 1991 Drama Desk and Outer Critic's Circle awards for Best Musical.

Lauren Caldwell directed it, with musical direction by Geraldine O'Mahoney and choreography by Sara Morsey. A cast of outstanding vocalists sang and danced their way across the stage, including a hilarious number where the actors tried to execute a Radio City Rockettes routine on roller skates.

"No mistaking it," Arline Greer wrote. "When you're hot, you're hot. The Hippodrome State Theatre's production of Kander and Ebb's musical *The World Goes 'Round* is so hot, it simmers, it sizzles, it flames with theatrical excitement.

"Itanza Wooden, Kathy Tyrell, Abby Lindsay, Tom Dusenbury, and Steve Wilkerson are the skilled performers and, in the course of performing the show's thirty songs, each has the opportunity to shine. Each of the songs, performed by a brilliant cast of five, is a small drama or comedy in itself. Witty, sad, ironic, kooky, wistful, torchy, romantic, these songs run the gamut of styles, and so do the performers who sing and dance to them. *The World Goes 'Round* moves with irresistible theatrical pizazz."[16]

The show ran from October 14–November 6.

(l-r) Kathy Tyrell, Tom Dusenbury, Itanza Wooden, Abby Lindsay, and Steve Wilkerson sing in *The World Goes 'Round*.

Same Scrooge, New Humbug

Hippodrome playwright-in-residence David Boyce wrote a new adaptation of Charles Dickens's *A Christmas Carol* for their seventeenth production. Gone were the singing and dancing of the musical version penned by Carlos Asse and Jim Wren, which they had staged annually since 1988. Rusty Salling still played Scrooge, but for the first time, audiences had to pay. An ad for the play said they would still collect food and toys for the underprivileged, but tickets cost ten bucks for adults and five for children.

After he found out they were charging admission, Hippodrome co-founder Greg von Hausch, who was no longer with the theatre, said, "Yeah, I know you need the money. But God, that was such a wonderful thing that you did for free. Everybody was just in the spirit of Christmas, and it generated a lot of goodwill."

Despite the charge for tickets, the show remained popular and ran a full month, from November 18–December 18. But like the two characters that come to Scrooge's workplace trying to solicit contributions, the Hippodrome management was back before the Alachua County Commission. As they had the previous December, they sought $75,000 from the Tourist Development funds immediately, to be followed by another $125,000 later. Like Scrooge's solicitors in their first attempt, they were rebuffed. Eventually, they got the money.

Donated food and toys surround a Christmas tree in the second-floor lobby.

1   Arline Greer, review of *Songs My Mother Taught Me*, by Melba Moore, David Boyce, Lauren Caldwell, and Mary Hausch, directed by Mary Hausch and Lauren Caldwell, Hippodrome Theatre, Gainesville, FL, *Gainesville Sun*, January 14, 1994.

2   Ibid.

3   Ibid.

4   "From the Mouth of Melba," *Gainesville Sun*, February 3, 1994.

5   Arline Greer, review of *Earthly Possessions*, by Frank Galati, directed by Mary Hausch, Hippodrome Theatre, Gainesville, FL, *Gainesville Sun*, February 25, 1994.

6   Ibid.

7   Dick Kerekes, review of *Lost in Yonkers*, by Neil Simon, directed by Lauren Caldwell, Hippodrome Theatre, Gainesville, FL, *First Coast Entertainer*, April 23, 1994.

8   Arline Greer, review of *Lost in Yonkers*, by Neil Simon, directed by Lauren Caldwell, Hippodrome Theatre, Gainesville, FL, *Gainesville Sun*, April 15, 1994.

9   Ibid.

10 Bill DeYoung, "Young Star on the Rise," *Gainesville Sun*, May 6, 1994.

11 Arline Greer, review of *Oil City Symphony*, by Mike Craver, Mark Hardwick, Debra Monk, and Mary Murfitt, directed by Mary Murfitt, Hippodrome Theatre, Gainesville, FL, *Gainesville Sun*, June 10, 1994.

12 Alycia Spector, "Adventures in Wonderland," *Gainesville Sun*, July 29, 1994.

13 Ibid.

14 Arline Greer, review of *Beau Jest*, by James Sherman, directed by Lauren Caldwell, Hippodrome Theatre, Gainesville, FL, *Gainesville Sun*, September 9, 1994.

15 Ibid.

16 Arline Greer, review of *The World Goes 'Round*, by John Kander and Fred Ebb, directed by Lauren Caldwell, Hippodrome Theatre, Gainesville, FL, *Gainesville Sun*, October 21, 1994.

1995

Broken Glass

After a year of musicals and comedies, Mary Hausch said, "We wanted to do a serious, challenging play. Audiences have asked for that." She chose to direct Arthur Miller's newest play. Mary said, "*Broken Glass* is one of the best plays we've read in years. It's a socially relevant drama and... relates to what's going on today in the world: the fragmentation of society; individual responsibility; should we become involved or not?"[1] Mary was referring to news reports of systematic ethnic cleansing in Bosnia during the 1990s.

Miller derived the play's title from "Kristallnacht," which translates as "Night of Broken Glass." It refers to the shards of broken glass that littered the streets after the windows of Jewish-owned stores, buildings, and synagogues were smashed in a night of violence and arson the Nazi party carried out against the Jews in 1938.

Photo: Michael Beebe/*Gainesville Sun*

Sara Morsey and David Shelton in *Broken Glass*.

Broken Glass is set in Brooklyn, New York, that same year. Phillip and Sylvia are a long-married Jewish couple. Although safely ensconced thousands of miles from Nazi Germany, Sylvia suddenly becomes paralyzed and confined to a wheelchair after reading about Kristallnacht in the paper. Ray Dooley and Sara Morsey played Phillip and Sylvia.

Their neighbor, a Jewish physician played by David Shelton, examines Sylvia and can find nothing physically wrong. He believes Sylvia's paralysis is psychosomatic, and though he's not a psychiatrist, he begins to treat her according to his diagnosis. In doing so, the doctor learns more about the problems Sylvia is having in her personal life, particularly in her marriage.

Then Phillip, who works on foreclosures in a Brooklyn bank, has a heart attack at work. While dying at home, he and Sylvia confront each other about their feelings. His final words are "Sylvia, forgive me!" Upon his death, Sylvia's paralysis is cured.

Once Arthur Miller was told that the Hippodrome is a special American theatre willing to risk mounting a work that challenges the mind, rather than going for easy entertainment, he agreed to be interviewed by phone from his home in Roxbury, Connecticut. "*Broken Glass*, basically, in one sense, is about the tendency toward denial and what that does to people on both a personal level and a political level," he said. "Sylvia is a very empathetic individual. She puts herself in the place of other people." At the same time, the playwright admitted, "It interested me that it [Sylvia's intuitive feeling] could travel over 3,000 miles of water. It implies a connection that's invisible."[2]

Miller ended the interview with a personal message to lovers of the theatre, and to the Hippodrome: "I'm glad people are as interested as you are. You can't give up hope. There's always tomorrow."[3]

Also in the cast were Rachel Tench as Sylvia's sister, Rusty Salling as Phillip's employer, and Robin Olson as the doctor's wife. Although many questions remained unresolved when the houselights came up after the final scene, audiences had watched with rapt attention. Reviews called it a riveting drama. The show, which opened January 13, had to be held over an extra week, closing on February 12.

Clair de Lune—French for Moonlight

Obie Award-winning New York actor Ray Dooley stayed on after *Broken Glass* to play Johnny in the Hippodrome's next play, *Frankie and Johnny in the Clair de Lune* by playwright Terrence McNally. Kate Hurd, also from New York City, was cast as Frankie.

Johnny, a physically fit, over-forty short-order cook, is certain he has found his soul mate in Frankie, a frumpy middle-aged waitress, when their first date ends in bed. She, convinced of her unattractiveness, is ready to write off the encounter as a one-night stand.

In the afterglow, they struggle over the possibility of falling in love. He's ready to leap. Frankie's disinclined to jump to conclusions. The interplay between them as they slowly reveal themselves to each other is poignant and sometimes hilarious.

In a romantic gesture, Johnny calls the radio station to request the disc jockey play "the most beautiful music ever written" for his lady. From the radio comes Claude Debussy's "Clair de Lune." Buoyant with love, Johnny beckons Frankie to join him at the window to bask in the moonlight. Hence, the title for the play.

Photo: Brian Lukanic

Ray Dooley as Johnny and Kate Hurd as Frankie in *Frankie and Johnny in the Clair de Lune.*

Arline Greer said in her review, "It probably goes without saying that the success of a two character play lies with the actors who portray the roles. Ray Dooley's Johnny is filled with passion, romance, humor and a desperation that underlies it all. He gives Johnny tenderness and sincerity. Kate Hurd... is a lovely actress. She moves her Frankie from guarded suspicion to curiosity, humor, resignation, and acceptance in a slow, steady development of her character. McNally's dialogue for the two is clever, witty and ultimately touching. The humor springs directly from the characters.... Lauren Caldwell has directed with spirited timing, respect for [the play's] subtleties and good taste."[4]

The show ran March 3–26. Ads warned, "Explicit language and nudity." But those who came for that got a moving, funny, romantic comedy as part of the bargain.

Swordplay, Sorcery, and Love

From April 21–May 14, the Hippodrome presented *The Illusion,* award-winning playwright Tony Kushner's adaptation of the 1636 play by Pierre Corneille.

The enchanting tale, filled with magic, sorcery, sword fights, lovestruck entanglements, and hilarious bravado, is set in seventeenth-century France. A repentant

Top: Robert Ellis. Bottom: (l-r) Robert Patrik Thompson, Caylen Clark, Sara Morsey, Peter Zachari, Carla Capps, and Timothy Altmeyer in *The Illusion*.

Photo: Julie Esbjorn

father, seeking news of his prodigal son, enters the cave of the magician Alcandre. There, he learns some powerful lessons about fathers and children, love and passion, and magic and art as the sorcerer conjures three episodes from the son's life. Plays within the play, each vignette shows the boy in different amorous relationships as he progresses in his development. The father watches, but only as the strange tale reaches its conclusion does he decide to re-embrace his son.

The *Gainesville Sun* review called it "a dazzling production" and said, "Under Lauren Caldwell's astute direction, the play moves like some great colorful kaleidoscope. The Hippodrome's cast for *The Illusion* is brilliant. Sara Morsey, who plays Alcandre, the magician, brings clarity and majesty to her role. Traber Burns, who plays Pridamant, the father, gives a believable performance, combining humor and skepticism. As the banished son, Timothy Altmeyer makes a wonderfully romantic, athletic, and, ultimately pathetic figure. Carla Capps, who plays the woman he loves in all the play's vignettes, gives a lovely, touching performance as ingénue, lover, and wronged wife."[5]

Sara recalls, "I was the first woman in the country to play Alcandre. I think I kind of talked my way into that role by suggesting that a woman could certainly play that part. It didn't have to be a man. And the kid was Tim Altmeyer. It was his first play at the Hippodrome. He was right out of school and he was nuts and it was great. He was a really good actor who did everything in rehearsal—you know, he didn't hold back."

For Tim, that included three days of sword fighting practice with Robert Patrik Thompson, who played his opponent in each vignette. Filling out the other roles were Robert Ellis, Caylen Clark, and Peter Zachari.

UFOs—a Florida Perspective

A play about an aviator in China who invented an airplane only six years after the Wright brothers was bumped from the Hippodrome schedule in favor of more bizarre aerial phenomena.

The theatre had managed to snag the Southeastern premiere of the wacky off-Broadway hit *The Sugar Bean Sisters*, which had just completed a very successful run and was being remounted in September. Within that window of opportunity, the Hippodrome got the rights to the play and the author, Nathan Sanders, came to Gainesville for the opening. "I'm more excited about this production than I was about New York, because Florida is my home," Sanders told the *Gainesville Sun.* "It's a thrill."[6]

The story is set in Sugar Bean, Florida—a fictional place about forty miles from Disney World. Two downright loony Mormon sisters, Faye and Willie Mae, watch the skies from the backyard of their home on the edge of the Watchalahoochee Swamp. Faye (Lauren Caldwell) is convinced space people will return on the twenty-fifth anniversary of a UFO landing that occurred in the sugar cane fields where the circular scar of their first visit is still visible. Willie Mae (Nell Page) is looking for an angel to lift her up to the celestial kingdom but wouldn't mind running off with Bishop Crumley (Brad Evans). Then a feathered creature wanders in from the swamps. She turns out to be Videllia Sparks, a dancer from New Orleans who performs dressed as a bird. Videllia, played by Diane Bearden, tries to con the sisters out of their fortune, which Willie Mae has buried somewhere in the backyard.

Photo: Wendy Kernodle

The Sugar Bean Sisters, Willie Mae (Nell Page) and Faye (Lauren Caldwell), watch for UFOs with exotic dancer Videllia Sparks (Diane Bearden).

Anyone who has driven through Florida has passed signs inviting tourists to visit reptile farms, so Sanders adds one more character, Reptile Woman (Bonnie Harrison), a person who runs Reptile World and rids homes of snakes with her uncanny ability to smell them.

Much of the play's fun comes from its zany banter. The play opens with the sisters' arrival home from an exasperating day trip to Disney World. Faye tells her sister, "I've got one nerve left, and you are danglin' from it."[7] But, Sanders told the *Sun*, "This play is not a laugh machine. These women are real. Although they're not educated, their lives are important. Listen to what they're saying, not how they're saying it."[8]

The critics thought otherwise, calling it, "an exuberantly wacky comedy."[9] Arline Greer said, "Sanders' dialogue for *The Sugar Bean Sisters* is laced with acid humor reflecting the love-hate relationship of the sisters. Sparkling hot one-liners follow hard on each other's heels as the sisters fight for their separate dreams. Interjecting yet a third dimension of humor with her inspired acting is Diane Beardon.... Mary Hausch's direction moves with inspired, unfailing, humor."[10]

Audiences loved the show, which opened June 9 and had its run extended two extra weeks, closing July 16.

Tangled Tales for Summer

For the second year of their Family Performance Series, the Hippodrome presented an original play scripted by co-founder and resident costume designer Marilyn Wall. *Tangled Tales: The Wolf, His Lunch, Her Grandmother and Some Pigs*, was just that—a hilarious mix of Little Red Riding Hood, Goldilocks and the Three Bears, Cinderella, and The Three Little Pigs.

A young girl visits her grandmother on a hot summer's day and shares an adventure as her grandmother weaves classic fairy tales into one magical fable. The Hippodrome ads called it "an enchanting romp." The show ran from July 25–August 13. The cast included Sara Morsey, Brad Evans, Jimmy Jay, Marcia Brown, and Patrick Lennon.

Red Riding Hood (Sara Morsey) and Grandma (Marcia Brown) in *Tangled Tales: The Wolf, His Lunch, Her Grandmother and Some Pigs*.

Season Twenty-three

Opening their twenty-third season was Wendy Wasserstein's *The Sisters Rosensweig*, which had won five Outer Critics Circle Awards, including Best Broadway Play. The Hippodrome had originally scheduled it for February, but the producers wouldn't release the rights until September, so *The Illusion* had been presented instead. Even with the delay, the Hippodrome became one of the first theatres to receive the rights to it.

The play was a comedy, but the Rosensweig sisters were as different from the Sugar Bean sisters as one could imagine and as different from each other as their first names. The eldest, Sara, played by Sara Morsey, is president of an international bank. The middle sister, played by Jennifer Pritchett, is named Gorgeous and hosts a radio call-in advice show. The youngest sister, Pfeni, played by Robin Proett Olson, is a famous travel writer.

The sisters gather in the sitting room of Sara's swanky London home, ostensibly to celebrate her fifty-fourth birthday. But Pfeni is also in town to rendezvous with her new lover (Mark Chambers), a bisexual theatre director whose gay side she hasn't come to terms with. Pfeni's lover brings his friend Merv (Dan Jesse), a purveyor of faux fur visiting from New York who instantly falls for Sara. Joining the party is Sara's daughter Tess (Tamerin Corn) and her dim-witted boyfriend (Heath Ward), a member of the Lithuanian resistance. Rounding out the cast is Rusty Salling as Sara's stuffy British companion.

Photo: Brian Lukanic

The Sisters Rosensweig and their men. Front (l-r): Robin Proett Olson, Sara Morsey, Jennifer Pritchett, and Tamerin Corn. Back: Rusty Salling, Mark Chambers, and Dan Jesse.

Between the many comical lines is an underlying contrast between Sara, who has spent her lifetime denying her Brooklyn Jewish roots, and Gorgeous, who has embraced them entirely. Arline Greer wrote, "The best reason to see the play is for the performances of Jennifer Pritchett as Gorgeous and Sara Morsey as Sara. Many actresses have had a field day with the stereotypical Gorgeous. It's hard to imagine or remember anyone funnier than Jennifer Pritchett. She lights up the stage. Morsey, at the other end of the spectrum, plays the cool, sophisticated, Sara with exquisite style that lets you know who's in control."[11]

Masters of humorous characters, Dan and Rusty were well-known to Hippodrome audiences, but with Mark Chambers's debut, director Lauren Caldwell introduced Gainesville to a comedic talent she would bring back again and again.

The Sisters Rosensweig opened September 8 and ran through October 8.

Of Maps and Chairs

Mary Hausch, director of the next play, *Lonely Planet*, called it an absurdist comedy—possibly because the script by Steven Dietz heavily references Eugène Ionesco's comedy *The Chairs*. But it has also been described as a compassionate two-character comedy about gay men dealing with friendship and fears during the AIDS epidemic.

Jody, played by Traber Burns, owns a small map store on the oldest street in an American city and is seemingly worldly and knowledgeable. Carl, played by Rusty Salling, is a frequent visitor to the store who has either held a lot of different jobs or is lying about his varied vocations.

The play opens with Jody finding that Carl has deposited a chair in his store. Soon, Jody's store is littered with mismatched chairs. In an argument between the two, it is revealed that every chair was owned by someone they knew in the gay community who died from AIDS. Carl, who helps empty the residences afterward, can't stand to see the chairs abandoned and alone, so he brings them to Jody's store. The play's humorous dialogue between Jody and Carl is laced with observations about human behavior, the serendipity of friendship, and the cruelty of the world.

Photo: Brian Lukanic

Rusty Salling and Traber Burns in a scene from *Lonely Planet*.

Arline Greer called it "a beautifully written, provocative, funny, absorbing play with an original perspective." She said, "It doesn't deal just with AIDS or gay men. *Lonely Planet*'s major focus is on friendship and the improbable ties that bring together people who seemingly are disparate types. Rusty Salling, the quirky Carl of multi careers, has never done finer acting than he does here. Traber Burns as Jody is no less so."[12]

Lonely Planet ran from October 20–November 12.

Another New *Christmas Carol*

For their eighteenth annual production of *A Christmas Carol*, Mary Hausch and Bonnie Harrison co-wrote a new script that Bonnie directed. It replaced the version David Boyce had penned just the year before.

"Some people really, really liked it last year, and some people didn't," Bonnie told the *Gainesville Sun*. "I've also heard some didn't like the musical version. And I'm sure some people won't like this version either.... It's important for us to change from year to year. For the actors, too—Rusty having done many, many a year, it gives him a little different leaning on the character."[13]

The production ran a full month, from November 24 through December 23. Rusty still played Scrooge. Traber Burns was the new Bob Cratchit. Nell Page played Mrs. Cratchit, her daughter Molly played Martha Cratchit, and son, Will, played Tiny Tim.

Scrooge purchases the "prize turkey" from the son of the poulterer (played by Michael McShane).

Photo: Randy Batista

1   Greer, Arline, "Curtain Up on the 1995 Season," *Gainesville Sun*, January 13, 1995.
2   Ibid.
3   Ibid.
4   Arline Greer, review of *Frankie and Johnny in the Clair de Lune*, by Terrence McNally, directed by Lauren Caldwell, Hippodrome Theatre, Gainesville, FL, *Gainesville Sun*, March 10, 1995.
5   Arline Greer, review of *The Illusion*, by Tony Kushner, directed by Lauren Caldwell, Hippodrome Theatre, Gainesville, FL, *Gainesville Sun*, April 28, 1995.
6   Arline Greer, "One Seriously Comic Play," *Gainesville Sun*, June 9, 1995.
7   Nathan Sanders, *The Sugar Bean Sisters*, Dramatic Publishing, Woodstock, IL.
8   Arline Greer, "One Seriously Comic Play," *Gainesville Sun*, June 9, 1995..
9   Arline Greer, review of *The Sugar Bean Sisters*, by Nathan Sanders, directed by Mary Hausch, Hippodrome Theatre, Gainesville, FL, *Gainesville Sun*, June 16, 1995.
10 Ibid.
11 Arline Greer, review of *The Sisters Rosensweig*, by Wendy Wasserstein, directed by Lauren Caldwell, Hippodrome Theatre, Gainesville, FL, *Gainesville Sun*, September 15, 1995.
12 Arline Greer, review of *Lonely Planet*, by Steven Dietz, directed by Mary Hausch, Hippodrome Theatre, Gainesville, FL, *Gainesville Sun*, October 27, 1995.
13 Bill DeYoung, "A Different Perspective on Ebenezer Scrooge," *Gainesville Sun*, November 24, 1995.

1996

Six One Acts

Although the Hippodrome had experienced mixed results presenting collections of one-act plays over the years, David Ives's *All in the Timing* was well received. First, unlike earlier attempts, all six plays were written by the same author—winner of the Outer Critics Circle Award for Playwriting. Second, they had a common theme, spoofing language and society's inability to communicate. Third, they were genuinely funny. The plays varied in length from eight to twenty minutes, never overstaying the joke.

The show had been a hit off-Broadway, winning accolades from New York critics for its witty wordplay, sentiments echoed by local reviewers. "*All in the Timing* is original, a rarity in contemporary theater. With Lauren Caldwell's sharp direction... the Hippodrome does it justice," wrote Arline Greer.[1] The Jacksonville reviewer raved, "The Hippodrome has opened 1996 by continuing its standard of excellence in professional theatre for the North Florida area."[2]

The six plays shared a common set consisting of a circular stage with two- or three-foot-tall letters of the alphabet suspended behind the actors. Each play had two to four characters, played by various combinations of Nell Page, Rusty Salling, Sara Morsey, Peter Zachari, and Damon Maida.

In the first play, *Sure Thing*, Nell and Damon's characters meet in a restaurant and strike up a conversation. But unfortunately, he turns her off by saying the wrong thing. Each time he does, a bell rings and the conversation starts over until, finally, they romantically connect.

Next, in *Words, Words, Words*, a research professor locks three monkeys in a room with typewriters until they can come up with *Hamlet*. They have no idea what *Hamlet* is, but they come up with some gems.

For *The Philadelphia*, Nell and Sara portray waitresses. Rusty's character has just ordered food using a very convoluted banter. His friend, played by Damon Maida, arrives frustrated by the day he's having. After he lists the odd things that have happened, Rusty explains that Damon is ensnared in an anomalous pocket of reality called a "Philadelphia," in which he can only get what he wants by asking for what he doesn't want.

The Universal Language is a funny play about a shy, stuttering woman and a con man running a language school to teach Unamunda, a univer-

All in the Timing actors (l-r) Damon Maida, Nell Page, Rusty Salling, Peter Zachari, and Sara Morsey illustrate various characters in six one-act plays.

Photo: Alan Campbell

sal language he claims to have invented. With rapid-fire patter, he strings together nonsense syllables. "It's strange how much I understand," she tells him. As the two begin to fall in love, he confesses his scam.

The playwright had received much praise for *Philip Glass Buys a Loaf of Bread*, a satire of the renowned composer's music that mimics Glass's unusual musical structure in the orchestrated language used by David Ives's four characters. Yes, Philip Glass is one of them, and he does indeed buy a loaf of bread from the baker.

The last play of the show is *Variations on the Death of Trotsky*, a series of comic vignettes that show revolutionary Leon Trotsky dying over and over again until he ultimately makes his final philosophical statements on human life before dying the last time.

All in the Timing ran from January 5–28.

New Management and Extra Venue

Also in January, the Hippodrome announced several changes. Lauren Caldwell was named Artistic Director, a position previously held only by the six founders and Marshall New. Lauren continued in this role until she left the company in 2018. Mark Sexton, who had been serving as Director of Development, became General Manager—a post he would hold until 2004.

The Hippodrome had also cemented a relationship with Florida Community College at Jacksonville to bring plays to its new 600-seat Wilson Center for the Arts slated for completion that spring. The college also planned to hire Hippodrome staff as adjunct faculty and set up an artist-in-residence program.

A Modern Classic

Next, the Hippodrome staged *To Kill a Mockingbird*, Christopher Sergel's dramatization of Harper Lee's classic Pulitzer Prize-winning novel. Set in 1935, a small Alabama town is caught up in racial tension created by a highly charged trial. The events are narrated by a grown-up version of Scout, the young daughter of defense attorney Atticus Finch.

A no-account white woman, Mayella Ewell, has falsely accused African American Tom Robinson of rape. Her drunken father backs up her lie. As Atticus prepares to defend Tom in court, townspeople direct increasing hostility toward the accused and the Finch family. Witnessing the turmoil are Scout, her older brother Jem, and their young friend, Dill, who are at the heart of the story.

To find the right three actors to play Scout, Jem, and Dill, director Lauren Caldwell auditioned 100 children. In the end, Elya Ottenberg, who had played Arty in *Lost in Yonkers,* was cast as Jem. Kjell Ryerson, who had previously played Tiny Tim in *A Christmas Carol,* got the part of Dill. The critical role of Scout went to eleven-year-old Alison Jim, who had played Marta in the Hippodrome Summer Spectacular production of *The Sound of Music.*

The cast of To Kill a Mockingbird poses on the set of Atticus Finch's house. Standing (l-r): Elya Ottenberg, Itanza Wooden, Gerald Rivers, Rachel Tench, Rusty Salling, Ellen Lau, Rhonda Wilson, Tracy Salter, Dan Jesse, and Heath Ward. Seated (l-r): Kjell Ryerson, Alison Jim, Traber Burns, Sara Morsey, Michael Beistle, Frank Edmondson, Nell Page, Patrick Lennon, and Damon Maida.

Photo: Brian Lukanic

The central themes of ignorance and fear of the unknown are paralleled in the children's pursuit of Scout and Jem's mysterious hermit neighbor, Boo Radley. Atticus fights his legal battle with a result that is part defeat and part triumph. Scout learns lessons that change her life forever, not only about human flaws but also about her father and human dignity.

The play opened on February 16, during Black History Month. The Hippodrome developed outreach programs for local schools, including a specialized curriculum based on the book. Following a Sunday matinee performance, the theatre hosted a panel of community leaders and activists in a forum to discuss racial division. County Commissioner Charles Chestnut moderated it.

Actress Itanza Wooden, who played Calpurnia, the Finch family's no-nonsense housekeeper, told the *Gainesville Sun* she believes *Mockingbird* carries a strong message for everyone "because racism is still there—it's disguised, but it's still out there today."[3]

The play proved immensely popular, exceeding all expectations and selling out almost every performance. Its run had to be extended twice, finally closing on March 24. According to General Manager Mark Sexton, it was "the most successful production in the Hippodrome's twenty-three-year history, with total attendance of more than 12,000 people."[4]

"This Mockingbird Sings," Arline Greer headlined her review.[5] She said, "The taut silence of a rapt audience totally engrossed in this moving play guarantees it. Not only do its historical truths pertain to contemporary thought, but it moves the mind and touches the heart in ways that only fine art can do.

"Outstanding actor Traber Burns plays the role of Atticus in the play, creating a character who is completely his own. Nell Page Sexton as the grown-up Jean

Louise carries us through the narrative with the voice of Harper Lee herself. The narration is skillfully interwoven with the play's action so that the dramatic flow is constant. At the same time, it offers insights into the behavior of the protagonists. Lauren Caldwell has taken her cast of 19 people and molded them into a small society, epitomizing the townfolk.... They come to life in a multidimensional set designed by Carlos Asse.

"The play's three children: Alison Jim's Scout, Elya Ottenberg's Jem, and Kjell Ryerson's Dill, give winning performances. Gerald Rivers as Tom Robinson, the accused rapist, gives a thoroughly convincing performance. As Mayella, the woman he is alleged to have attacked, Tracy Salter is white trash all the way, and Dan Jesse is fittingly obnoxious as Mayella's drunken father. Michael Beistle makes an authoritative Sheriff Heck Tate. Three neighbors are interpreted expertly by Sara Morsey, Rachel Tench and Ellen Lau, respectively."[6]

The rest of the cast, who also did fine work in the production, included Patrick Lennon, Rhonda Wilson, Frank Edmondson, Damon Maida, Rusty Salling as the judge, and Heath Ward as the elusive Boo Radley.

Not that things started smoothly. Lauren Caldwell recalls a funny story from opening night. "Dan Jesse and Mike Beistle were old-timers, and I was the new kid on the block," she said, recalling a scene where their characters had to shoot a rabid dog. I said to the stage manager and to Mike and Dan, 'Now, make sure that you test that rifle every night so that we make sure that it's going off.' And this is what they said to me, 'Don't you worry your pretty little head about it. We got it covered.'"

"Okay," she said.

Continuing the story, she recounted, "Then on opening night, sure enough, the gun doesn't go off, and I am just sitting there shaking my head, wondering if they had tested the darn thing, thinking that they probably had not. The story, the myth, goes that Dan Jesse went out in the vom and supposedly kicked the dog.... I don't remember that moment exactly, but I do remember that on opening night, that gun did not go off."

> **Vom?**
>
> The entrance aisles on either side of the Hippodrome's center seating area are called the "voms," a term dating back to Roman times. During productions, actors often use the vom to enter or exit a scene.

Another Bit of Simon's Past

For their next play, Neil Simon's *Laughter on the 23rd Floor*, director Mary Hausch cast five of the actors from *Mockingbird*: Traber Burns, Dan Jesse, Nell Page, Tracy Salter, and Heath Ward. Joining them were Pat Lennon, David Hopkins, Peter Zachari, and Gregg Jones in the role of Max Prince.

The script drew heavily on Neil Simon's memories of his time as a writer for Sid Caesar's *Your Show of Shows*, one of television's earliest and most popular comedy shows. In addition to Simon, Caesar's other brilliant writers included Woody Allen, Mel Brooks, Larry Gelbart, Carl Reiner, and the sole woman on the team, Selma Diamond. In the play, their names are changed, but their personalities are recognizable to those familiar with their later work.

Photo: Renee Benoist

Acting out an idea in a scene from *Laughter on the 23rd Floor* are (l-r) Patrick Lennon, Heath Ward, Gregg Jones, Tracy Salter, David Hopkins, and Nell Page.

The entire story takes place in the writer's room at NBC in New York City. The time is 1953, the height of McCarthyism. Max Prince is a comic genius, a tyrant, and a paranoiac with a heart of gold who vows not to bend to sponsors or NBC executives. His show, once the highest rated on TV, is no longer at the top, and the network is moving toward sitcoms. His writers, a team of brilliantly funny social misfits devoted to their boss, create joke after joke. The result is a play loaded with one-liners, mayhem, neuroses, nonstop gags, and constant one-upmanship.

"*Laughter on the 23rd Floor* has that commodity in abundance," wrote the *Gainesville Sun* reviewer. "It's not surprising then that Simon's *Laughter* is one long collection of jokes: one-liners, sight gags, and dipsy-doodle situations that go on nonstop all evening.... graced with a dynamic performance by Gregory Jones as the wild-eyed Max, whose political loyalties give rise not only to his comic genius but to his loyalty to the writers who nourish him. Jones gives a bravura performance, in the role of a lifetime. The others in the cast—particularly Dan Jesse and Traber Burns—are wonderfully fun."[7]

Not all the humor was scripted. Nell Page, who played the sole woman writer, recalls that the costume department had used a colander under her dress to make her look pregnant. "At one point Gregg's character comes up and hugs me and when he does, I heard this noise. I thought, 'Oh, my God, what's going on?' Well, he had pushed the colander in and I couldn't get it [to pop back] out. So here I was, I had this inverted baby."

Laughter on the 23rd Floor filled the theatre with laughs from April 12–May 5, 1996.

Photo: Jason Davis

Marion J. Caffey as Jelly Roll Morton in *Jelly Roll! The Music and The Man.*

Summer Shows

Opening June 7, and held over until July 14, was *Jelly Roll! The Music and The Man,* created by Vernel Bagneris from the music and lyrics of Jelly Roll Morton, arranged by musical director Morten Gunnar Larsen. It had won the Obie Award.

Marion J. Caffey, who starred in the Hippodrome production, had seen Vernel workshop the show and said it inspired him the way few others had. When Vernel called to say he was taking a break and offered the role to Marion, he jumped at it. By the time the Hippodrome presented the musical, Marion had performed it off-Broadway and toured North America for the preceding ten months, bringing to Gainesville a finely tuned performance.

Jelly Roll Morton was an American ragtime and jazz pianist, bandleader, and composer. Born and raised in the Creole world of New Orleans, he invented the jazz genre while playing dark, smoky backstreet bars in the early 1900s. Infinitely complex, gifted, foolish, superstitious, and enchanting, Jelly Roll Morton was the composer of some of the most memorable jazz ever written.

Accompanied by New York pianist Paul Asaro, Marion J. Caffey brought *Jelly Roll* to life in Gainesville with an exciting evening packed with music, song, dance, and stories of the unsung jazz genius. The *Sun* theatre critic praised it: "Under Lauren Caldwell's direction, *Jelly Roll* is a complete show, beautifully lighted by Robert P. Robins. And it's performed ever so joyously by the multitalented Marion J. Caffey and his brilliant pianist, Paul Asaro. [Caffey's] dancing is nothing less than inspired. He doesn't so much glide as slither. His movements are suave, smooth, humorous, acrobatic. When he dances, he's in a world by himself. It's almost as if the audience didn't exist."[8]

Five Days Later

Photo: Dede Smith

The Little Prince (Abby Lindsey) meets a downed aviator (David Shelton).

Hot on the heels of *Jelly Roll!* Was the Family Performance Series show *The Little Prince,* based on the famous book by Antoine de Saint-Exupéry, as adapted for the stage by Mark Brown and Paul Kiernan. Lauren Caldwell directed it. *The Little Prince* opened July 19 and ran through August 11, extended for an extra week.

Beloved by children and grownups alike, the story is told by a downed aviator (David Shelton) who recounts his encounter with a prince from a tiny planet no larger than a house. The prince's interplanetary travels have brought him into contact with a king, a businessman, a geographer, a lamplighter, a heavy drinker, a snake, and a fox. On Earth, he learns from the fox that what is really important in life is love and friendship.

Abby Lindsay, the star of *Ruthless!,* played the sweet little prince. Nell Page and Heath Ward played multiple characters the prince encountered on various planets.

(l-r) Dan Bright, Sara Morsey, Heath Ward, Traber Burns, Robin Bloodworth, and Abby Lindsay in *The Lion in Winter*.

Photo: Alan Campbell

Twenty-Fourth Season

The Hippodrome kicked off its new season with *The Lion in Winter*, James Goldman's portrayal of the volatile relationship between England's King Henry II and his politically powerful wife, Eleanor of Aquitaine. When they met, she was thirty and the former Queen of France. Henry was nineteen. Their marriage made them the dominant force in England and France and created three potential heirs to Henry's throne.

The play takes place at Christmastime in Henry's palace at Chinon, France. Henry II (Traber Burns) is with Eleanor (Sara Morsey), whom he has imprisoned for the past fifteen years. Their strong-willed sons, Richard the Lion Heart (Robin Bloodworth), Geoffrey (Dan Bright), and John (Heath Ward), who are all vying for his throne, have joined them.

Henry announces his plan to produce another heir with his young mistress, Alais (Abby Lindsay), whom Eleanor raised like a daughter but who is now her rival for Henry. To complicate matters, Alais is half sister of the King of France (Brik Berkes) and inconveniently is betrothed to Henry and Eleanor's son Richard. The holiday turns into a lustful, greedy, stormy quest for power, pitting husband against wife, brother against brother, and sons against parents.

New York set designer James Morgan created a cold medieval stone castle, populated by characters wearing elaborate period costumes designed by Marilyn Wall. Lauren Caldwell directed the play, which had two runs. From September 6–29, it played at the Hippodrome. Then, the set was struck and transported to the new Wilson Center for the Arts in Jacksonville, where the Hippodrome cast and crew restaged the show from October 4–20. It was the first play in the new facility and an auspicious beginning of a new relationship for the Hippodrome.

In another outreach gesture, the Hippodrome Education Department published *Perspectives,* a curriculum guide for *The Lion in Winter.* They made it available to students of the Alachua and Duval County School Systems as well as UF and Santa Fe Community College students. They continued to produce *Perspectives* curriculum guides for every show in the 1996–1997 season.

Man's Best Friend

What if your dog could talk? That is the premise behind A. R. Gurney's witty comedy *Sylvia,* directed by James Morgan. Greg, a New Yorker in the throes of a midlife crisis, finds stray dog Sylvia one day in Central Park and brings her home, much to the horror of his wife Kate. Sylvia, who can talk, gazes adoringly at her new master and declares, "I love you. I think you're God." Comedic fireworks ensue as Sylvia vies with Kate for Greg's affection, offering saucy comments and a unique "dog's eye view" of their twenty-two-year marriage.

Mark Sexton and Nell Page, real-life spouses at the time, played Greg and Kate. Lauren Caldwell happily set aside her director's hat for the role of the title character. "How many times does a woman get to play a dog?" she said. "They are few and far between."

Gregg Jones played three hilarious supporting roles: Tom, a macho dog owner who gives unsolicited advice about man's relationship with dogs; Leslie, an androgynous marriage counselor; and Phyllis, a socialite friend from Kate's years at Vassar.

(l-r) Gregg Jones as Phyllis, a socialite friend of Kate (Nell Page), is repulsed by Sylvia (Lauren Caldwell), the beloved mutt of Kate's husband (Mark Sexton).

Photo: Alan Campbell

One performance had an unintended hilarious improvisation. In the scene, the dog was supposed to jump onto Phyllis's lap. When she did, Gregg Jones's wig fell off. Lauren snatched it up, as a dog would, and began tossing it around the stage, playing "fetch." Nell finally retrieved it and put it back on him. But she got it on backwards.

Although Arline Greer called the script "a one-joke play," audiences laughed all the way through.[9] Still, she praised the acting: "Mark Sexton... makes the joke believable. Nell Page is sweetly annoyed as Kate. Gregg Jones is extremely funny. The laughs are courtesy of Lauren Caldwell... rambunctious, impudent, she's a bundle of animal enthusiasm."[10]

Sylvia ran for a full month, from October 25–November 24.

Yet Another New *Christmas Carol*

For its 1996 production, Mary Hausch wrote and directed another new adaptation of Charles Dicken's *A Christmas Carol*, replacing the version she and Bonnie Harrison had written the previous year. The show ran from December 3–22. According to General Manager Mark Sexton, the show "enjoyed an unprecedented box office and critical response."

1   Arline Greer, review of *All in the Timing*, by David Ives, directed by Lauren Caldwell, Hippodrome Theatre, Gainesville, FL, *Gainesville Sun*, January 12, 1996.
2   Dick Kerekes, review of *All in the Timing*, by David Ives, directed by Lauren Caldwell, Hippodrome Theatre, Gainesville, FL, *First Coast Entertainer*, January 13, 1996.
3   Bill DeYoung, "Mockingbird Still Sings True," *Gainesville Sun*, March 16, 1996.
4   Ibid.
5   Arline Greer, review of *To Kill a Mockingbird*, by Christopher Sergel, directed by Lauren Caldwell, Hippodrome Theatre, Gainesville, FL, *Gainesville Sun*, February 23, 1996.
6   Ibid.
7   Arline Greer, review of *Laughter on the 23rd Floor*, by Neil Simon, directed by Mary Hausch, Hippodrome Theatre, Gainesville, FL, *Gainesville Sun*, April 19, 1996.
8   Arline Greer, review of *Jelly Roll! The Man and the Music*, by Vernel Bagneris, directed by Lauren Caldwell, Hippodrome Theatre, Gainesville, FL, *Gainesville Sun*, June 14, 1996.
9   Arline Greer, review of *Sylvia*, by A. R. Gurney, directed by James Morgan, Hippodrome Theatre, Gainesville, FL, *Gainesville Sun*, November 1, 1996.
10 Ibid.

1997

Indiscretions

Reaffirming the Hippodrome's fondness for theatre of the absurd, they opened January 1997 with Jeremy Sams's translation of Jean Cocteau's dark comedy, *Indiscretions*, directed by Mary Hausch.

Theatre historians claim that Jean Cocteau wrote the play while on an eight-day opium binge. After it opened in 1938, the Council of Paris banned it for "being prejudicial to moral and public order." That, of course, made it even more popular. When Jeremy Sams's translation was produced on Broadway in 1995, it garnered nine Tony Award nominations. In Gainesville, the show had to be held over an extra week, running from January 10–February 9, 1997.

Set in 1938, it is a wildly twisting story of a bourgeoisie Parisian family. Traditional lines of love and lust become hopelessly confused and irreparably entangled in a whirlwind of infidelity, adultery, and mistaken identity. Yvonne is a hypochondriac mother so attached to her grown son, Michael, that she has pushed away her husband, George. The husband has taken a lover. Living with them is Yvonne's spinster sister, Leonie, who had once been engaged to George. When Michael's parents learn he has fallen in love with his girlfriend, Madeleine, they freak out—Yvonne because she's unwilling to let Michael go and George because he may have had a prior involvement with Madeleine.

Photo: Christine DeLano

Clockwise from top: Nell Page, Sara Morsey, David Hopkins, Ashley Homer, and Edmund J. Kearney in *Indiscretions*.

The *Gainesville Sun* called it "A great production and brilliant performance by the Hipp's cast of five.... Nell Page Sexton as [Leonie], the take-charge sister, gives a clipped, tart, and, ultimately, deadly performance that's chillingly funny. Sara Morsey, the flamboyant, destructive Yvonne, is all hysterics flouncing and pouting, the doting mother out of control. David Hopkins is funny and attractive as Michael.... Edmund J. Kearney is a blustery George.... Ashley Homer gives a lovely, believable performance as Madeleine, the girlfriend."[1]

In conjunction with the run of *Indiscretions*, the Hippodrome presented a series of discussions, lectures, films, and panels titled *Lovers, Lunatics and Poets: The Role of Arts in Social Change*. Panelists and lecturers included UF and Santa Fe Community College professors. A grant from the Florida Humanity Council funded the programs.

Streetcar

From February 28–March 30, the Hippodrome presented one of Tennessee Williams's best-known dramas, his Pulitzer Prize-winning tragedy *A Streetcar Named Desire*. The play, familiar to most theatergoers, tracks the decline of frail, self-destructive Blanche DuBois, who seeks refuge with her sister, Stella, and her brutish brother-in-law, Stanley.

Director Lauren Caldwell auditioned eighty actors for the lead roles, including many Hippodrome regulars. "People are amazed by the quality of talent that lives in this town," she said. "But I didn't have a Stanley in town. It was very important for me to capture the right actor for the right role, but I also had to find four people who I thought meshed together. So to find that Stanley that goes with that Stella that goes with that Blanche, it became a chemistry kind of thing."[2]

Photo: Jen Friedberg

Sherry Skinker as Blanche in
A Streetcar Named Desire.

In the end, she hired four New York actors for the leads. Sherry Skinker played Blanche, Karla Mason was Stella, John Dino was Stanley, and Timothy Joseph Ryan portrayed Blanche's suitor, Mitch. The supporting roles went to local actors Bonnie Harrison, Gregg Jones, Rusty Salling, LaVon Fisher, Sigue Hoffman, Richard Delia, and Rick Gonzalez.

Lauren's search paid off. Although Marlon Brando's Stanley remains ingrained in cinematic history, Arline Greer said, "The Hippodrome State Theatre's brilliant new production of *Streetcar* succeeds in supplanting those old images with talented new actors, and an absorbing production directed with spine-tingling intensity by Lauren Caldwell."[3]

Another local reviewer called it "Edge-of-your seat drama."[4] Reviewer Shamrock McShane wrote: "an indelible theatrical experience. Here the play is realized in sound, color, light, texture and performance so seamlessly, it's like a dream—an erotic, violent, cruel, yet somehow tender dream.... the must-see show of the season."[5] Dick Kerkles's review raved, "Truly marvelous talent from top to bottom."[6]

Lauren credited the playwright's genius. "It all goes back to honoring the text," she told the *Gainesville Sun*. "This play is dangerous, the stakes are very high for all the characters involved, and Mr. Williams writes with a very poetic quality. And if you don't run from it, and you honor the text the way it's written, it all begins to add up."[7]

A Streetcar Named Desire proved so popular that, of course, it had to be held over.

Another Big Score

In February, General Manager Mark Sexton announced that *A Midsummer Night's Dream*, scheduled for the April–May time slot, was being replaced by a new musical, *Always... Patsy Cline*.

"In the world of American theatre, procuring the rights to a play (especially a hot, new musical) can be a long, arduous process," Mark explained in the Hippodrome's newsletter. "But the work is always well worth it, and this season it has paid off big.

Photo: Jason Davis

(l-r) Starstruck housewife Louise Seger (Lauren Caldwell) watches Patsy Cline (Jessie Janet Richards) perform in *Always ... Patsy Cline.*

The remarkable new musical *Always... Patsy Cline* [is] an incredible, dramatic play based on the life of Patsy. The play has been playing to sold-out houses across the country and has been hailed as a critical masterpiece. We have to strike while the iron is hot and the rights to *Patsy Cline* are available."[8]

Always... Patsy Cline tells the story of Patsy Cline's career through the eyes of an adoring starstruck housewife, Louise Seger. It is based on their real-life relationship and is peppered with twenty-two of Cline's hit songs. The two women met at a concert in Texas and became fast friends, exchanging letters as the country singer's career escalated until her untimely death in a plane crash two years later.

Lauren Caldwell played Louise Seger, who narrated the story. Broadway actress Jessie Janet Richards portrayed Patsy Cline, singing with full voice and finely honed vocal technique, accompanied by a live four-piece band. The *Gainesville Sun* reported, "Clapping in appreciation, [the audience] rose to their feet, demanding encore after encore. A smiling, ever-gracious Jessie Janet Richards obliged—filling the theatre with the golden, velvety sound of her Patsy Cline renditions."[9]

The show, written by Ted Swindley and directed by Mary Hausch, opened April 25 and played through May 25. It then moved to the Wilson Performing Arts Center in Jacksonville, where it ran from May 28–June 1.

"It was a crowd-pleaser," Lauren said. "It's also a very difficult two-woman show. One has to have the pipes to sing all those Patsy Cline songs, and the other has forty-something pages of dialogue spoken directly to the audience because her and Patsy never exchange words."

Teen Playwrights

Also in May, on the Second Stage, the Teen Playwright Festival staged three winning plays written by teens: *P.I.* by Corey Elliot, *Best Half Foot Forward* by Daniel J. Gilfarb, and *The Procreation of Amoebas and the Meaning* by Mel McCarthy.

(l-r) Debra Walton and Ernestine Jackson play Alberta Hunter at different ages in *Cookin' at the Cookery.*

Summer Cookin'

The Hippodrome summer musical for 1997 was the world premiere of *Cookin' at the Cookery*, an original work written, directed, and choreographed by Marion J. Caffey. It was based on the life of blues and jazz legend Alberta Hunter, whose bold and sultry singing style bridged the gaps between classic blues, modern jazz, and cabaret-flavored pop. Hunter became the toast of American and European audiences from the Roaring Twenties until 1956, when she quit performing to become a registered nurse. Twenty years later, she reached mandatory retirement age of seventy—so her employers thought. Actually, she was eighty-two. She'd lied about her age to get into nursing school. Not ready for retirement, Alberta launched a spectacular comeback at a Greenwich Village

Photo: Erlinda V. Lopez

venue, the Cookery, and culminated her career with a performance at the White House during Jimmy Carter's presidency.

New York actress Ernestine Jackson, twice nominated for a Tony Award, played Alberta Hunter and sang most of the show's twenty songs. Debra Walton, who had appeared in previous Hippodrome shows *Six Women with Brain Death* and *From the Mississippi Delta*, portrayed Alberta Hunter as a young woman and also had several other roles.

Arline Greer wrote, "The actresses are extraordinarily good. The two have marvelous energy and rapport. They can punch out lines, deliver songs, and make the stage come alive." But, she complained, "The chronicle becomes tedious. Too much unnecessary detail is packed into the play."[10] Audience members disagreed and three of them wrote the newspaper telling anyone who hesitated about going to see *Cookin'* after reading the review to see it for themselves.

The review apparently didn't hurt. The show had to be extended an extra week, opening June 6 and running through July 6.

(l-r) Nell Page, Lauren Caldwell, Peter Fonda, Marilyn Wall, and Mark Sexton on the set of *Sylvia*.

Photo: Michael Rennie

A Hippodrome Cinema Premiere

Independent filmmaker Victor Nuñez had recruited Hippodromers to work on his film *Flash of Green* in 1983. Since then, Marilyn Wall had periodically left the Hippodrome costume department in the capable hands of Leslie Klein and others whenever Nuñez needed her assistance on his subsequent films. On June 21, he returned her loyalty by premiering their latest collaboration, *Ulee's Gold*, in the Hippodrome Cinema a week ahead of any Florida movie house and the weekend before its gala premiere in Los Angeles.

The film stars Peter Fonda, who was so appreciative of Marilyn that he came to the Hippodrome the previous fall and did a fundraiser for the theatre following the preview performance of *Sylvia*. Fonda was nominated for an Academy Award and won the Golden Globe Best Actor Award for his work in *Ulee's Gold*.

Family Performance Times Two

During the summer of 1997, the Hippodrome doubled the number of plays in its Family Performance Series and presented two original works on the mainstage from July 25 through August 10 with two or three performances a day in alternating time slots.

Lauren Caldwell adapted and directed Rudyard Kipling's *Just So Stories*, answering life's important questions like how the elephant got his trunk, the camel got his hump, the kangaroo got his hop, and why the alphabet was made.

Clockwise from top: Tamerin Corn, Daniel DeVito, Rochelle Douris, Ric Rose, Isa Garcia-Rose, Bonnie Harrison, Carl McNulty, and Keith Krutchkoff perform in *Just So Stories*.

Sara Morsey portrays author Marjorie Kinnan Rawlings in *An Enchanted Land.*

The second show was *An Enchanted Land,* a one-act, one-woman play based on the life and works of Marjorie Kinnan Rawlings. It was written and directed by Mary Hausch. Playing the part of Rawlings, Sara Morsey stalked the Spartan set pouring from her whiskey bottle and pecking at her typewriter as if the audience were just a group of friends who had dropped into her Cross Creek living room. The *Gainesville Sun* called it "a brilliant tour-de-force by Morsey, who inhabits the character of Rawlings and brings her to believable life."[11]

An Enchanted Land later toured schools as a Theatre for Young Audiences program, and it also went to Edinburgh, Scotland, to be presented at what is unquestionably the world's largest theatre festival.

Twenty-fifth Season

The Hippodrome began its twenty-fifth season with a coup. Obie Award-winning playwright Paula Vogel allowed them to premiere her newest play, *The Mineola Twins,* even before it opened in New York. Vogel was a big deal. She'd won the Drama Desk Award and been nominated twice for a Pulitzer Prize.

Director Mary Hausch said she "was thrilled when, despite all obstacles, Lauren got the rights for us to produce it and convinced Paula Vogel to come here to work on it with us."

"I had to bloody my knees to get it, but it's worth it," said Lauren Caldwell.

Vogel said she'd agreed to the Hippodrome because of its national reputation. But she never expected its grand, three-story beaux arts building.

Lauren recalled, "We rounded the corner, coming up to the Hippodrome, and she was flabbergasted."

"Good God! That's your theatre?" Paula said.

"Yep," Lauren replied.[12]

Playwright Paula Vogel (right) meets with actors Lisa Kay Powers and Nell Page and director Mary Hausch during a rehearsal for *The Mineola Twins.*

Photo: Tim Davis

Mary was a week into rehearsals and had all her actors off book by the time Paula arrived. As they worked through the script, Paula edited and revised scenes to make them better. Paula and the Hippodromers formed a fast friendship, and she returned in 1999 with another of her plays.

The Mineola Twins has been described as a loopy satire, but beneath its surface, Vogel looks at the political, social, and cultural changes that divided the US from the Eisenhower era through the Nixon years, and then during the Reagan-Bush era. These changes are personified by twin sisters who have opposite natures and politics. Mary Hausch cast one actress to play both women.

"In a multi-layered and altogether extraordinary performance, Lisa Kay Powers plays both twins," Arline Greer wrote. She continued, "The actress moves from Myrna's goody-two-shoes personality, ambitious to become the all-American wife and mother, to Myra, unconventional, rebellious, and promiscuous (she's slept with the entire first string of her school's football team). And she changes character with the speed of an eye blink, never making a false move."[13]

The playwright described it as "a comedy in seven scenes, four dreams and five wigs."[14] One of the funniest dreams was a lunatic ballet in a mental institution, choreographed by Ric Rose and performed by Daniel DeVito and Gillian Martin, playing psychiatric aides.

Photo: Gary Wolfson

A scene from *The Mineola Twins*. Foreground (l-r): Timothy Altmeyer, Lisa Kay Powers, and Nell Page. Back (l-r): Daniel DeVito and Gillian Martin.

Nell Page and Timothy Altmeyer also had dual roles. Nell was Myrna's boyfriend and later played Myra's lesbian lover. Tim portrayed both sisters' adolescent sons.

By the time the play reaches the Reagan-Bush era, Myrna has become the nation's most influential conservative talk show host while Myra works for women's reproductive rights.

The Mineola Twins ran from September 5–28. Greer called "this punchy and puzzling satire a humorous, provocative experience."[15]

Ring of Fire

Lauren Caldwell had nothing against General Manager Mark Sexton when she cast him as Renfield in Steven Dietz's adaptation of Bram Stoker's *Dracula*. In fact, she and Mark remained good friends even after she put his character in a cage surrounded by flames. Her innovative staging certainly wouldn't pass fire code today, but it was an attention grabber.

Mark recalls, "Lauren asked if I would shave my head and I did. She had our master set builders build a giant birdcage that was suspended in the air above the stage. It had a copper pipe around the edge of it with holes in it that was connected to a propane tank. At the right time in the play, fire would go up the side of this birdcage that I was in while I was writhing in agony."

Photo: Natalie Fesmire

Mark Sexton as Renfield in a cage of fire.

Dan Jesse was cast in the role of Van Helsing, Dracula's nemesis. It was the second time he'd played the part. The first was in the Hippodrome's 1978 production *The Passion of Dracula*, which was more of a spoof. This version addressed how complex, unexpected darkness strikes even the purest hearts.

In addition to Renfield's fiery cage, there were other pyrotechnic special effects. Dan remembers one in particular: "The set had been fireproofed like crazy, but there were a lot of fireworks going off in scenes of the vampire. One night, apparently a certain section had not been fireproofed enough and the special effects set a small amount of leaves on fire upstage. And I'm sure the stage manager is about ready to drop the fire curtain. [The fire] is very small, so staying in character, continuing to say my lines, I walked up there, stomped it out, and acted like, *Oh, this is just part of the ordeal we're going through in the story.*"

Joy Schiebel played Mina, a beautiful schoolmistress whose heart aches for Jonathan Harker (Tom Delling), the solicitor responsible for bringing Dracula (Danan Pere) to London. Mina's dearest friend, Lucy (Lisa Kay Powers), has three suitors. One of them is Dr. Seward (Charles Tucker). He runs an insane asylum where he is trying to "solve" Renfield, an inmate believed to be Dracula's servant. In the face of strange, frightening happenings, the doctor brings wise, eccentric Professor Van Helsing into the ancient fight between good and evil, light and darkness.

Also in the cast as various vixens, attendants, and maids were Daniel DeVito, Rebekah Durham, David Jenkins, and Jennifer Lindquist, with Lou Ensenat and Liz Nehls as understudies. Perfect for Halloween with plenty of blood and blood-sucking, the play was held over twice, running from October 17–November 23.

A Christmas Carol

In December, the Hippodrome staged its twentieth production of *A Christmas Carol*, which ran from December 2–21.

1 Arline Greer, review of *Indiscretions*, by Jeremy Sams, directed by Mary Hausch, Hippodrome Theatre, Gainesville, FL, *Gainesville Sun*, January 17, 1997.
2 Bill DeYoung, "Hippodrome's Streetcar Takes Maiden Trip Tonight," *Gainesville Sun*, February 28, 1997.
3 Arline Greer, review of *A Streetcar Named Desire*, by Tennessee Williams, directed by Lauren Caldwell, Hippodrome Theatre, Gainesville, FL, *Gainesville Sun*, March 7, 1997.
4 Shannon Colavecchio, review of *A Streetcar Named Desire*, by Tennessee Williams, directed by Lauren Caldwell, Hippodrome Theatre, Gainesville, FL, *Detours* (supplement to *Independent Florida Alligator*), March 6, 1997.
5 Shamrock McShane, review of *A Streetcar Named Desire*, by Tennessee Williams, directed by Lauren Caldwell, Hippodrome Theatre, Gainesville, FL, *Moon Magazine*, March 12, 1997.
6 Dick Kerekes, review of *A Streetcar Named Desire*, by Tennessee Williams, directed by Lauren Caldwell, Hippodrome Theatre, Gainesville, FL, *First Coast Entertainer*, March 8, 1997.
7 Bill DeYoung, "Hippodrome's Streetcar Takes Maiden Trip Tonight," *Gainesville Sun*, February 28, 1997.
8 Sexton, Mark, "A Midseason Lineup Dream Come True," *Ovation*, Hippodrome State Theatre, February 1997.
9 Arline Greer, review of *Always . . . Patsy Cline*, by Ted Swindley, directed by Mary Hausch, Hippodrome Theatre, Gainesville, FL, *Gainesville Sun*, May 2, 1997.
10 Arline Greer, review of *Cookin' at the Cookery*, by Marion J. Caffey, directed by Marion J. Caffey, Hippodrome Theatre, Gainesville, FL, *Gainesville Sun*, June 25, 1997.
11 Bill DeYoung, review of *Family Performance Series*, Hippodrome Theatre, Gainesville, FL, *Gainesville Sun*, August 1, 1997.
12 Bill DeYoung, "Totally Hipp: 25 Years On," *Gainesville Sun*, September 5, 1997.
13 Arline Greer, review of *The Mineola Twins*, by Paula Vogel, directed by Mary Hausch, Hippodrome Theatre, Gainesville, FL, *Gainesville Sun*, September 12, 1997.
14 Ibid.
15 Ibid.

1998

Three Tall Women

The Hippodrome opened 1998 with Edward Albee's Pulitzer Prize-winning psychological exploration of the female psyche, *Three Tall Women*. Three tall actresses, Sara Morsey, Joy Schiebel, and Jayne Heller played the women. Veteran New York stage actress Jayne had played her character twice before.

In the first act, Jayne played a wealthy, cantankerous elder reminiscing about the past. Sara played her middle-aged companion/caretaker. Joy's character was a young lawyer sent to help the old lady get her affairs in order.

Photo: Stephen Morton/*Gainesville Sun*.

Three Tall Women played by three tall actresses, Sara Morsey, Joy Schiebel, and Jayne Heller.

All that switched in the second act, when the three actresses portrayed the same woman at different periods in her life. Jayne's character is still in her nineties, but no longer demented. Sara plays the woman at middle age, strong and cynical. Joy is the woman when she was a young flapper. The only man in the cast is David Hopkins, who plays the elderly woman's estranged son. He arrives, sits at her bedside, and never says a word as the three women talk around him.

Arline Greer praised the Hippodrome's production: "*Three Tall Women* in its most potent interpretation... an absolute tour de force marvelously acted.... Directed impeccably by Mary Hausch, this *Three Tall Women* is simply splendid."[1]

The show ran from January 9–February 1, 1998. Two days later, they toured it to the Wilson Center for the Arts in Jacksonville, Florida, where it played for another five days.

Fragile Creatures

Immediately following the Jacksonville show, Sara, Joy, and David returned to the Hippodrome to rehearse their roles in the next play, Tennessee Williams's *The Glass Menagerie.* Actor Peter Giles joined them, playing the part of Tom Wingfield.

The story is set in a small St. Louis apartment where faded Southern belle Amanda Wingfield (Sara Morsey) guilt-trips and manipulates her grown children. Tom longs to be a writer while shy, fragile Laura (Joy Schiebel) mostly listens to records and plays with tiny glass animals.

Photo: Brendan Fitterer

By candlelight, Laura Wingfield (Joy Schiebel) shows her gentleman caller (David Hopkins) her glass unicorn in a pivotal scene of *The Glass Menagerie.*

The financially strapped Wingfields are living off Tom's job at a shoe warehouse. Amanda yearns for the comforts of her youth and also longs for her children to have the same comforts. She becomes obsessed with finding a suitor for Laura and pressures Tom to bring Laura a "gentleman caller" from work—Jim, played by David Hopkins.

When Jim arrives for dinner, Laura recognizes him as the boy she was attracted to in high school. Overcome by shyness, she feigns illness. But when the electricity goes out, she and Jim are left alone. By candlelight, she shows him her glass menagerie. He accidentally breaks the horn off her unicorn. They dance, they kiss. He then tells her he's engaged and departs. After Amanda learns Jim is to be married, she cruelly lashes out at Tom, who has had enough and leaves home for good.

One of Williams's most famous works, *The Glass Menagerie,* is the play that launched his success. The Hippodrome had done well with *Streetcar,* and this one proved equally favorable.

Critics loved it. "A beautiful, poignant play and the most accessible of all Tennessee Williams's works, *The Glass Menagerie* lights the Hippodrome stage with a glow that lingers in memory long after its stage candles are darkened," wrote Arline Greer. "The role of Amanda demands a great actress. The Hippodrome has one in Sara Morsey, who moves through the play dispensing the eclectic blessings of guile, innovation, anger, humor and determination. Morsey's extraordinary portrayal of Amanda Wingfield dominates the stage. Yet, she never detracts from the actors who support her."[2]

Greer called Peter Giles's portrayal of Tom "a gem of a performance." She also said, "Joy Schiebel, who plays Laura, transforms herself from a plain, neurotic girl into a glowing woman."[3]

Jacksonville reviewer Dick Kerekes said, "The scene between Laura and Jim, the gentleman caller, rates among the best-ever in theatre history."[4]

In conjunction with the show's run, the Hippodrome presented a month-long tribute to Williams. It included displaying his paintings in the gallery, a keynote address by his biographer, a panel discussion with two of his lifelong friends, and lectures by several professors from UF and Duke University. Events were spread over successive weekends throughout March 1998. *The Glass Menagerie,* directed by

Lauren Caldwell, opened February 27 and played for an extra week, not closing until March 29.

Another Dietz

For the third season in a row, the Hippodrome chose a play by Steven Dietz. Mary Hausch remembers seeing *Private Eyes* with Lauren Caldwell at the Humana Festival in Louisville, Kentucky, where thespians from across the country gather annually to see new works.

"Being at the Festival for a sneak preview allows us to negotiate rights on some terrific properties before they are snatched up by Broadway, Off-Broadway, film, or video producers," Mary said. "The runaway hit at last year's festival was Steven Dietz's *Private Eyes*. It was quite a treat since Dietz directed his play for the festival. Somehow Dietz was able to write the play that everyone who has experienced the inner workings of theatrical life has been dying to write."[5]

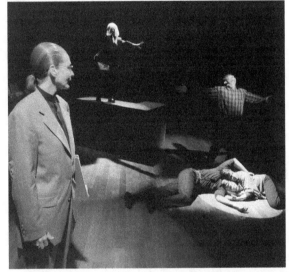

Photo: Alan Campbell

The play is a play-within-a-play-within-a-psychiatrist's office. It could be labeled a romantic comedy, a whodunit, or a psychological meditation. It's definitely a puzzle. The set is a bare stage where a play is being rehearsed. For the first time, audiences saw the back wall of the theatre. "I wonder if some of them will think it's a set we built," Mary said.[6] It wasn't. But perhaps it was the only thing in the play that was exactly what it seemed.

An actress, Lisa, is auditioning for the part of a waitress. She is having an affair with Adrian, her British director. Or maybe that's just in her husband Matthew's mind. A mysterious woman, Cory, is a waitress but also a private eye. Frank, a psychiatrist played by Sara Morsey, addresses the audience, trying to help them puzzle out what's going on.

Principal actors in *Private Eyes*. Standing (l-r) are Sara Morsey, Nell Page, and Timothy Altmeyer; lying on floor are Gregg Jones and Karla Mason.

"The Hippodrome State Theatre's production of *Private Eyes* sweeps from one surprise situation to another, with the audience caught off guard every step of the way," wrote Arline Greer.[7]

Mary told Shamrock McShane she'd started by casting Timothy Altmeyer as Matthew. She said, "I was aware that the character could come across as bland if I didn't cast an actor who had intensity. That was crucial. Tim's got incredible intensity. He's also intuitive. And he makes such big choices."[8]

For Lisa, she cast Karla Mason, who'd played Stella in the Hippodrome's *Streetcar* the previous season. "There is a vulnerability to Karla that an older man, a director like Adrian, could easily take advantage of," Mary said.[9]

The role of Adrian went to Gregg Jones. "Working with Gregg is always fun," Mary said. "He's so creative you practically have to tie him up."[10]

Nell Page played Cory. "Dietz never clarifies who she is or where she's going," Mary said. "She's got to be alluring and dangerous at the same time. Nell is so good at playing extremes, but always with dimension, with depth."[11]

Shamrock McShane's review called Nell's performance "quirky, witty, controlled, flamboyant, impetuous, charismatic, and funny, reason in itself to see *Private Eyes*."[12] The show ran from April 24–May 17.

Silver Anniversary Soiree

On Saturday, April 25, 1998, the Hippodrome celebrated its twenty-fifth anniversary at the home of UF President John Lombardi and his wife Cathryn. Featured among the entertainers was Jessie Janet Richards, who had stunned audiences with her singing in *Always.... Patsy Cline*.

Beehive

> **Amazing!**
>
> Guinness World Record for the tallest beehive hairdo: six feet, eleven inches high—created by stylist Marina Rodriguez.

After the soiree, Jessie Janet Richards stayed in town to choreograph and co-direct (with Lauren Caldwell) the Hippodrome's summer musical, *Beehive*. Created by Larry Gallagher, it was less of a play and more a revue of pop songs of the 1960s. It celebrated female vocalists from Lesley Gore and Petula Clark to Diana Ross, Tina Turner, Janis Joplin, and many more. Lauren calls these type of shows "jukebox musicals." An apt description because the show consisted of thirty-seven golden oldies loosely connected by smatterings of dialogue between tunes.

This musical journey back in time was fueled by six talented actresses. LaVon Fisher, Nadine Holloway, Hope Boynton, Rebekah Durham, Stephanie Roberts, and Cindy Thrall gave vocal performances on par with the original recording artists. Many of their show-stopping renditions brought applauding audiences to their feet. As the saying goes, "the crowd went wild"—repeatedly.

The musical's title comes from a hairstyle popular in the early to mid-1960s. To create a beehive, a woman's hair was teased up above her head, shaped into a smooth cone, and then lacquered firmly in place with abundant hairspray. If you're too young to have seen this style, imagine a soft-serve ice cream cone. To achieve this look, the Hippodrome called on the talents of Gainesville hairstylists Lester Smilowitz and Amber Waters. The pair designed more than thirty-five wigs for the show.

Photo: Randy Batista

Cast of *Beehive*. Front row (l-r): LaVon Fisher, Hope Boynton, and Stephanie Roberts. Back row: Nadine Holloway, Rebekah Durham, and Cindy Thrall.

In a reversal of their usual order for tours, *Beehive* played the Wilson Center for the Arts in Jacksonville May 26–31 before starting a month-long run at the Hippodrome from June 5–July 5.

Always... Patsy

Continuing to fill the summer with music, the Hippodrome remounted its 1997 hit, *Always... Patsy Cline* with Jessie Janet Richards and Lauren Caldwell reprising their respective roles as Patsy and Louise Seger. The show once more proved successful and ran from July 10–August 2.

Season Twenty-six

The Hippodrome began its twenty-sixth season with *The Last Night of Ballyhoo*, a Tony Award-winning play by Alfred Uhry, who had also written *Driving Miss Daisy*. Uhry created the play for Atlanta's Alliance Theatre company to perform during the 1996 Olympics games, which were held there.

The story is set in 1939. All of Atlanta is excited that *Gone with the Wind* is premiering there. Widowed sisters Boo (Sara Morsey) and Reba (Sherry Skinker) live in an upscale Christian neighborhood with their brother, Adolph, a successful Jewish businessman played by Anthony Newfield. Reba's daughter, Sunny (Andrea Studley), is a brainy student at Wellesley College. Boo's daughter, Lala (Tiffany Yates), is a college dropout. The girls compete for dates.

Ballyhoo is *the* social event of the year for young Jews from the "right kind" of Jewish society, and Lala desperately needs to get invited. Lala settles for Peachy (Kevin Blake), a Southern Jew with a perfect pedigree but an obnoxious personality. Sunny upsets the family when she falls for a New Yorker, played by David Silverman, because he's not their "kind of Jew."

The family's superior attitude toward other Jews echoes their Christian neighbors' anti-Semitism toward them. But *The Last Night of Ballyhoo* was mainly a comedy played for sweetness and romance. Directed by Mary Hausch, it opened September 7 and was held over an extra week, closing October 4.

Photo: Randy Batista

(l-r) Tiffany Yates, Kevin Blake, Anthony Newfield, and Sara Morsey in a scene from *The Last Night of Ballyhoo*.

Campy Horror

In October, the Hippodrome staged *The Rocky Horror Show*, an outrageous, campy musical by Richard O'Brien. Although the 1975 movie, *The Rocky Horror Picture Show*, became a midnight-movie cult favorite, the play actually came first and served as the basis for the film script.

It's a humorous parody of science fiction and horror B movies from the 1930s through the 1960s, with a score of rock songs, a wild plot, and even wilder characters. In brief, the car of wide-eyed innocents Brad and Janet breaks down in the middle of nowhere during a pouring rainstorm. The nearest place to telephone for help is the castle of cross-dressing bisexual mad scientist Dr. Frank N. Furter. Brad and Janet are greeted by his hunchback servant, Riff Raff (Billy Sharpe), and a bawdy maid, Magenta (LaVon Fisher).

Apprehensive and uneasy, Brad (Larry Alexander) and Janet (Cindy Thrall) are about to flee when Dr. Frank appears and invites them up to his laboratory. Wearing a black corset, fishnet stockings, and stiletto heels, Mark Chambers made a hilarious Dr. Frank. In his first song, he showed the audience that he also had a terrific singing voice.

On their way to the lab, Janet and Brad's clothes are taken to dry, leaving them in only their underwear. The doctor gives them lab coats to wear and shows them his

Photo: Randy Batista

Center is Dr. Frank N. Furter (Mark Chambers) surrounded by his minions from *The Rocky Horror Show*.

creation, Rocky, a tan, muscled specimen portrayed by Jon Townsend. That night, both Brad and Janet end up having sex with the doctor, believing they are having relations with each other.

The show is peppered with songs and dance numbers, of which "Time Warp" is probably the most remembered. Although it is difficult to imagine how, the plot grows more absurd. A biker named Eddie arrives, and a competing scientist soon after that. Then, dressed in space suits with ray guns, Riff Raff and Magenta reveal they are space aliens taking Dr. Frank back to their home planet. Brad and Janet escape the castle and watch as it blasts off into space.

Directed by Lauren Caldwell and choreographed by Cindy Thrall, the show was filled with raunchy dialogue, decadent costumes, and exuberant dance numbers by actors with strong singing voices. Rude, lewd, and crude, it wasn't the *Sun* reviewer's cup of tea, but audiences loved it, howling with laughter and applauding.

The reviewer for the more liberal-minded *Independent Florida Alligator* didn't mind. Krystal Outman wrote, "Franks shocking simulated sex, fellatio, and buggery scenes will entertain even the most repressed college freshmen, and he wears a thong pretty damn well."[13] After effusive compliments about the vocal talents of Cindy Thrall and LaVon Fisher, Outman turned her attention to the star: "The topper is definitely femme fatale Frank N. Furter. Mark Chambers, who plays the 'sweet transvestite from transsexual Transylvania,' works it hard as head diva of a stage full of twisted little underlings."[14]

The musical opened October 16 and had its run extended twice before closing November 22.

Tuna and Scrooge

In 1998, while continuing with their perennial production of *A Christmas Carol* for the twenty-first year, the Hippodrome added a second play to its Christmas schedule. The shows ran parallel December 1–20, alternating time slots.

A Tuna Christmas, by Jaston Williams, Joe Sears and Ed Howard, is one of those madcap farces the Hippodrome loves to produce, with two actors playing multiple roles, frantically changing costumes and personalities. In this case, Lauren Caldwell played nine characters and Mark Chambers eight, often having only seconds to change wardrobe and appear as someone else.

"That show will beat the hell out of you," Lauren said. "It is an extremely difficult show."

Challenging for Mark, too, because the extended run of *The Rocky Horror Show* overlapped rehearsals. "That dovetailed into the first year of *A Tuna Christmas* starring opposite Lauren Caldwell," Mark recalled. "We were such a wonderful team in that show, for many, many years."

"I have a very special relationship with Mark," Lauren said, "sharing those years together onstage." Her one obstacle was that the playwrights specified two male actors. "We had to ask [their] permission for a woman to do that show." Lauren became the first.

It is set in fictional Tuna, Texas, at Christmastime. The tiny town's annual Christmas Yard Display Contest is in turmoil because a mysterious phantom has been vandalizing the decorations. Strewn among the scenes are a half dozen or more subplots and hundreds of funny lines tossed off by characters with names like Helen Bedd and Inita Goodwin (waitresses at the local diner). Three behind-the-scenes dressers got the actors in and out of costume at warp speed.

Lauren Caldwell and Mark Chambers as two of the seventeen wacky characters they play in *A Tuna Christmas*.

"Under Mary Hausch's smooth direction, the actors create individual characters who go beyond comic stereotypes," wrote Arline Greer. "They are funny, to be sure, but they are also touching as well. Chambers isn't just good; he's superb. He has an instinctive knowledge of how women behave. Caldwell's portrayal of men is not as strong as her women, probably because of her diminutive stature, but she is funny all the same. *A Tuna Christmas* makes great fun of conservative, knuckle-headed values with such good nature, it lights up the holiday season more brightly than its Christmas yard display."[15]

Audiences so loved *A Tuna Christmas* that the Hippodrome reprised it for eight more years.

1 Arline Greer, review of *Three Tall Women*, by Edward Albee, directed by Mary Hausch, The Hippodrome Theatre, Gainesville, FL, *Gainesville Sun*, January 16, 1998.

2 Arline Greer, review of *The Glass Menagerie*, by Tennessee Williams, directed by Lauren Caldwell, The Hippodrome Theatre, Gainesville, FL, *Gainesville Sun*, March 6, 1998.

3 Ibid.

4 Dick Kerekes, review of *The Glass Menagerie*, by Tennessee Williams, directed by Lauren Caldwell, The Hippodrome Theatre, Gainesville, FL, *First Coast Entertainer*, March 7, 1998.

5 *Ovation*, The Hippodrome State Theatre, Gainesville, FL, April 1998.

6 Shamrock McShane, review of *Private Eyes*, by Steven Dietz, directed by Mary Hausch, The Hippodrome Theatre, Gainesville, FL, *Moon Magazine*, May 13, 1998.

7 Arline Greer, review of *Private Eyes*, by Steven Dietz, directed by Mary Hausch, The Hippodrome Theatre, Gainesville, FL, *Gainesville Sun*, May 1, 1998.

8 Shamrock McShane, review of *Private Eyes*, by Steven Dietz, directed by Mary Hausch, The Hippodrome Theatre, Gainesville, FL, *Moon Magazine*, May 13, 1998.

9 Ibid.

10 Ibid.

11 Ibid.

12 Ibid.

13 Krystal Outman, review of *The Rocky Horror Show*, by Richard O'Brien, directed by Lauren Caldwell, The Hippodrome Theatre, Gainesville, FL, *Independent Florida Alligator*, November 12, 1998.

14 Ibid.

15 Arline Greer, review of *A Tuna Christmas*, by Jaston Williams, Joe Sears and Ed Howard, directed by Mary Hausch, The Hippodrome Theatre, Gainesville, FL, *Gainesville Sun*, December 11, 1998.

1999

Learning to Drive

On January 8, 1999, the Hippodrome opened Paula Vogel's award-winning *How I Learned to Drive*. Director Lauren Caldwell had seen the play in the summer of 1997 before it won the New York Drama Critics and Outer Circle awards for Best Play—before it won the Pulitzer Prize. "It's a very powerful piece," Lauren told the *Gainesville Sun*.[1]

Photo: Randy Batista

In the foreground is Jennifer Hubbard as Li'l Bit in *How I Learned to Drive*; behind her is the Greek chorus, played by Nell Page, Timothy Altmeyer, and Bonnie Harrison.

The play deals with an inappropriate relationship between an uncle and his teenage niece as she grows up. That may sound like *Lolita*, but it's not. "It's a love story," Lauren explained. "This is a definition of love we all can't necessarily understand."[2]

The main character, Li'l Bit, played by Jennifer Hubbard, recalls her seemingly harmless relationship with Uncle Peck (Anthony Newfield) as it developed into something she knew was unhealthy but was reluctant to give up. Li'l Bit's memories with Uncle Peck span from the present backward through her development at ages eighteen, thirteen, and eleven, when he started teaching her to drive. The intervals are identified by songs of the sixties and punctuated with headings from the driver's manual read aloud by her family members, played by Nell Page, Bonnie Harrison, and Timothy Altmeyer.

"The issues it deals with are important, and the way in which they surface helps the audience come to terms with that type of relationship," Lauren said.[3]

"There's a complex situation here," added Jennifer Hubbard, "and we're going to look at it from a bunch of sides."[4]

"Vogel addresses the subject of incest with a minimum of after-school-special melodrama, with a tenderness that helps the viewer digest the experience. Vogel achieves this partly through non-linear storytelling, jumping through time without a crescendo to a foreseeable tragedy.... as well as a certain brand of wry, rural humor that flavors Li'l Bit's recollections."[5]

As they had with other socially relevant plays, the Hippodrome offered panel discussions on sexual abuse and post-performance discussions for audiences to share their reactions. *How I Learned to Drive* ran through February 9.

Oscar Wilde, Again

Ten years prior, the Hippodrome's February play had been Eric Bentley's *Lord Alfred's Lover*, which concerned the real-life trial and conviction of Oscar Wilde for his affair with Lord Alfred Douglas. Actually, there were three trials. Thus, the

Photo: Marianna Massey

Anthony Newfield (center) as Oscar Wilde in *Gross Indecency: The Three Trials of Oscar Wilde.*

title of the Hippodrome's 1999 production, *Gross Indecency: The Three Trials of Oscar Wilde* by Moisés Kaufman.

Irish playwright and poet Oscar Wilde lived during the Victorian era when homosexuality was illegal in the United Kingdom. He had a relationship with Lord Alfred Douglas, whose father, the Marquess of Queensberry, tried to end it by accusing Wilde of sodomy. Wilde sued the Marquess for criminal libel but didn't win.

In response, Wilde was charged with gross indecency. In this, his second trial, the jury failed to reach a verdict, so he was tried again. This time, he was convicted of committing acts of gross indecency with other male persons and sentenced to hard labor.

Kaufman created the play from extensive research and incorporated quotes from court documents, newspaper accounts, and books by and about Wilde. At various points, the play's narrator (David Schmidt) reads from them onstage. Additonal narrators were Cameron Francis and Kevin Blake.

Mary Hausch directed the production, casting Anthony Newfield in the role of Oscar Wilde. David Arrow played Wilde's attorney, and Mark Sexton portrayed the Marquess's attorney. John Felix played the Marquess and several smaller roles. Timothy Altmeyer played multiple characters.

The *Gainesville Sun* critic praised Anthony Newfield's "genuinely heartrending performance" and said, "*Gross Indecency* builds to a compelling climax with Newfield's tragic figure of Oscar Wilde. The emotional gripping conclusion transcends its frantic beginning."[6] The play opened February 26 and ran through March 21.

A Violent Thriller

The glorification of violence in movies and video games begetting violent behavior in society was the message playwright William Mastrosimone had in mind when he penned the Hippodrome's next production, *Like Totally Weird*. He wrote the play almost in its entirety during a two-hour plane ride. "I wrote fast and furious, leaving blanks for scenes I already knew," Mastrosimone said.[7]

Photo: Randy Batista

Kenny (Kevin Blake) holds a gun on Mindy (Jennifer Barton) and Russ (Mark Kincaid) while Jimmy (Cameron Francis) looks on in *Like Totally Weird*.

The story takes place in the ritzy bungalow of Russ Rigel (Mark Kincaid), a Hollywood filmmaker known for his violent action films. He and his live-in girlfriend, played by Mindy Feedham, are about to leave for a benefit when his home is invaded by two teenage fans, Jimmy and Kenny. The boys know every word of Rigel's violent films. All they want to do is talk to him, ask questions, and run dialogue from his movies. Things quickly go off the rails as the pair holds Rigel and his girlfriend at gunpoint.

Arline Greer called it "a totally tense, violent thriller." She said, "The Hippodrome pulls out all the stops in a pitch-perfect production. With Lauren Caldwell directing, the action moves from clammy unease to out-and-out terror. The boys, Kevin Blake as the crazed Kenny, and Cameron Francis as Jimmy, are nothing short of superb. They are funny, pathetic, mean, dangerous. And you can't take your eyes off them throughout the play."[8]

William Mastrosimone had previously written a one-act play about school shootings, *Bang Bang You're Dead,* and offered it without charge to schools around the country. The Hippodrome produced staged readings of that play twice during the run of *Like Totally Weird*, casting teens from their workshop program.

Then, on April 20, 1999, there was another school shooting in Littleton, Colorado. Coincidentally, it happened the same week as Hippodrome teens performed *Bang Bang You're Dead*. The theatre was packed, mostly with students from Gainesville area high schools. After each performance, the Hippodrome held "talkbacks" for the cast and audience to discuss the play and the latest incident—Columbine High School.

Like Totally Weird was held over for an extra week, running from April 16–May 16.

Quirky and Sweet

After three plays in a row dealing with heavy subjects, a little comic relief was in order. Director Mary Hausch filled the need with *Resident Alien*, a comedy written by Stuart Spencer about a UFO visitor.

Actor George Tynan Crowley played Michael, a Kierkegaard-quoting intellectual stuck working in a small Wisconsin town's K-Mart. His ex-wife, Priscilla (Caitlin Miller), runs a bar with her dim-witted second husband Ray, played by Tim Altmeyer.

Michael's problem is that aliens from outer space have abducted his and Pricilla's son, Billy. In their hurry to get away, the UFO left behind one of its crew. The alien, played by Kevin Blake, now spends his days on Michael's couch eating Cheese Doodles and watching reality TV.

Cameron Francis played a good-hearted sheriff who is investigating Billy's disappearance. Will Sexton, son of Mark and Nell (Page) Sexton, played the part of Billy.

Photo: Randy Batista

Ray (Timothy Altmeyer) sleeps on the bar as Priscilla (Caitlin Miller) interacts with Alien (Kevin Blake) in *Resident Alien*.

"Finally, a truly dysfunctional family that's truly funny!" wrote Arline Greer. "Every member of the six-person cast has a lock on the characters they play. Their ensemble acting is as good as it gets in the Hipp's long tradition of perfectly meshed ensembles. Blake... is nothing short of perfection as the green man from outer space who teaches lessons of self-acceptance and the need to belong in this gently lunatic comedy. *Resident Alien*... is a light, good-natured charmer, cool entertainment for a summer evening."[9]

Resident Alien ran for nearly the full month of June (4–27) and was followed in July by a remount of the previous summer's hit *Beehive*, which played from July 9–August 22.

Season Twenty-seven

The Hippodrome started its new season with Douglas Carter Beane's richly satiric comedy *As Bees in Honey Drown*. The script is filled with fast-talking, tongue-twisting dialogue spoken by quick-witted characters. "It's written in a wonderful, biting, hip style," said the play's director, James Morgan, who had previously directed *Sylvia*.[10] He'd also designed the sets for thirty-one Hippodrome plays following Carlos Asse's departure.

Nell Page starred as Alexa Vere de Vere, an absolutely fabulous whirlwind con artist who captivates and takes advantage of the almost-famous. Her co-star, Timothy Altmeyer, played writer Evan Wyler, whom Alexa convinces to write a screenplay based on her glamorous life. To do this, he must accompany her everywhere. Soon, he finds himself picking up the tab as she spends lavishly, always promising to pay him back. She never does. But once his credit card is maxed out, Alexa disappears. Evan finds past victims of her schemes and plans for them to confront her together, but she learns of the plot and spoils it.

Photo: Randy Batista

Alexa Vere de Vere (Nell Page) conning writer Evan Wyler (Timothy Altmeyer) in *As Bees in Honey Drown*.

The play's title is one of Alexa's catchphrases. One day, she passes a bookstore and sees it on the cover of an exposé Evan has published about her.

Timothy Altmeyer understood how his character becomes subverted by Alexa. He said, "As an actor living in New York, I identified with Evan Wyler's quest for fame, recognition, and financial reward. You start off pursuing your quest as an artist. Then you saw that there's money being made, and parties to go to, friends to be made. And all of a sudden you lose sight of why you do what you do."[11]

Arline Greer wrote, "It would be hard to refuse anything offered by seductive Alexa... played by Nell Page Sexton in what surely is one of her finest bravura performances."[12] Cameron Francis, Tiffany Yates, Sara Morsey, and Neal Utterback played Alexa's other victims, of whom Greer said, "All give performances that are wickedly funny and on the mark."[13]

As Bees in Honey Drown ran September 3–26, but in the middle of the run, Hurricane Floyd forced cancelation of the Wednesday, September 15 show. The powerful Category 4 storm struck the Bahamas and was forecast to strike Florida. More than one million Florida residents on the east coast were told to evacuate. However, thankfully, Floyd turned northward, missing Florida, and the Hippodrome schedule resumed the next day. Wednesday night ticket holders were contacted and given their choice of another performance.

Lease Renewed

They say time flies when you're having fun. It didn't seem like the Hippodrome had been in the old Post Office for twenty years, but they had, and the lease was up for renewal. On September 27, the City Commission approved a new twenty-year lease with the Hippodrome State Theatre. The city leased the building to the theatre for $250,000 a year and then gave the theatre an annual $250,000 grant for the lease payment. The renewed lease provided for a re-evaluation of rent levels every five years.

A *Frankenstein* Like No Other

From the outset, director Lauren Caldwell insisted her *Frankenstein* was not going to be a literal translation. Deconstructing Victor Gialanella's adaptation of the novel by Mary Shelley, she reimagined the play as a visually different and challenging nightmare.

"The coolest thing about Lauren is she doesn't tell you how to do stuff," said actress Joy Schiebel, who played Dr. Frankenstein's fiancée. "She always says, 'This is what I have in mind.'"[14]

For this show, what Lauren had in mind was to stage the well-known story like one long dream sequence performed like a ballet, interspersed with dialogue. Ric Rose, who choreographed the play, appeared as Dr. Frankenstein's doppelgänger. Arline Greer wrote, "Frankenstein's moments of agony are mirrored by his doppelgänger, danced by Rose with so much dramatic intensity that words seem unnecessary." But she didn't care for the script, adding, "This is probably a good thing as Gialanella's dialogue for *Frankenstein* is ponderous, filled with clichés and has little to recommend it."[15]

Mark Sexton played Frankenstein's creation as a victim of scientific meddling—no bolts in the neck or Boris Karloff stagger. Whenever the creature is enraged, Frankenstein's doppelgänger (Ric Rose) appears, and when the creature kills, it is depicted through a dance of death. Set on a mostly bare stage, actors enter as if floating from Frankenstein's subconscious in a dreamlike fashion. The cast also included Cameron Francis, Sara Morsey, Bonnie Harrison, Jade Servin, and Rusty Salling.

It was a *Frankenstein* like no other. Despite the *Sun*'s rather negative review, the show was held over an extra week, playing from October 15–November 20. During the run, the Hipp held a Halloween Ball in the Sun Center courtyard on Saturday, October 30, to benefit the Hippodrome. The well-attended event featured local bands The Usuals and House of Dreams.

Photo: Randy Batista

Multilevel *Frankenstein* like no other.

Christmas Shows

For the second year, the Hippodrome remounted *A Tuna Christmas* with Lauren Caldwell and Mark Chambers again playing the zany citizens of Tuna, Texas. It ran concurrently with *A Christmas Carol*, then in its twenty-first year, from November 30–December 19.

On Saturday, December 4, the cast of *A Christmas Carol* joined Dance Alive and other performers for the City of Gainesville's Historic Holiday/Festival of Lights. In costume, the cast made the short two-block walk from the Hippodrome to the Gainesville Community Plaza where the event was held.

1   Alisson Burke, "Learning to Drive: The Hippodrome's Drama that Dares," *Gainesville Sun*, January 8, 1999.

2   Ibid.

3   Ibid.

4   Ibid.

5   Ibid.

6   Arline Greer, review of *Gross Indecency: The Three Trials of Oscar Wilde*, by Moisés Kaufman, directed by Mary Hausch, Hippodrome Theatre, Gainesville, FL, *Gainesville Sun*, March 5, 1999.

7   Bill DeYoung, "A Walk on the Dark Side," *Gainesville Sun*, April 16, 1999.

8   Arline Greer, review of *Like Totally Weird*, by William Mastrosimone, directed by Lauren Caldwell, Hippodrome Theatre, Gainesville, FL, *Gainesville Sun*, April 16, 1999.

9   Arline Greer, review of *Resident Alien*, by Stuart Spencer, directed by Mary Hausch, Hippodrome Theatre, Gainesville, FL, *Gainesville Sun*, June 11, 1999.

10 Bill DeYoung, "Comedy with a Sting," *Gainesville Sun*, September 3, 1999.

11 Ibid.

12 Arline Greer, review of *As Bees in Honey Drown*, by Douglas Carter Beane, directed by James Morgan, Hippodrome Theatre, Gainesville, FL, *Gainesville Sun*, September 10, 1999.

13 Ibid.

14 Bill DeYoung, "Hippodrome Actress Here for 4th visit," *Gainesville Sun*, October 29, 1999.

15 Arline Greer, review of *Frankenstein*, by Victor Gialanella, directed by Lauren Caldwell, Hippodrome Theatre, Gainesville, FL, *Gainesville Sun*, October 22, 1999.

2000

Mega-church Rivalry

The January 2000 play was *God's Man in Texas* by David Rambo. It centers on a market-savvy mega-church with a congregation of ten thousand members. They come to worship and participate in a myriad of social activities. Many live on church property under the watchful eye of an all-powerful pastor, Reverend Gottschall. The charismatic-but-aging preacher is searching for the right man to eventually replace him. The front-runner, an up-and-coming evangelical idealist, Reverend Jerry Mears, ends up in a contest of wills with Gottschall, who eventually decides he doesn't want to leave. The two men are closely observed by Hugo, the church's sound technician, who wires them for their big Sunday sermons to crowds of ten thousand or more.

Photo: Randy Batista

(l-r) Reverend Jerry Mears (Mark Kincaid), Hugo (Scott Kealey), and Warren Hammack as Reverend Gottschall, who believes he is *God's Man in Texas*.

Mary Hausch directed the cast of three men. Arline Greer praised their performances: "Warren Hammack, as Gottschall, gives an uncannily accurate portrayal of the pastor drunk with his own power. It's an understated performance, simultaneously humorous and alarming.

"Mark Kincaid's Jerry [Reverend Mears] is totally sincere, a bit taken with himself, blinded and ultimately indignant in his voyage to redemption. Scott Kealey as Hugo is truly the comic relief of the play. His performance is ingenuous, appealing and without artifice."[1]

Greer called the three-hour play "ungodly long, but engrossing.... [Playwright] Rambo's words are seductive and, like the preacher calling the flock to walk the aisle in his mega-church, they make for mesmerizing theater."[2]

A week after the play opened, the *Gainesville Sun* elicited the opinions of four local pastors and a UF professor of religious history regarding the production and some of the issues it raised. Considering prior friction between the Hippodrome and the First Baptist Church over *Hair*, one might have anticipated a negative reaction. But the ministers (two Baptists, a Methodist, and an Episcopalian) did not object. Though they admitted they didn't expect to like the play, their general response was that it communicated well the tensions that come within a church.[3]

God's Man in Texas ran from January 7–30.

Hedda Gabler

In February, director Lauren Caldwell offered Hippodrome audiences a new adaptation of Henrik Ibsen's classic *Hedda Gabler* written by Jon Robin Baitz.

Hedda Gabler (played by Joy Schiebel) is a repressed, manipulative woman who craves excitement but is stuck in a marriage with a boring (and broke) academic,

George Tesman (played by Mark Kincaid). In response, she interferes with the lives of those around her. Ibsen wrote the original play in 1890, when women had few options. Lauren liked the idea of putting Hedda in the present day.

"What if Hedda had every option open to her in the year 2000 and still couldn't make the choices that she needed to make, in order to escape from this domestic straightjacket?" Lauren said. "Ibsen said the only thing that every director must understand is that Hedda was raised as a boy. All Hedda ever wanted was to be on top, and she cannot allow her femininity to come through that exterior that she's got."[4]

Photo: Randy Batista

(l-r) Mark Kincaid as George Tesman, Bonnie Harrison as Judge Brack, and Joy Schiebel as Hedda in an updated version of *Hedda Gabler*.

In a bit of gender-bending, Lauren cast a woman to play lascivious Judge Brack, who proposed to have an affair with Hedda. However, the actress cast for the typically male role, Adale O'Brien, fell down multiple flights of the backstage stairway during tech rehearsal the Sunday before previews were to open. She was hospitalized and was never able to return to the show. Lauren was heartbroken. Adale was a top talent at Actor's Theatre of Louisville and the annual Humana Festivals, and Lauren had been thrilled that Adale agreed to come to the Hippodrome. Bonnie Harrison stepped in and played Judge Brack for the entire run, from February 25–March 19.

Master Class

The next play was Terrence McNally's *Master Class*, which had won the Tony Award for Best Play. It is based on the life of opera diva Maria Callas, and the premise is that while teaching a series of opera master classes, she relates recollections about the glories of her life and career.

Maria Callas, an American-born Greek soprano who reigned over La Scala (the world's greatest opera house) throughout the 1950s. She was portrayed at the Hippodrome by Sara Morsey, who studied biographies and taped interviews of Callas in preparation for the role. "I fell in love with her," Sara said. "But I almost lost my mind. This is the hardest role I've ever had to prepare for. She's a terribly sympathetic character. But she was really a diva. She was very dedicated to her art, and a perfectionist."[5] Not unlike Sara herself, who had just completed a run of *Master Class* in Memphis, Tennessee, prior to starting rehearsals at the Hippodrome.

It paid off. "Sara Morsey, who plays Callas as if she *were* Callas," wrote Arline Greer. "Her performance as the legendary Greek soprano almost transcends that of the bravura tour de force.... On stage the entire evening—speaking, listening, miming a lyric, dancing to the music of an aria, mocking, rejoicing, mourning—Morsey is simply superb."[6]

Photo: Randy Batista

Maria Callas (Sara Morsey) chastises a soprano played by Niffer Clark in *Master Class*.

Doug Maxwell, who frequently served as musical director for Hippodrome musicals, played Manny, Maria's piano accompanist. The simple set contained only a grand piano and a desk, table, chair, and footstool. The production used the audience as the class.

The plot is a series of auditions by Maria's students, interspersed with monologs about the singer's past. She is alternately dismayed and impressed by the students, often speaking harshly to them. Sophie, a plump soprano played by Babe Root, is told she needs a new look. A second soprano, played by Niffer Clark, is also chastised. Then a determined tenor, played by Terry Gsell, manages to perform an entire aria for Maria.

Lauren Caldwell directed the production, which stayed onstage for a full month, from April 14–May 14.

Two Summer Musicals

That summer, there were two musicals—almost three. Marion J. Caffey was preparing a new show called *Let the Juke Joint Jump*, but it wasn't finished to his satisfaction in time. So, he took on the task of directing *Forever Plaid*, which was written by Stuart Ross with musical and vocal arrangements by James Raitt.

As the Four Plaids, Chad Hudson, Richard Rowan, Cameron Stevens, and Daniel Siford perform a parody of *The Ed Sullivan Show* in *Forever Plaid*.

Photo: Randy Batista

Forever Plaid is another of those "jukebox musicals" that became a popular choice for Hippodrome summer shows. This one featured four male vocalists, Daniel Siford, Cameron Stevens, Chad Hudson, and Richard Rowan, in tribute to harmony quartets of the 1950s. The songs, pop hits of the era by such groups as the Four Aces and the Four Freshmen, included "Three Coins in the Fountain," "Undecided," "Sixteen Tons," "Chain Gang," "Perfidia," "Cry," "Heart and Soul," "Lady of Spain," "Shangri-La," "Love is a Many-Splendored Thing," and more.

The Four Plaids are a high school quartet whose dream of recording an album is cut short when they die in a collision with a busload of Catholic school-girls who were on their way to see the Beatles perform on *The Ed Sullivan Show*. Unexplainably, the Plaids have returned to life for a final chance at musical glory (performing for the Hippodrome audience). In the process, the four recreate 1950s proms, TV shows like *The Perry Como Show*, and a manic parody of *The Ed Sullivan Show* with the typical eclectic assortment of opera singers, jugglers, and acrobats.

Each night during the Hippodrome run, an audience member was plucked from their seat to play piano for the show. Whether the victim knew how to play the piano wasn't relevant. The tune was the old standard "Heart and Soul," and he or she only had to hit one key repetitively in time, while a member of the Plaids played the rest. Usually, the embarrassed "volunteer" struggled to play along and get back to their seat as quickly as possible. But on occasion, the cast would be taken by surprise when the person selected was an accomplished pianist and took over the song. The actors never minded as it garnered an extra round of applause.

Forever Plaid was a hit and ran from June 2–July 9, with many audience members returning to see it a second time.

Five days after *Forever Plaid* closed, the Hippodrome remounted *Always... Patsy Cline* for the third year. Lauren Caldwell directed and Sara Morsey took over the role of Texas housewife Louise Seger, which Lauren had played in previous years. The part of Patsy Cline was performed by Melissa Swift-Sawyer, an actress from Denver with something unique to celebrate. She'd performed the show 1,499 times. Her first night at the Hippodrome marked her fifteen-hundredth performance. Opening night was July 14, and the show ran through August 13.

Photo: Randy Batista

Melissa Swift-Sawyer as Patsy and Sara Morsey as Louise in *Always . . . Patsy Cline*.

Season Twenty-eight

What would you say to your best friend if he had just blown forty thousand dollars on an abstract painting? That was the dilemma posed in the Hippodrome's season opener *ART*, a Tony Award-winning play by French playwright Yasmina Reza, translated by Christopher Hampton.

ART centers on the relationship between three friends and an all-white painting that looks like there's nothing on the canvas. Serge, played by James Donadio, has paid an indecent amount for it. Marc (Larry Larson) thinks Serge has lost his mind, flat-out calls the painting shit, and tries to persuade him that all contemporary art is a sham. Outraged, Serge turns to their mutual friend, Yvan, played by Scott Kealey. Yvan is ambivalent, trying to please one friend, then the other.

Photo: Michael Weimar

(l-r) Larry Larson plays Marc, with Scott Kealey as Yvan and James Donadio as Serge, in Yasmina Reza's *ART*.

The trio's reaction to the painting brings out hidden feelings, frustrations, and insecurities. Soon, the discussion about art turns into one about friendship and one's taste in women. Fueled by testosterone and adrenaline, the resulting battle is both a serious discussion of what constitutes art and an exploration of the balance of power in friendships.

Arline Greer's review summed it up: "Every moment of *ART* is loaded with ferocious, tantalizing humor. It is that rare theater bird: a comedy that keeps you thinking overtime."[7]

Mary Hausch directed the play, which ran from September 1–24, 2000.

Hysteria

The Hippodrome's next play, *Hysteria*, was an outrageous comedy based on an actual meeting between two of the twentieth century's greatest and most eccentric minds, Sigmund Freud and Salvador Dali. This historical meeting took place in 1938 in a quiet London suburb, where Freud had fled from Nazi-occupied Austria. Dali considered Freud one of the most vital influences in his life and art—the patron saint of surrealism. Freud, on the other hand, was of the opinion that the surrealists were complete fools, and considered Dali a lunatic... that is, until they met. Freud recognized in Dali a combination of passion and control, which he himself also possessed. Later, Freud wrote that Dali had indeed changed his view of modern art.

Those are the bare facts from which Terry Johnson's farce springs. Johnson added another historic figure, Dr. Abraham Yahuda, an Egyptian scholar who challenged Freud's controversial work and who, in Johnson's script, serves as Freud's doctor. The story is set in motion when a patient, Jessica, taps on Freud's window, demanding an analysis of her childhood. She, a conglomeration of Freud's real-life case studies, soon doffs her clothing.

Hysteria takes these conflicting forces and allows them to collide. Between Dr. Yahuda's physical and verbal jabs, the neuroses of the naked patient in his closet, and the babbling surrealist, Freud himself comes close to hysteria.

Director Mary Hausch cast Mark Chambers as Sigmund Freud, Gregg Jones as Salvador Dali, Peter Haig as Dr. Yahuda, and Joy Schiebel as Jessica. Emilee MacDonald played a minor role as Freud's daughter, Anna. The *Independent Florida Alligator* called it "a must-see production."[8] It played for a full month, from October 20–November 19.

Photo: Michael Weimar

The *Hysteria* cast includes (l-r) Peter Haig as Yahuda, Gregg Jones as Dali, Mark Chambers as Freud, and Joy Schiebel as Jessica.

Gregg Jones, whom Arline Greer said "makes a sublimely deranged figure of the self-worshipping Dali," had his own fantastic experience on opening night.[9] He said, "I had read Dali's biography. I'd been to the Dali Museum in St. Pete for two consecutive days and spent like four hours a day communing with his paintings. I was really immersed in the world of Dali. I was down in the basement by myself opening night of *Hysteria*, warming up my voice, doing the accent, which was a combination of French and Spanish. I was working on the dialect and saying some of my lines out loud. I heard this voice behind me say, 'Ah, don't worry, you will be fine.' And I turned around and Salvador Dali was standing there. He said, 'Don't worry, you put in the work. You're going to be fine. Thank you for being me.' That's all he said. Then it was over. But it was chilling."

Christmas Plays

December 1–23, Gregg Jones made his own apparition as the ghost of Jacob Marley in the annual production of *A Christmas Carol*. Mark Chambers traded Freud's beard for his eight wacky characters in *A Tuna Christmas*.

1   Arline Greer, review of *God's Man in Texas*, by David Rambo, directed by Mary Hausch, Hippodrome Theatre, Gainesville, FL, *Gainesville Sun*, January 14, 2000.
2   Ibid.
3   Gary Kirkland, "Assessing *God's Man in Texas*," *Gainesville Sun*, January 15, 2000.
4   Bill DeYoung, "Hedda Opens Tonight," *Gainesville Sun*, February 25, 2000.
5   Bill DeYoung "A Date with La Diva," *Gainesville Sun*, April 14, 2000.
6   Arline Greer, review of *Master Class*, by Terrence McNally, directed by Lauren Caldwell, Hippodrome Theatre, Gainesville, FL, *Gainesville Sun*, April 21, 2000.
7   Arline Greer, review of *Art*, by Yasmina Reza, translated by Christopher Hampton, directed by Mary Hausch, Hippodrome Theatre, Gainesville, FL, *Gainesville Sun*, September 8, 2000.
8   Jessica Arnold, review of *Hysteria*, by Terry Johnson, directed by Mary Hausch, Hippodrome Theatre, Gainesville, FL, *Independent Florida Alligator*, October 26, 2000.
9   Arline Greer, review of *Hysteria*, by Terry Johnson, directed by Mary Hausch, Hippodrome Theatre, Gainesville, FL, *Gainesville Sun*, October 27, 2000.

2001

The Blue Room

The Hippodrome kicked off 2001 with *The Blue Room*, David Hare's adaptation of *Reigen* by Arthur Schnitzler. "Reigen" means "round dance," and in the play, characters of different ages and social strata follow a round-robin of sexual encounters. Its 1921 production scandalized Vienna. The police closed it and the actors were tried for obscenity. Hare's version is set in modern times yet remains faithful to the original.

Photo: Michael Eaddy

Jason Marr and Joy Schiebel in *The Blue Room*.

The play, according to director Lauren Caldwell, "is an examination of the primitive sexual appetites in all social strata."[1] Two actors, Joy Schiebel and Jason Marr, played five roles each. These include a married woman, a student, a playwright, a model, an actress, a cab driver, a husband, a politician, and more. Through a sexual daisy chain, the play explores the twilight world of its characters' sexual desires and the dangerous adventures that might result should one follow every stirring of the heart or flow of inexplicable emotions.

"*The Blue Room*," Arline Greer wrote, "makes no compromises with Hare's tongue-in-cheek depiction of men and women caught in an ongoing search for sexual satisfaction, a search that ultimately leads to emptiness. The two [actors] come together and come apart, each assuming different distinct identities, changing accents, intonations and body posture.... Nudity in the show is never gratuitous, and because it lacks erotic feeling, most likely isn't a turn-on for audiences. It's a tour de force by this couple who not only can do it all, but bare it all."[2]

"Of course," Lauren told the *Gainesville Sun*, "There will be people who say 'Let's go see that nude play at the Hippodrome,' and then there'll be other people who do not like the form and style because it's not conventional."[3] But in the end, there weren't any protesters or letters to the editor about nudity. The show ran from January 12–February 4.

Macbeth

The Scottish play, as superstitious thespians refer to William Shakespeare's *Macbeth*, is a dark, brooding tale of ambition and greed, unchecked by a moral code, which ultimately ends in the self-destruction of its principal characters. It begins with a group of witches predicting that a Scottish general named Macbeth will become king. Consumed by ambition and spurred to action by his wife, Lady Macbeth, he murders King Duncan and takes the Scottish throne. Although he is racked with guilt and paranoia, Macbeth must commit more murders to protect his reign. All of which leads him and Lady Macbeth into madness and death.

This was the Hippodrome's second rendition of *Macbeth*. The first had been staged at their Hawthorne Road location twenty-six years before and was directed by Marilyn Wall on a bare-bones budget. Recalling his role as Macbeth in the 1975 production, Rusty Salling said, "Early in the run, the actor playing Duncan showed up wearing under his costume, a protective breastplate fashioned by his wife, to guard against what was apparently my youthfully overenthusiastic vigor during the murder scene."[4]

Scene with the witches in *Macbeth*.

In 2001, it was Rusty's turn to die when director Lauren Caldwell cast him as Duncan. Scott Kealey played Macbeth and Sara Morsey was Lady Macbeth. Lauren had technical resources that the earlier Hippodrome lacked. With them, she created a spellbinding spectacle that opened with a fierce thunderstorm, out of which emerged an unholy family of witches. The set's ceiling was a forest of trees. An eerie light refracted through its branches. Waves of fog emanated from the forest floor.

Lauren left the time and place undefined but leaning toward futuristic. Costumer Marilyn Wall dressed Lady Macbeth in blood-red velvet and Duncan's army in sadomasochists' leather and chain. Where Shakespeare's script had three witches, Lauren added a fourth—Mark Chambers, who *Moon Magazine* said "twists the weird sisters into sexual ambiguity, keeping an elfin gamin, winningly portrayed by the nimble Alison Jim, on the end of a leash."[5]

The *Independent Florida Alligator* said, "Caldwell's vision of deviancy run amok makes the show a must-see."[6]

In addition to Alison Jim, who had debuted in 1996 as Scout in *To Kill a Mockingbird*, the other witches were played by Joy Schiebel and Bonnie Harrison. Filling out the large cast were veterans of previous Hippodrome plays—Jason Marr, Timothy Altmeyer, Dana Panepinto, Neal Utterback, and Niall McGinty— and a compliment of UF theatre majors—Melvin Huffnagle, Rory Lambert, Steven White, Stephen Vendette, Alan Jeans, and James McAndrew.

"A spectacular performance of William Shakespeare's *Macbeth* fills the stage at the Hippodrome State Theatre," wrote Arline Greer. "Notable for its use of stage effects, this is a *Macbeth* that resonates with the sound of drums and dazzles the eye with brilliant lighting, balletic movements, waves of vapor emanating from a trap door, gorgeous costumes, and swashbuckling swordplay. As a spectacle, the Hippodrome's *Macbeth* is gripping theater. But the moral of the tale told in Shakespeare's immortal words tends to get short shrift. Shakespeare's words may take a second seat to the action in this Hippodrome production of *Macbeth*, but as spectacle alone, it makes a fierce impression."[7]

Macbeth opened March 2 and ran through April 1.

Anton in Show Business

Next up was Jane Martin's comedic look behind the curtain of regional theatre. *Anton in Show Business* tells the story of three struggling actors cast in an ill-fated production of Anton Chekhov's *The Three Sisters* in San Antonio, Texas.

Cast of *Anton in Show Business*: (l-r) Bonnie Harrison, Nell Page, Sara Morsey, Joy Schiebel, Merideth Maddox, Sonya Cole, and Dana Panepinto.

Photo: Dave Cone

Seven women played fifteen characters (both male and female). Leads Merideth Maddox, Sara Morsey, and Joy Schiebel played the (lucky?) actors who won the Chekhov parts. Their madcap excursion takes the actors through the typical regional theatre mire of funding crises, impossible critics, eccentric directors, and inept producers—portrayed by Bonnie Harrison, Nell Page, and Sonya Cole. Dana Panepinto played an annoying, outspoken audience member who criticizes the sisters' performances during the play.

A Texas native and graduate of Baylor University, Lauren Caldwell knew the world the play satirized. "I am particularly excited about directing this play for the Gainesville audiences," she said. "One reason is that Martin's play strikes a very vivid chord. Her depiction of these eccentric characters is wonderful and so true to life. We are able to hold them close to our heart as they struggle through the trials and tribulations of the nonprofit arts scene in America. And finally, even though the play is a comedy, perhaps the audience will embrace the difficulties that artists go through to keep us intrigued and entertained."[8]

The play, which the *Gainesville Sun* called "a boisterous romp,"[9] ran from April 20–May 13.

Two Summer Musicals

The Hippodrome kicked off summer with a month-long run of *Hedwig and the Angry Inch* from June 1–July 1. Director Lauren Caldwell hadn't heard of the two-person musical until her annual trip to New York searching for unique, original works. Boy, was it ever.

Written by John Cameron Mitchell with music and lyrics by Stephen Trask, it is set in the world of 1980s muddled gender glam-rock—think David Bowie. Hedwig relates her story of surviving a botched sex change operation to escape communist East Berlin and become a rock star in America. Mark Chambers, who dazzled audiences with his bodacious Frank N. Furter in *Rocky Horror*, was a natural for Hedwig.

The unlikely inspiration for the story was Plato's *Symposium*, which describes Zeus's plan to split humanity in half so humans would not be a threat to the gods. The playwright conceived Hedwig as one such creature, constantly on the search for her other half. She finds it in the form of Yitzak, performed by Cindy Thrall, who had previously sung with Mark in *Rocky Horror* and belted out rock tunes in 1998's *Beehive*.

Photo: Lee Ferinden

Mark Chambers as Hedwig in *Hedwig and the Angry Inch.*

The *Independent Florida Alligator* said, "The casting of this dynamic duo was right-on, and both musically trained actors hit all the high notes with oooomph."[10]

These sentiments were echoed by Arline Greer: "There probably isn't another actor with greater gifts than Mark Chambers... a one-man show, on stage for 90 minutes without intermission. He does have a sidekick, Yitzak... and he also has The Angry Inch band, a rock group composed of Tané DeKrey, Richy Stano, Edward Roses, Devin Moore, and Tom Hurst. They, too, are on stage for the entire show. The Angry Inch is not small potatoes. They play very well."[11]

After Lauren first saw *Hedwig and the Angry Inch*, it won the Obie Award, the Outer Critics Circle Award, and was about to become a major motion picture. But somehow, the Hippodrome had been one of the few select theatres granted rights to produce *Hedwig* before its big release on the silver screen.

Forever Plaid Again

On July 13, the Hippodrome followed the glam-rock of the 1980s with a trip back to the 1950s in a remount of the previous summer's hit *Forever Plaid*. This time Daniel Siford, who reprised his role as Frankie, also directed and choreographed the show. The other three cast members were accomplished musicians appearing in *Forever Plaid* for the first time. Billy Sharpe played Sparky, Allie Laurie was Jinx, and Joe Pedulla was Smudge. The show ran through August 12.

Season Twenty-nine

The Hippodrome opened the new season with a Pulitzer Prize winner, *Dinner with Friends* by Donald Margulies. It was directed by Mary Hausch and starred Scott Kealey as Gabe, Sara Morsey as Karen, Nell Page as Beth, and Gregg Jones as Tom. The story is about two couples who have been best friends for twelve years, sharing their lives over dinners and vacationing together. All is well in their worlds until Beth reveals that her marriage to Tom is ending. The news rocks the equilibrium of the couples' long-term friendship.

Gabe and Karen are shocked. Karen immediately sides with Beth. But Gabe waits to hear Tom's side. It isn't complicated. Tom's found a new, younger woman.

Photo: Lee Ferinden

(l-r) Sara Morsey, Nell Page, Gregg Jones, and Scott Kealey in a scene from *Dinner with Friends*.

Out of their rage and frustration, passion bursts from the divorcing couple. They attack each other sexually as well as psychically. "This is some of the best work Gregg has ever done," Nell said. "Gregg and I both tend toward roles that take us over the top. So for us to play these parts, where everything is pulled back, it makes for such a productive stretch internally."[12]

Beth, refusing to play the poor, bereft, abandoned wife, announces to a shocked Karen that she has a new love. "Page and Morsey play off each other with consummate skill that lifts the play to a high moment of honest revelation," wrote Arline Greer.[13]

Tom and Beth go their separate ways, and Gabe and Karen are left to examine their marriage. In the play, Karen says, "You go along, and you think you're on solid ground, and all of a sudden the earth cracks open."[14]

Playwright Donald Margulies told NPR, "It's really about the aftershocks that we all experience when certain constants in our lives, things that we perceive to be constant, suddenly shatter and are no longer dependable."[15]

The play opened on August 31. "Attendance was gangbusters the first week," said Hippodrome General Manager Mark Sexton.[16] Then, on September 11, terrorists crashed two passenger jets into the New York City World Trade Center. "After the attacks," Mark said, "the bottom dropped out. We've never felt a punch like this one. The first week after the attacks, attendance dropped 75 percent. It's coming back a little, but it's still light."[17] To help recover some of its losses, the Hippodrome extended *Dinner with Friends* for another week, closing September 30.

Misery

From October 19–November 19, the Hippodrome presented *Misery*, British writer-director Simon Moore's adaptation of the Stephen King novel about a psychotic fan.

King drew the story from personal experience. He'd posed for a Polaroid photo with a man who described himself as King's number one fan. Sometime later, this fan made front-page news as Mark David Chapman, the man who shot John Lennon after asking for his autograph.

In the play, like the novel, famous author Paul Sheldon (Jason Marr) is injured when his car goes off the road in a snowstorm and crashes. Luckily, Paul is rescued by a former nurse and his number one fan, Annie Wilkes (Sara Morsey). He awakens to find himself in an old farmhouse cut off from the rest of the world. His crushed legs and excruciating pain make him a prisoner to Annie, who insists that she will nurse him back to health but refuses to tell anyone of his whereabouts. To make matters worse, this schizophrenic fan is not happy that Paul has killed off her favorite character in his latest novel. She makes him burn it and start over, propelling Paul into a living hell.

"Unlike the novel and the movie, the stage version focuses on the conflict of two players: celebrity and fan," said director Lauren Caldwell.[18] To get the stunts right, she brought in a movement expert from Alabama who coached the actors on things like transfer from a bed to a wheelchair, Annie chopping off Paul's leg with an ax, and the fight scene where they try to kill each other on the bed.

In one of her rare expressions of displeasure, the *Gainesville Sun* critic dismissed the play out of hand, citing Lauren's directing as lacking the fundamental ingredient of tension and said that neither actor displayed much passion. The reviewer for *First Coast Entertainer* took the opposite position: "Ms. Morsey and Mr. Marr are excellent in these demanding roles, and both are quite believable.... *Misery* is the most intense play I have seen in many a moon. If you are a Stephen King fan, this is a must see. If you like outstanding acting, with definitive direction (thank you, Lauren Caldwell), you will love this show."[19]

Photo: Michael Eaddy

Annie Wilkes (Sara Morsey), number one fan of author Paul Sheldon (Jason Marr), forces him to rewrite his novel in Misery.

Sharpe Substitute

In 2001, Mary Hausch directed the Hippodrome's twenty-fourth production of *A Christmas Carol* as well as its fourth production of *A Tuna Christmas*. In the latter, Lauren Caldwell still portrayed her share of the wacky residents of Tuna, Texas. But the six characters played by Mark Chambers in previous years were performed by Billy Sharpe (*Forever Plaid*). Mark was working at another theatre that year. Both shows ran from November 30–December 23.

1 *Ovation*, The Hippodrome State Theatre, Gainesville, FL, January 2001.
2 Arline Greer, review of *The Blue Room*, by David Hare, directed by Lauren Caldwell, Hippodrome Theatre, Gainesville, FL, *Gainesville Sun*, January 19, 2001.
3 Bill DeYoung, "Red Hot and Blue," *Gainesville Sun*, January 12, 2001.
4 Rusty Salling, "Macbeth: The Prequel," *Ovation*, The Hippodrome State Theatre, Gainesville, FL, March 2001.
5 Shamrock McShane, review of *Macbeth*, by William Shakespeare, directed by Lauren Caldwell, Hippodrome Theatre, Gainesville, FL, *Moon Magazine*, March 7, 2001.
6 Jessica Arnold, review of *Macbeth*, by William Shakespeare, directed by Lauren Caldwell, Hippodrome Theatre, Gainesville, FL, *Independent Florida Alligator*, March 15, 2001.
7 Arline Greer, review of *Macbeth*, by William Shakespeare, directed by Lauren Caldwell, Hippodrome Theatre, Gainesville, FL, *Gainesville Sun*, March 9, 2001.
8 Lauren Caldwell, "From the Artistic Director," *Ovation*, The Hippodrome State Theatre, Gainesville, FL, April 2001.
9 Arline Greer, review of *Anton in Show Business*, by Jane Martin, directed by Lauren Caldwell, Hippodrome Theatre, Gainesville, FL, *Gainesville Sun*, April 27, 2001.
10 Jessica Arnold, review of *Hedwig and the Angry Inch*, by John Cameron Mitchell, directed by Lauren Caldwell, Hippodrome Theatre, Gainesville, FL, *Independent Florida Alligator*, June 7, 2001.
11 Arline Greer, review of *Hedwig and the Angry Inch*, by John Cameron Mitchell, directed by Lauren Caldwell, Hippodrome Theatre, Gainesville, FL, *Gainesville Sun*, June 8, 2001.
12 Shamrock McShane, "Who's Hungry?" *Moon Magazine*, September 5, 2001.
13 Arline Greer, review of *Dinner with Friends*, by Donald Margulies, directed by Mary Hausch, Hippodrome Theatre, Gainesville, FL, *Gainesville Sun*, September 7, 2001.
14 Donald Margulies, *Dinner with Friends*, Dramatists Play Services, New York, NY.
15 *Ovation*, The Hippodrome State Theatre, Gainesville, FL, September 2001.
16 Bob Arndorfer, "Economic Impacts of War Questionable," *Gainesville Sun*, September 30, 2001.
17 Ibid.
18 Lauren Caldwell, "Number One Fan," *Ovation*, The Hippodrome State Theatre, Gainesville, FL, October 2001.
19 Dick Kerekes, review of *Misery*, by Simon Moore, directed by Lauren Caldwell, Hippodrome Theatre, Gainesville, FL, *First Coast Entertainer*, October 27, 2001.

2002

Musical Beds

In January 2002, the Hippodrome staged Patrick Marber's award-winning play *Closer*, in which four characters play musical beds. Although it contains no nudity, it is a very sexy play where the characters tell each other intimate details of their sexual encounters. But they never truly learn to merge their physical acts of love-making with the emotional truths that beckon them to move closer.

Photo: Michael Eaddy

Anna (Sara Morsey) and Larry (Dan Leonard) meet in *Closer*.

Dan, a thirty-five-year-old obituary writer, meets Alice, a twenty-three-year-old stripper. They become lovers. The couple meets professional photographer Anna when she shoots the cover of Dan's first novel. Anna also photographs Alice and uses photos of her in an exhibition.

On an internet porn site, Dan, pretending to be Anna, makes a date with Larry, a dermatologist with strong sexual proclivities. Dan cons Anna into meeting Larry, and the two fall in love and marry. Then Dan has an affair with Anna and Larry with Alice. Sexual fantasies, betrayal, guilt, and destructive emotions inhabit all four characters as they search for love in all the wrong places. Sex and love become weapons to hurt and scar. The couples break up and regroup over and over through a vicious cycle of love and lust. The script has clever lines and humorous moments, but it's not a happy play.

Arline Greer said, "There's precious little love to be found in *Closer*, but the sex? It's good. Offensive, perhaps, but good." Lauren Caldwell, who directed this Hippodrome production like a well-oiled machine, has assembled an altogether brilliant cast to play at Marber's sexual games. Marguerite Stimpson as the waif-like Alice gives a striking performance, alternating toughness with fragility. She moves with the grace of a dancer.

"Christopher Franciosa as Dan—ingratiating, naive, duplicitous, young—makes Dan all but irresistible. As Anna, Sara Morsey gives another stellar performance. Of all the characters, Morsey's Anna has the most insight into what she is doing, whom she is hurting, what she wants at any given moment in contrast to what she wants at another moment. Dan Leonard gives a stiletto-sharp interpretation of Larry."[1]

Closer ran from January 11–February 3, but not everyone loved it. There were letters to the *Gainesville Sun* both for and against the artistic director's choices. One called the play "dismal, vulgar, and depressing." Others praised the Hippodrome for not being afraid to address controversial subjects. Patrons continued to debate the merits in the Letters to the Editor section well into March, when the issue was quelled by Lauren's stunning production of *The Diary of Anne Frank*.

The Diary of Anne Frank

When the Hippodrome performed *The Diary of Anne Frank*, director Lauren Caldwell chose Wendy Kesselman's new adaptation of a previous version by Frances Goodrich and Albert Hackett. The story comes from a diary given to a young Jewish girl for her thirteenth birthday. What began as a simple entry on that day marks the beginning of a unique account of three years spent hiding from the Nazi regime. Anne's diary, published by her father after she died in a concentration camp, is the true story of an ordinary girl in extraordinary circumstances, and her voice erupts on the page with brilliance. Anne's words, beautiful and haunting, hold universal themes and are embedded with humor, love, fear, and startling clarity.

Actors on *The Diary of Anne Frank* set, a factual replica of the Frank's hiding place: (l-r) Scott Kealey, Dan Jesse, Marguerite Stimpson, Bonnie Harrison, Sara Morsey, and Emilee MacDonald; foreground with back to camera, Niall McGinty.

Photo: Michael Eaddy

Transferred to the Hippodrome's intimate stage, the conclusion of Anne's tale moved audiences to tears at every performance. The set, designed by Mihai Ciupe, was a factual replica of the annex of the Amsterdam office building where the family hid. The actors portraying the eight Jews remained in character, never leaving the stage, even during intermission. Outside the annex (offstage) were heard Nazi troops marching and shouts of "Heil Hitler."

"The Hippodrome's production of the play is remarkable in every way," wrote Arline Greer. "The story of everyday happenings is told by an irrepressible Anne, who bounds across the stage with childlike energy and enthusiasm. Played by Marguerite Stimpson with an uncanny feeling for the adolescent girl, she imbues the play with humor, sadness, joy, anger and love. She creates a small world on the Hippodrome stage in which each protagonist is brought to vivid life. Stimpson's Anne is incandescent."[2]

Her performance was equaled by the rest of the skilled cast. Scott Kealey and Bonnie Harrison played Anne's parents and Emilee MacDonald her older sister. Sara Morsey and Dan Jesse played fellow Jews Mr. and Mrs. Van Daan with Niall McGinty as their adolescent son. Dan Leonard played a Jewish dentist hiding with them. Their Dutch protectors were played by Robin Thomas and Stephen Vendette.

"From the moment audiences enter the theater and hear the names of those murdered... on to the very end of the play," Greer wrote, "director Lauren Caldwell never allows the tension to go limp. When the ending comes and each character is illuminated by a spotlight, frozen in time, we are transfixed, held there as Anne's words are heard yet again, exhorting us to be our better selves.... *The Diary of Anne Frank* is a rare theater experience, theater that takes you right out of yourself. It's not to be missed."[3]

Yet, even in 2002, the generation that remembered the unspeakable horrors of World War II was disappearing. Lauren Caldwell recalls sitting on the porch of the theatre when she overheard a young college student ask, "Who is Anne Frank?"

"My first reaction was, *Has he been living under a rock?* My next reaction was *Oh my God, how proud I am to preserve the memory of this wise and brave girl on our stage.*"[4]

Pieter Kohnstam talks to a Hippodrome audience on March 30, 2002, about his childhood with Anne Frank.

In conjunction with the play, Hippodrome dramaturg Tammy Dygert brought together bookstore owners, members of the Alachua County School Board, Alachua County District Library, UF professors and librarians, local radio personnel, and representatives from B'nai Israel (a local synagogue) and Hillel (a Jewish campus organization), to ask, "What if all of Gainesville rallied together to read the same book at the same time?" Out of it came a program called "One City, One Story," through which community members read *The Diary of Anne Frank* in schools, book clubs, and individually. Author Shelley Fraser Mickle featured the book in a series of newspaper columns throughout February and March. The Hippodrome also hosted a series of free lectures and a touring exhibit from the Anne Frank Center. UF broadcast readings on its PBS radio station.

The Diary of Anne Frank ran March 1–31.

Proof

If the letter writers who threatened to cancel their subscriptions back in January needed further convincing than *Anne Frank* to retain them, they got it with the next play, *Proof* by David Auburn. This was another case of the Hippodrome scoring rights to an amazing work. *Proof* had just won the 2001 Pulitzer Prize, three Tony Awards, including Best Play, and every other major theatre award. Its Broadway run continued even as it opened in Gainesville. How did that happen?

"We are recognized nationally as a theatre that produces the highest quality artistic work and that has the support of a diverse and discriminating audience," said Mary Hausch, the play's director.

For her cast, Mary brought in Yale-trained actress Ibi Janko to play the lead, Catherine, and Eb Thomas, a veteran of the New York Shakespeare Festival, as her father, Robert. They were joined by Hippodrome regulars Niall McGinty as Hal and Marguerite Stimpson as Claire.

The play begins after Robert's death. Catherine has to deal with losing her father. She also has to deal with her estranged sister, Claire, who arrives from New York with her own agenda, and with Hal, her father's former student, who is desperately searching for a glimpse of brilliance and clarity in the 103 notebooks Robert left behind.

Robert, a brilliant innovator in the field of mathematics, was known to have penned the most elegant, perfect mathematical proofs. But like other geniuses, he became plagued with a mental illness that forced Catherine to give up her life and her education to take care of him.

The play flashes backward in time so that we see Catherine and Robert at various stages in their lives. This creates an emotional background for Catherine's own ongoing struggle. She, too, has her father's passion for the poetry of numbers but is afraid her inherited genius might lead her to share Robert's fate.

Hal, eager to understand the inner workings of Robert's mind, tries to decipher the notebooks despite Catherine's protests. Along the way, a

Photo: Michael Eaddy

Proof cast: (l-r) Eb Thomas, Ibi Janko, Niall McGinty, and Marguerite Stimpson.

budding romance develops between them. Then, Hal discovers a brilliant theorem about prime numbers in an old notebook. "Something mathematicians have been trying to prove since... since there were mathematicians," he tells the sisters.[5] Questions about its authorship heighten the plot until it is finally revealed that the proof in the notebook is Catherine's, not Robert's.

Proof ran from April 19–May 12. About it, Arline Greer wrote, "It's a beautifully crafted play that's part psychodrama and part family drama. It's funny, stimulating and emotionally satisfying.... The word 'elegant' is used by mathematicians to describe theories of uncommon distinction, the right word for this production of *Proof*."[6]

Honky Tonk Angels

The Hippodrome had much previous success with jukebox musicals, so for the summer of 2002, they presented *Honky Tonk Angels*. The play, penned by Ted Swindley, who wrote *Always... Patsy Cline*, hangs thirty-two well-known country songs on a skeletal plot. Director Lauren Caldwell summarized the story thus: "Three women from three corners of the U.S. of A. meet on a Greyhound bus headed for Nashville and along with a lot of baggage (and I don't mean suitcases), they sing their way to the top with tunes that take you down memory lane."

Honky Tonk Angels: (l-r) Jessie Janet Richards, LaVon Fisher, and Christina Parke.

Photo: Michael Eaddy

To play the three wacky women, Lauren cast Jessie Janet Richards (*Always... Patsy Cline*), LaVon Fisher (*Beehive* and *Rocky Horror*), and newcomer Christina Parke, whose voice harmonized perfectly with the others. Accompanied by a live band, they sang ninety minutes of familiar country hits from "Stand by Your Man" to "Coal Miner's Daughter," and of course, Kitty Wells's "It Wasn't God Who Made Honky Tonk Angels."

The *Gainesville Sun* called it a "fun and musical romp" and said LaVon Fisher's performance was "a hoot, a very talented hoot. The same could be said of the other two actresses who perform in this fast-moving show, whose songs and scenes flow seamlessly, one into the other. [Jessie Janet] Richard's performance of 'Stand by Your Man' catches Tammy Wynette's every inflection. The threesome blend voices into a variety of songs."[7]

These summer musicals often brought audiences from outlying counties who didn't regularly come to the Hippodrome. Many returned to see the show again, bringing friends or family. This was the case with *Honky Tonk Angels*, which opened June 7 and was held over an unprecedented five times, closing August 11. In July, Kim Stout took over for Jessie Janet Richards as the show played on. General Manager Mark Sexton estimated that 16,000 people attended the show.

Thirtieth Season

On August 30, the theatre kicked off its thirtieth season with *Stones in His Pockets*, an award-winning British comedy by Marie Jones. After a lot of long-distance communication with the London agents, the Hippodrome became the first US regional theatre to be granted production rights.

This play tells the story of Hollywood invading a small, sleepy Irish village to make a motion picture. The production brings some much-needed revenue, but locals who work on the film also learn that big business is a bit dodgy. The first act begins with two actors portraying movie extras Charlie Conlon (Mark Ellmore) and Jake Quinn (Paul Taviani). But as the play proceeds, the actors take on additional roles as various men and women from the Tinsel Town cast and crew. These include the film's assistant directors, an accent coach, a leading lady and her bodyguard, and assorted Irish villagers.

Under Mary Hausch's direction, Mark Ellmore and Paul Taviani accomplished all of this without changing costumes. Altering only their hairstyles, body language, accents, and vocal inflection, the two played a combined total of fifteen characters.

While the *Sun* critic said the play had "a lot of charm," she also said it lacked cohesion: "Although Ellmore and Taviani indeed morph effortlessly from one character into another, there is confusion, particularly in the play's first act. Here, it's almost impossible to tell who the players are and what they're about. In *Stones* second act, the character switches become much clearer but there are new problems as Jones' comedy has turned to tragedy."[8]

Stones in His Pockets ran through September 22.

Photo: Michael Eaddy

Mark Ellmore and Paul Taviani portray fifteen characters in *Stones in His Pockets*.

Bat Boy: The Musical

In the prior five years, the Hippodrome had selected plays for October to fit the mood of Halloween: *Dracula, Frankenstein, Misery,* and the campy *Rocky Horror Show.* For their thirtieth season, they found *Bat Boy: The Musical.*

Inspired by a trashy tabloid story about a half-boy, half-bat creature discovered in a West Virginia cave, authors Keythe Farley, Brian Flemming, and Laurence O'Keefe created a musical comedy that is also a supernatural thriller with a moral. When the rights became available to regional theatres, director Lauren Caldwell pounced. "This show contains some of the best music I have ever heard, and a book that is clever and simply one of a kind," she said.[9]

The score, a mix of rock and roll, beautiful ballads, and a little rap music, required a cast who could really sing, and Lauren stacked the deck with proven vocal powerhouses: Mark Chambers (*Rocky Horror, Hedwig,* and others); Catherine Fries Vaughn (*Nunsense*); Chad Hudson, Billy Sharpe, and Daniel Siford (three-fourths of *Forever Plaid*); and Christina Parke (*Honky Tonk Angels*). Alongside them were Diana Preisler, Katrina Griffin, Leannis Maxwell, and Hippodrome company members Brian Natale, Carl Holder, and Stephen Vendette.

"The entire cast of *Bat Boy* is irresistible," wrote Arline Greer. "All the many characters in *Bat Boy* can sing. Their blended voices resonate throughout the theater. They are accompanied by a fine band led by the show's musical director, Tané DeKrey. Every scene in *Bat Boy* is filled with robust music and eye-catching

(l-r) Mark Chambers, Chad Hudson as Bat Boy, and Stephen Vendette in *Bat Boy: The Musical*.

Photo: Michael Eaddy

choreography. Ric Rose, the show's choreographer, has created some engaging dance sequences."[10]

In the story, three teens discover Bat Boy (Chad Hudson) in a cave and bring him to the home of Dr. Parker, a Jekyll and Hyde-type veterinarian. The creature is renamed Edgar, taught to speak English, and learns social customs and manners. Parker's wife and daughter develop affection for the boy, and the doc resents it.

When a traveling preacher (Mark Chambers) brings a tent revival to town, Bat Boy begs to make his first foray into society. Parker is against it and creates trouble for the boy, who ends up having sex with the daughter.

"Go to this show with an open mind and leave your small children at home," actor Billy Sharpe told the *Independent Florida Alligator*.[11] The *Alligator* reporter added, "There's lots of blood sucking, gore, incest, and even an interspecies orgy thrown in for your amusement."[12] As for the moral of the musical, which played from October 18–November 10, the reporter said, "Besides being wildly entertaining, *Bat Boy* could infect you with a concept still needed in this world—tolerance and acceptance."[13]

Holiday Plays

The theatre reprised its annual *A Christmas Carol* for its twenty-fifth run, this time with Sara Morsey as director. They also offered a new holiday play for 2002, *The Santaland Diaries*. Director Joe Mantello adapted it from a story in the best-selling book *Holidays on Ice* by National Public Radio humorist David Sedaris. The sardonic tale is based on Sedaris's stint working as an elf in Santaland at Macy's.

Mark Chambers played Crumpet the elf in the one-man show. Filled with wry insight, four-letter words, and abundant sexual references, the play explores the collision of Christmas and American consumerism at that popular Santa stop: the department store. Crumpet joins other elves-in-training and gets caught in the Yuletide lunacy that brings out the best and worst in people—including Santa.

Mark noted that he brought firsthand experience to the play. He said, "When I first moved to San Francisco, I was out of work. I called the Equity Hotline and became Santa at a big department store. I had to go to Santa school and learn [friendly phrases] in all different languages. I had to take psychology lessons too. It wasn't what I expected. It was really an acting job. The costume was so exquisite.

"*Santaland* just cracked me up because I was a Santa. I encountered the same things: the sad adults who just needed some sort of attention, the child who peed on me. I felt like I was holding a little Chihuahua, who got too excited. I did it [for] two years and was voted the favorite, sweetest Santa by the elves."[14]

The Santaland Diaries opened November 29 and *A Christmas Carol* opened the following day. Both plays ended their runs on December 22.

Mark Chambers as Crumpet the elf in *The Santaland Diaries*.

Photo: Michael Eaddy

1   Arline Greer, review of *Closer*, by Patrick Marber, directed by Lauren Caldwell, Hippodrome Theatre, Gainesville, FL, *Gainesville Sun*, January 18, 2002.

2   Arline Greer, review of *The Diary of Anne Frank*, by Wendy Kesselman, directed by Lauren Caldwell, Hippodrome Theatre, Gainesville, FL, *Gainesville Sun*, March 8, 2002.

3   Ibid.

4   *Ovation*, The Hippodrome State Theatre, Gainesville, FL, February 2002.

5   David Auburn, *Proof*, Dramatists Play Service, New York, NY.

6   Arline Greer, review of *Proof*, by David Auburn, directed by Mary Hausch, Hippodrome Theatre, Gainesville, FL, *Gainesville Sun*, April 26, 2002.

7   Arline Greer, review of *Honky Tonk Angels*, by Ted Swindley, directed by Lauren Caldwell, Hippodrome Theatre, Gainesville, FL, *Gainesville Sun*, June 14, 2002.

8   Arline Greer, review of *Stones in His Pockets*, by Marie Jones, directed by Mary Hausch, Hippodrome Theatre, Gainesville, FL, *Gainesville Sun*, September 9, 2002.

9   *Ovation*, The Hippodrome State Theatre, Gainesville, FL, October 2002.

10 Arline Greer, review of *Bat Boy: The Musical*, by Keythe Farley, Brian Flemming, and Laurence O'Keefe, directed by Lauren Caldwell, Hippodrome Theatre, Gainesville, FL, *Gainesville Sun*, October 25, 2002.

11 Amy Sowder, "This Just in: Bat Boy Could Reverse Hatred of Musicals," *Independent Florida Alligator*, October 17, 2002.

12 Ibid.

13 Ibid.

14 "A Q&A with Mark Chambers," *Ovation*, The Hippodrome State Theatre, Gainesville, FL, December 2002.

2003

The Play About the Baby

The Hippodrome's first play for 2003, Edward Albee's *The Play About the Baby*, directed by Lauren Caldwell, opened January 10 and ran through February 2. The play is not so much about a baby as it is about the human condition. There is an unseen baby—of sorts—at the show's center, but Albee's four characters are there to probe the crevices between innocence and devastating personal loss. He has named them generically: Boy, Girl, Man, and Woman.

Photo: Lee Ferinden

Cast of *The Play About the Baby*: (l-r) David Shelton, Niall McGinty, Marguerite Stimpson, and Sara Morsey.

Boy and Girl are newlyweds frolicking in their own Eden somewhere between innocence and experience—an Adam and Eve of the twenty-first century. Offstage, Girl gives birth. Despite the occasional interruption of their newborn's cries, they continue living a blissful existence peppered with lustful outbursts.

Enter Man and Woman, a comic duo bouncing off each other like a well-timed vaudeville team. With witty repartee, they introduce a relationship's darker elements to the squirming Boy and Girl. Like serpents in the Garden, these intruders suggest alternative truths to the reality in which Boy and Girl have lived. Soon, doubt begins to wash over Boy and Girl and they begin to question everything—including the existence of their baby.

Is the baby real or imaginary? Originally, that wasn't left so up in the air. Lindsay Beacham, Hippodrome stage manager for *The Play About the Baby*, had worked with Albee when he directed the play's preview in Houston, Texas. She said, "Albee envisioned a real baby, but a monstrous one, disproportionate, to be operated by an actor inside it, almost like a puppeteer. The baby that appeared at the end of the show and that was tried in previews... it was me in costume," she said. "We could never work it out. I was practically blind inside the thing and had to be directed through a headset. All I could see were patches of light. And then, just before we opened, Albee decided to cut it."[1] He rewrote the ending.

"Be warned!" Arline Greer said in her review. "If you're looking for the answer to what Edward Albee's *The Play About the Baby* is about, you won't necessarily find it here.... The baby is not just a baby but a symbol of hope, a dream, a goal.

"David Shelton, who plays the very urban, tongue-in-cheek Man, has never appeared to better advantage on a local stage. He is very funny and, even in his cruelest moments, brings to life vaudeville quality that cuts the anguish down to the absurd. His counterpart, Sara Morsey as Woman, is equally funny, with her stories of a lovestruck artist and her youthful 'milk pink hips.'

"Marguerite Stimpson and Niall McGinty are charming and beautiful as Girl and Boy. Their naked and half-naked frolicking never seems offensive. They are sweetly innocent, full of exuberance and totally endearing. When the play ends with its sad reckoning, it's difficult not to feel emotionally bereft for the young twosome."[2]

Romeo and Juliet

It had been seventeen years since the Hippodrome had staged William Shakespeare's *Romeo and Juliet*. Director Lauren Caldwell thought it was time to weave moody, modern theatrics into Shakespeare's classic dialogue. "The story itself is completely intact," Lauren told the *Gainesville Sun*. "What will be surprising (to audiences) is how we executed that."[3] Instead of a realistic Verona, the two-level set was black wrought iron stairs and scaffolding. Marilyn Wall gave the costumes contemporary touches—Juliet in a short pink skirt and sneakers.

The well-known tale begins with a street brawl between servants of enemy families, the Capulets and Montagues. The ruling prince (Kelley Guarneri) intervenes and declares that any further breach of peace will be punished by death.

Count Paris (Steven Blackwell) asks Capulet (Mark Sexton) about marrying his daughter, Juliet (Marguerite Stimpson). Capulet suggests Paris wait until Juliet is older and invites him to attend a Capulet ball. Lady Capulet (Robin Thomas) and Juliet's Nurse (Bonnie Harrison) try to persuade Juliet to accept Paris's courtship.

Romeo (Niall McGinty), son of Montague (Gregg Jones), is depressed over an unrequited infatuation. His cousins Benvolio (Emilee MacDonald) and Mercutio (Charlie Kevin) convince him to sneak into the ball. There, Romeo meets and falls in love with Juliet. After the ball, Romeo sneaks into the Capulet orchard and overhears Juliet at her window, vowing her love to him in spite of her family's hatred of the Montagues. Romeo climbs up to her balcony, and they agree to be married.

With the help of Friar Lawrence (Sara Morsey), who hopes to reconcile the two families through their children's union, they are secretly married the next day. Then Juliet's cousin Tybalt (Kevin Blake) fatally wounds Mercutio in a duel; Romeo slays him and is exiled by the prince. Romeo and Juliet secretly consummate their marriage before he leaves.

Juliet (Marguerite Stimpson) and Romeo (Niall McGinty) kiss.

Capulet arranges Juliet's marriage to Paris, so she fakes her death. When Romeo learns she has died, he buys poison, enters her crypt, and joins her in death. Juliet then awakens, discovers Romeo is dead, and stabs herself with his dagger.

Arline Greer didn't care for Lauren's interpretation. "The general feeling of the Hippodrome's production of *Romeo and Juliet* is one of commotion. What is lost in this spectacle is Shakespeare's beautiful language. Nor is the love story entirely believable. The passion that should explode between these two lovers never seems to ignite. The best performances are given

Photo: Michael Eaddy

by the warring Montague and Capulet, played by Gregory Jones and Mark Sexton, respectively. Each speaks with clarity, and brings dramatic nuance to his role. This Hippodrome production is altogether dazzling to the eye and ear. It is totally original, will remind you of no *Romeo and Juliet* you have seen before."[4]

Additional cast members were Brian Natale, Kirt Taylor, Stephen Vendette, Sandra Dietel, Paige Burt, Carl Holder, Christina Parke, Lisa Vendette, and Clay Smith. The show ran from February 28–March 30, during which they again sponsored a One City One Story project with great success. This time, students from local elementary schools, middle schools, high schools, and colleges performed scenes from the play throughout the community.

The Carpetbagger's Children

In April, Mary Hausch directed Horton Foote's *The Carpetbagger's Children*, casting powerhouse actors Sara Morsey, Nell Page, and Catherine Fries Vaughn as sisters Cornelia, Grace Anne, and Sissie.

The three sisters are direct decedents of a soldier in the Union Army who was stationed in Confederate Texas during the Civil War. After the war, he returned to Texas, carpetbag in hand, as the appointed County Treasurer and Tax Collector. The sisters grew up in one of the finest houses in town, obtained at the expense of the bankrupt farmers whose land he'd procured for pennies on a dollar.

In the play, Grace Anne says, "I always dreaded the day when the Civil War was brought up and someone would point to me and say, as if it had never been said before, 'her Papa was a Carpetbagger.'"[5]

Photo: Michael Eaddy

The Carpetbagger's Children are played by (l-r) Nell Page, Sara Morsey, and Catherine Fries Vaughn.

The sisters tell their stories in monologs that vividly bring to life the townsfolk and events of their lives from Reconstruction through World War II. Cornelia, the matriarch, wants viewers to understand why she took over Papa's business affairs and ran the household with an iron fist. Grace Anne, the renegade, wants the audience to know that she has no regrets about rebelling against the family, marrying a chronic loser, and being ostracized from the family. Sissie, the melodious dreamer, wants to lift everyone's spirits with her beautiful singing voice and just wants the audience to like her.

The Carpetbagger's Children was nominated for the Pulitzer Prize for Drama and won the American Theatre Critics Association Award for Best New Play and the Steinberg New Play Award. Foote also received the National Medal of Honor for the play.

Arline Greer called it a "small dramatic gem" and asked, "How could anyone not stand in utter admiration of these three remarkable actresses?"[6]

The Carpetbagger's Children ran from April 18–May 11.

Shear Murder

The 2003 summer play wasn't one of the jukebox musicals that had been so successful for the previous five years. That might seem like sheer madness. No, it was *Shear Madness*, a farcical murder mystery that, as of 2023, still holds the Guinness Book of World Records title for the longest-running non-musical play in the history of American theatre.

Getting the rights to perform it wasn't easy. The show's owners, Marilyn Abrams and Bruce Jordan, refused the Hippodrome's first request. "It is very rare we let any director other than a *Shear Madness*-trained director do the show," said Bruce Jordan. "But we got such good reports about the Hippodrome, and Mary [Hausch] in particular, we decided to give it a shot."[7]

Abrams and Jordan had bought the rights to a German murder mystery written by Paul Pörtner, which they turned it into a farce featuring interactive audience participation. By 2003, it had been seen by six million people. Gainesville was the smallest market it had ever played. Mary had to go to the Kennedy Center in Washington, D.C., to attend *Shear Madness* School. There, she spent time watching multiple daily showings, studying the comedy's nuances and audience questions.

Shear Madness is set in a unisex hairstyling salon. Out of the audience's sight, a famous pianist is murdered in the upstairs apartment with a pair of barber's shears while the entire cast seems to be in the shop. The investigation (and audience questions) is handled by police detective Nick Rossetti (Gregg Jones) and his vacuous assistant Mikey (Stephen Blackwell). Both happen to be there getting a shave at the time of the murder.

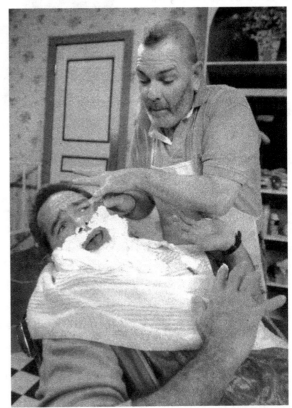

The suspects are salon owner Barbara Demarco (Lauren Caldwell), uninhibited gay stylist Tony Whitcomb (Mark Chambers), society matron Mrs. Shubert (Sara Morsey), and shifty antiques dealer Eddie Lawrence (Cameron Francis). The dialogue is peppered with lowbrow jokes—and, in the Hippodrome production, localized with Alachua County references. At the end of the first act, the houselights come up and the audience is invited to question the suspects. During intermission, Detective Rossetti joins theatergoers in the lobby, listens to their theories, and presents them in the second act. At the play's end, audience votes decide the killer, and the actors adjust the ending accordingly.

The show opened on June 6 and played to packed houses through August 10. Hippodrome Marketing Director Adam Sternefeld told the *Gainesville Sun*, "People have returned two or three times in a row."[8]

Photo: Lee Ferinden

Detective Nick Rossetti (Gregg Jones) being shaved by stylist Tony Whitcomb (Mark Chambers) in *Shear Madness*.

Season Thirty-one

The new season opened with a wacky musical comedy, *The Big Bang*, directed by Lauren Caldwell. Mark Chambers and Billy Sharpe played Jed and Boyd, two playwrights with the same names as the show's creators: Jed Freur, who wrote the music, and Boyd Graham, who wrote the book and lyrics.

Accompanied by their keyboard player (Tané DeKrey), the two are in a Fifth Avenue apartment pitching their latest creation to potential backers (the audience). Their epic musical spans the history of the world from the Big Bang to the present. They tell the audience that since the proposed extravaganza runs twelve hours, they will only be performing the highlights.

Billy Sharpe and Mark Chambers act out scenes for a new musical, *The Big Bang*, accompanied by musical director/keyboard player Tané DeKrey.

Photo: Michael Eaddy

The two men snatch the apartment's furnishings for makeshift props and costumes as they perform the biggest names in history: Adam and Eve, Attila the Hun, Julius Caesar, Nefertiti, Plato, Jesus, the Virgin Mary, Napoleon, Mrs. Gandhi, and even Cher.

Arline Greer called it "inspired and marvelously funny." She said, "Sharpe and Chambers are brilliant actors who never miss a beat. They sing; they dance; they clown; they engage the audience.... It would be impossible to find funnier people than Mark Chambers and Billy Sharpe. Their performances make *The Big Bang* one of the Hippodrome's most enjoyable productions in years."[9]

The show ran from August 29–September 28.

Jekyll and Hyde

On a stark set of metal scaffolding, with plenty of spooky fog roiling on the stage floor, the Hippodrome presented *The Strange Case of Dr. Jekyll and Mr. Hyde*. Adapted by Jean Lafayette from the novel by Robert Louis Stevenson, the play takes the form of a coroner's inquest. Detective Newcomen (Sara Morsey) makes a chronological examination of the diary of Dr. Jekyll, whose rush to advance medical research unleashes his darker side by drinking a potion that transforms him into homicidal madman Mr. Hyde.

Photo: Lee Ferinden
Dr. Jekyll (Cameron Francis) holding the potion that transforms him into Mr. Hyde in *The Strange Case of Dr. Jekyll and Mr. Hyde*.

Cameron Francis played Jekyll and Hyde without makeup changes, just shifting his demeanor. Ibi Janko, last seen in *Proof*, returned to play Rachel, the woman who wants to marry Jekyll. Billy Sharpe played Jekyll's longtime friend Dr. David Lanyon with Robin Thomas as the maid who witnessed Hyde's crime.

"Man, at the most fundamental level, is not one but two," says the character Rachel.[10] And that is the theme in a nutshell—the duality of human nature expressed as an inner struggle between good and evil. The play adds a dash of substance abuse when Jekyll/Hyde can't stop drinking his dangerous concoction.

Unfortunately, as Arline Greer noted, "there isn't much that is frightening about Lafayette's adaptation…. The production is fine, but the play itself tends to be old hat and not up to the Hippodrome's high standards."[11]

The show, directed by Lauren Caldwell, ran from October 17–November 16.

Christmas Duo

Like the opposites Jekyll and Hyde, the Hippodrome again alternated the sweet, kid-friendly *A Christmas Carol* with the foul-mouthed elf of *The Santaland Diaries*. Mark Chambers reprised his role as Crumpet the elf while siblings Emyrs and Aegis Duensing took turns playing Tiny Tim on alternate nights. Both shows opened November 28 and played through December 21.

1 Shamrock McShane, *New Moon Magazine*, December 30, 2002.
2 Arline Greer, review of *The Play About the Baby*, by Edward Albee, directed by Lauren Caldwell, Hippodrome Theatre, Gainesville, FL, *Gainesville Sun*, January 17, 2003.
3 Dave Schlenker, "Shakespeare's New Look," *Gainesville Sun*, February 28, 2003.
4 Arline Greer, review of *Romeo and Juliet*, by William Shakespeare, directed by Lauren Caldwell, Hippodrome Theatre, Gainesville, FL, *Gainesville Sun*, March 7, 2003.
5 Horton Foote, *The Carpetbagger's Children*, Dramatists Play Service, New York, NY.
6 Arline Greer, review of *The Carpetbagger's Children*, by Horton Foote, directed by Mary Hausch, Hippodrome Theatre, Gainesville, FL, *Gainesville Sun*, April 25, 2003.
7 Dave Schlenker, "Stay Sharp at Shear," *Gainesville Sun*, June 6, 2003.
8 Dave Schlenker, "*Pajama Game* Opens, *Madness* Held Over," *Gainesville Sun*, July 11, 2003.
9 Arline Greer, review of *The Big Bang*, by Boyd Graham, directed by Lauren Caldwell, Hippodrome Theatre, Gainesville, FL, *Gainesville Sun*, September 5, 2003.
10 Dave Schlenker, "Man's Dark Side," *Gainesville Sun*, October 17, 2003.
11 Arline Greer, review of *The Strange Case of Dr. Jekyll and Mr. Hyde*, by Jean Lafayette, directed by Lauren Caldwell, Hippodrome Theatre, Gainesville, FL, *Gainesville Sun*, October 24, 2003.

2004

French Farce

In January 2004, Mary Hausch directed *Life x 3*, a farce written by French playwright Yasmina Reza and translated by Christopher Hampton. Mary had previously directed Hampton's translation of Reza's play *ART,* back in 2000.

In the story, Henry and Sonia are putting their son to bed and settling in for a quiet evening at home when an unexpected knock at their door throws their lives into chaos. Henry's colleague Hubert and his wife Inez show up for an important business dinner—a day early!

(l-r) Ibi Janko, Richard Warner, Nell Page, and Cameron Francis in *Life x 3*.

Photo: Michael Eaddy

With no food in the house, Henry and Sonia serve an impromptu feast of Cheez-Its, cookies, and lots of wine. Their (offstage) son's crying sets off the couple's competitive parenting skills. Marital spats erupt. Inez discovers an ever-growing run in her pantyhose. Hubert drops the unsettling news that another research team is about to publish a paper bearing a remarkable resemblance to Henry's work—news that could make Henry's past three years of research obsolete.

The script repeats the first act twice more, varying the characters' reactions. Hubert makes lecherous advances in response to Sonia's shameless flirtation, and the evening quickly and comically spirals down toward a catastrophic unraveling of normal civilized behavior.

"The Hippodrome's production is smart and funny, moving with the speed of light for ninety minutes without intermission," said the *Gainesville Sun*. "It is worth seeing, if only, to enjoy Nell Page as Inez, who is very funny as she slides into drunkenness. Richard Warner plays Hubert, Inez's condescending husband and accomplished academician, with an endless supply of smarminess. Ibi Janko as Sonia gives a versatile performance, easily moving from arrogance to coyness and displeasure during the play's three spins. Cameron Francis, the woe-begone Henry, is comical in his confused efforts to please his wife, child, and mentor."[1]

Life x 3 ran from January 9–February 8.

The War of the Worlds

Following *Life x 3*, Lauren Caldwell tried her hand at science fiction, adapting and directing the H. G. Wells novel *The War of the Worlds*. Hippodrome dramaturg Tammy Dygert set up another One City One Story program encouraging the community to read Wells's classic. Events also included local actors reading excerpts from Orson Welles's 1938 radio program about an alien invasion that created mass hysteria when it was originally broadcast.

Perhaps if the script had followed the novel, or even been a story about the radio show, it would have been better received. Instead, it was a series of strangely disconnected elements ranging from Robert Oppenheimer to Adam and Eve. Seven actors, Cameron Francis, Sara Morsey, Stephen Blackwell, Bill Irwin, Charlie Kevin, Robin Thomas, James Webb, Jr., and J. Salome Martinez, Jr., played multiple roles. The closest the play got to its source material was the opening, where a solitary survivor sat atop a mound of dead bodies.

Photo: Michael Eaddy

An actor stands on a heap of bodies as attack rays strike the rest of the cast in *The War of the Worlds*.

Enormous Prop

To create the mound of bodies, the Hippodrome turned to ThemeWorks, a firm in nearby High Springs that fabricates large, lifelike pieces for zoos and theme parks. The completed prop consisted of eight 300–400 pound sections.

Trying not to seem too harsh, Arline Greer said the "adaptation veered off course." She called it "a curious blend of imagery and language presented in an episodic structure with no central focus.... a play that relies too much on image rather than on substance."[2]

"I don't fancy myself a playwright," Lauren Caldwell admitted in an interview with Shamrock McShane. "What I can do is create a collage." She shrugged, "This play may not be for everybody."[3] She was right about that. *War* only survived its minimum run, February 27–March 21.

Rounding Third

Mary Hausch directed the next play, Richard Dresser's *Rounding Third*. This quirky comedy teams up two of the most mismatched men ever to coach Little League baseball.

Don is an affable, beer-swilling ex-jock with a win-at-all-cost philosophy. Every year, Don gets help from an assistant coach. This year, the man filling those shoes is Michael, a wide-eyed newcomer who wears a suit, packs a cell phone, drinks Starbucks cappuccinos, and believes that the fun is in the playing, not in winning or losing.

Photo: Michael Eaddy

Charlie Kevin and Cameron Francis play dads coaching Little League in *Rounding Third*.

Michael's son can neither hit the ball nor field it, is nearly blind without his glasses, and can't remember Don's coaching tips from one game to the next. Don's son is the team's star pitcher and every dad's dream. Don and Michael disagree on everything, especially as they coax their struggling young team closer and closer to the playoffs.

With a kinder eye toward this show than the prior one, Arline Greer praised the actors, director, and script: "As the two coaches vie for the kids' attention, audiences come to think there really is a team of players on the field. Charlie Kevin as Don and Cameron Francis as Michael are very good at creating that illusion. In one glory moment toward the end, the audience holds its collective breath, hoping a kid will catch a game-deciding fly ball. Director Mary Hausch makes the production come alive in this good-natured Hippodrome production. Dresser's one-liners are very funny, but even though they keep us laughing, they also give us something to think about after we leave the theater."[4]

Rounding Third played from April 16–May 16.

Summer Smash

In the summer of 2004, The Hippodrome found another smash hit with *I Love You, You're Perfect, Now Change*. It played for over two months, from June 4–August 8. At the time, it was billed as the longest-running off-Broadway musical revue in New York history with over 2,500 performances. The book and lyrics are by Joe DiPietro and the music is by Jimmy Roberts.

(l-r) Billy Sharpe, Felecia Harrelson, James Webb, Jr., and Meghan Lowery in *I Love You, You're Perfect, Now Change.*

Photo: Michael Eaddy

Four actors take on over forty roles in a collection of scenes and songs about the difficulties and joys of dating, engagement, marriage, parenthood, divorce, widowhood, and everything in between. The Newark *Star-Ledger* described it as "*Seinfeld* set to music."

I Love You, You're Perfect, Now Change celebrates the humor and poignancy of relationships through original songs in a wide variety of musical styles, including ballads, tango, rock and roll, and country and western. It was directed by Heidi Cline, a guest director who had directed the show three times in Atlanta. Her musical director was Tané DeKrey. The cast paired Billy Sharpe (*The Big Bang*) and James Webb, Jr. (*The War of the Worlds*) with UF Theatre Department graduate students Meghan Lowery and Felecia Harrelson.

"The energy of the cast members rivals that of any Broadway production," said the reviewer for *InSite Magazine*. "Every detail of every scene has been well designed and is articulated so well through each actor. From driving a car on stage, to exploring how men and women first came to love, *I Love You, You're Perfect, Now Change*, will astound you with laughter."[5]

"No matter how old you are or where you are in your relationships, you will identify with these most enjoyable musical send-ups of situations most of us have had more than a nodding acquaintance," wrote Arline Greer. "Nothing needs to change in the Hippodrome's likeable musical that goes to the heart of relationships."[6]

Change in Management

One relationship did change. Hippodrome General Manager Mark Sexton resigned. He'd held the position since 1996 and was ready to do something else. The parting was amicable, and Mark remains a close friend and staunch supporter of the Hippodrome.

Looking back at his stint as General Manager, Mark said, "I was still doing plays, and that was important for my sanity. The balance between acting and being the manager worked pretty well, but during that particular period, the theatre was humming. There were over fifty people on staff. That $20,000-a-week payroll was formidable and there were there were several times when Mary, Lauren, and I would be sitting in the office on Monday wondering how we'd make that payroll on Friday. But I'm very proud that we never missed a payroll while I was the general manager. It got to the point where it was getting more and more difficult for me to even think about doing a play because running the business was really intense. So, I, like many, did my turn at the Hippodrome, made my contribution, and then I moved on."

Season Thirty-two

Steve Martin, known to many as a movie star, standup comedian, or early cast member of *Saturday Night Live*, is also a novelist and playwright. *The Underpants*, presented by the Hippodrome from August 27–September 19, is Steve Martin's adaptation of a 1911 German farce, *Die Hose* by Carl Sternheim.

This send-up of bourgeois snobbery and conformity is set in the early 1900s, when a woman's underwear was held up by a drawstring around her waist. Louise (Christine Sellers) is standing on a chair on tiptoe watching Kaiser Wilhelm passing by on parade when her underpants come untied and fall to her feet. Suddenly, the crowd's attention switches from the king's carriage to the lady's privates.

Her boorish husband, Theo (Mark Kincaid), a government clerk, fears the incident may damage his career. Meanwhile, her exposure brings a stream of men to rent rooms in the couple's home and compete for Louise's attention—a fact that goes over Theo's head. Among them is Versati (William Irwin), a poet seeking inspiration by getting Louise between the sheets, and Cohen (Bryan Garey), a Jewish barber lusting for her. A third gentleman is an elderly scientist (Rusty Salling) who knows nothing of the lady's faux pas and is only looking for peace and quiet. Middle-aged spinster Gertrude (Sara Morsey), who lives upstairs, yearns to live vicariously through Louise's sexual adventures and attempts to orchestrate Louise's affair with one of the men. Louise morphs into a vamp in a heartbeat, and the chase is on.

Photo: Michael Eaddy

Louise (Christine Sellers) shocks Herr Klinglehoff (Rusty Salling) in *The Underpants*.

"You can almost hear Steve Martin in between the door slams," said Rusty Salling.[7]

"A really good farce takes the most unlikely premise and, after a scant ten minutes, has you totally engrossed, identifying with its characters, and, laughing helplessly," observed Arline Greer. "Steve Martin's *The Underpants* is a very, very good farce. The cast is first rate, with each actor mastering the show's deadpan humor. And Martin is clearly present here: Versati proclaims, 'I want to make love to you. It won't take a minute.'"[8]

"This is a first-rate farce with excellent acting and comic timing," wrote theatre critic Dick Kerekes. "Director Lauren Caldwell has selected a picture-perfect cast and they deliver lots of laughs and physical comedy."[9]

Nickel and Dimed

Instead of trying for a Halloween-themed show that October, the Hippodrome opted for an insightful social commentary, *Nickel and Dimed*. The award-winning play by Joan Holden is based on Barbara Ehrenreich's critically acclaimed national bestseller.

Wondering how anyone could survive, let alone prosper, on six to seven dollars an hour, journalist Barbara Ehrenreich decided to find out. She moved from Florida to Maine to Minnesota, taking the cheapest lodgings available and accepting work as a waitress, hotel maid, house cleaner, nursing home aide, and Walmart employee. She compiled her findings into a *New York Times* bestseller, which revealed low-wage America in all its tenacity, anxiety, and surprising generosity. The Hippodrome again created a One City One Story program centered on Barbara Ehrenreich's book, which was featured in seven weekly newspaper columns by Shelley Fraser Mickle.

(l-r) Sara Morsey, William Irwin, Brenda Porter, Adrienne Lovette, Christine Sellers, and Laura Rohner in the *Nickel and Dimed* diner scene.

Photo: Michael Eaddy

Director Lauren Caldwell retained Sara Morsey, Christine Sellers, and William Irwin from *The Underpants* and filled out the rest of the cast with newcomers Brenda Porter, Adrienne Lovette, and Laura Rohner. Everyone played multiple characters except Sara, who portrayed the journalist, Barbara.

The set included a restaurant table, a shopping cart, and a clothing rack beneath a bright overhead sign reading, "America the land of opportunity." Old shoes, bottles, and cans covering the arch of the proscenium symbolized America's throwaway society.

The story opens in a bustling, understaffed diner in Key West. A reporter from the *Gainesville Sun* noted that while "*Nickel and Dimed* is peppered with high humor, it's of the truth-is-stranger-than-fiction variety. And as the laughter subsides, the powerful, real-life story of a well-to-do journalist who intentionally dives below the poverty level echoes with a modern urgency."[10]

2004 was an election year. "Running this show during the presidential election was no coincidence," Lauren Caldwell told the *Gainesville Sun*. "Fact is, Ehrenreich wrote her book in better economic times, but the human struggles that surface in this work remain and are more critical today."[11]

Nickel and Dimed ran from October 15–November 7. Reviewers from multiple local newspapers praised the socially conscious play and its actors.

Senior Playwright Festival

November 6–8 the Hippodrome inaugurated its Senior Playwright Festival with performances of the three winning plays: *The Postman Roulin* by James Sunwall, *The Cell Phone* by Marjorie Abrams, and *Lost in Cyber-Space*, by Kal Rosenberg. The festival was the brainchild of Hippodrome dramaturg Tammy Dygert and was produced in conjunction with the Institute of Learning in Retirement. In July, the festival had issued a call for original short plays written by senior residents of Florida, and Tammy conducted a series of workshops for the playwrights. The winning plays were selected from twenty-five entries. The Senior Playwright Festival became an annual affair that continued through 2009.

Tuna Returns

Following two seasons of *The Santaland Diaries*, the Hippodrome brought back the popular *A Tuna Christmas*, with Lauren Caldwell and Mark Chambers reprising their multiple characters. Alternating with *Tuna* was the annual production of *A Christmas Carol*, now in its twenty-seventh year. Both plays ran from November 26–December 19.

1   Arline Greer, review of *Life x 3*, by Yasmina Reza, translated by Christopher Hampton, Hippodrome Theatre, Gainesville, FL, *Gainesville Sun*, January 16, 2004.
2   Arline Greer, review of *The War of the Worlds*, by Lauren Caldwell, directed by Lauren Caldwell, Hippodrome Theatre, Gainesville, FL, *Gainesville Sun*, March 5, 2004
3   Shamrock McShane, "The War of the Worlds," *Satellite Magazine*, March 2004.
4   Arline Greer, review of *Rounding Third*, by Richard Dresser, directed by Mary Hausch, Hippodrome Theatre, Gainesville, FL, *Gainesville Sun*, April 21, 2004.
5   Laura Storey, review of *I Love You, You're Perfect, Now Change*, by Joe DiPietro, directed by Heidi Cline, Hippodrome Theatre, Gainesville, FL, *InSite Magazine*, June 2004.
6   Arline Greer, review of *I Love You, You're Perfect, Now Change*, by Joe DiPietro, directed by Heidi Cline, Hippodrome Theatre, Gainesville, FL, *Gainesville Sun*, June 11, 2004.
7   Dave Schlenker, "Much Ado about Underpants," *Gainesville Sun*, August 27, 2004.
8   Arline Greer, review of *The Underpants*, by Steve Martin, directed by Lauren Caldwell, Hippodrome Theatre, Gainesville, FL, *Gainesville Sun*, September 3, 2004.
9   Dick Kerekes, review of *The Underpants*, by Steve Martin, directed by Lauren Caldwell, Hippodrome Theatre, Gainesville, FL, *EntertainingU*, September 2004.
10 Dave Schlenker, "Life on a 'Living' Wage," *Gainesville Sun*, October 14, 2004.
11 Ibid.

2005

Two Grand Pianos

Mary Hausch didn't have to do much to direct the January play, *2 Pianos, 4 Hands*. The two actors she hired, Richard Todd Adams and Tom Frey, had performed the show hundreds of times, and the set basically required two concert grand pianos.

The play is a clever, laugh-out-loud comedy about the journey of two promising child prodigies learning piano, following them through their awkward teenage years of experimenting with jazz and then their retrospection in adulthood. It is based in part on the lives of the play's authors, Richard Greenblatt and Ted Dykstra.

The show is anything but a dull piano recital. An eclectic assortment of piano music from Bach to Billy Joel, with some Jerry Lee Lewis thrown in for good measure, is played live on-stage on the concert grand pianos. The actors portray multiple characters in hilarious vignettes that recount the characters' endless hours of repetitious practice while other kids are outside playing, along with pushy parents dreaming of celebrity for their children and the eccentric music teachers they encounter along the way.

Audiences and critics loved it. The show, which opened January 7, had to be held over an extra week, closing February 6.

Photo: Michael Eaddy

(l-r) Tom Frey and Richard Todd Adams play the authors of *2 Pianos, 4 Hands*.

Our Town

Next, the Hippodrome presented Thornton Wilder's Pulitzer Prize-winning classic, *Our Town*. The somewhat dated play had become the quintessential choice for high school drama departments and community theatres, but in the hands of the Hippodrome Theatre's professional actors, it once again sparkled. Director Lauren Caldwell, who sometimes turned classics into futuristic spectacles, stayed with Wilder's time period and set directions.

A portrait of small-town America in the early 1900s, the play celebrates the underlying beauty in everyday living—birth, love, marriage, aging, and death. Thornton Wilder called it the "magic of the mundane." Told by a narrator named simply "the Stage Manager," the story follows the lives, loves, and losses of two families in a New Hampshire hamlet called Grover's Corners.

The Stage Manager was played by David Shelton, whom *Satellite Magazine* called "An actor's actor." The reviewer said, "Shelton brooks no sentimentality and his role gives us a god-like view of things, where time, in a sense, has ceased to exist."[1]

The Hippodrome's seventeen-member cast was not as large as the cast for some productions of *Our Town*, but all the key characters were there and, unlike amateur theatres, the Hippodrome paid its actors. Equity actors Bryan Garey and Nell Page played Dr. and Mrs. Gibbs. Sara Morsey and Gregg Jones were Mr. and Mrs. Webb.

The Stage Manager, played by David Shelton (center), narrates the story of families in Grover Corners, New Hampshire.

Photo: Michael Eaddy

Lara Briney and Justin Tolley played Emily and George, the young couple whose courtship, marriage, and death carry the thread of the story.

Matthew Crider, Matt Cippaghila, and Randall Moring played multiple parts, eliminating the expense of extra actors. Jonathan Stewart was a theatre student and Jenny Fleck a recent graduate. Susan Moring had acted in the Hippodrome Senior Playwright Festival. The role of the youngest character was shared by four elementary school boys, Edward Bonhaue, Matthew Craig, Owen O'Grady, and Evan Robins, who took turns playing Wally Webb. All four were veterans of either *A Christmas Carol* or the Hippodrome Summer Spectacular plays.

To dress the cast appropriately for the period, Marilyn Wall designed twenty-seven costumes, sewn with the help of Doris Edwards, Dena Thue, and Shawn Fleck. Upstairs in the third-floor costume shop, after fitting actress Lara Birney with her character's wedding dress, Marilyn had her try on a pair of closed-toe flats that strapped around the ankle. "Show me some of your movement," she said. Lara ran a few steps back and forth and decided the shoes would do fine. "You have to set an actor free to tell a story," Marilyn told *Sun* reporter Elena Velkov. "Shoes are the foundation."[2]

Their work didn't go unnoticed by the *Sun* theatre critic, who wrote, "One aspect of this production that merits particular acclaim is the costume design and execution. Marilyn A. Wall's beautiful garments and attention to detail are stellar. The Hippodrome State Theatre's sparkling production of this classic drama presents the play in the period called for by the script. We should thank the Hippodrome for giving us the opportunity to visit *Our Town* and find new significance in the ordinariness of everyday things."[3]

Our Town ran from February 25–March 20.

Anna in the Tropics

The Hippodrome followed *Our Town* with another Pulitzer Prize winner, *Anna in the Tropics* by Cuban playwright Nilo Cruz. In this case, the setting is Ybor City, a neighborhood in Northeast Tampa founded by Cuban cigar makers in the 1880s.

Photo: Michael Eaddy

Cast of *Anna in the Tropics*. (l-r) Armando Acevedo, Jessica K. Peterson, Javi Mulero, Rosalinde Milan, Petrus Antonius, Jennica Carmona, and Timothy Andres Pabon on the cigar factory set.

The play is set in 1929 in a family-owned business that makes hand-rolled cigars. To ease the tedium of their craft, cigar workers traditionally hired a lector, a well-dressed, well-spoken man who read aloud to them while they toiled. Things are set in motion with the arrival of a new lector (Timothy Andres Pabon), who chooses to read them Tolstoy's *Anna Karenina*.

"This book will be the end of us,"[4] says the eldest daughter's unfaithful husband, Palomo, played by Armando Acevedo. He's not wrong. Days of immersion in *Anna Karenina's* themes of betrayal, family, marriage, and infidelity cause the workers to examine their own lives.

"The characters' lives are forever changed, for better or for worse, because of the transformative powers of literature on the human mind and soul," wrote Gainesville theatre critic Sherwin Mackintosh. "*Anna in the Tropics* features an excellent ensemble cast, all strong performers, functioning as one complete unit. Every character is well developed in the writing, which gives each actor a moment to shine. Prop designer Lorelei Esser must have done a lot of research to recreate the process of making cigars and how the factory looked in 1929."[5]

The play, directed by Mary Hausch, ran from April 15–May 8. In conjunction with the play, the Hippodrome Art Gallery exhibited colorful paintings by Ferdie Pacheco depicting the Cuban lifestyle in South Florida in the early 1900s.

Musical Memories of 8-Track Tapes

Long before there were streaming services, iPods, or even CDs, the only option for listening to music in automobiles was the radio. Then along came the 8-Track, a stereo tape cartridge that played a full album of music on a continuous loop. From the late 1960s until 1980, it was the dominant form of portable music. So it made perfect sense to the next show's creator, Rick Seeber, to name a jukebox musical featuring songs from that period *8-Track: The Sounds of The '70s*. The Hippodrome's chosen summer show, it opened June 3 and ran through July 31.

Photo: Michael Eaddy

Stars of *8-Track: The Sounds of The '70s*. Standing (l-r): Armando Acevedo, Rachel Anton, Kelly Atkins. Kneeling: Chad Hudson.

Forget plot—*8-Track* tells, entirely through hit songs of the seventies, the story of four young people as they navigate that tumultuous decade. The actors/singers change wigs and period clothing—bell bottoms, leisure suits, halter tops, and platform shoes—as they sing their way from the final years of the Vietnam War through the rise of feminism and finally enter the Disco Era with its legendary party scene. More than fifty tunes from the likes of The Carpenters, Labelle, Barry Manilow, Marvin Gaye, the Doobie Brothers, the Bee Gees, Helen Reddy, the Eagles, and KC and the Sunshine Band make up the show's vast songbook.

Director Lauren Caldwell cast four strong singers to perform the show and hired Dance Alive founder Judy Skinner to choreograph them. Cast member Armando Acevedo, who had just appeared in *Anna in the Tropics,* was also a Disney performer and moonlighted in nightclubs. Chad Hudson had been one of the *Four Plaids* and played the title character in *Bat Boy: The Musical.*

New to the Hippodrome, but not to musical theatre, were the female leads, Rachel Anton and Kelly Atkins. Rachel, a native New Yorker, had among her credits *A Chorus Line*, *Fiddler on the Roof*, and the lead in *Evita.* Kelly had trained to be a classical singer, but she'd fallen in love with musical theatre and switched fields. Given a solo, Kelly could out-sing most anyone—a talent the Hippodrome would tap repeatedly, bringing her back year after year for future summer musicals.

Arline Greer wrote, "Atkins sings 'You Light Up My Life' so beautifully she dims all memory of Debbie Boone." But Greer also noted that the entire cast "is equally at home singing duets, trios, quartets and solos in which they shine individually. Because they are a likeable foursome, they get the audience going almost immediately, clapping, singing and dancing in the aisles." Summing up, Greer said, "The Hippodrome's *8-Track* is a rip-roaring roller coaster of a musical revue."[6]

The second act was a scorcher—focusing mainly on disco, with songs like "Saturday Night Fever," "Stayin' Alive," and "Y.M.C.A." The Hippodrome set builders had recreated a disco dance floor—colored Plexiglas squares lit from below. "It was just gorgeous," recalled Kelly Atkins, "but dancing on that floor in those shoes, I will never forget it. We had 70s clothes, and the shoes were, like, crazy—these super high platform shoes. I don't think any of us ever fell, but just the precariousness of working that floor in those shoes I will always remember."

Audiences so loved *8-Track* that the show had to be extended an extra month beyond its scheduled run.

New Manager

The Hippodrome had been without a general manager for the past year. In August, Rocky Draud was named to fill the post vacated by Mark Sexton. Rocky had been working with the theatre doing sound design for productions since 2000 and had served as Business Manager earlier in 2005.

Thirty-third Season

Director Lauren Caldwell described the Hipp's season opener, *Mere Mortals,* as "a meeting of *The Twilight Zone* and *The X-Files*." Rather than a single play, the show consisted of six short literate, comedic one-acts written by David Ives. "It gives audiences what they expect from television comedies with an added punch of meaningful insight," Lauren said.[7] Back in 1996, the Hippodrome had presented another production of six short Ives plays, *All in the Timing*, which had received good reviews. So, why not try him again?

Six veteran Hippodrome actors portrayed a total of twenty characters. The show was divided into two acts of three plays each.

Act one opens with *Foreplay or: The Art of the Fugue*, which features all six actors and serves as a great icebreaker that gives the audience a sense of the plays that follow. Cameron Francis, Garrett Bantom, and Bryan Garey took turns playing the character Chuck at different stages of his life. His dates with characters played by Sara Morsey, Christine Sellers, and Marcia Brown take place at a miniature golf course, where innuendo from golf terms eventually creates a fugue of sexually charged discussions.

Photo: Michael Eaddy

In *Mere Mortals*, cast members play different characters in six plays. Standing at back: Sara Morsey and Cameron Francis. Seated: Bryan Garey and Christine Sellers. Foreground: Marcia Brown and Garrett Bantom in a scene from *Captive Audience*.

This is followed by the title piece, *Mere Mortals*, where three macho construction workers eat lunch sitting on a girder fifty stories up. The guys bare their innermost secrets, and their revelations challenge each other's ability to believe and their capacity for one-upmanship.

The first act ends with *Time Flies*, in which two mayflies realize they are the subjects of a David Attenborough nature documentary and, even more horrifying, that they only live for one day. They decide to live it with eagerness, and their carpe diem attitude makes an analogy to humankind with humor and grace. Marilyn Wall's costumes for mayflies Christine Sellers and Bryan Garey were hilarious.

Act two begins with *Captive Audience*, a cautionary fable about the effect of television. Like the opening of act one, the play featured all six actors. Garrett Bantom and Marcia Brown played Rob and Laura, a married couple whose living room television talks back to them and threatens to swallow them. The rest of the cast played personalities on TV, which become interchanged with the couple. Was it a coincidence that Rob and Laura were the names of the main characters on *The Dick Van Dyke Show*?

Next up was *Dr. Fritz or: The Forces of Light*. Cameron Francis played an American tourist south of the border, who was seeking medical attention. Sara Morsey was a wacky souvenir seller and voodoo witch doctor who channels an even wackier German doctor to help him. Arline Greer described it as "working with a quasi-metaphysical theme that's just outside the realm of the ordinary."[8]

The final play, *Degas C'est Moi*, explores a fascination with famous figures from the past as well as our desire to leave our own significant thumbprint for future generations. In this piece, Bryan Garey played a jobless New Yorker who convinces himself that he is Edgar Degas and then sets out on a daylong odyssey as the painter. It ends with a feel-good epiphany that being yourself isn't so bad, especially when you notice the beauty around you.

"Mere Mortals?" asked Arline Greer, summing up her review. "Not one of these characters accepts being 'mere.' Neither does this Hippodrome production, unless it's said to be merely, well done."[9]

Ives' collection of funny one-acts opened August 26 and ran until September 18.

Photo: Michael Eaddy

Jonathan Harker (Armando Acevedo) drives a stake into Count Dracula (Robin Bloodworth).

Bram Stoker Blood-fest

Eight years had passed since Lauren Caldwell had directed a modernized version of Bram Stoker's *Dracula*. "There are just certain myths we keep coming back to," Lauren told the *Gainesville Sun*.[10] But this time she turned to a more traditional script. In fact, the granddaddy of them all, written by Hamilton Deane and John L. Balderston back in the 1920s. And who better to cast as the bloodsucking count that an actor named Robin *Blood*worth?

Robin, who previously appeared in *The Lion in Winter*, brought a family connection to the role. His father, movie actor Robert Bloodworth, had played a vampire in a 1984 film.

The Hippodrome's 2005 version returned to the classic gothic set and costumes. Each performance required over a half-gallon of very real-looking stage blood. The show was not only bloody but also dark, brooding, and sexy.

"*Dracula* is not for the timid and definitely not for kids," noted the *Independent Florida Alligator*.[11] "It's as sexy as it is bloody,"[12] said Ryan Burbank, who played Mina, an undead muse who uses her beauty as bait. In fact, "there is much temptation throughout this classic tale, as the savvy Count relies as much on lust as he does on fangs."[13]

Other key roles included Rachel Roberts as Lucy Seward, who, after being bitten by Dracula, tries to turn her fiancé, Jonathan Harker (Armando Acevedo). Arline Greer said, "[Rachel Roberts is] a perfect Lucy, pliant and weak in the early stages, willful, cunning and sensual when she exerts her bloodthirsty power. Mark Chambers makes a serious, take-charge Professor Van Helsing. Mark Kincaid's Dr. Seward is every inch the concerned, beleaguered parent.... Tom Nowicki, as the lunatic Renfield, gives an outstanding performance, bringing both pathos and humor to the many-sided character. The play's major figure, the blood-sucking Count Dracula, is given a vibrant, compelling performance by Robin Bloodworth. He simply dominates the stage."[14]

Two other Hippodrome actors, Garrett Bantom (*Mere Mortals*) and Loren Omer (*The Lion in Winter*), played multiple smaller parts.

Photo: Michael Eaddy

Playing a girl child bitten by Mina were two teenage veterans of *A Christmas Carol* and Hippodrome Summer Spectaculars, Kelsey Salazar and Kayla Robins. The latter is the daughter of Hippodrome lighting designer Bob Robins, who said, "Her mother was really concerned about the actress gnawing on [Kayla's] neck. She didn't like watching that at all." For Kayla, the worst part was getting drenched in blood while operating a special effect in the final scene. Kayla was hidden under the coffin, pumping stage blood to squirt from Dracula as a stake was driven into his heart. Some nights the bag would break and she'd end up covered in it.

Dracula opened October 14 and was held over an extra week, closing on November 13.

Mina (Ryan Burbank) bites actress Kayla Robins in *Dracula*.

Holiday Shows

A Tuna Christmas and *A Christmas Carol* played alternate show times from November 25 through December 18.

1 Shamrock McShane, review of *Our Town*, by Thornton Wilder, directed by Lauren Caldwell, Hippodrome Theatre, Gainesville, FL, *Satellite Magazine*, March 2, 2005.
2 Elena Velkov, "Details are Key in Creating Costumes for *Our Town*," *Gainesville Sun*, March 6, 2005.
3 Dick Maxwell, review of *Our Town*, by Thornton Wilder, directed by Lauren Caldwell, Hippodrome Theatre, Gainesville, FL, *Gainesville Sun*, March 3, 2005.
4 Nilo Cruz, *Anna in the Tropics*, Dramitists Play Service, New York, NY.
5 Sherwin Mackintosh, review of *Anna in the Tropics*, by Nilo Cruz, directed by Mary Hausch, Hippodrome Theatre, Gainesville, FL, *Gainesville Sun*, April 21, 2005.
6 Arline Greer, review of *8-Track: The Sounds of The 70s*, by Rick Seeber, directed by Lauren Caldwell, Hippodrome Theatre, Gainesville, FL, *Gainesville Sun*, June 9, 2005.
7 Arline Greer, "Hipp Opens Season Friday," *Gainesville Sun*, August 25, 2005.
8 Arline Greer, review of *Mere Mortals: Six One-act Comedies*, by David Ives, directed by Lauren Caldwell, Hippodrome Theatre, Gainesville, FL, *Gainesville Sun*, September 2, 2005.
9 Ibid.
10 Dave Schlenker, "Dracula Flutters Back into the Hipp," *Gainesville Sun*, October 13, 2005.
11 Gabriella Vigier, "Dracula Sucks at the Hipp," the *Independent Florida Alligator*, October 13, 2005.
12 Ibid.
13 Dave Schlenker, "Dracula Flutters Back into the Hipp," *Gainesville Sun*, October 13, 2005.
14 Arline Greer, review of *Dracula*, by Hamilton Deane and John L. Balderston, directed by Lauren Caldwell, Hippodrome Theatre, Gainesville, FL, *Gainesville Sun*, October 20, 2005.

2006

Polar Opposite of the Cartoon

With the antics of *A Tuna Christmas* and Tiny Tim's "God Bless us every one," behind them, the Hippodrome turned serious, opening January with Bryony Lavery's *Frozen*. It's a grim tale of child abduction and murder—as polar opposite of Disney's film of the same name as one could imagine.

The play has three main characters. Sara Morsey played the mother whose ten-year-old daughter lost her life at the hands of a murdering pedophile. Timothy Altmeyer played the child killer, and Jessica Peterson portrayed a forensic psychologist researching serial killers. Denis McCourt had a non-speaking role as a prison guard.

Cast of *Frozen*: (l-r) Jessica Peterson as a forensic psychologist, Denis McCourt as a guard, Timothy Altmeyer as the child killer, and Sara Morsey as the child's mother.

Photos: Michael Eaddy

Arline Greer's review suggested that the drama posed the following questions: "Do serial murderers ever come to feel contrition for their acts? Can we, as a society, understand and forgive the perpetrators, if not their acts? In addressing these questions and others, *Frozen* gives audiences a long, hard look into the lives of a family dealing with loss, the serial killer who caused their anguish, and a criminal psychologist who attempts to still the conflict that ties the two together.

"Sara Morsey represents every mother who has lost her child to murder. She lives in hope for a while, confronts despair, gives way to anger and thinks about revenge. Ultimately, she confronts the killer of her child with that knotty question of forgiveness. It's a tour de force for Morsey, whose anguished wails of loss fill the house. As a counterpoint, Altmeyer's Ralph is no less compelling as he is forced to look at what he's done. Peterson, Morsey, and Altmeyer make a letter-perfect ensemble. They have a gift for handling Lavery's humorous lines without losing the solemnity of the play's questions."[1]

Director Lauren Caldwell had an even bigger question in mind. Could the production serve as a springboard for a community campaign dedicated to keeping children safe from predators? The Hippodrome elicited participation of the Gainesville Police Department, Alachua County Crisis Center, Guardian ad Litem, Parents of Murdered Children, the Chief Assistant State Attorney, and professors from UF. Panel discussions followed each Sunday matinee.

Sadie Darnell, who was with the Gainesville Police Department at the time and later became Alachua County Sheriff, was involved in the production of *Frozen* almost from the very start. She said she was skeptical of the content at first. But once Darnell saw the play, she said she realized the positive impact it could have on the community. By bringing the subject to the forefront and offering discussions with professionals who have dealt with abductions, the public may realize it does have power to prevent harm to children.[2]

Frozen ran from January 6–29.

Family-friendly Comedic Fable

The Hippodrome followed the somber *Frozen* with the premiere of a fanciful children's fable that held a deeper meaning for adults. *A Very Old Man with Enormous Wings* is Nilo Cruz's adaptation of a short story by Nobel Prize-winning author Gabriel García Márquez. Cruz had written the prior season's *Anna in the Tropics*. This play was completely different. "The magical realism elements and the wonderful, universal story make this a story for everyone," Director Mary Hausch told the *Gainesville Sun*.[3]

Two children, Fefe and Momó, discover a very old man with enormous wings in their backyard, who has apparently fallen from the sky; they believe him to be an angel. The angel, old, sick, and decrepit, cannot speak, but the children read his thoughts by looking into his eyes. When they learn that, after eons of time, he no longer remembers his name, they name him Afar.

Children Fefe and Momó find *A Very Old Man with Enormous Wings*, played by Ric Rose.

Their parents, Pelayo and Elisenda, say that if Afar truly is an angel, let him cure their sick baby. When Afar doesn't, they think Fefe and Momö are wrong. All the same, Pelayo sees a way to make money using Afar as an attraction. Soon, Pelayo is charging admission to see the angel. Ordinary workers, a woman who has been crying endlessly, and a girl with a box of prayers all come to him with hope or pleas. For a price, spectators even can pluck a feather or an eyelash, leaving the angel in worse condition than when he was found.

Photo: Michael Eaddy

Backstage, it must have felt like a cast of thousands. Mary Hausch had ten principal actors:

Ric Rose, Armando Acevedo, Tanya Perez, Jessica Peterson, Usman Ally, Justin Redfern, Laura Rohner, Marisol Sanchez Baez, Stephen L. Schmitz, and Samantha Walsh. In addition, there were six school-age actors ranging from third through tenth grade who alternated performances. Rachel Coffman Abrams and Kelsey Salazar played Fefe. Ryan Leopold and Manny Marichal took turns as Momó, while Isabel Luvalle-Burke and Mana Handel traded off as the girl with the box of prayers.

If that wasn't enough, Mary decided to incorporate into the show the music and movement of capoeira, a Brazilian martial art and cultural expression. While that was a first in the history of Gainesville theatre and brought a thrilling dimension to the show, the capoeira group added fifteen more performers: Borracha, Aimee Green, Lydia Mitchell, Malia Blanchard, Stephanie Nixon, Alex Britto, James Overstreet, Adrian Gonzales, James Sanders, Derrick Irving, Jordan Simpson, Litira Kokkas, Nikki Torres, Brianna Letouneau, and Megan Young.

UF dance professor Ric Rose choreographed the show. He also played the old man, wearing a pair of wings designed by Carlos Asse, which were indeed enormous.

"Truth and kindness triumphs with this shining production geared especially for children," wrote Arline Greer. "The twin themes of redemption and innocence run through the play. The journey to see Afar is marked with song and dance. The lyrical songs are sung to a guitar accompaniment. Nathan Wang has written original music for the show with sound by Rocky Draud and Anna Gramlich. The dancing with its exciting capoeira theme is led by Borracha. The story is told in whimsical language with enchanting music, electrifying dance and colorful visual images that will keep young eyes glued to the stage."[4]

In addition to the live professional stage production of *A Very Old Man with Enormous Wings*, the Hippodrome again created a One City One Story program and held many community events at local public libraries and bookstores throughout the month of March. The play ran from February 24–March 19.

A Satire on Terrorist Hysteria

From April 14 through May 7, the Hippodrome presented the East Coast premiere of Catherine Butterfield's *The Sleeper*—only the second time the play had been produced. The *Independent Florida Alligator* called it "a sexy comedy with timely political undercurrents... unafraid to poke fun at society's all-encompassing fear and mistrust."[5]

The hysterical fear of terrorists following the events of 9/11 is personified in Gretchen (Laura Rohner), a housewife in a loveless marriage to foul-mouthed workaholic Bill (Bryan Garey). Her main activity outside the home is helping with Terrorist Alert Day at her children's school.

Despite his vastly different political viewpoints, she is swept off her feet by her son's tutor, Matthew (Bryant Smith). Their sex scene plays out against Madonna's song "Like a Virgin." As her extramarital affair heats up, Gretchen goes to a dippy psychiatrist (Sara Morsey) to confess her guilt, but the psychiatrist's advice is "Enjoy!" But how can she? Matthew's politics are not those of a conformist American patriot, and the people arriving at his apartment (Paul Deines and Christafer Ivan Sobbing) don't resemble all-American boys. Then a lecture by a terrorist expert (Rusty Salling) on recognizing "sleeper" terrorists among us pushes Gretchen to the edge of paranoia.

Photo: Michael Eaddy

From time to time, the actors break the fourth wall and speak directly to the audience. Bill claims Gretchen's behavior couldn't be his fault, and Gretchen's sister, Vivian (Christine Sellers), comments on Gretchen's dull marriage and Bill's flaws.

Gretchen (Laura Rohner) discusses her dull marriage with her sister (Christine Sellers) in *The Sleeper*.

Most of the cast members had performed together in previous plays. "I cast the same people for a reason," director Lauren Caldwell told the *Gainesville Sun*. "It's like playing in a band where you jam together.... Timing is the key to any comedy, and having actors who have all worked together before helps immensely with their timing and delivery."[6]

"*The Sleeper* is a smart, entertaining show," wrote Arline Greer, "enjoyable from the moment you walk into the theater to see Carlos Asse's gorgeous set. The entire professional cast deserves praise for peerless ensemble work. *The Sleeper* is as funny and mind-blowing a play as the Hippodrome has produced in a long time, a thoroughly enjoyable experience."[7]

Starke Onstage?

Director Lauren Caldwell was in New York City looking for plays when she heard that *The Great American Trailer Park Musical* playing off-Broadway was set in Starke, Florida. She saw it and said, "It was an incredibly fun night." Although the play received mixed reviews from New Yorkers, Lauren realized the natural appeal a musical set in the local area would have in Gainesville. "I think it's a great story with a great sense of humor about it," she said. "And I think people love to see stories about themselves, or at least, about things they recognize."[8]

Perhaps not Starke mayor Steve Futch, who told the *Gainesville Sun* he worried how the play would affect his city's reputation. The Hippodrome Marketing Department devoted weeks of public relations efforts to assuage Starke residents' fears about the play and offered them ten-dollar tickets throughout the entire run. Opening night, the mayor, his wife, and about fifty of his constituents attended the show and said they found it hilarious.

Pippi, a stripper fleeing her Magic Marker-sniffing boyfriend, Duke, finds herself living in a Starke trailer park after making a wrong turn on US 301. She isn't there long before she's having an affair with Norbert, a toll collector who lives in the single-wide next door with his agoraphobic wife, Jeannie. Trailer park gossips Pickles, Lin, and Betty make up a Greek chorus, bringing the audience up to date on their neighbors' history. Pickles is married to a "fancy" man in Jacksonville who delights in community theatre. Betty inherited the mobile home park after the convenient death of her late husband, and Lin's husband is on death row at the nearby prison.

Photo: Michael Eaddy

(l-r) Mark Chambers, Cindy Thrall, and Kelly Atkins, three members of *The Great American Trailer Park Musical* cast.

"Make no mistake," wrote Dave Schlenker in the *Gainesville Sun*, "*The Great American Trailer Park Musical* is, indeed, a musical comedy. For all the satiric pokes at small-town South, there are also the big voices of Broadway and the dreamy eyes and outstretched arms of the show-stopper…. There is the happy ending, the second-act surprise, and the big musical-ensemble finale. And, as with most musicals, there is a sincerity and old-fashioned sweetness among these characters."[9]

Kelly Atkins (*8-Track*) played Pippi and gave an amazing performance belting out a song while upside down doing a pole dance. Mark Chambers, as Norbert, has a rich bass-baritone and sang with emotion that made his character real rather than a caricature. Catherine Fries Vaughn (*Nunsense*) was his wife, Jeannie. Cindy Thrall (*Hedwig* and *Rocky Horror*) as Betty was joined by Mackenzie Curran as Pickles and Jennifer Anderson as Lin. Last to appear was Pippi's ex-boyfriend, played by Ted Stephens III.

Bryan Mercer was the musical director—the first of many musicals he would do at the Hippodrome. "Bryan is a wonderful musical director," said Catherine Fries Vaughn, "because he approaches everything both from a musical standpoint but also an acting point of view. You never lose the character or the intention of the character. So it's not ever just about singing notes with Bryan. It's always what you can bring to the music as an actor."

Set Designer Mihai Ciupe tossed in a few Starke landmarks—a motel sign, the water tower, and a Brahma bull statue anyone who has passed through Starke on US 301 would remember. The script also makes reference to the nearby state prison's electric chair.

The show's authors, David Nehls and Betsy Kelso, had never been to Starke. They'd just used the name at the suggestion of a friend who came from Jacksonville. They got a few things wrong. Norbert wouldn't be a toll collector on the Turnpike—that's eighty-seven miles from Starke. Also, Pippi's place of work wouldn't have been in Starke, which had an ordinance against strip clubs. But David Nehls did help the Hippodrome get the regional premiere. "Most of what I know of the theatre itself comes from friends of mine who have worked there and had positive experiences," he said. "I know they've done some offbeat shows… and our rowdy little show fits in with that company very well."[10]

Very well indeed; it sold 21,548 tickets. *The Great American Trailer Park Musical* became the Hippodrome's best-selling, longest-running show in thirty-three years. It opened June 2 and played for twelve weeks, closing August 20. That was two weeks longer than *Honky Tonk Angels*, which had set the previous record at ten weeks.

Season Thirty-four

In September, guest director Jim Wren reimagined Hollywood in 1939 with Ron Hutchison's award-winning comedy *Moonlight and Magnolias*. The play is based on the true story of when legendary movie producer David O. Selznick (Cameron Francis) halted production of *Gone with the Wind* to have a new screenplay written. Selznick yanked director Victor Fleming (Gregg Jones) off the set of *The Wizard of Oz* and brought in famed screenwriter Ben Hecht (Bryan Garey). But Hecht had never read the novel, so Selznick and Fleming acted out scenes while Hecht typed. Mackenzie Curran played an office assistant, Miss Poppenghul.

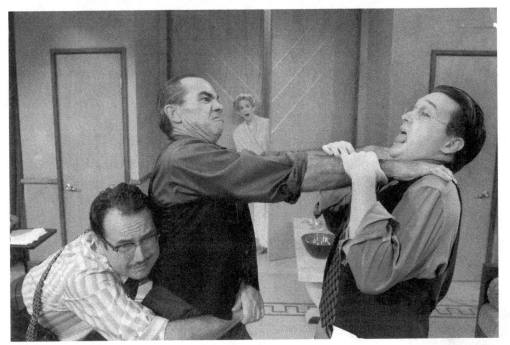

(l-r) Screenwriter Ben Hecht (Bryan Garey) restrains director Victor Fleming (Gregg Jones) from strangling David O. Selznick (Cameron Francis) as a stunned Miss Poppenghul (Mackenzie Curran) watches from the doorway in *Moonlight and Magnolias*.

Photo: Michael Eaddy

Hutchison's play includes many tidbits of old Hollywood garnered from gossip columnists like Hedda Hopper. However, he toyed with the facts a bit to increase dramatic tension. In the play, Selznick locks Fleming and Hecht in his office and gives them five days to create a brand-new script, feeding them only bananas and peanuts. In reality, they had two weeks. They worked a demanding pace of eighteen-hour workdays but could go home to sleep. Selznick *was* under intense pressure. Keeping the cast and crew idle was costing $50,000 a day.

"Everybody can relate to what it's like to pull an all-nighter," Bryan Garey told the *Gainesville Sun*. "Well, this is like pulling five of them. The characters are absolutely crazy at the end of it."[11]

"This is one of the most physically exhausting plays I've done here," said Cameron Francis.[12]

"There's a fine line between commitment and pain," Gregg Jones added.[13]

Theatre critic Dick Maxwell said, "[Cameron] Francis's inspired performance is the engine that drives the show. One minute, he offers impersonations of Scarlett and her drunken father and the next delivers a paean on the wonder and beauty of movies and their importance to the public. The play is one-half slapstick comedy and one-half serious consideration of the business, joy, and torment of making movies.... The funniest parts of the piece are easily the shenanigans of Selznick and Fleming as they portray the characters from the story, but... one should not go to this show anticipating sidesplitting one-liners and jokes at every turn. While there are some hilarious moments, there are also thought provoking passages."[14]

Moonlight and Magnolias ran from September 8–October 1.

Adult-only Wonderland

"I bet you're not going to see any *Alice in Wonderland* like this anywhere else," Hippodrome dramaturg Tammy Dygert told a reporter when discussing the Hippodrome's next production.[15] To begin with, Anne Coulter Martens's script envisions an adult Alice. Director Lauren Caldwell imagined Alice trapped in a nightmare. "What would happen if we fell so far down we couldn't get back up? People often get caught up in the bizarre realities of inner darkness and cannot escape," Lauren said.[16]

The cast wore white face makeup with black-rimmed eyes reminiscent of 1970s shock-rocker Alice Cooper. Except for Alice (Kelly Atkins), the Cheshire Cat (Sara Morsey), and the Queen of Hearts (Mark Chambers in red stilettos with six-inch heels), the rest of Lewis Carroll's storybook characters were absent. In their place was a sextet of sirens that tempted, teased, and tormented Alice: Jennifer Anderson, Elizabeth Arnold, Robyn Berg, Ryan Burbank, Kate Kertez, and Catherine Fries Vaughn.

Kelly Atkins as Alice falls down the rabbit hole in an unusual version of *Alice in Wonderland*.

Photo: Michael Eaddy

"The costumes are remarkable," said *Sun* critic Dick Maxwell. "The women in the chorus are dressed in colorful flowing gowns that are so versatile they can be twisted, tucked and rearranged to serve a number of different purposes. The costuming for the Queen of Hearts is a sight to behold."[17]

Not much on plot, the show focused on dance and movement choreographed by Judy Skinner. "Catherine Fries Vaughn is terrific as a tap-dancing, trash-talking cupcake," Maxwell said. Kelly Atkins provides a stunning, highly emotional, very physical performance as she is subjected to various abuses at the hands of the inhabitants of Wonderland. Her role is extremely demanding and calls for almost constant activity and stage presence on her part during the 80-minute show, which is performed without an intermission."[18]

Alice was one of Kelly's most physically demanding roles. She had to hang upside down from the rungs of a ladder. "The still poses are more exhausting than the movement," Kelly recalled. "I don't think I've ever done anything as violent before." It's a tossup whether she was referring to the butcher knives, the ax-wielding queen, or being strapped to a table and struggling to escape. An ambiguous ending leaves open the possibility that Alice was insane and her descent wasn't into a rabbit hole but into the maddest asylum.

It may come as a surprise that none of the reviewers disliked the show and generally gave the Hippodrome credit for taking a risk. The play ran from October 20–November 12.

Christmas

For the seventh time, Lauren Caldwell and Mark Chambers performed *A Tuna Christmas* while Rusty Salling made his seventeenth appearance as Scrooge in *A Christmas Carol. Tuna* opened November 24 and *A Christmas Carol* the following day. Both shows ended on December 22.

1 Arline Greer, review of *Frozen*, by Bryony Lavery, directed by Lauren Caldwell, Hippodrome Theatre, Gainesville, FL, *Gainesville Sun*, January 12, 2006.
2 Alice Wallace, "Play Puts Spotlight on Child Abduction," *Gainesville Sun*, January 5, 2006.
3 Travis Atria, "On the Wings of a Fable," *Gainesville Sun*, February 23, 2006.
4 Arline Greer, review of *A Very Old Man With Enormous Wings*, by Nilo Cruz, directed by Mary Hausch, Hippodrome Theatre, Gainesville, FL, *Gainesville Sun*, March 2, 2006.
5 Katie Burns, review of *The Sleeper*, by Catherine Butterfield, directed by Lauren Caldwell, Hippodrome Theatre, Gainesville, FL, *Independent Florida Alligator*, April 20, 2006.
6 Travis Atria, "Life, Lust and Hysteria," *Gainesville Sun*, April 13, 2006.
7 Arline Greer, review of *The Sleeper*, by Catherine Butterfield, directed by Lauren Caldwell, Hippodrome Theatre, Gainesville, FL, *Gainesville Sun*, April 20, 2006.
8 Alice Wallace, "Starke-inspired Play Finishes Run on Weekend," *Gainesville Sun*, August 18, 2006.
9 Dave Schlenker, "Secrets, Songs, and Single-wides," *Gainesville Sun*, June 1, 2006.
10 Ibid.
11 Travis Atria, "When Hollywood Was Golden," *Gainesville Sun*, September 7, 2006.
12 Ibid.
13 Ibid.
14 Dick Maxwell, review of *Moonlight and Magnolias*, by Ron Hutchinson, directed by Jim Wren, Hippodrome Theatre, Gainesville, FL, *Gainesville Sun*, September 15, 2006.
15 Kelly Sereikas, "'Alice' Opens with New Twist," *Independent Florida Alligator*, October 2006.
16 Ibid.
17 Dick Maxwell, review of *Alice in Wonderland*, by Anne Coulter Martens, directed by Lauren Caldwell, Hippodrome Theatre, Gainesville, FL, *Gainesville Sun*, October 26, 2006.
18 Ibid.

2007

Desperate Suburbanites

By January 2007, the television show *Desperate Housewives* was at the peak of its popularity. So why not start the year with a dark comedy about three wealthy suburban women who want to kill their husbands? *The Smell of the Kill* by Michele Lowe is exactly that.

Photo: Michael Eaddy

(l-r) Cady West Garey, Laura Rohner, and Nell Page portray wives willing to take desperate measures in *The Smell of the Kill*.

Three women are talking in the kitchen after dinner while their husbands are in another room. The women are rich, living in multimillion-dollar homes in a fashionable Chicago suburb, but the wives are shallow and can be violent. Nicky (Laura Rohner), for example, shoots holes in her walls to blow off steam because her husband has dragged their family through a painful public trial for embezzling millions.

Debra (Nell Page) has a husband who can't keep his hands off other women, and she's just learned from his mistress that he is planning a divorce that will force Debra out of the lavish home she designed and built.

Molly (Cady West Garey) is an alcoholic trapped in a childless marriage with an obsessive husband who wants to know where she is at all times but who won't have sex with her.

All three marriages are in decay. The never-seen husbands are just male voices offstage being rude, arrogant, and self-absorbed. Later, the men accidentally lock themselves in a walk-in freezer and pound on the door for help. As the thumping diminishes and then ceases, the women realize the potentially lethal situation the men have gotten themselves into. The question for the women is whether to rescue the men and continue in problematic marriages or should they take a stroll to the local Baskin-Robbins for dessert before "discovering" a tragic accident? With more than a little convincing of each another, the wives decide to let the husbands chill.

The show's director, Rob Satterlee, visiting from Chicago's famous Steppenwolf Theatre, told the *Gainesville Sun*, "The play works so well because it mixes moments of levity and humor with ones of intensity and seriousness. If you don't play those serious parts, the comedy won't work."[1]

Theatre critic Dick Maxwell wrote, "In real life, marital infidelity, embezzlement and frustration are not that funny. The ability to turn these dour topics into humor lies in the fortunate combination of good writing by playwright Michele Lowe, tight direction by Robert H. Satterlee, and superb acting by Cady West Garey, Nell Page and Laura Rohner.... The burden of carrying the evening rests with the actors who are masters at controlling the action, and in creating and holding our interest."[2]

"If you like your comedy on the dark side with exceptionally good acting, make plans to catch this gem," wrote Jacksonville critic Dick Kerekes.[3]

The Smell of the Kill ran from January 12–February 4.

The Chosen

The Hippodrome offering for March was *The Chosen*, an adaptation of the best-selling novel by Chaim Potok. "I think this is one of the better adaptations from book to play that I've come across," director Lauren Caldwell said.[4] Chaim Potok himself co-wrote the script with Aaron Posner.

The story takes place in the Williamsburg neighborhood of Brooklyn, New York, after World War II and follows two adolescent boys from different factions of Judaism. Danny Saunders (Elya Ottenberg) is the son of a strict Hasidic rabbi, Reb Saunders, who is preparing Danny to someday take over his followers. Young Reuven Malter (Michael Littig), on the other hand, comes from the more secular Conservative Jews who have begun to assimilate into American culture. He and his father, David Malter (David Brummel), openly exchange ideas on what it means to be a friend and what it means to be a Jew in the time of the Holocaust. This is in sharp contrast to Danny's home, where silence rules and his father only speaks to him when they study Talmud together.

(l-r) Elya Ottenberg, Howard Elfman, Michael T. Toth, Michael Littig, and David Brummel in *The Chosen*.

Photo: Michael Eaddy

The boys meet as rivals in a baseball game where Danny's line drive strikes Reuven's eye, hospitalizing him. Danny visits him and apologizes. The two become fast friends, and it is their relationship that is at the center of the play. Reuven's father describes it as "two bodies with one soul." Against the backdrop of the Holocaust and the movement to create the nation of Israel, there are larger ideas, too.

"You've got two plays going on here," said Howard Elfman, who portrayed Danny's father. "You've got the families and the Zionist movement."[5]

"We thought this one had a lot to say about what's going on in the world today," Lauren Caldwell said, referring to the ongoing Middle East situation. "It brings up questions of our responsibility to other people and other nations."[6]

"*The Chosen* does what good dramas do," wrote Arline Greer. "It creates a world rich with ideas. And it's all good. Key to the success of the play's dramatic intensity is the performance of Michael T. Toth, who plays a grown up Reuven. Toth narrates the story with fluidity of a natural storyteller. He makes the play's words come alive."[7]

The Chosen ran March 2–25, and the Hippodrome created its sixth One City One Story program, this time featuring Chaim Potok's novel.

The Memory of Water

(l-r) Sara Morsey, Kate Kertez, and Catherine Fries Vaughn play sisters in *The Memory of Water*.

Photo: Marvin Halelamien

The next play, Shelagh Stephenson's *The Memory of Water*, is a comedy about three sisters reuniting at their mother's funeral and coming to terms with their differing memories. Its curious title refers to a homeopathic theory that water is capable of retaining the memory of particles dissolved in it.

The play's action unfolds over a couple of days in the mother's bedroom, which serves as a battleground, therapy session, and memorial for the sisters. The three siblings have little in common other than their shared childhood, and they may have false memories as each remembers personal events from her childhood only to discover those events actually happened to another sister.

"It's very serious subject matter, but if you've been to a funeral you know funny things can happen," said Catherine Fries Vaughn, who played the middle sister, Mary. She is a doctor in love with a married man (Bryan Garey). The recently deceased mother (Jan Wikstrom) appears to Mary as a restless spirit.

Sara Morsey played eldest sister Teresa, who runs a health food store with her second husband, Frank (David Brummel), and took care of their mother in her final years with dementia. Kate Kertez played Catherine, an immature, pill-popping, pot-smoking, overly dramatic youngest sister who has affairs with unsuitable men and inevitably gets dumped by them.

"Secrets among the sisters stem from their relationship with their mother, relationships that never were solid for any of them," wrote Arline Greer. "*The Memory of Water* is that rarity in theatre, a well-written play that's both funny and touching. It will make you laugh even as you think about memories, both shared and personal."[8]

The Memory of Water was directed by Lauren Caldwell and played from April 20–May 13.

England Swings

In 2007, the summer show was *Shout! The Mod Musical*, created by Phillip George and David Lowenstein with dialogue by Charles Morris and Phillip George. Like previous summer jukebox offerings, this one consisted of a string of recognizable "oldies" loosely connected by a weak storyline.

It is set in London during the swinging Mod era (mid-1960s to early 1970s). Five women, identified in the playbill only by the color of their apparel, sing popular tunes from the British Invasion period. The songs are interspersed with amusing readings of unhelpful advice penned by a starchy ultraconservative columnist and published in *Shout! Magazine*.

Photo: Michael Eaddy

Cast of *Shout! The Mod Musical*: (l-r) Lauren Hathaway, Mackenzie Curran, Rachel Anton, Jennifer Anderson, and Kelly Atkins.

Blue Girl is gorgeous and wealthy, and while she can go on and on about how perfect her life is, she has questions regarding her sexuality. Green Girl is racy, sexually charged, always throwing around innuendos, and frequently hooking up with men. Orange Woman is married, in her forties, and starting to suspect her husband is cheating on her. Yellow Girl is an American who has traveled to Britain in order to see Paul McCartney. Red Girl is the youngest and a bit hopeless in the beginning, stating she is not good-looking like other girls, until the man of her dreams comes along.

Director Lauren Caldwell needed five strong female vocalists. She started with her female leads from *8-Track*, Kelly Atkins and Rachel Anton, then added Jennifer Anderson and Mackenzie Curran, who had both appeared in *Trailer Park*. For the fifth role, she hired Lauren Hathaway, who had performed the leading roles in *Gypsy* and *The Sound of Music* in New York and Los Angeles.

The five harmonized together on some songs, and on solo songs brought audiences to their feet with show-stopping vocals. Frequent costume changes complemented the progression of years through songs. Audiences recognized every tune, from Petula Clark's "Downtown" to Nancy Sinatra's "These Boots Are Made for Walking." Of course, a show titled *Shout!* couldn't very well end without the entire cast singing the Isley Brothers' "Shout."

Arline Greer raved, "Carlos Francisco Asse has designed a set for the show that can rival anything seen in the flower-child era of the '60s with multi-levels of lights and flowers, patterned floors and two revolving columns in which the actresses spin, sing and dance.... Marilyn A. Wall's costumes are a show in themselves, ranging from short, belted trench coats to svelte, shimmering dresses and outfits resembling England's Union Jack. Bryan Mercer, the show's musical director, has arranged songs that show off the skills of each actress, singly and in unison. *Shout!* It's pure entertainment, fun all the way through."[9]

Kelly Atkins recalled, "That was another one of those super-high-levels-of-singing-tight-harmony, constantly moving, dancing-in-very-demanding-footwear kind of shows. A handful of performers, onstage for the entire show, singing forty songs, and dancing the whole time, are the most physically demanding performances. And Rachel Anton and I ended up choreographing that show. Our choreographer was supposed to be Judy Skinner. On the second day of rehearsals, Judy blew her knee out. Rachel had been in *8-Track* with me and we had an understanding of how we each moved and danced, so we talked with Lauren and decided that we would take on the show. Neither one of us would consider ourselves professional-level choreographers on any scale, but you get in a situation like that, you just do what you have to do. I think it worked really well."

Shout! opened June 8 and entertained audiences all the way through August 5.

Season Thirty-five

To open their thirty-fifth season, the Hippodrome produced *Doubt* by John Patrick Shanley. The intense drama had won the Pulitzer Prize for Drama and the Tony Award for Best Play and ran for 550 performances on Broadway. This was before allegations of sexual wrongdoings by Catholic priests made headlines, so the show's central conflict left more room for doubt than it would if presented today.

The play is set in 1964 at a Catholic School in the Bronx. Father Flynn, a beloved and progressive parish priest, finds himself at loggerheads with the school's principal, Sister Aloysius, a rigidly conservative nun. The two come into direct conflict after she learns from a young, impressionable nun, Sister James, that the priest met in private with twelve-year-old Donald, the school's first African American student.

Photo: Michael Eaddy

Sister Aloysius (Sara Morsey) confronts Father Flynn (Michael Stewart Allen) in *Doubt*.

Aloysius, in the presence of Sister James, openly confronts Flynn with her suspicions. He angrily denies wrongdoing, insisting that he was disciplining Donald for drinking altar wine. Aloysius, dissatisfied with Flynn's story, meets with Donald's mother, who ignores Aloysius's accusations and says she supports her son's relationship with Flynn.

Father Flynn eventually threatens to remove Aloysius from her position if she doesn't back down. Aloysius informs him that she telephoned the last parish he was assigned to, discovering a history of past infringements. After declaring his innocence, the priest begins to plead with her, at which point she blackmails him and demands that he resign immediately, or else she will publicly disgrace him. She leaves the office, disgusted. Flynn calls the bishop to apply for a transfer; later, he receives a promotion and is instated as pastor of a nearby parochial school.

Learning this, Aloysius reveals to Sister James that she'd fabricated the story about calling Flynn's previous parish and she has no evidence of past wrongdoing. In the end, Aloysius wonders if the doubt is in herself or the Church. With no proof that Father Flynn is or is not innocent, the audience is left with its own doubt. If staged in 2023, audiences might be less willing to give Flynn the benefit of doubt.

Jacksonville theatre critic Dick Kerekes compared it to the Hippodrome's 2002 production of *Proof*: "Both plays are challenging to audiences as they command your absolute attention and both amply reward you."[10]

Arline Greer called it "a dazzler, not to be missed. The Hipp's smart and sensitive production [is] directed by Mary Hausch with a knowing eye toward its ever-shifting nuances.... Sara Morsey gives the performance of her career as Sister Aloysius. She doesn't so much play the part as live it. Michael Stewart Allen as Father Flynn gives a touching performance that combines the priest's outwardly bluff, genial personality with his inner fragility. He's a fine foil for Morsey's Sister Aloysius. As Sister James, Kate Kertez enlists our sympathies with her humorous confusion and her very real desire to arrive at an understanding. Alecia Robinson plays Donald Muller's mother as if she was born to the role. The play is gripping for the entire ninety-five uninterrupted minutes of its running time."[11]

The subtitle of *Doubt* is "a parable." The Hippodrome's outstanding production of *Doubt* ran September 7–30.

Zombie Parody

Hippodrome Artistic Director Lauren Caldwell looked for a play to fill the October–November slot and settled on a script by Lori Allen Ohm, *Night of the Living Dead*, based on the George Romero film.

In *Night of the Living Dead*, while surrounded by zombies, Sara Morsey as Alachua County Sheriff Sadie Darnell is interviewed by TV20 news anchor Paige Beck (Nell Page).

"The question I asked is, 'Can you create horror onstage?'" Lauren said. "The answer is no, I don't think you can. So we made it a little absurd and ridiculous."[12] She also localized it for Gainesville. In Romero's story, a group of strangers hide in a farmhouse fending off zombies and watching television reports from a sheriff and a local newscaster. So, Lauren approached Alachua County Sheriff Sadie Darnell for permission to have actress Sara Morsey impersonate her in the play.

"My first thought was how wonderfully fun that is and how typical it is of the Hippodrome to think of something like that," Sheriff Darnell told the *Gainesville Sun*. "I hope they recognize that I've got a sense of humor and that I'm not all stuffy."[13] She even lent them an Alachua County Sheriff's uniform.

For the newscaster, Lauren turned to Channel 20's evening news anchor, Paige Beck, who also agreed to go along with the joke. Hippodrome veteran Nell Page studied Beck's vocal inflections and delivery and how she did her makeup.

Photo: Michael Eaddy

Costume designer Lorelei Esser found a wig identical to Beck's haircut, and Nell did an amazing impersonation.

Lauren also peppered the script with dozens of references to Gainesville and the Gator football team. She allowed her cast of twenty actors to freely ad-lib anything they thought was funny. The eight cast members in the farmhouse fighting off the zombies were Armando Acevedo, Robyn Berg, Kate Kertez, Matthew Lindsay, Marjorie Kammerlohr, Denis McCourt, Jessica Ires Morris, and Ted Stephens III. Ten brain-hungry zombies—more humorous than scary—were played by Libby Arnold, Kate Daub, Dan Kahn, Bobby McAfee, Jorgia McAfee, Kristin Mercer, Alex Mrazek, Loren Omer, Kellie Palladino, and Es Swihart.

"*Night of the Living Dead* is by turns creepy, violent, bloody, ridiculous, self-referential, and slapstick. It is full of screaming, shooting and, naturally, zombie dance sequences," said the *Gainesville Sun*.[14] The zombie attack lasted from October 19–November 11.

Christmas

The Hippodrome's recurring Christmas show *A Tuna Christmas* opened November 23 and *A Christmas Carol* opened the next day. Both closed on December 23.

1 Travis Atria, "The Roar of the Scheming," *Gainesville Sun*, January 11, 2007.
2 Dick Maxwell, review of *The Smell of the Kill*, by Michele Lowe, directed by Robert Satterlee, Hippodrome Theatre, Gainesville, FL, *Gainesville Sun*, January 18, 2007.
3 Dick Kerekes, review of *The Smell of the Kill*, by Michele Lowe, directed by Robert Satterlee, Hippodrome Theatre, Gainesville, FL, *EntertainingU*, January 2007.
4 Travis Atria, "An Exploration of Fathers, Sons and Faith," *Gainesville Sun*, March 1, 2007.
5 Ibid.
6 Ibid.
7 Arline Greer, review of *The Chosen*, by Aaron Posner and Chaim Potok, directed by Lauren Caldwell, Hippodrome Theatre, Gainesville, FL, *Gainesville Sun*, March 8, 2007.
8 Arline Greer, review of *The Memory of Water*, by Shelagh Stephenson, directed by Lauren Caldwell, Hippodrome Theatre, Gainesville, FL, *Gainesville Sun*, April 26, 2007.
9 Arline Greer, review of *Shout! The Mod Musical*, by Phillip George and David Lowenstein, directed by Lauren Caldwell, Hippodrome Theatre, Gainesville, FL, *Gainesville Sun*, June 14, 2007.
10 Dick Kerekes, review of *Doubt*, by John Patrick Shanley, directed by Mary Hausch, Hippodrome Theatre, Gainesville, FL, *EntertainingU*, September 2007.
11 Arline Greer, review of *Doubt*, by John Patrick Shanley, directed by Mary Hausch, Hippodrome Theatre, Gainesville, FL, *Gainesville Sun*, September 13, 2007.
12 Travis Atria, "Zombies Invade Gainesville," *Gainesville Sun*, October 18, 2007.
13 Marisa Spyker, "Look Out for Zombies, Familiar Characters," *Gainesville Sun*, October 20, 2007.
14 Travis Atria, "Zombies Invade Gainesville," *Gainesville Sun*, October 18, 2007.

2008

The Dead Guy

When the Writers Guild of America strike from November 2007 to February 2008 halted production of most scripted television shows, networks filled the gap with a flurry of "reality" TV. The sudden change in TV programming perfectly underscored the Hippodrome's January play, *The Dead Guy*, Eric Coble's satirical stab at the entire culture surrounding television reality shows.

Eldon Phelps, an unemployed, pot-smoking, booze-addled slacker with no future, agrees to die on a new TV reality series. In exchange, he'll receive one million dollars to spend any way he chooses for one week before he's contractually obligated to die. A TV cameraman will film him as he blows through the fortune. Episodes will be broadcast nightly, and at the end of the week, TV viewers will vote on the means of Eldon's death. Tim Altmeyer, who played the hapless loser, said he enjoyed playing up the inherent absurdity: "There is a cartoon aspect about the role."[1]

Director Lauren Caldwell tried something that hadn't been done before. She gave the actor playing the cameraman (Michael T. Toth) a working camera and displayed his live video feed on five overhead TV screens. This gave audiences two things to watch: the actors onstage and the footage being captured by the cameraman. Lauren said, "The presence of a television screen on stage allows the audience to detach from what happens to Eldon in the same way people do when watching actual TV shows. The tragedy is on the screen because that's where we're used to looking at tragedy, not right in front of us."[2]

Of course, the play isn't a tragedy; it's a dark comedy that points out the absurdity of reality TV. Jessica Ires Morris played the producer who signed Eldon up and moderates the nightly broadcasts. "In [the producer's] quest for ratings, she's single-minded and ruthless, not a woman you want to mess with," wrote Arline Greer. "Morris is quite simply amazing in a role that dominates the play. She meets her match with Tim Altmeyer... perfect as Eldon, who becomes the unlikely hero of a morbid reality show. Sara Morsey is funny as Eldon's mother. Bobby McAfee is right-on as Eldon's half-witted brother. Playing Christy, the girlfriend who sticks by Eldon, Libby Arnold gives a winning performance. Nell Page is amusing doing double duty as both a hooker and a doctor."[3]

TV viewers vote to have the producer shoot Eldon. After she does, she promises the audience there will be more dead guys in the future.

Photo: Michael Eaddy

Tim Altmeyer (on floor), Jessica Ires Morris, Libby Arnold, and Nell Page with cameraman Michael T. Toth in a scene from *The Dead Guy*.

Greer said, "Eric Coble makes a damning observation of American culture epitomized by the reality show."[4]

The Dead Guy ran from January 11–February 3.

Tennessee Williams's Dead Guy

The subject of death was the only thing the Hippodrome's next play, Tennessee Williams's *Suddenly Last Summer*, had in common with *The Dead Guy*.

"Tennessee Williams has set one of the great horror stories of the last century," wrote Arline Greer. "A macabre, decadent story, it tells of the dubious pleasures of cannibalism, homosexual procuring, old-age vanity, mother love gone awry, and a lobotomy."[5]

The character at the center of the story, Sebastian Venable, is dead before the play begins. Although he's never seen, his reputation looms over the tale. Sebastian was a poet and world traveler, but also a homosexual in the 1930s, when homosexuality was considered a mental illness and a shameful secret that families kept hidden.

The action takes place in a lush garden behind a New Orleans mansion on a gorgeous set designed by Carlos Asse. Sebastian's mother, Mrs. Violet Venable, meets with a doctor from the private mental asylum where she is paying to confine her niece, Catharine.

Photo: Michael Eaddy

(l-r) Scott Hudson as Dr. Sugar, Sara Morsey as Mrs. Venable, and Beth Hylton as Catharine in *Suddenly Last Summer*.

After waxing nostalgic about her son, who died under mysterious circumstances, Mrs. Venable offers to make a generous donation to support the doctor's psychiatric research if he will perform a lobotomy on Catharine to stop her from babbling about Sebastian's homosexuality and his violent death in Spain. The doctor is reluctant to agree to such a drastic action without examining her.

Catharine is brought to the mansion and sees her mother and brother for the first time since being admitted to the asylum. Violet is holding up the probate of Sebastian's will, from which they stand to inherit. They plead with Catharine to say whatever Violet wants, as they need the money. But the doctor has injected Catharine with truth serum and she can only speak the truth.

Catharine proceeds to give a scandalous account of the events leading up to Sebastian's death. How he used her to procure young men for his sexual exploitation, just as his mother had previously done. How he was set upon, mutilated, and partially devoured by a mob of starving children in the street. Mrs. Venable lunges at Catharine but is prevented from striking her and is taken offstage, screaming, "Cut this hideous story from her brain!"[6] Far from being convinced of Catharine's insanity, however, the doctor concludes the play by stating he believes her story could be true.

In her review, Arline Greer praised the cast, director, and playwright: "Sara Morsey, as Violet, is every inch the patrician lady. She means to show she's in charge. Beth Hylton's Catherine commands the stage.... [During] her monologue in which she relives Sebastian's bloody, awful death... a wave of nausea and shock fills the theatre.

"Scott Hudson gives a strong performance as the immaculate doctor.... Smaller roles are well handled by Nell Page, who plays Catharine's mother, and Michael T. Toth as George, her greedy brother. Kate Kertez plays Violet's servant, and Libby Arnold is Sister Felicity, a nun in charge of Catharine. Lauren Caldwell's taut direction keeps the story's suspense mounting until its final moments. *Suddenly Last Summer* [is] the grande dame of horror stories told with Tennessee Williams' particular brand of poetic imagery."[7]

The show ran from February 29–March 23.

The Pursuit of Happiness

In April, Mary Hausch directed Richard Dresser's comedy *The Pursuit of Happiness*, which concerns a husband and wife trying to send their reluctant daughter off to college. Gainesville being a college town, Mary said, "I felt like it was very resonant for this community." Dresser had also written *Rounding Third*, which she had directed in 2004.

Libby Arnold played the daughter, Jodi, who sees that workday struggles have sapped the joy out of her father's life. Nell Page and David Sitler played her parents, Annie and Neil. Jodi's not wrong. Neil loathes working in a faceless corporation and sees promotions as simply shifting from one tiny cubical to another. He makes friends with an equally unhappy coworker (played by Cameron Francis).

Annie remembers college as the happiest time in her life and wants the same for her daughter. But Jodi has procrastinated on sending in her application until it's too late. So Annie visits an unhappily married admissions officer (Kevin Rainsberger) who had a crush on her in college and sleeps with him to get Jodi admitted.

While it has dark undertones, the play is basically a light comedy. "One of the delights of *The Pursuit of Happiness* is the variety of characterizations offered by the actors," wrote theatre critic Dick Maxwell. "The play belongs to Nell Page. She is completely delightful as Annie, the obsessed mother who is not to be swayed from her goal of making her daughter happy, even if [her] daughter doesn't want to go along with the program. David Sitler is excellent in giving us a man trying to come to grips with the demons.... Sitler portrays [Neil] appropriately with a sense of bitter humor overlying anger. Libby Arnold's Jodi is the most rational member of this crew. She approaches

Photo: Michael Eaddy

Cast of *The Pursuit of Happiness*. Standing: Kevin Rainsberger and Cameron Francis. Kneeling: Nell Page, Libby Arnold, and David Sitler.

her role with a restraint that contrasts nicely with the havoc wreaked by the so-called adults. Cameron Francis is perfect as this klutzy but endearing soul. Some of the funniest moments in the show involve Francis's interaction with the family over tea and ice cream.

"Kevin Rainsberger.... and Page fit perfectly in their scenes together, exhibiting the professionalism and competence that makes them both fine actors.

"Mary Hausch... deftly balances the unbalanced personalities existing on stage during the course of the show to afford a light comedy that is as enjoyable as it is timely."[8]

The Pursuit of Happiness played from April 18–May 11.

Thirty-fifth Anniversary

By its thirty-fifth anniversary, an astounding five million people had seen Hippodrome plays and TYA performances. The theatre had become a beacon, a landmark, and a trendsetter, not only in North Florida but for theatres throughout the South. For the occasion, co-founder Kerry McKenney wrote:

"The celebration of the Hippodrome Theatre Thirty-fifth Anniversary invites a recollection of its inception and context within theatre nationwide. The Hippodrome began at a special moment. New York had been the undisputable center for theatre. However, with the support of the National Endowment of the Arts, a new form of theatre emerged all over the country—experimental, political and poetic. Astonishing work and innovation appeared in places like the Steppenwolf Theatre in Chicago, Empty Space Theatre in Seattle and . . . the Hippodrome Theatre in Gainesville! It was a time of legendary theatre companies and extraordinary writing. Writers included Harold Pinter, Tom Stoppard and Sam Shepard. These avant garde companies and writers inspired the Hippodrome. It was visual, physical, and provocative. The spirit was young and daring. We had big ideas. We improvised, failed, and succeeded. We produced good work—Shakespeare, Voltaire, biting satires, outrageous comedies. Sometimes it transcended and was great work. Amazingly, we drew a dedicated audience. We had generous help from friends, actors, designers, benefactors. We are thankful to have shared such a moment in time. Who would imagine such a thing would happen in Gainesville and go on for thirty-five years! Kudos to the hundreds of people who made it happen."

College: The Musical

For their summer musical, the Hippodrome premiered *College: The Musical* written by Drew Fornarola and Scott Elmegreen, two recent Princeton graduates who had lived their subject matter. Director Lauren Caldwell brought in musical director Bryan Mercer and choreographer Ric Rose to help shape the play, which was having its world premiere at the Hipp. Drew and Scott came to Gainesville and remained in residence, collaborating with Lauren as the play was developed, rewriting or adding scenes at her suggestion.

Photo: Michael Eaddy

A scene in the dorm of *College: The Musical*. Clockwise from left: Bryant Smith, Ted Stephens III, Kim Mead, Nicholas Barnes, Casey Ford Alexander, Mary Elizabeth Runyon, Jorgia McAfee, Jennifer Shorstein, and Jake McKenna on the couch.

The show was about six guys and six girls trying to make their way through a college semester while dealing with typical parties, roommates, and video games. It had a large cast of young people in that age range. Some were veterans of other Hippodrome shows, and some were new. All were excellent singers. Praising her cast, Lauren said, "I've got some voices in the show that will peel the paint off the wall." (In a good way.)

In the cast were Casey Ford Alexander, Jennifer Anderson, Nicholas Barnes, Kimberly Bates, Marty Austin Lamar, Jorgia McAfee, Jake McKenna, Kim Mead, Mary Elizabeth Runyon, Jennifer Shorstein, Bryant Smith, and Ted Stephens III.

One might have expected that in a university city, a play about student tribulations and hijinks would go over well. Cast member Ted Stephens said, "Whether you are in college or beyond, everyone can relate." [9] Yes, but perhaps not in the same way. Parents that might not have wanted to know learned what their darlings were up to when the cast sang "Boot and Rally," a song about drinking until you puke, then returning to drink more. As for the student population, they were living it, so why come see a show about it? The show opened June 6 and had its run extended once, closing on July 13. Other summer musicals had been extended two or three times.

The Hippodrome tried to attract the kind of interest prior summer musicals had received by hosting a July Fourth block party in front of the theatre. They also sent the cast out to the Haile Village Farmer's Market to perform songs from the show. A Haile resident said, "Not many people from this side of town go downtown. When we go downtown, we look like we're looking for our kids."[10]

Season Thirty-six

Photo: Michael Eaddy

Gutenberg! The Musical! (clockwise) actors Kirt Bateman and Jay Perry with musical director/accompanist Brian Hargrove.

After *College: The Musical*, it seemed like the only thing to do was to satirize blockbuster musicals. What better vehicle than the Southeastern premiere of *Gutenberg! The Musical!* written by Anthony King and Scott Brown.

Arline Greer described it as "a goofy, funny, often hilarious two-man show in which actors Kirt Bateman as Doug and Jay Perry as Bud play the authors of a new musical. Hoping to find Broadway backers for their show, the twosome acts out the entire production for the audience. Bud and Doug are conceivably the worst writers who ever attempted to create a musical. As the show goes on and they engender more and more laughter at their well-intentioned but off-the-wall efforts."[11]

The setup is that they believe the Hippodrome audience is full of Broadway producers. "It's almost a jab at commercial theatre," director Lauren Caldwell told the *Gainesville Sun*. "It's very clever."[12] Musical director Brian Hargrove provided the piano accompaniment. Both actors had previously performed the show in Salt Lake City.

"What makes the show work so well is the acting of Kirt Bateman as Doug and Jay Perry as Bud," Greer said. "They are so genuinely thrilled with what they've written, they barely can contain their excitement.... That makes you want to root for them. The low-key satire of *Gutenberg! The Musical!* may not make it in the annals of great musicals, but it does make it a laugh-filled, easy-to-enjoy evening."[13]

The show ran September 5–28.

A Spooky Play

Photo: Aaron Daye

David Shelton and Tim Altmeyer tell the story of *The Woman in Black*.

It had become something of a trend for the Hippodrome to try a spooky play for their October slot. In this case, it was *The Woman in Black: A Ghost Play*, which playwright Stephen Mallatratt adapted from the novel of the same name written by Susan Hill. "This play has been running for 18 years in London," said director Lauren Caldwell. "We've had our eye on it for a long time."[14]

Tim Altmeyer played Arthur Kipps, a young British solicitor called to settle the estate of solitary and friendless Alice Drablow. The recently deceased woman lived in a dreary house surrounded by marsh and quicksand, which, at high tide, was cut off from the mainland. His story of the woman in black is told by an older version of himself, now retired. He's enlisted an actor (David Shelton) to help him tell it in hopes that this will allow him to finally put the memory behind him.

The two men meet on a rehearsal stage, where the actor takes Kipps's written account of what happened and whittles it from five hours to ninety minutes. During the performance, the actor becomes Kipps, and Kipps takes on six roles. The woman in black, portrayed by Kellie Palladino, does make an appearance. She has no lines in the play, but without her presence, there is no ghost story to tell. "I don't like being scared and I don't watch scary movies," Kellie said, "But it's great fun to be the scary thing."[15]

"It's a tour de force for Altmeyer and Shelton, who create a full set of believable characters from just two," wrote the *Sun* theater critic. She said, "The Hippodrome's production of *The Woman in Black* is a first rate thriller."[16]

The Woman in Black spooked audiences from October 17–November 9.

Rusty's Ghost Tour

The Hippodrome Ghost Tour started in October 2008, conducted by Rusty Salling, who also wrote the tour script. The idea was for Rusty to lead a gullible group through the building, behind the scenes, and into places audiences never get to see—and do so in the dark while he told them about spirits that may or may not haunt the building from its days as a courthouse. It was a one-man show, assisted by Hippodrome Marketing Director Jessica Hurov and actor Matthew Lindsay.

The night began with Matthew, as a sort of majordomo, shepherding the tour group into the third-floor rehearsal room where Rusty had hidden himself in a walk-in vault that once held court documents. The group took seats and waited pensively, wondering what was about to happen. After about ten minutes, Rusty quietly stepped out and slammed the vault shut, startling everyone. Dressed in all black, he slowly circled the group like a modern Vincent Price.

The legend, he told them, dated back to 1914 when a young man, who may or may not have committed a murder, was being held in a cell there awaiting hanging. While a makeshift gallows was constructed in the courtyard, he wrote a heartfelt letter to his mother, begging her to come help him. The mother made the difficult journey to Gainesville by train, over thousands of miles, only to find out her son had been hanged the day before she arrived. Distraught and overwhelmed with emotion, she went insane. "She still haunts the Hipp to this day," Rusty said as he led the group down a dark hallway and shined a flashlight toward the women's restroom, where he said she can sometimes be heard weeping. Jessica, hiding in the restroom, wept.

When the tour reached the mainstage, the theatre was completely dark except for the "ghost light," a simple floor lamp with a single bulb that by tradition most theatres leave on when the stage is empty. Rusty gave an elaborate reason for the ghost light. Then, it suddenly flickered and went off. Matt would shake a box containing old silverware to produce a clanking. The audience would scream. Rusty would flick the ghost light back on and Jessica, wearing a turn-of-the-century dress from the play *Our Town*, ran across the far backstage. The audience caught only a hint of movement, a glimpse of her skirt. She would proceed down the back stairs to hide in the basement.

Eventually, the tour reached the then-unfinished basement and included a peek into the mechanical room of the Hippodrome elevator. Installed in 1911, the original uncovered panel of electrical relays will crackle and shoot sparks whenever the

Photo: Michael Eaddy

In 2008, Cameron Francis and Matthew Lindsay take over the roles of *A Tuna Christmas*.

elevator operates. Although it is safe for passengers above, it does remind one of a scene from *Frankenstein*.

Rusty told the story well, feeding out morsels crumb by crumb, leading up to the tour's climax. The prop department had rigged a man-sized dummy that dropped into view as Rusty opened the doors to the costume storage area. Matt edged the group closer to Rusty. Jessica came out of hiding, slipped up behind them, and let out a blood-curdling scream that pierced the darkness and echoed throughout the basement.[17]

Rusty conducted sold-out ghost tours at Halloween for four years.

Christmas Favorites

For 2008, the Hippodrome brought back the hysterical, much-loved *A Tuna Christmas*. This time, it had a new cast. Cameron Francis played the multiple roles previously performed by Mark Chambers, and Matthew Lindsay portrayed the characters formerly played by Lauren Caldwell. Mary Hausch directed. The *Gainesville Sun* called the new cast "entirely brilliant and wonderful."[18] *A Tuna Christmas* opened November 28 and *A Christmas Carol* opened the next day for its thirty-first year. Both shows closed on December 21.

1 Travis Atria, "Better Off Dead," *Gainesville Sun*, January 10, 2008.
2 Ibid.
3 Arline Greer, review of *The Dead Guy*, by Eric Coble, directed by Lauren Caldwell, Hippodrome Theatre, Gainesville, FL, *Gainesville Sun*, January 17, 2008.
4 Ibid.
5 Arline Greer, review of *Suddenly Last Summer*, by Tennessee Williams, directed by Lauren Caldwell, Hippodrome Theatre, Gainesville, FL, *Gainesville Sun*, March 6, 2008.
6 Tennessee Williams, *Suddenly Last Summer*, Concord Theatricals, New York, NY.
7 Arline Greer, review of *Suddenly Last Summer*, by Tennessee Williams, directed by Lauren Caldwell, Hippodrome Theatre, Gainesville, FL, *Gainesville Sun*, March 6, 2008.
8 Dick Maxwell, review of *The Pursuit of Happiness*, by Richard Dresser, directed by Mary Hausch, Hippodrome Theatre, Gainesville, FL, *Gainesville Sun*, April 24, 2008.
9 Jeremiah Stanley, "Haile Hears about *College*," *Gainesville Sun*, June 1, 2008.
10 Ibid.
11 Arline Greer, review of *Gutenberg! The Musical!*, by Anthony King and Scott Brown, directed by Lauren Caldwell, Hippodrome Theatre, Gainesville, FL, *Gainesville Sun*, September 11, 2008.
12 Travis Atria, "Patently Ridiculous Musical," *Gainesville Sun*, September 4, 2008.
13 Arline Greer, review of *Gutenberg! The Musical!*, by Anthony King and Scott Brown, directed by Lauren Caldwell, Hippodrome Theatre, Gainesville, FL, *Gainesville Sun*, September 11, 2008.
14 Travis Atria, "Halloween Spook-tacular," *Gainesville Sun*, October 16, 2008.
15 Ibid.
16 Arline Greer, review of *The Woman in Black*, by Stephen Mallatratt, directed by Lauren Caldwell, Hippodrome Theatre, Gainesville, FL, *Gainesville Sun*, October 23, 2008
17 Jon Silman, "Ghost Tour Reveals Past," *Independent Florida Alligator*, October 29, 2009.
18 Arline Greer, review of *A Tuna Christmas*, by Ed Howard, Jaston Williams, and Joe Sears, directed by Mary Hausch, Hippodrome Theatre, Gainesville, FL, *Gainesville Sun*, December 4, 2008

2009

The Glass Menagerie

Bankruptcy of several major brokerage firms in the fourth quarter of 2008 crashed the stock market, put the global economy in a tailspin, and forced a US government bailout of the banking, insurance, and auto industries. The arts were not so fortunate. Federal, state, and local grants for arts organizations were cut. This included the Hippodrome, which lost a half-million in state grant money. Mary Hausch told the *Gainesville Sun* the cuts and the economy were the worst she'd seen in her thirty-five years with the Hipp.

Measures were taken to keep the theatre alive, including cutting production staff and the number of paid interns. She also reduced the number of days the cinema was open and lessened the box office hours. "It was tempting to raise ticket prices," she said, "but because of the tough economy we really didn't want to make it more difficult for people to come."[1]

Another change was to replace the scheduled musical, *Tick, Tick, Boom*, with Tennessee Williams's *The Glass Menagerie*. Mary explained, "Producing a musical costs at least $150,000. So we opted for a show that is a wonderful classic and is a beautiful piece of theatre, but that really was less expensive to produce."[2]

The Hippodrome had previously staged *The Glass Menagerie* in 1998 to critical acclaim. The story is of shy, fragile Laura, whose mother, Amanda, a faded Southern belle, pressures her son to fix Laura up with a suitor.

Lauren Caldwell, who had directed the play's prior production, again cast Sara Morsey as Amanda. To play the son, Tom, she chose Niall McGinty, and Michael Littig played Laura's gentleman caller. For the key role of Laura, she hired Philadelphia-based actress Marybeth Gorman. The play opened January 9 and ran through February 1.

The *Sun* theater critic praised the 2009 version, calling it "fine theater craft" and a "jewel-studded Hippodrome production."[3]

Valentine Poetry

On Valentine's Day, Third-Eye Spoken, a poetry performance group, presented a program of passionate poetry on the Hippodrome mainstage. Poems were divided into two classes, love poetry and erotic poetry. The program also included belly dancing and live music. "The goal is to make poetry theatrical," said the evening's host, Lacy Nagy. "This is not your mama's poetry."[4]

Photo: Michael Eaddy
(l-r) Marybeth Gorman, Niall McGinty, and Sara Morsey play Laura, Tom, and Amanda Wingfield in *The Glass Menagerie*.

Modernizing a Greek Myth

After *The Glass Menagerie*, Marybeth Gorman stayed on to play the lead in *Eurydice*, Sarah Ruhl's updating of the myth of Orpheus, with Niall McGinty as Orpheus. In Greek legend, the poet Orpheus's grief over the death of his wife, Eurydice, led him to write such depressing, sorrow-filled music that he was allowed into the underworld to bring her back.

In the opening scene, Eurydice and Orpheus frolic on the beach and speak poetically of their love for each other. Then, on their wedding day, she is lured into the land of death by Hades, Lord of the Underworld (Rusty Salling), who has disguised himself as a man claiming to have letters from her deceased father. Separated in death from the love of her life, Orpheus, she reconnects with the first man any girl ever loves, her father, played by D. Christopher Wert.

Sarah Ruhl's Eurydice is a modern woman who has a choice of returning to life and marriage or staying below. Director Lauren Caldwell's vision had the actors play out surface-world scenarios on twelve-foot-tall scaffolding and the underworld scenes underneath the scaffold. Special elements of the set included a working water pump and an elevator that rained inside. The soundtrack ranged from Pachelbel's "Cannon in D" to the hard rock of Guns N' Roses. Three talking stones comprised a Greek chorus that barked out the rules of the land of the dead: Big Stone (Kevin-Michael Chu), Little Stone (Jorgia McAfee), and Loud Stone (Sara Morsey).

(l-r) Marybeth Gorman plays the title role in *Eurydice* with Hades (Rusty Salling), Big Stone (Kevin-Michael Chu), Loud Stone (Sara Morsey), and Little Stone (Jorgia McAfee).

Photo: Michael Eaddy

"As the stones, we mirror a lot of the characters in the play," said Jorgia McAfee. "I represent, as Little Stone, a lot of the attributes of Eurydice, and I'm very little girlish."

"And I'm just old," said Sara about her role as Loud Stone.[5]

Eschewing togas and clothing of ancient Greece, Marilyn Wall's costumes for Eurydice included a black-and-white formal dress, an electric pink jacket, and a

1950s-style bikini. For the Lord of the Underworld, she created a dramatic red costume trimmed in silver with a cowboy hat. Rusty also had his toenails painted red and rode around the stage on a Segway scooter.

Actor Marybeth Gorman said, "The play is a wild ride and the audience shouldn't try so hard to figure it out. It's a play that works best on an emotional level, not an intellectual level."[6]

Critic Arline Greer concurred: "*Eurydice* is an emotional play that will stay with many who see it. The play exudes a gentle charm that should be experienced to be appreciated. Marybeth Gorman handles the difficult role of Eurydice skillfully. As the play's central character, Gorman deals quite well with the challenge, offering us a portrayal that is rich in variety and nuance."[7]

Eurydice opened on February 27, but the US economic picture seemed to be getting worse, so the following Tuesday, the Hippodrome cut the price of tickets for seats in the side sections to fifteen dollars. "We think that theater is a great thing to do, especially when times are hard," Lauren Caldwell told the *Gainesville Sun*. "But the most important thing we wanted to do is make it affordable to our public."[8] The show continued through March 22.

The Greatest Liar

In April, the Hippodrome presented *Shipwrecked!*, Donald Margulies's fact-based adaptation of Louis de Rougemont's memoirs. It is a rambunctious adventure that follows de Rougemont's thirty years at sea, complete with scurvy pirates, giant killer octopi, hostile Aborigines, deserted islands, a shipwreck, and more. De Rougemont actually made up much of what he claimed had happened, so his readers dubbed him the greatest liar on Earth.

It was a three-actor play with a ton of sound effects. Tod Zimmerman portrayed Louis de Rougemont. With split-second costume changes, Cameron Francis and Tara Vodihn played over thirty characters de Rougemont allegedly encountered. On a minimalist set with an octagon-shaped platform, the actors had over one hundred props. "I think it's the most exhausting role I've ever done," Tod told the *Gainesville Sun*. Cameron agreed: "It's challenging, energy wise."[9]

Arline Greer called *Shipwrecked!* "a winner—hands down."[10] She also said Cameron Francis's performance as a dog named Bruno "all but steals the show. As Francis wiggles his nose, stretches his neck and douses Louis with big, wet slurpy licks of love, the thought comes

Photo: Michael Eaddy

Tod Zimmerman (center) portrays Louis de Rougemont. Cameron Francis and Tara Vodihn play the thirty characters he meets in *Shipwrecked!*

to mind that Francis has been studying 'Dog' all his life. His performance is both funny and heartbreaking.

"The storyteller/hero of the tale is played with the charm and charisma of a Sean Connery by Tod Zimmerman, who inhabits the stage as boy and man for the entire evening, seemingly tireless as he narrates his tale. This fun-loving, charming production of *Shipwrecked!*, directed by the fun-loving Lauren Caldwell, takes us away in our imaginations to where anything is possible."[11]

Shipwrecked! played from April 17–May 10.

Back to the Trailer Park

In uncertain economic times, having a sure thing for a summer musical was a wise move. So the Hippodrome brought back its longest-running, best-selling show, *The Great American Trailer Park Musical* written by David Nehls and Betsy Kelso. And they'd save money on production costs because they still had the original set and costumes in storage.

Director Lauren Caldwell again cast Kelly Atkins, Mark Chambers, and Catherine Fries Vaughn to play leads Pippi, Norbert, and Jeannie. Bryan Mercer returned as musical director and Judy Skinner as choreographer. Veterans of recent Hippodrome musicals, Jorgia McAfee and Kim Mead, played two of the remaining trailer park residents. Rachel Lomax and Tim Norton filled the final two roles, making their Hippodrome debuts. Stealing scenes and charming audiences was a fresh addition to the trailer park, Chula, an eight-inch-tall Chihuahua that belonged to Kim Mead. The pup had made her first appearance on the Hippodrome stage in *College: The Musical!* The tiny diva lived up to her name, which means "hot" in Spanish.

Photo: Michael Eaddy

The 2009 cast of *The Great American Trailer Park Musical*. Standing (l-r): Catherine Fries Vaughn, Mark Chambers, Kelly Atkins, and Tim Norton. Kneeling (l-r): Rachel Lomax, Chula (the Chihuahua), Kim Mead, and Jorgia McAfee.

The show opened June 5 and was extended repeatedly through August 16, nearly matching the original's record-breaking run. Nightly, audiences leaped to their feet in standing ovations following the grand finale. The reviewer was effusive, too.

"There are some things in this world that just get better the second time around," wrote Arline Greer. "*The Great American Trailer Park Musical* onstage at The Hippodrome State Theatre, is one of them, not that it wasn't hilariously perfect when The Hipp performed it originally. Caldwell's *Trailer Park* brings back some of the actors who made the show a hit originally and introduces four new performers—every one of them a gem. Every one of these actors gives a dynamic performance, singing, dancing, playing their roles to the hilt. And yes, it really is more fun to see the second time around."[12]

Season Thirty-seven

Back in the 1980s, a man fulfilled his lifelong dream of flying when he tied helium-filled weather balloons to a lawn chair and soared sixteen thousand feet up. How things played out for him after his real-life exploit was the subject of the Hippodrome's September play, appropriately titled *Up*.

The script is fiction. Playwright Bridget Carpenter based it on the true story but changed the character's name and imagined his life fifteen years after his historic flight. Walter Griffin (Tod Zimmerman) plans to fly again, this time in an aircraft of his own making, and spends his days tinkering with shoddy contraptions. He has imaginary conversations with a French tightrope walker famous for his daring 1974 tightrope walk between New York City's World Trade Center towers. Matthew Lindsay played the famed Frenchman.

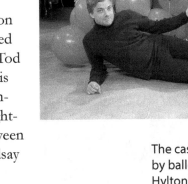

Photo: Michael Eaddy

The cast of *Up!*, surrounded by balloons. Back: (l-r) Beth Hylton, Dylan Kammerer, Jennifer Smith, Tod Zimmerman, and Sara Morsey. Front: Matthew Lindsay.

The wonderful actress from *Suddenly Last Summer*, Beth Hylton, played Walter's frustrated wife Helen, who struggles to keep the family afloat on her paycheck. Sara Morsey had dual roles as Helen's mom and the aunt of new girl Maria (Jennifer Smith), who befriends Walter's son, Mikey (Dylan Kammerer). As the friendship between Maria and Mikey deepens, both families are affected.

"I think it's a real interesting piece for nowadays," said director Lauren Caldwell, "how the dark cloud of the economy can cause sort of dysfunction in your lives. It shows both sides so clearly. You root for Walter because he has such soul and his heart is so large and his aspirations are so big, but you also understand Helen in saying 'You've got to put some bread on the table.'"[13]

One side of the set had a yellow chrome-legged Formica kitchen table and chairs that represented the Griffins' home. On the other side, a burgundy armchair and coffee table denoted Maria and her aunt's living room. There was, of course, Walter's latest lawn chair with a window fan strapped to it. Video by Shirley Lasseter and Michael Eaddy was projected on the stage throughout the play, creating an open-sky motif, and a platform upstage served actor Matthew Lindsay as he pantomimed walking the tightrope.

The *Sun* reviewer said the "direction is excellent in *Up*" and the "cast is lively, witty and sharp... the balance between the different threads of the story is maintained to the end allowing the actors to shine and carry the audience up with them."[14]

Up ran September 4–27.

Psychological Thriller

The cover photo of the *Gainesville Sun*'s October 15, 2009, issue of *Scene* showed actor Tod Zimmerman strapped into a straightjacket. The stark image was from the Hippodrome's next show, *Mindgame*, written by British playwright Anthony Horowitz and directed by Lauren Caldwell. It was a good score for the Hippodrome; the play had just ended its off-Broadway run the prior December.

The set, designed by Carlos Asse, was the office of Dr. Farquhar, the man in charge of an asylum for the criminally insane. It had a desk and office chair upstage, and also a wooden chair with arms at mid-stage. David Sitler played the doctor and Sara Morsey his nurse, Plimpton.

The play opens with true crime writer Mark Styler (Tod Zimmerman) waiting to meet the doctor in his office. Styler has come to interview a notorious serial killer being held there. The doctor arrives and the men talk, but things don't seem right. Farquhar is reluctant to let Styler see the inmate and encourages Styler to leave. Styler, however, refuses with the excuse of a long car journey. In the end, he stays, and Farquhar offers him dinner. His assistant, Nurse Plimpton, seems frightened and anxious. She tries to slip Styler a note, but Farquhar burns it.

Plimpton reluctantly makes liver sandwiches and a pot of tea for Styler. After she leaves, Styler and Dr. Farquhar discuss the book further. Styler is desperate for the interview. It is suggested that the killer could be put in a straightjacket to keep him from damaging anything. Farquhar retrieves a straightjacket from a closet and offers to show what it is like. Styler reluctantly agrees. Once Styler is strapped in, Farquhar taunts him about being mad and threatens him with a scalpel. Then, Nurse Plimpton returns and knocks Farquhar unconscious with a wine bottle. She explains that Farquhar is actually an inmate who killed most of the staff during a psychiatric drama session. Nurse Plimpton is, in fact, Dr. Carol Ennis. She cannot undo the straightjacket straps, and as she bends down to get the scalpel to cut them, the killer awakens, grabs her, and then stabs her behind a curtain.

Photo: Michael Eaddy

(l-r) Sara Morsey, Tod Zimmerman, and David Sitler play in *Mindgame*.

The two men talk. It turns out they used to be neighbors, and perhaps Styler's motives for visiting are not as they appeared to be. Dr. Ennis suddenly awakens and cries out for help. She is then strapped to the chair. Styler is tricked into thinking he is the killer and must suffocate Ennis. Once the deed is done, he feels guilt, but then Ennis comes to and now assumes the role of Dr. Farquhar. Styler is told he is really the inmate and Styler was just his assumed name. He tries to prove them wrong; however, his car is gone and the letter he sent to Farquhar is blank. In the end, Styler is forced to believe he is the inmate, although it is never explicitly revealed to the audience who is actually who.

"Director Lauren Caldwell has put together an incredible ensemble cast," wrote reviewer Sherwin Mackintosh. "Just when you begin to feel that one of them is your favorite, the game shifts, the costumes change, and suddenly, you are drawn to another. All three have their 'aha' moments, but Morsey stands out in her role as Nurse Plimpton. As the troubled, inappropriately dressed nurse, Morsey continues to develop her character to its final chilling metamorphosis. This thriller will keep you guessing until the final seconds."[15]

Mindgame played from October 16–November 8. Sara Morsey fell on stage near the end of the run and, thinking she'd sprained her ankle, performed the final five shows on crutches, not knowing she'd broken it.

Holliday Plays

Photo: Michael Eaddy

Rusty Salling as Scrooge (center) pretends to scare the 2009 cast of *A Christmas Carol*, which ran concurrent with *A Tuna Christmas* from November 28–December 20.

1   Lashonda Stinson Curry, "Stage Fright," *Gainesville Sun*, January 2, 2009.

2   Ibid.

3   Arline Greer, review of *The Glass Menagerie*, by Tennessee Williams, directed by Lauren Caldwell, Hippodrome Theatre, Gainesville, FL, *Gainesville Sun*, January 15, 2009.

4   Travis Pillow, "Spoken-word Group to Heat Up the Hipp," *Gainesville Sun*, February 14, 2009.

5   Lashonda Stinson Curry, "Love Lost in Worlds Apart," *Gainesville Sun*, February 26, 2009.

6   Ibid.

7   Arline Greer, review of *Eurydice*, by Sarah Ruhl, directed by Lauren Caldwell, Hippodrome Theatre, Gainesville, FL, *Gainesville Sun*, March 5, 2009.

8   Bill Dean, "Hipp Cuts Select Ticket Prices to $15," *Gainesville Sun*, March 4, 2009.

9   Travis Atria, "Rambunctious Adventure," *Gainesville Sun*, April 16, 2009.

10 Arline Greer, review of *Shipwrecked*, by Donald Margulies, directed by Lauren Caldwell, Hippodrome Theatre, Gainesville, FL, *Gainesville Sun*, April 23, 2009.

11 Ibid.

12 Arline Greer, review of *The Great American Trailer Park Musical*, by David Nehls and Betsy Kelso, directed by Lauren Caldwell, Hippodrome Theatre, Gainesville, FL, *Gainesville Sun*, June 11, 2009.

13 Lashonda Stinson Curry, "Theater on a New Level," *Gainesville Sun*, September 3, 2009.

14 Arline Greer, review of *Up*, by Bridget Carpenter, directed by Lauren Caldwell, Hippodrome Theatre, Gainesville, FL, *Gainesville Sun*, September 10, 2009.

15 Sherwin Mackintosh, review of *Mindgame*, by Anthony Horowitz, directed by Lauren Caldwell, Hippodrome Theatre, Gainesville, FL, *Gainesville Sun*, November 1, 2009.

2010

Dead Man's Cell Phone

For their January play, the Hippodrome selected *Dead Man's Cell Phone* written by Sarah Ruhl, author of last season's *Eurydice*. Director Lauren Caldwell said, "Ruhl is the hot, new contemporary playwright in theater now... her pieces... are flavored with imaginative scenes and dark humor."[1]

Photo: Michael Eaddy

Cast of *Dead Man's Cell Phone*: (l-r) Tim Altmeyer, Sara Morsey, Teniece Divya Johnson, Matthew Lindsay, Jessica Ires Morris, and Nichole Hamilton.

Dead Man's Cell Phone starts with Jean (Nichole Hamilton) finishing her lunch in a restaurant when she becomes irritated that the man at the next table refuses to answer his ringing cell phone. She goes over to him and realizes the man is dead. Jean calls 911 and sits with him until the ambulance arrives. In her panic, she continues to answer the persistent phone without telling the callers what has happened, just saying she'll take a message. One of the calls is from his mother, Mrs. Gottlieb (Sara Morsey), from whom Jean learns the dead man's name is Gordon.

Jean leaves the restaurant—taking the dead man's cell phone with her and continuing to answer his calls. She even attends his funeral, during which a mysterious woman calls and asks to meet. The woman, played by Teniece Divya Johnson, turns out to be Gordon's sexy mistress and wants to know his dying words. Jean lies and says his last words were declarations of love for her.

Mrs. Gottlieb calls and invites Jean to her home, where she begins asking intrusive and bizarre questions. Jean ends up pretending she's one of Gordon's coworkers. This alarms Mrs. Gottlieb for a moment. Jean placates her with another lie and is invited to come back for dinner. That night, she meets Gordon's widow (Jessica Ires Morris) and his brother, Dwight (Matthew Lindsay). Dwight owns a stationery store and takes her there after dinner. They connect. She and Dwight kiss.

"It's got nice, warm themes to it about love and the commitment that we need to make in terms of loving people for who they are, but then it's also got this bizarre, skewed humor to it, too," Lauren said.[2]

The bizarre twist is when dead Gordon (Tim Altmeyer) steps on stage and addresses the audience, outlining what happened the day he died and confessing he was in the unsavory business of selling human organs.

The scene reverts to Jean and Dwight, who confesses he loves her but gets angry when she answers the cell phone and tells the caller Gordon is dead. He forbids her to use it anymore. She ignores him and continues to take calls, further involving herself with Gordon's mother and widow. A stranger demands that Jean give her the phone because it has all of Gordon's business contacts. Jean refuses and is struck in the head. The stranger takes the phone, and when Jean comes to, she is back in the restaurant with Gordon, who tells her she is now his pipeline into the world of the living.

Jean tells Mrs. Gottlieb that she's seen Gordon in Heaven and that he's waiting for her. Overjoyed, Mrs. Gottlieb runs into a bonfire in the backyard so that she can be with Gordon. Jean is horrified, but Dwight is happy his mother and his brother are together again.

"It may leave you a bit perplexed at the end," wrote reviewer Dick Kerekes, "but it is a fast paced show and you never lose interest in the 90 minutes of action.... Don't miss the unusual and truly interesting theatre experience that *Dead Man's Cell Phone* promises and delivers."[3]

The show ran January 8–31.

Defiance

Mary Hausch took over directing chores for *Defiance* by playwright John Patrick Shanley, the author of *Doubt*, which she had also directed.

After a series of racial conflicts at Camp Lejeune, base commander Lt. Col. Littlefield (David Sitler) promotes a Black officer (Ryan George) to captain solely based on race. The newly promoted captain just wants to be seen as a Marine officer, not a Black officer. But the focus shifts from race relations to morals and ethics with the arrival of a new chaplain (Matthew Lindsay) and the revelation that the colonel has had an affair with the wife of a private (Jason Weiss). Actor Carolyn Popp played Littlefield's spunky, supportive wife and Aaron Ganas played a gunnery sergeant.

Photo: Michael Eaddy

Cast members Carolyn Popp, David Sitler, Ryan George, Matthew Lindsay, Jason Weiss, and Aaron Ganas line up in *Defiance*.

"I think the core conflict deals with responsibility and the responsibility that you have to yourself, to an institution, to your friends, to your supervisors and the structure of things,"[4] said Ryan George, who made his Hippodrome debut in *Defiance*. Although Ryan moved to New York City after graduating UF later that spring, he has occasionally returned to act in and direct Hippodrome plays up through 2023.

Mary Hausch described *Defiance* as "powerful and explosive. The actors successfully carry out the play's high drama factor, but without being overtly dramatic. I think that's one of the things we worked really hard for.... We did a lot of research and did a lot of preparations. We talked to the Marines, a military lawyer, and some other people to get a feeling of what it was like in that time."[5] She had Marine veterans visit the theater to help the Hipp get everything right, from protocol to costumes.

Arline Greer called it "a moving piece of theater that engages the audience from start to finish, commands our attention and wages a successful campaign for our hearts and minds."[6]

Defiance opened February 26 and played through March 21.

Around the World in 80 Days

Jules Verne wrote the novel *Around the World in 80 Days* in 1872, a time when that seemed like an impossible feat, although Nellie Bly, famed journalist for the *New York World*, made the entire trip in seventy-two days in 1889.

A lavish film adaptation released in 1956 won five Academy Awards, including Best Picture. In 2001, playwright Mark Brown adapted the book for a five-actor stage production. This was the version Lauren Caldwell chose for the Hippodrome's next play, which ran from April 16–May 9.

Photo: Michael Eaddy

Jessica Ires Morris, carried by fellow cast members Kevin-Michael Chu, D. Christopher Wert, Ric Rose, and Brendan Powers (who plays Phileas Fogg), in *Around the World in 80 Days*.

The story begins when a finicky, wealthy Englishman, Phileas Fogg, bets the members of his club that he can travel completely around the world and return to London in eighty days. Accompanied by his manservant and pursued by an inept detective who has mistaken him for a bank robber, Fogg crosses continents and seas, rides elephants and trains, saves a young Hindu widow, and makes it home in time to win the bet. Along the way are mishaps and misadventures.

Lacking Hollywood's special effects budget and cast of thousands, Lauren had to use all of the Hippodrome's ingenuity. Actor Brendan Powers played Phileas Fogg, but the other four cast members, Ric Rose, Jessica Ires Morris, D. Christopher Wert, and Kevin-Michael Chu, had to collectively take on twenty-six roles. The cast simulated riding an elephant by bouncing on a trampoline. Riding a train was accomplished by holding glow-in-the-dark Hula-Hoops. And the actors used every part of the stage, including "a couple of places we've never used," Lauren said. "The result is a show in constant flux, with the action moving from the stage to the wings to the audience to the production booth and back."[7]

"Everything has to be so fast and fluid," Brendan Powers said.[8]

"I can honestly say that I have never seen a more engaging, creative venture than this," wrote Sherwin Mackintosh in his review. "The cast and crew were at their very best, and every detail was in place. It was truly magical. Lauren Caldwell's vision is endless and her production staff is perfect in the execution of this resourceful, raucous, ridiculous romp."[9]

Summer—Madness Again

While the Great Recession, as it was called, was easing, future grant money remained uncertain. So, the logical thing to do was to bring back Paul Pörtner's *Shear Madness*. It had been a hit "with legs," as they say in the theatre world. It had its run in 2003 extended through most of the summer.

Shear Madness 2010, featuring (l-r) Gregg Jones, Sara Morsey, Cameron Francis, Jennifer Smith, Kevin-Michael Chu, and Matthew Lindsay.

Photo: Michael Eaddy

Since the play's owners stipulated directors must have attended *Shear Madness* School and Mary Hausch already had, she took on the directing duties. Three of her 2003 cast members were available: Gregg Jones as Detective Rossetti, Sara Morsey as Mrs. Schubert, and Cameron Francis, although he switched to the role of Tony this time.

Kevin-Michael Chu stepped into the part of Eddie, which Cameron had vacated. Joining him were recent Hippodrome favorites Jennifer Smith as Barbara DeMarco, the saucy stylist, and Matthew Lindsay as Mikey, the detective's assistant.

The show ran from June 4–July 11. It had good attendance and received great reviews. *Sun* theater critic Dick Maxwell wrote, "The place to go for a good laugh is the Hippodrome State Theatre, which opened its summer show *Shear Madness* last Friday. The theatre was packed the night I saw the show and everyone was having a wonderful time. Director Mary Hausch has assembled a particularly bright and skilled group of actors... Francis is delightful in his role as the campy salonista, Tony. He is a bundle of energy with immaculate comic timing. Smith turns in another sterling performance as the anti-ingenue DeMarco, a saucy tart. Chu interacts well with members of the audience who seek to throw suspicion on him. Morsey is a versatile actor who is so believable in every role she assumes; the range of her acting talent is remarkable. Jones, as Rossetti, is a force to be reckoned with. He holds the play together and puts it through its paces. Lindsay, who does a great job as Mikey, gets a laugh with almost every move he makes."[10]

Season Thirty-eight

The Hippodrome's thirty-eighth season took flight with *Boeing Boeing*, a Tony Award-winning farce adapted by Beverly Cross and Francis Evans from a French play by Marc Camoletti. The story takes place in the stylish 1960s-era apartment of Bernard (Jason Weiss), an American architect (and playboy) living in Paris. He is successfully juggling three airline hostesses, each of whom believes she is his fiancée. Bernard manages this by monitoring international flight schedules to know when each is arriving and departing. Bernard's French housekeeper, Bertha (Sara Morsey), helps keep the whole sham organized and running smoothly, against her better judgment.

(l-r) Nichole Hamilton, Jason Weiss, Sara Morsey, Candace Clift, Cameron Francis, and Kim Mead in *Boeing Boeing*.

Photo: Michael Eaddy

Marilyn Wall's costumes for the three women wouldn't fly today but were exactly the kind of thing stewardesses had to wear at the time—stiletto heels, miniskirt suits, and tight blouses. They also nicely complimented the figures of actresses Nichole Hamilton, Candace Clift, and Kim Mead, who played flight attendants from three different countries.

Carlos Asse designed a gorgeous two-level set of a mod apartment with seven doors on the upper level. These are integral to the comedy, which arises after Bernard's friend Robert (Cameron Francis) arrives in Paris unexpectedly and catches on to Bernard's scheme. When a flight cancellation causes an overlap in the women's itineraries, there is much dashing in and out of the upstairs doors as Bernard tries to convince each woman that the other women are with his friend. Robert is blindsided by the American Gloria, charmed by the voluptuous Italian Gabriela, and kissed by the lovestruck German Gretchen—not once, but twice.

Director Lauren Caldwell said nailing the door choreography was an important factor in keeping the high energy and fast rhythm of the show, which moved swiftly with witty dialogue. Aside from the doors, the actors also had to master their accents. "I don't think I've ever been in a play with this many accents," said Sara Morsey, who played Bertha with a heavy French accent. "It's a challenge because you have to keep yourself from falling into the accent of the person you're talking to."[11]

Arline Greer called it a "sure laugh-getter. It's been said that timing is everything in a good farce. Luckily, Lauren Caldwell ... has the timing set perfectly. Morsey as the maid, Francis as the beleaguered Robert, and Mead, playing Gretchen as if she had leapt straight out of Richard Wagner's 'Die Walkyrie,' all shine. If you love farce, *Boeing Boeing* is your cup of tea ... a well-played farce and a happy, laughter-filled beginning to the new Hippodrome season."[12]

The hilarious farce soared from September 1–26.

Passing of a Comic Great

Mike Beistle, a much-beloved actor who had appeared in over thirty-five Hippodrome plays, passed away on September 30, 2010, due to complications from diabetes. Mike was seventy. A memorial was held for him on the Hippodrome mainstage on November 28.

"Mike Beistle was just as larger-than-life as the characters he played on the Hippodrome State Theatre's stage," said the *Gainesville Sun*.[13]

Rusty Salling added, "Future actors may ask, 'Who was Mike Beistle?' And then, old people like me can say, 'Well, let me tell you...'"[14]

Yet Another *Dracula*

The Hippodrome had already staged *Dracula* thrice before—each adaptation by a different playwright. But the wildly popular *Twilight Saga* novels and the HBO series *True Blood* had created a modern obsession with vampires. So Lauren Caldwell found a script by Mac Wellman and brought the undead Count back to the stage for a fourth time, telling the story in a non-linear way. "We know that audiences know the story of *Dracula*," Lauren said. "What makes this particular version so appealing is our chance to offer a different way of telling that story."[15]

Lauren retained five of her *Boeing Boeing* cast members: Nichole Hamilton as Lucy, Cameron Francis as Dr. Seward, Jason Weiss as Jonathan Harker, Candace Clift as Mina, and Kim Mead as a Vampyrette. The role of Dracula went to Justin Sease, with Eric Mendenhall as Van Helsing, Matthew Lindsay as Quincey, and Filipe Valle Costa as Simmons. Isa Garcia-Rose and Jennifer Smith brought the total of dancing Vampyrettes to three.

Although the characters' names were familiar, scenic designer Kent Barrett's set of two parallel multi-level scaffolds and numerous ladders was not. Actress Jennifer Smith called it "a jungle gym for adults."[16]

"It's hard not to let this set upstage you," said Nichole Hamilton.[17] The physical aspect of the show, which involved constantly climbing up and down ladders and jumping from level to level, provided an extra challenge. "It's an actor's dream, but,

Justin Sease plays the title character in *Dracula*. Behind him are (seated) Isa Garcia-Rose, Nichole Hamilton, Jennifer Smith, Candace Clift, Kim Mead, (standing) Cameron Francis, Matthew Lindsay, Filipe Valle Costa, Eric Mendenhall, and Jason Weiss.

Photo: Michael Eaddy

remembering the lines while exploring the space is a challenge," Nichole said.[18] Not to mention avoiding the IV bags of stage blood wrapped around the scaffold's dingy bars.

"Interestingly enough, for a story called *Dracula*, the actual character of Dracula is felt more than seen," wrote the reporter from the *Gainesville Sun*. "This requires a commanding physical presence from Justin Sease, who plays Dracula. It is a testament to the entire cast that the ominous presence of Dracula permeates each scene, even though Sease is at the back of the stage for much of the play."[19]

"It's kind of great that I get to sit up there and pretend like I control everything," Justin said.[20]

When Dracula finally takes action, Jennifer Smith told the *Independent Florida Alligator*, "It's going to be raining blood—literally."[21]

Dracula ran from October 15–November 17. In the middle of the run, Dance Alive National Ballet put on a dance production of *Dracula*. The Hippodrome joined them in offering a two-for-one deal, giving patrons the opportunity to see both performances.

Something Different for Christmas

In addition to their thirty-third annual production of *A Christmas Carol*, the Hippodrome presented *This Wonderful Life*, a unique one-man version of the classic Frank Capra film *It's a Wonderful Life*. The play, conceived by Mark Setlock and written by Steve Murray, recreates the entire holiday movie with one actor playing George Bailey and all thirty-one characters. And it worked.

If you are among the few who don't have this film indelibly imprinted in your mind, it is about a desperate man who attempts to end his life by jumping off a bridge. An apprentice angel stops him and helps him to see how different the world would have been if he'd never existed.

Photo: Michael Eaddy

Christopher Swan plays George Bailey and thirty-one other characters in *This Wonderful Life*.

Reviewer Sherwin Mackintosh wrote: "Five minutes into the show, when veteran actor Christopher Swan delivered a perfect Jimmy Stewart imitation... this critic was hooked... [Swan] cleverly channels more than thirty characters. Christopher Swan seamlessly weaves the characters together as we watch the movie in our mind come to life on stage. At the conclusion of Swan's ninety-minute performance, the entire audience rose, en masse as on cue, recognizing a tour de force with a standing ovation. What a wonderful way to welcome the holiday season with a unique retelling of a classic story. Don't miss it. You'll become a believer too."[22]

This Wonderful Life, directed by Lauren Caldwell, opened on November 26, and *A Christmas Carol*, directed by Sara Morsey, opened the following day. Both shows played through December 19.

1 Lashonda Stinson Curry, "Stranger on the Phone," *Gainesville Sun*, January 7, 2010.

2 Ibid.

3 Dick Kerekes, review of *Dead Man's Cell Phone*, by Sarah Ruhl, directed by Lauren Caldwell, Hippodrome Theatre, Gainesville, FL, *EntertainingU*, January 11, 2010.

4 Lashonda Stinson Curry, "Loyalty, Duty, Put to the Test," *Gainesville Sun*, February 25, 2010.

5 Ibid.

6 Arline Greer, review of *Defiance*, by John Patrick Shanley, directed by Mary Hausch, Hippodrome Theatre, Gainesville, FL, *Gainesville Sun*, March 4, 2010.

7 Travis Atria, "Long Trip with Many Characters," *Gainesville Sun*, April 15, 2010.

8 Ibid.

9 Sherwin Mackintosh, review of *Around the World in 80 Days*, by Mark Brown, directed by Lauren Caldwell, Hippodrome Theatre, Gainesville, FL, *Gainesville Sun*, April 22, 2010.

10 Dick Maxwell, review of *Shear Madness*, by Marilyn Abrams and Bruce Jordan, directed by Mary Hausch, Hippodrome Theatre, Gainesville, FL, *Gainesville Sun*, June 6, 2010.

11 Lashonda Stinson Curry, "Mod-era Airplane Antics," *Gainesville Sun*, September 2, 2010.

12 Arline Greer, review of *Boeing Boeing*, by Beverly Cross and Francis Evans, directed by Lauren Caldwell, Hippodrome Theatre, Gainesville, FL, *Gainesville Sun*, September 9, 2010.

13 Jackie Alexander, "Late Actor, Teacher Honored at Hipp," *Gainesville Sun*, November 29, 2010.

14 Ibid.

15 Lauren Caldwell, *Dracula* playbill, Hippodrome Theatre, Gainesville, FL, 2010.

16 Benjamin Evans, "There Will Be Blood," *Independent Florida Alligator*, October 14, 2010.

17 Ibid.

18 Travis Atria, "Revamping a Classic Tale," *Gainesville Sun*, October 14, 2010.

19 Ibid.

20 Ibid.

21 Benjamin Evans, "There Will Be Blood," *Independent Florida Alligator*, October 14, 2010.

22 Sherwin Mackintosh, review of *This Wonderful Life*, by Steve Murray, directed by Lauren Caldwell, Hippodrome Theatre, Gainesville, FL, *Gainesville Sun*, December 9, 2010.

2011

Happy Days

Photo: Michael Eaddy

End Days cast. Clockwise from Elvis: Filipe Valle Costa, David Sitler, Jennifer Smith, Sara Morsey, and Mark Woollett (as Jesus).

End Days, written by Deborah Zoe Laufer, would appear to be a comedy about religion, but its real message is that you can be happy if you've a mind to. The action takes place in the New York City apartment of the Stein family sometime after the destruction of the World Trade Center. The head of the family, Arthur, worked in the building and slipped into a depression after the incident, never leaving home. His wife, Sylvia, is a former Orthodox Jew who has turned Christian evangelist and walks and talks with Jesus (literally). Their petulant, hostile teenage daughter, Rachel, wears Goth makeup and eschews both religions. Sylvia believes the "end days" are at hand, and she's ready to ascend in the rapture so long as she can bring Rachel.

Into this scene comes Nelson, an adolescent Elvis impersonator with such a hopeless crush on Rachel that he wants to convert from Christianity to Judaism. Nelson gives Rachel some books by Stephen Hawking, and the scientist makes a brief appearance.

If it all sounds wacky, it pleased Arline Greer, who wrote: "Lauren Caldwell has given her usual expert direction to a fine group of ensemble actors, however. Credit David Sitler for playing the morose-but-salvageable Arthur with a slowly awakening zest for life. Sara Morsey, as Sylvia, gives a moving performance as she struggles to choose between faith and family. Jennifer Smith, as Rachel, is totally delightful both when she's a brat and when she's daddy's little girl. Mark Woollett is very funny in the dual roles of Jesus and Stephen Hawking.

"But the show's treat is Filipe Valle Costa, who plays Nelson. Costa makes Nelson a completely loveable character; inquisitive, accepting, giving, passionate, kind. Speaking with the author's voice, he is saying that it's all good: Christianity, Judaism, science, faith. Whatever road you take, you can choose to be happy."[1]

End Days played January 7–30.

Monkey Business

Not since 1986's *Little Shop of Horrors* had puppets been characters in a mainstage production. That changed with the regional premiere of David Zellnik's *Serendib*. But whereas *Little Shop*'s Audrey II was an overgrown potted plant who stayed in one place, *Serendib*'s puppet monkeys hopped around the stage and interacted in monkey fashion.

Photo: Michael Eaddy

The cast of *Serendib*. Top: Kim Mead and Justin Sease. Middle: Wayman Ezell and Trenell Mooring. Bottom: Michael Gill, Indika Senanayake, and Matthew Lindsay.

Set in the jungles of Sri Lanka, in impressive temple ruins designed by Kent Barrett, one female and two male scientists are studying the behavior of toque macaque monkeys to see if they can document whether the creatures are happy. They have agreed to be joined by a BBC video crew making a nature show. However, when the videographers arrive, they bring with them a Russian researcher with diametrically opposed views. They do this to stir things up with the intention of turning the documentary into a sensationalized reality show.

The male scientists vie for the affections of their Sri Lankan peer, Dr. Anna Sunilagatte, played by New York actress Indika Senanayake, a native of Sri Lanka. In a parallel plot, the actors use puppets to portray monkeys in the midst of their mating season. The monkeys convey their thoughts through lines spoken by the actors manipulating them.

New York puppet designer Emily DeCola created realistic-looking life-size monkey puppets. The Hippodrome brought in master puppet choreographer Jessica Scott to train the actors to make the puppets act realistically. "We're the first regional theatre in the country to do [*Serendib*]," said director Lauren Caldwell, "so this is only the second time it's ever been done so it's a coup for us."[2]

Playwright David Zellnik also came down to conduct a writing workshop and answer questions from the theatre audience following a Sunday matinee performance of the play. Cast member Indika Senanayake had consulted on the off-Broadway production. The roles of her fellow scientists were played by Matthew Lindsay and Wayman Ezell. Trenell Mooring played the research team's cook. Michael Gill was the Russian antagonist. Justin Sease and Kim Mead played the BBC video crew. All of them, except Kim Mead, had dual roles as monkey puppeteers.

Actor Michael Gill, who had worked with puppets before, said, "I've never worked with a puppet like this ever and I've never had to be as physically contorted with a puppet like this for that long of a period of time. It's very physically exhausting."[3]

The play deals with several issues, including how the influx of human activity affects the study's monkey subjects. It compares how the group of mixed-gender humans and the troop of monkeys react under stress, and which group winds up having the most influence. The Hippodrome's performance also left the audience wondering who is studying whom when, at the end of the play, a spotlight illuminated a monkey on the wall slowly gazing around the audience.

"Acting by the diverse cast is excellent," wrote theater critic Dick Maxwell.[4]

Serendib ran from February 25–March 20. During its run, on March 3, the Hippodrome lent its mainstage to professional ballerina Ani Collier to showcase her latest contemporary dance installment, *The Nightingale and the Rose*, based on an Oscar Wilde fable of the same name. She cleverly worked her choreography to make use of the *Serendib* set.

Monty Python Hitchcock

The Hippodrome's next play was Patrick Barlow's parody *The 39 Steps*, which he had based on Alfred Hitchcock's film version of the novel by John Buchan. Although Barlow replicated the film almost scene by scene, he did it for laughs. Director Lauren Caldwell said, "It's a combination of two iconic things: Alfred Hitchcock and Monty Python."[5] Barlow's adaptation had won the Drama Desk Award and two Tony Awards.

Photo: Michael Eaddy

Jessica Ires Morris, Justin Sease, Jason Weiss, and Ric Rose in a scene from *The 39 Steps*.

Unlike the large-cast movie, the play called for three actors, Justin Sease, Ric Rose, and Jessica Ires Morris, to play dozens of roles. Switching costumes and accents in split seconds, they portrayed everything from a Scottish hotelier to a thorn bush. The fourth actor, Jason Weiss, played the hero, Richard Hannay, and stayed in the same role throughout. The actors had to simulate all the elements of an action thriller—jumping from bridges, dashing atop a moving train, plunging out windows. "There's no respite," said Jason Weiss. "It's a killer. I've been acting professionally since 1998, and this is by far the most strenuous show I've ever done."[6]

The play begins when Richard Hannay, a bored gentleman of leisure with comical, suave good humor, finds himself at a local music hall. There, he meets a beautiful spy who agrees to go home with him for the night. The next morning, he finds her murdered. Fearing he could be blamed, he flees to Scotland with police, secret agents, and suspicious characters on his trail. After ninety minutes of theatrics, the chase winds up back in the music hall where Hannay's adventure began.

Arline Greer summed it up: "Shots are fired. The bad guys get theirs and the good guys still have a surprise or two left. The technical work by all involved is sheer wizardry and although there are more giggles than belly laughs in the Hippodrome's *The 39 Steps*, the show makes for an entertaining evening.... Rose and Sease get completely inside every role they play, no matter how silly or ridiculous. The truth of their acting brings the audience along with them, breathless, even as they giggle at the foolishness on stage."[7]

The 39 Steps ran from April 15–May 8.

Summertime

Summer at the Hippodrome often meant a musical. In 2011, that was *Suds,* created by Melinda Gilb, Steve Gunderson, and Bryan Scott. It was directed by Lauren Caldwell, with Jean McCormick as musical director and Ric Rose as choreographer. It was billed as "The rockin' 60's musical soap opera." In other words, a jukebox musical loaded with forty-eight golden oldies like "Please Mr. Postman," "Are You Lonesome Tonight," and "It's My Party."

Lauren brought back singers Kelly Atkins and Billy Sharpe, who had performed in many previous Hippodrome musicals. Rounding out the cast of four were New York City actresses Wendi Stoltzfus and Lia Sumerano. Though they were making their Hippodrome debut in *Suds*, both had performed some of the same musicals elsewhere as Kelly and Billy had at the Hipp.

Suds cast: Wendi Stoltzfus, Lia Sumerano, Billy Sharpe, and Kelly Atkins.

Photo: Michael Eaddy

The lighter-than-soap-bubble plot concerns a laundromat employee, Cindy, who has been dumped by her pen-pal boyfriend and notified by the IRS that she owes thousands of dollars. She has also learned her beloved cat has been run over. What's a girl to do but commit suicide in a washing machine? She is saved by two angels who are assigned to awaken her lust for life and hope for love. This is accomplished by singing songs that topped the charts in the 1960s and have lyrics that support the storyline.

"It's nostalgic," said Lauren Caldwell. "It brings home memories if you know this music.... You can't escape the fact that they're all classics. They're just good, good songs."[8]

Carlos Asse designed a pink-and-turquoise set, complete with three working washing machines and three dryers. Marilyn Wall costumed the women in bright full skirts with Billy in a postal uniform and later a white tux. She also outfitted the whole cast in gold for the finale. Once he did his turn as the postman, Billy returned in the second act to sing "Secret Agent Man" and other tunes.

Although she said "*Suds* is all fluff," Arline Greer also called it "good fun in the best tradition of the Hippodrome's summer musical shows. Blessed with strong voices to match their strong bodies, all three actresses make the story move along from one circumstance to the next. All four performers are talented singers and move well to Ric Rose's athletic choreography."[9]

Suds opened June 3 and was a success, held over through July 31.

Season Thirty-nine

To open their thirty-ninth season, Mary Hausch chose to direct *God of Carnage* by Yasmina Reza, translated by Christopher Hampton. It had won the Tony Award for Best Play and was the third Hampton translation of a Reza play that Mary had directed. The prior two were *ART* and *Life × 3*.

Photo: Michael Eaddy

(l-r) Tim Altmeyer, Kim Mead, Benjamin Burdick, and Jessica Ires Morris in a scene from *God of Carnage*.

On a set recreating an upscale yuppie apartment, two couples meet to discuss a playground scuffle between their sons that got out of hand. Alan and Annette Raleigh's child had hit the son of Michael and Veronica Novack with a stick and knocked out two of his teeth.

Tim Altmeyer and Kim Mead played the Raleighs. He is an obnoxious lawyer more attached to his cell phone than to his family, and she is in wealth management. Michael Novack (played by Benjamin Burdick) is a wholesaler and his wife Veronica (Jessica Ires Morris) is writing a book about genocide in the Darfur region of Africa.

The intent of the couples' meeting is to discuss the matter in a civilized manner and write out what the boys need to do to accept responsibility. But as the evening goes on, Veronica exaggerates the harm, claiming her son has been disfigured and his face bashed in. The parents become increasingly childish and exacerbate the situation. Calm discussion suddenly turns into screaming, and the meeting degenerates into dark comic chaos—leaving no book un-thrown, no vase standing.

"It's almost like choreography, in a way,"[10] said Mary Hausch, describing how she mapped out the placement of various props to ensure a seamless flow for the actors' moments of rage and hysteria.

"It's a much more detailed, technical approach to acting," noted actor Benjamin Burdick. "You have to make it feel natural, but you have to make sure every book or pillow is in the right place at the right time."[11] Benjamin, a Yale graduate and L.A.-based actor, was making his Hippodrome debut. Playing his wife, Jessica Ires Morris was also based in L.A., but this was her sixth Hippodrome play. She and Benjamin were a couple in real life, which, she said, "makes tense onstage moments easier. It also brings an added level of believability. When you're actually with someone, you can be more brutal on stage because you trust them."[12] Undoubtedly, Jessica referred to a moment in the play when her character leaps on her husband's back in frustration.

Equal in talent to their L.A.-based cast members were Kim Mead and Tim Altmeyer. Kim was a Cal State and UF graduate based in New York and had frequently returned to Gainesville to play roles in a half dozen Hippodrome plays since 2008's *College: The Musical*. Tim was a Hippodrome regular and a professor of theatre at UF. He'd done his turn on Broadway performing with such luminaries as Al Pacino, Dianne Wiest, David Strathairn, Marisa Tomei, Valerie Harper, and Kathleen Turner.

Together, the foursome's portrayal of civilized adults' reversion to primitive childhood behaviors underscored Reza's point that there is a savage element buried within even grownups. *God of Carnage* played at the Hippodrome September 2–25.

Ghost Story from Henry James

For a Halloween-spirited thriller, Lauren Caldwell settled on *The Turn of the Screw*, which is based on a novella by Henry James. This adaptation by Jeffrey Hatcher had premiered in Portland, Maine, in 1996 and was produced off-Broadway in 1999.

Photo: Michael Eaddy

Nichole Hamilton and Christopher Swan in *The Turn of the Screw*.

The two-actor play starred Nichole Hamilton and Christopher Swan. She portrayed a young, pretty governess hired to look after two orphan children in a remote manor house. But the governess learns she is not alone. The ghosts of two people once familiar at the manor haunt the house and the children. Christopher Swan played four characters: the master, the housekeeper, the ten-year-old boy, and the ghostly Quint—not much of a challenge after playing thirty-two parts in *This Wonderful Life*.

Henry James intentionally left the end of his story enigmatic. Lauren Caldwell asked, "Did the governess see the ghosts? Were the ghosts real or were they a fabrication of her tilted imagination?" Lauren added, "If the audience leaves the show and debates its meaning over a glass of wine, she's done her job."[13]

"I fell in love with [the show]," Nichole said, "because it's so complex and ambiguous and leaves you with so many questions."[14]

Reviewer Dick Maxwell pointed out that "the greatest source of fear still remains the human imagination. [Director Lauren Caldwell] has been able to meet the challenge by guiding exceptional actors and capturing the attention and imagination of the audience. The result is an unforgettable evening of theater."[15]

The Turn of the Screw ran from October 14–November 6.

Christmas Shows

For 2011, the Hippodrome reprised the previous season's production of *This Wonderful Life* with actor Christopher Swan once again performing all the roles. It opened November 25 and ran through December 23.

A Christmas Carol had a shorter run that year, opening November 26 and closing December 17. It was their thirty-fourth production of the show.

1 Arline Greer, review of *End Days*, by Deborah Zoe Laufer, directed by Lauren Caldwell, Hippodrome Theatre, Gainesville, FL, *Gainesville Sun*, January 13, 2011.
2 Lashonda Stinson Curry, "Stage Full of Monkeys," *Gainesville Sun*, February 24, 2011.
3 Ibid.
4 Dick Maxwell, review of *Serendib*, by David Zellnik, directed by Lauren Caldwell, Hippodrome Theatre, Gainesville, FL, *Gainesville Sun*, March 3, 2011.
5 Travis Atria, "Characters on the Climb," *Gainesville Sun*, April 14, 2011.
6 Ibid.
7 Arline Greer, review of *The 39 Steps*, by Patrick Barlow, directed by Lauren Caldwell, Hippodrome Theatre, Gainesville, FL, *Gainesville Sun*, April 21, 2011.
8 Alexandra Hamilton, "Learning to Have Lust for Life, Hope for Love," *Gainesville Sun*, June 2, 2011.
9 Arline Greer, review of *Suds*, by Melinda Gilb, Steve Gunderson, and Bryan Scott, directed by Lauren Caldwell, Hippodrome Theatre, Gainesville, FL, *Gainesville Sun*, June 9, 2011.
10 Sara Watson, "Adults Behaving Badly," *Gainesville Sun*, September 1, 2011.
11 Ibid.
12 Ibid.
13 Ibid.
14 Ibid.
15 Dick Maxwell, review of *The Turn of the Screw*, by Jeffrey Hatcher, directed by Lauren Caldwell, Hippodrome Theatre, Gainesville, FL, *Gainesville Sun*, October 19, 2011.

2012

Siren's Song

In Greek mythology, Sirens were feminine beings with voices so alluring that their song caused sailors to crash their ships on rocky islands. At the Hippodrome, *Sirens* was the January play. It is a modern rom-com—with a twist—written by Deborah Zoe Laufer, author of the prior January's play, *End Days*.

Sam, a songwriter, has lost his creative muse, and his twenty-five-year marriage to Rose has lost its spark. When they first met, Sam wrote a song about her that became a mega-hit. He's written others since then, but none that have equaled his first success. To rekindle things, they celebrate their anniversary with a cruise of the Greek Isles.

Aboard the ship, Rose learns that to find inspiration, Sam has been "friending" young women on Facebook and meeting up with them. "Only for coffee," he protests. She declares that their marriage is over. While she is giving him a piece of her mind, he hears the Siren's song and jumps overboard.

Sam washes up on the island of a pretty but bored Siren who has no interest in middle-aged Sam and only sings when a ship comes near. She's also vacuous—a battery-operated box given to her by the gods occupies all the space in her small brain. Soon Sam realizes youthful passion isn't everything. He offers her new batteries for her box in exchange for returning him to Rose.

Sam arrives at their apartment to find Rose dressing for a date with Richard, her high school crush. Richard is smarmy, so the date doesn't go well. But her subsequent reconciliation with Sam inspires him to write a new song.

Underlying the humorous and witty dialogue is a story of love lost and regained between two people who have already shared a lifetime together. Laufer's script also provides an interesting comparison between the spark of love and that of artistic creativity.

Filipe Valle Costa, who had played Elvis-impersonator Nelson in *End Days*, played Rose's unfortunate date, Richard. New York actress Lauren Nordvig was the Siren.

Photo: Michael Eaddy

The Siren (Lauren Nordvig) finds Sam (Michael Crider) washed up on shore in *Sirens*.

Michael Crider and Nell Page portrayed Sam and Rose. They had last shared the stage twenty-one years earlier in *Les Liaisons Dangereuses*. Michael had spent the intervening years appearing on television series in New York and L.A. and, although Nell had seemed to be a part of every Hippodrome season, she was actually making her return after three years away.

"The best news of the evening is that Nell Page is back at the Hipp," wrote Arline Greer. "Laufer has taken the serious theme of marriage monotony between a long-married couple and turned it into a light-hearted comedy ... with the actors

Lauren Caldwell has directed so skillfully ... *Sirens* gives audiences an evening of fun and good-natured comedy."[1]

When *Sirens* opened on January 13, patrons had the opportunity to meet the playwright. She had also attended the previous night's preview and answered audience questions in a session following the performance. *Sirens* played until February 5.

Move Over, Neil Simon

The Hippodrome's next comedy, *Over the Tavern* by Tom Dudzick, has been called the Catholic equivalent of Neil Simon's *Lost in Yonkers* and *Brighton Beach Memoirs*.

Scene from *Over the Tavern* featuring (l-r) Whitney Humphrey, Cameron Francis, Taylor Badri, Sara Morsey, Filipe Valle Costa, Paxton Sanchez, and Nichole Hamilton.

Photo: Michael Eaddy

The story is set in 1959 in Buffalo, New York, where twelve-year-old Rudy lives with his family in a tiny apartment above his father's tavern and attends Catholic school. Rudy was played by real-life eighth grader Paxton Sanchez. Another eighth grader, Whitney Humphrey, portrayed Rudy's mentally challenged brother, Georgie. Both boys were veterans of Hippodrome Summer Spectacular camps and multiple productions of *A Christmas Carol*.

Rudy is a smart, wise-cracking kid who upsets his ruler-wielding, palm-whacking teacher, Sister Clarissa (Sara Morsey). When he tells her he'd rather shop around for a more fun religion, she decides a home visit is in order. But there's a lot going on in the family's cramped apartment.

Rudy's father, Chet (Cameron Francis), is a physically and psychologically wounded man who comes home from work in a bad mood and yells at his kids and long-suffering wife, Ellen (Nichole Hamilton). A running joke is that Chet constantly forgets to bring home the spaghetti for dinner. Besides Georgie, whom it's Rudy's responsibility to care for, he has two other siblings. Annie (Taylor Badri) is shy and confused by sexual awakening. Oldest brother Eddie (Filipe Valle Costa) is in adolescent rebellion.

All hell breaks loose when Sister Clarissa's visit puts Chet in opposition to his own children and their fiercely protective mother. "Centuries-old dogma becomes pitted against mother love, and Sister Clarissa had best move to the side of the angels who always win out in this cheerily recognizable conflict," wrote Arline Greer. "Audiences grin ear-to-ear at this Hippodrome production of *Over the Tavern*. It's a happily-ever-after show directed like a swiftly moving train by Lauren Caldwell."[2]

Over the Tavern was a hit. With its run extended an extra week, it played March 2–25.

Thoroughly Modern Willie

William Shakespeare's words are so revered that people forget he wrote for all levels of society. Along with lofty passages, he also tossed in sexual innuendo, rude humor, and fart jokes. Nowhere is that more evident than in *A Midsummer Night's Dream*, the Hippodrome production from April 11 through May 13.

"The great thing about Shakespeare is you can put your own stamp on it; you can update it," said director Lauren Caldwell. That is especially true of *A Midsummer Night's Dream*, which, unlike most of the Bard's plays, doesn't rely on historical places or characters. "This one appeals to so many ages," she said.[3]

A Midsummer Night's Dream cast in the hybrid piano/ sports car. Front left: Isa Garcia-Rose. Row two: Sara Morsey, Mark Woollett, and Cameron Francis. Row three: Candace Clift, Alaina Manchester, and Filipe Valle Costa. Row four: Matt Mercurio, Ryan George, and Matthew Lindsay.

The Hippodrome had last staged *A Midsummer Night's Dream* in 1975. This time, they used a script adaptation by Cass Foster with added music and dance numbers. Lauren also added iPads, Facebook, Twitter, and a hybrid piano/sports car. Even with the modern touches, Shakespeare's words weren't altered. Although the script abridged his text, the plot remained intact.

The play is a romantic comedy that interweaves subplots involving a wedding and three groups of characters. One subplot concerns the lovers who are to be wed and two friends whose love is being thwarted. A second plotline follows a group of amateurs rehearsing a play they are to perform at the wedding. Both groups are in a forest inhabited by the third group, fairies whose king and queen are estranged and using the humans in their domestic squabble.

The Hippodrome's 1975 production had a cast of twenty. This time, Lauren had ten actors, with eight of them playing dual roles. Sara Morsey, Mark Woollett, Filipe Valle Costa, Matthew Lindsay, Ryan George, Alaina Manchester, Matt Mercurio, and Candace Clift each played a human and a fairy character. Isa

Photo: Michael Eaddy

Garcia-Rose and Cameron Francis each played one part. She was an elegant dancing fairy, and he was Puck—a mischievous sprite with magical powers.

"Lauren Caldwell has assembled a terrific cast and incorporated modern technology in an imaginative way that rewards the audience with an absolutely delightful evening of theater," wrote Dick Maxwell. "The Hipp's production ... emphasizes comedy throughout. There is a great deal of physical humor, stage combat, dancing (choreographed by Ric Rose), magic tricks, special effects, and music from opera to rock 'n' roll ... All of this entertainment is crammed into a condensed format that omits some of the original text but leaves enough of it intact that you don't feel slighted."[4]

Marvelous Summer Musical

The Hippodrome musical that summer was *The Marvelous Wonderettes* written by Roger Bean. "We've found that Gainesville really loves revues," director Lauren Caldwell told the *Gainesville Sun*. "We've had this one on the short list for a long time."[5] Bean wove thirty-three hit songs from the 1950s and 1960s into a story about four high school girls who form a group called The Marvelous Wonderettes, perform at their prom, and, ten years later, perform again at their class reunion.

Although the plotline was razor-thin, the script cleverly used song lyrics to drive the tale. But what ultimately kept audiences coming back throughout its eight-week run (June 1–July 29) were the four wonderful Wonderettes.

Cast members Kelly Atkins and Wendi Stoltzfus had performed together the previous year in *Suds*. Katrina Asmar and Diany Rodriguez were new to the Hipp, but both had appeared in musicals elsewhere. Together, they sang intricate four-part harmonies while dancing and keeping a sense of comedic timing.

The Marvelous Wonderettes: (l-r) Katrina Asmar, Wendi Stoltzfus, Kelly Atkins, and Diany Rodriguez.

Photo: Michael Eaddy

"The goal is to make it look easy," Wendi said. "While on the veneer it looks like a cute show, it's one of the most challenging shows I've ever worked on."[6]

Musical director Bryan Mercer started by having them learn the harmonies, then Rachel Anton, who had choreographed *Shout!*, got them doing the dance routines. Once they had all that down, they worked on the comedy bits. These included audience participation when a Wonderette would come up to the seating area and sing a solo to/about some soon-to-be embarrassed patron.

It's no surprise that the *Sun* reviewer wrote, "*The Marvelous Wonderettes* is an irresistible jukebox smash. This cheeky, self-deprecating puff of cotton candy is truly hilarious, with laugh-out-loud moments throughout. By the end of the evening you are thoroughly endeared to these girls and will be best friends forever. Not only are they great individual performers, they also work well as a tight musical ensemble, easily handling the close harmonies, while not missing a beat and keeping us engaged in the story."[7]

Season Forty

On August 31, the Hippodrome led off its fortieth season with *Other Desert Cities* by Jon Robin Baitz. It was another major score for the theatre. *Other Desert Cities* had just finished its Broadway run, where it had been nominated for five Tony Awards and the Pulitzer Prize.

The story takes place at Christmastime, which in Florida's August heat might stretch the imagination, but then again, the play is set in Palm Springs, California, where December temperatures reach ninety degrees. The city is one of the state's wealthiest, and the Wyeth family's parents (Sara Morsey and Peter Thomasson) are among its most politically conservative. Holding directly opposite views are their liberal children and an alcoholic pot-smoking aunt (Lauren Caldwell).

Everything is set in motion when daughter and novelist Brooke arrives home from New York with the news that her next book is a tell-all memoir concerning her deceased brother's involvement with the radical underground and his subsequent suicide. Her parents freak out. Another brother (Matthew Lindsay) and her aunt support her. Eventually, her parents reveal the secret they've been keeping. The brother she thinks is dead is living in Canada; they had helped him escape and faked his suicide note.

Gainesville Sun reviewer Bill Dean wrote, "Rabin's script, balancing early, hilarious barbs with later straight-faced self-disclosures, is true and fair to his characters, offering brimming moments to all. *Other Desert Cities* works as a metaphor of a country that's as divided and torn apart as the family it portrays, yet it primarily pinpoints a family's de facto group therapy session. Their accidental, self-delivered session leads to self-deliverance."[8]

"The play is about love and redemption,"[9] said UF graduate student Michelle Bellaver, who was making her Hippodrome debut as Brooke.

Peter Thomasson, who played the father, Lyman Wyeth, was also new to the Hippodrome but brought decades of acting experience, including film work with Candice Bergen and Christian Slater. In 2010, he'd been named Atlanta's Actor of the Year.

Tim Altmeyer, an assistant professor at UF, had acted in fourteen previous Hippodrome productions, but *Other Desert Cities* was his first turn to direct there. Lauren Caldwell, who traded places with him by taking a role on stage, said, "I've known Tim for a long time. I trust him. We have a keen respect for each other as artists."[10] The show played through September 23.

Photo: Michael Eaddy

Other Desert Cities cast. Front: Lauren Caldwell, Michelle Bellaver, Matthew Lindsay. Back: Sara Morsey and Peter Thomasson.

Audience members in the front row were given umbrellas to protect their clothes when *Carrie* actress Chelsea Sorenson (below) was drenched in blood.

Both photos: Michael Eaddy

Time to Get Bloody

Lauren Caldwell took back the directing reins in October for *Carrie*, Erik Jackson's spoof on the famous novel by Stephen King. The story is about shy social misfit Carrie White, whose mother never told her about the birds and bees until she got her first period and then sent her directly to the prayer closet to purge herself of sin. The mean popular clique makes Carrie the victim of a diabolical prank at the prom that drenches her in blood. When the blood bath finally came, its splash could reach those seated in the front rows. During the second act, cast members passed out umbrellas to patrons in the "splash zone."

Chelsea Sorenson, the actress who played Carrie and was on the receiving end of the blood bath, told the *Gainesville Sun*, "I'm excited. I expect to be pink for a couple of weeks. But I've got my Carrie survivor pack with my shampoo and face soap so I can shower right after."[11]

The show's production staff worked long and hard to get the blood formula just right. It couldn't stain because they had to launder costumes after each show. It couldn't contain soap in case it got into the actress's eyes. And, of course, it had to look like real blood. Once they had the recipe right, they created a vat of the stuff for use throughout the play's run (October 12–November 4). Technical director Michael Eaddy estimated they needed at least a gallon and a half per show.[12]

Ericka Winterrowd played Carrie's nemesis and Sara Morsey was Carrie's uptight, overprotective mother. Other members of the cast included Katrina Asmar, Candace Clift, Matthew Lindsay, Chase Milner, Diany Rodriguez, and Filipe Valle Costa.

Ric Rose choreographed the prom dance consisting of nonstop 1970s disco pop songs.

Popular Christmas Hits

From November 24–December 22, the Hippodrome presented its thirty-fifth production of *A Christmas Carol*. By popular demand, they brought back *A Tuna Christmas* for its eleventh run, starring Matthew Lindsay and Cameron Francis for the third time.

1 Arline Greer, review of *Sirens*, by Deborah Zoe Laufer, directed by Lauren Caldwell, Hippodrome Theatre, Gainesville, FL, *Gainesville Sun*, January 19, 2012.

2 Arline Greer, review of *Over the Tavern*, by Tom Dudzick, directed by Lauren Caldwell, Hippodrome Theatre, Gainesville, FL, *Gainesville Sun*, March 1, 2012.

3 Travis Atria, "Hipp Stages a Modernized *Midsummer Night's Dream*," *Gainesville Sun*, April 12, 2012.

4 Dick Maxwell, review of *A Midsummer Night's Dream*, by William Shakespeare, adapted by Cass Foster, directed by Lauren Caldwell, Hippodrome Theatre, Gainesville, FL, *Gainesville Sun*, April 19, 2012.

5 Travis Atria, "Wondrous Rhythms for Summer," *Gainesville Sun*, May 31, 2012.

6 Ibid.

7 Sherwin Mackintosh, review of *The Marvelous Wonderettes*, by Roger Bean, directed by Lauren Caldwell, Hippodrome Theatre, Gainesville, FL, *Gainesville Sun*, June 14, 2012.

8 Bill Dean, review of *Other Desert Cities*, by Jon Robin Baitz, directed by Tim Altmeyer, Hippodrome Theatre, Gainesville, FL, *Gainesville Sun*, September 13, 2012.

9 Travis Atria, "In Search of the Truth," *Gainesville Sun*, August 30, 2012.

10 Ibid.

11 Rick Allen, "Blood Bath at the Hippodrome," *Gainesville Sun*, October 14, 2012.

12 Ibid.

2013

Venus in Fur

The Hippodrome promised its January play, *Venus in Fur*, written by David Ives, would raise more than a few eyebrows with its discussion of men, women, the struggle for power, and what each sex values in the other. "It's not your everyday play,"[1] said director Lauren Caldwell.

A Broadway hit, the two-character play is about a playwright/director who has adapted an erotic novella for the stage and the actress who auditions to play the lead. The story begins with Thomas (Tim Altmeyer) lamenting the inadequacies of the actresses who have shown up that day to audition when a new actress, Vanda Jordan (Lauren Nordvig), knocks on the door and lets herself in. She's brash, vulgar, and unschooled, and it's hard to imagine that she will please the very particular and exasperated director. But his main character is also named Vanda, so she convinces him to let her try out for the part.

Photo: Michael Eaddy

In *Venus in Fur*, Tim Altmeyer and Lauren Nordvig play a director and actress caught up in the characters they rehearse.

For her audition, Thomas reads the male character's lines—a man so enamored by a woman that he desires to be her slave. Vanda gives a terrific reading and shows astonishing insights into the novel and her character. She has brought a bag of costumes and, beneath her dress, she's wearing a black leather corset. They both become caught up in the characters they are reading. The balance of power is reversed and the actress establishes dominance over the director. As the story continues, the two characters take turns attempting to seduce and manipulate each other.

"It's imperative to him that this thing gets made, and it gets made well," Tim said, explaining his character's motivation. "This guy thinks he knows everything, and in the course of the play, he realizes he does not."[2]

Tantalizing Lauren Nordvig, last seen as the Siren in *Sirens*, said, "I think Vanda is one of those roles every girl will want to play. She's a diamond. She has so many sides to her."[3]

"This play isn't about pornography or S&M," wrote the *Gainesville Sun* reviewer. "More than anything, *Venus in Fur* explores the many ways—both real and imagined—in which love can mess with your mind. Not many small-town theaters have the gumption—some might call it audacity—to produce a Tony Award-winning play like *Venus in Fur*. Of those that do, only a rare few possess the talent and stagecraft to pull it off. Fortunately for us, the Hipp just happens to be one of those rare gems."[4]

The show was a success and held over an extra week, playing from January 11– February 10.

> **Fact:**
>
> *Venus in Furs* is an actual 1870 novel written by Leopold von Sacher-Masoch, from which the word "masochism" is derived.

Family Reunion

Photo: Michael Eaddy

King O' the Moon continues the Pazinski family story with (l-r) Michael Crider as Walter, Ericka Winterrowd as Maureen, Thaddeus Walker as Rudy, Logan Wolfe as Georgie, Josh Price as Eddie, Lauren Roth as Annie, and Nichole Hamilton as Ellen.

Their next play, *King O' the Moon*, was written by Tom Dudzick, whose *Over the Tavern* had been a hit the prior season. The story features the same family a decade later during the 1969 Apollo moon mission. Rudy, who as a child doubted Catholicism, is now in seminary and is involved in peace marches. His brother Eddie is about to be shipped off to Vietnam. Their sister, Annie, is married but on the verge of that Catholic no-no, divorce. Their father has died and their widowed mother, Ellen, runs the tavern in his stead. Mentally challenged Georgie still lives at home. Two new characters in this sequel are Maureen, Eddie's wife, and Walter, Ellen's tavern employee and would-be suitor.

UF theatre professor David Shelton directed, and the entire cast were David's former students. Nichole Hamilton (reprising the role of Ellen) and Michael Crider (who played Walter), had finished their degrees ages ago. Other cast members—Logan Wolfe (Georgie), Josh Price (Eddie), Lauren Roth (Annie), and Ericka Winterrowd (Maureen)—were more recent graduates. Thaddeus Walker (Rudy) was still at UF, but all were experienced theatre professionals. "There is a maturity to them that they have developed,"[5] David said.

The title *King O' the Moon* has a double meaning: the brothers' childhood rivalry over who was king o' the tree house and the moment when the family and all of America watched in awe as the first man stepped onto the surface of the moon. "It was the culmination of the 60s," David said. "All that turmoil, and suddenly there was this heroic event that lifted everyone up for a while."[6]

"It's such a magical thought to put a man on the moon,"[7] said actor Lauren Roth, who had yet to be born when the Eagle landed.

The *Gainesville Sun* reviewer said, "This fast-paced tale, which is well told and well acted, will make you laugh. The exception comes in those small moments when it will strike you mute with awe over the sheer weight of the emotional baggage these people are hauling around with them.... If you couldn't laugh along with these wonderfully eccentric characters, they would make you cry. In the hands of director David Shelton and his cast of talented actors, comedy wins hands down in *King O' the Moon*. This is a finecast and a great emotional stew of a family saga."[8]

The show ran from February 22–March 17.

Robin Hood for Laughs

Lauren Caldwell took Greg Banks's script for *Robin Hood* and injected it with slapstick humor, live music, and modern references. Marilyn Wall costumed the Sherriff of Nottingham in a tasseled cowboy shirt. Robin Hood's sword was a swatch of silk. They played it for laughs but kept its language suitable for family audiences.

"This is a fast-paced laugh fest interrupted only by occasional lapses into Looney Tunes-like action sequences and flickering surrealism," wrote *Sun* critic Ron Cunningham.[9]

Beneath the hijinks of the performance, the well-known story plays out. The greedy are getting the better of the peasants, who are getting poorer; the dashing hero takes from the rich and redistributes it to the destitute. "What I like about this character," said Ric Rose, who played Robin Hood, "is that he may never have existed in real life, but we want him to."[10]

Photo: Michael Eaddy

"If there is an irony here," said the *Sun* critic, "it is that Robin fits Rose so well that Ric could play the part convincingly in a straightforward retelling of the legend. The fair Maid Marian [Nichole Hamilton] does deadpan like she's got the patent on it. Cameron Francis is the hardest-working actor on the set, playing no fewer than four characters, including a very campy Prince John, and a foppish Will Scarlet [also Friar Tuck and Little John]. Matthew Lindsay does a glib turn as the Sheriff of Nottingham. Logan Wolfe in the role of 'a gaggle of evil villains,' Hannah Benitez, and Kenneth Smoak play pretty much everybody else."[11]

Cast of *Robin Hood*: (l-r) Logan Wolfe, Hannah Benitez, Cameron Francis, Ric Rose, Nichole Hamilton, Matthew Lindsay, and Kenneth Smoak.

The untraditional rendering of the outlaw tale, which played from April 12–May 5, inspired audience members to write letters to the *Gainesville Sun* praising its energy, charm, and good, clean entertainment that kept children and adults alike completely enthralled.

Fortieth Anniversary

On May 18, the Hippodrome celebrated its fortieth anniversary with a party. "Over all forty years, we've touched four and a half million people," said Mary Hausch. "We're inviting all of them."[12]

"It's an iconic moment—not just for the Hipp, but for any regional theatre," Lauren Caldwell said. "The fact that we've reached the forty-year mark is truly special ... this anniversary is proof of the bond between the theatre and its audiences."[13]

Sara Morsey added, "Theatres are closing down across the country because of the hostile climate we have toward the arts. It's a celebration of huge tenacity on the part of those who have kept the theatre open."[14]

Certainly foremost responsible for keeping the Hipp alive was Mary Hausch, who, while announcing the fortieth-anniversary party, also revealed that she and General

Manager Rocky Draud would retire after the fortieth season concluded with the next play, *Avenue Q*.

The cast of their summer musical, *Avenue Q*, which was in rehearsal at the time, provided entertainment at the party.

Controversial Puppets

Two weeks after the anniversary party, the Tony Award-winning hit Broadway musical *Avenue Q* opened at the Hippodrome on May 31. The show, produced in partnership with UF, was co-directed by Lauren Caldwell and Charlie Mitchell. Bryan Mercer was musical director and Stephanie Lynge the choreographer. It was the first time in forty years that UF and the Hipp had collaborated on a play—but it would not be the last.

Written by Jeff Whitty, with music and lyrics by Robert Lopez and Jeff Marx, *Avenue Q* combined real-life performers with puppet characters à la *Sesame Street*. But this was no kids' show. These puppets cursed, lauded pornography, and copulated on stage. The playbill contained a legal disclaimer that the show "has not been authorized or approved by the Jim Henson Company or Sesame Workshop."[15] Still, much of the show's ironic humor derives from its contrasts with *Sesame Street*.

Cast of *Avenue Q* human and puppet characters. Standing: (l-r) Brian (Joseph London), Christmas Eve (Grace Choi), puppet Princeton, Michael Hull, puppet Kate Monster, Jennifer Lauren Brown, Gary Coleman (Juanita Green), David Collins, puppet Nicky, and Joel Gennari. Kneeling: Joel Oramas, puppet Trekkie Monster, David Leppert, Marissa Toogood, Bad Idea Bears puppets, and Daniel Fuentes.

Photo: Michael Eaddy

Three of the cast members, dressed in colorful street clothes, portray young people one might see on *Sesame Street* acting as if the puppets are sentient beings. The characters they play are a Japanese therapist named Christmas Eve (Grace Choi); her laid-back fiancé, Brian (Joseph London); and 1960s sitcom star Gary Coleman (Juanita Green), who is now an apartment building superintendent. They sing, dance, and treat the puppets as real while ignoring the puppeteers who, garbed in dark monochrome clothing, share the stage unconcealed.

The majority of puppet characters represent other young adults. Kate, a kindergarten teaching assistant, and Lucy, a sultry vamp, were handled by Jennifer Lauren Brown. Michael Hull controlled the puppets named Princeton, a recent college graduate, and Rod, a gay Republican who lives with Nicky (handled by Joel Gennari).

Animal-like puppets included Trekkie Monster (Joel Oramas), a surly proponent of internet porn, and the Bad Idea Bears, two cute teddy bears who consistently give bad advice. The bears were handled by Daniel Fuentes and Marissa Toogood, who also managed a second puppet, Mrs. Thistletwat. Actors David Collins and David Leppert were also part of the ensemble.

The story concerns young people navigating early adulthood and discovering that real-world problems don't have the happy resolutions found on the children's programs they grew up watching. It begins with Princeton moving into the Avenue Q apartment building and meeting his neighbors. Several songs address adult themes, such as racism, pornography, and homosexuality.

Princeton and Kate go on a date to a club where he meets Lucy, who performs a steamy number. (This required a quick switch of puppets since Jennifer Lauren Brown had both characters.) The Bad Idea Bears get Kate and Princeton drunk, who then end up having enthusiastic, high-decibel sex. To which *Sun* reviewer Ron Cunningham noted, "It needs to be said that sex between puppets is not pretty. It's pretty funny, though."[16]

The next morning, Kate misses her class, gets scolded, and quits her job. Christmas and Brian get married. At the wedding, Nicky outs Rod as gay and gets kicked out of their apartment. Kate catches the wedding bouquet, Princeton panics, and she breaks up with him. Lucy, looking for a place to crash, seduces the rebounding Princeton, upsetting Kate. But just like the happy resolutions promised by their childhood TV, everything works out.

"Never mind that these kids can sing and dance, and that they wear their roles as comfortably as their own skins. The real marvel is that they manage to do all of the above while simultaneously breathing life and personality into the puppets," Cunningham wrote. "*Avenue Q* is an anthem for a generation; the TV-raised millennials who come out of college loaded down in debt only to discover that the careers they assumed would be waiting have gone AWOL."[17]

The run of *Avenue Q* was extended repeatedly that summer, playing for nine-and-a-half weeks until finally closing on August 4.

Mary and Rocky Retire

Mary Hausch and Rocky Draud's retirement became effective August 31. She, a Hippodrome co-founder, had remained at its helm for over forty years. Rocky had worked there for thirty-two years, the last eight as General Manager/Managing Director.

Mary had directed over 120 Hippodrome productions and acted in 50 of its plays. She wrote and directed *An Enchanted Land*, which won Best of the Fringe at the

Edinburgh Festival in Scotland in 1999. Her adaptation of Charles Dickens's *A Christmas Carol* had played annually for sixteen years.

In addition to running the Hippodrome, Mary served as a panelist and reviewer with the National Endowment for the Arts and the Florida Division of Cultural Affairs and was honored numerous times:

- The *Gainesville Sun*'s Star Business Award (1991).

- The *Gainesville Sun*'s Arts Person of the Year Award (1993).

- The National Park Service Award (1998).

- Selected by the *Gainesville Sun* as one of fifty men and women of "notable achievement" in the past 100 years (2000).

- Woman of the Arts by the Gateway Girl Scout Council (2001).

- Volunteer of the Year Award for creating a HITT pilot program in the Caribbean (2003).

- Award for Excellence in Professional Theatre from the Florida Professional Theatre Association (2004).

- Outstanding Alumni Achievement Award from the University of Florida (2004).

- Lifetime Achievement Awards from the City of Gainesville and Alachua County (2008).

- The Florida Theatre Conference Distinguished Career Award (2008).

- University of Florida's Distinguished Alumnus Award (2013).

- Spirit of Gainesville Award (2013).

Rocky told the *Gainesville Sun*, "Mary has the amazing combination of being an incredibly creative, artistic person, as well as a great business mind. And from the very beginning she has understood the way to make a business sustainable."[18] In an earlier interview, he'd said, "Without her financial guidance, the Hipp might not be so hip."[19]

Season Forty-one

The Hippodrome kicked off its forty-first season with *Don't Dress for Dinner*, a madcap sequel to *Boeing Boeing*, which had been a hit three years earlier. Robin Hawdon adapted it from a farce by Marc Camoletti, who had also authored *Boeing Boeing*. Jim Wren directed.

In *Don't Dress for Dinner*, *Boeing Boeing* playboys Bernard and Robert are back. This time, Bernard is married to Jacqueline (Rachel Burttram) but is having an affair with Suzanne (Molly Coyne). Unbeknownst to him, Jacqueline is cheating on him with his best friend Robert. Matthew Lindsay reprised his role as Bernard from

Boeing Boeing. Brendan Powers, last seen as Phileas Fogg in *Around the World in 80 Days*, played Robert.

The action begins when Jacqueline is scheduled to be away for the weekend. Bernard invites Robert and Suzanne to join him at a converted French farmhouse. When Jacqueline learns Robert is coming, she cancels her trip. So Bernard has to get Suzanne to pretend to be the cook, while Suzette (Michelle Bellaver), the real cook, masquerades as Robert's mistress. Enter Suzette's jealous husband, George (Russell Schultz), demanding to know what's going on, forcing everyone to improvise their way through a collision course of assumed identities and outrageous infidelities. Calamity rains down and hilarity reigns.

(l-r) Molly Coyne, Brendan Powers, Rachel Burttram, Michelle Bellaver, and Matthew Lindsay in *Don't Dress for Dinner*.

Photo: Michael Eaddy

The *Sun* theater review called it "a delightful French farce. There are so many tangled webs to weave, doors to slam, tracks to cover, prats to fall, lies to carry, egos to mollify and identities to shift in this fast-moving comedy of indelicate errors that it is a wonder the actors aren't prostrate on the floor by the final act."[20]

Rachel Burttram credited the writing: "It inherently lends itself to the proper delivery of the joke. And when we're galloping, it's wild fun. It feels like we're on a train together—a freight train."[21]

Dinner lasted from August 30–September 22.

New Boss

With Mary Hausch retired, Marilyn Wall was the last co-founder remaining at the theatre, but she hadn't been on the administrative side of things for nearly four decades and had no interest in taking it on. She had an artistic nature and was content to remain Costume Designer-in-Residence. So the Board of Trustees began a search for someone new to replace Mary as Producing Director. They found Thomas Eldon Anderson, who started on October 8.

Michael Curry, chairman of the board, headed up the search committee. They needed to find someone with a unique skill set. "Tom really fit the bill," Mike said. "I knew, first and foremost, the Hipp is a complicated and complex business."[22] He spoke from experience, having been the Hippodrome's business manager in the 1990s.

Tom and his wife, actress Cristine McMurdo-Wallis, had previously lived in Gainesville and acted at the Hipp in 1992's *Prelude to a Kiss*. He'd also appeared in *Lend Me a Tenor* and *Lips Together, Teeth Apart* under his stage name, Thomas Eldon. Since leaving Gainesville in 1992, he'd gained extensive business experience in development, planning, sales, marketing, and venture capital.

In his role as Hippodrome Producing Director, he said he would be an ambassador of the arts to the business community and an ambassador of business to the arts. "One of the things I specialize in is building the bridges," he said. He planned to spend his first few months gathering information to chart a new course for the theatre. Then, in January 2014, he would present a three-to-five-year strategic plan to the board and launch capital campaigns in September of that year.[23]

Zombie Town

For years, October had meant one thing to the Hippodrome: present a Halloween play. However, the *True Blood* and *Twilight Saga*-fueled popularity for vampire tales had started to fade. By 2013, zombies were the rage. "I've never seen such an obsession with zombies," said Lauren Caldwell. "I think they have made a comeback and are [at] the height of their popularity. We are hitting this at a good time."[24] She was referring to Tim Bauer's *Zombie Town: A Documentary Play*, which opened October 11 and played through November 3.

The story follows a group of San Francisco documentarians trying to reconstruct the details of a night when corpses climbed from their graves and terrorized the residents of a tiny Texas town. It's told in a non-linear fashion as different characters recount the zombie attack. Although Bauer's script didn't call for actual zombies, Lauren added them anyway. "I can't imagine a play called *Zombie Town* without zombies," she said.[25] Actors Annelih Hamilton, Joshua Hamilton, Nichole Hamilton, Kenneth Smoak, and Marissa Toogood played the zombies.

The threatened townsfolk were portrayed by Matthew Lindsay, Michelle Bellaver, Christopher Swan, Josh Price, and Logan Wolfe, with each actor performing four or five roles. Ric Rose choreographed the zombies, who danced as though attending a rave—albeit a brain-eating rave.

"In our popular culture, there are basically two ways to spin zombies; for laughs or for gore," wrote theater critic Ron Cunningham. "The Hippodrome Theatre is spinning strictly for

Photo: Michael Eaddy

Cast of *Zombie Town: A Documentary Play*. Standing: Christopher Swan, Marissa Toogood, Matthew Lindsay, Kenneth Smoak, and Josh Price. Sitting: Annelih Hamilton, Logan Wolfe, Nichole Hamilton, Michelle Bellaver, and Joshua Hamilton.

laughs.... Nothing scary about this apocalypse, save the appalling sight of the walking dead rocking out to Led Zeppelin.... All in all, *Zombie Town: A Documentary Play* makes for a thoroughly amusing evening of gore-lite fare."[26]

Christmas Players Switch Roles

2013 was the final year the Hippodrome performed Mary Hausch's adaptation of *A Christmas Carol.* Gregg Jones gave up his long-standing role as Jacob Marley's ghost to direct the show, which ran from November 30–December 21.

The theatre also presented the ever-popular *A Tuna Christmas,* which opened November 29 and ran through December 22. Lauren Caldwell directed Matthew Lindsay and Brendan Powers, who played multiple characters each. This was Brendan's first year in *Tuna.*

1 Tyler Francischine, "When Push Meets Pull," *Gainesville Sun,* January 10, 2013.

2 Ibid.

3 Ibid.

4 Diana Tonnessen, review of *Venus in Fur,* by David Ives, directed by Lauren Caldwell, Hippodrome Theatre, Gainesville, FL, *Gainesville Sun,* January 10, 2013.

5 Travis Atria, "From the Tavern to the Moon," *Gainesville Sun,* February 21, 2013.

6 Ibid.

7 Ibid.

8 Ron Cunningham, review of *King O' the Moon,* by Tom Dudzick, directed by David Shelton, Hippodrome Theatre, Gainesville, FL, *Gainesville Sun,* February 28, 2013.

9 Ron Cunningham, review of *Robin Hood,* by Greg Banks, directed by Lauren Caldwell, Hippodrome Theatre, Gainesville, FL, *Gainesville Sun,* April 18, 2013.

10 Travis Atria, "A Comedic Adventure," *Gainesville Sun,* April 11, 2013.

11 Ron Cunningham, review of *Robin Hood,* by Greg Banks, directed by Lauren Caldwell, Hippodrome Theatre, Gainesville, FL, *Gainesville Sun,* April 18, 2013.

12 Tyler Francischine, "Hitting 40 in Stride," *Gainesville Sun,* May 11, 2013.

13 Ibid.

14 Ibid.

15 *Avenue Q* playbill, Hippodrome Theatre, Gainesville, FL, 2013.

16 Ron Cunningham, review of *Avenue Q,* by Robert Lopez, Jeff Marx, and Jeff Whitty, directed by Lauren Caldwell and Charlie Mitchell, Hippodrome Theatre, Gainesville, FL, *Gainesville Sun,* June 6, 2013.

17 Ibid.

18 Bill Dean, "Mary Hausch Steps Down from Hipp after 40 Years," *Gainesville Sun,* May 10, 2013.

19 Rick Allen, "Blood Bath at the Hippodrome," *Gainesville Sun,* October 14, 2012.

20 Ron Cunningham, review of *Don't Dress for Dinner,* by Robin Hawdon, directed by Jim Wren, Hippodrome Theatre, Gainesville, FL, *Gainesville Sun,* September 5, 2013.

21 Travis Atria, "Serving Up Romance and Adultery," *Gainesville Sun,* August 29, 2013.

22 Jennifer Waters, "Bridging the Arts, Business," *Gainesville Sun,* October 20, 2013.

23 Ibid.

24 Travis Atria, "Brains Over Braun," *Gainesville Sun,* October 10, 2013.

25 Ibid.

26 Ron Cunningham, review of *Zombie Town: A Documentary Play,* by Tim Bauer, directed by Lauren Caldwell, Hippodrome Theatre, Gainesville, FL, *Gainesville Sun,* October 17, 2013.

2014

Good People

For January, the Hippodrome snagged one of Broadway's recent hits, the Tony-nominated *Good People*, written by David Lindsay-Abaire. The play alternates between moments of comedic whimsy and tense drama while exposing social issues plaguing minimum-wage workers with few marketable skills.

The play is set in Southie, a blue-collar Boston neighborhood where this month's paycheck barely covers last month's bills. Margaret, a.k.a. Margie, has just lost her job for chronic tardiness caused by caring for her special-needs daughter.

Faced with eviction by Dottie, her landlord, Margie goes to see Mike, an old high school boyfriend. He made it out of the neighborhood to become a successful doctor and has tried to forget his origins. Margie wangles an invitation to his birthday party, where she hopes to find employment among his rich friends.

Both Dottie and Margie's best friend, Jean, encourage Margie to tell Mike that her daughter is his so he will pay child support. When Mike informs her the party's been called off, she assumes he's disinviting her because he's embarrassed to have his well-to-do friends meet her. So, she decides to crash the party.

Standing: Kevin Rainsberger and Felecia Harrelson. Seated (l-r): Matthew Lindsay, Sara Morsey, Cristine McMurdo-Wallis, and Nell Page in *Good People*.

Photo: Michael Eaddy

She arrives and discovers the party really was canceled, but his wife Kate invites Margie to stay and reminisce about Mike's past. During their discussion, Mike tells Margie her financial problems are her own fault for not trying hard enough. Margie tries to explain to Mike that he had lucky breaks that most people from Southie didn't get. Finally, she attempts the illegitimate child ploy her friends suggested, but Mike and Kate bully her into admitting the child isn't his, and she leaves in shame.

Later, Dottie receives an envelope of cash marked for Margie's rent, and Margie, thinking it came from Mike, intends to return it. But at Bingo, she learns the money came from her former boss, Stevie. She agrees to accept it as an indefinite "loan." In a final twist, one of Margie's friends asserts that "everybody knows" her baby was Mike's.

"*Good People* is a jarring yet often hilarious account of how the bottom half of the other 99% must hang on by their fingernails," wrote the *Gainesville Sun* reviewer. He added praises for the entire cast. "Sara Morsey is near perfect as Margaret... Nell Page nearly steals the show as Jean... Kevin Rainsberger turns in an absorbing performance [as Mike]... Felecia Harrelson is excellent as Kate... Cristine McMurdo-Wallis' Dottie is a brittle penny-pincher... Stevie, a good guy forced to be the heavy [is] played with surprising sweetness by Matthew Lindsay."[1]

Letters to the *Gainesville Sun* called *Good People* "Brilliant" and "One of the Best."[2] It played from January 10–February 2. During the run, the Hippodrome lent the mainstage to Dance Alive National Ballet, who gave a stunning dance performance on January 20.

New Management

After barely four months at the helm, the Hippodrome's new head, Thomas Anderson, left the position on February 14. "My immediate task when I arrived was to provide the transition board a producing director's review of the theatre's operations within ninety days," Anderson wrote in a press statement. "The discovery process upon my arrival took me and others by surprise, and I feel that my resignation, and now salary savings, will help the theatre focus on its immediate needs."[3]

Anderson made a series of recommendations based on his findings, one of which led to the elevation of the Hippodrome's Marketing and Communications Director, Jessica Hurov, to the role of Managing Director. "During the process, one thing he [Anderson] came to realize is that the talent, skillset, and knowledge to lead the theatre was already here," Jessica told the *Gainesville Sun*.[4]

"I love the Hipp, and call on everyone to support Lauren Caldwell and Jessica Hurov as they address the immediate needs and artistic mission of the theatre,"[5] Anderson's statement concluded.

Jessica began her career at the Hippodrome as Director of Marketing in 2005, a position she held for seven years. She left for a brief stint running PR for Dean Lavelli's office at UF but returned to the Hipp after receiving a call from Rocky and Mary. "Please come back," they said. "You know we're going to be leaving."

Jessica told Rocky and Mary, "I don't want my communication with our audiences to stop when they enter the front door of the building. I want to work with our front of house, our bar, box office; and be able to really understand the customer experience once they are physically here."

So, they developed a new position for Jessica at that time: Director of Marketing and Communication. In addition to marketing and public relations, the new role gave her expanded administrative responsibilities in the areas of fundraising, subscriptions, membership, and patron relations. These experiences made her the natural choice to become Managing Director on February 12, 2014.

While Jessica, as Managing Director, teamed with Artistic Director Lauren Caldwell to run the theatre, Nicole Daenzer, the Hippodrome's accountant and Director of Operations, took on the additional task of writing grant applications. The board decided they no longer needed a Producing Director and eliminated the position rather than seek a replacement for Anderson.

A week after stepping into her new role, Jessica announced the Hippodrome was launching a capital campaign to raise $750,000 over the following six months. The theatre's funding had suffered since the start of the Great Recession in 2008, when state and federal grant money all but disappeared. Since then, the Hippodrome had eliminated fourteen positions through layoffs and attrition, and the theatre's annual budget had dropped from $2.3 million to $1.7 million.

Leveling Up

For those who haven't spent as much time gaming as the characters in Deborah Zoe Laufer's *Leveling Up*, the title refers to progressing to the next level in role-playing video games. The story is about four basement-dwelling twenty-somethings who are addicted to video games and live on ramen noodles, beer, and weed. Director Lauren Caldwell's cast members were all of that age. Josh Price and Marissa Toogood were becoming Hippodrome regulars, last seen together in *Zombie Town*. Making their Hippodrome debut were out-of-town actors Daniel Schwab and Brett Mack. Daniel had been working at the Asolo Repertory Theatre in Sarasota and the freeFall Theatre in St. Petersburg. Brett's experience included stage, film, and television roles.

The three male characters Ian, Chuck, and Zander, spend their days and nights glued to their game consoles, living virtual lives. All three are drawn to the same woman, Jeannie, who has an actual life beyond the digital world. If that sounds like the sitcom *The Big Bang Theory*, it's not.

"Rather it is a tragicomedy that will put you in stitches and then make you feel a bit tacky for having laughed at these wretched descendants of Peter Pan's lost boys," wrote critic Ron Cunningham. "Together and apart they are living Thoreau's 'lives of quiet desperation.' The four young actors who bring *Leveling Up* to life look, move, and talk as though they have been there themselves."[6]

Jeannie is forever trying to coax the guys out of their electronic reality. Chuck is a mellow slacker who seduces Jeannie's avatar in a virtual Las Vegas. Zander gets by on charm, using his friends in a vitamin-supplement Ponzi scheme that eventually

(l-r) Marissa Toogood, Brett Mack, Daniel Schwab, and Josh Price in *Leveling Up*.

Photo: Michael Eaddy

blows up. Ian, the most skilled of the gamers, is so good with a joystick that he's eventually hired by the National Security Agency to fly drones. It is then when he realizes that, unlike his gaming kills, his victims are real people.

With a play so much about gaming, it was necessary to share the gamers' experiences with the audience. For that, the Hippodrome turned to UF's Digital Worlds Institute, which designed the digital imagery, projection, and sounds for the production. "It was a great partnership," Lauren told the *Gainesville Sun*. "We have a special kind of projector with a special kind of lens."[7] It made the Hipp the first theatre in the country to feature multimedia along with the performance.

Leveling Up ran from February 21–March 16.

A Second *Tempest*

The Hippodrome had last produced William Shakespeare's *The Tempest* in 1977 with Mike Beistle playing the lead, Prospero. When director Lauren Caldwell cast the 2014 version, she decided a little gender-bending was in order and made slight modifications to the characters' names. Prospero became Prospera, played by Sara Morsey. The usurping brother Antonio became a sister, Antonia, portrayed by Emily Green. And a man, Michael Littig, played the role of Ariel.

Financial constraints being what they were, the Hippodrome cut the total number of characters from twenty-two to fourteen essential roles. In addition to Prospera, Antonia, and Ariel, they kept: Ferdinand (Brett Mack), Miranda (Ericka Winterrowd), Stephano (Logan Wolfe), Caliban (Ryan George), Trinculo (Kenneth Smoak), Alonso (Robert Cope), Gonzalo (Charlie Mitchell), Sebastian (Matthew Lindsay), and Ariel's spirits (Stephen Ruffin, Marissa Toogood, and Laine Evans Nelson).

Top: Sara Morsey as Prospera is shown with the other thirteen cast members of *The Tempest*.

Photo: Michael Eaddy

Although the set design and the gender of the leads changed, the plot did not. A noble of Milan, betrayed by a sibling and exiled to a desolate isle with daughter Miranda, becomes a magician and gets comeuppance by conjuring a storm that shipwrecks her enemies on the island.

"The cast is lively," said the *Sun* review. "Michael Littig's interpretation of Ariel is as unorthodox as it is fun to watch. Hipp veteran Sara Morsey turns in her usual A-list performance … Ryan George's Caliban … moves about the stage with the grace of a crouching panther and projects an aura of barely contained fury that threatens to burst from his taut body. If there is a disappointing flatness to this production, it is the absence of chemistry between Morsey's Prospera and Emily Green's Antonia … when the two finally do come face-to-face, what passes between them feels more akin to indifference. That said, there are sufficient sparks and sparkling exchanges in this Hipp production…. The Hipp's backstage crew deserves much credit for creating an appropriately dreamy environment—moody lighting, enchanting music, water that alternatively falls gently from the heavens and boils furiously from the depths."[8]

The Tempest played from April 1–May 4.

Christmas in Summer?

The Hippodrome had twice done exceedingly well staging David Nehls and Betsy Kelso's *The Great American Trailer Park Musical* set in a trailer park in Starke, Florida.

(l-r) Stephanie Lynge, Susan Haldeman, Grace Choi, Alec James, Mark Chambers, and Marissa Toogood in *The Great American Trailer Park Christmas Musical*.

Photo: Michael Eaddy

So, when the playwrights came up with a holiday-themed play, *The Great American Trailer Park Christmas Musical*, it seemed worth doing even though the play's run, from May 30–August 3, wasn't anywhere near Christmas.

Both plays are set in Armadillo Acres trailer park, but Betty, Lin, and Pickles, who served as a Greek chorus in the previous play, become main characters in the new play. Mark Chambers, the only cast member who appeared in the Hipp's earlier *Trailer Park* musicals, returned, but as a new character. This time he played Jackie, the owner of a Hooters-like pancake restaurant.

The story takes place twelve days before Christmas. Betty (Susan Haldeman), owner of the trailer park, is trying to get the place showcased by a magazine that pays a cash prize. But Darlene (Grace Choi), the trailer park Scrooge, won't let anyone decorate her side of the Christmas tree. When she catches Rufus (Alec James) stealing her cable, her attempt to disconnect him pulls the decorations down. Ditzy blonde Pickles (Marissa Toogood) still believes in Santa, and Lin (Stephanie Lynge) wears a vial around her neck containing the ashes of her husband, who died in the electric chair. But the Hippodrome cast sang and danced through it all with marvelous voices that wouldn't quit.

Ron Cunningham called it "*Christmas Carol* meets *The Exorcist*, only with a lot more cussin'…. This is all great fun, but it's not exactly family-friendly holiday fare…. It is wicked funny. If your toe isn't tappin' you're likely dead … or maybe just terminally prudish."[9]

Directed by Lauren Caldwell, with Bryan Mercer as musical director and Ric Rose as choreographer, the show ran for nine weeks—unarguably a success.

Forty-Second Season

The Hippodrome and the UF School of Theatre and Dance teamed up for a second year to produce *Clybourne Park*, Bruce Norris's Pulitzer Prize- and Tony Award-winning play about race and real estate. UF theatre professor Ralf Remshardt directed it. He drew his cast of eight evenly from veteran Hippodrome actors Christopher Swan, Stephanie Lynge, Matthew Lindsay, and Emily Green and UF theatre students Oluchi Nwokocha, Sean Cancellieri, Javon Johnson, and Michael Pemberton.

Ralf called *Clybourne Park* "a drama that, in a manner both breathtakingly funny and ruthlessly profound, seemed to bring to the surface all of those aspects of America's ongoing, ever-unfinished conversation about race and class we would rather politely avoid."[10]

Cast members (l-r) Stephanie Lynge, Christopher Swan, Javon Johnson, Oluchi Nwokocha, Emily Green, Matthew Lindsay, and Sean Cancellieri on the set of *Clybourne Park*.

Photo: Michael Eaddy

The story is set in a fictional neighborhood and is told in two acts fifty years apart. The first act takes place in the segregated Chicago of the 1950s when a Black family buying a house in all-white Clybourne Park creates an uproar. In act two, half a century later, poorer neighborhoods throughout the city are targets for gentrification, and a white family tries to buy the same house in the now all-Black Clybourne Park, much to the consternation of its residents.

Norris's dialogue is intended to make the audience squirm. "Which is not to say *Clybourne Park* isn't funny. It's hysterical at times," wrote Ron Cunningham in the *Gainesville Sun*. "Even when the joke hits a little close to home. *Clybourne Park* is a biting commentary on why Americans can't seem to have an honest conversation about race. What makes *Clybourne Park* such a pleasure to watch is the easy ability of this capable cast to reverse roles—to change from discriminators to discriminated as smoothly as they change their clothes."[11]

"On some levels, the play has to offend," Ralf told the *Sun*. "And, as the cast seems to agree, it's much easier to look at racism in the past than to admit it is still an entrenched part of the present."[12]

Clybourne Park played September 5–28.

Less Creepy Than Campy

To mount something appropriate for Halloween, the Hippodrome came up with *Slasher*, Allison Moore's send-up of films of the *Texas Chainsaw* ilk. It was the play's Florida premiere.

Matthew Lindsay played Marc, a washed-up Hollywood director who returns to the tiny Texas town where he'd filmed his only cinematic success in hope of making another hit. All he lacks are money, time, and talent. At a greasy diner, he meets young waitress Sheena (Marissa Toogood) and casts her as the female lead.

Photo: Michael Eaddy

Desperate to escape her demanding mother (Sara Morsey) and dependent younger sister (Stefanie Anarumo), Sheena accepts the role, reasoning that as the lead, she'll be the last girl to die.

Matthew Lindsay, Marissa Toogood, and Logan Wolfe in a scene from *Slasher*.

Logan Wolfe played a film student/production assistant who also dons a rubber mask as the film's slasher when necessary. Emily Green played eight characters, including a news anchor and the slasher's first victim, a real estate agent. Sean Cancellieri played an unnamed creepy character known only as "The Man."

Although Ron Cunningham's theatre review had kind words for the actors, he was critical of the play: "Lauren Caldwell has peppered her production with a cast of familiar faces who know their business and are certainly capable of delivering a punch line with real punch. If only there were more punches in the material these actors have to work with, it would be perfect. Matthew Lindsay is in his element as Marc. [Marissa] Toogood is at her best when she is emoting like nobody's business. Sara Morsey is wonderful. The hardest-working member of this cast is Emily Green." He was referring to Emily having to dangle in a harness. But, he carped, "*Slasher* is: More amusing and less laugh-out-loud than you might expect. More campy and less creepy.... More smarmy and less scary.... More pink froth and less blood red."[13] Although blood did gush profusely in the second act.

Slasher ran from October 17–November 9.

Christmas Musical

In addition to the traditional production of *A Christmas Carol*, starring Rusty Salling in his twenty-fifth turn as Scrooge, the Hippodrome offered a new musical. *Winter Wonderettes* revisits the characters of *The Marvelous Wonderettes*, and both shows were created by Roger Bean.

Photo: Michael Eaddy

Winter Wonderettes played by (l-r) Susan Haldeman, Catherine Fries Vaughn, Yael Reich, and Katrina Asmar.

Katrina Asmar reprised her role as Cindy Lou. Catherine Fries Vaughn stepped in as Missy. Susan Haldeman was Betty Jean, and newcomer Yael Reich played Suzy. The production, directed and choreographed by Ric Rose, is a typical jukebox musical, except this time it's built around twenty-five holiday songs. Bryan Mercer served as musical director. The women sang four-part harmonies and solos over a wide selection of tunes from "Jingle Bell Rock" to "Santa Baby."

"Even though they are jukebox musicals," Catherine Fries Vaughn said, "the underlying theme is about the friendship between the women."

"Of course, the best thing about *Winter Wonderettes* is the music," said the *Gainesville Sun* review. "Betty Jean's tortured version of 'O Tannenbaum' is painfully funny. If Asmar's soulful rendition of 'All Those Christmas Clichés' doesn't break your heart, you probably haven't got one. *Winter Wonderettes* is a nicely wrapped present all tied up with a big red bow. Go to the Hipp and unwrap it."[14]

Winter Wonderettes was on stage November 28–December 21. Running in tandem November 29–December 20 was a new version of *A Christmas Carol* with a script by Janet Allard and Michael Bigelow Dixon, directed for the first time by Lauren Caldwell.

1 Ron Cunningham, review of *Good People*, by David Lindsay-Abaire, directed by Lauren Caldwell, Hippodrome Theatre, Gainesville, FL, *Gainesville Sun*, January 16, 2014.
2 Letters to the Editor, *Gainesville Sun*, January 20, 2014.
3 Carla Vianna, "Hippodrome's Producing Director Exits after 4 Months," *Gainesville Sun*, February 15, 2014.
4 Ibid.
5 Ibid.
6 Ron Cunningham, review of *Leveling Up*, by Deborah Zoe Laufer, directed by Lauren Caldwell, Hippodrome Theatre, Gainesville, FL, *Gainesville Sun*, February 27, 2014.
7 Travis Atria, "A Digital Connection," *Gainesville Sun*, February 20, 2014.
8 Ron Cunningham, review of *The Tempest*, by William Shakespeare, directed by Lauren Caldwell, Hippodrome Theatre, Gainesville, FL, *Gainesville Sun*, April 24, 2014.
9 Ron Cunningham, review of *The Great American Trailer Park Christmas Musical*, by David Nehls and Betsy Kelso, directed by Lauren Caldwell, Hippodrome Theatre, Gainesville, FL, *Gainesville Sun*, June 5, 2014.
10 *Clybourne Park* playbill, Hippodrome Theatre, Gainesville, FL, 2014.
11 Ron Cunningham, review of *Clybourne Park*, by Bruce Norris, directed by Ralf Remshardt, Hippodrome Theatre, Gainesville, FL, *Gainesville Sun*, September 11, 2014.
12 Travis Atria, "A Look at Race, Class, in America," *Gainesville Sun*, September 4, 2014.
13 Ron Cunningham, review of *Slasher*, by Allison Moore, directed by Lauren Caldwell, Hippodrome Theatre, Gainesville, FL, *Gainesville Sun*, October 23, 2014.
14 Ron Cunningham, review of *Winter Wonderettes*, by Roger Bean, directed by Ric Rose, Hippodrome Theatre, Gainesville, FL, *Gainesville Sun*, December 4, 2014.

2015

Chekhov in a Blender

The names of characters in the Hippodrome's January play, *Vanya and Sonia and Masha and Spike*, come from Anton Chekhov's classics. But this comedy by Christopher Durang, incorporating Chekhov themes, doesn't require knowledge of the Russian playwright. "My play is not a Chekhov parody," said Durang. "I take Chekhov scenes and characters and put them into a blender."[1]

The story centers on three middle-aged siblings. Vanya (Tom Foley) and Sonia (Sara Morsey) spent their adulthood caring for their now-dead parents while their absent movie star sister, Masha (Nell Page), paid the bills. Like an old married couple, the two squabble over petty things, like whether the nine cherry trees on their property constitute an orchard, while bemoaning their lost chances to live their own lives:

Sonia: "I dreamt I was fifty-two and I wasn't married."

Vanya: "Were you dreaming in the documentary form?"[2]

Lauren Caldwell yielded the job of director to David Shelton and took on the role of Cassandra, the family's live-in housekeeper who makes dire prophecies that no one believes.

Masha arrives with a gorgeous but vacuous boy toy, Spike (Ryan George), and tells her siblings she's returned to attend a costume party at an influential neighbor's home. She's going as Snow White and has brought costumes for them to be her

Dressed for a costume party are characters from *Vanya and Sonia and Masha and Spike* played by (l-r) Sara Morsey, Nell Page, Ryan George, Lauren Caldwell, Tom Foley, and Megan Wicks.

Photo: Michael Eaddy

dwarfs. Sonia refuses. "I want to play the evil queen as portrayed by Maggie Smith on her way to collect an Oscar,"[3] she tells Masha.

Vanya tries to keep the peace between his sisters, but as a gay man, he's repeatedly distracted by the preening Spike, who takes every opportunity possible to strip down and show off his muscular body. The neighbor's pretty niece, Nina (Megan Wicks), comes over. She's an aspiring actress who provokes envy in Masha, lust in Spike, and sympathy in Vanya. While everyone is getting ready for the party, Masha, who owns the farmhouse where they all grew up, announces that she intends to sell it. Vanya, Sonia, and Cassandra are devastated.

The day after the party, Cassandra uses a voodoo doll on Masha, trying to erase thoughts of selling the house. Nina convinces Vanya to let her read to the others a play he is secretly writing. During the reading, Spike is rudely texting on his phone, angering Vanya, who launches into an impassioned rant.

Masha discovers Spike is texting her personal assistant, with whom he's having an affair. She kicks him out of the house and announces she no longer intends to sell it. The play ends with the siblings sitting together listening to the Beatles song "Here Comes the Sun."

"*Vanya and Sonia and Masha and Spike* is interesting stuff indeed," wrote *Gainesville Sun* reviewer Ron Cunningham. "But more than that, this Hipp production is a rare opportunity to watch three very funny, very talented women exchange barbs and brickbats like the old pals and pros they are. Foley may be eclipsed by the terrific trio through much of this production, but comes into his own toward the end of the play when he delivers a sidesplitting soliloquy that Hamlet himself might have envied."[4]

The play, which had won the Tony Award for Best Play and the Drama Desk Award for Outstanding Play, ran at the Hippodrome from January 9–February 1.

Reinventing *The Simpsons*

The Hipp's next production was the Florida premiere of *Mr. Burns, A Post-Electric Play*, a musical comedy with book and lyrics by Anne Washburn and music by Michael Friedman. It was directed by Lauren Caldwell. The show's musical director, Bryan Mercer, and choreographer, Stephanie Lynge, both played characters as well.

Not an upbeat musical, this dark comedy is the story of a bedraggled band of apocalypse survivors trying to retain their lost culture by taking turns recounting the "Cape Feare" episode of *The Simpsons* around a campfire. In act two, seven years later, the group has evolved into a traveling theatrical troupe that performs complete episodes, including commercials.

Bryan Mercer said it raises the question of how our culture would hold on to its identity without electricity: "To ruin our culture, all you'd have to do is pull the plug. Other cultures sing folk songs. We sing TV themes."[5]

"There are not many things that keep our civilization from being barbaric," said Lauren. "But there's nothing like the arts." Ultimately, the play's message is that if we hold on to arts and culture, we can hold on to our humanness, even in the face of an apocalypse.[6]

An ensemble cast of Hippodrome regulars (Matthew Lindsay, Stephanie Lynge, Katrina Asmar, Marissa Toogood, Charlie Mitchell, Logan Wolfe, Bryan Mercer, and Marissa Williams) played dual roles as apocalyptic survivors and *Simpsons* characters.

Whether you liked the play depended on several factors, foremost whether you liked *The Simpsons* in the first place. *Sun* theater critic Ron Cunningham noted, "On the night I attended, there were noticeably more vacant seats during Act Two than Act One. This, the result of patrons voting with their feet, that *Mr. Burns* was nothing like they anticipated. But leaving early was a mistake. Because the best was yet to come.... What happens on the Hippodrome stage after the intermission in *Mr. Burns* is visually stunning, emotionally absorbing, bitingly funny, oddly lyrical, and—yes—even electrifying."[7]

Photo: Michael Eaddy

Cast of *Mr. Burns, A Post-Electric Play*: (l-r) Charlie Mitchell, Stephanie Lynge, Bryan Mercer, Katrina Asmar, Marissa Toogood, Marissa Williams, Logan Wolfe, and Matthew Lindsay.

Mr. Burns, A Post-Electric Play opened February 20 and ran through March 15.

World Premiere

On April 10, the Hippodrome presented the world premiere of Jon Jory's *The Two Musketeers!*, which ran through May 3. In a story perhaps too close to real life, a fictional theatre troupe staging Alexandre Dumas's *The Three Musketeers* doesn't have the budget to pay three actors after funding for the arts gets cut. But the show must go on, so the only thing to do is eliminate one of them and present *The Two Musketeers!*

Directed by Lauren Warhol Caldwell strictly for laughs, it still needed plenty of swordplay. For that, she brought in UF Associate Professor Tiza Garland, who happened to be a certified teacher with the Society of American Fight Directors, the British Academy of Stage and Screen Combat, and Dueling Arts International. Tiza started by having the actors sword fight in slow motion and then ramped things up as they got better. She also joined the cast, playing three of the female characters: Milady, Queen Anne, and Jussac.

David Patrick Ford played D'Artagnan, the provincial bumpkin who comes to join the musketeers. Except for David, the rest of the cast members played multiple roles with split-second costume changes.

Matthew Lindsay played Cardinal Richelieu, Porthos, De Treville, a servant, a messenger, D'Artagnan's father, and even an abbess. Nick Clark Tanner played Athos,

Lauren Warhol Caldwell?

Lauren's explanation for her name change is that once upon a time she met the artist Andy Warhol while hanging out with Liza Minnelli at a bar in New York City. "I told him he had a really cool name, and he said 'Take it.'" She didn't right away, but after his death, "I just started using it."[15]

Photo: Michael Eaddy

The Two Musketeers!
performed by (l-r) Nick Clark
Tanner, Caitlin Hargraves,
David Patrick Ford, Matthew
Lindsay, Tiza Garland, and
Michael Stewart Allen.

the King, Bonacieux, a jeweler, and a boatman. Michael Stewart Allen was Aramis, Buckingham, a man in black, and a servant. Caitlin Hargraves portrayed Constance, Kitty, an innkeeper, a guard, and an assassin.

Ron Cunningham's review summed it up: "*The Two Musketeers!* is a veritable orgy of leaping, sword-crossing, prancing, cross-dressing, role-switching, word-mincing, history-bending, pillow-fighting, plot-thickening nonsense featuring possibly the hardest-working small cast of multiple personalities ever to elbow each other aside on the Hipp's small stage."[8]

In the spirit of the musketeers' motto, "All for one and one for all," the Hippodrome held eight Community Partner Nights during the play's run, each benefiting a different nonprofit organization. For eight performances of *The Two Musketeers!*, patrons could get a ticket for half price if they donated cash or a requested item to the charity designated for that show. For example, one night it was canned goods and healthy snacks for the Southern Legal Counsel's Food4Kids Backpack Program. On another night, it was tube socks and toiletries for Grace Marketplace.

Hippodrome Managing Director Jessica Hurov told the *Gainesville Sun* that the theatre had seen a lot of community support over the years and was grateful to be able to give back. Additional nonprofits that benefited from the Community Partner Nights were Meridian Behavioral Healthcare, March of Dimes, Guardian ad Litem, Bread of the Mighty Food Bank, Three Rivers Legal Services, and the Child Advocacy Center.

Honky Tonk Summer

The Hippodrome had done well with Ted Swindley's *Honky Tonk Angels* in 2002, so they brought it back for the summer of 2015. Lauren Warhol Caldwell, who had directed it last time, did so again, this time with a different musical director, Bryan Mercer, and a different choreographer, Stephanie Lynge.

Katrina Asmar, who had sung in *The Marvelous Wonderettes* and again in *Winter Wonderettes*, played Sue Ellen. Darlene was played by Marissa Toogood from *The Great American Trailer Park Christmas Musical*. Juliana Davis as Angela was new to the Hippodrome but an experienced

Photo: Michael Eaddy

The *Honky Tonk Angels* arrive in Nashville, played by Katrina Asmar, Marissa Toogood, and Juliana Davis.

professional with numerous musical plays on her resume. The show opened May 29 and played through July 26.

Ron Cunningham wrote, "These new angels are fun and funny. And they sing and dance every bit as well as the country star wannabes they are playing. Heck, these actresses could be country stars in their own right if they set their minds to it."[9]

Season Forty-three

In their third year co-producing a play, UF and the Hippodrome chose *Peter and the Starcatcher*, a musical comedy by Rick Elice with music by Wayne Barker. It is based on a novel Florida humorist Dave Barry co-authored with Ridley Pearson, and it purports to tell how Peter Pan and the Lost Boys came to be when two ships collided on the stormy seas, causing a clash between pirates and orphans. Lauren Warhol Caldwell directed the play. Bryan Mercer served as musical director and played two of the characters.

> According to this prequel, Molly grows up to become Wendy's mother.

"A stream-of-consciousness comedy with many actors playing multiple roles flitting frenetically about the stage while alternately rattling off one-liners and telling the audience what's going on in straight-faced narrative" was how Ron Cunningham described it. "There are moments of hilarity, interrupted by minutes of tedium, revived by cold water plunges into absurdity."[10] He equated it with the prior season's *The Two Musketeers!*

Cunningham continued, "David Patrick Ford is amazing as Captain Black Stache. Not to be upstaged by Ford's farce and facial hair is Marissa Toogood, the most reliably versatile weapon in Caldwell's arsenal of regulars.... [Marissa portrays] the insatiably curious thirteen-year-old Molly. [Logan] Wolfe's Smee—second banana to Stache—is as engaging as Walt's cartoon version. And Niall McGinty plays the much-abused orphan Peter."[11]

Photo: Michael Eaddy

David Patrick Ford as Captain Black Stache holds Molly (Marissa Toogood) captive in Peter and the Starcatcher.

Hippodrome regular Matthew Lindsay was also in the cast, and UF cast members included Jason David Collins, Wesley Huffman, Jake Lesh, Orlando Mendez, Andrew Quimby, and Charlie Mitchell. The play ran September 2–27.

All Girl Halloween

All Girl Frankenstein, Bob Fisher's adaptation of Mary Shelley's novel, opened October 16 and played through November 8. As the title implies, all characters, male and female alike, were played by women, with Candace Clift as Victor Frankenstein and Nichole Hamilton as the Creature. Jorgia McAfee played Victor's assistant, Clerval. Sara Morsey was the Hunchback.

Originally staged by a troupe in Chicago, the Hippodrome was only the second company to take on the all-female adaption of *Frankenstein*. "It's an interesting experiment in female empowerment," said Stephanie Lynge, who played Frankenstein's mother. "It's not your parents' Frankenstein."[12]

Photo: Michael Eaddy

In *All Girl Frankenstein*, Nichole Hamilton as the Creature looms over (top row) Sara Morsey, Ariel Reich, Stephanie Lynge, (middle row) Emily Norcia, Candace Clift as Victor Frankenstein, Melanie Sholl, (seated on floor) Marissa Toogood, and Jorgia McAfee.

The story veers in a more seductive direction from standard horror fare with a dash of campiness, homosexuality, bondage, and necrophilia. Victor Frankenstein is still the mad scientist who reanimates lifeless matter into a creature desperate for a mate and ready to kill. Meanwhile, Victor is unable to sexually satisfy his girlfriend, Elizabeth (Ariel Reich).

Marissa Toogood played Victor's brother, William, and Lauren Warhol Caldwell directed. UF students Melanie Sholl and Emily Norcia played busty, bawdy maids in tight corsets.

The *Sun* reviewer wasn't enamored: "It is just campy enough to be funny. It is not quite frightening enough to be horrifying. *All Girl Frankenstein* is cursed with its share of tedium, and occasionally wanders annoyingly astray. Still, it is just wicked enough to put one in the proper Halloween mood."[13]

A Nordic Queen and a New Ebenezer

For its holiday offering, the Hippodrome presented a new play, *The Snow Queen*, written and directed by Charlie Mitchell, alongside the thirty-eighth annual production of *A Christmas Carol*.

Charlie adapted the story by Hans Christian Andersen, blending the characters and magic of the Nordic folktale with contemporary characters' problems. Astrid (Stephanie Lynge) thinks love has passed her by. Next-door neighbor Karl (David Patrick Ford), a failed storyteller-turned-office drone, fancies her but has trouble putting his feelings into words.

Astrid has an adolescent daughter, Gerta (Sami Gresham), who retreats into fantasy and urges Karl to spin his yarns of the Snow Queen (Grace Abel) and Kai (Jeremy Martinez), the boy in the ice palace waiting for Gerta to rescue him. Gerta's grandmother (Karel Wright) narrates the play.

Grace Abel and David Patrick Ford in a scene from The Snow Queen.

Christie Robinson played a bandit queen who learns she can't steal friends. David Leppert portrayed multiple characters, including a talkative cabby who spoils the mood of Astrid and Karl's date. Both actors also took on minor parts: talking statues, a crow, a goblin philosopher, and an overstuffed reindeer.

"Mitchell's dialogue is crisp and witty," wrote Ron Cunningham. "His songs are funny. And every one of his interwoven, 'once upon a time' stories comes with a moral all its own.... *The Snow Queen* is funny, thought provoking and even mind-bending."[14]

The Snow Queen ran from November 27–December 20, concurrent with Janet Allard and Michael Bigelow Dixon's adaptation of *A Christmas Carol* directed by Niall McGinty, which opened a day later and closed a day earlier than *The Snow Queen.* The big difference in this year's *Christmas Carol* was the actor who played Scrooge.

Rusty Salling, who had appeared in every Hippodrome production of *A Christmas Carol*—the last twenty-five as Ebenezer Scrooge—probably would have rather died than given up a role he had so finely honed. But that year, he was fiercely battling cancer and his illness had reached a stage where he couldn't perform. So Gregg Jones, who had played Jacob Marley opposite Rusty for sixteen years, stepped in as Scrooge.

Rusty's best friend, Dan Jesse, recalls that year. He said, "Rusty had become synonymous with that show. I mean, he had become such an institution that Gregg was really nervous about taking over the role. After Rusty came to see Gregg do the show, Gregg said to him, 'Well, what did you think?' Rusty said, 'Gregg, you were so good that when I come back to do this show next year, I'm going to steal some of your bits.'"

1   Harry Haun, "Christopher Durang, in a Russian Mood by Way of Bucks County, Lands on Broadway," *Playbill*, December 12, 2013.

2   Christopher Durang, *Vanya and Sonia and Masha and Spike*, Dramatists Play Service, New York, NY, 2014.

3   Ibid.

4   Ron Cunningham, review of *Vanya and Sonia and Masha and Spike*, by Christopher Durang, directed by David Shelton, Hippodrome Theatre, Gainesville, FL, *Gainesville Sun*, January 15, 2015.

5   Tyler Francischine, "Pop Culture Unplugged," *Gainesville Sun*, February 19, 2015.

6   Ibid.

7   Ron Cunningham, review of *Mr. Burns, A Post-Electric Play*, by Anne Washburn and Michael Friedman, directed by Lauren Caldwell, Hippodrome Theatre, Gainesville, FL, *Gainesville Sun*, February 26, 2015.

8   Ron Cunningham, review of *The Two Musketeers!*, by Jon Jory, directed by Lauren Warhol Caldwell, Hippodrome Theatre, Gainesville, FL, *Gainesville Sun*, April 16, 2015.

9   Ron Cunningham, review of *Honky Tonk Angels*, by Ted Swindley, directed by Lauren Warhol Caldwell, Hippodrome Theatre, Gainesville, FL, *Gainesville Sun*, June 4, 2015.

10 Ron Cunningham, review of *Peter and the Starcatcher*, by Rick Elice, directed by Lauren Warhol Caldwell, Hippodrome Theatre, Gainesville, FL, *Gainesville Sun*, September 10, 2015.

11 Ibid.

12 Erin Jester, "She's Alive!," *Gainesville Sun*, October 17, 2015.

13 Ron Cunningham, review of *All Girl Frankenstein*, by Bob Fisher, directed by Lauren Warhol Caldwell, Hippodrome Theatre, Gainesville, FL, *Gainesville Sun*, October 29, 2015.

14 Ron Cunningham, review of *The Snow Queen*, by Charlie Mitchell, directed by Charlie Mitchell, Hippodrome Theatre, Gainesville, FL, *Gainesville Sun*, December 3, 2015.

15 Ron Cunningham, "Longtime Hipp Artist Explores Life After Theater," *Gainesville Sun*, February 7, 2019.

2016

Collected Stories

Upon hearing the title of the Hippodrome's January play, *Collected Stories*, longtime subscribers might have assumed it was a production of one-act plays similar to those the Hippodrome had periodically mounted in the past. They'd be wrong. The comedic drama by Donald Margulies is about creative ambition, entitlement, and an evolving relationship between mentor and protégée.

Photo: Michael Eaddy

Collected Stories starring Sara Morsey and Juliana Davis.

Sara Morsey played Ruth Steiner, a haughty professor and established writer of some note. Juliana Davis, who had appeared in the previous summer's *Honky Tonk Angels*, played Lisa Morrison, an anxious grad student willing to work as Ruth's personal assistant just to learn from her. The stories referred to in the title are those that Lisa gets Ruth to share about her life during the Beat Era. Over the course of six years, Lisa gradually evolves from student to acolyte to Ruth's superior. It all comes to a head when Lisa bases her successful first novel on stories Ruth shared in confidence about her fling with a famous Beat poet. Outraged, Ruth calls Lisa a literary vampire. She says, "You didn't ask. You skulked like a thief scavenging through my personal effects."[1]

Ron Cunningham wrote: "Congratulations to Lauren Warhol Caldwell for taking a chance on this sparse play with a tiny cast and profound message. That two hours of conversation between just two actors can add up to an absorbing evening of theatre is itself a tribute. And not just to Margulies' witty, acidic, and tightly written script, but to the considerable talents of Sara Morsey and Juliana Davis."[2]

Collected Stories ran January 8–31.

Wacky Whodunit about Women in Their 40s

Women in Jeopardy! by Wendy MacLeod made its Southeastern premiere at the Hippodrome on February 19 and played through March 13. Director Lauren Warhol Caldwell called it a play "created by a woman for women. The women in this are not just mothers or wives, they're independent women. They have their own stories to tell."[3] They are witty, protective, sexual beings who have reached middle age and aren't looking back.

Longtime gal pals Liz, Jo, and Mary are over-forty divorcées whose social lives have pretty much been reduced to sharing glasses of chardonnay. But there is hope as Liz rushes into Mary's Utah kitchen, giddy about how revitalized she feels due to her new love affair with a creepy dentist. She says, "There has been a renaissance of my nether parts."[4]

(l-r) Matthew Lindsay, Lija Fisher, Carolyn Pool, Stephanie Lynge, Logan Wolfe, and Michele Dalia in a scene from *Women in Jeopardy!*

Photo: Michael Eaddy

Although the dentist may have murdered his hygienist, Liz can't see him the way Jo and Mary do. Worried that Liz or her busty teenage daughter, Amanda (Michele Dalia), may be in jeopardy, Mary and Jo enlist a clueless cop to investigate.

The cop, who happens to look exactly like the dentist, awkwardly flirts with Mary, and Amanda's snowboarder boyfriend, Trenner, somehow gets it into his head that Mary is coming on to him. Although the hygienist's murder never gets solved, there are plenty of hilarious one-liners.

"Listen, there's no subtlety in this production," said the *Sun* review. "Everybody is having so much fun onstage that one suspects there's real wine in all those bottles. Stephanie Lynge plays Mary with a long-suffering inner serenity that perfectly deflects Carolyn Pool's dagger-eyed Jo. Lija Fisher's Liz does everything but physically chew the scenery. Which says something about Michele Dalia that she manages to out-Liz Liz in the guise of Amanda. These women are in jeopardy precisely because they surround themselves with strange men. And nobody does strange better than Hipp regulars Matthew Lindsay and Logan Wolfe. Lindsay is at his schizophrenic best in the look-alike roles of the skin-crawling dentist and the clueless cop. Wolfe is likewise nicely cast as Trenner, Amanda's vacuous beau."[5]

The play doesn't try to make any large sweeping statements; rather, it inspires conversation through its laughter. But, as the character Mary sagely advises young Trenner, "Never, ever tell a woman they still look good for their age."[6]

The Elephant Man

Thirty-five years prior, the Hippodrome had inaugurated its new home in the restored beaux arts Federal Building with a lauded production of *The Elephant Man*. In 2016, they restaged it under the direction of Lauren Warhol Caldwell, starring Bryan Mercer in the title role.

Nichole Hamilton, Joe
Ditmyer, and Bryan Mercer
in *The Elephant Man*.

Photo: Michael Eaddy

In addition to Bryan Mercer as John Merrick, the new cast featured Nichole Hamilton as Mrs. Kendal and Joe Ditmyer as Dr. Treves. Juliana Davis played Princess Alexandria and three other characters. Mark Chambers, Logan Wolfe, Niall McGinty, and Drew Michele each had multiple parts.

"But, really, who among us is normal?" asked theater critic Ron Cunningham in his review. "*The Elephant Man*, now playing at the Hippodrome Theatre, is an exploration of the paper-thin line between the grotesque and the normal. Lauren Warhol Caldwell takes full advantage of the play's approach to forgo elaborate makeup. Instead, there is an utterly fascinating sequence early on in which a seemingly unremarkable man, Bryan Mercer, playing the title character, stands in front of an image of the real Merrick and then slowly begins to contort his body and twist his facial expressions into a convincing imitation. That Mercer is able to maintain these no doubt painful contortions for the entire running time of the show is itself remarkable. That he somehow manages to remain in such unnatural physical form while also transforming himself from barely lucid sideshow freak to witty, erudite companion to the rich and famous, is extraordinary. Mercer is simply amazing."[7]

The Elephant Man played from April 8–May 1.

Green Slime for Summer Laughs

A rock musical about an earth scientist's attempt to clean up a toxic waste site in New Jersey? That could only be *The Toxic Avenger* by Joe DiPietro and David Bryan, based on Lloyd Kaufman's 1984 low-budget horror movie of the same name. Joe DiPietro, who wrote the book and lyrics, had also penned the Hippodrome's 2004 summer hit, *I Love You, You're Perfect, Now Change*. David Bryan, a founding member of the band Bon Jovi, wrote the music and lyrics. The pair, both New Jersey natives, had won Tony Awards for their musical *Memphis*.

The play's setting is Tromaville, New Jersey, site of a toxic waste dump. Aspiring earth scientist Melvin Ferd the Third informs the town's beautiful, blind librarian, Sarah, that horrible vats of toxic goo have appeared all over Tromaville. He also tells her he is determined to find out who's responsible and stop them. She directs him to the town records, where he discovers Mayor Babs Belgoody is behind the toxic goo. When he confronts her, the mayor promises to change her ways. To prove it, she makes Melvin her deputy. But as soon as he leaves, she sends her goons to toss him into a drum of toxic waste.

While passing by the toxic drum on her way home, Sarah is sexually harassed by the goons. Out of smoking green slime, Melvin emerges as the Toxic Avenger—a large, green mutant with a hideously deformed face but a ripped superhero body. He makes quick work of the goons and carries Sarah to her apartment, where she nicknames him Toxie. Smitten by Sarah, he comes home to his disappointed mother, Ma Ferd, and later sees a doctor who refers him to a mad scientist.

In *The Toxic Avenger*, (l-r) Jordan Silver plays a goon for Mayor Belgoody (Kelly Atkins), Dave Schoonover is Melvin Ferd the Third, Maria Kerrigan is Sarah, and Nathanial Tenenbaum is the mayor's other henchman.

When the mayor supervises the unloading of a huge shipment of toxic waste at the Tromaville docks, Toxie foils her plan and reveals that he's actually Melvin Ferd the Third. The mayor vows to destroy him. Determined to find his whereabouts, she confronts his mother and the two women have it out in a song titled "Bitch/Slut/Liar/Whore."

Actress Kelly Atkins played both women and delivered a hilarious performance of the number in a two-sided costume, which depicted Ma Ferd when Kelly turned in one direction and Mayor Babs when she turned the other way.

The mayor incites a drunken lynch mob to chase Toxie, who is cornered and dissolved with bleach. Sarah weeps. Ma Ferd rushes in with the one thing that can save him—a glass of contaminated water from the Hudson River. Melvin is restored, and he vows to kill polluters and end global warming. He marries Sarah and is elected governor.

The Toxic Avenger played from June 3–July 13. It was directed by Lauren Warhol Caldwell with musical direction by Bryan Mercer and choreography by Stephanie Lynge. Dave Schoonover played Melvin Ferd the Third. Maria Kerrigan was Sarah. Nathanial Tenenbaum and Jordan Silver played everyone else: goons, folksingers, cops, soul sisters, hipsters, mobsters, and more.

Rusty Salling

Rusty Salling, one of Gainesville's great and best-loved talents, took his final bow June 12, 2016, after battling cancer for more than a year. Rusty was sixty-seven. He had graced the stage of the Hippodrome Theatre from its earliest years, wowing audiences with some of the best performances in the theatre's history, and was renowned for his brilliant portrayal of Ebenezer Scrooge.

Nell Page and Kevin Rainsberger wrote: "His work was so good, so pure, so clean, so well thought out, that as a member of any ensemble of which Rusty was a part, you were equally inspired and compelled to be your best as well—to put the work in, because Rusty did. It was evident in every role he played in over forty years at the Hippodrome."[8]

In addition to acting, Rusty had worked tirelessly for the theatre he loved, from managing the box office to keeping the Hipp's computer systems running as Information Systems Director.

Season Forty-four

In their fourth collaboration with the UF School of Theatre and Dance, the Hippodrome presented Sarah Ruhl's *Stage Kiss*. Billed as a new romantic comedy with plenty of drama, it is a charming tale about two actors who haven't seen each other in twenty years.

Photo: Michael Eaddy

Gregg Jones plays a director, Michael Krek is Husband, David Patrick Ford plays He, and Stephanie Lynge is She in *Stage Kiss*.

"The first act is sort of a silly farce about the staging of love and the imagination," director Tim Altmyer said, "and the second act is sort of a more serious examination of trying to love somebody in real life."[9]

Two former lovers, simply called She and He, are cast opposite each other as romantic leads in a long-forgotten 1930s melodrama. She is now married and has a teenage daughter. He is dating a sweet schoolteacher. But they quickly lose touch with reality when a stage kiss morphs into a backstage romance.

"The Hipp has kicked off its new season with a wicked comedy about an off-again, on-again romance played out on the successive stages of two atrocious plays. It's extremely funny. If not laugh-a-minute, then pretty darn close," wrote theater critic Ron Cunningham. "[Stephanie] Lynge is on fire as the central character in this comedy of the absurd. She's husband [is] played with a pleasing Sad Sack sweetness by Michael Krek.... Then there's David Patrick Ford as He who brings on the bacon.... Andrew Quimby is hysterical as Kevin. And then there's Gregg Jones' understated turn as the most clueless director in the history of theatre. Brittney Caldwell and Summer Pliskow round out this impressive cast as, respectively, a passive-aggressive fiancée and an annoyingly profane teenager."[10]

The Hippodrome had previously produced two of Sarah Ruhl's other plays, *Eurydice* in 2009 and, in 2010, *Dead Man's Cell Phone*, which Tim Altmyer had also directed. *Stage Kiss* played from September 2–25.

Halloween Fare

As they had been wont to do in recent years, the Hippodrome followed a trend of their own making and tried a parody of something creepy for the Halloween play. This time, it was *Whatever Happened to Baby Jane?*, Dale Gutzman's parody of a 1962 film that was itself a parody of Hollywood's obsession with stars.

Photo: Michael Eaddy

Bryan Mercer as Baby Jane, who imprisons paraplegic sister Blanche (Mark Chambers) in *Whatever Happened to Baby Jane?*

Set in an old Hollywood mansion, the plot of both the film and the play is about an aging former child star, "Baby" Jane Hudson, who torments her paraplegic sister, Blanche, a former movie star who had a far more successful career. The film gained fame by pitting Joan Crawford against Bette Davis, whose intensely bitter rivalry was legendary. Lest Hippodrome audiences miss the point, the theatre projected flickering black-and-white images of Crawford and Davis over the players on stage.

Director Lauren Warhol Caldwell cast Bryan Mercer as Jane and Mark Chambers as Blanche. However, the two men didn't have the rivalry of Crawford and Davis; they were actually friends. But both could do campy queens like nobody's business.

Jane, an increasingly unstable alcoholic, is believed to have caused the car accident that paralyzed Blanche. Jane now keeps wheelchair-bound Blanche trapped upstairs because the mansion purchased with Blanche's earnings lacks an elevator. After Blanche drags herself down the stairs trying to escape, Jane ties Blanche to her bed and kills their nosy housekeeper. Later, Blanche, starved, dehydrated, and near death, tells Jane that she was not responsible for the accident.

As a straight psychological thriller, the play might have made better Halloween fare, but the *Sun* reviewer said Gutzman's script of dark comedy and sight gags "unfortunately turns out to be rather thin gruel."[11] Not that he faulted the leads. "These guys playing faded dolls are the best.... Bryan Mercer does lurching, intoxicated, menacing Jane with perfection.... Yeah, Mercer is that good. Mark Chambers' Blanche doesn't stand a chance.... Still, Chambers nails Crawford's aristocratic intonation. Expectations are simply too high for Mercer and Chambers to soldier on alone. Other cast members flit on and off screen like bystanders looking for something useful to do.... But Jane and Blanche seem to be the only ones having any fun. Audience included."[12]

The other cast members were Sara Morsey, Niall McGinty, Logan Wolfe, Ariel Reich, Maya Handa Naff, Jake Lesh, Madeline Smyth, and Christie Robinson. *Whatever Happened to Baby Jane?* ran from October 14–November 6.

Ultimate Christmas

Gregg Jones settled into his second year as Scrooge for the Hippodrome's thirty-ninth annual production of *A Christmas Carol*. The Dickens tale, adapted by Janet Allard and Michael Bigelow Dixon and directed by Niall McGinty, played November 26–December 18.

It alternated performance times with a wacky musical, *The Ultimate Christmas Show (Abridged)*, written by Reed Martin and Austin Tichenor. Stephanie Lynge got her

Photo: Michael Eaddy

(l-r) Matthew Lindsay, David Patrick Ford, and Mark Chambers throw everything into *The Ultimate Christmas Show*.

first turn to direct a show at the Hippodrome. Bryan Mercer served as musical director.

The premise is that a blizzard has prevented the cast of a church's variety pageant from arriving, but the audience is already there. So, three members of the congregation must perform the entire thing. The show is densely packed with sight gags, politically incorrect monologues, parodies of Christmas songs, and audience participation.

Although the characters they play are amateurs, the actors who played them were seasoned professionals: Mark Chambers, David Patrick Ford, and Matthew Lindsay. In a comic bit, the men performed an ad-libbed performance of "The Twelve Days of Christmas," with audience suggestions taking the place of the gifts conventionally mentioned in the song.

"It adds an extra layer of enjoyment because the audience doesn't just sit back passively," Stephanie Lynge told the *Gainesville Sun*. "It's just another fun way to kind of celebrate the season."[13]

The Ultimate Christmas Show (Abridged) played from November 25–December 18.

1 Donald Margulies, *Collected Stories*, Dramatists Play Service, New York, NY, 1998.
2 Ron Cunningham, review of *Collected Stories*, by Donald Margulies, directed by Lauren Warhol Caldwell, Hippodrome Theatre, Gainesville, FL, *Gainesville Sun*, January 14, 2016.
3 Tyler Francischine, "Independent—With Stories to Tell," *Gainesville Sun*, February 18, 2016.
4 Wendy MacLeod, *Women in Jeopardy!*, Dramatists Play Service, New York, NY, 2016.
5 Ron Cunningham, review of *Women in Jeopardy!*, by Wendy MacLeod, directed by Lauren Warhol Caldwell, Hippodrome Theatre, Gainesville, FL, *Gainesville Sun*, February 24, 2016.
6 Wendy MacLeod, *Women in Jeopardy!*, Dramatists Play Service, New York, NY, 2016.
7 Ron Cunningham, review of *The Elephant Man*, by Bernard Pomerance, directed by Lauren Warhol Caldwell, Hippodrome Theatre, Gainesville, FL, *Gainesville Sun*, April 21, 2016.
8 Kevin Rainsberger and Nell Page, "Rusty Salling: A Life in the Theatre," *Gainesville Sun*, June 19, 2016.
9 Gabrielle Calise, "Kisses Sweeter Than Time," *Gainesville Sun*, September 1, 2016.
10 Ron Cunningham, review of *Stage Kiss*, by Sarah Ruhl, directed by Timothy Altmyer, Hippodrome Theatre, Gainesville, FL, *Gainesville Sun*, September 8, 2016.
11 Ron Cunningham, review of *Whatever Happened to Baby Jane?*, by Dale Gutzman, directed by Lauren Warhol Caldwell, Hippodrome Theatre, Gainesville, FL, *Gainesville Sun*, October 20, 2016.
12 Ibid.
13 Jordan Milian, "The Show Must Go On," *Gainesville Sun*, November 24, 2016.

2017

Demonic Puppet

The Hippodrome's January play was *Hand to God*, a Tony Award-nominated dark comedy about Christian-ministry puppets, often described as a humorous mix of *Avenue Q* and *The Exorcist*. "It's a southern regionalism that's fairly unknown in the North,"[1] explained the play's author, Robert Askins. Fundamentalist Christian congregations in the Bible Belt often use puppets to teach children how to follow the Bible and avoid Satan.

Margery (Kelly Atkins), a recent widow, is the play's central character. To keep her occupied, her minister, Pastor Greg (Charlie Mitchell), asks her to run the puppet club. Its teenage members include her son Jason (Jon Kovach); Jessica, the girl next door, whom he has a crush on (Ariel Reich); and Timothy, the neighborhood troublemaker (Ryan George).

As the puppet club prepares for a Sunday performance, the characters become sexually attracted to each other. Jason's hand puppet, Tyrone, takes on a life of his own, announces that he is Satan, and, over the course of the play, leads everyone into sin. Pastor Greg's attempted exorcism of Tyrone fails. Jason finally bludgeons the puppet. Just when the audience thinks Tyrone is finally dead, he reappears, larger than ever, in an epilogue in which he mocks the audience for wanting to see him again and summarizes humanity's thousands of years of solving their problems by putting horns on them.

About her choice of the play, director Lauren Warhol Caldwell said, "The reviews were really and truly unanimously off the charts about how funny it is."[2] She expected that some would be offended by the play. Despite the colorful hand puppets, there are episodes of violence, sexual situations, and vulgar language throughout the show. "You can't be afraid," she said. "You can't be an artist and try to please everybody."[3]

Photo: Michael Eaddy

Hand to God cast. Bottom: Pastor Greg (Charlie Mitchell), Mom (Kelly Atkins), and Timothy (Ryan George). Top: Jason (Jon Kovach), Jessica (Ariel Reich), and demonic puppet Tyrone.

One who was not offended was theater critic Ron Cunningham, who wrote: "It may be the funniest play ever about unfunny things; mental illness, mutilation, demonic possession, take your pick. Jon Kovach is simply amazing as sweet-tempered Jason and his evil alter ego Tyrone. Kelly Atkins plays Margery with a winsome wholesomeness mixed with just the right measure of spice and sass. Ryan George does Timothy with a wide-eyed kinetic energy. More than a match for the mouthy Tyrone is Ariel Reich, with her miles-over-the-top performance as Jessica. *Hand to God* is worth seeing, if only for Tyrone's irreverent musings." But, Cunningham warned readers, "When Tyrone opens his neon-blue, teeth-studded pie hole, the F bombs fall as thick as hailstones on a Texas prairie."[4]

Hand to God played from January 13–February 5.

A Birthday Present Shared

The Hippodrome's next play, *Becky's New Car* by Steven Dietz, had two unusual audience members. Charlie and Benita Staadecker drove from their home in Naples, Florida, to see the production. Ten years earlier, Charlie had commissioned the play as a gift for Benita's sixtieth birthday instead of giving her a cruise or a lavish party. "Why not invest in a work of art that continues beyond your years?"[5] he said.

"It's my gift to everyone to be able to enjoy this work,"[6] Benita said.

Since the play's original opening in Seattle, the couple had traveled to at least thirty-five playhouses to see the show. "What we didn't realize," Charlie said, "is the play can take on different facets; different prisms to look through as the director finds the words can be nuanced in a way we didn't see before."[7] Hippodrome General Manager Jessica Hurov and Lauren Warhol Caldwell met with the couple and gave them a tour of the theatre before they attended a Friday evening performance.

Director David Shelton brought the production to the stage just two-and-a-half weeks after *Hand to God* closed. Knowing five of the seven actors prior to producing the play helped him reduce their learning curve. "You kind of have this trust already built in," said Nichole Hamilton, who had the lead role as Becky Foster. "While a comedy at heart, *Becky's New Car* tackles some tough situations. It borders on the existential—what life is, how we come to discover our purpose."[8]

Players in *Becky's New Car*: (l-r) Gregg Jones, Chelsi Stancil, Niall McGinty, Nichole Hamilton, Adam Lishawa, Catherine Fries Vaughn, and Bryan Mercer.

Photo: Michael Eaddy

Becky is the middle-aged wife of laid-back husband Joe (Adam Lishawa) and mother of tightly wound, still-living-at-home college student Chris (Niall McGinty). She works at a car dealership with fast-talking salesperson Steve, played to the hilt by Bryan Mercer. One night, Becky is the sole person at work when widowed millionaire Walter Flood (Gregg Jones) walks in and buys nine new cars as party favors.

Walter is taken with Becky and soon begins to woo her, which interferes with the plans of a destitute trust fund heiress (Catherine Fries Vaughn) who has her eye on Walter's money. Also, Walter's daughter, played by Chelsi Stancil, dislikes Becky at first sight. Meanwhile, Becky's straight life takes twists and turns, speeding toward a midlife collision.

"*Becky's New Car* is engaging, flawed, and improbably convoluted," said the *Sun* theater review. "But let's not quibble over plot holes and unexplained motivations. Played strictly for laughs, *Becky's New Car* is in gear and rolling. Adeptly performed by Hipp regular Nichole Hamilton, Becky establishes instant rapport with the audience. Bryan Mercer gets to do what he always does best on the Hipp stage: Over-the-top angst of the head-exploding variety. Always a pleasure to watch Mercer wear his emotions like a cheap suit."[9]

The show ran from February 24–March 19.

Hamlet with a Hashtag

Now in their forty-fourth year, it seemed unfathomable that the Hippodrome hadn't done William Shakespeare's *Hamlet* multiple times, but the list of their past productions reveals April 2017 was the first.

Possibly the best known of the Bard's plays, it needs but the briefest synopsis. Hamlet, a prince, returns home to discover that his mother has married his uncle, who now sits on the throne. Seeing the ghost of his father, Hamlet believes they murdered him and plots revenge. The king, fearing Hamlet, sends him to sea with a letter asking the English king to execute Hamlet, but pirates attack the ship. Hamlet escapes and returns home. While he's away, his love interest, Ophelia, dies. His planned revenge involves a play within the play and a duel with a poisoned sword. It goes awry, and in the end, everybody dies.

Photo: Michael Eaddy

Gravedigger (Charlie Mitchell) listens as Horatio (Bryan Mercer) and Hamlet (Michael Littig) ponder deceased jester York.

Director Lauren Warhol Caldwell decided they wouldn't change Shakespeare's words but would set the play in contemporary times with modern electronics, business suits, riot gear, and automatic rifles. The National Endowment for the Arts awarded the Hippodrome a grant to collaborate on Hamlet with the international Workcenter of Jerzy Grotowski and Thomas Richards, bringing them to Gainesville for a two-week residency in the fall of 2016. (Grotowski was considered one of the most influential theatre practitioners of the twentieth century.) Lauren said she had worked on the *Hamlet* production for nearly two years.

The cast featured Michael Littig as Hamlet, V Craig Heidenreich as his uncle (Claudius), and Sara Morsey as Hamlet's mother, Gertrude. Bryan Mercer was Horatio and Lauren Nordvig played Ophelia. Niall McGinty played Laertes, Guildenstern, and Lucianus. Logan Wolfe was Rosencrantz plus three other characters. Charlie Mitchell was wise Polonius, and Matthew Lindsay had four roles.

The *Sun* reviewer said, "The Hippodrome's current production of *Hamlet* is graced with the sort of strong performances one expects from the theater's troupe of seasoned professionals."[10] His issue was that "the liberal insertion of pop culture symbolism—iPhones, laptops, selfies, vaping, switchblade in lieu of sword—threatens to trivialize rather than modernize. This production has all the star power it needs to make *Hamlet* an unforgettable evening of theatre. In flirting with #HamletFarce the Hipp forsakes the wise counsel of Polonius: 'To thine own self be true.'"[11]

Hamlet ran from April 17–May 7.

Photo: Michael Eaddy

2017 cast of *Forever Plaid*: (l-r) Matty Colonna, Charles Logan, Nick Endsley, and James Gish.

Thrice Plaid

For their summer musical, the Hippodrome reprised *Forever Plaid* for a third go-round. This time it had a new musical director, Bryan Mercer, a new cast, and a new director, Steven Flaa, who had directed sixteen productions of *Forever Plaid* at other theatres across the state. Playing the Four Plaids were Nick Endsley, Matty Colonna, Charles Logan, and James Gish. Lightning struck again, and the show had an extended run from June 2–July 30.

Season Forty-five

Continuing what was now a tradition, the Hippodrome collaborated with the UF School of Theatre and Dance to present *1984*, Andrew White's adaptation of George Orwell's classic dystopian novel.

The story is about a totalitarian surveillance state that eliminates privacy, replaces it with disinformation, and wages psychological warfare on its citizens through state-sanctioned media. Niall McGinty played the central character, Winston, a low-ranking member of the party that rules the militaristic superpower Oceania. His job is to forge and alter documents to make it appear as if the party's current claims have always been true. Winston, however, holds a secret disdain for the party and keeps an illegal diary he purchased from an antiques dealer named Charrington, played by Sara Morsey.

Photo: Michael Eaddy

Winston (Niall McGinty) and O'Brien (V Craig Heidenreich), leader of the Brotherhood in *1984*, where Big Brother is always watching.

Winston receives a love note from Julia (Maya Handa Naff) and they engage in a love affair, which is a crime against the state. The couple joins a secret resistance called the Brotherhood, and the organization's leader, O'Brien (V Craig Heidenreich), gives them an illegal book to study. When Winston and Julia are captured, tortured, and brainwashed, Charrington and O'Brien are revealed to be agents of the Thought Police.

The oft-used term for government spying, "Big Brother," originated in Orwell's novel as Oceania's omniscient ruler who watches and dictates everything people must do and think. The book also introduced "newspeak," where nice-sounding, easily pronounceable contractions mask their ideological content. In contemporary politics, "newspeak" is sometimes used as an allegation that a politician is introducing new meanings of words to suit his or her agenda.

A *Sun* article said, "According to Lauren Warhol Caldwell, the play's artistic director, the Hippodrome decided to start their season with *1984* because of its recent resurgence in pop culture. Since the election of Donald Trump as president, the book has resurfaced on bestseller lists. 'With all the hype over the novel, we started researching plays.' ... Sara Morsey, who plays Charrington, said that she remembers reading *1984* when she was in college and now realizes how Orwell's depiction wasn't too far from today's technological advancements."[12] V Craig Heidenreich added, "Back in the '80s, nobody was talking about global warming as if it were a real thing, and yet Orwell had imagined a world where it was 84 degrees in December."[13]

Other members of the cast of twelve included theatre professionals Laura Shatkus, Thiago Palma, and six UF theatre students: Jeff Drushal, Amanda Hayter, Michael Krek, Kristina Johnson, Orlando Mendez, and Diego Zozaya.

The play opened September 1, but Hurricane Irma forced cancellation of the Sunday performances a week later. The theater reopened the following Tuesday and shows continued through September 24. The headline of the *Gainesville Sun* review read, "Seven decades on, *1984* still makes gripping theatre."[14] In conjunction with the play, the Hippodrome promoted a One City One Story communitywide reading initiative of the book, which included reading events on the Hippodrome steps and at the Library Headquarters branch.

From Big Brother to Drag Queen

Breaking with the previous decade's trend of presenting a horror or horror-parody in October, director Stephanie Lynge said the Hipp decided to "go with something a little more costume and pizzazz, rather than horror, since *1984* was a heavy trip itself."[15] And you couldn't go much further afield than a drag queen dive bar in Panama City, Florida, the setting for *The Legend of Georgia McBride* by Matthew

To keep his job, Casey (Jon Kovach) transforms from Elvis impersonator to drag queen with help from Miss Tracy (Mark Chambers) in *The Legend of Georgia McBride.*

Photo: Michael Eaddy

Lopez. Stephanie, who also choreographed the show, added that she was "excited for audiences to come in and be blinded by all the sparkle."[16]

The plot revolves around Casey (Jon Kovach), a down-on-his-luck, desperately broke Elvis impersonator whose wife Jo (Caroline Strang) is expecting. His gig at a rundown dive isn't drawing any crowds, so the bar owner, played by Charlie Mitchell, fires Casey and replaces his act with a B-level drag show. If he wants to keep working there, Casey has to learn a whole new side of show business. And there's nobody better than Miss Tracy Mills (played by Mark Chambers) to teach him. Tracy is an older drag queen who mentors him. "Take off your clothes. We're turning you into a girl," Tracy tells him.[17]

Casey's competition is Rexy (Kevin Kantor), a jealous, alcoholic drag queen who tells Casey that drag "is not a night job" and "it's not for sissies."[18] That's not Casey's only problem. He must keep his wife Jo from finding out about his new act. With Tracy's help, Casey turns out to be pretty great at it.

"It's OK to flee reality for a bit and go see *The Legend of Georgia McBride*," Ron Cunningham wrote. "And leave with no regrets. Because Matthew Lopez's script is tightly written, fast-paced, and wickedly funny. The songs are spirited, and the strutting is stupendous."[19]

The Legend of Georgia McBride played from October 13–November 5.

Love Letters

On October 24, Kevin Rainsberger and Nell Page gave a benefit performance of A. R. Gurney's *Love Letters* to raise money for Southern Legal Counsel—a not-for-profit public interest law firm that is committed to the ideal of equal justice for all and the attainment of basic human and civil rights. The play was a finalist for the Pulitzer Prize in Drama.

In the play, Andrew and Melissa, both born to wealth and position, are childhood friends whose lifelong correspondence tells the story of their lives. They sit side by side at tables and read the notes, letters, and cards in which, over nearly fifty years, they have discussed the hopes and ambitions, dreams and disappointments, and victories and defeats that have passed between them throughout their separated lives.

Holiday Shows

Niall McGinty directed the Hippodrome's fortieth production of *A Christmas Carol*, which ran from November 25–December 22. For their alternate play, they tried something different. While it was not a holiday-themed play, *A Year with Frog and Toad* charmed audiences of all ages. The whimsical musical, with book and lyrics by Willie Reale and music by his brother Robert, is based on the children's stories by Arnold Lobel. Clint Thornton, who also played the curmudgeonly Toad, directed it. Musical direction was by Bryan Mercer, who played the easygoing Frog.

Cast of *A Year with Frog and Toad*: (l-r) Bryan Mercer, Marissa Toogood, Maya Handa Naff, Nick Lerew, and Clint Thornton.

Photo: Michael Eaddy

The show had broken new ground by bringing professional children's theatre to Broadway and was nominated for three Tony Awards: Best Musical, Best Book of a Musical, and Best Original Score.

The musical follows the woodland adventures of the two friends and their assortment of colorful, hopping, crawling, and flying companions over the course of a year. Marissa Toogood played Bluebird, Turtle, Young Frog, Squirrel, and a mole. Maya Handa Naff was Robin, Mouse, Mother Frog, Squirrel, and a second mole. They were all great. But Nick Lerew stole every scene in which he hilariously scurried around the stage on a scooter as Snail, delivering messages between Frog and Toad. Nick also played Father Frog, Cardinal, Lizard, and a mole. The show ran from November 24–December 17.

1 Beth Stevens, "*Hand to God* Playwright Robert Askins on Being a Title Fetishist, Losing the Texas Tragedy & What Opens Doors," broadway.com, April 14, 2015.
2 Gabrielle Calise, "*Hand to God* Opens Friday at the Hippodrome," *Gainesville Sun*, January 12, 2017.
3 Ibid.
4 Ron Cunningham, review of *Hand to God*, by Robert Askins, directed by Lauren Warhol Caldwell, Hippodrome Theatre, Gainesville, FL, *Gainesville Sun*, January 19, 2017.
5 Deborah Strange, "Gift of Theater," *Gainesville Sun*, March 4, 2017.
6 Ibid.
7 Ibid.
8 Alejandro López, "*Becky's New Car* Zooms Down the Road of Life's Challenges," *Gainesville Sun*, February 23, 2017.
9 Ron Cunningham, review of *Becky's New Car*, by Steven Dietz, directed by David Shelton, Hippodrome Theatre, Gainesville, FL, *Gainesville Sun*, March 2, 2017.
10 Ron Cunningham, review of *Hamlet*, by William Shakespeare, directed by Lauren Caldwell, Hippodrome Theatre, Gainesville, FL, *Gainesville Sun*, April 20, 2017.
11 Ibid.
12 Sara Marino, "The World of Big Brother," *Gainesville Sun*, August 31, 2017.
13 Ibid.
14 Ron Cunningham, review of *1984*, by Andrew White, directed by Lauren Warhol Caldwell, Hippodrome Theatre, Gainesville, FL, *Gainesville Sun*, September 7, 2017.
15 Sara Marino, "From Elvis Impersonator to Drag Queen," *Gainesville Sun*, October 12, 2017.
16 Ibid.
17 Matthew Lopez, *The Legend of Georgia McBride*, Dramatists Play Service, New York, NY, 2017.
18 Ibid.
19 Ron Cunningham, review of *The Legend of Georgia McBride*, by Matthew Lopez, directed by Stephanie Lynge, Hippodrome Theatre, Gainesville, FL, *Gainesville Sun*, October 26, 2017.

2018

The Royale

The Hippodrome's first play of the new year was Marco Ramirez's *The Royale*. It is set in 1905 during the Jim Crow era, and its fictional character Jay (Bryce Michael Wood) is modeled after Jack Johnson, the first African American World Heavyweight champion boxer. The play tells the story of a racially charged fight of the century, in which an African American boxer takes on the Caucasian heavyweight champ.

(l-r) E. Stanley Richardson, Dylan Kammerer, Bryce Michael Wood, Ryan George, and Renata Eastlick in *The Royale*.

Photo: Michael Eaddy

Jay strives to use his boxing abilities to prove that race is nothing more than the color of someone's skin. Helping him through his journey are his sparring partner, Fish (Ryan George); his fight promoter, Max (Dylan Kammerer); and his trainer, Wynton (E. Stanley Richardson). On the night before the big fight, his sister, Nina (Renata Eastlick), tries to warn him against it. She says, "What do you think will happen if you win? The price of the white resentment that will ensue will be paid in blood and broken bones by other black people." He responds, "Did you come all the way up here to tell me to lose?"[1]

Ryan George, who co-directed the play with Lauren Warhol Caldwell, said, "There are things now that we're very far past ... but still the tension and angst of race relations or sexual orientations, those things are still bubbling up under the surface of society, and it's important to remember that you have to visit your past and learn from it."[2]

"From start to finish a pounding, gutty rhythm pulses through the Hippodrome's production," said the *Sun* review. "This fast-moving tale from the early turn of the last century about a black boxer trying to punch, jab, and jaw his way into a white world, is set to the thunder-clap rhythm of smashing hands and the brutal thump of pounding feet.... Raw athleticism, pugnacity, and attitude ripple from every sinew of Bryce Michael Wood's finely sculpted boxer's body. But it is the vulnerability and torment flashing across Jay's world-weary face that establishes Wood's acting chops."[3]

The play opened January 12 and ran through February 11. Almost weekly during its run, the *Gainesville Sun* printed letters from audience members wowed by the show. One writer lived as far away as North Carolina. Closer to home, Mark Sexton wrote: "If you want a once-in-a-lifetime experience that will leave you changed, inspired, and uplifted by the sheer artistry of the event, *The Royale* is a knockout."[4]

Chapatti

On January 29, the Hippodrome Theatre presented *Chapatti* by Christian O'Reilly in a benefit for the Bonnie J. Addario Lung Cancer Foundation in memory of actor and choreographer Ric Rose who passed away November 18, 2017, and to honor the Hippodrome's earliest benefactor Caren Gorenberg, a cancer survivor.

The play concerns two lonely animal lovers living in Dublin. When forlorn Dan and his dog Chapatti cross paths with the amiable Betty and her nineteen cats, an unexpected spark begins. A warm and gentle story unfolds about people rediscovering the importance of human companionship. The cast featured Nell Page and Kevin Rainsberger.

Premiering *Ripcord*

Next up was the Florida premiere of *Ripcord*, a comedy by Pulitzer Prize-winning playwright David Lindsay-Abaire, who also wrote *Good People,* which the Hippodrome had produced four years earlier. *Ripcord* centers on two women sharing a room in a retirement home. A harmless bet results in an escalating game of one-upmanship reminiscent of Neil Simon's *The Odd Couple* or the more recent Netflix comedy *Grace and Frankie.*

Two of the Hippodrome's most experienced grande dames, Nell Page and Sara Morsey, played Marilyn and Abby. Marilyn is a happy, active senior while Abby prefers to read quietly and be left alone. Although Abby cares a great deal about some things, she often keeps those things to herself. In many ways, the story is about Abby's growth and acceptance of people. Director V Craig Heidenreich said, "It's astonishingly and excruciatingly funny and surprising and imaginative, while also being a heartfelt and honest portrayal of transformation and of hope in a world that needs more of it."[5] This was Craig's first time directing at the Hippodrome, but he had acted in and directed over two hundred productions elsewhere in Florida.

Photo: Michael Eaddy

Nell Page and Sara Morsey play incompatible roommates in *Ripcord*.

Critic Ron Cunningham summed up the tension between the two women: "One won't shut up to save her life, and the other wouldn't open up if her life depended on it.... Sara Morsey and Nell Page were born to play Abby and Marilyn. The parts could have been written for them.... What follows between these two spry combatants is an increasingly improbable series of unfortunate events involving zombies, kidnapping, parachutes, invasion of privacy, mugging, rope tricks and—perhaps most shocking of all—one filling in the other's Sudoku puzzles."[6]

The supporting actors were all Hippodrome veterans adept at comedy. Bryan Mercer portrayed Abby's son. Laura Shatkus played Marilyn's daughter, and Niall McGinty was Marilyn's son-in-law. Both Laura and Niall played additional characters as well. Rounding out the cast was Logan Wolfe as a facility employee who'd rather be an actor.

The play proved popular and had its run extended an extra week, playing from March 2–April 1.

The Christians

V Craig Heidenreich stayed on to play a character in Lucas Hnath's *The Christians*, which opened April 20 and ran through May 13. This off-Broadway hit centers on a pastor who worked for twenty years to build his church from a modest storefront to a mega-church with a baptistry the size of a swimming pool and a congregation of thousands. One day, he delivers an unexpected sermon that rejects the traditional Fundamentalist Hell as a construct of our own making and not God's. Pastor Paul (Joe Ditmyer) points out that the Bible never mentions such a place.

Photo: Michael Eaddy

(l-r) Renata Eastlick, V Craig Heidenreich, Joe Ditmyer, Juliana Davis, and Marquis Gibson in *The Christians*.

This prompts his associate pastor, Joshua (Marquis D. Gibson), to take the pulpit and challenge him in a faceoff that ultimately leads to a vote by the congregation on whether to fire Joshua. Sitting on the dais watching the two men go head-to-head is the pastor's wife, played by Juliana Davis, and a church Elder, Jay (V Craig Heidenreich).

Throughout the play, Pastor Paul struggles to communicate his beliefs to his wife, his friends, and the congregation of thousands who trust and believe him. As the pastor and associate pastor debate, a congregant (played by Renata Eastlick) raises her hand to ask if Pastor Paul had waited until the church's debts were paid off to adopt this new, more inclusive, and universalist Christianity. But the play was not anti-Christian or anti-religion. Nor was it like *God's Man in Texas*.

"The play is about good, kind, decent, loving humans trying to bridge that insurmountable gap to be able to communicate with each other," said V Craig Heidenreich. "There's an effort being made by the playwright to insist on people trying to listen to each other."[7]

Director Lauren Warhol Caldwell added, "Both sides are embraced so beautifully, everybody wins. There's not a loser in the house because somewhere in this story you, as an individual, are being represented."[8]

Atypical of most Hippodrome plays, the actors used microphones to create the feel of a mega-church. "Because it does take place in a church, most people can't put themselves into the shoes of the characters," said Joe Ditmyer. So the actors break the fourth wall and let the audience take on the role of the congregation.

Renata Eastlick added, "The storytelling becomes much more realistic because we have the opportunity to engage with the audience." She described the play as being "thought-provoking theatre."[9]

During its run from April 20–May 13, the *Gainesville Sun* published several letters to the editor praising the play. The *Sun* review called the cast steller and said the play made a point worth pondering.

Summer Jukebox

Summer—time to drop a coin in the Hippodrome jukebox and enjoy some oldies. For 2018, that was *The Bikinis*, the story of four Jersey girls from a former '60s pop group known as The Bikinis. In a typical jukebox musical plot, the four women reunite decades after their heyday to put on a benefit performance to keep greedy developers from turning their childhood trailer park into a beachfront condo. This sets up a lively, lighthearted retrospective of thirty-five hits from the 1960s and 1970s. Of course, that repertoire has to include Brian Hyland's 1960 novelty hit "Itsy Bitsy Teeny Weeny Yellow Polka Dot Bikini."

Photo: Michael Eaddy

The Bikinis, played by Wydetta Carter, Catherine Fries Vaughn, Melanie Souza, and Kelly Atkins.

The show was created by Ray Roderick and James Hindman with additional music by Joseph Baker. Lauren Warhol Caldwell directed it. Bryan Mercer was the musical director and Stephanie Lynge the choreographer.

The cast of four featured Kelly Atkins, Catherine Fries Vaughn, Melanie Souza, and Wydetta Carter. Kelly and Catherine had sung together in both Hippodrome productions of *The Great American Trailer Park Musical*. Melanie and Wydetta were new to the Hippodrome, but both were professionals who had appeared in plenty of musicals elsewhere.

Catherine, who had previously done *The Bikinis* at a theatre in Alabama said, "What I liked about The Bikinis is it's sometimes hard to find vehicles for women *of an age* and I enjoyed the fact that show was fun and comedic and an opportunity for women who are more mature."

The Bikinis opened June 1. Audiences loved the old girl-group songs performed by four superior vocal talents, and the show had an abundance of one-liners, dancing, kitsch, and glitzy costumes. Its run was extended repeatedly, finally closing on July 29.

Managing Director Takes New Position

In August, the Visitors and Convention Bureau announced that Jessica Hurov had been hired as the Alachua County Tourism Manager. Jessica had spent twelve years at the Hippodrome, the last four as Managing Director, during which time she oversaw its two-and-half million-dollar budget. She told the *Gainesville Sun* her new position was "a dream job."

The Hippodrome board did not name a Managing Director to replace Jessica, and the theatre entered its next season with Lauren Warhol Caldwell continuing as Artistic Director and Nicole Daenzer as Director of Operations.

Season Forty-six

The Hippodrome started its forty-sixth season with money troubles. On opening night of Sarah DeLappe's *The Wolves*, Chairman of the Board of Trustees Michael Curry stood at center stage next to the play's director, Lauren Warhol Caldwell, and announced to the audience, "Congratulations. The Hippodrome is no longer a ward of the state." The Florida legislature had whittled the Hipp's funding to the bare minimum. In the 1990s, the Hipp could count on the state for about $250,000 a year. The state's most recent cuts dropped that to $9,941. Lauren called it "humiliating, a clear message from the state that it doesn't value artists."[10]

Photo: Michael Eaddy

Clockwise from top: Emma McAvoy, MaRah Williams, Marissa Toogood, Ariel Reich, Gloria Halsell, Jordan Sison, Isabella Werber, Suzy Weller, and Melanie Sholl play *The Wolves*, a soccer team.

To cut costs, the Hippodrome reached an agreement with the union to reduce actors' pay and perform seven shows a week instead of eight. The bare Astroturf set for *The Wolves* was another example of frugality. Jointly producing the play with the UF School of Theatre and Dance helped, too. UF theatre students or recent graduates made up half of the all-female cast: Gloria Halsell, Emma McAvoy, Jordan Sison, Melanie Sholl, and MaRah Williams. The other half were Hippodrome company members or theatre professionals from New York: Stephanie Lynge, Marissa Toogood, Ariel Reich, Suzy Weller, and Isabella Werber. Only seven of the ten actors were union members.

"Whatever we have to do, wherever this leads us," Lauren said, "the art is not going to suffer. I'm not willing to offer anything up but excellence."[11]

The Wolves had won the 2017 Obie Award and was a finalist for the Pulitzer Prize. The characters are nine teenage girls who make up the Wolves, a high school soccer team. They are identified only by the numbers on their uniforms. The set is an indoor soccer facility. Throughout the play, the girls converse during their warm-ups before each game. Topics range from the sentencing of an elderly participant in the Cambodian genocide to social gossip about each other and unseen characters, their bodies, their coach's obvious hangovers, their desire to play soccer in college, and speculations about Number 46, a new girl on the team who is homeschooled.

Their inappropriate conversations often cause conflict amongst the teammates. Number 00, the goalie, suffers from social anxiety attacks and runs outside to vomit before each game. Number 7 is a profanity-spouting sexual adventuress who suffers a career-ending skiing injury before the second-to-last game, leaving the team hanging.

When Number 14 is killed in an auto accident a week before the final game, Number 00 breaks down in grief and leaves the stadium. Her teammates assume that the others will also ditch the game and they will have to forfeit. However, the surviving team members all show up. The deceased Number 14's mom (played by Stephanie Lynge) doesn't appear in the play until the end when she gives the team a rallying speech. Stephanie's monologue stole the show.

Among the cast members, only Melanie Sholl had ever played soccer. So Lauren brought in a trainer from UF's Department of Recreational Sports, Katelyn Peterson, who had been a starter on an NCAA Women's Soccer team for all four years of her collegiate career. She taught the cast basic soccer stretches and drills so they could look like real soccer stars.

"First and foremost, we wanted to start attacking the footwork," said Marissa Toogood. "It's a lot to be doing all at once when you think about the choreography, the drills, and what you have to say on top of it."[12]

Although the things adolescent girls talk about and the level of profanity when adults aren't around shocked some audience members, theater critic Ron Cunningham thought the play had merit. He said, "Sarah DeLappe's *The Wolves*, a sometimes hilarious, sometimes excruciating, and not occasionally heart-rendering breakdown of who says what and why in the moments leading up to game on. *The Wolves* gives us much to talk about. From the petty to the profound to the pitiable, it is a conversation worth having."[13]

The Wolves ran from August 31–September 23.

Gala

Somehow, the Hippodrome had missed holding a forty-fifth-anniversary party. But needing to do some serious fundraising, they held a benefit on September 28 that they called "A Gala in Three Acts." The event featured cocktails, hors d'oeuvres, and dinner, followed by live entertainment from the Scott Wilson Trio, Kelly Atkins, Matthew Morgan, and Bryan Mercer, for the low price of $150 per person.

Halloween Production

The Hippodrome had taken a breather from its Halloween routine with the prior year's drag queen comedy, *The Legend of Georgia McBride*. But for 2018, vampires were back. *Let the Right One In* combines a coming-of-age romance with a vampire story about a lonely twelve-year-old boy and the girl next door.

Playwright Jack Thorne based the play on a novel by Swedish author John Ajvide Lindqvist, which had also been made into a Swedish film.

Oskar, a shy, bullied boy, meets Eli, a pale girl who appears to be his age and has just moved in next door. Eli lives with Håkan, an older man who seems to be her dad. Initially, she tells Oskar that they cannot be friends. However, the two ex-

Photo: Michael Eaddy
Cast of *Let the Right One In*.
Front (l-r): Stephanie Lynge,
Niall McGinty, Bryan Mercer,
and Charlie Mitchell. On
scaffold: Ben Tracy, Clint
Thornton, Marissa Toogood,
Gregory Buckheit, and
Orlando Mendez.

change Morse code messages by tapping on their adjoining apartment wall, and over time, they develop a close relationship. Eli helps Oskar stand up for himself against his tormentors.

Later, she is spotted killing a man and drinking his blood after Håkan, who usually procures blood for her, has failed. After another failure, Håkan offers his neck to Eli for feeding, and Eli drains him of his blood. Eli goes to Oskar's apartment and spends the night with him, during which time they agree to go steady, although Eli tells him she isn't a girl. It turns out she was changed into a vampire during adolescence and has retained the appearance of an adolescent even though she's 228.

Ben Tracy played Oskar, Marissa Toogood was Eli, and Stephanie Lynge played Oskar's mother. Clint Thornton was Håkan, and Bryan Mercer was the unfortunate man who got killed. Charlie Mitchell played the teacher. Niall McGinty, Gregory Buckheit, and Orlando Mendez were the school bullies.

Lauren Warhol Caldwell decided to intertwine powerful movements throughout the show to better display the characters' emotions and inner turmoil. "If you were to just watch the movement, without dialogue, you would know what the play was about," she said. "I wanted it to be more married to the actual text."[14]

That doesn't mean the *Sun* critic liked it. He said, "*Let the Right One In* overdoses on leaden, piano- and violin-induced gothic fugue-like states, in which time itself slows and everyone begins to drift across the stage like a troop of synchronized zombie dancers stuck in molasses. You understand why it's happening. But that doesn't stop these dim, mass mood swings from growing tedious, distracting, and even counterproductive.... and enough stupor-inducing ennui to make you glance at your watch occasionally."[15]

Let the Right One In opened October 12 and ran through November 4.

Holiday Shows

In addition to the annual presentation of *A Christmas Carol*, directed for the fourth year by Niall McGinty, the Hippodrome offered up *Every Christmas Story Ever Told (And Then Some)*, written by Michael Carleton, Jim FitzGerald, and John K. Alvarez, and directed by Stephanie Lynge.

In the play, three actors start out preparing for yet another performance of *A Christmas Carol*. But they are fed up with Dickens's old saw and decide to create a brand-new play with help from the audience that includes everyone's holiday favorites, while adding their own twisted touches. Logan Wolfe told the *Gainesville Sun* he was particularly excited to interact with the audience during the performance. "In live theatre, you never know what's going to happen. But when you bring in a total wild card out of the audience, you *really* never know."[16]

Ali Foley, Mark Chambers, and Logan Wolfe in *Every Christmas Story Ever Told (And Then Some)*.

Photo: Michael Eaddy

Reviewer Ron Cunningham noted it was "as overstuffed with alliteration, innuendo, and double-entendres as last year's Christmas turkey. Logan Wolfe and Mark Chambers, two of the most reliable jokers in the Hipp's marked deck, try their best to cram in as many BHC (Beloved Holiday Classics) as time and physics allow. And with the able assistance and boundless energy of Hipp newcomer Ali Foley, they very nearly pull it off."[17]

The play opened November 23, and *A Christmas Carol* opened the day after. Both plays closed on December 23.

1   Marco Ramirez, *The Royale*, Samuel French Inc., New York, NY, 2017.
2   Sara Marino, "Taking a Swing at History," *Gainesville Sun*, January 11, 2018.
3   Ron Cunningham, review of *The Royale*, by Marco Ramirez, directed by Lauren Warhol Caldwell and Ryan George, Hippodrome Theatre, Gainesville, FL, *Gainesville Sun*, January 18, 2018.
4   Mark Sexton, letters to the editor, *Gainesville Sun*, January 26, 2018.
5   Rebecca Santana, "Pulling the *Ripcord*," *Gainesville Sun*, March 1, 2018.
6   Ron Cunningham, review of *Ripcord*, by David Lindsay-Abaire, directed by V Craig Heidenreich, Hippodrome Theatre, Gainesville, FL, *Gainesville Sun*, March 8, 2018.
7   Rebecca Santana, "Acclaimed Drama *The Christians* Opens at the Hipp," *Gainesville Sun*, April 19, 2018.
8   Ibid.
9   Ibid.
10 Scottie Andrew, "Hipp Deep," *Gainesville Sun*, September 23, 2018.
11 Ibid.
12 Kristen Altus, "Running with the Pack," *Gainesville Sun*, August 30, 2018.
13 Ron Cunningham, review of *The Wolves*, by Sarah DeLappe, directed by Lauren Warhol Caldwell, Hippodrome Theatre, Gainesville, FL, *Gainesville Sun*, September 6, 2018.
14 Catie Wegman, "Won't You Be My Neighbor?," *Gainesville Sun*, October 11, 2018.
15 Ron Cunningham, review of *Let the Right One In*, by Jack Thorne, directed by Lauren Warhol Caldwell, Hippodrome Theatre, Gainesville, FL, *Gainesville Sun*, October 18, 2018.
16 Catie Wegman, "A Comedic Christmas Story," *Gainesville Sun*, November 22, 2018.
17 Ron Cunningham, review of *Every Christmas Story Ever Told (And Then Some)*, by Michael Carleton, Jim FitzGerald, and John K. Alvarez, directed by Stephanie Lynge, Hippodrome Theatre, Gainesville, FL, *Gainesville Sun*, November 29, 2018.

2019

Lauren's Third Act

Readers of the *Gainesville Sun* who noticed a small three-paragraph blurb in the January 22, 2019, issue were shocked: "The Hippodrome Theatre announced Monday in a news release that artistic director Lauren Warhol Caldwell has left the theatre after twenty-eight years. The theatre's board of directors has appointed Stephanie Lynge, who's been with the Hipp for four years, as interim artistic director."[1]

In a follow-up article, Ron Cunningham wrote, "She arguably became the single most influential figure in the Hippodrome State Theatre's artistic evolution; choosing and directing most of its offerings ... putting her own imprimatur on the Hipp's unique brand."[2]

"I provoked as much as I could," Lauren told him. "I loved my stories. I had a lot of freedom there in terms of the kind of shows I wanted to do."[3]

Cunningham continued, "[Lauren] is taking her leave and embarking on a ...well, let's just call it a third act. And she's quite ready to leave it to others to sum up her legacy there."[4]

Gregg Jones, Lauren's friend since she began with the Hippodrome, offered his opinion: "When Jessica Hurov left, Lauren couldn't do the art and business at the same time. She thought she could, and I think to save money, she was trying to wear both hats. The theatre fell way into the red, and then her health started to suffer because of that."

Stephanie Lynge, who was appointed interim artistic director, has since said, "Trying to run the theatre single-handedly is not a job that one single person or even two people can do in the long run. We have to be able to grow our staff in order to grow the Hippodrome so that we're not asking one person to work eighty hours a week, because that's not sane in the long run for anyone."

Looking back on her twenty-eight years there, Lauren said, "I had fallen deeply in love with the Hippodrome. I put it first before everything, my family, my social life, and as I reflect back now that I'm gone, I also put it before my career and that was not good. I think that was probably my tragic flaw in my career growth. The Hippodrome is not the core of my existence any longer."

Lauren still resides in Gainesville, remains active in theatre, directs UF plays, and is an adjunct professor at the UF School of Theatre and Dance.

The Season Must Go On

Lucas Hnath's debut Broadway play, *A Doll's House, Part 2*, was already scheduled to open January 11. So, Charlie Mitchell directed it in place of Lauren.

Hnath had written last season's *The Christians*. The subject matter this time was an imagined extension of Henrik Ibsen's *A Doll's House*. Ibsen's play concerns Nora, a married woman struggling to find self-fulfillment in the male-dominated world of 1879 Norway. In Ibsen's final scene, Nora leaves her keys and wedding ring and slams the door shut as she exits.

A Doll's House, Part 2 begins with a knock on the same door, and Nora enters after fifteen years. While away, she has become a successful feminist novelist. The reason for her return is to get her estranged husband, Torvald, to sign legal papers that will finalize their divorce. The family and the children's nursemaid question Nora about what she has been doing and express their disapproval.

A Doll's House, Part 2 featured (l-r) MaRah Williams, V Craig Heidenreich, Sara Morsey, and Tess Hogan.

Photo: Michael Eaddy

"You don't have to have seen *A Doll's House*, which premiered in 1879, to get it," Charlie Mitchell said. "The play stands on its own. Back in the day, *A Doll's House* was revolutionary. For a woman to walk out on her life and not just her husband, but her children—it was called the 'door slam heard all around the world.'"[5]

Tess Hogan, who played Nora, said, "At this political and social moment, it points out how much has changed, and how much has not changed."[6] In real life, Tess is married to V Craig Heidenreich, who played Nora's husband, Torvald. It was the first time in fourteen years the two had performed together in a play. Craig noted, "Some of the stuff [in the play] hits a little close to home."[7]

Sun critic Ron Cunningham praised all four actors and commented, "The best scenes in this play are the explosive exchanges between Hogan and Heidenreich. They literally collapse to the floor in their emotional exhaustion and then, remarkably, manage to laugh at their own excesses." He called it Craig's "finest performance to date."[8]

Sara Morsey played the nursemaid, Anne Marie, who greets the returning Nora with "You're looking older, and a little fatter."[9]

Hnath's script also introduced a character that never appeared onstage in Ibsen's version, Emmy, one of the three children Nora had abandoned. MaRah Williams portrayed the now-grown daughter who wants the kind of marriage that Nora rejected.

The play proved popular and its run was extended an extra week, closing on February 10.

A Jocular Miracle

V Craig Heidenreich stayed on to direct the next show, *Miracle on South Division Street*, a comedy by Tom Dudzick, who had penned earlier Hippodrome successes *Over the Tavern* and *King O' the Moon*. Craig had also directed last season's *Ripcord*.

The play is set in Dudzick's favored place, Buffalo, New York, with yet another Catholic family. Clara Norwak's children, Jimmy, Ruth, and Beverly, have been raised to revere the family's miracle. It seems that during World War II, the Virgin Mary appeared in the barbershop owned by Clara's father, and he was so moved by the experience he had a statue made to commemorate it.

Jacki Schram, Laura Shatkus, Nell Page, and Niall McGinty play the Norwak family in *Miracle on South Division Street*.

Photo: Michael Eaddy

A strict Catholic to her toes, Clara's only issue is that the pope has refused to recognize the family's miracle. Later in the play, the family discovers the statue might not be of Mary. In typical comedic form, humor comes from interactions between family members. Beverly prays to improve her bowling score while hoping something will happen with a cute guy who almost became a priest. Ruth wants to leave Buffalo for a stage career in New York City. And Jimmy, well, the girl his heart is set on marrying is Jewish, but he knows the idea will make his mother's head explode.

"Clara is played with no-nonsense perfection by the marvelous Nell Page," said the *Sun* review. "But Ruth is her mother's daughter, and in Jacki Schram, Page has met her match.... Niall McGinty and Laura Shatkus nicely round out the cast as squabbling siblings Jimmy and Bev.... They say family miracles are made of this."[10]

"This show is fun and heartwarming; it's about family and accepting each other for who we are," said the Hippodrome's new artistic director, Stephanie Lynge. "The audience should go away with joy and laughing."[11]

Miracle on South Division Street ran from March 1–24.

Changes

In addition to naming Stephanie Lynge as interim artistic director, the board also made the Hipp's accountant and operations director, Nicole Daenzer, interim managing director. Education director Gabrielle Byam became the third member of a triumvirate to run the theatre. The board eventually dropped "interim" from Stephanie and Nicole's titles.

"We all knew that things had been difficult," Stephanie recalled. "Trying to figure out and find our path through Nicole, and Gabby, and I, all three agreed that first thing we would address was the culture of our institution. We felt it was extremely important to be transparent with everyone and ask them to be the same about everything. We wanted to stabilize the Hippodrome's finances and even before the pandemic, we were able to pay off half of the debt that was on the books when we started. We tightened the belt. We started making fiscal decisions that would help us continue forward and survive and grow."

That included changing the play scheduled for April, Ayad Akhtar's Pulitzer Prize winner, *Disgraced*. "When we did our number crunching, we realized that we could not do that play in the way it deserves to be done. The cost of set, costumes, and rehearsal process for that show would not have been a fiscally good idea at that moment," Stephanie said. "We replaced it with a two-person show with a simpler set and costumes so that we could do a professional high-quality production. That was *Sex with Strangers*. Great title," she added.

At the same time, they needed to finalize their summer musical, announce the 2019–2020 season, and get the subscriber renewal forms in the mail. They dubbed the new season "Breaking Boundaries."

Sex with Strangers

Stephanie Lynge directed Laura Eason's *Sex with Strangers*, casting a Hippodrome favorite, Nichole Hamilton, opposite Marquis Gibson, who had played the associate pastor in *The Christians*.

Photo: Michael Eaddy

Nichole Hamilton and Marquis Gibson in a scene from *Sex with Strangers*.

Sex with Strangers is not as salacious as the title makes it sound. Although the two characters, Olivia and Ethan, do end up in bed, what they have in common is a shared passion for writing. She's a thirty-something struggling novelist. He started a blog that evolved into two bestsellers, and he's constantly on Twitter. The play is described as a smart and sexy exploration of the conflict between the life you live online and the life you try to live in the world.

"At the end of the day, it's not about sex," Stephanie said. "It's about connection, about striving and grasping after what you want. *Sex with Strangers* is a beautifully nuanced script with a powerful, very emotionally packed story that we could do right."[12]

Ron Cunningham wrote: "Nichole Hamilton and Marquis D. Gibson are accomplished and appealing actors who hold up their respective ends in this two-person dramady very well, thank you very much. They are good enough at what they do to make you care about their characters.... In truth *Sex with Strangers* is less about sex—indeed what passes for physical lust on this stage is pretty tame stuff in our *Shades of Grey* age—and more about the literary ties that bind these two would-be lovers."[13]

Even with Cunningham calling it tame, the play didn't draw huge numbers. Its title may have put off conservative theatergoers. The show opened April 19 and closed May 12.

Million Dollar Quartet

If *Sex with Strangers* didn't draw big audiences, *Million Dollar Quartet* did. "We just absolutely fell in love with it," Stephanie Lynge recalled. "It was on the docket. We were already working on trying to make that happen when I took over, so I continued along that path and got the rights and the production elements."

It didn't hurt that the Hipp was able to save on costs for *Million Dollar Quartet*, thanks to the Florida Repertory Theatre in Fort Myers. When Hurricane Irma hit Florida in 2017, residents of Fort Myers were ordered to evacuate the area. The Hippodrome had helped Florida Repertory Theatre by housing its actors and crew in Gainesville and allowing them to use the Hippodrome space to continue rehearsals for an upcoming production.

Returning the favor in 2019, Florida Repertory loaned the Hippodrome instruments, costumes, and other materials they had used in a recent production of *Million Dollar Quartet*. That saved the Hipp thousands of dollars.

It also helped that the lead actors had all been in the show elsewhere, including Hugh Hysell, who, in addition to directing the show, also reprised the part of Sam Phillips, which he had played on the national tour.

The musical is described as a memory play of a true event in rock and roll history. A twist of fate brought four rock and roll legends back to the same studio where each of them had been discovered by Sam Phillips.

Carl Perkins, Johnny Cash, and Jerry Lee Lewis were in a recording session on Tuesday, December 4, 1956, when Elvis Presley dropped by to see Sam. Elvis ended up jamming with his old friends. Luckily, the session that followed was recorded by Sam Phillips and retains its historical significance as a landmark event. At the end of the night, someone at the studio took a photograph, which the Hipp projected at the play's conclusion.

Colin Escott and Floyd Mutrux wrote the book for the musical and used the songs from the recording session for the music. Bryan Mercer was the musical director for the Hippodrome production. Unlike many previous summer musicals that had used prerecorded tracks, these actors played the instruments live on stage.

Million Dollar Quartet featured (l-r) Brady Wease, Sam Jones, Justin Bendel on bass, Joe Boover, Colin Barkell, Benny Cannon on drums, Cali Newman, and Hugh Hysell.

Photo: Michael Eaddy

Sam Jones played Carl Perkins, Colin Barkell was Johnny Cash, and, except for the preview shows, Brady Wease played a wild Jerry Lee Lewis. Joe Boover portrayed Elvis Presley, with Cali Newman as his sexy girlfriend, Dyanne. Justin Bendel played standup bass and Benny Cannon drums. Every one of them sang like their respective stars with amazing accuracy—no small feat since these iconic songs are burned into America's collective memory.

With a more substantial plot than a jukebox musical, Sam Phillips takes the audience back in time to the exact moments when each of the four legends discovered their own unique sound. It is also a tale of passion, broken promises, secrets, and celebrations where the facades of fame are peeled back to show the men behind the music that influenced every rock and roller who followed.

"Not to give into hyperbole," wrote Ron Cunningham, "but this reimagining of what happened on a freezing day in Memphis when four future rock legends came together and proceeded to blow the mercury out the thermometer is ... well, simply electric. *Million Dollar Quartet* works on two levels. The rock, blues, and gospel standards are superb. Whether these are four talented musicians who also act, or vice versa, is beside the point. Beyond the music, however, the backstory is equally compelling. Each of [Sam's] protégés would ultimately find both success and misery. And for these precious few hours their collective hopes, doubts, and vulnerabilities are playing out at high volume."[14]

The show had a couple of quick substitutions with equally capable actors/singers/musicians. Brady Wease was injured in an auto accident a week before opening night, so Brian Michael Henry flew in to play Jerry Lee Lewis until Brady could go on. The second replacement was due to the show's popularity. The play, which opened May 31, kept being extended. Colin Barkell was under contract for another play and finally had to leave. James Penca replaced him as Johnny Cash until August 4, when the show closed.

Season Forty-seven

Season forty-seven began with *The Curious Incident of the Dog in the Night-Time* by Simon Stephens, based on the novel by Mark Haddon. The Hipp also revived the One City One Story program, which encouraged people in Gainesville to read and discuss the book. Related events started with an open mic night on August 22 and continued through the run of the play.

The story revolves around Christopher, played by Kyle Brumley. He's a young man whose characteristics, which resemble autism spectrum disorder, shape the plot. "Through Christopher, we get to experience life through the eyes of someone who processes and experiences the world differently than many of us," said Stephanie Lynge.[15]

The Curious Incident of the Dog in the Night-Time revolves around Christopher (center), played by Kyle Brumley. Other cast members: (kneeling) Gloria Halsell, (standing l-r) J. Moliere, Shayna Silverman, Virginia Marie Martinez, James Dennis, Nick Bublitz, Cynthia Beckert, Clint Thornton, and Niall McGinty.

Photo: Michael Eaddy

Fifteen-year-old Christopher has an extraordinary mind but is out of sync with the world. When he falls under suspicion for killing his neighbor's dog, he sets out on a life-changing journey to find the true culprit and uncovers family secrets that turn his world upside down. The play, which explores what it truly means to love and be loved, won five Tony Awards, including Best Play. Lighting designer Robert Robins and sound designer Amanda Nipper used noise, light, and motion to give audiences a sense of how Christopher perceives the world. The Hippodrome collaborated with UF's Center for Autism and Related Disorders, to ensure authenticity.

The play was co-produced with UF's Theatre of School and Dance and directed by Ralf Remshardt. The joint venture offered UF students Nick Bublitz, James Dennis, Zachary Gropper, Gloria Halsell, Virginia Marie Martinez, J. Moliere, and Shayna Silverman an opportunity to work in an Equity theatre. Sharing the stage were professional actors Kyle Brumley, Cynthia Beckert, Niall McGinty, and Clint Thornton.

The Curious Incident of the Dog in the Night-Time ran from August 30–September 22.

Blameless

When *The Blameless* was selected for the new season, the Hippodrome didn't foresee its unfortunate timeliness. Nick Gandiello's script about the repercussions of gun violence only had one prior production, and the Hippodrome would be its East Coast premiere. But by the time it opened on October 11, the country had experienced seven new incidents of school shootings since the Hipp had chosen the play.

Stephanie Lynge, who directed the tense drama, said in a letter to the *Gainesville Sun*, "This play is not about the politics of guns or the bills and activism from both sides. It is about what happens afterward. How do the families survive, heal, and move forward after the media has moved on to the next story?"[16]

The play begins with the lively Garcia family, who has always tackled life with humor and tough love. But on the anniversary of their son's death in a mass shooting, their strength is put to the test. Drew Davis (Tim Altmeyer), father of the shooter, wants to meet with the families of his son's victims, but only the Garcias will oblige. They invite him to dinner.

Grief is still fresh for all the characters. Parents Diana and Alex Garcia (played by Maryann Towne and Alberto Bonilla) remember their son through his jacket. The deceased boy's sister (Hannah Benitez) and her boyfriend (Oghenero Gbaje) create music to honor him. But his aunt (Maylin Castro) resents Davis for his son's actions.

The play's subject matter is gun violence, but at its core are forgiveness and empathy. The play focuses on humanity and people living with the aftereffects of losing

Actors Alberto Bonilla, Maryann Towne, and Maylin Castro prepared a meal on stage during every performance of *The Blameless.*

Photo: Michael Eaddy

their children to gun violence. Ultimately, the characters realize that both sides lost children—the victim's parents, certainly, but the parents of the shooter have also lost their son forever.

The set is the Garcia home, and the Hippodrome's production included a fully functioning kitchen. Much of the dialogue takes place while the family prepares dinner. This provided a real challenge for the properties designer. First, they had to decide what to cook that the actors could eat. Were any of them vegetarian or gluten intolerant or didn't eat dairy? Next, what could they prepare within the length of the scenes before they had to sit down to eat? Finally, with the Hipp's financial straits, what could they afford, given that they were literally preparing a meal seven shows a week? They settled on making a three-bean salad and heating up a leftover casserole in the microwave. Even so, to accomplish that, the assistant stage manager, Karina Ortega, had to cook a fresh casserole in her apartment daily and bring it to the theatre before the show.

The *Sun* reviewer called the cast strong but the script weak. The *Independent Florida Alligator* disagreed: "*The Blameless* is a show that is as emotional as it is enjoyable, discussing a controversial topic in a domestic, personal way that cannot be found in the news. The show doesn't offer answers, but instead provides closure, and it is this hope for the future that best characterizes the journey of the play."[17]

The Blameless ran through November 3.

Holiday Cheer

After two challenging dramas in a row, audiences were due some holiday merriment. Niall McGinty wrote a new adaptation for the Hippodrome's annual production of *A Christmas Carol*. At its heart are all the familiar elements of the classic, but Niall's version starts with a party of Victorians passing among themselves small books of the Charles Dickens tale. Someone brings out a trunk of props. Gregg Jones dons his Scrooge costume and the cast slips into the familiar story, directed by John Gray.

The Cratchit family in a new adaptation of *A Christmas Carol* by Niall McGinty (far right), who also plays Bob Cratchit.

Photo: Michael Eaddy

Then, for its companion holiday show, the Hippodrome presented *Scrooge in Rouge*, a merry musical farce with book by Ricky Graham, Jeffery Roberson, and Yvette Hargis and music by Jefferson Turner. Clint Thornton directed it, with musical direction by Bryan Mercer and choreography by Stephanie Lynge.

Done in the style of a Victorian-era British Music Hall, this quick-witted, cross-dressing show abounds in bad puns, bawdy humor, and witty songs that were delivered by Kelly Atkins, Matthew McGee, David Patrick Ford, and Bryan Mercer. There is even an appearance by Queen Victoria in the form of a puppet.

Photo: Michael Eaddy

Scrooge in Rouge starred (l-r) Matthew McGee, David Patrick Ford, Kelly Atkins, and Bryan Mercer.

The plot is that the Royal Hall Music Players have come to perform *A Christmas Carol*, but most of the company got food poisoning, leaving only three actors to perform all the parts. (In the Hipp production, they were accompanied by Bryan on the piano.) However, this is not a family-friendly version of *A Christmas Carol* with crotchety Ebenezer learning heartwarming lessons. With quick costume changes, each actor played multiple characters and delivered countless double entendre and crude jokes.

Scrooge in Rouge opened November 22, and *A Christmas Carol* opened November 30. The plays alternated time slots, and both ran through December 22.

1   "Hippodrome Loses Longtime Director," *Gainesville Sun*, January 22, 2019.

2   Ron Cunningham, "Longtime Hipp Artist Explores Life after Theater," *Gainesville Sun*, February 7, 2019.

3   Ibid.

4   Ibid.

5   Gabriella Paul, "Nora Returns After 15 Years in *A Doll's House Part 2*," *Gainesville Sun*, January 10, 2019.

6   Ibid.

7   Ibid.

8   Ron Cunningham, review of *A Doll's House, Part 2*, by Lucas Hnath, directed by Charlie Mitchell, Hippodrome Theatre, Gainesville, FL, *Gainesville Sun*, January 17, 2019.

9   Lucas Hnath, *A Doll's House, Part 2*, Dramatists Play Service, New York, NY, 2018.

10 Ron Cunningham, review of *Miracle on South Division Street*, by Tom Dudzick, directed by V Craig Heidenreich, Hippodrome Theatre, Gainesville, FL, *Gainesville Sun*, March 8, 2019.

11 Alexandria Ng, "Relating to Each Other, Family Style," *Gainesville Sun*, February 28, 2019.

12 Alexandria Ng, "'Sex with Strangers' Explores Relationships Starting Today at the Hippodrome," *Gainesville Sun*, April 18, 2019.

13 Ron Cunningham, review of *Sex with Strangers*, by Laura Eason, directed by Stephanie Lynge, Hippodrome Theatre, Gainesville, FL, *Gainesville Sun*, April 26, 2019.

14 Ron Cunningham, review of *Million Dollar Quartet*, by Colin Escott and Floyd Mutrux, directed by Hugh Hysell, Hippodrome Theatre, Gainesville, FL, *Gainesville Sun*, June 14, 2019.

15 Julia Campitelli, "Creating a Book Club for the Community," *Gainesville Sun*, August 15, 2019.

16 Stephanie Lynge, letter to the editor, *Gainesville Sun*, October 6, 2019.

17 Marlena Carrillo, review of *The Blameless*, by Nick Gandiello, directed by Stephanie Lynge, Hippodrome Theatre, Gainesville, FL, *Independent Florida Alligator*, October 9, 2019.

2020

A New Partnership

In an innovative cost-saving move, the Hippodrome partnered with freeFall Theatre in St. Petersburg, Florida, to do two plays in 2020. Each theatre would produce one play and then swap them, allowing them to realize savings in rehearsal and costume costs. "In this new fiscal situation that theatre finds itself in, we have to get more and more creative in order to produce high quality professional theatre," said Stephanie Lynge.[1]

The two companies collaborated on scenic design to make sure the sets would transfer with relatively little modification between the two different stages. Upon transfer to the other theatre, the main work would be lighting design and adjusting the actors' blocking. The Hippodrome presented Josh Tobiessen's *Lone Star Spirits* January 24–February 16. Meanwhile, freeFall Theatre was staging *Marie and Rosetta* in St. Petersburg.

Stephanie Lynge directed *Lone Star Spirits*, a fast-paced comedy with hairpin turns that takes a hilarious and sympathetic look at family, spirituality, those who stay and those who leave their hometowns, and the ghosts that haunt us either way.

Marissa Toogood played Marley, who hopes a trip to her Texas hometown with her hipster fiancé, Ben (Niall McGinty), will be quick. But the moment she enters her estranged father's failing liquor store, she's immediately set upon by her football

Jessica (Brooke Tyler Benson) looks skeptical as Drew (Haulston Mann), Walter (Bryan Mercer), Marley (Marissa Toogood), and Ben (Niall McGinty) hold a séance in *Lone Star Spirits*.

Photo: Michael Eaddy

hero ex-boyfriend, Drew (Haulston Mann). He's looking to relight a romance with the only girl he never cheated on.

By the time Marley reveals to her father, Walter, (Bryan Mercer), the reason for her visit—to announce her engagement—things are wildly out of hand. Upon learning Marley is engaged, Jessica (Brooke Tyler Benson), her former high school hellion classmate and now a single mom, wants to drag Marley out for a two-woman bachelorette party. Then there's the ghost of the bear-wrestling pioneer who founded the town and used to live in the store, and with whom Drew and Marley's father speak on a daily basis.

"We chose this show because it's funny, and it is honest, and it is completely relatable," Stephanie said.[2]

"It's a comedy, but there's also a lot of moments of real human connection—moments that we have all had in our lives that kind of hurt," Brooke Tyler Benson added.[3]

After a successful run and receiving good reviews in both the *Gainesville Sun* and *Independent Florida Alligator*, the Hipp packed up the whole kit and caboodle and headed south.

Something Bad Might Be Coming

At the beginning of February, the *Gainesville Sun* reprinted a *Washington Post* article about a strain of coronavirus spreading from China. It asked, "Are we on the verge of our next global pandemic?"[4] Little did they know.

The Godmother of Rock and Roll

Following a successful run at freeFall Theatre in St. Petersburg, *Marie and Rosetta* swapped venues with *Lone Star Spirits*. Director Lydia Fort brought her actors, stage manager, and technical crew to Gainesville and opened at the Hippodrome on February 28.

The play tells the story of legendary Sister Rosetta Tharpe, an acclaimed vocalist and guitarist who pioneered a sound that influenced the first generation of rock and roll legends: Elvis Presley, Johnny Cash, Jimi Hendrix, Ray Charles, and others. Breaking new ground in the world of gospel music, she was a force of nature—a Black woman who boldly proclaimed her worth in a time when America fiercely denied it. She is now considered by musicians to be the Godmother of Rock and Roll, though she had been all but forgotten until 2017, when she was inducted into the Rock and Roll Hall of Fame.

George Brant's jubilant play gives the audience a fly-on-the-wall seat to the first rehearsal between Sister Rosetta and her protégée, Marie Knight, a pure washed-in-the-blood-of-the-Lamb wife of a preacher. It takes place in a funeral home basement—the only place that will let them rehearse. It is the eve of their debut show together in a Mississippi warehouse and, ultimately, the tour that would establish them as one of the most important duos in American popular music. Both actors

(l-r) Illeana Kirven and Hillary Scales-Lewis play the title characters in *Marie and Rosetta*.

Photo: Michael Eaddy

sang and played the songs made famous by Sister Rosetta as they told the heart-warming story of faith, sisterhood, and rock and roll.

"*Marie and Rosetta* is at once a musical jubilee, a gal-pal road trip, a lesson in the evolution of swing into gospel into rock," wrote *Sun* theater critic Ron Cunningham. "Illeana Kirven as the legendary Sister Rosetta all but explodes by the time she hits full throttle. Capable of shattering glass with her voice or her guitar, Rosetta is at the top of her game. Marie, Hillary Scales-Lewis, underwhelms at first. But there is a method to this reticence. Scales-Lewis shrewdly draws Marie out of her shell in measured beats. And, oh my, can that girl sing and play when she gets her head on right."[5]

Although *Marie and Rosetta* continued to the end of its scheduled run, March 22, it wasn't easy. The virus, now labeled COVID-19, was spreading rapidly. Deaths associated with the virus continued to rise. The Hippodrome took precautions, purchasing an electrostatic sterilizer and sanitizing the theatre seating, lobby, and restrooms before every performance. Anyone not feeling well or exhibiting cold or flu symptoms was asked to stay home.

By the time the show finished its run, the world was in a global pandemic, though President Donald Trump and Florida's governor, Ron DeSantis, were stalling on taking action. Finally, on April 1, Governor DeSantis issued a statewide stay-at-home order closing most public places and businesses. The Hippodrome canceled the rest of its season and shut its doors.

Pandemic Time

All but essential businesses like grocery stores and pharmacies were shuttered. Congress passed measures to stabilize the economy for what everyone hoped would be a brief duration. One of those was the Payroll Protection Plan (PPP), a loan that enabled businesses to keep employees paid. The Hippodrome applied for and received the money.

"We all cried with relief and gratitude," Stephanie Lynge said when she received the news. "We are beyond grateful that the Hipp continues forward, keeping our full-time staff on payroll and planning a way to bring professional theatre to our community as we start to come out of this. We're going to make it because we are creative people, and we have to get creative."[6]

Health Department orders required wearing masks in stores, offices, and public places; limited the number of people allowed in buildings at one time; and decreed minimum distances between those people. The Hippodrome wardrobe department, having no plays to make costumes for, set about sewing 150–175 masks a week from home.

On June 4, the governor issued a new order easing restrictions and allowing movie theaters, bars, and playhouses to reopen at half capacity. The governor's order came on the heels of a Health Department report that Florida had hit its greatest single-day total of COVID-19 cases since the pandemic started. But the Hippodrome didn't reopen. The Actor's Equity Association had issued strict rules to protect actors from COVID-19 that made live rehearsals and performances impossible. Instead, the Hipp focused on planning the next season, which traditionally opened at the end of August.

Broadway announced it would remain closed until September 6, worrying many actors, directors, designers, and patrons about the decline of theatre. However, Broadway veteran and Gainesville native Malcolm Gets told the *Gainesville Sun* he was not worried about the state of theatre: "Every year, people express their worry about the future of theatre, yet it continues on due to the passion of those involved. Singers want to sing. Dancers want to dance. Actors want to act."[7]

Above: Malcolm Gets as Cosmé McMoon.

Below: Kelly Atkins as Florence Foster Jenkins.

Souvenir

The pandemic dragged on. It became apparent that live performances at the Hippodrome would not be taking place any time soon. It was time to go virtual. After weeks of negotiation with Equity, the Hippodrome became one of the first theatres to be granted a unique contract that allowed them to produce a play, record it, and stream it remotely online.

The play they chose was Stephen Temperley's *Souvenir*, a sidesplitting celebration of the life of Florence Foster Jenkins, the real-life singer whose voice made her a legend—for her complete lack of pitch and rhythm. Kelly Atkins starred as Florence Foster Jenkins and Malcolm Gets as her accompanist, Cosmé McMoon.

Director Stephanie Lynge and twelve collaborators put the show together without breaking social distancing guidelines. She rehearsed the actors over Zoom calls and built identical sets in each of the actors' homes, where the show was videoed. Kelly and Malcolm delivered lines to each other over phone calls. The recordings were edited together, and the play went online from July 19–26. "It was an exhausting blur of fantastic fun," Stephanie recalled.

A Virtual Season

Back in February, when the Hipp planned for the 2020–2021 season, they had chosen "Remember and Reimagine" as its theme. By summer, they hoped to produce at least a hybrid season that offered both socially distanced live shows and high-quality online versions for patrons who would feel safer enjoying the show from home.

When it came time to start rehearsals, however, it still wasn't safe to bring artists together to rehearse and perform live—even with the extensive safety protocols the Hippodrome had in place. Newscasts said a COVID-19 vaccine was in the works, but it wouldn't be available until the end of the year. The Hippodrome canceled its fall shows and hoped for a better 2021. The PPP money ran out, and they had to lay off staff.

Virtual Shakespeare

Charlie Mitchell conceived and directed *Shakespeare Thou Art Translated*, a video mash-up of lines from ten classic Shakespeare plays transported to present-day Gainesville. Its intent was to explore how universal Shakespeare really is. Recorded mostly outdoors, it featured Hippodrome favorites Kelly Atkins, Sabrina Blackney, Bruce Cornwell, Cameron Francis, David Patrick Ford, Ryan George, Nichole Hamilton, Haley Johnson, Gregg Jones, Matthew Lindsay, Greg Mallios, Bryan Mercer, Katie Medved, J. Moliere, Niall McGinty, Nell Page, E. Stanley Richardson, Clint Thornton, Ryan Travis, and Zöe Wilde. The show streamed October 9–15.

Keeping a Hipp Holiday Tradition

In an effort to at least keep their yuletide tradition, the Hippodrome streamed a new production of Steve Murray's *This Wonderful Life*. The one-man play, directed by Stephanie Lynge, featured David Patrick Ford playing every character from the iconic movie *It's a Wonderful Life*. Since it had only one actor, they could safely record it. The play streamed from December 4–10.

However, safely recording a production with the large ensemble cast of *A Christmas Carol* wasn't feasible. Bah humbug. Fortunately, there was an archive video of an earlier year's production with Gregg Jones as Ebenezer Scrooge and a cast of dozens. They streamed it from December 11–24.

1	April Rubin, "*Lone Star Spirits*—Comedy with a Heart," *Gainesville Sun*, January 19, 2020.
2	Ibid.
3	Ibid.
4	Tom Frieden, "We're Unprepared for the Next Pandemic," *Gainesville Sun*, February 1, 2020.
5	Ron Cunningham, review of *Marie and Rosetta*, by George Brant, directed by Lydia Fort, Hippodrome Theatre, Gainesville, FL, *Gainesville Sun*, March 9, 2020.
6	Douglas Ray, "Lessons and Questions as Gainesville Reopens," *Gainesville Sun*, May 31, 2020.
7	Laura Chiarello, "Critical Funds," *Gainesville Sun*, June 4, 2020.

2021

False Hope

The Hippodrome planned for a reopening. In addition to using their electrostatic sprayer to quickly and thoroughly sanitize all surfaces between performances, they also planned to minimize audience occupancy by leaving multiple empty seats between patrons. But the pandemic persisted.

Artistic director Stephanie Lynge thought that with proper precautions, the Hipp might be able to stream its January 2021 play, *The Revolutionists*. Then a cast member caught COVID-19 and the production had to be canceled. *The Revolutionists* was postponed to the following season and the rest of the mainstage plays scheduled for the 2020–2021 season were canceled.

Marilyn Wall

On March 9, Hippodrome co-founder Marilyn Wall died. Although there have been over a million deaths in the US from COVID-19, Marilyn's wasn't one of them. She had suffered Parkinson's disease for almost fifteen years, and for the last several, her worsening condition had forced her to turn costume design over to her successors. Then, in February 2021, she fell and broke her femur. While recovering from hip surgery, she developed pneumonia. Marilyn was seventy-two.

Marilyn Wall with costumes.

During her almost-fifty-year association with the Hippodrome, Marilyn had acted, directed, and even written a play, but her love was costume design. Throughout her career, she designed and built costumes for more than 350 professional productions for the stage and film. In the movie world, she designed costumes and make-up for *A Flash of Green*, *Shimmer*, *Ruby in Paradise*, *Gathering Evidence*, *Miami Hustle*, and *Ulee's Gold*. She rubbed elbows with movie stars Sally Field, Ed Harris, Mary Beth Hurt, Ashley Judd, Angelina Jolie, Kathy Ireland, Peter Fonda, and Patricia Richardson. She did makeup for Bill Clinton, Al Gore, and Phil Donahue. Marilyn twice won Emmys for her work on the national children's television series *Salsa*.

"She was truly outstanding,"[1] said Hippodrome co-founder Gregory von Hausch, who first met Marilyn when they were both theatre majors at UF.

"There was sort of a magnet inside of Marilyn that drew people toward her," Lauren Warhol Caldwell said. "Our relationship started out as director to costume designer, but it evolved into probably one of the richest friendships I've ever had in my life."[2]

Proof of Love

Their next virtual play, Chisa Hutchinson's *Proof of Love*, was performed and recorded in New York City and streamed May 7–16. The one-woman play was directed by Hippodrome company member Ryan George.

Joy Lynn Jacobs played Constance, a wife in an upper-class Black family who thinks she has a happy life and a loving husband until a tragic accident forces her to face uncomfortable truths about her marriage and herself. Set in a hospital room, Constance sits next to her comatose husband and delivers a stirring monologue that touches on fundamental issues of race, class, love, and fidelity.

A Show Must Go On

After sixteen months in the dark, the Hippodrome staged its first live performance in the theatre during the summer of 2021. It turned out that the Equity ruling preventing union members from doing live performances during the pandemic didn't apply to cabaret shows. Multi-award-winning singer, actor, and improv artist Laura Hodos wrote a script for *By the Light of the Silvery Screen* with musical arrangements by Bryan Mercer. Stephanie Lynge directed, and they put the show together in six days.

Bryan Mercer and Laura Hodos perform in *By the Light of the Silvery Screen*.

The cabaret performance, which ran from June 4–6, celebrated love, hope, and happiness. It featured Bryan playing piano and trading quips with Laura, who sang a variety of tunes from the movies.

Audiences were pleased with the show and happy to be back in the theatre. After the show closed, the Hippodrome extended the cabaret concept with Hippodrome actors singing at free pop-up shows at various locations around town.

A Good Turn

The prolonged pandemic forced Actors' Warehouse, a Gainesville playhouse founded and run by Steven Butler, to give up its building. In his youth, Steven had acted in Margaret Bachus's TYA plays. From June 4–6 and July 30–August 8, the Hippodrome lent him the Hipp Cinema to stage the one-man play *How I Learned What I Learned* by August Wilson.

Later in the year, the Hipp again opened the Cinema to present an important play about a tragedy that had taken place only twenty miles west. *New Berry* relates how five African Americans were hanged from a single oak tree by a mob of two hundred white men in 1916. A sixth was hanged a month later, after being found guilty by an all-white jury. The play was a collaborative effort by Ryan Travis, Ryan George, Bakari Garvin, and E. Stanley Richardson.

Paul Helm and Brady Wease star in *Murder for Two*.

Season Forty-nine

When the Hippodrome opened its mainstage to live audiences in September, patrons were instructed to wear masks. Empty seats, reserved to keep people socially distanced, bore circular blue signs. Although a full house meant only half full, people were glad to be back.

The opening play was *Murder for Two*, a wild musical by Jo Kinosian and Kellen Blair. Stephanie Lynge directed it with Bryan Mercer serving as musical director.

Described as the perfect blend of music, mayhem, and murder, the two-actor show featured Paul Helm and Brady Wease. Paul played policeman Marcus Moscowicz, who really wants a promotion to detective. Brady played a dozen suspects.

The set was a living room parlor where the body of a murdered author lay on the floor. The novelist had a propensity for revealing family members' and neighbors' secrets in his books, making everyone he knew a suspect. To impress the chief of police and earn his promotion, Moscowicz has only one hour to interrogate the suspects and solve the crime before the department detective arrives to take over the case. Brady Wease instantly switched characters to portray different suspects using only accents and body language.

Both actors were skilled piano players who gave killer musical performances and sometimes traded off in the middle of a song.

Murder for Two ran September 17–October 3.

DeShawn White as Camae and Chaz Rose as Dr. Martin Luther King, Jr. in a scene from *The Mountaintop*.

Photo: Michael Eaddy

The Mountaintop

Ryan George directed the Hippodrome's next production, Katori Hall's *The Mountaintop*, which reimagines the events that took place the night before civil rights leader Reverend Dr. Martin Luther King, Jr., was assassinated. The play takes place in King's room at the Lorraine Motel.

Dr. King is hoarse from giving his sermon "I've Been to The Mountaintop." He craves a Pall Mall cigarette and has sent someone to get him a pack. A storm rages outside. He orders room service and thinks about what he will preach the next day.

Camae, a maid, knocks on his door. She has brought his order—the cigarettes—and also a flask of whiskey. They have a conversation that is initially filled with flirtation but slowly progresses into a deeper discussion of King's hopes and fears and the fight for civil rights. But this is no rom-com. In a sudden turn, Camae reveals she is an angel sent by God to collect him and bring him to Heaven. When he pleads and bargains for more time so he can continue his work, she explains that his baton will be passed on.

King forces Camae to telephone God, hoping he can convince God to give him more time. However, the call ends with King understanding his fate is set in stone and his death is arriving shortly. In the last minutes, King has a vision filled with significant names who grab the baton to continue the fight for civil rights. His vision finishes with a monologue to motivate people to continue the fight in the hope that one day we will reach the Promised Land on Earth. The play ends with King handing the baton to whoever is willing to take it next.

The story and the acting stunned audiences. Theater critic Ron Carpenter wrote: "Chaz Rose is pitch-perfect as King. He's got the rhythm, he's got the cadence, he's got the passion.... DeShawn White is nobody's shrinking violet as Camae. She is sassy and irreverent. She will not stand in King's shadow. Suffice it to say that what seemed to start out as a classic bedroom farce suddenly becomes an otherworldly experience that may send chills down your spine before the final bows."[3]

The Mountaintop played from October 22–November 7.

Live Holiday Shows

The Hippodrome was once again able to perform holiday shows before live audiences. Niall McGinty's adaption of *A Christmas Carol*, which debuted in 2019 only to go on hiatus during the quarantine, was back on the mainstage, with Gregg Jones continuing his role as Ebenezer. The show ran December 2–23.

Cast members of Niall McGinty's adaptation of *A Christmas Carol* toast at the end of the play.

Photo: Michael Eaddy

The second Hippodrome holiday show that season, *Miracle on 34th Street*, takes place a hundred years after the time of Scrooge. It reenacts a 1947 *Lux Radio Hour* broadcast of *Miracle on 34th Street*. Lance Arthur Smith and Jon Lorenz took the radio script from that historic show and adapted it into a stage play.

The Hipp audience became the studio audience as the play's six actors prepared and broadcasted a program from the Golden Age of Radio, commercials and all. Each actor had dual roles—as both a radio actor and as the part the radio actor plays. For example, David Patrick Ford played radio star Grady Williams, who was playing the role of Fred Gailey on the radio. David Carey Foster played Kristofer Van Lisberg, who was Kris Kringle on the radio show. Laura Hodos played

Reenacting a 1947 radio play of *Miracle on 34th Street* are (top) Bryan Mercer and Carson Holley. Bottom: (l-r) David Patrick Ford, Laura Hodos, David Carey Foster, and Sophia Young.

Photo: Michael Eaddy

Cordelia Ragsdale, whose character was Doris Walker. Fictional child star Gracie Demarco played Doris's daughter, Susan, on the radio show. In real life, Gracie/Susan was portrayed by twelve-year-old Carson Holley from Orlando. Recent UF graduate Sophia Young played Olivia Glatt, who was the radio show's "female character actor."

Miracle on 34th Street alternated show times with *A Christmas Carol* from November 26 through December 23. It was directed by Stephanie Lynge. Bryan Mercer was the play's musical director and also portrayed the radio announcer, piano player, and foley artist Alex Mialdo. (The foley artist makes sound effects—a door opening, footsteps in the snow, a car engine starting.) The audience enjoyed seeing how the sound effects were made.

1 Danielle Ivanov, "Hippodrome Founder, Designer, Marilyn Wall Dies at Age 72," *Gainesville Sun*, March 12, 2021.

2 Ibid.

3 Ron Cunningham, review of *The Mountaintop*, by Katori Hall, directed by Ryan George, Hippodrome Theatre, Gainesville, FL, *Gainesville Sun*, October 25, 2021.

2022

As You Like It, Again

In January, the Hippodrome co-produced William Shakespeare's *As You Like It* with the UF School of Theatre and Dance. These joint productions were especially helpful for plays with large numbers of characters. Filling the cast with UF's most talented theatre students saved the Hippodrome money. It also gave the students an opportunity to work with professional actors and add a professional theatre credit to their resumes.

Although the Hippodrome hadn't staged *As You Like It* since 1980, it is one of Shakespeare's oft-performed romantic comedies. In it, the Bard uses many of his favorite comic contrivances—gender switching, cross-dressing, mistaken identities, and abundant misunderstandings. The play also contains one of his most famous monologues, which begins, "All the world's a stage."

Shakespeare set the play in seventeenth-century France, but director Charlie Mitchell moved it to more modern times. Charlie envisioned the all-powerful Duke as a mid-twentieth-century European dictator. Costume designer Erin Jester gave him fringed shoulder boards like the doorman at a swanky hotel. She dressed poorer inhabitants of the forest like depression-era farmers.

Charlie told the *Gainesville Sun*, "This is a good time for a Shakespeare comedy.... There's lovers escaping from a practically fascist court into a world where everybody jumps when somebody sneezes."[1]

In *As You Like It*, Duke Frederick (Matthew Lindsay) banishes Rosalind (Katie Medved), and she flees to the forest dressed like a man. She's accompanied by her

Cast of *As You Like It*: (l-r) Niall McGinty, Bryan Mercer, Zöe Wilde, Germainne Lebron, Katie Medved, K. P. Powell, Christian Carlson, Steven Butler, Sophia Paige, Seth Greenberg, Amber Coleman, Nyq Smith, Matthew Lindsay, and Clint Thornton.

Photo: Michael Eaddy

cousin Celia (Zöe Wilde), the duke's daughter. There, they meet a variety of memorable characters and fall in love—Rosalind with Orlando (K. P. Powell) and Celia with Oliver (Germainne Lebron)—but not before several identity mix-ups. The timeless will-they-won't-they tale of love ends in happiness against all odds.

Additional cast members included professional actors Bryan Mercer, Niall McGinty, Clint Thornton, and Steven Butler. Joining them were UF theatre students Amber Coleman, Christian Carlson, Lukas Chaviano, Emma Friedman, Seth Greenberg, Nyq Smith, and Sophia Paige. The production opened January 19 and ran through February 6.

A Comic Clash of Egos

Next up was *Living on Love* by Joe DiPietro, who had penned two prior Hippodrome hits, 2004's *I Love You, You're Perfect, Now Change* and 2016's *The Toxic Avenger*. DiPietro based *Living on Love* on Garson Kanin's *Peccadillo*.

The Hippodrome billed it as a romantic comedy of operatic proportions. Scenic designer Tim Dygert came up with a gorgeous set mimicking a glorious Manhattan penthouse, and costume designer Erin Jester created lavish, opulent costumes any diva would die for. To fill those costumes, director Stephanie Lynge hired actors who could perform an operatic aria (Kelly Atkins) and deliver over-the-top comedy with a straight face (Alberto Bonilla).

Photo: Michael Eaddy

The cast of *Living on Love*. Standing: (l-r) Alberto Bonilla as Maestro, Jaden Waz and Noah Yager as comical servants, and Kelly Atkins as the diva (holding Nugget). Seated: Melissa Macleod and Kyle Brumley play ghostwriters.

Audience members knew Kelly could sing from her many summer musicals. What they perhaps didn't know was that she also performed with the Opera Theater of Connecticut and as a soloist for the Jacksonville Symphony. In this play, she portrayed demanding diva Raquel De Angelis. Playing her famous conductor husband, Vito, was Broadway actor Alberto Bonilla, last seen at the Hipp as the father in *Blameless*.

Vito, or "Maestro" as he likes to be called, has accepted a huge advance from a major publisher to deliver his autobiography, but he's just fired his fifth ghostwriter. Knowing that Vito is a sucker for the ladies, the publisher sends lovely Iris Peabody (Melissa Macleod) to gain his cooperation. When diva Raquel perceives a romantic connection forming between her husband and his new scribe, she hires her own handsome young ghostwriter (Kyle Brumley) to write her story. Battle lines are drawn, and no blow is too low to see who comes out on top. The result is a delightful and hilarious romantic comedy.

And yes, Kelly sang—almost every time she entered the room. Then, near the end, UF musical theatre students Jaden Waz and Noah C. Yager, who played anonymous comical servants, suddenly sang out in perfect harmony and nearly stole the show. But not quite. That honor went to a small rescue Shih Tzu mix named Nugget that the diva carried throughout the show.

At the opening night party, Nugget's owner brought her to the lobby to meet her fans, and the friendly pup was just as charming offstage as on.

"Everyone's falling in love with everyone else, and of course, at the end, everybody ends up with who they are supposed to end up with," said Stephanie Lynge. "Our season this year is just about re-finding our joy, and this one just makes me laugh."[2]

Living on Love ran March 11–27.

French Revolution

Four beautiful, badass women lose their heads in Lauren Gunderson's dark comedy *The Revolutionists*. Set during the French Revolution's Reign of Terror, the irreverent historical fiction puts former queen Marie Antoinette, Charlotte Corday (Jean-Paul Marat's assassin), playwright Olympe de Gouges, and Haitian rebel/spy Marianne Angelle together in one room. The women want feminist playwright Olympe to write their stories.

This darkly sophisticated satirical farce dances on the guillotine blade's edge between violence and legacy, art and activism, and feminism and terrorism. Compatriots and chosen sisters, they try to figure out how to change the conscience of a society undergoing an upheaval. "The Reign of Terror was not a good time to be a woman," Stephanie Lynge said. "These characters are based on real women who went through it, but it doesn't pretend to be a history lesson. It is an exploration of their spirit and courage."[3]

Photo: Michael Eaddy

The Revolutionists features four historical French women: Marie Antoinette (Elise Hudson), playwright Olympe de Gouges (Laura Hodos), rebel/spy Marianne Angelle (Danea Osseni), and assassin Charlotte Corday (Marissa Toogood).

"*The Revolutionists* is a crisp and extremely funny exploration of the forces that to this day conspire to keep women in their place," said the *Gainesville Sun* review. "Much credit to Stephanie Lynge for her keen casting eye. Call it chemistry, mutually assured empathy, or common cause convictions, these sisters in sedition clearly get each other. And the audience knows it. It is a sheer joy to see Marissa Toogood return to the Hippodrome as spit-fire assassin Charlotte. Danea Osseni's Marianne is the center of gravity that keeps the others from flying off into space. 'Nobody wants a musical about the French Revolution,' she explains to Olympe.... Laura Hodos keeps Olympe changing and evolving, seemingly without breaking a sweat. Elise Hudson must be seen to be believed as Marie Antoinette.... But Hudson's Marie also possesses inner steel."[4]

The Revolutionists played from April 29–May 15.

Honky Tonk Summer

With the pandemic somewhat under control, the summer jukebox musicals could return. Roger Bean, who had written *The Marvelous Wonderettes* and *Winter Wonderettes,* collaborated with music arranger Jon Newton to create *Honky Tonk Laundry*, and the Hipp snapped it up.

Tara Kromer, a former Hippodrome stage manager, directed it. Bryan Mercer served as musical director and Stephanie Lynge choreographed the two-woman cast.

Photo: Michael Eaddy

Emily King Brown and
Allie Seibold in *Honky Tonk
Laundry.*

Honky Tonk Laundry is set in the Wishy Washy Washateria, a laundromat owned by Lana Mae. She needs help because her previous employee can't make bail—so she hires Katie. Soon, they find themselves up to their elbows in soap, suds, and cheatin' hearts as they churn their way through twenty-three country songs.

Emily King Brown, who played Lana Mae, and Allie Seibold, who played Katie, were new to the Hippodrome, but both had extensive musical theatre experience in cities from Boston to L.A.

Audiences knew the songs, and they clapped, cheered, and stamped their feet June 4–July 10.

Season Fifty

A lot of playwrights adapt plays from books, but award-winning author Ray Bradbury wrote both the novel and the play *Fahrenheit 451*, which the Hippodrome selected to kick off its fiftieth season. The science fiction play about a future when books are banned and burned was co-produced with the UF School of Theatre and Dance.

Ray Bradbury's classic dystopian story explores a world turned away from science, art, and individuality. In 2022, when the news reported on school districts banning books like *The Diary of Anne Frank*, the play's subject seemed to resonate even more than it had when the novel was originally published in 1950.

"It's very clear that the book and the play are absolutely relevant to our moment," said director Ralf Remshardt. "There is a whole new generation that needs to hear some of the things this play has to say."[5]

Set in a totalitarian world that obliterates individuality, imagination, and books, it is up to an unlikely hero to expose the truth. Montag (Niall McGinty) is a young fireman who forsakes his world and struggles to regain his humanity as he battles his mentor, fire captain Beatty, played by David Patrick Ford. The firemen's job isn't to extinguish fires; it is to incinerate outlawed books that people have hidden and burn the homes in which those books are discovered.

Montag's wife, Mildred (Katelyn Crall), spends her days in a drug-addled state watching propaganda on a large-screen TV. Then, Montag meets waifish Alice (Jacqueline St. Pierre). Her innocent questions set him on a mission to save and read the books he's supposed to destroy. Caught between social conformity and the desire to express his own thoughts, he breaks free of a regimented existence and risks everything for the right to think. Also in the cast were Roxanne Fay, David Carey Foster, Rose Horton, Jack McKinney, and Jay Nixon.

Photo: Michael Eaddy

Niall McGinty and David Patrick Ford play firemen in *Fahrenheit 451*.

"The Hipp's ensemble delivers up Bradbury's dystopian drama about government book burners with verve and, yes, fire," said the *Sun* review. "The production values with all of the sound, light and fury are up to Hipp standards."[6]

The title *Fahrenheit 451* refers to the temperature at which paper burns. Certainly, no one at the Hippodrome wanted to find out at what temperature a sweater burns.

"We were at our first preview for *Fahrenheit 451*," Stephanie Lynge recalled. "A woman in the front row—her sweater slid off her lap. Unbeknownst to her, the sleeve fell onto the halogen lights. While David Patrick Ford was giving his speech about 'burn this, burn that,' the sweater caught on fire; at which point I vaulted over a bunch of chairs. But one of our amazing ushers beat me to the stage. As I was opening my mouth to yell 'HOLD!' the usher picked up that sweater and ran down the vom with it. I ran after her. We took it outside and put it out."

The show played September 2–18. During that time, the theatre and district library sponsored a poetry contest and a One City One Story program to encourage the community to read the novel.

Family Politics

With politicians vying for local and congressional offices, October 2022 seemed like a good time to present Beth Kander's *Running Mates*. Coming off the dystopian drama *Fahrenheit 451*, director Stephanie Lynge said, "Something a bit lighter and more engaging seemed in order. We are swinging into a fall election season that is heavy and tense with a lot of conflict. We decided on a family comedy that makes fun of politics."[7]

Sam Storm has been the mayor of a small town for the past twenty years. He is beloved by the community and by his doting wife, Sofia, a middle-aged former beauty pageant queen who takes yoga classes in her home with her best friend Liddie.

Sam's is usually the only name on the ballot, but after an embarrassing video is leaked, his seat in office is threatened. Mischief ensues when the last person he ever expected as an opponent decides to run against him—his wife, Sofia, with

Cast members play political opponents in *Running Mates*. Seated: Joy Lynn Jacobs and Matthew Lindsay. Standing: (l-r) Nicholas Perez-Hoop, Michelle Bellaver, Maggie Cramer, and André Sguerra.

Photo: Michael Eaddy

Liddie as her campaign manager. Now it's down and dirty as husband and wife duke it out. Political fisticuffs threaten their marriage. Then, an unexpected third candidate enters the race—their grown daughter, Savannah, in a write-in campaign being run by Sofia and Liddie's yoga teacher.

Political shenanigans, witty banter, and slapstick humor abound in this mildly amusing comedy. In the end, when Savannah wins, it's all about family.

Matthew Lindsay, who played Sam, and Michelle Bellaver, who played Liddie, had appeared together a decade earlier in three Hippodrome plays: *Other Desert Cities, Don't Dress for Dinner*, and *Zombie Town*. Michelle, who had been working in New York as an actor, director, and playwright, was back in town as a Visiting Professor at UF.

Joy Lynn Jacobs, who played Sam's wife, Sofia, was a Broadway actress who had also performed in the Hippodrome's one-woman play *Proof of Love*, which streamed during the pandemic. André Sguerra, another New York actor, played the yoga instructor.

Minneapolis-based actor Maggie Cramer played Savannah. Nicholas Perez-Hoop, who split his time between Philadelphia and Tampa, portrayed Sam's assistant, J. B.

Running Mates ran October 14–30.

New Works Festival

Back in 2020, the Hippodrome had conceived an annual New Works Festival to support narrative voices through the development and exploration of plays in traditional and experimental formats. The idea was to support innovative or thought-provoking material representing the diverse landscape of Florida artists and their stories. Then the pandemic put everything on hold.

In 2022, the New Works Festival became a reality. Michelle Bellaver was the show's producer. She, along with four Hipp employees and two artistic interns, read scripts submitted by forty-five playwrights and winnowed the number down to three winners. "The stories feel like stories we've never heard before," Michelle told the *Independent Florida Alligator*.[8]

The winning playwrights worked with directors, actors, and producers to develop and workshop their plays before they were showcased in staged readings in front of a live audience. A post-show talkback following the productions allowed the authors to get feedback directly from the audience.

The first play, *The Ultimate Cheeseburger* by Jena Rashid, was performed on November 4. The story takes place at Chicken & Roots, a chain restaurant where, like most working Americans, everyone is just trying to make ends meet. But when the district manager comes in to give a spiel about how everyone at Chicken & Roots is "family" and they're all "team" members who need to work together, one person is finally pushed too far.

Photo: Michael Eaddy

Actors perform a reading of *Suture Bowl*, one of three winning scripts in the Hippodrome's New Works Festival.

On November 5, the next two plays were presented. In *Evie & Loren* by Bethany Dickens Assaf, the title characters look like a perfect match when they find each other on Tinder—but it turns out she's his former mother-in-law.

Following that show was Irene L. Pynn's *Suture Bowl*. The action takes place in the final episode of the highest-rated reality series ever, a game show where top surgeons face off to battle it out with higher stakes than they ever imagined.

Holiday Murder and Tiny Tim

The Hippodrome's first live play in 2021, *Murder for Two*, returned in 2022 with a festive twist as *Murder for Two Holiday Edition*. Paul Helm reprised his role as the police officer investigating a murder, and Brady Wease again played all thirteen suspects. What made it a *Holiday Edition*? Not much. The show is a musical, so they slipped a few bars of Christmas songs into the score, a couple of references to the season, a little mistletoe, and even a self-deprecating admission that it was basically the same play. Nonetheless, audiences said they had a good time. And perhaps because the original production had only 50 percent seating due to social distancing, many hadn't seen the prior year's performances.

Photo: Michael Eaddy

Brady Wease and Paul Helm perform in *Murder for Two Holiday Edition*.

Stephanie Lynge directed it, and Bryan Mercer was the musical director. *Murder for Two Holiday Edition* opened November 25.

Niall McGinty's adaptation of *A Christmas Carol*, directed by John Gray, opened the following day, and both shows closed on December 23.

1 Ron Cunningham, "Theaters Offer January Shows to Bemuse, Befuddle and Delight," *Gainesville Sun*, January 17, 2022.
2 Ron Cunningham, "Comedy at Hipp Among 4 New Plays Opening in Gainesville," *Gainesville Sun*, March 6, 2022.
3 Ron Cunningham, "Plays Opening Touch on Revolution, Family Tragedy and Lost Generation," *Gainesville Sun*, April 24, 2022.
4 Ron Cunningham, review of *The Revolutionists*, by Lauren Gunderson, directed by Stephanie Lynge, Hippodrome Theatre, Gainesville, FL, *Gainesville Sun*, May 4, 2022.
5 Ron Cunningham, "Relevant Plays Part of Scaled-back Theater Season," *Gainesville Sun*, August 30, 2022.
6 Ron Cunningham, review of *Fahrenheit 451*, by Ray Bradbury, directed by Ralf Remshardt, Hippodrome Theatre, Gainesville, FL, *Gainesville Sun*, September 7, 2022.
7 Ron Cunningham, "Three New Plays Showing This Month in Gainesville," *Gainesville Sun*, October 12, 2022.
8 Averi Kremposky, "Hippodrome Theatre to Unveil 3 Plays at New Works Festival," *Independent Florida Alligator*, November 3, 2022.

The Wizards Behind the Curtain

Sit in a silent, pitch-black room and imagine actors pantomiming a play offstage that you cannot see, mouthing dialogue you cannot hear. That would be your theater experience without the people behind the curtain who manage the sets, props, sound, lights, and scene changes.

Heretofore, this book has discussed fifty years of plays, plots, actors, and directors. It has rarely mentioned those whose work behind the scenes makes the Hippodrome shows as wonderful as they are. Although it would be impossible to name every person who swung a hammer or sewed a stitch, some description of backstage tasks, and a few of those who performed them, is appropriate.

In the early days, the Hippodrome founders and their friends did everything. The director for one play might run the lights on the next. Everyone would pitch in to build sets or find props. Marilyn Wall usually did costume design, but she was the first to admit she wasn't a great seamstress. So, Doris Edwards and Leslie Klein did much of the actual sewing. Leslie also designed costumes sometimes while Marilyn was on a movie shoot.

Director

When we see a play, we are seeing the director's conceptual vision of how to tell that story. The Hippodrome licenses the right to perform a script, but most contracts stipulate that the playwright's dialogue cannot be cut or changed. Very few scripts contain more than a modest description of the set, clothing, or blocking (the actors' movements). The director creates their own interpretation of the play. Then, collaborating with the scenic, lighting, sound, and costume designers, they design those elements as a team.

The director casts the show, finding actors who will bring the characters to life. They do this by auditioning new actors and ones they've worked with before. Rehearsals begin, and the director tries to draw from each actor their best. Directors, including Stephanie Lynge and Lauren Warhol Caldwell, are open to letting actors try different ways of delivering a line or an action. Stephanie said she sketches little diagrams, like the kind football coaches draw, to describe actors' movements across the stage. "I probably end up using only about 20 percent of it," she said, "but it helps me see it in my head."

Musical Director

For musicals, there are two versions of the play: the book (which contains the dialogue and text of the lyrics) and the score (which contains the music, orchestral arrangements, and lyrics the singers will perform). The musical director is responsible for all musical aspects of a production. If the show features a live band, the musical director will probably be the conductor. If the Hippodrome pre-records the instrumental tracks, as it often does for its jukebox musicals, the musical director hires the musicians and studio, and also supervises the recording and mixing of the tracks.

Hippodrome musical directors also act as the rehearsal pianist and vocal coach, working with the singers in the cast. Bryan Mercer has been the musical director for most productions since 2006, but a few of the other musical directors in the Hipp's history include William Hays, Doug Maxwell, Eddie Gwaltney, and Tané DeKrey.

Choreographer

The choreographer designs the dances, steps, and movement for a show. Plays like *West Side Story* have iconic choreography. Other musicals, like *Shout!*, didn't have a choreographer when rehearsals began, but the actresses needed to dance while they sang, so Kelly Atkins and Rachel Anton made up the choreography.

UF dance professor Ric Rose and the founder of Dance Alive, Judy Skinner, were often called upon to choreograph for the Hipp. Choreography isn't limited to musicals. For instance, the director of a Shakespeare play might add music and have the actors do a contra dance. In the case of *Frankenstein*, Ric turned the doppelganger scenes into a ballet. For *Night of the Living Dead*, the director decided the zombies should dance to Michael Jackson's "Thriller" and asked Rachel Anton to choreograph it. Since 2015, Stephanie Lynge has also choreographed many of the musicals.

Stage Manager

Once the play opens, the director, musical director, and choreographer are finished with their work and the stage manager takes over. "I'm not allowed to change anything or give any notes. It's all hers," said Stephanie Lynge. "I use 'she' because most of the Hipp's stage managers lately have been women."

During rehearsal, the stage manager communicates with the actors, writes down all the blocking, coordinates with wardrobe and properties, and makes sure union rules are followed. Once the show is running, the stage manager is in charge. Sitting in the booth (above and behind the audience), the stage manager calls the cues, telling the lighting and sound technicians "go" when it's time to change the lights or start a sound effect or music. The stage manager is also the person making safety calls if needed.

Because the Hippodrome is a professional theatre, its stage managers are Equity members. For many years, an actor who wasn't cast in a particular play served as the stage manager for that production. Doing so helped them earn the Equity points required to keep their health benefits. In 1997, however, Adam Cohen became the first resident stage manager to stay at the Hipp for a prolonged time. He was followed in 2002 by Liz Nehls, who stage managed for six seasons.

While earlier stage managers had been actors, Liz wasn't. Although she'd studied acting at UF before switching to stage managing, she really didn't want to be on

Photo: Michael Eaddy

Liz Nehls waves pool noodles while trying to stage manage *Shipwrecked!*

stage. But for *Shipwrecked!*, Lauren Caldwell wanted her to play the octopus. "The booth was actually on stage, in full view of the audience," Liz recalled. "I had [to wave] these two pool noodles while I was calling the show. It was insane."

Liz left to take a job at UF in 2010. Tara Kromer took her place, and served as stage manager through 2012. In 2013, Amber Wilkerson became the resident stage manager and has continued in the position. Previously, Amber had spent two seasons as a property intern, assistant stage manager, and then stage manager for *A Christmas Carol* in 2005 and 2006.

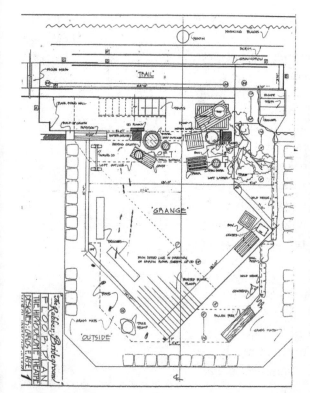

Carlos Asse's set design floor plan for *The Robber Bridegroom*.

Scenic Designer

The scenic designer designs the set by collaborating with the director and analyzing the script. Together, the two arrive at an overall visual concept for the production. The scenic designer then develops a complete set of drawings that are used by the scenic shop to construct and decorate the set. These include all elements from the stone façade of a castle exterior to the wallpaper pattern in a Victorian play. At the Hippodrome, this also involves designing around two immovable steel pillars upstage that support the building. For most plays, the space backstage is usually tight, so the design must not only show the onstage position of movable scenic elements but also their storage position offstage. Carlos Asse has been the most frequently mentioned Hippodrome scenic designer, but there have been others. A few, but by no means all, include James Morgan, Tim Dygert, Mihai Ciupe, and Michael Eaddy.

Costume Designer

Many actors say that once they put on the costume—whether that's a corset or a military uniform—they begin to feel their character. In other words, the costume changes the actor's posture and bearing. Collaborating with the director, the costume designer establishes the play's time period and tone with clothing and shoes.

"I focus on the actor's journey through the piece and ask, 'How can I visually help them make that journey?'" said Marilyn Wall. "I always try to design for an actor, build their costume, and then set them free so they can do their work."

Marilyn excelled at costume design, but there have also been many other costume designers at the Hipp, including Leslie Klein and Lorelei Esser. More recent costume designers include Alyssa Couturier, Jessica Nilacala Kreitzer, Lori Gann-Smith, Stephanie Parks, and Erin Jester.

Marilyn Wall's costume design for the lead actress in *The Underpants*.

Properties Designer

The property designer designs or finds props—any objects handled by the actors, such as a bottle of wine, a book, or a phone. But not a purse or hat—that's wardrobe/costume. Sometimes there is a fine line between props and "set dressings." In these cases, the various designers collaborate to produce the result. For example, in *Fahrenheit 451*, the big bookcase was part of the set, but the firehose that dropped from the ceiling was a prop, and the lead electrician rigged the electromagnetic system that held the hose overhead. There have been many property designers at the Hipp, but one of the earliest was Lorelei Esser.

Actor Petrus Antonius, scenic designer Carlos Asse, dramaturg Tammy Dygert, and properties manager Lorelei Esser discuss tobacco leaves for *Anna in the Tropics*.

Technical Director

The technical director is in charge of the physical world of the play. Responsibilities include making sure the scenic design is on time and within budget and that the set is built properly and safely. The technical director makes the budget, orders all the materials, and is then in charge of building the set. At the Hippodrome, that person may also oversee creating or acquiring properties, but not always. Often, the Hipp's technical director is also the theatre's master carpenter, master electrician, production manager, or even the scenic designer. Although Hippodrome playbills sometimes failed to credit the technical director, there always was one. For many plays, that person was Michael Eaddy, and before him, Carlos Asse and Tim Dygert. As of late, the technical director has been Warren Goodwin. For a long time, the Hipp's technical director also served as production manager, but since 2019, the production manager's responsibilities have been shifted to the Hipp's lighting designer, Bob Robins.

Lighting Designer

The lighting designer works with the scenic designer and director to support the director's vision for the play. Lighting creates atmosphere, indicates time of day, and establishes the environment of the characters' physical world. It determines if the actors stand out against the physical set or meld into it.

Bob Robins, the Hippodrome's longtime lighting director, cites two productions from 2022 as contrasting examples: "Are the actors living in a realistic living room, like *Running Mates*, or are they living in a non-realistic living room like *Fahrenheit 451*? Both had living rooms, but the lighting color and technique created two radically different-looking shows."

The costume designer's choice of clothing colors and fabrics are also factors the lighting designer must consider. For example, a red light would make a green dress look brown.

Today, the Hippodrome uses a computerized light board, which the lighting director is responsible for programming. Elsewhere, larger theatres have begun using video projection effects in stage productions—the Hipp acquired new equipment in 2022. Implementation of videos also comes under the purview of the lighting director.

Tech rehearsal for *Collected Stories*: (l-r) sound designer Amanda Nipper, lighting designer Bob Robins, and stage manager Liz Nehls.

Photo: Michael Eaddy

Sound Designer

Thunder rumbles, a dog barks, the wind howls, spooky music fills the stage, and then the phone rings. All of these effects are products of the sound designer. In the early days, at the theatre on Hawthorne Road, someone backstage shook a piece of sheet metal or turned the crank on a wind machine. In modern times, the sounds are prerecorded and played back by a sound technician who pushes a button in the control booth. Among the first Hippodrome sound designers was Peter Theoktisto. Later, the job belonged to Rocky Draud and then Risa Baxter, followed by Amanda Nipper.

Stagehands and Dressers

Not to be overlooked are those unobtrusive persons, usually dressed in black, who scurry onto the stage at scene breaks to rearrange furniture or add and remove props. The show couldn't happen without them.

With plays like *A Tuna Christmas* where actors playing multiple characters must make split-second costume changes, one or more assistants (called dressers) help the actor remove the previous costume and don the new one.

Brendan Powers and Matthew Lindsay show off the many costumes they must change in *A Tuna Christmas*.

Photo: Michael Eaddy

Dramaturg

Few outside the theatre world know the term dramaturg—let alone know what that person does. A dramaturg is a theatre company's literary advisor who reads, researches, and interprets scripts. The first person listed in a Hippodrome playbill as the dramaturg was Sidney Homan, a UF English professor and Shakespeare scholar. He co-directed *The Comedy of Errors* with Kerry McKenney in 1985 and directed *Talk Radio* in 1989.

In the 1990s, David Boyce became the theatre's second dramaturg. He began his association with the Hippodrome as a performer in the Hippodrome's Theatre for Young Audiences (TYA) shows. David was also a playwright. He co-authored *EcoHeroes* with Lauren Caldwell and adapted *Alice in Wonderland* for TYA to tour in schools.

Tamerin (Tammy) Dygert held the longest tenure as the Hipp's dramaturg. Her expanded role included attending actor auditions, negotiating rights for plays, and researching the historical period and/or location where a play is set. Tammy adapted this material into booklets that were distributed to school children. She also wrote articles for the Hippodrome newsletter, started the One City One Story program in Gainesville, produced the Senior Playwriting Festival, and so much more.

Beyond the Mainstage

This text has concentrated on the theatre's mainstage and a few Second Stage productions, but there are two spaces located on the theatre's first floor that contribute to the Hippodrome's reputation as the focal point of Gainesville's artistic culture: the Hippodrome Cinema and Hippodrome Art Gallery.

Hippodrome Cinema

In a world of multiscreen cineplexes showing the same blockbuster in five auditoriums, there's no room in local theatres for foreign, independent, or art house films, and nowhere in Gainesville to see a documentary or a black-and-white classic from the 1940s—that is, until January 21, 1982, when the Hippodrome Cinema lit the screen for the first time.

Under the direction of Shirley Lasseter, the cinema began with a simple 16mm projector. Audiences sat on couches and folding chairs. Now, the couches and chairs have been replaced by seventy-five plush, rocking stadium-style seats. In 1995, the projection system was upgraded to 35mm with surround sound. The system was updated again to a new digital projection system in 2013. A Hippodrome Cinema renovation in 2023 included new seating, a new screen, new lighting, flooring, and wall treatments.

The Hippodrome Cinema is the region's only film and video arts program for first-run artistic films, providing a center for the presentation and examination of independent films. It also provides a venue for annual short film and animation festivals and premieres of new works by independent filmmakers and documentarians. The cinema space is also used for the Hipp Unplugged series of staged readings and is home to the Hippodrome Second Stage plays.

Art Gallery

Photo: Michael Eaddy

Artist Ferdie Pacheco stands next to an exhibit of his paintings in the Hippodrome Art Gallery.

Adjacent to the Cinema is the Hippodrome Art Gallery, which offers visual artists a beautiful space to showcase their talent. A lofted ceiling and tall windows bring an airy feeling to the charming Art Gallery. Historic wood moldings and elegant marble provide a culturally rich atmosphere.

The Hipp makes its art gallery available, by invitation, for exhibits by Florida artists at no charge. The exhibits change regularly and are often tied to themes of the current mainstage production. The Hippodrome Art Gallery has long been a favorite stop on Gainesville's monthly Artwalks.

The Hippodrome Theatre Lower Level

The Hippodrome Theatre Lower Level, as the basement has tactfully been re-named, was for many years used to store props and costumes. In 2008, the props and costumes were moved, the floor was tiled, and an outside elevator was installed. Later, acoustic sound-deadening panels were added. The basement now provides a versatile space that is used for opening night parties, as a venue for musicians, and is also available to rent for private gatherings.

Bar

Both the first floor and the basement have full-service bars that offer alcoholic and non-alcoholic beverages during Hippodrome events. The first-floor bar, adjacent to the cinema, also sells popcorn. What's a movie without popcorn?

2023 and Beyond

Elaborate Entrance

On January 27, the Hippodrome began the second half of its fiftieth season with *The Elaborate Entrance of Chad Deity* by Kristoffer Diaz. The play, winner of the 2011 Obie Award for Best New American Play, is about the economic-driven theatrical aspects of professional wrestling.

While pro wrestlers' athleticism is real, the sport has developed a strong kinship to theatre in that there are heroes and villains, and the matches are scripted and rehearsed. In the play, Mace (Alexis Suarez), despite being the superior wrestler, is relegated to playing the masked villain inevitably defeated by the champion, Chad Deity (Jonathan Bangs). Both men are under contract with the wrestling promotion company and controlled by its CEO (David Patrick Ford).

Chad makes an elaborate entrance at each bout, laden with gold jewelry, wearing a fur coat, and displaying his gigantic championship belt. The promoters capitalize on racial stereotypes to win support from the audience. Mace, tired of being the guy who loses to make the winners look good, recruits an Indian actor, Vigneshwar (Rahul Joshi) to join them.

Alexis Suarez and Jonathan Bangs play competing pro wrestlers in *The Elaborate Entrance of Chad Deity*.

Photo: Michael Eaddy

The CEO initially refuses, but eventually hires him as "The Fundamentalist," changes Mace's name to Che Chavez Castro, and advertises the pair as anti-American extremists. They quickly become wrestling fans' favorite villains, defeating other wrestlers, Billy Heartland and Old Glory (both played by Jose DeGracia, who had thirteen years' experience in pro wrestling). The CEO chooses the Fundamentalist to defeat Chad and become the next champion in a super match, but Vigneshwar decides to leave wrestling. Mace is asked to step in, and finally gets to perform as himself without a mask, but loses to Chad Deity.

Alberto Bonilla directed the show, which ran through February 12. Alberto is a Broadway, film, and television actor who appeared at the Hippodrome in *The Blameless* and *Living on Love*.

Native Gardens

For their next show, *Native Gardens* by Karen Zacarias, guest director Kristin Clippard cast veteran Hippodromers Nell Page and Kevin Rainsberger as Virginia and Frank, a well-heeled couple in an old, established, Washington, D.C. neighborhood.

Marco Adiak Voli, and Emmy-winning producer, Aléa Figueroa made their Hippodrome debut as new neighbors, Pablo and Tania. Pablo, a high-powered lawyer, and Tania, a very pregnant doctoral candidate, are realizing the American dream when they purchase a house next to Virginia and Frank.

At first, Virginia and Frank are excited to have new neighbors because the previous owner had let the place run down, which caused Frank to lose the city flower garden contest for the past three years. When Pablo and Tania ask if they can replace a rusted chain-link fence with a new wood one, Frank is elated, sure that will improve the look of his flowerbeds. Tania promises to plant flowers on her side of the fence.

Not everything is rosy. Tania is a proponent of native plants, which Frank calls weeds. Also at issue is a magnificent old oak tree which Pablo and Tania love, but Virginia and Frank think should be cut down. Then, in preparation for the new fence, a survey finds the true property line cuts smack through the middle of Frank's precious flowerbed. And time is running out. Pablo has invited colleagues to a back yard barbeque the following weekend. The disagreement soon spirals into an all-out war of class, privilege, and entitlement. But in the end, everyone makes up and good neighbors become friends.

(l-r) Kevin Rainsberger, Nell Page, Marco Adiak Voli, and Aléa Figueroa star in *Native Gardens*.

Photo: Michael Eaddy

Hippodrome co-founders Bruce Cornwell, Kerry McKenney Oliver-Smith, and Gregory von Hausch cut the cake at the Hippodrome's birthday party.

Student actors Alexandra Lopez, Allen McBride, and Andrea Acevedo had non-speaking roles as gardeners and construction workers. *Native Gardens* ran from March 10–26.

The Big Five-O

On April 15, 2023, the Hippodrome held a fiftieth anniversary celebration of its founding on April 18, 1973. The event included an open house, tours of the historic building, live musical and dance performances—even a circus act in front of the steps. Attendees included cast members from some of the Hippodrome's earliest plays: Dan Jesse, Jon Schwartz, Dana Moser, Chad Reed, Christina Palacio, Sandy Scott, Gerry Munn, Martha Williams, Jennifer Pritchett, Nell Page, Kevin Rainsberger, and many others. Caren Gorenberg, Marshall New, and Carlos Asse were there along with co-founders Bruce Cornwell, Kerry McKenney, and Gregory von Hausch. And, like any good birthday party, there was a cake.

Silent Sky

In April, the Hippodrome brought to the stage *Silent Sky*, the true story about nineteenth-century astronomer Henrietta Leavitt. Playwright Lauren Gunderson (author of *The Revolutionists*) explores a woman's place in society during a time of immense scientific discoveries, when women's ideas were dismissed until men claimed credit for them.

When Henrietta begins work at the Harvard Observatory in the early 1900s, she isn't allowed to touch a telescope or express an original idea. Instead, she joins a group of women "computers," charting the stars for a renowned astronomer who calculates projects in "girl hours" and has no time for the women's theories. Henrietta, in her free time, attempts to measure the light and distance of stars. She must also take measure of her life on Earth, trying to balance her dedication to science with family obligations and the possibility of love. Henrietta believes in both.

Below: cast of *Silent Sky* (l-r) Cynthia Beckert, Tim Dowd, Elise Hudson, Savannah Simerly, and Laura Shatkus.

Photo: Michael Eaddy

Social progress, like scientific progress, can be hard to see when one is trapped among earthly complications. In an exquisite blend of science, history, family ties, and fragile love, a passionate young woman must map her own passage through a society determined to keep a woman in her place. With music by Jenny Giering bursting forth onstage, Henrietta and her female peers change the way we understand both the heavens and Earth.

Directed by Stephanie Lynge, the show ran April 21–May 7. The cast featured Elise Hudson, Laura Shatkus, Cynthia Beckert, Savannah Simerly, and Tim Dowd.

Summer Musical

The Hippodrome wrapped up its fiftieth season with the Tony Award-winning musical *A Gentleman's Guide to Love and Murder*. A musical comedy, with book and lyrics by Robert L. Freedman and music and lyrics by Steven Lutvak, it is based on the 1907 novel *Israel Rank: The Autobiography of a Criminal* by Roy Horniman.

It is the uproarious story of Monty Navarro (Lukas Poost), an heir to a family fortune who sets out to jump the line of succession by eliminating the eight pesky relatives who stand in his way. Monty also has to juggle his mistress (she's after more than just love), his fiancée (she's his cousin, but who's keeping track?), and the constant threat of landing behind bars! Of course, it will all be worth it if he can slay his way to his inheritance . . . and be done in time for tea.

Unlike "jukebox" musicals that regularly filled the Hippodrome summer slots with "oldies," *A Gentleman's Guide to Love and Murder* is more traditional in that its twenty-four original songs are about the actual story and serve to further or explain the plot. The director was Stephanie Lynge, musical director was Caryl Fantel, and the choreographer was John Gray. The show was scheduled to run June 2–July 9.

A Gentleman's Guide to Love and Murder cast:
Kelly Atkins
Emily Chaviano
Sean Cunningham
David Patrick Ford
Skylar Geraghty
Alia Munsch
Connor Neun
Lukas Poost
Olivia Sargent
Nicole Simpkins
Noah Yager

Looking Beyond

The daring band of six Hippodrome co-founders could never have foreseen that their fledgling theatre would eventually evolve into one of the most respected and beloved Gainesville institutions. Now, at the fifty-year mark, can anyone predict what further growth the next five decades will bring? Perhaps not, but Artistic Director Stephanie Lynge has shared some thoughts about the more immediate future.

"Over the next fifty years, I see the Hippodrome offering an even wider variety of artistry," Stephanie said. "We have our Hipp Unplugged—a series of staged readings. We want to restart our Second Stage series. We have our New Works Festival that we want to grow to eventually be able to send our participating playwrights to other theatre festivals. The idea behind all of those is to do edgier work. To present work by underrepresented playwrights, to bring in new audience members, and to challenge ourselves as well as to find ways to funnel that work onto our mainstage.

"We want to not only create art—we want to support art with our gallery. How can we continue to use that space for artists in our community, and how can that space help them take the next step, whatever that is for them? Maybe we'll change our gallery exhibits more often, or hold more events in the gallery.

"We will continue to support our Education Department. It does amazing work out in the community, and it does amazing work right here. We want to grow those programs with staffing.

"In my perfect world, the Hippodrome grows not only in what we create and the expansion of our audience, but also by supporting our local talent and giving them space for their creative ventures. One of our marketing employees created the Basement Sessions. It's another platform for locals, generally young musicians, to come and say, "Here's a space." Let's attract these audiences, get their music out there, and have it heard.

"The Hippodrome is a space for everyone, and we want to grow all of those areas so that we are supporting everyone at every stage, including professional actors and directors. One of the reasons this theatre was created was to bring contemporary plays in a professional manner to this community. That's how it started and certainly, as I look back through everything, I see that's very true. We will continue to provide amazing professional theatre at a level that you'd have to drive four to six hours in any direction to match."

Actor Gregg Jones speaks to its intrinsic merit: "The real-time connection with living, breathing bodies is one of the essences of theatre and what separates it from other art forms. It has the ability for us as a culture to connect collectively, just like we did in prehistory.

"When we were tribal, we did storytelling with the shaman around the campfire in the middle of the wilderness. The modern-day campfire for transmission of culture and oral history is the theatre. In place of the fire, we have the lit stage, and that becomes the sanctified space.

"I think that purpose and function gained importance the more we became married to digital screens. Separated from the interpersonal relations, we become more disconnected and less connected.

"Real interaction is so valuable, where audience members are feeling and vibrating in the space common to the actors. We exchange vibrations in that space. And that moves the needle—not only culturally but societally—about who we are as human beings. I think the theatre has great value, and I think the Hippodrome is part of that."

Echoing Gregg's passion for theatre, Stephanie Lynge said, "The people who choose to work here are passionate about what they do. I mean, you can feel that energy coming out of the building."

Clearly, the Hippodrome is more than just another playhouse. Speaking of the magnificent historic beaux arts building, former Managing Director Jessica Hurov said, "It is their greatest asset and their greatest responsibility. The building needs to be fed, it wants to be fed. What does it want to be fed with? People and money. Getting patrons in here for programming of any kind, whether jazz shows in the basement or movies or art gallery or education camps for kids.

"The service of the building is to the public, and the building wants more of it— no matter what the function or event. And when the people come, it starts from there. You build affinities to donors or business sponsors or get new people interested in doing programs or attending them or bringing their children.

"This place needs constant evolution. It needs time and attention. We talk about wild spaces needing public funding. I remember Caren Gorenberg saying to me, 'This is a public space *and* a wild space. It needs to be constantly tended to, and there's never a time that you can sit back, cross your arms, put your feet up, and say, "We're done." You're *never* done.'"

Theater of Dreams. 1993 by Margaret Ross Tolbert photographed by Michael Eaddy

About the Author

Richard Gartee, a longtime subscriber and patron of the Hippodrome, is honored to contribute to the preservation of its history. Richard is an award-winning novelist who has had six novels, five collections of poetry, and fifteen nonfiction books published. *The Hippodrome Theatre First Fifty Years* is his twenty-seventh full-length book. Learn more about his writing career and books by visiting www.gartee.com.

BOOKS BY RICHARD GARTEE PRESENTLY AVAILABLE:

HUMOROUS FICTION
Ragtime Dudes at the World's Fair

Ragtime Dudes in a Thin Place

Ragtime Dudes Meet a Paris Flapper

METAPHYSICAL FICTION
Atlantis Dying

Lancelot's Grail

Lancelot's Disciple

NONFICTION
Skating on Skim Ice

The Hippodrome Theatre First Fifty Years

POETRY COLLECTIONS
Mountain Breathing

Watching Waves

Canyon Falls

Index